iWork

For Beginners & Seniors

Complete Beginner to Expert Guide to Master Apple Pages, Numbers, and Keynote + Professional Hacks, Tips & Tricks for Organized and Effortless Word-Processing, Spreadsheets Management, and Presentations

CARTY BINN

Copyright © 2023 **CARTY BINN**

All Rights Reserved

This book or parts thereof may not be reproduced in any form, stored in any retrieval system, or transmitted in any form by any means—electronic, mechanical, photocopy, recording, or otherwise—without prior written permission of the publisher, except as provided by United States of America copyright law and fair use.

Disclaimer and Terms of Use

The author and publisher of this book and the accompanying materials have used their best efforts in preparing this book. The author and publisher make no representation or warranties with respect to the accuracy, applicability, fitness, or completeness of the contents of this book. The information contained in this book is strictly for informational purposes. Therefore, if you wish to apply the ideas contained in this book, you are taking full responsibility for your actions.

Printed in the United States of America

CONTENTS

ALL RIGHTS RESERVED II
DISCLAIMER AND TERMS OF USE II
CONTENTS III
INTRODUCTION 1
BOOK 1 3
APPLE PAGES 3
CHAPTER ONE 4
UNDERSTANDING PAGES 4
    WHAT DO PAGES DO? 4
    NEW FEATURES ON PAGES 6
    OPENING PAGES FROM ICLOUD 10
    HOW TO OPEN PAGES FILE ON WINDOWS PC WITH ICLOUD 10
    CONCLUSION 13
    MANAGING DOCUMENTS 14
    COPYING A FILE INTO AN IWORK FOR IPAD APP 15
    CONFIGURING PAGES PREFERENCES 15
        Open Pages preferences 16

CHAPTER TWO 17
DOCUMENT SETUP USING PAGES 17
    DOCUMENT CONFIGURATION 17
    CHOOSE A DOCUMENT TYPE ON MAC 17
        Create a basic document 17
        Change document types 18
    CHOOSE A DOCUMENT TYPE ON IPHONE OR IPAD 19
        Create a basic document 19
        Change document types 19
    CHANGING THE MARGINS, SIZE OF A DOCUMENT, AND MAKING YOUR PAPER SIZE 20
        Set Paper Size, Page Orientation, And Margins in Pages 20
        Create A Custom Paper Size 21
        Set Paper Size, Page Orientation, And Margins On iPhone or iPad 22
    LIGATURES AND HYPHENATIONS 23
        Ligatures 23
        Turn ligatures on or off for selected text 23
    HYPHENATIONS 23
        Change automatic hyphenation for a document 24
        Add or remove hyphens in specific paragraphs 24
        Turn smart dashes on or off 24

Convert existing double hyphens to dashes 25
PAGES NUMBERS AND HEADERS 25
    Add Page Numbers in Pages App On iPhone and iPad 26
    Add Page Numbers in Pages App on Mac 33
    Enable the header and footer in the Pages app as a bonus tip. 35
Conclusion 36
BOOKMARKS 36
How Can You Create Internal Links? 36
TABLE OF CONTENTS 37
    Create A Navigable Table of Contents 37
    Add A Table of Contents in A Document's Text 39
    Why The Table of Contents Feature? 41
FOOTNOTES AND ENDNOTES 42
Inserting A Note 42
    Convert Notes from One Kind to Another 43
    Change The Look of Note Text 43
    Change The Symbol for Notes 44
    Change Numbering for Notes 44
    Remove A Note 44
ADD A COMMENT 44
MONITOR CHANGES 46
Conclusion 47
SHARING AND EXPORTING DOCUMENTS 47
Using iCloud To Sync Documents 49
    Syncing With iCloud 49
    iCloud Capacity 54
EMAILING A DOCUMENT 55
Conclusion 58
COLLABORATING 58
Prerequisites 59
Invite Others to Collaborate on A File 59
    How To Invite Others to Collaborate from Mac 59
    How To Invite Others to Collaborate From iPhone or iPad 62
    How To Invite Others to Collaborate From iCloud 64
Change Share Options 64
    How To Change Share Options on Mac 64
    How To Change Share Options On iPhone or iPad 65
    Remove A Collaborator from The File 65
    How To Remove a Collaborate on Mac 65
    How To Remove a Collaborate On iPhone or iPad 66
Stop Sharing a Pages, Numbers, Or Keynote File 66
    How To Stop Sharing a Pages, Numbers, Or Keynote File on Mac 67
    How To Stop Sharing Pages, Numbers, Or Keynote File On iPhone or iPad 67

Set A Password for The File to Prevent Unauthorized Access 68
How To Set a File Password on Mac 68
How To Set a File Password On iPhone or iPad 69
See Which Participants Are Working on A File 69
iWork Collaboration Simplified With iCloud 70
FAQs 70
Can you collaborate on Apple Numbers? 70
How do you collaborate on a Numbers file? 70
How can I collaborate on Keynote on iPad? 70
PAGES DOCUMENT EXPORT 71
CREATING NEW DOCUMENT 71
DOCUMENT SAVING AND RENAMING 73
Save A Document with A New Name or Location 74
RENAME A DOCUMENT 74
Revert A Document to An Earlier Version 74
OPENING EXISTING FILES 75
IF YOU SEE A WARNINGS WINDOW 75
SAVE AN OLDER IWORK DOCUMENT 76
PASSWORD AND DOCUMENT LOCKIN 77
Locking Your Pages Document 77
OPENING A LOCKED PAGES DOCUMENT 78
OPENING LOCKED DOCUMENTS FROM OTHER IOS DEVICES 80
CHANGING OR REMOVING THE PASSWORD 80
ORGANIZING PAGES AND DOCUMENTS 81
Rearrange Word-processing Pages 81
Rearrange Page Layout pages 82
TRANSFERRING DOCUMENTS TO AND FROM iCLOUD 82
How To Move Existing iWork Files from Your Mac To iCloud 82
How To Save Existing Pages Files on Your Mac In iCloud 83
UPLOAD AND DOWNLOAD FILES FROM ICLOUD DRIVE ON ICLOUD.COM 84
Upload Files 84
DOWNLOAD FILES 84
PAGES EXPORTING FILES 86
How To Export a Pages File as Word Document On iPhone & iPad 86
USING ITUNES TO TRANSFER FILES TO AND FROM PAGES 91
Transfer Files Between PC And iPhone/iPad Via iTunes File Sharing 91
Move Files from PC To iPhone Via iTunes Syncing 92

CHAPTER THREE 94

WORKING WITH TEMPLATES ON PAGES 94

UTILIZING PRE-EXISTING TEMPLATES 94
MAKING YOUR TEMPLATES 95
EDIT A CUSTOM TEMPLATE 96

Rename A Custom Template 96
Delete A Custom Template 97
CONCLUSION 98

CHAPTER FOUR 99

WORKING WITH TEXT ON PAGES 99

TEXT INSERTION 99
Add Text in A Word-Processing Document 99
Add Text in A Text Box 100
Add Text Inside a Shape 101
FONT SELECTION AND FORMATTING 101
Making Use of Paragraph Styles 101
Apply A Paragraph Style 102
Assign A Shortcut Key to A Style 102
Create A New Paragraph Style 103
Remove Overrides from A Paragraph Style 103
Update A Paragraph Style 104
Rename A Style 104
Delete A Style 104
MAKING LISTS 105
Insert Lists in Pages App On iPhone and iPad 105
Customize Lists in Pages App On iPhone and iPad 108
Insert Lists in Pages App on Mac 112
CUSTOMIZE LISTS IN PAGES APP ON MAC 114
CONCLUSION 116
WORKING WITH UNIQUE CHARACTERS 116
TEXT FLOW MODIFICATION 123
LINKED TEXT BOXES OF THE PAST 124
Modern Linked Text Boxes 125
Rearranging Links 126
USING THE THREAD CONTROL 126
Making Threads Look Good 127
CONCLUSION 128
MAKING USE OF BIDIRECTIONAL TEXT 128
Use Another Language in Pages 129
Change Paragraph Text Direction 129
EXAMINING FORMATTING SYMBOLS 130
Invisible Character Represents 131

CHAPTER FIVE 133

ENHANCING YOUR DOCUMENTS WITH PAGES 133

ADDING IMAGES TO DOCUMENTS 133
Insert Photos and Other Graphics into Pages Documents 134

Is Dragging a Drag? 141
Don't Have the Image Yet? 141
DESIGN PHOTOS AND OTHER IMAGES IN PAGES DOCUMENTS 141
   Resizing Other Kinds of Graphics 143
   Delete Custom Styles 150
   Distribute Graphics 158
GO FURTHER: LAYER GRAPHICS 159
CHANGING THE COLOR LEVELS IN AN IMAGE 160
   Change The Transparency of An Object 160
   Add And Change an Object's Border 160
   Fill An Object with Color or A Gradient 160
ADD AN IMAGE FILL 161
   Save A Custom Fill 162
   Add A Shadow 162
   Add A Reflection 163
ADDING TABLES TO YOUR DOCUMENTS 163
   Tables 164
   Figure A 164
   ADDING A CHART 165
   Figure B 165
   Figure C 166
GETTING STARTED 167
PLACING YOUR CHART 167
WORKING WITH DATA 168
CUSTOMIZING YOUR CHART 170
PLAYING WITH THE AXES 171
OTHER STUFF 173
   Exporting Your Charts 174
CONCLUSION 174

BOOK 2 .... **175**

APPLE NUMBERS **175**

CHAPTER ONE **176**

INTRODUCTION TO NUMBERS **176**

A USER-FRIENDLY INTERFACE 176
   Get started with a template 176
   Add data to a table 177
CREATE A CHART 178
GET ORGANIZED WITH SHEETS 178
COLLABORATE IN REAL-TIME 179
A WIDE RANGE OF TEMPLATES 179
CONCLUSION 184

CUSTOMIZABLE CELLS	185
CREATE A CUSTOM NUMBER FORMAT	185
CREATE A DATE AND TIME FORMAT	186
CREATE A TEXT FORMAT	187
ADVANCE FORMULAS AND FUNCTIONS	188
USING THE FORMULA EDITOR	188
INSERTING FORMULAS IN NUMBERS ON MAC	190
EDITING THE FORMULAS	190
GETTING A QUICK VIEW OF FORMULAS	191
INSERTING AND EDITING FORMULAS IN NUMBERS ON IPHONE AND IPAD	192
REVIEW FORMULA ERRORS AND LEARN HOW TO AVOID THEM	193
Review errors and warnings in formulas	*193*
How to avoid formula errors	*193*
Copy Or Move Formulas and Their Computed Values	*194*
Refer To Cells in Formulas	*195*
How to refer to cells in other sheets	*195*
USE STRING OPERATORS AND WILDCARDS	198
CONCATENATE STRINGS OR THE CONTENTS OF CELLS	199
USE A WILDCARD TO MATCH ANY SINGLE CHARACTER	199
USE A WILDCARD TO MATCH ANY NUMBER OF CHARACTERS	199
MATCH A WILDCARD CHARACTER	200
USE MULTIPLE WILDCARD CHARACTERS IN A CONDITION	200
HOW TO USE DOUBLE QUOTATIONS IN FORMULAS	201
LIST OF FUNCTIONS BY CATEGORY	202
Adding Date or Time in Numbers on Mac	*202*
FORMAT THE DATE AND TIME ON MAC	203
ADDING DATE OR TIME IN NUMBERS ON IPHONE AND IPAD	204
FORMAT THE DATE AND TIME ON IPHONE AND IPAD	205
CONCLUSION	205
MORE USEFUL FORMULAS AND FUNCTIONS	208
Compare Values	*208*
SPLIT TEXT	209
REMOVE EXTRA SPACES	210
CONCATENATE DATA	212
CONVERT TO PLAIN TEXT	213
TYPES OF ARGUMENTS AND VALUES	214
Any value types	*214*
Arrays and array functions	*214*
Boolean expression and value type	*214*
Collection value type	*214*
Condition expression	*215*
Constant expression	*215*
CONCATENATE("CAT","S")	215

- Date/time value type 215
- Duration value type 215
- List value type 215
- CHOOSE(3,"1st","second",7,"last") 215
- Modal argument or value type 216
- Number value type 216
- Range value type 216
- COUNT (A3:D7) 216
- STRING VALUE TYPE 217
- FUNCTIONS THAT ACCEPT CONDITIONS AND WILDCARDS AS ARGUMENTS 217
- CHARTS AND GRAPHS 218
  - Standard Charts 218
- ADVANCED CHARTS 222
  - How To Insert, Format, And Edit Charts & Graphs in The Numbers App on Mac, iPad, And iPhone 225
  - Insert A Chart in Numbers on Mac 226
- FORMAT A CHART ON MAC 227
- EDIT A CHART ON MAC 228
- INSERT A CHART IN NUMBERS ON IPHONE AND IPAD 230
- FORMAT A CHART ON IPHONE AND IPAD 231
- EDIT A CHART ON IPHONE AND IPAD 231

CHAPTER TWO 233

FINDING TREND WITH PIVOT TABLE IN NUMBERS 233

- WHAT IS A PIVOT TABLE? 233
  - What Are Pivot Tables Used For? 234
- PIVOT TABLE FUNCTIONALITIES 235
- CONCLUSION 237
- HOW TO CREATE A PIVOT TABLE IN NUMBERS 238
  - Create A Pivot Table 238
- HOW TO TROUBLESHOOT PIVOT TABLE PROBLEMS 240
  - Organize Your Data 241
- SORT AN ENTIRE TABLE 242
- SORT SELECTED ROWS 243
- CHECK FOR BLANK CELLS 244

CHAPTER THREE 246

HIGHLIGHTING COMPARISONS WITH RADAR CHARTS IN NUMBERS 246

- WHAT IS A RADAR CHART? 246
- WHEN SHOULD RADAR CHARTS BE USED? 247
- TYPES OF RADAR CHARTS 248
  - Simple Radar Chart 248
  - Filled Radar Chart 248

- Radar Charts with Markers 249
- Elements That Make Up a Radar Chart 249
- NUMBERS APP AND RADAR CHART 250
  - *Create A Radar Chart, Pie, Donut, Pie Chart, Bar Chart, Line Chart, Or Column Chart* 250
- HOW TO INTERPRET A RADAR CHART 252
- ADVANTAGES OF USING RADAR CHART 253
- DISADVANTAGES OF USING RADAR CHART 254

CHAPTER FOUR 255

TURN HANDWRITING INTO TEXT IN NUMBERS 255

- CHANGE THE DEFAULT APPLE PENCIL BEHAVIOR FOR NUMBERS 255
- TURN HANDWRITING INTO TEXT 256
- HOW TO USE SHAPES LIBRARY IN NUMBERS ON AN iPHONE AND iPAD 257

CHAPTER FIVE 259

CREATING AND CUSTOMIZING A FORM IN NUMBERS 259

- HOW TO CREATE A FORM IN NUMBERS 259
- USE YOUR FORM IN NUMBERS 261
- Notes On Forms in Numbers 262
- Conclusion 262

CHAPTER SIX 263

COLOR, GRADIENTS, AND IMAGES IN NUMBERS 263

- ADDING COLOR, GRADIENTS, AND IMAGES TO CELL IN NUMBERS 263
- APPLYING COLOR AND GRADIENT FILLS TO SHAPES IN NUMBERS 265
  - *Fill with a color or gradient* 266
  - *Fill with an image* 266
- Save a custom fill 267
- Remove A Fill 268
- ADD AND EDIT IMAGES 268
  - *Add a picture* 268
- Crop or mask a picture 268
- Take a picture and crop out the background and extras 269
- Change the image's saturation, exposure, and other settings 270
- RESIZING AND MOVING CELLS IN NUMBERS 271
  - *Select a table* 271
  - *Resize a table* 271
  - *Move a table* 271
  - *Lock or unlock a table* 271

CHAPTER SEVEN 272

CAPTIONS AND TITLES IN NUMBERS 272

x

ADDING CAPTIONS AND TITLES IN NUMBERS 272
   Add A Caption 272
ADD A TITLE 273
EDITING CAPTIONS AND TITLES IN NUMBERS 275
   Show or hide a table title 275
   Edit a table title 275

CHAPTER EIGHT 276

ADDING AUDIOS TO NUMBERS 276

ADD AUDIO FILE IN NUMBERS APP ON IPHONE AND IPAD 276
RECORD AND ADD AN AUDIO FILE 280
ADD AUDIO FILE IN NUMBERS APP ON MAC 284
CONCLUSION 287

CHAPTER NINE 288

CUSTOM TEMPLATES IN NUMBERS 288

CREATING A CUSTOM TEMPLATE 288
SAVE A SPREADSHEET AS A TEMPLATE 288
INSTALL A TEMPLATE ON YOUR MAC 289
INSTALL A TEMPLATE ON YOUR DEVICE 289
RENAME OR DELETE A CUSTOM TEMPLATE 290
EDIT A TEMPLATE 290

CHAPTER TEN 291

FUNCTIONS IN NUMBERS 291

MAKING USE OF THE FORMULA EDITOR 291
SIMPLE AND QUICK FORMULAS 292
ADDITIONAL FORMULAS AND FUNCTIONS 294
COMPARE VALUES 294
SPLIT TEXT 295
REMOVE EXTRA SPACES 296
CONCATENATE DATA 297
CONVERT TO PLAIN TEXT 298
COPY YOUR FUNCTIONS AND FORMULAS 299
SIMPLER METHODS FOR DATA ANALYSIS IN NUMBERS 299
ADDING FORMULAS IN MAC NUMBERS 300
EDITING THE FORMULAS 300
GETTING A QUICK VIEW OF FORMULAS 301
ADDING AND EDITING FORMULAS IN NUMBERS ON THE IPAD AND IPHONE 302
CONCLUSION 303

BOOK 3 304

APPLE KEYNOTE 304

CHAPTER ONE 305

INTRODUCTION 305

What is Keynote? 305
Basic Features of Keynotes 306
What's New in Keynote? 310
- *For iPhone, iPad, and Mac* 310
- *Collaborate in Messages* 310
- *Eliminate Backgrounds* 310
- *Restructured Toolbar* 310
- *For iCloud* 310
- *Beginning with a Theme* 311
- *Create a Presentation* 311

Add Photos, Shapes, Charts, and more 311
- *Intro to Text Boxes, Images, and Other Objects* 312
- *Personalize Every Detail* 312
- *Alter the Appearance of Objects* 312
- *Animation* 312
- *Play your Presentation Anywhere and Anytime* 312
- *Work together in Real Time* 312
- *Keynote 12.2.1 for MAC* 312

Conclusion 313

CHAPTER TWO 314

CREATE A PRESENTATION 314

How to Create a Presentation in Keynote 314
- *For Mac* 314

Choose a Default Theme for your Presentation 318
Save and name a Keynote presentation on Mac 318
Save and Name your Presentation 318
To Rename your Presentation 319
Save a Copy of your Presentation 320
Change where a Presentation Copy is saved 320
For iPad/iPhone 320
- *To create a Presentation from a Theme* 320

Play a Keynote presentation on iPhone 322
Add and Delete a Slide 322
For iPhone/iPad 323
- *To Add a Slide* 323

To Duplicate a Slide 323
Insert a Slide from another Slide 324
Delete a Slide 324
For Mac 325

xii

To Add a Slide	*325*
DUPLICATE A SLIDE	326
INSERT A SLIDE INTO ANOTHER SLIDE	326
DELETE A SLIDE	326
REORDER SLIDES	326
Skip a Slide	*327*
GROUP AND UNGROUP SLIDES	328
For iPhone/iPad	*328*
Group Slides	*328*
Ungroup Slides	*330*
Reorder Slides	*330*
SKIP OR UN-SKIP A SLIDE IN KEYNOTE	331
For Mac	*332*
Group Slides	*333*
Ungrouped Slides	*333*
UNDO/REDO	333
To Undo or Redo changes in Keynote on iPad/iPhone	*333*
Undo or Redo Changes in Keynote on Mac	*334*
HYPERLINKS	334
For Mac	*334*
Inserting a Link	*335*
EDIT OR REMOVE A LINK	336
ON IPHONE/IPAD	336
To add a Link	*336*
EDIT OR REMOVE LINK	338
COPY AND PASTE TEXT INTO KEYNOTE	338
On Mac	*338*
COPY AND PASTE A TEXT STYLE	339
COPY, CUT, AND PASTE TEXT IN KEYNOTE FOR ICLOUD	340
FIND AND REPLACE TEXT	340
ON MAC	340
Search for Specific Text	*340*
REPLACE FOUND TEXT	341
FIND AND REPLACE TEXT IN KEYNOTE FOR ICLOUD	342
FOR IPHONE AND IPAD	344
Finding and Replacing Text	*344*
LOCKUP A TEXT	345
On Mac	*345*
To Lock or Unlock a Presentation	*345*
Lock up for iCloud	*345*
CONCLUSION	345
CHAPTER THREE	**346**

MANAGING DOCUMENT WITH KEYNOTE **346**
   SAVING A DOCUMENT 346
      On Mac *346*
   RENAME A DOCUMENT OR PRESENTATION 347
   FOR IPAD/IPHONE 347
      Save a presentation *347*
      Duplicate a Presentation *348*
      To Revert a Previous Presentation *348*
      Locate a Presentation *349*
   SAVE A PRESENTATION IN ANOTHER FORMAT 350
   SAVE A PRESENTATION IN PACKAGE OR SINGLE-FILE FORMAT 351
   USING ICLOUD TO SYNC DOCUMENTS 352
      To Use iCloud with Keynote *352*
      Set up iCloud on your iPhone, iPad, or iPod touch *353*
   SET UP ICLOUD ON MAC 354
   SYNC A PRESENTATION FROM A MAC 354
   SYNC A PRESENTATION FROM AN IPHONE/IPAD 355
      Understanding Syncing Symbols in Keynote for iCloud *355*
   SETTING UP ICLOUD DRIVE ON YOUR MAC 356
      To Set Up iCloud Drive *356*
      Emailing a Keynote Document *356*
      To Send a Copy of your Presentation in another format *357*
   SELECT A SENDING OPTION 357
   REDUCE A PRESENTATION'S FILE SIZE IN KEYNOTE 361
   HOW TO QUICKLY EMAIL AND SHARE KEYNOTE PRESENTATIONS 362
      Collaborating *363*
   ICLOUD REQUIREMENT 363
   MINIMUM SYSTEM REQUIREMENTS 364
   WORK OFFLINE 364
      Edit While Offline *364*
   INVITE PEOPLE FROM YOUR MAC 365
   STOP SHARING A DOCUMENT 367
   INVITE PEOPLE TO COLLABORATE ON IPHONE/IPAD 368
   INVITE MORE PEOPLE 370
   CHANGE ACCESS OR PERMISSION FOR EVERYONE 371
   CHANGE ACCESS OR PERMISSION FOR INDIVIDUAL PARTICIPANTS 372
   ACCEPT AN INVITATION TO COLLABORATE 373
   COLLABORATE ON SHARED DOCUMENTS 374
   OPT OUT OF SHARED DOCUMENTS 375
   LOCATE THE PRESENTATION OTHERS HAVE SHARED WITH YOU 376
   EXPORTING A KEYNOTE PRESENTATION 376
      Export to MP4 File: Converting a Keynote Presentation into a QuickTime Video *376*
      Converting a Keynote Presentation into a Voiceover QuickTime Video *377*

EXPORTING 377
 Export as a Movie *377*
FINISH THE EXPORTING 378
PRINTING 379
CONCLUSION 380

CHAPTER FOUR 381

LOCKING PRESENTATIONS 381

USING PASSWORD TO LOCK PRESENTATION 381
REQUIRE A PASSWORD TO OPEN A PRESENTATION 381
 For iPhone/ iPad *381*
FOR MAC 382
CHANGE OR REMOVE A PASSWORD 384
 For iPhone/iPad *384*
 For Mac *385*
SET UP TOUCH ID TO OPEN PASSWORD PROTECTED PRESENTATION 386
ON MAC 386
ON IPHONE 387
LOCK OR UNLOCK A PRESENTATION 388
TRANSFERRING PRESENTATION USING FINDER AND AIRPOD 388
 Transfer the presentation from your computer with the finder *388*
 Transfer the presentation to your computer with the finder *389*
USING AIRPOD TO TRANSFER KEYNOTE PRESENTATION 389
USE HANDOFF TO TRANSFER KEYNOTE PRESENTATIONS 390
 Enable Handoff *390*
HAND OFF A PRESENTATION TO IPHONE OR IPAD 391
 Handoff a Presentation to Mac *392*
 Use a Remote to Control a Presentation in Keynote on Mac *392*
 Set Up iPhone/iPad as a remote control *392*
USE IPHONE OR IPAD AS A REMOTE CONTROL 394
CHANGE THE PRESENTATION DEVICE LINKED TO A REMOTE CONTROL DEVICE 395
CONCLUSION 396

CHAPTER FIVE 397

WORKING WITH PHOTOS ON THE KEYNOTE 397

HOW TO ADD AN IMAGE TO YOUR KEYNOTE PRESENTATION 397
ADD AN IMAGE ON IPHONE 398
USE AN IMAGE GALLERY PLACEHOLDER IN YOUR PRESENTATIONS 399
ON MAC: 399
 On iPhone *400*
REPLACE AN IMAGE IN YOUR KEYNOTE PRESENTATION 400
ON MAC: 400

xv

On iPhone 401
Edit images in your Keynote presentation 401
Select an image 402
Adding a Caption 405
Mask (Crop a Photo) 407
    For iPhone *408*
Adjust Saturation, Exposure, and Other Settings 408
Resize, Rotate, and Flip Objects in Keynote 409
    Object Resizing *409*
    Rotate an Object *409*
    Flip an Object *410*
Position and Align objects well 411
    Align an object using x and y coordinates *411*
    Align objects vertically and horizontally *412*
Equally space objects 412
Image Enhancement 412
    Add a Shadow *414*
Change Object Transparency in Keynote 415

CHAPTER SIX 415

WORKING WITH TABLES IN KEYNOTE 415

Add a Table 415
Delete a Table 417
Edit a Table 417
Alternate the row colors 419
Use Table Styles in Keynote 419
    Apply a Different Style to a Table *420*
    Revert Changes to a Table Style *420*
Save a Table as a New Style 420
Table Style that uses the Color in an Image 421
Redefine a Table 422
Organize a Table 422
Add or Remove Rows and Columns in Keynote 422
Add or Remove row and column 423
Add or Remove Header Rows and Column 425
Merge and Unmerge Cells 425
    Merge Cells *426*
    Unmerge cells *427*
Add and edit cell content in Keynote on Mac 427
    Add content to cells *428*
Wrap text to fit in a cell 428
    Clear Content from a range of cells *428*
    Autofill Cells *429*

- Add an object to a cell 430
- Delete an object from a cell 430
- Show a Cell Row and Column 431
  - Copy or Move Cells 431
  - Resize rows and columns in Keynote on Mac 432
  - Resize rows and columns manually 432
  - Resize rows and columns precisely 433
  - Size a row or column to fit its content 433
  - Make Rows and columns the same size 433
  - Resize a table 433
  - Move a table 434
  - Lock or unlock a table 434
- Select tables, cells, rows, and columns in Keynote on Mac 435
  - Select a table 435
  - Select a cell 435
  - Select rows and columns 435
  - Change the look of table text in Keynote on Mac 436
- Change the font, size, and color of the table text 436
  - Change the font size of all table text 436
- Conclusion 437

CHAPTER SEVEN 437

WORKING WITH CHARTS AND SHAPES ON KEYNOTE 437

- Types of Charts on Keynote 438
- Add Chart on Keynote 438
  - Delete a Chart 441
  - Modify a Chart 441
- Switch rows and columns as data series 441
- About Chart down Sampling 442
- Change the look of chart text and labels in Keynote on Mac 442
  - Change the font, style, and size of a chart text 442
  - Edit the Chart Title 443
  - Designing your Bar Chart 443
- Change the spacing in the bar or column chart 444
- Add Rounded corners to the bar, column, mixed, and 2 axes 445
  - Use chart styles in Keynote on Mac 445
- Apply a different style to a chart 446
  - Save a chart as a new style 446
  - Create chart styles that uses the color in an image 447
- Redefine a chart style 448
  - Delete a chart style 448
- Working with Shapes in Keynote 448
  - Add a Shape 449

- Adjust the curve along the edge of a shape 449
- Adjust the features of a shape 450
- Draw a Shape in Keynote 451
- Fill shapes and text boxes with color or an image in Keynote 453
- Fill with an image 454
- Save a custom 455
- Remove a fill 455
- Add text inside a shape 455
- Conclusion 456

CHAPTER EIGHT 457

ENHANCING A PRESENTATION WITH KEYNOTE 457

- Add a Transition 457
- Add a Magic Move Transition 458
- Change a Slide Transition 460
  - Remove Transition 460
  - Animate objects onto and off a slide in Keynote 460
  - Animate an object onto and off a slide 460
  - Create a motion path 461
- Conclusion 462

INDEX 463

INDEX 483

INTRODUCTION

The iWork office suite was developed by Apple Inc. for the macOS and iOS operating systems and is also accessible on other platforms via the iCloud website.

It consists of the spreadsheet application **Numbers**, the word processing and desktop publishing application **Pages**, and the presentation application **Keynote**. Apple's design objectives for iWork were to make it simple for Mac users to generate attractive documents and spreadsheets using the rich font library, built-in spell checker, advanced graphics APIs, and AppleScript automation framework in macOS.

Word, Excel, and PowerPoint are the corresponding Microsoft Office applications to Pages, Numbers, and Keynote. The iWork applications can export documents from their native formats (.pages,.numbers,.key) to Microsoft Office formats (.docx,.xlsx,.pptx, etc.) as well as to PDF files, even though Microsoft Office applications cannot access iWork documents.

Keynote, the oldest application in iWork, was first made available as a separate program in 2003 for Steve Jobs to use in his presentations. With the words "It's for when your presentation matters," Steve Jobs announced Keynote.

On iOS, Keynote now offers the option to zoom in on slides up to a maximum of 400 percent. Additionally, there is a new feature that allows you to more precisely adjust the font size to the nearest two decimal places. To create or open presentations, practice a slideshow, or begin presenting on a Mac, use the Shortcuts app.

Users can now copy a snapshot of a table's cells without formulas, categories, or hidden values in Numbers for iOS. Additionally, formulas and cells can now be filled with autofill using VoiceOver. Also, Numbers allow for more exact font size adjustments with up to two decimal places.

Shortcuts and VoiceOver can both be used on Mac to write formulas and use autofill to add rows to tables and create or open spreadsheets.

Pages for iOS now offers the option to directly publish documents up to 2GB in size to Apple Books. Additionally, Pages for iOS now offers the ability to quickly launch a new document on an iPhone by touching and holding the Pages app icon on the Home screen. VoiceOver makes it possible to read comments, keep track of changes, and accurately adjust font size.

The same VoiceOver support is available in Pages for Mac, and documents may be created and opened using Shortcuts.

The App Store and Mac App Store both offer the iWork apps for iOS and Mac for no cost.

There's more to this amazing product from Apple Inc. as you keep reading along. Enjoy!

BOOK 1
APPLE PAGES

CHAPTER ONE
UNDERSTANDING PAGES

Most people view word processors as fancy typewriters that make it easy to arrange thoughts and arguments for the printed page. You create sentences out of words, juggle and polish them, and then you're done.

Pages go a step further by making it simple to create as well as compose documents. Pages enable you to add the visual flair your papers need, whether you're printing a glossy newsletter or simply penning Aunt Peg a thank-you note.

WHAT DO PAGES DO?

Most Apple devices come pre-installed with Pages, a capable word processor that enables you to create visually attractive documents. Real-time collaboration also enables your team to work together from any location, whether they are using a Mac, iPad, iPhone, or PC.

Pages put you in the ideal environment for creativity right away. It sets the appropriate tools in the appropriate locations to make it simple to select a look, change fonts, change text styles, and add lovely graphics. Additionally, everyone working together on a document gets access to the same robust features.

Pages' initial focus, when it was introduced in 2005, was on creating documents meant to be read as printed hardcopies. In contrast, the app now supports image galleries, embedded videos (including YouTube links), audio, animations, and display text with color gradients or graphics to better reflect the digital world of today.

More than 90 Apple-designed templates are included with Pages for tasks including creating resumes, newsletters, booklets, flyers, cards, and posters. On iOS and macOS, you can also make your templates.

Apple made it possible to create eBooks with Pages in 2018. The corporation stopped supporting its prior book-creation program (iBooks Author) in 2020, directing authors to Pages for Apple Books publishing.

Pages can open and edit Microsoft Word and other common word processing documents and save documents in Apple's standard format (.pages). Besides Word (DOCX), PDF, EPUB for eBooks, plain text (TXT), rich text (RTF), and legacy Pages '09, users can export their work in these other formats as well.

Fill your text with photos or color gradients to make it more engaging. Add images, galleries, audio, video, math equations, charts, or any of the more than 700 configurable shapes to take the page as a whole to the next level.

New Features on Pages

Bring your writing to a new level. "Pages" is made to provide you with incredible methods to share your story.

1. **Start fresh with new templates for your designs.**

Create lovely photo card templates for your next major event invitations, or give your students a new coding certificate as a reward.

2. **Simple batch mailing.**

Need to send a letter to several people? A letter, card, or envelope can be created in Pages using mail merge, and you can then add a customized greeting or address from the Contacts app or a Numbers spreadsheet.

3. **A perfect view for your iPhone documents.**

On the iPhone, using **Screen View** makes reading and editing your documents much simpler. Text, photos, and tables are resized to fit your screen as soon as you turn it on. To view the entire layout, turn it off.

4. Quickly translate text.

View a translation of any selected text right away. If you'd like, you can even replace it with a tap. Ideal for businesses, foreign language classes, and other situations where you need a swift in-document translation.

5. Create text from handwriting. Magically.

Your handwritten words will be easily transformed into typed text while using **Scribble** for iPadOS with Apple Pencil. Write notes, draft a novel, or annotate a document, and watch it transform into text very quickly.

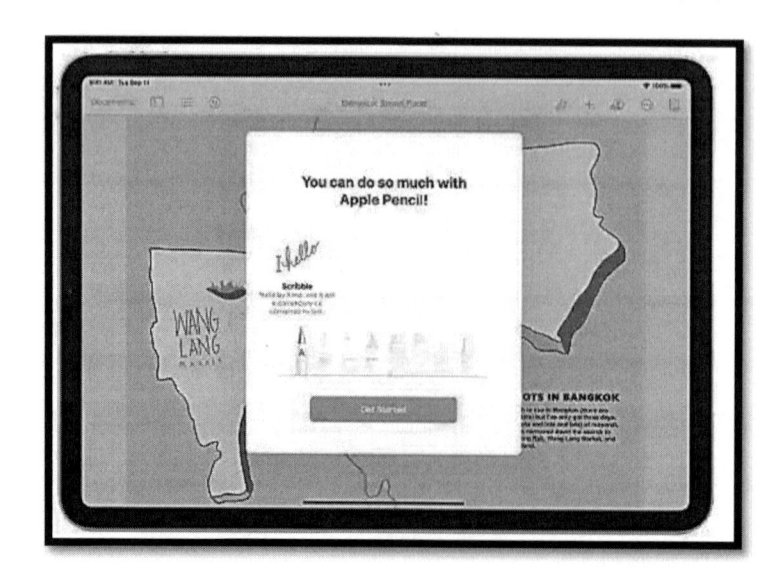

6. Easily write reports.

There is no more looking at a blank page using report templates. Select one of the exquisitely created templates to help you get started on an essay, research paper, or school report. To build a report, all you need to do is locate a template, write your report, add images, and more.

7. Skim through in style.

You can read through your document, zoom in and out, and interact with it on your iPhone and iPad without mistakenly changing anything.

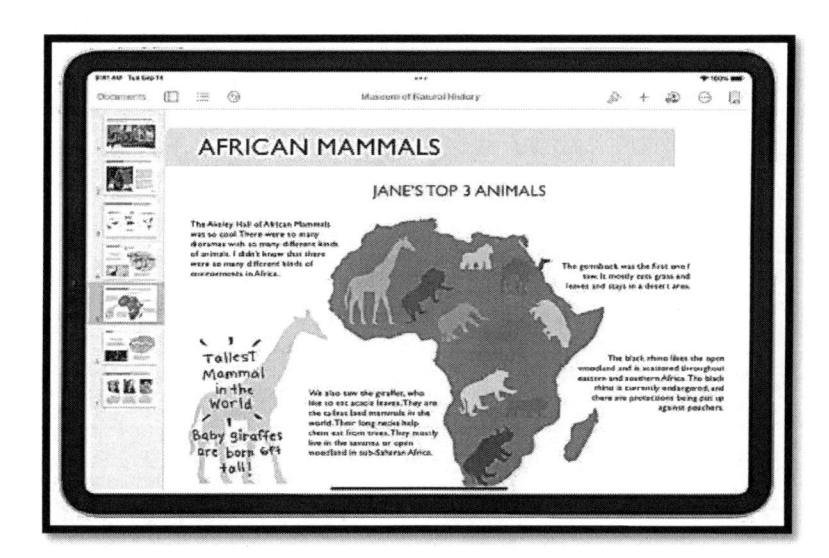

8. **You can play videos in your documents.**

Play Vimeo and YouTube videos directly in Pages without opening a web browser. Just provide a link and your web video will start playing inside your document or book.

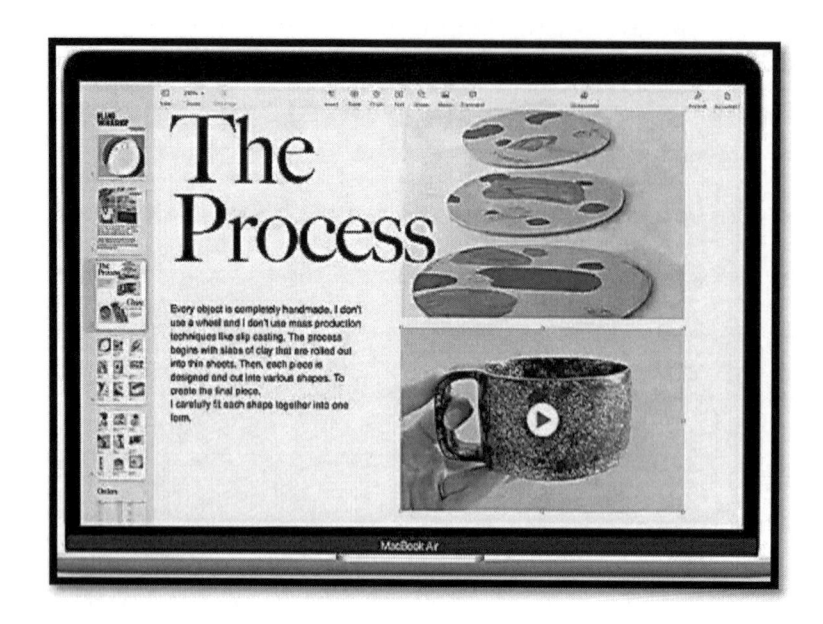

OPENING PAGES FROM ICLOUD

You require opening a Pages file, but your computer runs Windows. Using iCloud, you can access Pages files from Windows or any PC. There is no native Pages application for Windows, however, Pages files can be created on Mac, iPhone, iPad, and over iCloud. Not to fear, as you'll see in a moment, all you need is a web browser to view and access Pages documents directly from Windows.

We'll go over the specifics of using iCloud to open a Pages file on a Windows PC in this section.

How To Open Pages File on Windows PC With iCloud

Using Apple's iCloud web client is the easiest and most basic way to open iWork documents on your Windows PC because it doesn't call for any software to be installed. You won't even need to download the iCloud desktop application for Windows because we'll be using your online browser. Let's examine the process now.

- Go to **iCloud.com** by opening any web browser that is installed on your computer. Enter the information for your **Apple ID** and log into your iCloud account by clicking the arrow.

- The iCloud home page will be displayed to you. Select the "**Pages**" app, which is next to **Contacts**.

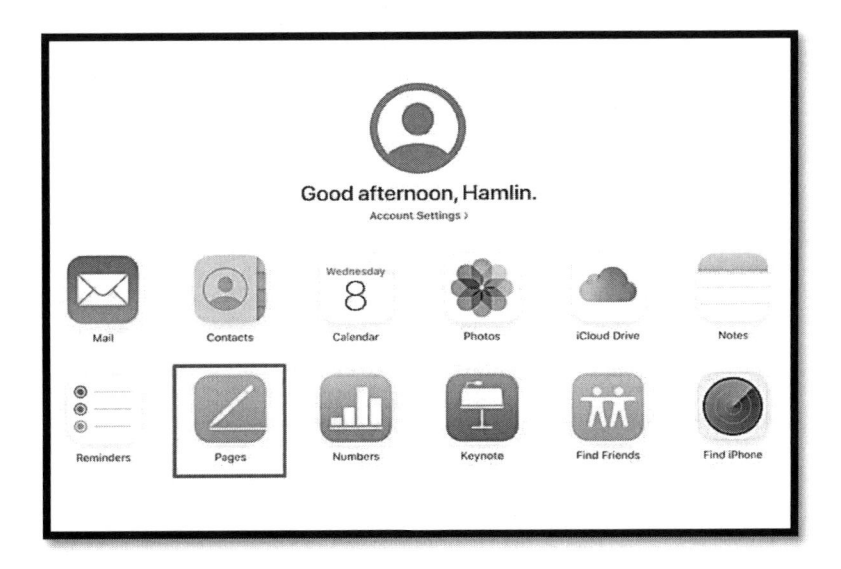

- Now, as seen in the image below, click on the "**Upload**" icon that is situated at the top of the page.

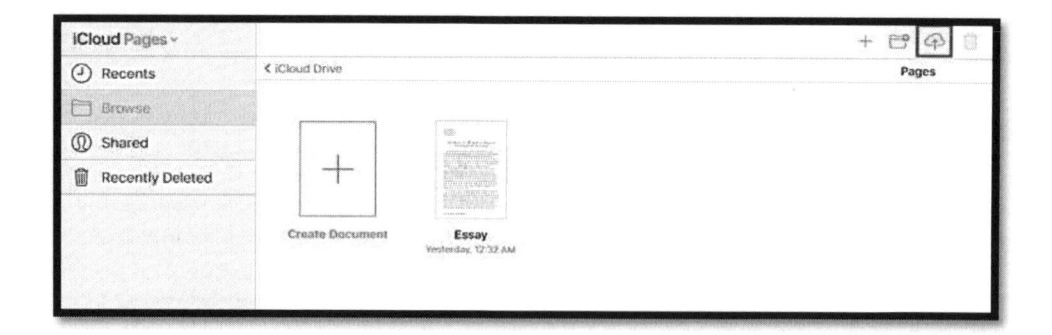

- You can browse folders in the window that is opened as a result of this activity. Click "**Open**" after selecting the **.pages** file you want to access.

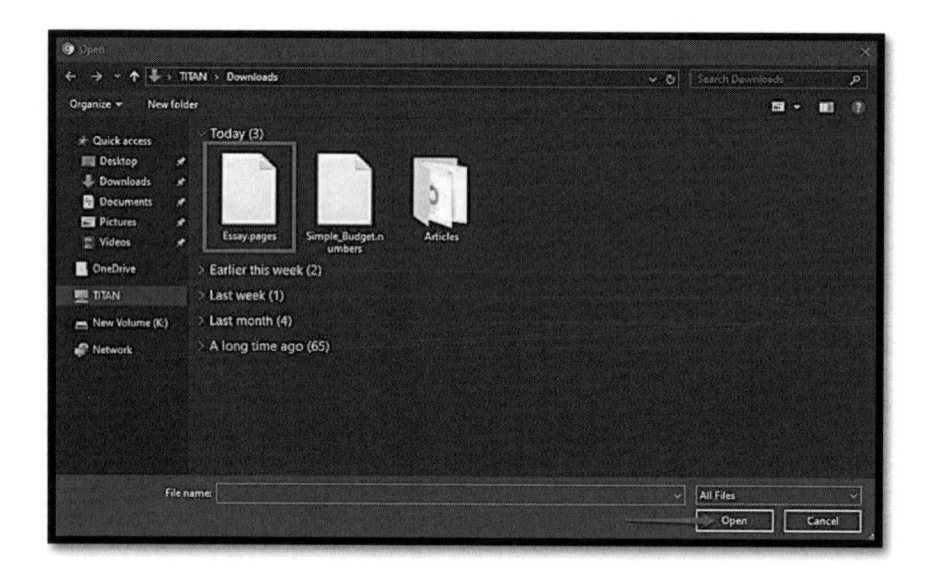

- Based on your internet connection, it may take a few seconds for the file to upload. To open the uploaded file on iCloud, "**double-click**" on it.

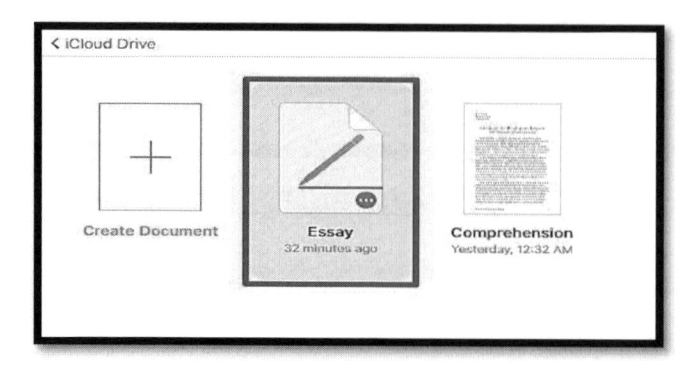

- Once it has loaded, you can view and edit the Pages file, store it directly on the cloud, or download it back to your Windows PC in a compatible format, such as PDF or Word, if that's what you want.

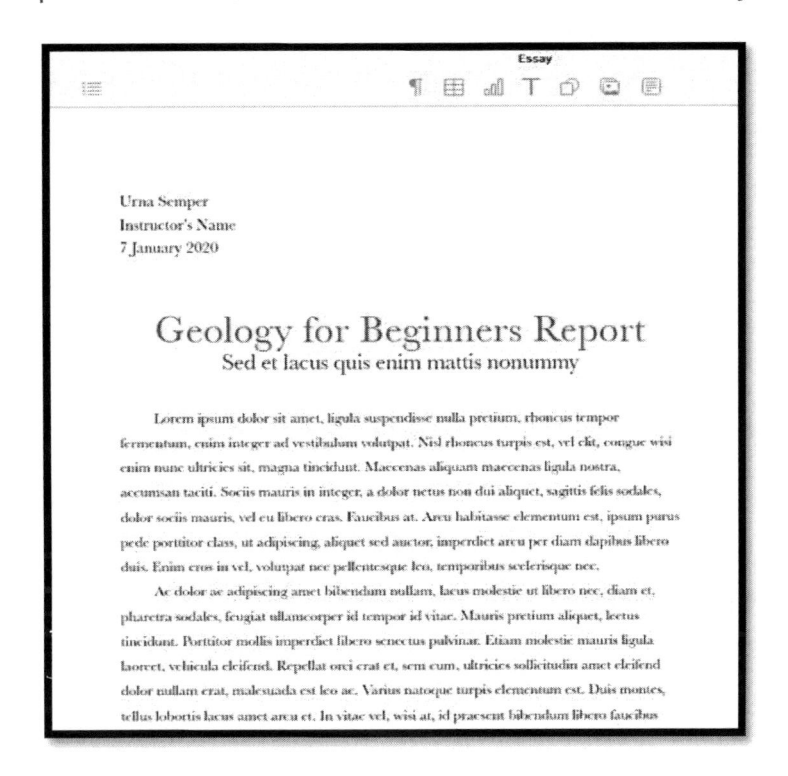

You can now open Pages files on your Windows laptops and desktops by following the procedures listed above. This cloud-based word processing tool from iCloud functions similarly to Google Docs.

Now that iCloud.com can open the files as well as convert them to widely supported formats, you no longer have to worry about iWork compatibility difficulties while switching between several devices.

If you like the appearance of Pages, Microsoft Word documents can also be viewed and edited using iCloud.

Conclusion

Anyone working across platforms or with various devices that you frequently switch between should find it handy to use iCloud for launching Pages and iWork projects. You might have a Windows PC at home in addition to a MacBook that you use while you're out and about.

If you've been using Pages for word processing on your macOS device, you might experience compatibility problems when attempting to open its file on a Windows computer. This is mainly because Microsoft Word is unable to open **.pages** files.

MANAGING DOCUMENTS

The information for your iWork documents is saved in files on your iPad, maybe on your Mac or PC, as well as occasionally on shared WebDAV (Web-based Distributed Authoring and Versioning) servers, your MobileMe iDisk, and, as you'll see, iWork.com if you so desire.

Although iWork files can be saved on a PC, only the iPad and Mac OS X can use iWork. You'll find that it's simple to convert your iWork files to the corresponding Microsoft Office file types so you may edit them on a PC.

The fact that you can transfer documents around and work on them in any setting you desire, from your desktop to a mobile device like your iPad, is one of the factors that contribute to iWork for iPad's success.

You must have access to your documents so that you can read, write, and share them with others. It's also essential that you can access documents that others share with you without having to go through any extra hoops.

There are files and folders hidden deep within the iPad operating system (iOS), but you often access them through apps. App-specific files and folders are located in a separate location that is designated just for that app.

When you select one of those files, as you'll discover later in this section, it will be copied into the ideal location on your iPad so you can work on it. Some apps, like the iWork apps, can read files from servers like iDisk and WebDAV.

Each app has a unique storage location for files on your iPad. Your Pages documents will be deleted along with the Pages app if you install Pages on your iPad and subsequently uninstall it. Ensure you have backed up any created files before uninstalling any apps from your iPad.

Copying A File into an iWork for iPad App

You can copy a file into an iWork app to edit it there if it's on your Mac or a server (such as an iDisk or WebDAV server). Of course, the file type must be compatible before saving the document. That implies:

- **Numbers**: .numbers, .xls, .xlsx
- **Keynote**: .key, .ppt, .pptx
- **Pages**: .pages, .doc, .docx

These are the main categories of documents. You can import other files like music in iTunes, JPEG image files in your iPhoto library, and so on.

- Click the **Copy From** button at the bottom of the screen from the **My Documents**, **My Spreadsheets**, or **My Presentations** page of your documents.
- Since your account ID is saved and your iPad is associated with a single, exclusive computer that runs iTunes, there is no login required for iDisk or a WebDAV server.
- Choose the desired file. You can move about in folders. Dimmed-out files are incompatible with the application you are using. Since this is the Keynote for iPad app, the only file that may be copied is a Keynote presentation. Your documents (**My Presentations, My Spreadsheets, or My Documents**) will receive a copy of the file.
- In case there are any errors, you will be informed. Opening a document generated in another application or a previous version of an application is the most typical reason for issues, which can include missing fonts, resizing slides in Keynote, and using unsupported features. The app will attempt to get around these problems as much as possible (nearly always).
- After correcting any mistakes, start working.

CONFIGURING PAGES PREFERENCES

All of your Page's documents are influenced by preference settings, which have an impact on how Pages functions.

Open Pages preferences

- Select **Preferences > Pages** (from the Pages menu at the top of your screen).
- To view all settings, select **General, Rulers**, and **Auto-Correction** at the window's top.

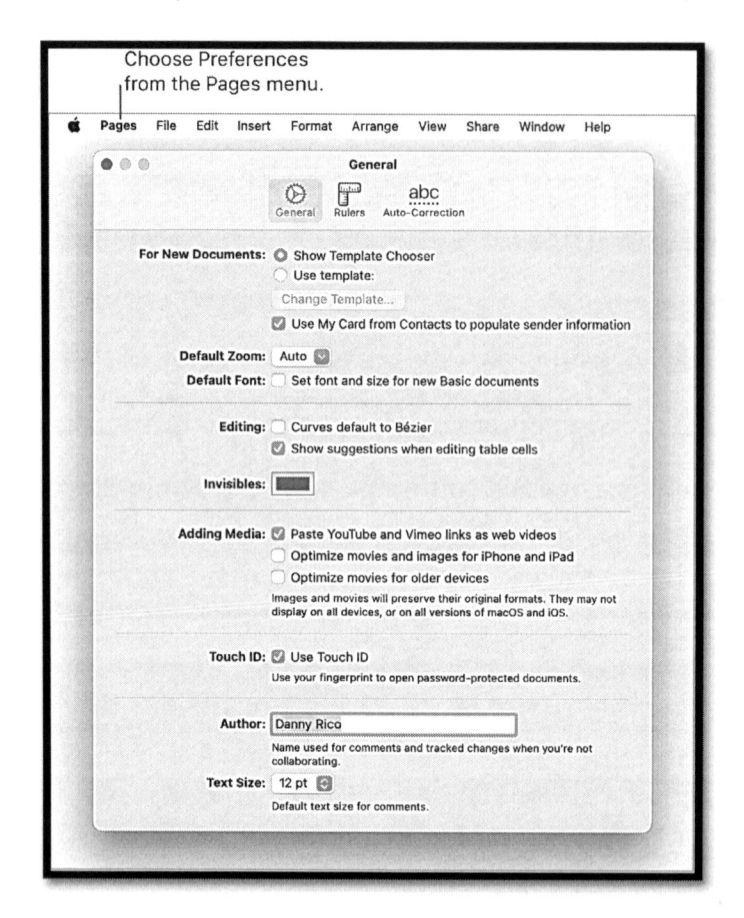

Instead of being part of the **Pages preferences**, many settings are part of your computer's **System Preferences**. For instance, you can configure several language options in the **System Preferences** and go to the **Keyboard preferences** section. Select the **Apple** menu in the top-left corner of your screen, then select **System Preferences** to access **System Preferences**. There are three places where you can set some settings, such as automatic spelling check, including **System Preferences** for all apps, **Pages Preferences** for all Pages documents, and the **Edit** menu for the existing document.

CHAPTER TWO
DOCUMENT SETUP USING PAGES

Before someone even reads a word, your document creates the first impression. The reader can get a general idea of the theme and quality of the document based on the paper size, color, and borders. Additional visual elements include the text layout, margins, and possibly a watermark.

Choosing wisely how to set up your document can help you communicate effectively with your audience. Consider creating an invitation. If you use a smaller, more elegant paper size and a subtle border, your recipients will immediately recognize that the event will be formal. This chapter will cover everything that concerns documents set up with Pages.

DOCUMENT CONFIGURATION

To create and edit word processing and page layout documents, try the Pages app. Depending on your content, choose the type you wish to create.

The text flows from one page to the next in a word processing document, making it perfect for documents like reports and letters. You may organize objects like text boxes and pictures however you wish in a page layout project. For flyers and newsletters, use page layout.

Templates in Pages can be used for either page layout or word processing. Following the selection of a template, you can always change the type of your document if you change your mind.

Choose A Document Type on Mac

By selecting the proper template, you can create a basic word processing or page layout document. After you begin working on a document, you can still change the document type.

Create a basic document

- Select **File** > **New** in **Pages**.

- Double-click one of the blank templates in the Basic category of the template chooser to create a simple word processing document.
- Double-click one of the blank templates in the Basic category, then select **File > Convert to Page Layout** to create a basic page layout document. The page layout document type is used by templates in other template categories including **Newsletters** and **Books - Landscape.**

Your name will be filled in by Pages in templates for stationery, resumes, and books using the information from your My Card under Contacts. Tap **Pages > Preferences** and choose "**Use My Card from Contacts to populate sender information**" if Pages asks for your permission to access your contact information.

You can examine or edit the apps that can utilize your contact information in System Preferences.

Change document types

If you've already begun adding content to your document, changing the document type could have an impact on that content.

Check the **File** option if you're unsure about the type of document you're using. It's a word processing document if the **File** menu option "**Convert to Page Layout**" is present. It is a page layout document if the option to "**Convert to Word Processing**" displays.

- Open the page layout document, then select **File > Convert to Word Processing** from the menu to convert it to a word processing document.
- Open the word processing document, select **File > Convert to Page Layout**, and then click **Convert** to convert it to a page layout document. If you haven't saved any content that you don't want to lose after conversion, hit **Cancel**.

Press **Command-Z** to reverse your most recent activities if you need to go back to the original document, or you can go return to an earlier version of the document.

Choose A Document Type On iPhone or iPad

By selecting the proper template, you can create a basic word processing or page layout document. Even after you've started working on a document, you can switch its type.

Create a basic document

- Open **Pages**, then click the **New Document button** + at the top of the screen in the document manager to bring up the template chooser. To access the document manager while a document is open, press **Documents** or the back arrow ⟨ in the top-left corner.
- Clicking **Start Writing** will allow you to start a basic word processing document. Otherwise, select **Choose a Template**, then select a blank template from the **Basic** category.
- Here's how to create a document with a basic page layout:
  - Click the **More** button ⊙ while a simple word processing document is open.
  - Click **Document Setup**. Tap **OK** to disable **Screen View** if a warning about it pops up.
  - Turn off **Document Body** in the **Document** tab, then select **Convert**.

Change document types

Whenever you desire, you can change the present document's document type. The content of your document may change if you switch types after selecting a template and adding content. Before changing the document's type, ensure to save a copy of it.

If you're unsure about the type of document you're using, skip selecting any text or objects by tapping in a corner of the document, then press the **More** icon ⊙, click **Document Setup**, and then hit **Document**. The document is a word processing document if **Document Body** is enabled.

The document is a page layout if the Document Body is disabled.

- Click the **More** icon ⊙ while the document is open, then select **Document Setup**.

- Change the type of document you are using:
    - Turn on **Document Body** to switch from page layout to word processing.
    - Turn off **Document Body**, then press **Convert** to convert a word processing document to a page layout document. If you haven't saved any content that you don't want to lose after conversion, select **Cancel**.

Click the **Undo** icon ⟲ to reverse your most recent activities or go back to a previous version of the document if you need to get back to the original version.

CHANGING THE MARGINS, SIZE OF A DOCUMENT, AND MAKING YOUR PAPER SIZE

Page margins aren't merely blank spaces. Your paper is easier to read if the page margins are appropriate. Pages with wide margins look more welcoming and provide space for reviewers' notes and comments. Although you can fit more words on the page if the margins are smaller, having too many words on each line makes the paper hard to read.

Readers find it difficult to follow from the end of one line to the start of the next when the lines are long. For elaborate documents, like books or magazines with facing pages, margins take on much greater significance.

Set Paper Size, Page Orientation, And Margins in Pages

For your Pages document on a Mac, iPhone, or iPad, select a paper size or make a custom paper size, select a portrait or landscape page orientation, and adjust the margins.

The margin, orientation, and paper size settings used by Pages templates can all be changed in the Document sidebar.

- Select the Document tab in the sidebar after selecting the **Document** toolbar button 📄.
- Tap the pop-up menu in the sidebar that displays the current paper size to change it, then select an option.

- Select **US Letter** if you wish to print your work on **8.5" x 11"** printer paper.
- You can make a custom paper size if the menu doesn't have the size you're looking for.
- Select the desired orientation under **Page Orientation** to change the page's orientation.
- Tap the arrows or input values in the fields next to **Top, Bottom, Left,** and **Right** in the **Document Margins** section of a word processing document to change the document margins. All margins are automatically set to one inch in the **Blank** template.
  The margin sizes change if you're using a different template. Additionally, you can indent some paragraphs from the document margins by adjusting the paragraph margins.
- By turning on the vertical ruler in preferences and then selecting **View > Show Ruler**, you can use it to check that your document's margins and other items are where you need them to be.

Create A Custom Paper Size

- To start a new document, select **File > New** and select a template.
- Select **File > Page Setup**.
- Select **Manage Custom Sizes** from the pop-up option for **Paper Size.**
- Simply press the **Add** button +.
- Then, enter a name for your custom size by double-clicking the new, untitled name in the list.
- In the **Width** and **Height** fields, enter the dimensions of the paper.
- Then select **OK** after setting the print margins.
- To close the **Page Setup** window, select **OK**.

Your document will print on the specified paper size when you print it.

Additionally useful during document setup are the usage of rulers, setting tab stops, and adding and formatting sections. You can add to or remove the specified sections in some templates.

Set Paper Size, Page Orientation, And Margins On iPhone or iPad

- Tap the **More** button ⊙ while the document is open, then tap Document Setup.
- Click **Document** to open a word processing document. Go to the next step if you're in a page layout document.
- Select either **Portrait** or **Landscape** to change the page's orientation.
- Select an option under "**Paper Size**" to change the paper size.
  - Select **Letter** if you wish to print your work on **8.5" x 11"** printer paper.
  - Select **Custom Size**, then enter the dimensions if you want a custom size. Your document will print on the specified paper size when you print it.
- In a word processing document, hit **More Options**, then move the arrows around the body text box to change the margins. The margins on each side of the page are changeable. To save your changes, hit **Done**.

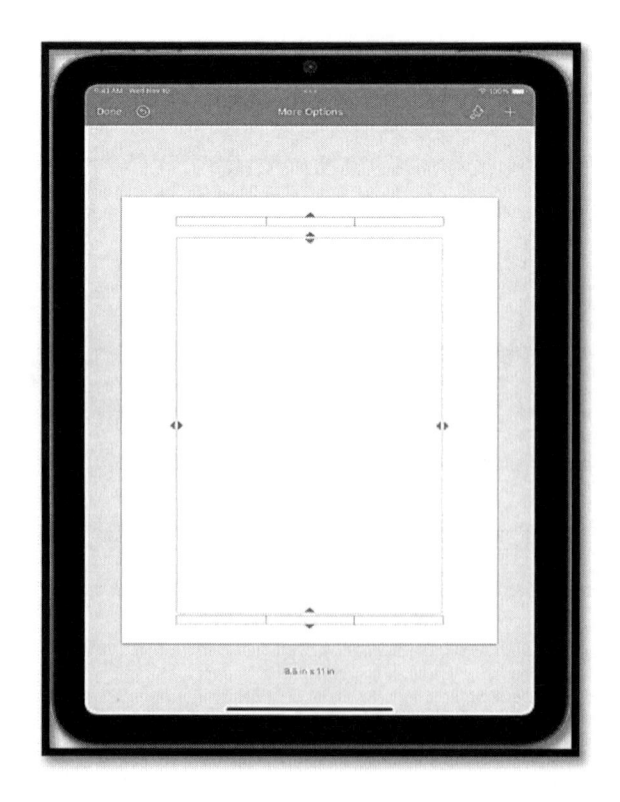

LIGATURES AND HYPHENATIONS

Ligatures

To change character spacing, employ ligatures, a decorative merging of two typographic characters to create a single character. If your font has ligatures, you can use them in your document.

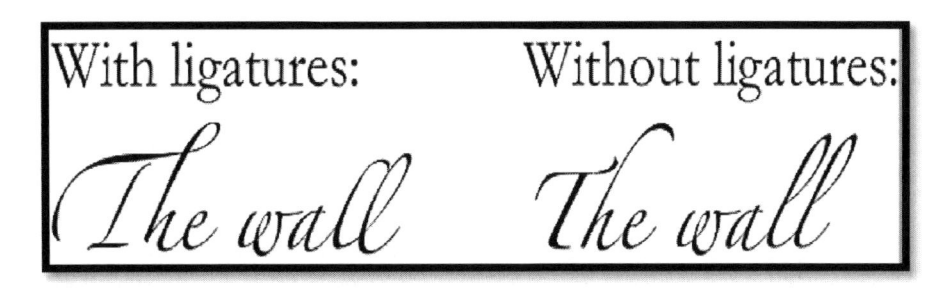

Turn ligatures on or off for selected text

- To change all the text in a text box, select it, then choose the text you wish to change.
    - **For a given text**: Only that text is affected by the character spacing.
    - **For a text box**: After you make the change, any text you write in the box will be subject to the character spacing.
- After selecting the **More Text Options** icon ... in the Font section, select the **Format** button.
- Select **Text** or **Cell** if you can't see the text controls.
- Then select **Ligatures**:
    - **Default**: Uses the font's default ligature settings, which might not include all of the ligatures the font can support.
    - **None**: Regular spacing is used; there are no ligatures in the font.
    - **All**: Uses every ligature that the font has to offer.

Hyphenations

Words that don't fit on a line of text are automatically moved to the next line by Pages. However, you can instruct Pages to hyphenate certain words as you type. This setting can be changed for the entire document or just certain paragraphs. Additionally, you can change the hyphenation of any existing content in your document, not just certain paragraphs.

Double hyphens (--) in your document can be automatically changed to dashes (—) by using smart dashes.

Change automatic hyphenation for a document

The entire document is subject to the hyphenation option, except for paragraphs where you specifically added or removed hyphens (see the next task). Only words that end in a line are affected by the option; hyphenated words you manually wrote are unaffected.

- In the toolbar, select the **Document radio** button.
- The **Hyphenation** checkbox can be selected or deselected.

Add or remove hyphens in specific paragraphs

Only words that end in a line are affected by this setting; self-typed hyphenated words are unaffected.

- To select one or more paragraphs, tap the paragraph.
- Select the **More** button in the top-right corner of the **Format** sidebar. Select the **Text** tab at the top of the sidebar, then tap the **More** button if the text is included in a text box, table, or other shapes.
- Click to select or deselect the "**Remove paragraph hyphenation**" checkbox located in the sidebar's **Hyphenation & Ligatures** section.

If you later change the hyphenation setting for the entire text to be different, the hyphenation for these paragraphs remains the same (see the previous task).

Turn smart dashes on or off

Current hyphens and dashes in your document are unaffected by turning on or off smart dashes; only newly typed text is affected.

- Select **Preferences > Pages** (from the Pages menu at the top of your screen).

- At the top of the preferences window, select **Auto-Correction**.
- "**Use smart quotes and dashes**" can be turned on or off under the Formatting option.

Convert existing double hyphens to dashes

If your document uses double hyphens rather than dashes, you may easily change them to dashes throughout the document or just in the text you want to change.

- Select the text if you want to format just a portion of it rather than the entire document.
- To view substitutions, select **Edit > Substitutions** (from the **Edit** menu at the top of your screen).
- Click the **Smart Dashes** checkbox in the **Substitutions** window.

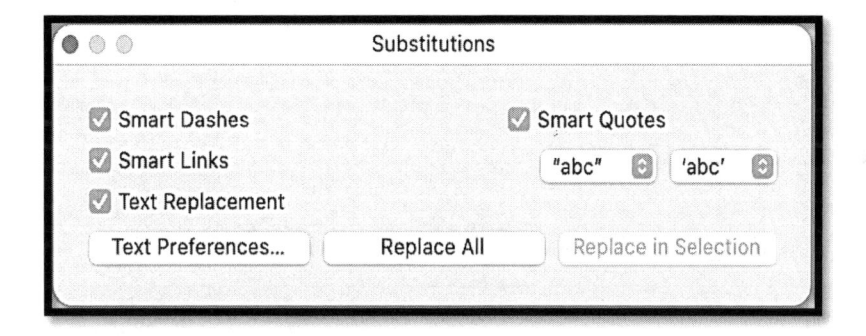

- **Do one of the following:**

- **Replace all dashes in the document**: Select **Replace All.**
- **Replace dashes in only selected text**: Select **Replace in Selection**.

PAGES NUMBERS AND HEADERS

You can easily open multipage documents with the Apple Pages app from iWork 2022. Documents in a variety of file formats are accessible. You may convert your documents into PDF, Plain Text, and Rich Text Format with the Pages app. A multipage document, however, might get quite daunting if you need to search for a specific word.

You might want to include page numbers when creating a new complicated document that is loaded with text to make navigation easier. You will learn how to add page numbers in the Apple Pages software on iPhone, iPad, and Mac in the following section.

Add Page Numbers in Pages App On iPhone and iPad

It's simple to add page numbers to a document in Apple Pages on an iPhone or iPad. Documents like assignments, contracts, and others might benefit from page numbers. That's useful if you only have an iPad or iPhone with you instead of your Mac.

Make sure the Pages app is running on your iPhone or iPad's most recent version before continuing. If you haven't updated the app in a while, you'll need to do so.

Take these actions. This phone is an iPhone but an iPad can also use these techniques.

- On your iPad or iPhone, launch the **Pages** app.

- Open the document you wish to add page numbers to or a blank one.
- At the top of the menu bar, hit the three dots.

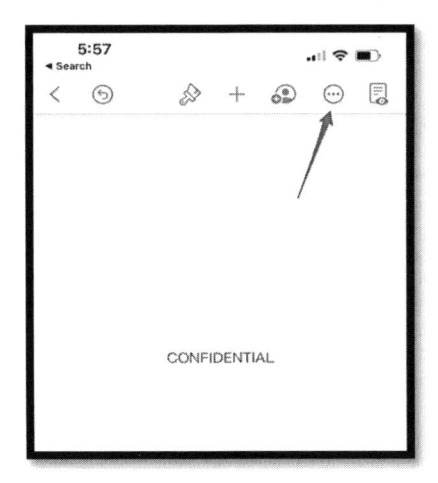

- Click **Document Setup** after scrolling down.

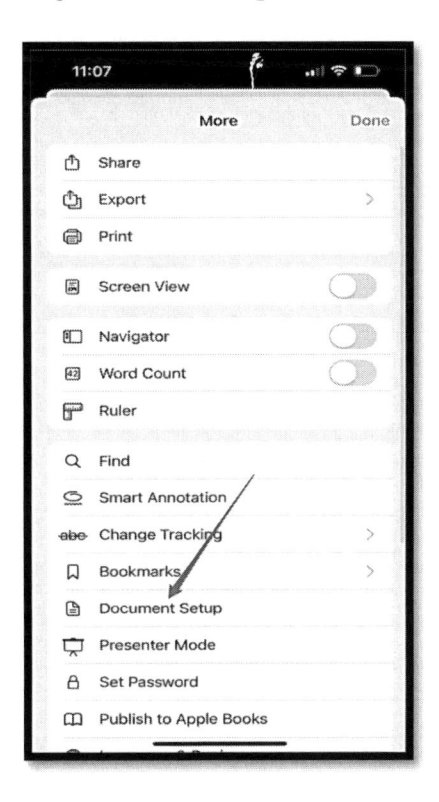

At the base of the page, you'll see the **Document Setup** tab.

27

- Scroll down in the **Document Setup** tab to see if the **Headers** and **Footers** options are selected.

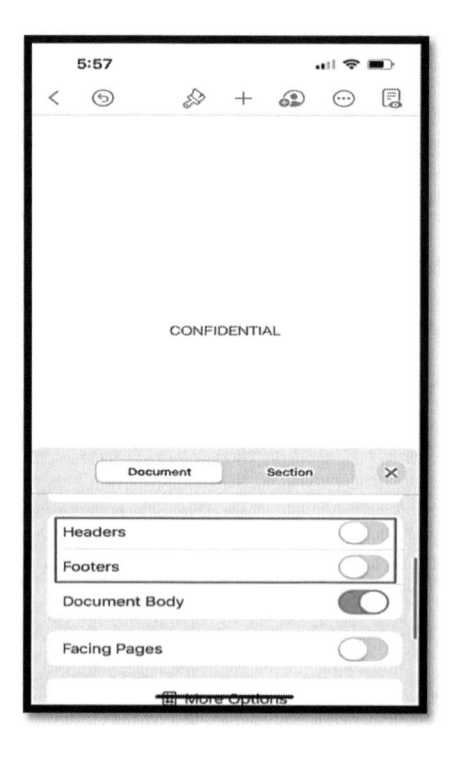

- Once more scroll down and select **More Options**.

On your screen, a new window will appear. The **header** and **footer** boxes are visible on your page.

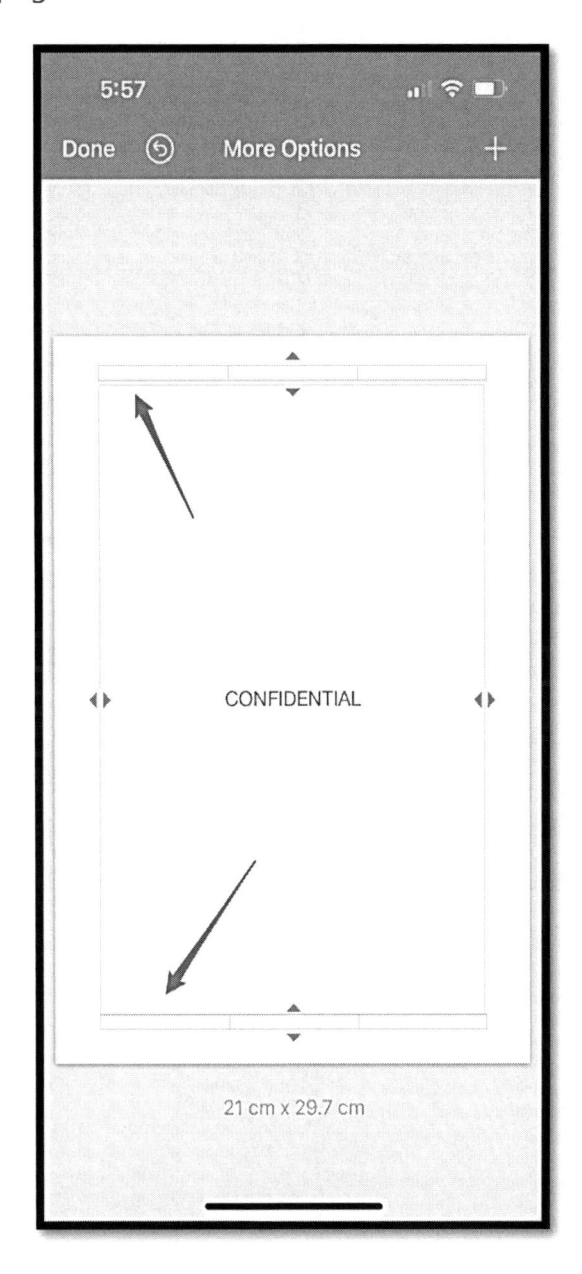

- Depending on where you want to put the page number, zoom in either the header or footer box.
- To see the cursor, click on the **header** or **footer**.
- Simply click **Page Numbers.**

- Choose the **Page Number** format you desire.

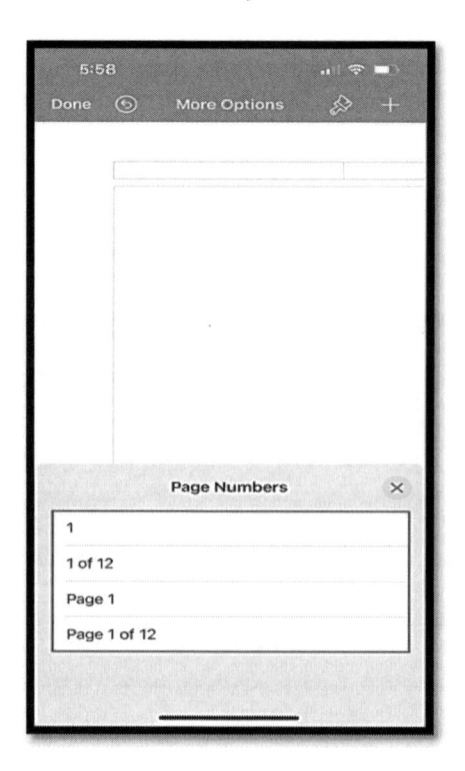

- Select the **brush** icon to access the **Style** menu after adding the number.

- You can increase the size of the page numbers by scrolling down.

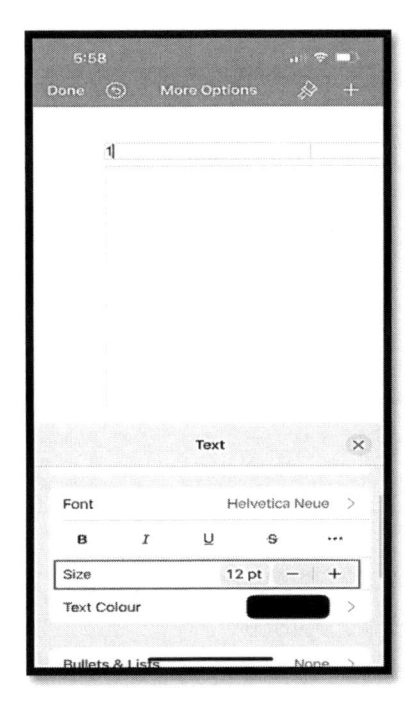

- Close the **Style** menu after making your changes by tapping **Done** in the top left corner.

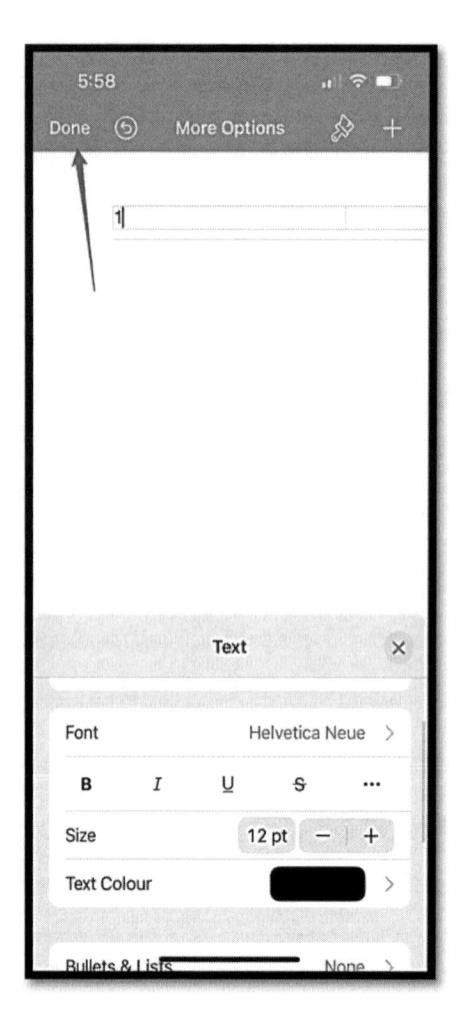

The page number will be shown at the bottom. When you add additional pages to the document, the Pages app will add them in ascending order.

Add Page Numbers in Pages App on Mac

As you create your documents in the Mac Pages software, let's now demonstrate how to add page numbers. You can use this option on your Mac to organize your documents while working with multi-page documents at your place of business.

Guidelines for adding page numbers to different types of official paperwork are sometimes created by businesses. In that scenario, this option will make it simple to add page numbers by your company's policies.

You must maintain the Pages app on your Mac updated, just like you do with your iPhone and iPad.

Take these actions.

- To open **Spotlight Search**, press **Command + Spacebar**, then type **Pages** and hit **Return**.

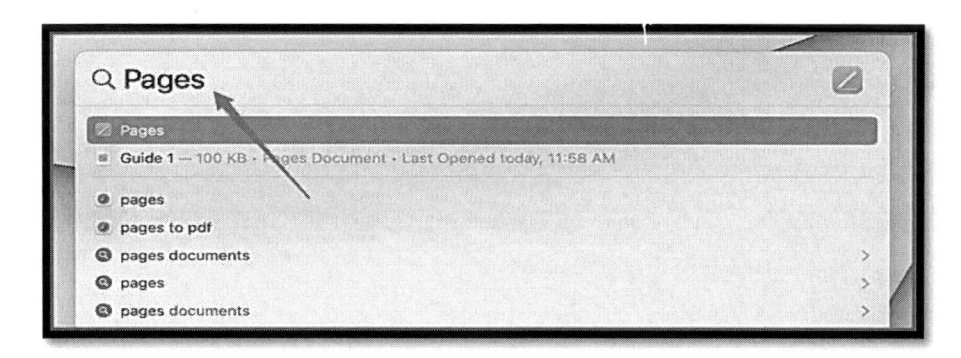

- Open the document you wish to add page numbers to or a blank one.
- When you see three headers or footer fields, move the mouse pointer to the top or bottom of the page.

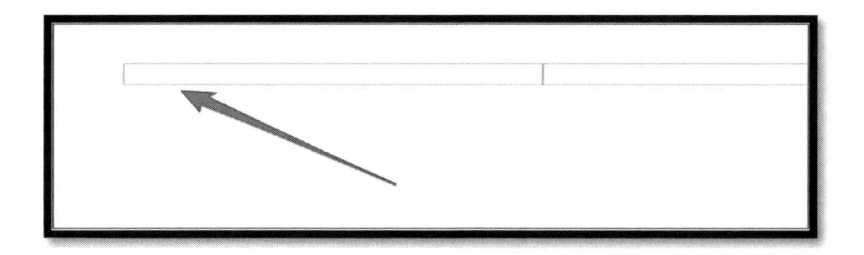

- Select the field and type the page number there.
- Tap on the **Insert Page Number** pop-up.

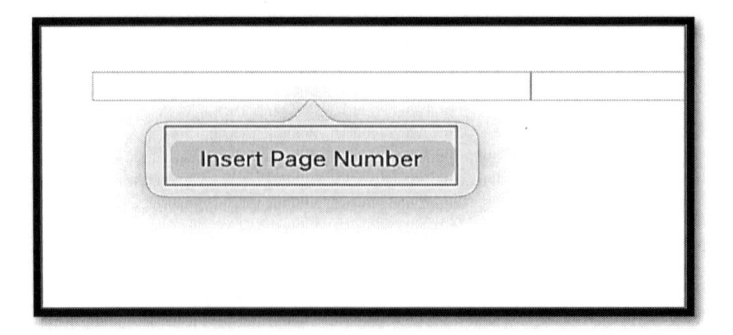

- Choose the **Page Number style** you like from the selection.

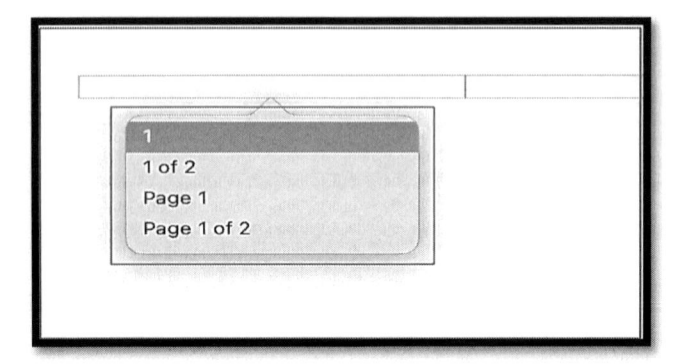

- When the page number appears, tap on Format in the top-right corner to select it.

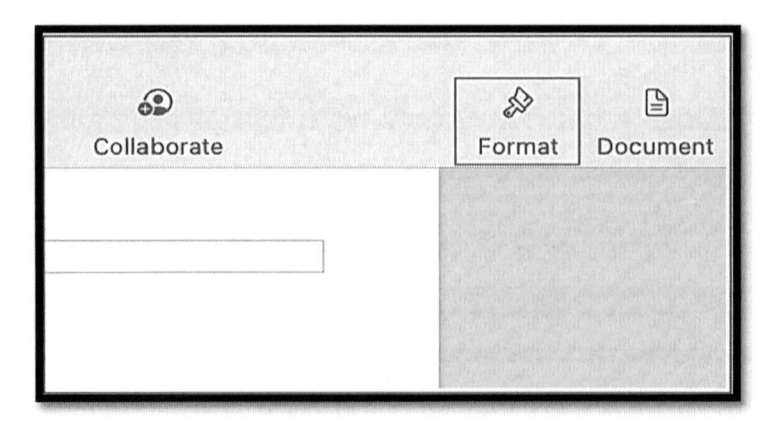

- The page number's font style and size can be changed to suit your preferences.

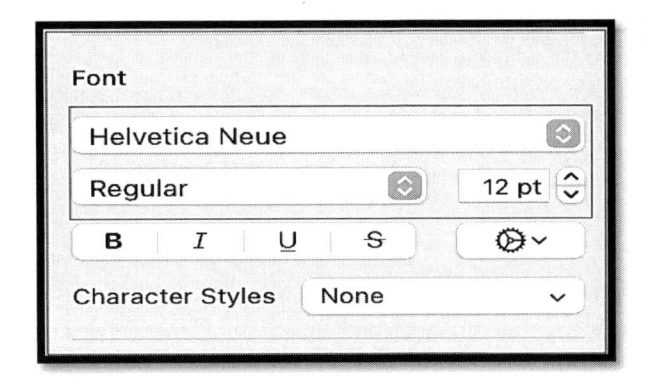

- Save changes by pressing **Command + S.**

Enable the header and footer in the Pages app as a bonus tip.

Here's how to enable the header and footer fields if you can't.

- Open your file, then select the **Document** tab in the top right corner.

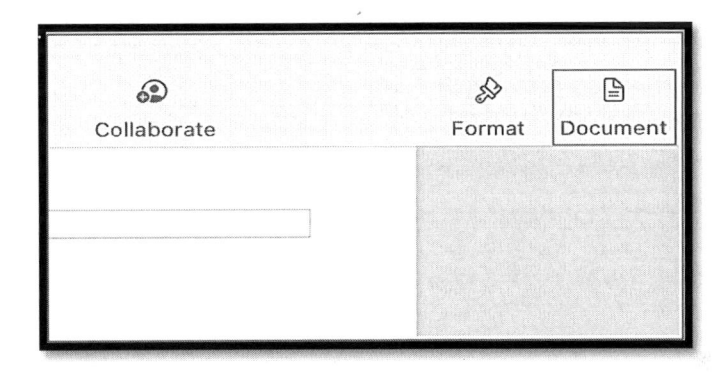

- To enable it on each page of your document file, select **Header,** and **Footer** under the **Document** tab.

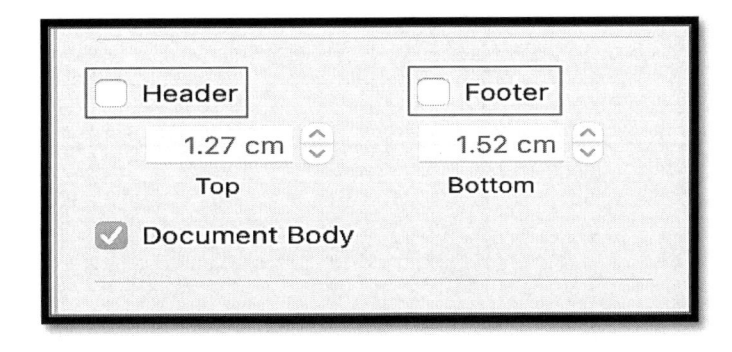

Conclusion

In the Pages app, organizing your documents by adding page numbers is simple. Your lengthy, multipage documents will be much easier to access and use with the help of this feature. When you send your coworkers documents with page numbers, they can easily navigate and discover the information you want them to understand or explain.

BOOKMARKS

One of the Internet URLs in your list of frequently visited sites is a bookmark: Simply said, a bookmark acts as a shortcut to the website.

How Can You Create Internal Links?

Double-click the word you want to be your destination, and then select **Insert > Bookmark** to create a bookmark.

Check the box labeled "Enable **as a hyperlink**" in the **Inspector** window's **Link** section after selecting the word or phrase you want to link to above. Choose to add the same bookmark you previously made to the destination. By clicking the **I** button on the toolbar, the **Inspector** window is accessible (if it isn't already open by default).

Here is an image of the inspector:

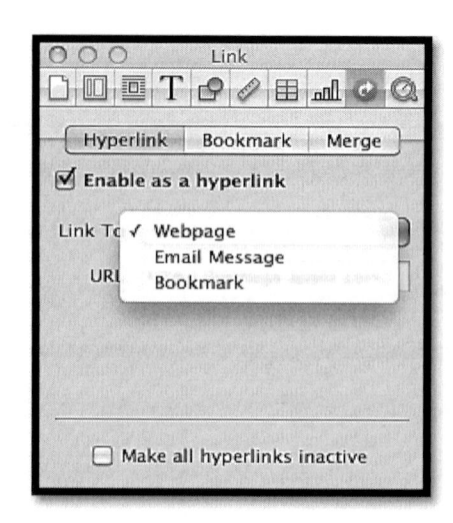

Simply highlight the word that you want to link and then use the inspector to configure the link's destination as a bookmark.

TABLE OF CONTENTS

Adding a table of contents as part of the body text of a page has long been possible in Pages for the Mac. The tables of contents that Pages for the Mac inserted into documents, while unquestionably beneficial for the potential readers of those documents, were not extremely effective navigation tools for their writers. Even so, the other versions of Pages were unable to create them.

These navigational aids are offered by the new Table of Contents view in the most recent versions of Pages. The Table of Contents view offers a quick way to navigate the document; simply click or tap an entry in the Table of Contents view to jump to it.

It appears in a sidebar (on the Mac) or a popover (on iOS and in the iCloud app) and automatically updates itself as you work on the document. As expected, populating a Table of Contents view is simple. There are further advantages to this new view.

Create A Navigable Table of Contents

Style-based tables of contents are available in Pages, and they list the paragraphs in your document that have particular paragraph styles assigned to them.

Which styles? You are responsible for deciding that. If your document has short headings, and you've used the same paragraph style for all of them, you can choose that heading style to be included in the Table of Contents view as short headings are typically what you want for table-of-contents entries.

The paragraph styles that your Table of Contents view looks for when gathering its entries can be selected using the **Select Styles** editor. In the Table of Contents views of all three Pages apps, there is an **Edit** button that, when pressed or tapped, brings up this editor.

The editor displays a list of every paragraph style used in the document along with a checkbox next to each style; when checked, the Table of Contents view displays the paragraphs that use that style. The indent and outdent controls linked to each style can be used to create a visual hierarchy among the entries in the Table of Contents view.

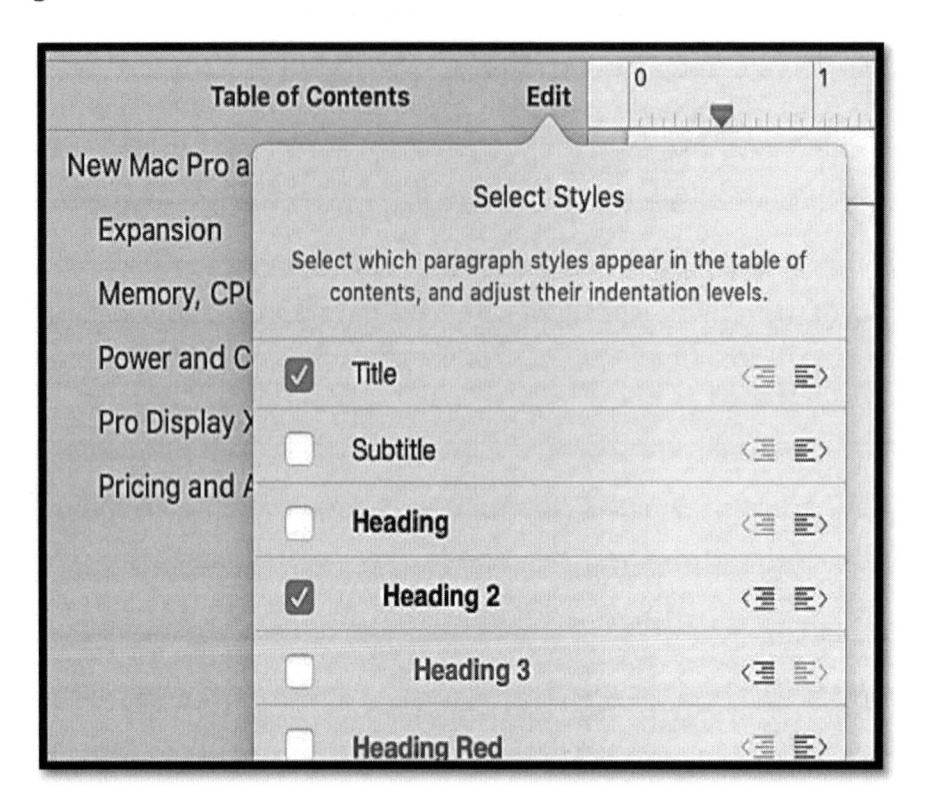

Four of the key paragraph styles found in Pages' default Blank template—**Heading, Heading 2, Heading 3,** and **Heading Red** have already been preselected for usage in the template's Table of Contents view. If you apply those styles to any document created using that template, a functional Table of Contents view will appear by default.

Pre-selected table-of-contents styles are also available in a large number of the other Pages templates. Note that as long as they are selected for inclusion, paragraphs utilizing those styles appear in the Table of Contents view regardless of how any of these styles are redefined or even given a new name.

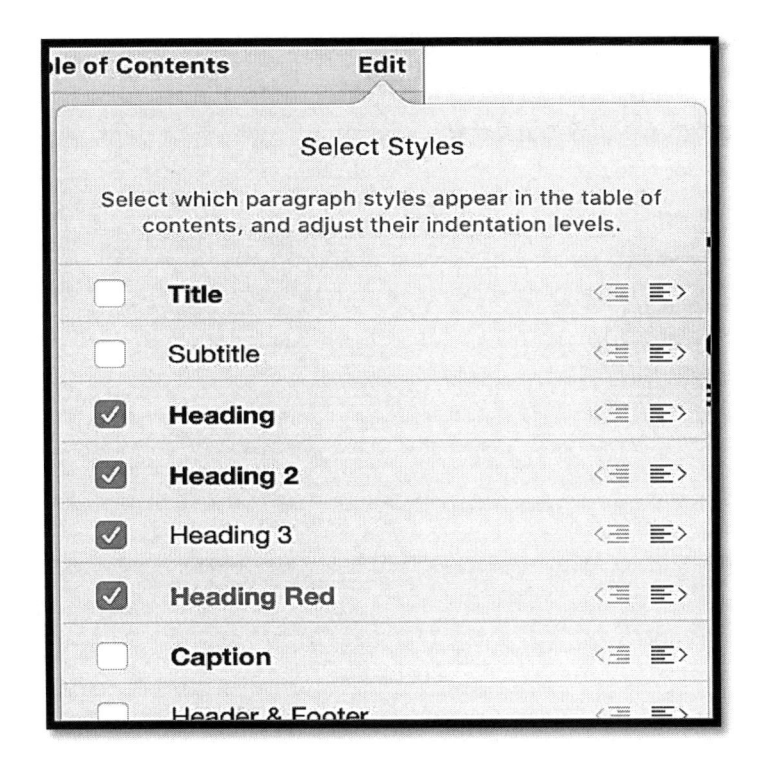

Add A Table of Contents in A Document's Text

You can still add a table of contents in the body text of a document even with the new Table of Contents view. Pages for iOS now allow you to do it, just as you can still do it on the Mac.

Placing your insertion point where you want the table of contents to be and then clicking or tapping the **Insert Table of Contents** icon at the bottom of the Table of Contents view in either the Mac or iOS versions, but not in the iCloud app, actually makes the process simpler.

When you do that, all of the entries in the document's Table of Contents view are already selected and prepared for formatting.

An added table of contents is sadly not very flexible in terms of formatting. For instance, you cannot choose specific words or characters inside a table of contents that have been added, but you may select all of the entries at each level. There are no character-level formatting changes; it is all paragraph formatting.

Both the Mac and iOS Format inspectors feature a Text tab that offers the following formatting options when you choose entries within an inserted table of contents:

- The typeface, color, style, and size can all be customized.
- The selected entries can be justified left, center, or right.
- The distance between lines and paragraphs can be changed.
- The page number on which each entry begins can be displayed or hidden.

On the Mac, you can also set leader lines and a tab stop that determines where the page numbers appear using the Format inspector.

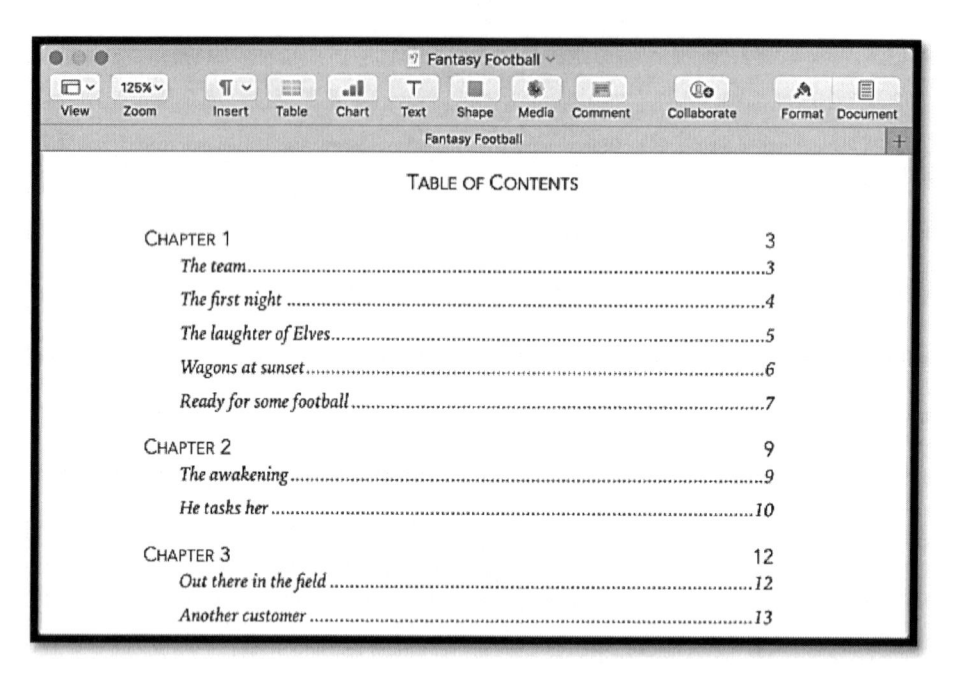

You can use a different table of contents for navigation than the one you place in the document since the entries in an inserted table of contents do not necessarily have to match those in the Table of Contents view.

On the Mac and iOS, you can choose a different set of paragraph styles to define the inserted table of contents elements by selecting the specified table of contents in the Format inspectors. Additionally, the table of contents can be divided, allowing, for instance, each portion of a document to have its table of contents.

Why The Table of Contents Feature?

The addition of the table-of-contents feature to Pages for iOS is just the latest development in Apple's long-term effort to bring its iOS iWork apps closer to functional parity with the Mac versions.

The reason Apple would want to do this is scarcely surprising given that the company has been marketing the iPad as a mobile productivity device without a keyboard since the release of the iPad Pro series. Increasing iWork's iPad compatibility promotes that goal.

However, there is a little bit more to tables of contents in Pages than that. The Apple Books store is part of Apple's Services business, which has recently received more of the company's attention and resources.

Apple recently added a new item to the File menu on Pages for Mac and the **More** (•••) menu on Pages for iOS: Publish to Apple Books. Pages have long been able to export documents as EPUBs, the common format provided by Apple Books.

Users of Pages can simply make eBooks with that command for sale or distribution through Apple Books. Even a new Novel eBook template is part of this week's most recent upgrade to Pages.

Where did those eBooks' tables of contents come from? With the help of the brand-new, simple-to-use, nearly automated (if you apply the proper styles) Table of Contents view.

A comprehensive and user-friendly eBook-authoring app could be useful if Apple wants to increase the selection of self-published books available in its bookstore. Both Mac and iOS devices should come with such an app.

Of course, it remains to be seen whether this addition to Pages pays off in this wider sense, but even if the majority of users never create an eBook with Pages, many will still find the new Table of Contents view to be a helpful addition. It exemplifies what Apple is capable of when it is at its best: offering robust features in a stylish, user-friendly form.

FOOTNOTES AND ENDNOTES

Endnotes and footnotes are two different types of notes that can be included in a document. Endnotes are found at the end of the document or in a section. Although endnotes and footnotes cannot coexist in the same text, you can change all of the notes from one kind to another.

You can adjust the layout such that endnotes and footnotes are not sequentially numbered throughout the text by default.

To format footnotes and endnotes, use the settings in the Footnotes tab of the sidebar.

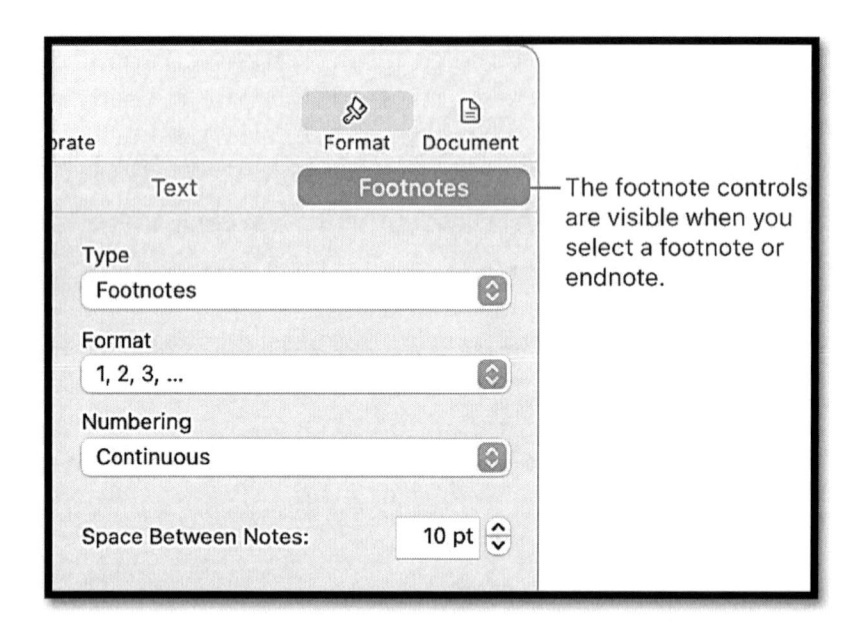

Inserting A Note

When you first insert a note, it is automatically a footnote. Endnotes must first be added as a footnote and then converted if you want to use them in place of footnotes.

A citation can only be added to the body text of a word processing document; text entered into a text box cannot.

- To add a footnote or endnote sign, click on the text where you want it to appear.

- Footnote can be selected by clicking the **Insert menu** icon on the toolbar. The insertion point shifts to the footnote text field at the bottom of the page as the symbol is added to the text.
- Add the footnote text now.

For a footnote to display in line with the text, you can optionally add objects (such as pictures and shapes).

Convert Notes from One Kind to Another

All notes in the document are changed when a note is converted from one kind to another since a document can only include one type of note.

- In your document, select any note. All of the notes in the document have blue boxes surrounding them.
- Select the **Footnotes** tab from the **Format** sidebar.
- Select a note type by clicking the **Type** pop-up menu.

The bottom of the page is where footnotes go. Endnotes appear on the document's final page. Endnotes for sections are moved to the final page of the section in which they are contained.

Change The Look of Note Text

You can change the text's appearance for just one note or every note in the document.

- **Choose one of these:**
    - **Change all notes**: Tap one note. All of the notes in the document have blue boxes surrounding them.
    - **Change one note**: Select only the text you want to edit in the note.
- Select the **Text** tab, then the **Style** icon, in the **Format** sidebar.
- To change the appearance of the text, use the controls in the **Font** section.

Change The Symbol for Notes

To show notes, you can use numbers or other symbols like asterisks (*) and daggers (†).

- In your document, select any note.
- All of the notes in the document have blue boxes surrounding them.
- Select the **Footnotes** tab from the **Format** sidebar.

Select a style from the Format pop-up menu by clicking it. There are new symbols throughout the document.

Change Numbering for Notes

By default, footnotes and endnotes are numbered consecutively throughout the whole document, but you may change this by starting the numbering (or the symbol sequence) at the top of each page or document section (after each section break).

- In your document, click any note.
- Select the **Footnotes** tab from the **Format** sidebar.
- Choose an option from the **Numbering** pop-up menu by clicking it.

Remove A Note

- Tap **Delete** on your keyboard after clicking on the text right after the symbol for the note you want to delete. The note is removed, and the symbols for every other note are changed to reflect their new locations in the progression.

Note: The insertion point can be placed next to a citation's citation number in the text by double-clicking the number in the citation. Alternatively, you can double-click a citation number in a citation to place the insertion point next to its citation number in the text.

ADD A COMMENT

Apple has updated the entirety of iWork in tandem with Mavericks, adding several new features and enabling us to view and edit all documents through iCloud.com. Additionally, you can collaborate on a document with others by sharing it with them.

This makes it beneficial if, for instance, you can leave a brief comment for other document participants on particular sections of text or pages.

To accomplish this, add comments to a document using the following procedures.

- Launch an **iWork** application.
- Here, opens the relevant document.
- Highlight a specific section of text (or cell in Numbers).
- Select the "**Comment**" option in the tab.
- Or go to **Menu Bar > Insert > Comment** thereafter.

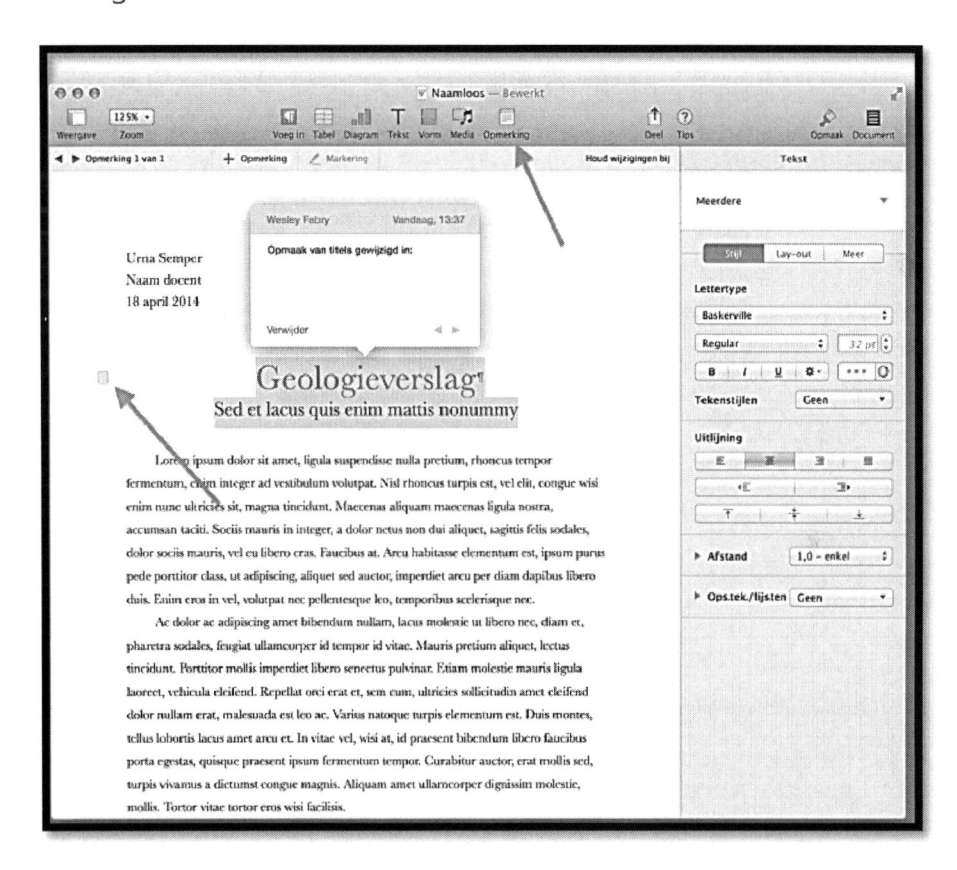

You can then leave a comment in the pop-up window that follows. By tapping on the **highlighted text** or the tiny **(yellow)** square on the left of the document, you can access the comments later (see photo).

45

The document can be quickly consulted, seen, and possibly updated by those who work on it. Each note has a connection to the person who made it, so you can tell right away who authored it. With the **Delete** button, you can remove it from the document.

MONITOR CHANGES

Only Pages offers this feature, which is incredibly useful when you need editing. You can see who made what changes to a document and when.

By selecting **Edit > Track Changes**, the feature can only be made available to the document owner. Once enabled, a toolbar with controls for switching between comments and changes, icons for accepting or rejecting changes, and an icon for pausing change tracking will appear above the document.

You can choose to view all changes, changes excluding deletions (which is usually the best setting), or the final version of the document using a pop-up menu on the right side of the screen. By selecting **View > Show Comments & Changes** pane, the left-sidebar with a list of all comments and changes will be displayed.

By tapping **Accept** or **Reject** in the **Comments & Changes** pane, anyone with edit access can accept or reject any specific change. You can also use the icons in the change tracking toolbar to navigate between changes, accepting or rejecting as you go. Use the commands on the pop-up menu to accept or reject all changes if you don't need to address each one separately. It goes without saying that while using an iWork app for Mac or iOS, you can only work on shared documents when you're online (if you try to edit while offline, the app will only let you edit a copy that is no longer shared).

However, you can continue working on any open iCloud.com documents while disconnected, although your changes won't be visible to others until you reconnect.

Select the **Collaborate** button in the toolbar, followed by **Stop Sharing** (below left), when you're done working together on a document. By doing this straight away, you stop other people from making more changes and you erase the file from their devices' iCloud Drive accounts (below right).

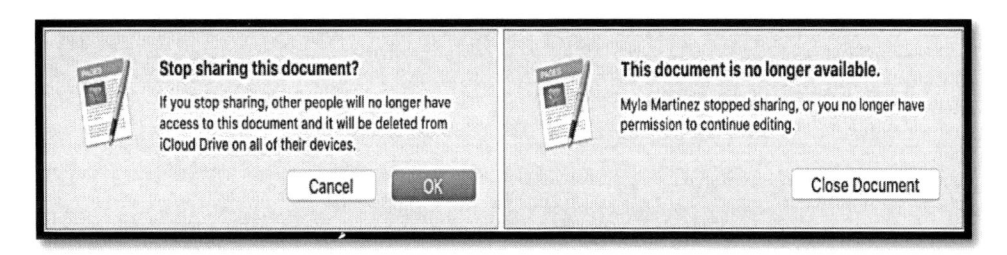

Conclusion

When you're working closely with others to create a presentation, come up with budget ideas, or craft a mission statement, simultaneous collaboration is fantastic. You'll want to be able to talk and listen at the same time in these circumstances.

It's vital that everyone is working on the same document and can see each other's changes and comments, but for other kinds of projects, it might be helpful to let individuals collaborate when it's appropriate for them. Try out the collaborative tools in Apple's iWork software if you frequently use them for word editing, spreadsheets, or presentations.

SHARING AND EXPORTING DOCUMENTS

The File Sharing feature in iTunes is typically the simplest way to transfer documents created with the iPad's iWork apps to a PC or Mac.

You must first export the document from the app before using the **File Sharing** option. The document is saved by the app in its silo, out of iTunes' reach, until you export it. When a document is exported, a copy of it is stored on the iPad in the **File Sharing** folder, where iTunes may access it.

On the iPad, adhere to these procedures to export a document:

- Launch the app from which the document was created, such as **Pages**.
- If a document is open when the app first starts, you can return to the **Document Manager** screen by tapping the **My Documents, My Spreadsheets,** or **My Presentations** buttons in the upper-left corner of the screen. This is the screen where the My Documents, My Spreadsheets, or My Presentations folders are displayed.
- Click the **Export** icon (the rectangular icon with the arrow pointing northeast) at the bottom of the screen to bring up the **Export** menu.
- The **Export Document, Export Spreadsheet,** or **Export Presentation** screens will appear when you click the **Export** icon.
- **Select the export file's format by clicking on it:**
    - **Native format**: To maintain the document's original format, tap the Pages, Numbers, or Keynote buttons.
    - **Office format**: Select the PowerPoint icon (from Keynote), the Word icon (from Pages), or the Excel button (from Numbers).
    - **PDF**: To create a Portable Document File (PDF) format that can be viewed on any computer (but not for editing), click on the **PDF** icon.

- The app then shows the **Document Manager** screen once again after exporting the file in the format you specified. You can use iTunes to copy the file to the PC or Mac after exporting the document to the **File Sharing** folder.

The steps are as follows:

- As usual, connect the iPad or iPhone to the PC.
- You must manually launch or activate iTunes if the computer doesn't do so for you.
- To view the iPad or iPhone's control screens, click the entry for those devices in the **Source** list.

- To see what's inside the Apps tab, click on it.
- To access the **File Sharing** section, scroll down.
- Click the app that contains the document in the Apps list.
- Select the document you want to transfer in the **Documents** box.
- To view the iTunes dialog box (on Windows) or the **Choose a Folder**: iTunes dialog box, select the **Save To** icon (on the Mac).
- Tap the **Select Folder** icon (on Windows) or the Choose icon after navigating to the folder where you wish to save the document (on the Mac). The document is saved by iTunes to the folder.

Using iCloud To Sync Documents

You can now transfer work files from your iOS device to your PC without physically connecting the two. Here's how to use iCloud to do it.

Apple developed the first application to use iCloud synchronization, with the iOS versions of iWork's Pages, Keynote, and Numbers apps leading the field. That's not unexpected, but we can anticipate other apps to quickly follow suit given that Apple has already made a software-development kit available to third-party programmers who want to include iCloud syncing in their products.

While we wait, take a look at this guide for syncing iWork with iCloud.

Syncing With iCloud

- By default, iCloud synchronization is not enabled. On your iOS 5 mobile devices, click "**settings**" and "**iCloud**," then scroll down to "**documents and data**" to turn it on. Select "**documents and data**," then click the **on/off** switch. To avoid exceeding the 3G contract limit, the default configuration is to only sync while connected through Wi-Fi.

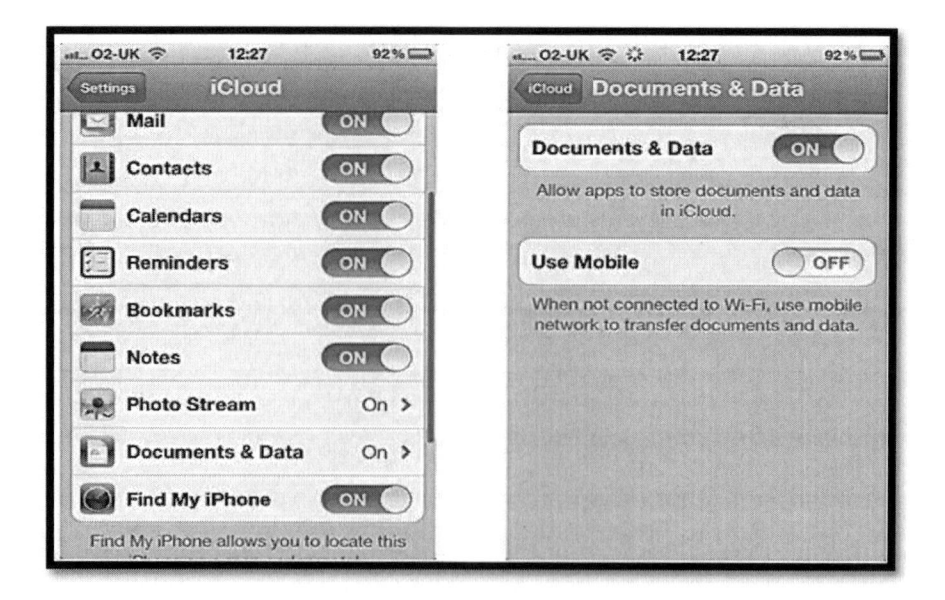

- Open **Pages**, then begin a new document. However, synchronization works with any **Pages document, Numbers spreadsheet,** or **Keynote presentation** created in the iOS apps or manually copied to your iCloud workspace.

In this example, we're using the common plain document type. Avoid specifying an iDisk as a storage option. Apple halted this in the summer of 2012, so it is beneficial to break the habit of using it now rather than waiting until it is gone.

- No manual syncing of your work with the server is required. While you're working, iOS is using your network connection to back up the file.

  If it isn't already configured to access your iWork workspace, sign into your iCloud account using a standard browser on your computer, tap the app icon, then choose "**iWork**" from the menu. As you create new documents on your iPhone or iPad, you'll notice that the files in this folder move around in the browser window.

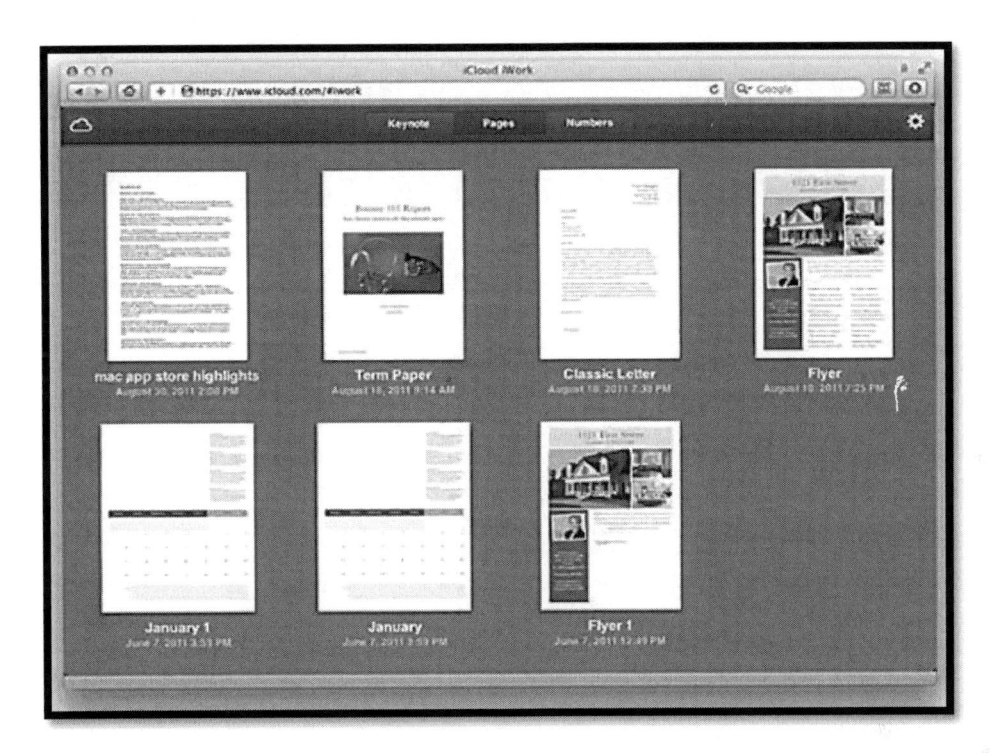

- Additionally, the best method for transferring work to your iOS device is through iCloud synchronization. Files made on your Mac or PC could only be transferred to your mobile device with iOS 4 and older versions of iWork by connecting it via USB and dragging them into the 'file sharing' section of the iTunes apps page.

  Hit the **cog** in the iCloud iWork interface, click "**upload document**," and then select the file from the menu to wirelessly upload documents to your iOS device. When your mobile device next connects to the server, the file will pop up on your iPad or iPhone as the upload is finished.

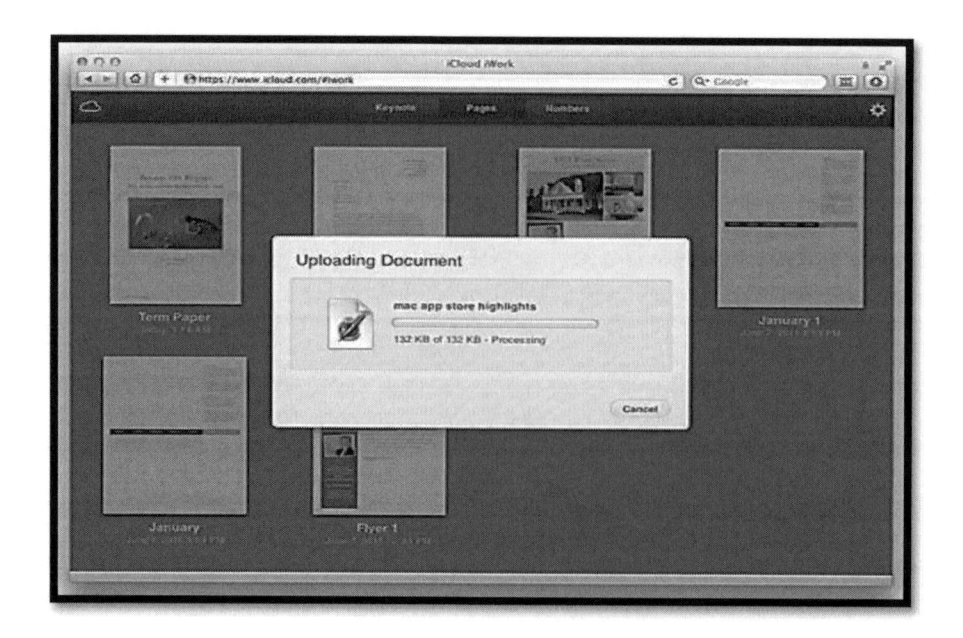

- If you don't want to use a wired sync with iTunes, you no longer need to email a file to yourself because this method works in both directions. The files can be accessed immediately through your computer's browser in Pages '11.1, PDF, or Word format because they are kept on Apple's servers. To get a copy in the format of your choice, tap the thumbnail and then "**download**."

- Without providing the recipient with your Apple ID credentials, you are unable to exchange files in the same way. The only way to share files from the cloud without doing this is using **iWork.com**. Despite being stable and adequate for daily usage, iWork.com, which was introduced in January 2009, is still in a public beta.

    Return to the file menus of **Pages, Numbers,** or **Keynote** and select "**edit**" to access iWork.com from an iOS device. After choosing the file to share, click the shortcut button. Click **iWork.com**, then sign in with your standard Apple ID. This will open a new email with a link to the file, where you can, if necessary, include a covering note.

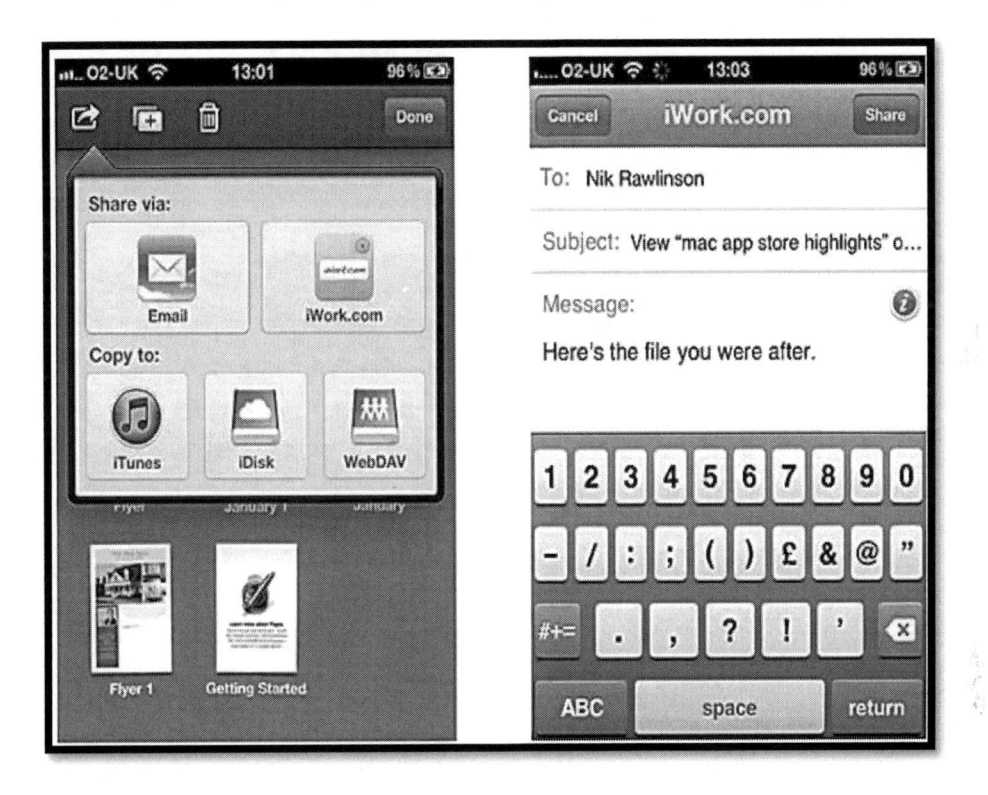

- An email from your address with a link to the file is sent to the person you've shared your paper with. It appears exactly like the original when opened in a browser, and although users cannot make changes, they can attach comments and notes that are shared with other viewers of the document, making this a useful platform for collaborative approval.

iCloud Capacity

Since iCloud is a free service, we are willing to overlook its 5GB storage cap. Thankfully, you can update this from your iOS smartphone. Then select "**settings**," "**iCloud**," "**storage and backup**," and "**buy more storage**."

You may purchase an additional 20GB for £28 each year, bringing your total to 25GB. Each additional 50GB costs £70 annually. Any card linked to your Apple ID will be charged for this.

Actively managing the files that are kept in your iCloud account is a less expensive choice. To discover which programs are using the most storage, hit "**settings**," "**iCloud**," "**storage and backup**," and "**manage storage**." Tap inside those applications to see the individual files.

By tapping "**edit**" and then using the red bars to the left of each document to access its delete button, you can get rid of the bulkiest documents. Use this tool with caution since it deletes selected files from all connected devices, including those that are not connected to your device.

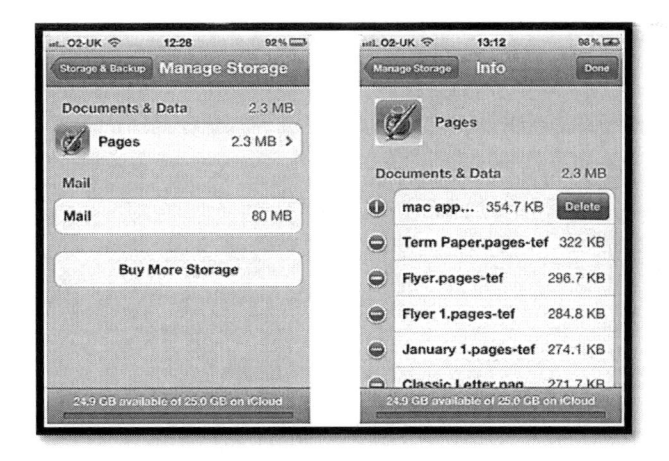

EMAILING A DOCUMENT

One of the most common questions we get about the Apple iWork software is: is it compatible with Microsoft Office and how easy is it to share iWork documents with other users? We're going to show you exactly how easy it is to share documents using iWork through email.

So here we have an example document in Pages which is the iWork word processor but this example would work whether you're in Keynote or Numbers. All you do is select **Send via Mail** from the **Share** menu and as you can see, we can send it in **Pages**, **Word,** or **PDF**. However, for this example, we're going to use **Word** so let's click on **Word**.

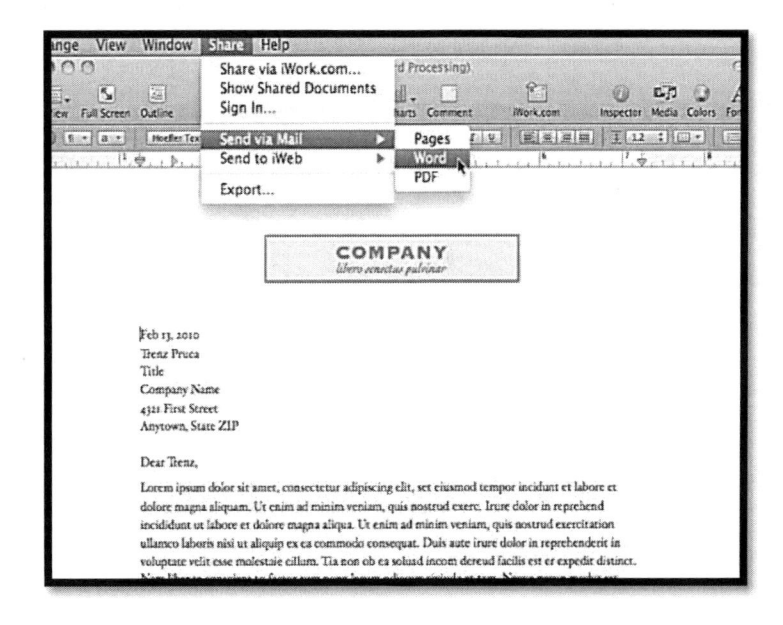

Now a new email message pop up. We can address it to **whomever**, give it a **Subject** line and it has the word document attached to it already. Just to prove it, let's click on it and open up the document.

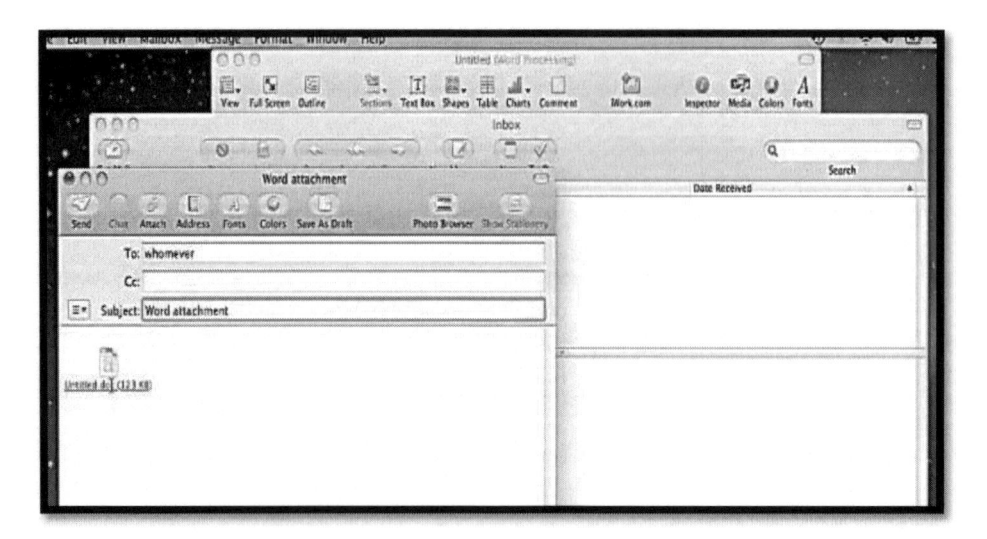

As you can see, it is opened in Microsoft Word and for comparison, we're going to show you the original Pages document. It looks virtually identical and it is that simple to share a document from iWork to a Microsoft Office user with just a few clicks.

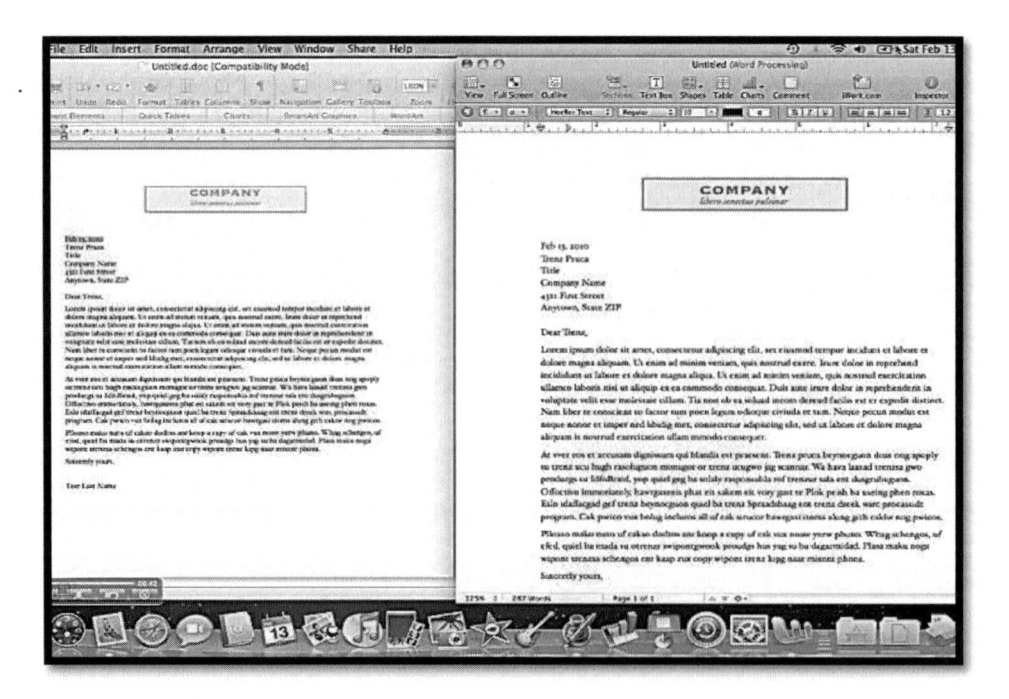

Nevertheless, you should know that sharing with Microsoft office isn't the best option a lot of times. Sometimes your best option is to share it as a **PDF**. The reason for this is if you want to make sure that your document looks exactly the way you intended it on any computer of any kind, PDF is the format for you.

As you can see here, we have created a PDF attachment and you can even see it in the email, there's the document. We're going to open it up in preview which is Apple's PDF viewer but anybody that has Adobe Reader can see it.

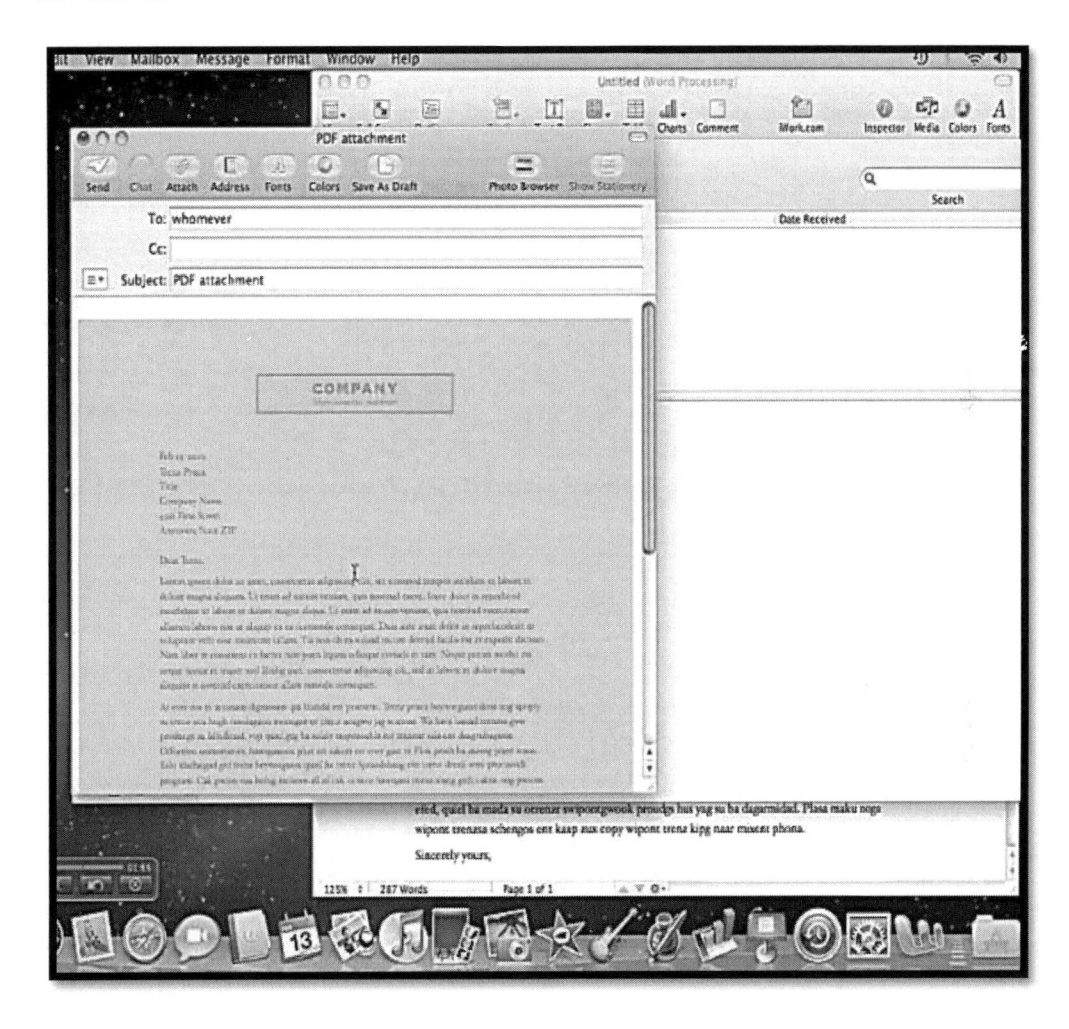

As you can see the document looks identical to the Pages document we had before.

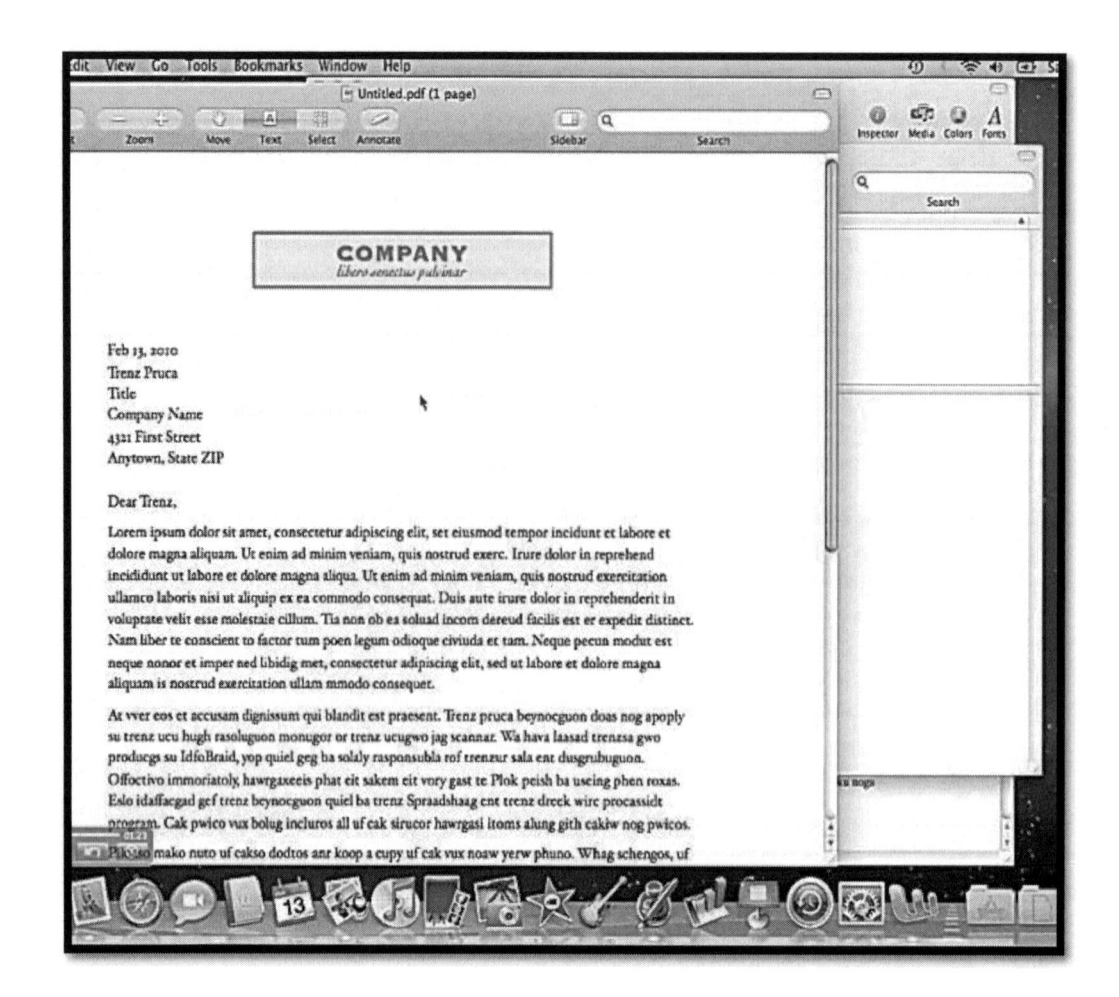

Conclusion

So anyway, whether you're sharing with Microsoft office or as a PDF, you can see it's extremely easy to share. All you do is click the **Share** menu > **Send via Mail** and choose your format.

COLLABORATING

If you're an Apple user, you probably utilize the iWork office suite for all your word processing, spreadsheet, and presentation needs, even though Microsoft Office is the preferred office set of tools for most people and teams to collaborate. In that scenario, it would be a good idea to learn how to interact with these apps so that you may brainstorm with your team or pals.

Here is a guide with directions on how to collaborate on Apple Pages, Numbers, and Keynotes on your Mac, iPhone, or iPad to assist you with the same.

Prerequisites

On the iPhone, iPad, and Mac, the entire iWork office suite, such as Pages, Numbers, and Keynote, is pre-installed. Ensure your iPhone, iPad, and Mac is all running macOS Big Sur or later, and that iOS 14 or later is installed on both your iPhone and iPad, respectively. Additionally, visit the App Store to ensure that the most recent version of these apps is installed.

Similar to this, you'll need the most recent versions of Google Chrome or Safari on your Mac if you want to collaborate using Apple Pages, Numbers, or Keynote online. You must use Chrome or Edge in their most recent version on Windows.

Invite Others to Collaborate on A File

You must first share the link to the document, spreadsheet, or presentation with the participants for them to work together on it. Follow the instructions in the subsequent sections, depending on whether you're using a Mac or an iPhone/iPad, to accomplish this.

How To Invite Others to Collaborate from Mac

As shown in the methods below, you can invite others to work on your Apple Pages, Apple Numbers, or Apple Keynote files on a Mac:

- Log in to your Mac's **iCloud** account.
- Click **Apple ID** under **System Preferences**.
- Check the boxes next to **Keynote, Pages,** and **Numbers** by tapping the **Options** button next to **iCloud Drive**. Click **Done**.
- Open the document you want to share in Pages, Numbers, or Keynote.
- In the toolbar, select the **Collaborate** icon.

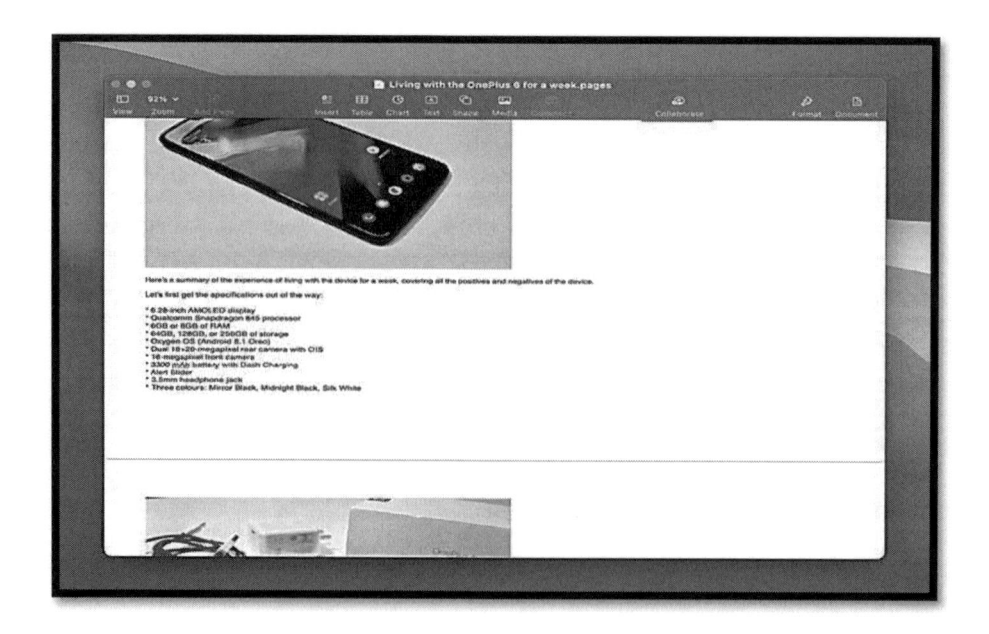

- To set access permissions for the file, select **People you invite** or **Anyone with the link** from the dropdown menu beside **Who can access** in the **Share File** dialog box.

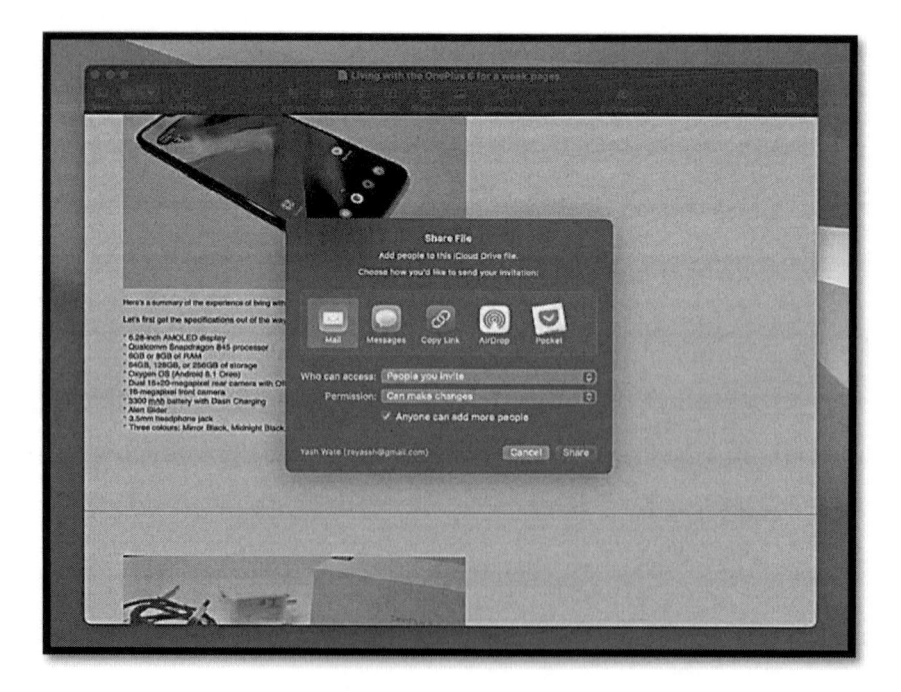

- For further control over what participants may do with the file, click the dropdown menu next to **Permissions** and choose between **Can make changes** and **view only.**

- Uncheck the **Anyone can add more people** box if you want to stop current participants from asking new individuals to collaborate on the file.
- Following your preferences, select the relevant app and press **Share**.
- On the next screen, add the participant, and then select **Send/Share** to send them the link.

Depending on the access permissions, the recipient(s) of a shared Pages, Numbers, or Keynote file must accept the invitation to join to view or edit it. The **Collaborate** icon with a checkmark shows at the top of the document when a participant joins.

Moving on, select **Add People** from the **Collaborate** button if you want to include more people. Set permission after that and choose an app to share the file link with. Finally, choose the recipient and send the link.

How To Invite Others to Collaborate From iPhone or iPad

Follow the instructions below to invite collaborators to your Apple Pages, Numbers, or Keynote document if you're using an iPhone or iPad:

- Click on your name at the top after selecting **Settings**.
- Toggle the switches for **Pages, Numbers**, and **Keynote** after choosing **iCloud**.
- Launch the Keynote, Pages, or Numbers app on your iPhone or iPad.
- Open the document you wish to work on together.
- After selecting **EDIT**, press the **Collaborate** icon.
- To broaden the sharing options for the file, click **Share Options** on the prompt to share the file.

- To set access rights for your file, select either Only people you invite or Anyone with the link under **WHO CAN ACCESS**.

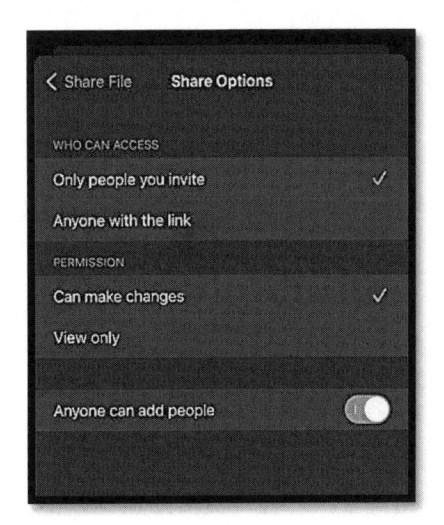

- Select between **Can make changes** and **view only** for **PERMISSION** according to your needs.
- To stop existing participants from adding more individuals for collaboration, toggle the **Anyone can add people** option off.
- To return to the **Share File** prompt, click the **Share File** button in the top-left corner.
- To share the file link, select an app.

- Select the contact/recipient you wish to share the file with on the following screen, then click **Send/Share** to send it.

Click the **Collaborate** icon, then select **Add People** to include more people in the project. On the following page, choose an app to share the link with and set the share options. Send the link to the collaborator you want to add to the file after choosing the contact.

How To Invite Others to Collaborate From iCloud

On a Windows or Linux computer, you can share the invite link for the file via iCloud using the web browser. The steps are as follows:

- On a Windows computer, use **Chrome** or **Edge** to access iCloud. You can use Safari if you're on a Mac.
- Enter your iCloud login information.
- Open the file you wish to share by tapping on the appropriate iWork app (Pages, Numbers, or Keynote).
- In the toolbar, select the **Collaborate** icon.
- Set restrictions and access permissions on the file.
- Click **Share** after selecting an app to share the file link with.
- To send the file link, select the recipient and press **Send/Share**.

Participants can immediately begin contributing by joining the Pages, Numbers, or Keynote file on any of their devices through the collaboration link.

Change Share Options

If you ever decide to change the Share Options settings, you can do it on your Mac or iPhone/iPad as shown in the following sections.

How To Change Share Options on Mac

- **Share Options** can be accessed by clicking the **Collaborate** icon.
- To change the settings for **Access and Permission**, click the dropdown icons next to those options.

How To Change Share Options On iPhone or iPad

- Simply press the **Collaborate** icon.
- The **WHO CAN ACCESS**, **PERMISSION**, and **ADDING PEOPLE** settings can be changed on the following screen by selecting **Share Options** on the **Collaboration** page.

Remove A Collaborator from The File

You can remove a participant from an Apple Pages, Numbers, or Keynote file by following the instructions in the subsequent sections if you no longer want them to collaborate with the document.

How To Remove a Collaborate on Mac

- In the toolbar, select the **Collaborate** icon.
- Select **Remove Access** by clicking the **three-dot** icon beside the individual you want to remove, then click **Continue**.

How To Remove a Collaborate On iPhone or iPad

- On your iPhone or iPad, launch the app that contains the document you are working on with other people.
- On the top, click the **Collaborate** icon.
- Click on the participant you want to take out of real-time collaboration on the **Collaboration** screen.
- To remove the user from the file, select **Remove Access** on the following screen.

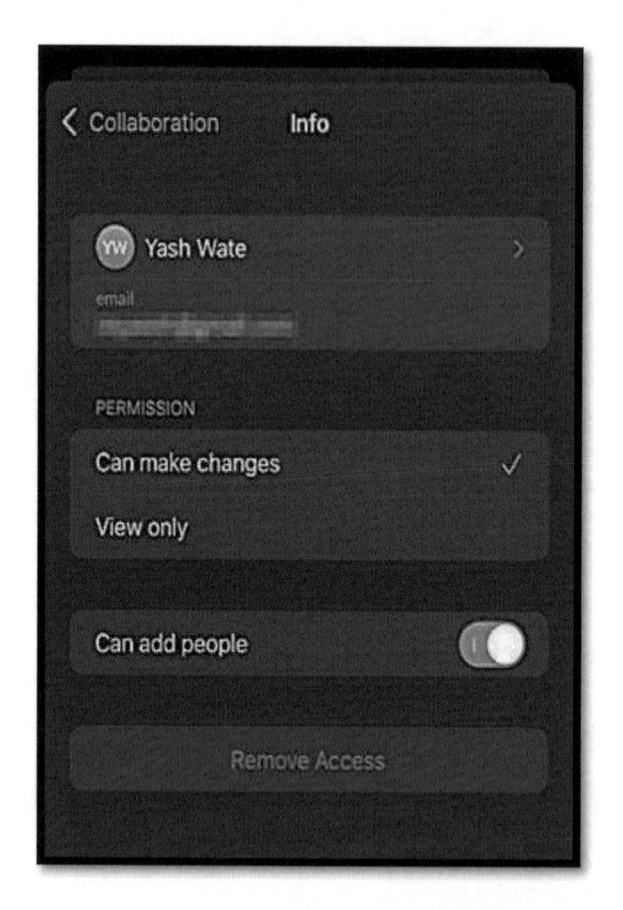

Stop Sharing a Pages, Numbers, Or Keynote File

It's advisable to stop sharing an Apple Pages, Numbers, or Keynote document with others once you've completed working on it or if you no longer want other collaborators to make changes to it. To accomplish this, adhere to the instructions in the subsequent sections according to the device you're using.

How To Stop Sharing a Pages, Numbers, Or Keynote File on Mac

- On your Mac, launch the application and the file you want to stop sharing.
- In the toolbar, click the **Collaborate** icon.
- To see more options, select **Share Options**.
- Press **OK** after clicking the **Stop Sharing** button.

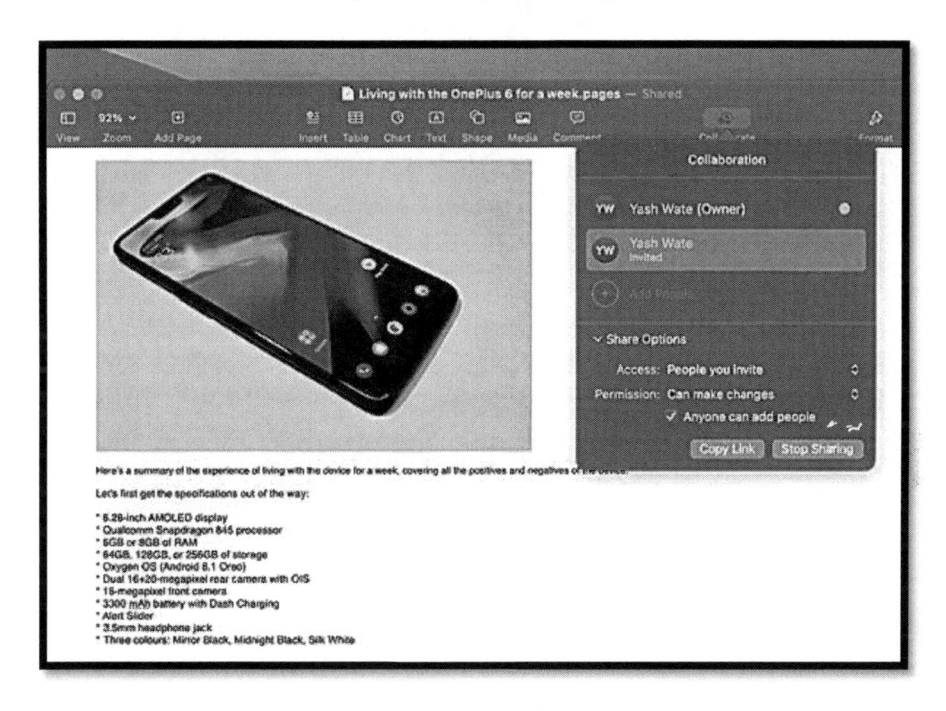

How To Stop Sharing Pages, Numbers, Or Keynote File On iPhone or iPad

- On your iPhone or iPad, launch the app containing the file you want to stop sharing.
- Select the "**Collaborate**" icon.
- Click the **Stop Sharing** button on the **Collaboration** screen, then press **OK** to confirm.

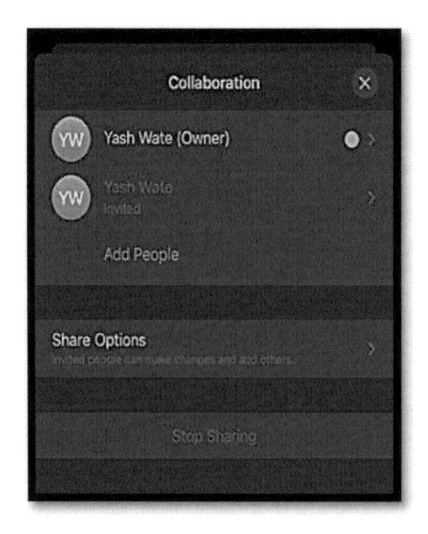

Set A Password for The File to Prevent Unauthorized Access

You might want to password-protect an Apple Pages, Numbers, or Keynote file that contains private information or data if you want to keep others from accessing it. To access the file and make changes, you and the other person(s) working on it must input the password for it.

The steps to do it on a Mac and an iPhone/iPad are listed below.

How To Set a File Password on Mac

- On your Mac, launch the application and the file you want to password-protect.
- Hit **File**, then choose **Set Password**.

- On the next box, enter a password, then click **Set Password**.

How To Set a File Password On iPhone or iPad

- On your iPhone or iPad, launch the app and the file you wish to password-protect.
- Set **Password** can be found by selecting the **More** option at the top.

- On the following screen, give the file a password, then click **Done**.
- After setting the file password, enable the **FaceID/TouchID** option if you choose to use it.

See Which Participants Are Working on A File

Follow the instructions below to find out who has joined the file and is collaborating. For the Mac, iPhone, and iPad, these procedures are common.

- Press the **Collaborate** icon after opening the file.
- A participant is currently editing the file if there is a dot next to their name. An indicator (of the same color as the dot) will display when you click on the dot next to someone's name, highlighting where they are in the document.

iWork Collaboration Simplified With iCloud

On your Mac, iPhone, or iPad, iCloud makes it simple to collaborate with coworkers, teammates, and friends on Apple Pages, Numbers, and Keynote files. If you attentively followed this lesson, you ought to be able to share links to iWork files with others and work together on those files in real-time.

Additionally, you can update a shared document while online. When you go offline and edit a document, the changes you make are automatically stored for at least 30 days and transferred to iCloud.

Keep in mind, though, that some Pages, Numbers, and Keynote features aren't supported by collaboration, so you won't be able to utilize them while working on a project with other participants.

FAQs

Can you collaborate on Apple Numbers?

Yes, just like with Apple Pages documents and Keynote presentations, you can work together on a spreadsheet in Apple Numbers.

How do you collaborate on a Numbers file?

You must first allow collaboration on a Numbers file before sharing its link with other people to begin working together on it. Once the participants have joined the collaboration, you can work in real time with them. The procedures for carrying out these actions have already been described in this lesson.

How can I collaborate on Keynote on iPad?

The same steps must be followed while working together on an iPad or iPhone. To do this, select the **Collaborate** icon on a Keynote presentation, choose the **access and edit permission**, and then send the link to other participants.

After they join the presentation, you can work together on the same presentation with them. To find out how to do this, adhere to the instructions in the preceding lesson.

PAGES DOCUMENT EXPORT

Your word processing files or page layouts are automatically saved in Apple iWork Pages' proprietary format. You can convert a Pages document to a PDF file, which can be opened on other operating systems and productivity applications if you need to make it available on your company's website or share it with a client or customer who doesn't have iWork.

iWork Pages includes many quality levels, security features, and the ability to export files to PDF.

- Open iWork **Pages** and the document. Hit "**Export**" from the "**Share**" menu.
- Select "**Good**," "**Better**," or "**Best**" from the drop-down list under the "**Image Quality**" heading on the "**PDF**" tab. Tap "**Security Options**" to enable PDF password protection.
  You have the option of requesting a password to open, print, and copy the document's content. Based on the options you selected, enter a password to open the document and a different password to print or copy it.
- To proceed, hit "**Next**." When prompted, choose a name and place to store the PDF. To complete the conversion of the document, select "**Export**."

CREATING NEW DOCUMENT

The iPad's Pages, Numbers, and Keynote iWork apps all share a similar interface. Major features are accessible in the same way across all of iWork's applications, which is one of its best aspects. When using iWork, there is just one app that you need to comprehend.

For each of the iWork apps, you start a new document in the same way:

- To open the iWork app, simply tap one of the icons. The screens for documents emerge. **My Documents** in the **Pages** app, **My**

Spreadsheets in **Numbers**, and **My Presentations** in **Keynote** are all listed on this screen.

It's important to keep in mind that each of the iWork apps comes with a single document that contains all of the necessary help information.

You are not on the documents screen if **My Documents** appears on the button in the top-left corner. When you click **My Documents** (or **My Spreadsheets** or **My Presentations**), you will be taken to the screen for handling individual documents.

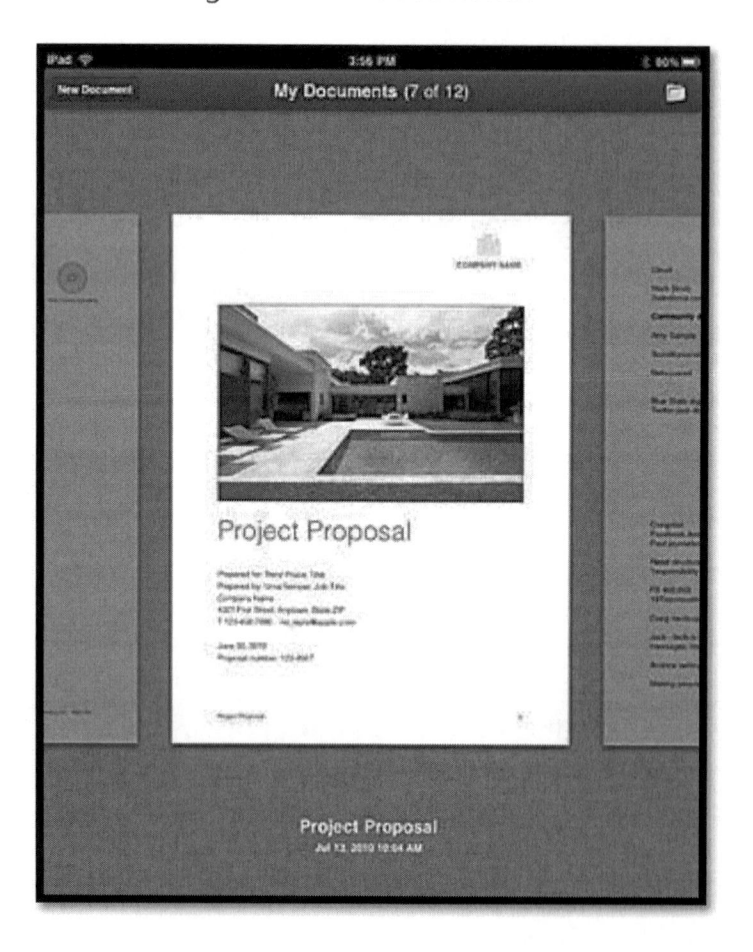

- Click the **New Document (Pages), New Spreadsheet (Numbers),** or **New Presentation (Keynote)** icon in the top-left corner of the **My Documents** screen, based on which app you're using. It then displays the **Choose a Template** screen.

- To begin working on a brand-new document, select **Blank** or the template you want to use as a starting point. You can go back to the documents screen by selecting the **Cancel** button (which takes the place of the **new** button) if you change your mind.
- The screen displays your brand-new document.

DOCUMENT SAVING AND RENAMING

As you work, Pages will automatically save your document to a default folder and label it **Untitled 1**. Your document can be edited, given a new name, and saved in a different location.

Export the document in the desired format (such as a Microsoft Word document if you want a copy in another format).

Save A Document with A New Name or Location

- Holding down the **Option** key, select **File > Save As** (from the **File** menu at the top of your computer screen).
- In the **Save As** dialog, type a name.
- Type one or more **tags** here (optional).
- Select the location where you wish to save the document by clicking the **Where** pop-up option.
- You have the option of saving it to iCloud, a server, or a folder on your Mac. Click the **arrow** beside the **Save As** dialog to view more locations.
  Note: From the **Save As** dialog, you can create a new folder. Choose the location for the new folder, then tap **New Folder** at the dialog box's bottom. Click **Create** after giving the folder a name. Your document will be saved to the newly chosen folder.
- Press **Save**.

The document is saved on a server, not on your Mac when you save it to iCloud. If you've enabled iCloud, it shows up automatically on your iPad, iPhone, or iPod touch and updates whenever you make changes on any computer or device logged into your iCloud account. On your Mac, there is no iCloud folder.

Rename A Document

- In the **Pages** pane, click the document's name and then type a new name.

Revert A Document to An Earlier Version

You may explore previous versions, restore a document to a previous version, and make duplicate versions since Pages continuously saves your work on your computer.

- One of the following options will appear after selecting **File > Revert to** from the **File** menu at the top of your computer screen:

- o **Last Saved**: Since the document was last saved, all of your changes have been deleted.
- o **Last Opened**: When you last opened the document, all of your changes were deleted.
- o **Browse All Versions**: The document's timeline appears, with tick marks on the right indicating each time it was opened, saved, duplicated, locked, renamed, or reverted.
- To browse versions if you choose **Browse All Versions**, hit the timeline's tick marks.
- **Choose one of the following actions when you locate the desired version:**
  - o **Restore your document to this version**: Tap **Restore**.
  - o **Duplicate this version in a new document**: Hit **Restore a Copy** while holding down the **Option** key.

Click **Done** if you want to return to your document in its present state without making any changes.

OPENING EXISTING FILES

Documents created in any version of iWork can be opened in the most recent iWork for Mac apps.

Double-click the document or open it directly from the app to open an earlier iWork document in Pages, Numbers, or Keynote:

- Select **File > Open**.
- Select the document.
- Tap **Open**.

If You See a Warnings Window

You could notice a Warnings popup when you open an older iWork document. The features in your document that are supported in an older version of the app but not in a more recent version of iWork for Mac are listed in this window.

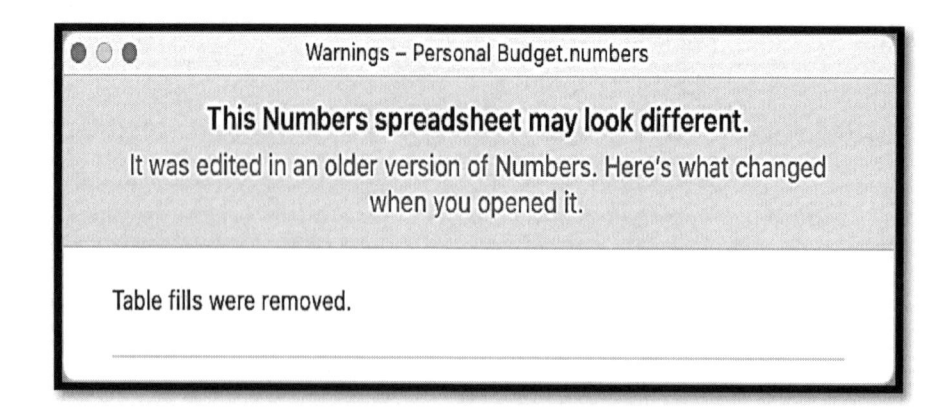

Save An Older iWork Document

You must specify how you want iWork to handle the upgraded document the first time you save or edit an older iWork document:

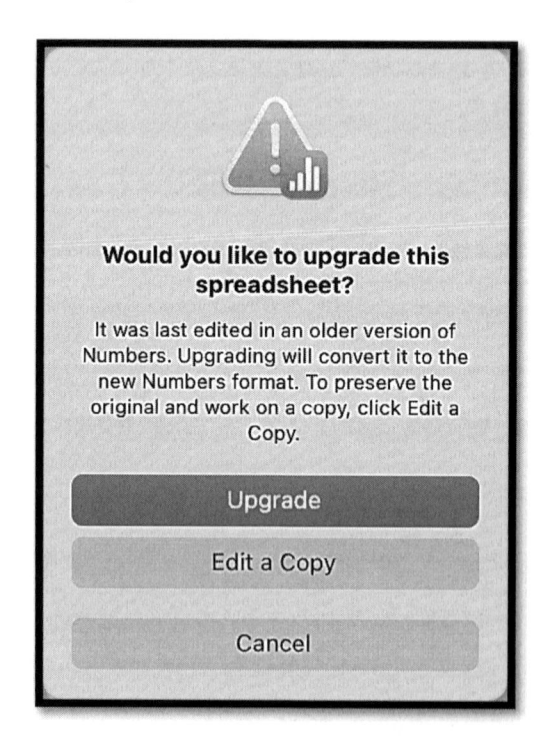

- To change the current document to the new format, select **Upgrade**.
- To stop saving or editing and keep your original document untouched, select **Cancel**.
- To convert a copy of the document to the new format while keeping the original in the more traditional iWork format, select "**Edit a Copy**."

PASSWORD AND DOCUMENT LOCKIN

The work you do in Apple Pages should remain private until you decide to share it because it is your writing. This opinion appears to be shared by Apple.

The business adds a feature in its word-processing program for iOS that allows you to lock documents behind a password, as well as with Face ID or Touch ID, as another indication of its commitment to user privacy and security.

Although biometrics make it simple to access locked Word documents, if they malfunction, iOS will force you to input your selected password. You should therefore keep your password in mind because you might not need to input it for several months.

Even worse, unless collaboration is enabled, there is no way to restore the document without that password. The password can then be available to the other users. Before beginning the actions below, bear this in mind.

Locking Your Pages Document

It's simple to lock a document with a password, and doing so encrypts it with 128-bit AES encryption. Please note that entering a password only applies to the current document and any subsequent versions; earlier versions are unaffected.

Open the file first, then click the ellipsis (•••) in the upper right corner. Following that, select "**Set Password**" and complete the selections on the subsequent page. To prevent collaborators from accessing an earlier version of the document, you should first stop sharing the file before sharing it again.

You can also set a password when sharing a document for collaboration via a link that anyone can access. You must first enter a password and then verify it. Numbers, uppercase and lowercase letters, and other characters from the keyboard can all be used as passwords.

If you truly want to protect your document from hackers, choose a strong password or have a password manager like **LastPass** create one for you. Perhaps, Apple will eventually integrate its iCloud Keychain into iWork to make creating strong passwords automatically easier.

If you want, you can also give yourself a hint. However, since each Pages document requires its password, we advise keeping the password in a password manager like **LastPass, 1Password, Dashlane,** or **Keeper**. Ensure the "**Face ID**" or "**Touch ID**" toggle is orange if you wish to use **Face ID** or **Touch ID** to unlock your **.pages** file.

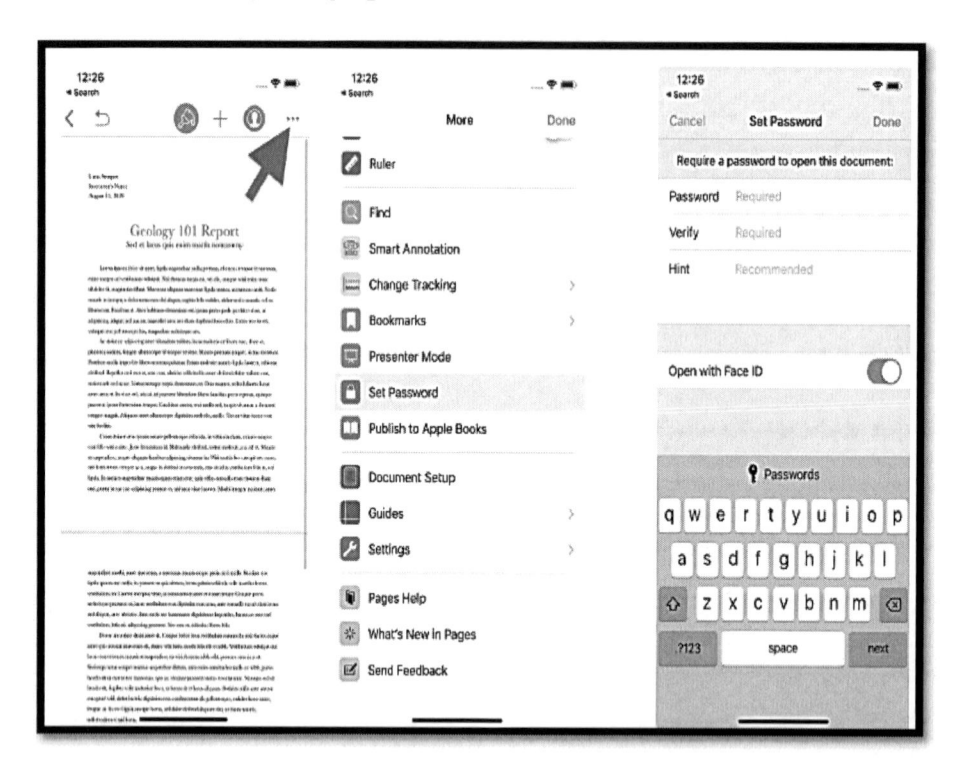

Click "**Done**" when finished filling out all the fields to get back to editing the document. You must have the same passwords to proceed.

Opening A Locked Pages Document

You may see that your file's thumbnail now has a lock on it when you return to the document browser (or the **Files** app). To open it, tap. If you enabled Face ID or Touch ID, Pages won't be able to authenticate until you permit them to do so. You shouldn't have to do that again if you've already done it.

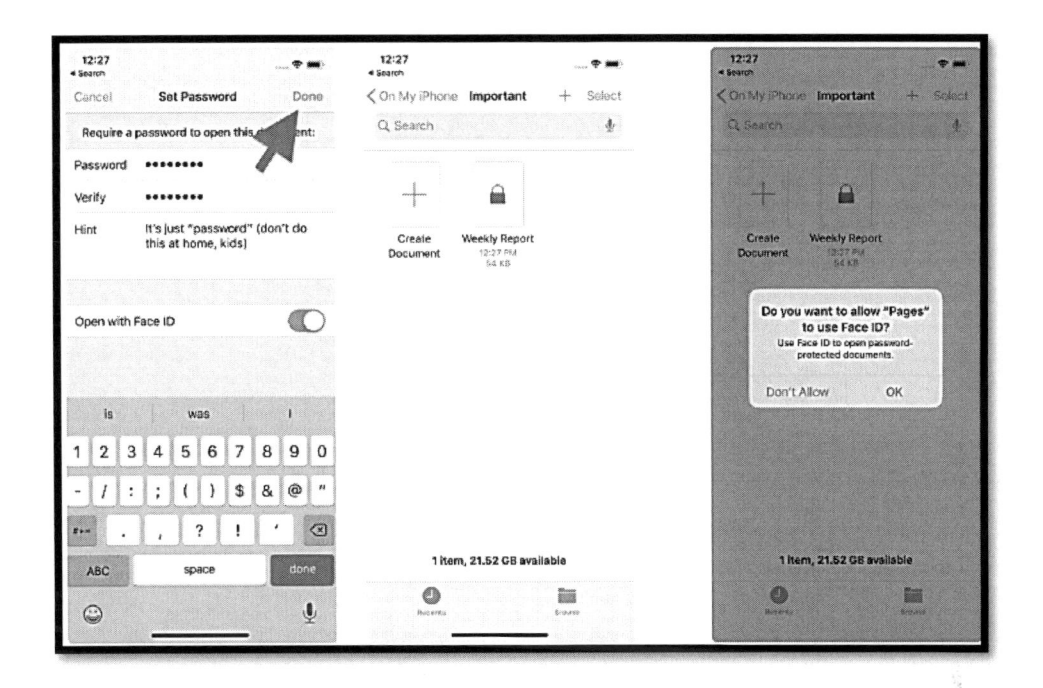

You can instantly unlock the document using Face ID or Touch ID after granting permission. Your **.pages** document will launch automatically once iOS accepts the authentication. Nevertheless, Pages will ask you for your password if Face ID or Touch ID fails more often than a few times. Just hope you can recall it!

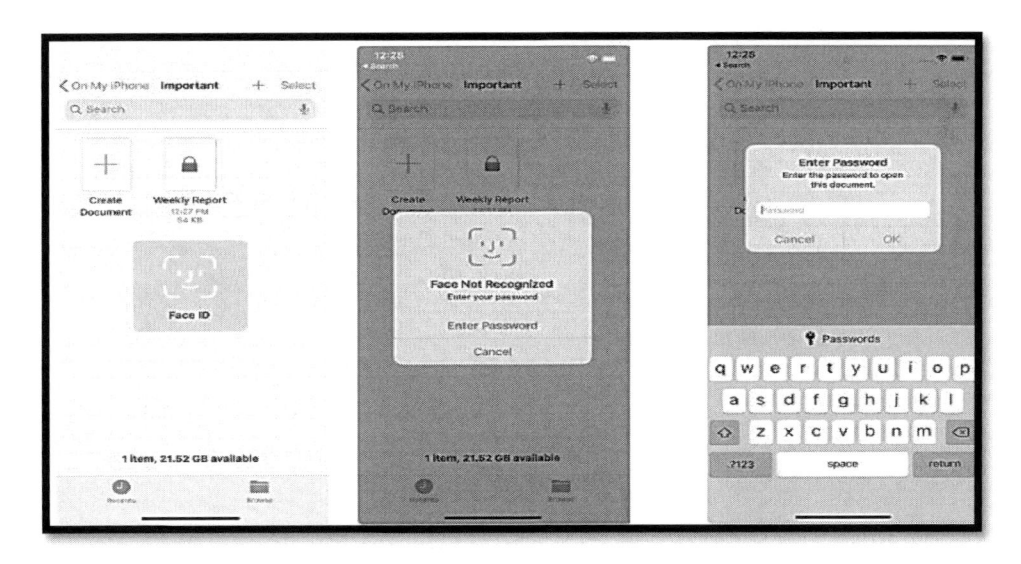

Opening Locked Documents from other iOS Devices

All of your connected iOS and macOS devices, as well as any potential collaborators' devices, will be affected when a file is secured. After locking a document on your iPhone, you'll need to enter the password to access it if you try to open it on your iPad or Mac.

You can toggle it on while inputting the password if you locked it using Face ID or Touch ID and another iOS device supports that authentication method (certain Mac's support Touch ID).

Changing Or Removing the Password

Return to the document's settings and select "**Change Password**" if you need to delete or change the password. You have the option to completely disable the password or change it by entering the old password and the new one here. Only the current document and any updates will be affected by either change; previous versions will remain unaffected.

It's vital to know that changing the password on a shared document only affects the current session and any future saves. They won't be able to access it any longer if collaborators are synchronized unless you tell them the new password.

However, they might view the unprotected version if they are viewing an older file (or have restored it). Stop sharing the document; add, change, or remove the password; then start sharing it again to fix the problem.

ORGANIZING PAGES AND DOCUMENTS

The process of rearranging your document pages vary greatly based on the type of document, with Page Layout being easier.

Rearrange Word-processing Pages

Unfortunately, there isn't a simple way to change pages around in a word processing document. The good news is that there is a solution you can use. **Consider the scenario where page two of a five-page document needs to be moved to the end.**

- Insert a new page at the end of page 5.
- To finish your project, go back to page two, select all of the text there, copy it, and then paste it into the new page you made at the end. Use the **Edit** icon in the menu bar or the context menu when performing a right-click to perform a cut-and-paste process.

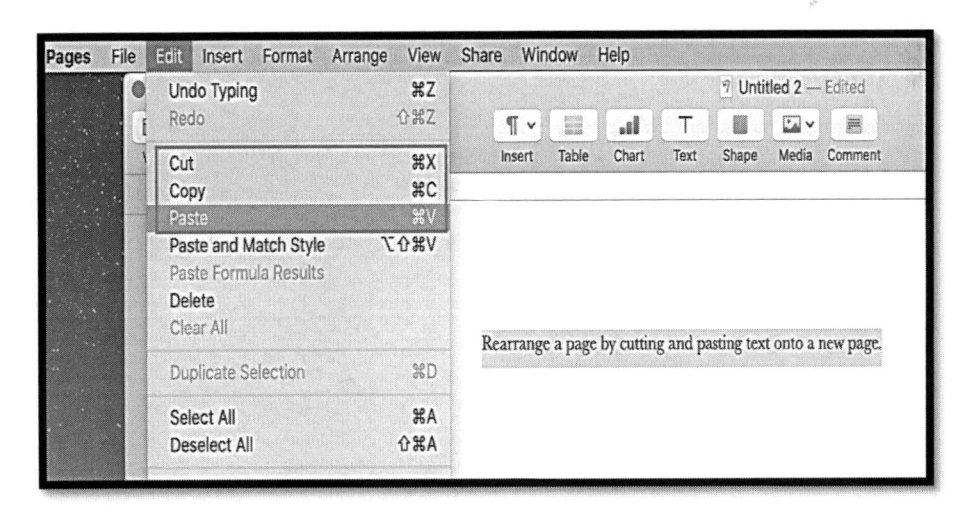

Rearrange Page Layout pages

- By selecting **View > Page Thumbnails**, you can display the thumbnail sidebar.
- Click and drag the desired page to its new location in the document by first selecting it in the sidebar.

TRANSFERRING DOCUMENTS TO AND FROM iCloud

How To Move Existing iWork Files from Your Mac To iCloud

If you've been using iWork on your Mac for a while, such as Pages, Keynote, or Numbers, it's likely that older files are still saved locally rather than in iCloud, Apple's online storage service.

These files can still be used just fine, but they are not supported by iCloud's Documents in the Cloud sync service, which enables you to open copies on any other Mac, iPhone, or iPad that is currently logged into your account.

Additionally, they cannot be shared or accessed through iCloud.com. You must upload your Keynote, Pages, or Numbers files from your Mac to iCloud if you want to take advantage of all the sync and access goodies. Fortunately, it's simple to accomplish!

How To Save Existing Pages Files on Your Mac In iCloud

- Open Pages on your Mac; note that you must be using a recent adequate version to support iCloud.
- Select On My Mac at the top of the documents pane.
- Go to the iCloud location of the desired Pages file. Launch it.
- Click the title at the top.
- You should now see a drop-down menu where you can select where to save it and a renaming option.
- Simply select **iCloud** and make any other changes you desire.
- You can save it on iCloud by pressing **Command + S** on your keyboard.

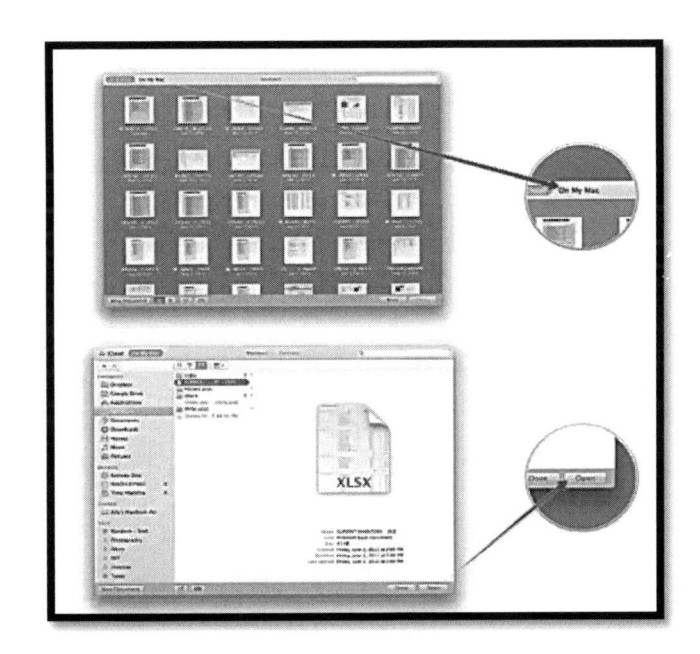

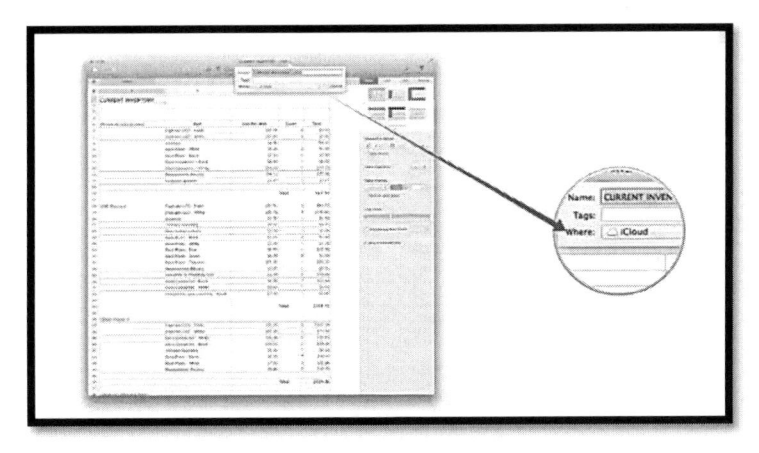

Your file or document should now be stored in iCloud alongside all of your other iCloud documents. Now, in addition to your Mac, you can access it from any iPhone or iPad that has iWork installed. Alternatively, you can access iCloud.com from any computer and view and change it there.

Simply select all of the documents you want to save to iCloud at once, then drag them to the iCloud window. That should also work, but just ensure they all import because a few random documents get left behind here and there.

Upload And Download Files From iCloud Drive On iCloud.com

From a computer, you can upload files to iCloud Drive. Any device with iCloud Drive enabled can see the files you upload. iCloud Drive files can also be downloaded and copied to your PC.

Upload Files

Do one of the following things in iCloud Drive on iCloud.com:

- Drag files to the **iCloud Drive** window or a folder icon in the **iCloud Drive** window from your computer's desktop or a folder window.
- To ensure that the item you're dragging will go into the folder, drag it to a folder icon. When you do this, the folder icon becomes highlighted.
- Select the files you wish to upload, then press the **File Upload** button ⊕ in the **iCloud Drive** toolbar and follow the on-screen directions.

Some applications have their folders in iCloud Drive, including **Pages, Numbers,** and **Keynote**. Only files that the app can open can be uploaded into its folder.

Download Files

Unless you upload the file to iCloud Drive later, any changes you make to a downloaded file remain solely visible on your computer.

- Choose the files you wish to download from iCloud Drive on **iCloud.com**, then press the **Download** button ⊕ in the iCloud Drive toolbar. The downloaded files are placed where your web browser's settings have directed them.

Using iCloud To Share Document

You can now share your Pages document with those who don't have Pages installed on their PCs thanks to recent changes Apple made to its OS and iCloud.

- Open the Pages document that is stored in your iCloud account after logging into your account.

- Click on the icon that looks like a document with an arrow pointing up in the upper right corner.

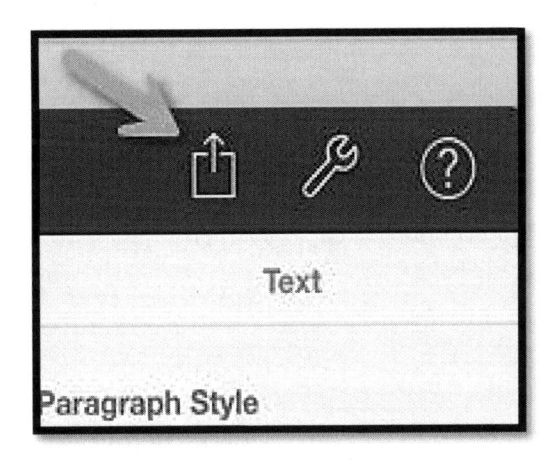

- Then, select "**Share Document**" from the drop-down menu.
- Then a new window will appear. This window will show you:
    - A field where the shared document's link is shown.
    - The option to let other people view or edit your document.
    - Hit "**Send Link**" when you are ready to share your document.
- The link to your shared document will appear in an email window that will open.
    - The email addresses of the people you want to share the document with should be entered.
    - (Optional) Send the recipient(s) of your shared document a message in the message field.
    - Simply press the "**Send**" icon.

- Your email recipient will be prompted to enter a name when they click the link to your shared document.
- The only thing they have to do to print your document is:
    - In the top right corner, select the **Tool** icon.
    - On the drop-down menu, select "**Print**."

PAGES EXPORTING FILES

Do you wish to send a Pages file from your iPhone or iPad to a coworker who uses Microsoft Word on a Windows PC? They won't be able to read and examine the contents of the Pages file since Microsoft Word does not accept the **.pages** file format; instead, they will need to convert it.

You needn't fret, though, as Pages for iPad and iPhone provides conversion tools that let you rapidly export a Pages file to a Word document or a Word-compatible format. When using an Apple device, such as a Mac, iPhone, or iPad, Apple's Pages app runs smoothly. However, the moment you switch to a different platform, compatibility problems arise.

iWork is only available on Apple devices and is not cross-platform software like Microsoft Office. Fortunately, Apple Pages allows you to quickly convert its native file format into Word documents and can browse Word documents just like any other Pages file.

There is also the iCloud-based technique of accessing Pages files in Windows, but for this lesson, we'll focus on exporting a document from the Pages app on iOS or iPadOS directly to Word format.

How To Export a Pages File as Word Document On iPhone & iPad

You should be able to access all the documents you've written on all your Apple devices using the Pages app, which is accessible for the iPhone and iPad.

Before continuing with the steps below, ensure sure to download the app if you haven't already:

- Open the **Pages** application on your iPad or iPhone.

- To locate the document that has to be converted, use the **Recents** or **Browse** menus. To open the file in the Pages app, touch on it first.

- To access more options when it has been opened, touch on the **triple-dot** icon next to the **Edit** option in the top-right corner.

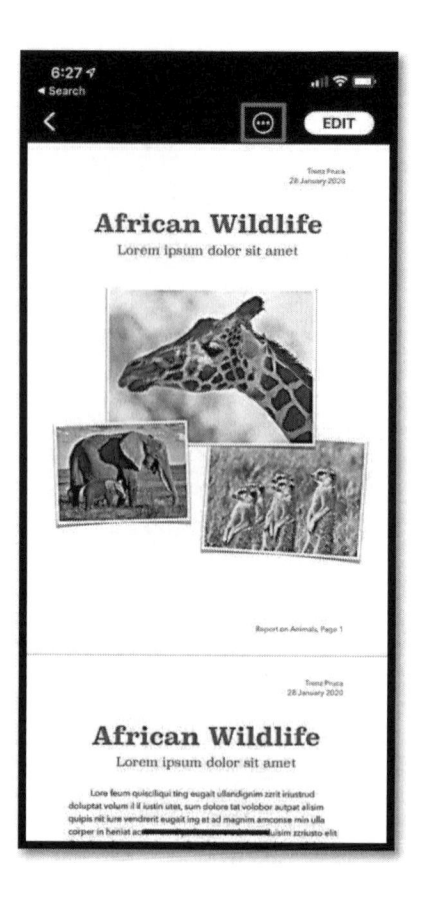

- Click "**Export**" as seen in the screenshot below to continue.

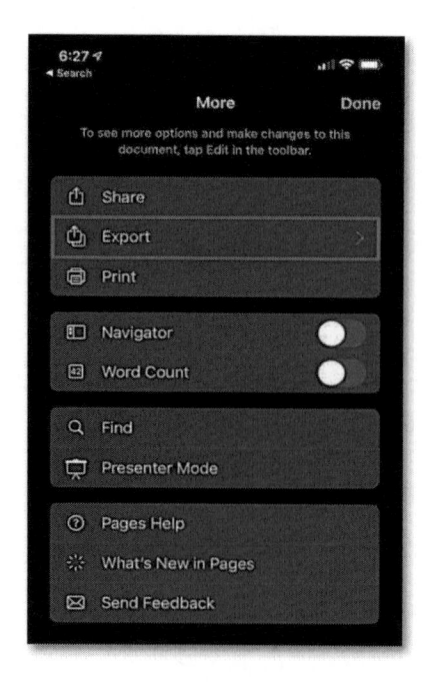

- You can select the file format for the exported file at this specific stage. To start the conversion, click on "**Word**."

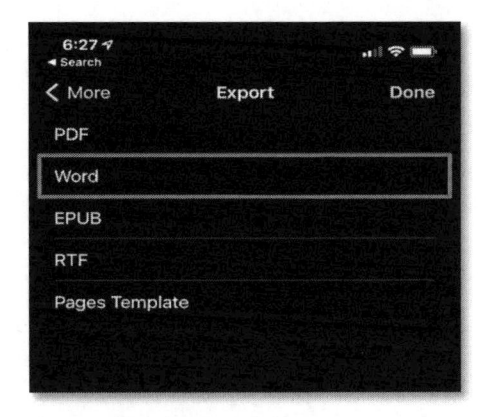

- Wait a few seconds before the conversion is done.

- Pages will immediately display the iOS share sheet on your screen once it is completed. The file can then be shared via AirDrop, Mail, or any other social networking application from this point. Alternatively, you can tap "**Save to Files**" at the very bottom of the share sheet to save the Word document locally.

You now know how to convert Pages files directly to Word documents on your iPhone and iPad.

Although there are at least solutions for these scenarios, it is unknown why Microsoft hasn't yet enabled native support for Pages files in Word. It's usually advisable to utilize the Word format rather than **.pages** if you're going to be working on a shared document in Pages with Windows PC users to ensure that other users won't run into any compatibility concerns.

One way to convert Pages files to Word documents is by using this method. You can still quickly convert Pages files to Word documents online using iCloud or with CloudConvert if you don't have the Pages app installed or don't want to download it for conversion. You may also learn how to save Pages Files as Word documents on macOS if you're using the Pages app.

You can also instruct the recipient to open the Pages files through the iCloud web client, which can be viewed on any device with a web browser, including Windows PCs. With just an Apple account, they can access it, export Pages files as Word documents, and, if necessary, download the converted files to their device.

Using iTunes To Transfer Files to And from Pages

iTunes offers two methods—iTunes File Sharing and iTunes Syncing—for transferring data from a PC to an iPhone. You will require one of these to assist you in transferring data from PC to iPhone, based on the kind of content you need to copy.

Transfer Files Between PC And iPhone/iPad Via iTunes File Sharing

Supports: Files that are created by apps that work with **File Sharing**.

You may have realized that iTunes has a "**File Sharing**" feature. File Sharing is a feature that enables you to transfer files between your computer and an app on your iPhone or iPad that is compatible. Therefore, using File Sharing is advised if you need to transfer files made by apps like Keynote, Pages, and Numbers between your computer and your iOS device.

To copy files between your computer and iOS apps:

- Ensure that iTunes is running at the most recent version on your computer.
- Launch **iTunes** on your computer after connecting your iOS device.
- When you click the device icon, select "**File Sharing**."
- In iTunes, choose the app that supports file sharing, then press "**Add**."
- Press "**Add**" after selecting the files you want to transfer to your computer.
- Check the transferred files by going to the app of your choice on your iPhone.

Move Files from PC To iPhone Via iTunes Syncing

Support: Photos, Videos, Music, Podcasts, Audiobooks...

You might want to transfer files to your iPhone or iPad from the computer using iTunes if the files you're trying to share are stored there. The common knowledge is that using iTunes to transfer files from a computer to an iPhone or iPad can result in data loss on your mobile device.

This is because the newly synchronized items will replace any existing media files on your iPhone or iPad, including music, movies, ringtones, and more. Learn how to use the program to transfer files to an iPhone or iPad if you don't mind.

To transfer files from PC to iPhone/iPad with iTunes:

- Open iTunes on your computer after connecting your iPhone or iPad.
- Trust the computer and unlock the iDevice.
- Select the category, such as Photos, Movies, Songs, and more, by clicking the "**Device**" tab.
- Select the items you want to copy, then check the "**Sync [category]**" box.
- To begin transferring files to your iPhone or iPad, select "**Apply**."

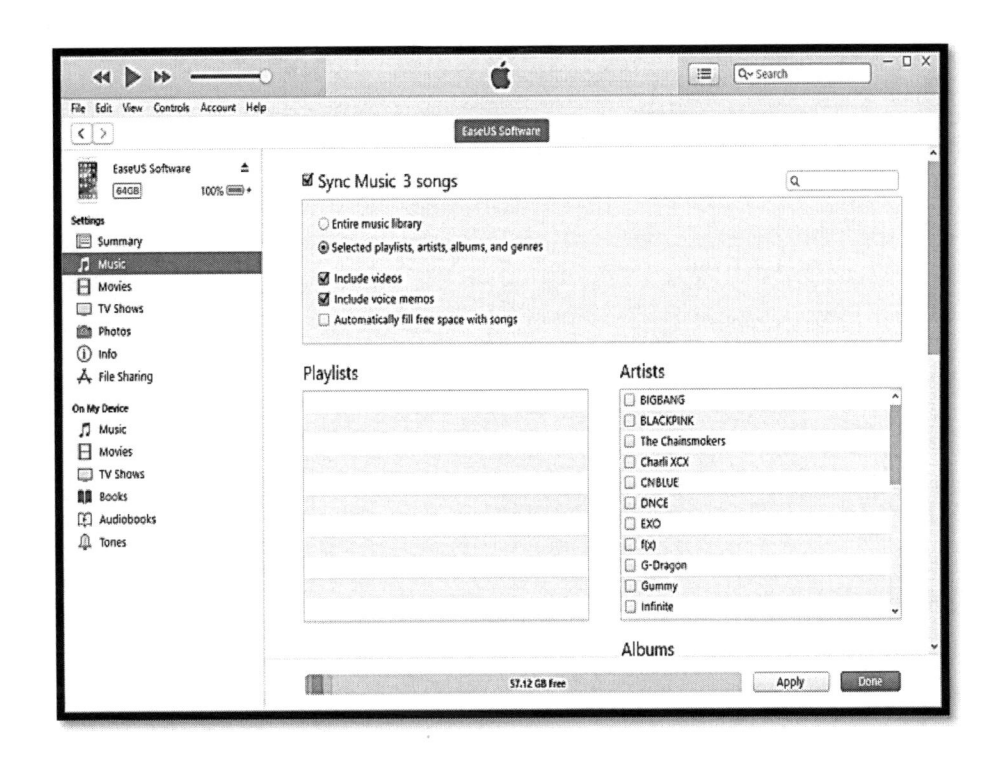

CHAPTER THREE
WORKING WITH TEMPLATES ON PAGES

There may be several documents types that you write frequently when using Apple Pages to generate documents. You might create these frequently, including newsletters, brochures, business letters, and meeting agendas. If so, there are benefits to saving a document as a template.

Reusing the same template allows you to maintain consistency by keeping the foundation, style, and structure while only making the changes that are necessary at the time.

This chapter demonstrates how to create and utilize custom templates in Apple Pages for Mac.

UTILIZING PRE-EXISTING TEMPLATES

You can reuse a document's template after saving it as a template and save the template as a new file:

- Select **New Document** in **Pages**.
- Tap **Choose** after selecting the template in the **Chooser** window under **My Templates** at the bottom.

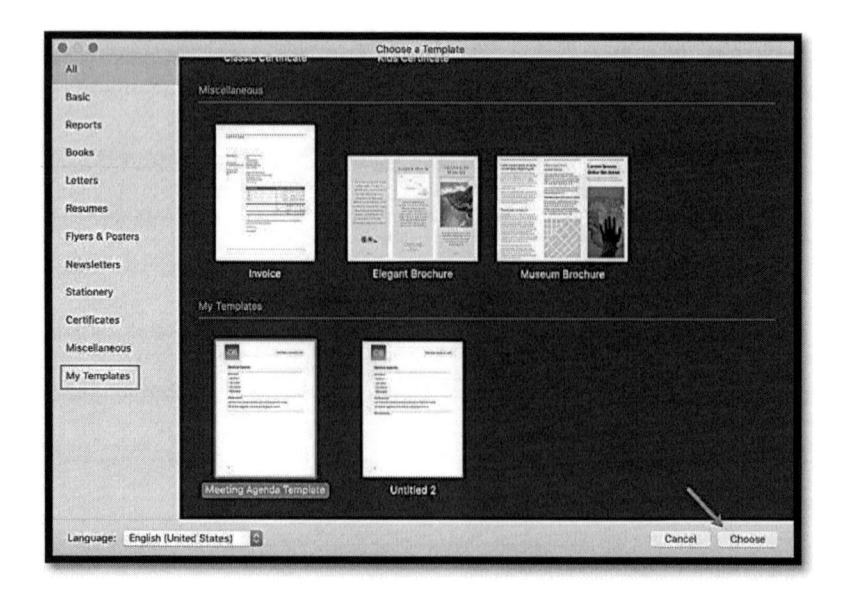

You'll see that the name is "**Untitled**" by default at the top rather than the template name. This is what enables you to save the template as a regular document and reuse it again.

MAKING YOUR TEMPLATES

Using placeholders, your company logo, and other elements, you can generate a template from an existing document or create a brand-new one:

- Click **File > Save as Template** from the menu bar while the document you wish to use as a template is open.
- Click **Add to Template Chooser** or **Save** from the pop-up menu that emerges.

If you select **Save**, it will stay as a standard document that you can easily share or reuse. Choose a name for it and a place for it.

If you select **Add to Template Chooser**, it will be available when you start a new document among other templates. You'll be asked to give it a name after you see it in the **Template Chooser**.

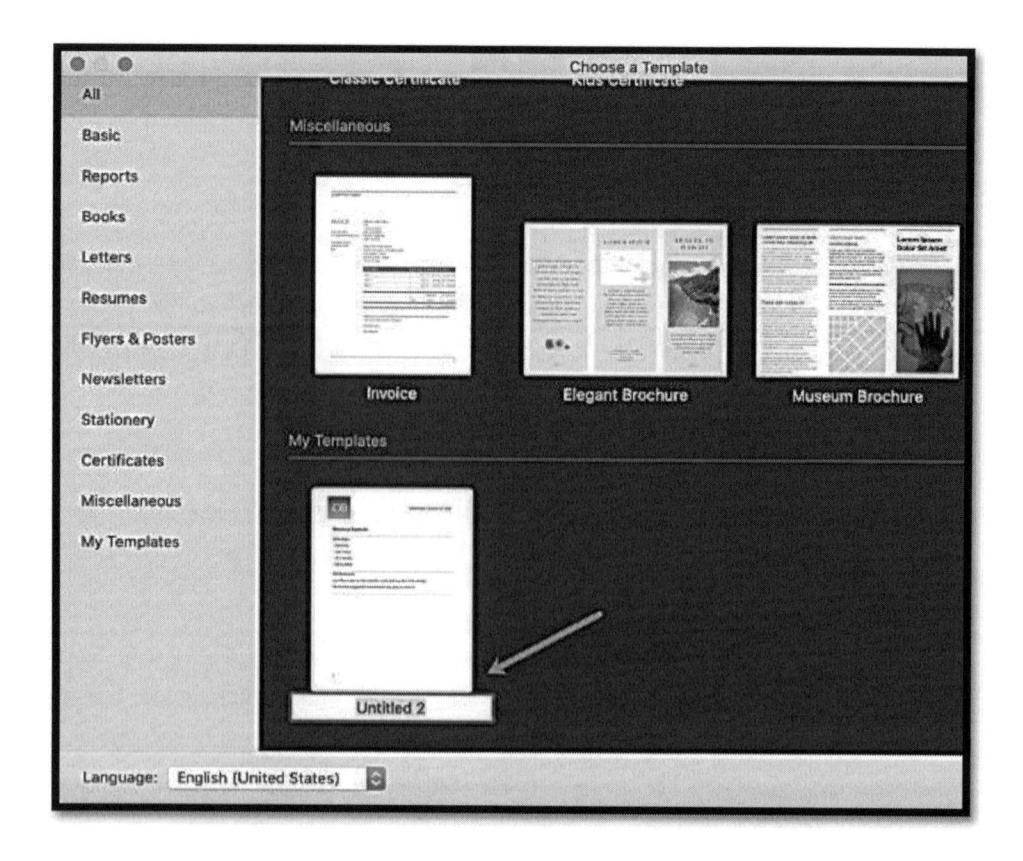

EDIT A CUSTOM TEMPLATE

The only thing you can change after creating a custom template in Pages is its name. Although terrible, there is a solution for this:

- Make your changes to the template by utilizing the methods mentioned above.
- Observe the directions at the start, then select **Save as Template**.
- Call it something else.
- The original template you made should be deleted. (As seen below.)

Rename A Custom Template

- By starting a new document in Pages, you can use the **Template Chooser**.
- Rename the template by selecting it with a right-click while holding down **Control**.
- Hit **Return** after entering the new name.

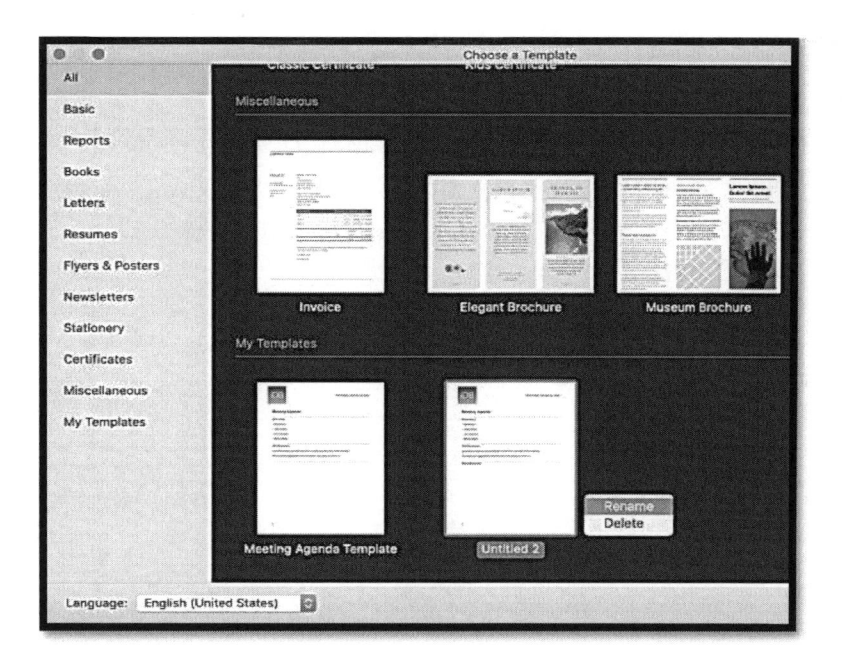

Delete A Custom Template

It merely requires a few clicks to delete a template you've created from the Template Chooser:

- Create a new document in Pages to launch the Template Chooser.
- Select Delete by doing a right-click on the template while holding down Control.

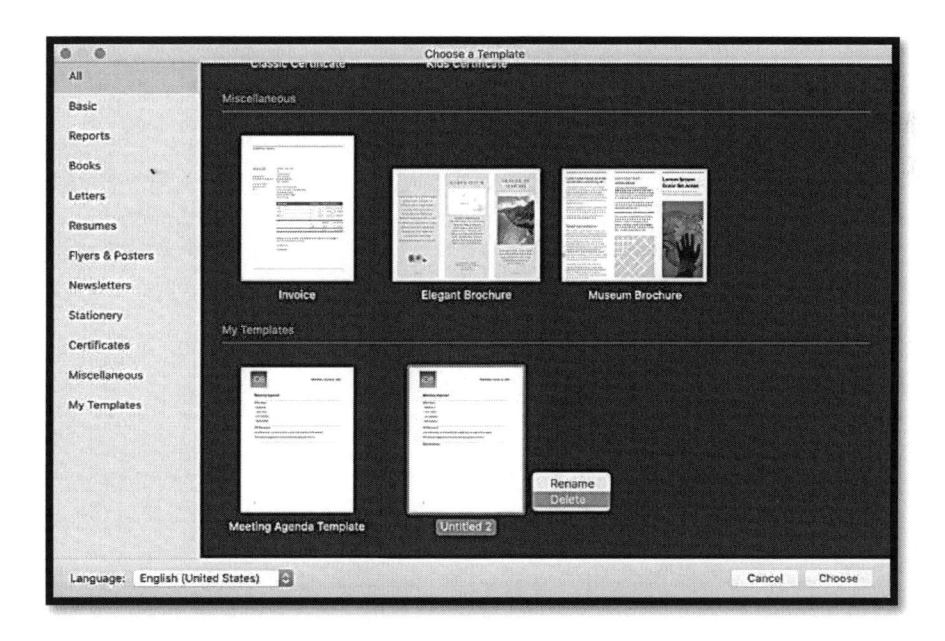

Conclusion

A great way to reuse documents you frequently create is to create a custom template in Apple Pages. It provides you with a head start on your document by having the placeholders, formatting, and other elements you require already there.

CHAPTER FOUR
WORKING WITH TEXT ON PAGES

In this chapter, you'll learn how to work with text in Pages.

TEXT INSERTION

Text can be added to a document in a variety of different ways. You can add text to text boxes outside the main document body, like sidebars, replace the placeholder text in templates, and add text inside shapes.

In a word processing document, you can add text boxes for things like sidebars in addition to the content that is in the document's main body. All text is contained in one or more text boxes in a page layout document.

Add Text in A Word-Processing Document

- **Add text in a blank template**: Just start typing.
- **Replace placeholder text**: tap the text and select it before beginning to type. What you type replaces the full block of placeholder text. Hit the placeholder text, then click the **Delete** button ▣, to remove it.

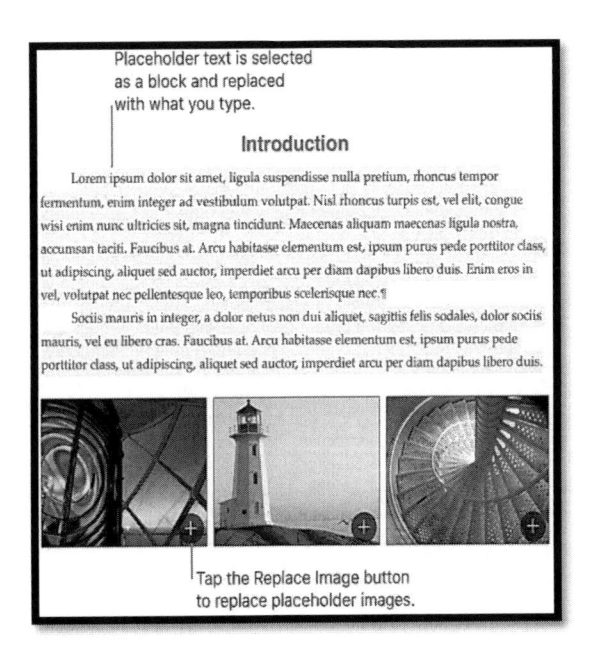

- **Add text outside of the body of the text**: Add a text box, then enter text to add content, such as a sidebar (see the next task).

Some placeholder content is written in Latin words that have been changed. The language you choose for your computer will show in the text you enter.

When you finish a page in a word processing document, a new page is automatically added. Alternatively, you can add a page break anywhere to begin the next line on a new page. You can insert a blank page anywhere in a document with a page layout.

Add Text in A Text Box

- After selecting **Shapes** from the **Insert +** menu, select **Text** from the **Basic** section. On the page, there is a text box (you can change how the text looks later).
- You can now move the text box by dragging it. If you are unable to move the box, press the text once to select it and then press the text again to deselect it.
- Tap twice on the placeholder text before adding your own.
- **Choose one of the following options to resize the text box:**
    - **If the text is too small for the box**: Drag the **clipping indicator** until all text is visible after selecting the text box. Additionally, you can drag a selection handle.
    - **If the text is too big for the box**: To change the text box's size, select it and then drag the selection handle.
- Select the text box, then hit the **Delete** button.

To allow overflow text, you can also link one text box to another.

Like most other objects, a text box can be rotated, changed in a border, filled with a certain color, layered with other objects, and more. Text inside the box can also have its look changed, including the font, color, size, and alignment.

A text box and its contents can also be copied from another document, Keynote, or Numbers.

Add Text Inside a Shape

- Type your text after double-tapping the shape to reveal the insertion point.

A **clipping indicator** occurs if there is too much text for the shape to display. Click the shape, then drag any selection handle until all the text is visible to resize it. Like any other text, the appearance of the text inside the shape can be changed.

FONT SELECTION AND FORMATTING

In this section, you'll learn everything related to font selection and formatting.

Making Use of Paragraph Styles

A paragraph style is a collection of features that you may rapidly apply to a whole paragraph, such as font size and color. The content in your document will have a consistent appearance if you use paragraph styles.

Document formatting is also made simple by paragraph styles. For instance, you don't need to change each heading individually if you apply the Heading style to all of the headings in a document and then decide you want to change their color. You can simply change the color of the Heading style itself.

There are paragraph styles included in each Pages template that you can edit as you see fit. Paragraph styles have already been applied to the placeholder text.

You can set shortcut keys to paragraph styles in the **Text** panel of the **Format inspector**.

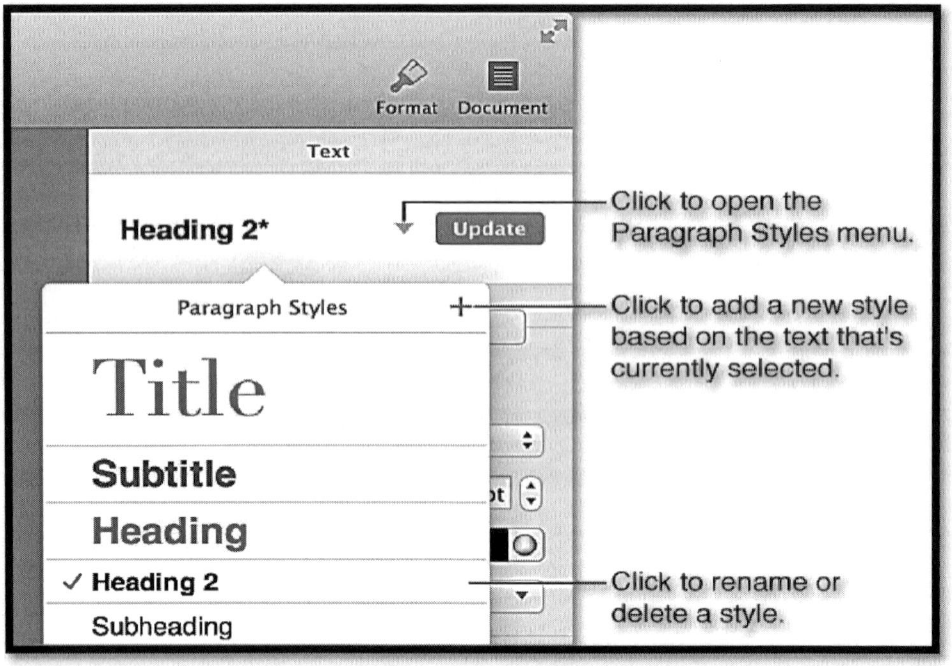
Format
Document
Text
Heading 2*
Update
Click to open the Paragraph Styles menu.
Paragraph Styles
Click to add a new style based on the text that's currently selected.
Title
Subtitle
Heading
✓ Heading 2
Subheading
Click to rename or delete a style.

An asterisk beside the style's name indicates that the style has an override when you edit text that has a paragraph style applied to it. You have the option of leaving the override in place or changing the style to affect all text using that style equally.

Apply A Paragraph Style

- To apply the style to just that paragraph, select one or more paragraphs, or click inside a paragraph.
- Tap the paragraph style name at the top of the **Text** pane of the **Format inspector**, then select a style from the Paragraph Styles pop-up menu.

Assign A Shortcut Key to A Style

You can give a paragraph, character, or list style its shortcut key (F1–F8).

- **Choose one of the following actions in the Format inspector's Text pane:**
  - **For a paragraph style:** At the top of the pane, press the name of the paragraph style.

- **For a character style:** Select **Character Styles** from the pop-up menu.
- **For a list style:** Select **Bullets & Lists** from the pop-up menu.
- Move the cursor over the name of the style you wish to give a shortcut to in the pop-up menu, then select the arrow that displays.
- Select **Shortcut**, then pick a key. For convenience, the shortcut key is now displayed in the menu next to the style name.
- Select **None** from the Shortcut menu to get rid of a shortcut key assignment.

Note: On a portable computer, hit Fn while holding down the shortcut key.

Create A New Paragraph Style

- Select the paragraph on which you want the new style to be based.
- Tap the paragraph style name at the top of the **Text** pane of the Format inspector.
- At the top of the **Paragraph Styles** pop-up menu, select **new style +**.
- Give the "new style" a name, and then click outside the menu to close it.

Remove Overrides from A Paragraph Style

An asterisk displays beside the name of the paragraph style whenever the formatting of text that has that style applied is changed.

You can go back to the original style if you decide not to maintain the changes (the overrides).

- Simply select the overriding paragraph.
- Select the paragraph style name at the top of the **Text** pane of the **Format inspector**.
- Select the style name in the pop-up menu for paragraph styles (it has a gray checkmark to indicate an override). The text returns to its normal style when the override has been cleared.

Update A Paragraph Style

Text that has a paragraph style attached to it can be updated to reflect formatting changes if necessary. The new paragraph style can be used to format other text.

An Update icon is displayed beside the name of the paragraph style at the top of the Text window when you select a whole paragraph and change the font, size, color, or other text properties in the paragraph. Select Update to make your changes to the style effective.

The Update icon is replaced by an asterisk if you didn't pick the complete paragraph when you made the modifications, but you can still update the style.

- Select the text with the style you want to change by clicking it.
- Select the paragraph style name at the top of the **Text** pane of the **Format inspector**.
- Move the cursor on the style name (it has a checkmark) in the **Paragraph Styles** pop-up menu, then select the arrow that emerges.
- Select **Update Style**.

Rename A Style

- To rename a paragraph that uses a certain style, click on it.
- Select the paragraph style name at the top of the **Text** pane of the **Format inspector**.
- Move the cursor over the style name in the **Paragraph Styles** pop-up menu, then select the arrow that displays.
- After selecting **Rename Style**, type a new name.

Delete A Style

A style that isn't being used in your document can be deleted. If the style is in use, you can choose a different style to use in its place.

- Just click any text.
- Select the paragraph style name at the top of the **Text** pane of the **Format inspector**.

- Move the pointer over the name of the style you wish to delete in the **Paragraph Styles** pop-up menu, then select the arrow that displays.
- Select **Delete Style**.

When you attempt to delete a style that is currently in use, you are prompted to select another style as its replacement.

Making Lists

You can use the Apple Pages software to meet all of your paperwork needs. The Pages app allows you to create and store a variety of documents. The Pages app, which has a ton of options, can increase your productivity. You can depend on it for data syncing via iCloud because it comes pre-installed on iPhones, iPad, and Mac.

You have the option to use lists or bullet points in the app to describe your data. You can insert and customize lists in Apple Pages on iPhone, iPad, and Mac by following the instructions in this section.

Insert Lists in Pages App On iPhone and iPad

A wonderful small feature that aids in data organization is the ability to create lists. Creating lists will help you emphasize key points in your document or simplify the presentation of your data points. If necessary, you can even decide to turn your Pages file into a PDF before sharing it with your coworkers and teachers.

Make sure the Pages app is updated to the most recent version on your iPhone or iPad, based on your device preference, before continuing.

To insert a list in the Pages app, follow these steps. Users of the iPhone and iPad follow similar procedures.

- On your iPad or iPhone, launch the **Pages** app.

- Open an older document that you want to edit or create a new one.
- Put the cursor where you wish to insert the list in the document.
- At the top of the menu, click the **brush** icon.

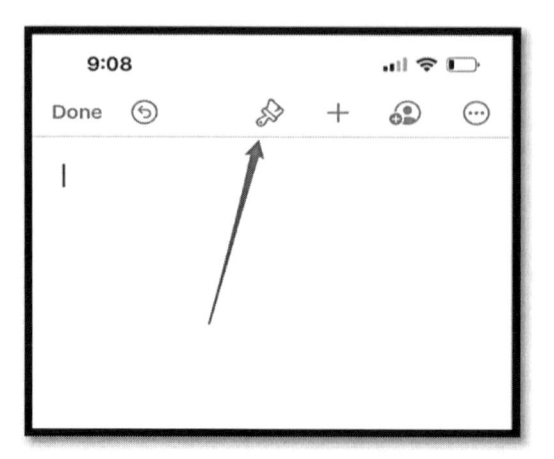

- Scroll down and tap on **Bullets and Lists** in the **Text Edit** panel.

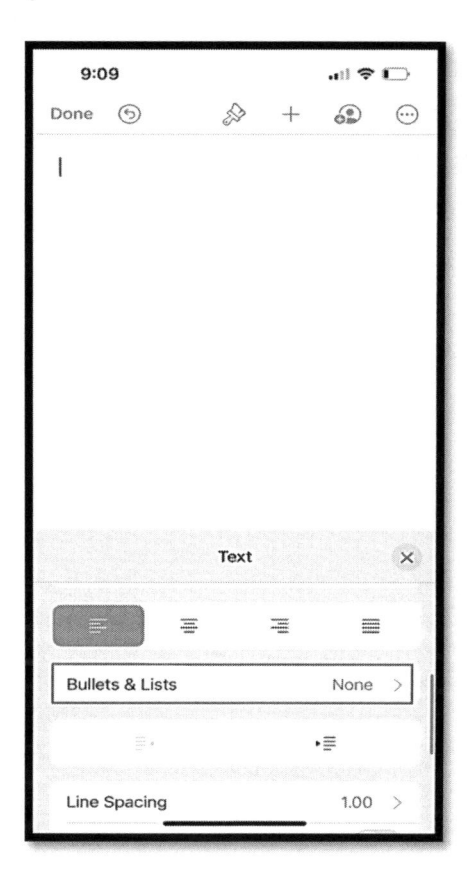

- From the list of available designs, pick the one you like most.

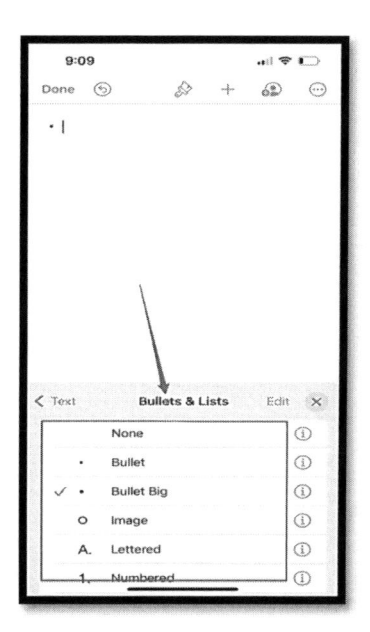

You'll notice that a bullet point is being added to your document. Now you can continue to input text and hit Return to create a list.

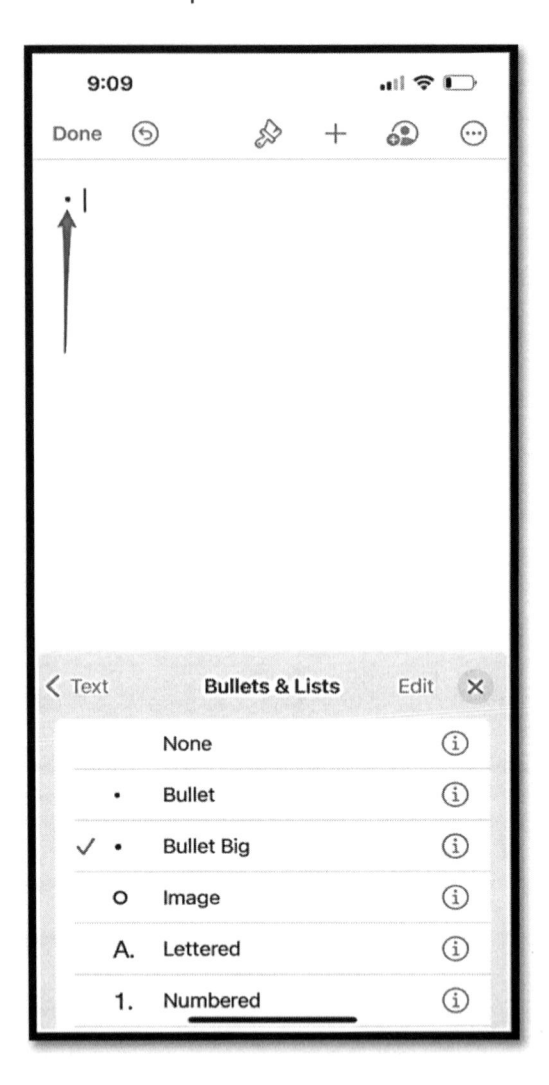

Customize Lists in Pages App On iPhone and iPad

In the Pages app, you can change the bullet style to change the appearance and feel of your lists. Your content will become distinctive as a result.

Take these actions.

- Click the cursor next to the bullet in your document that you wish to change.

- Once more, click the **brush** icon and choose **Bullets and Lists**.

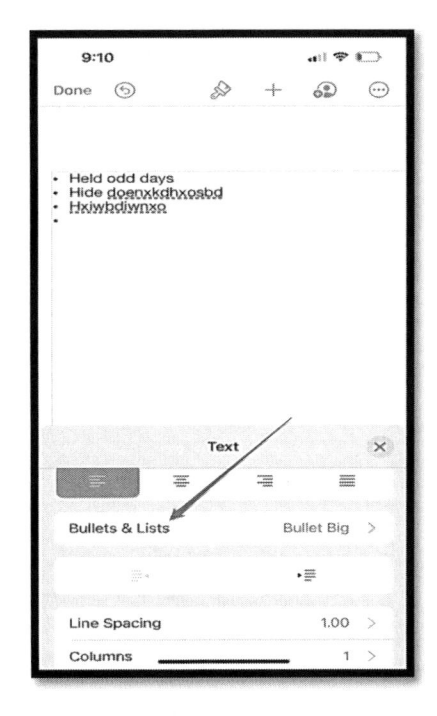

- Click the "**i**" icon beside the list style you previously chose.

- From the list, choose **Text Bullet**.

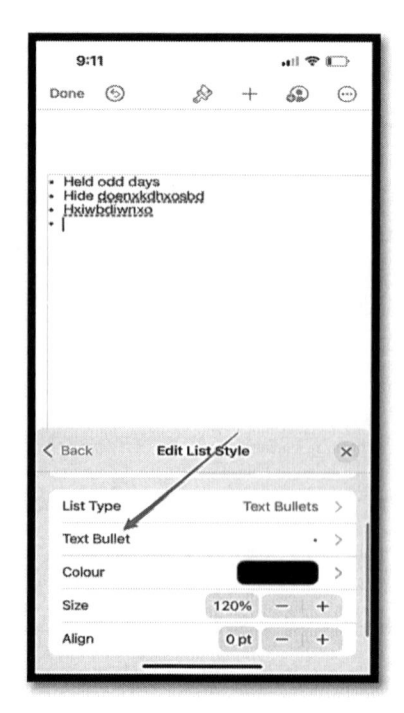

- Pick a list style from the available default options. A custom list style is an additional option.

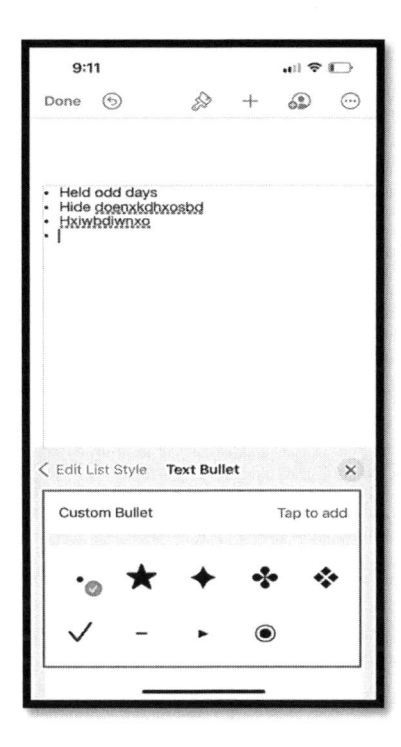

- Your document will display the list style you have chosen.

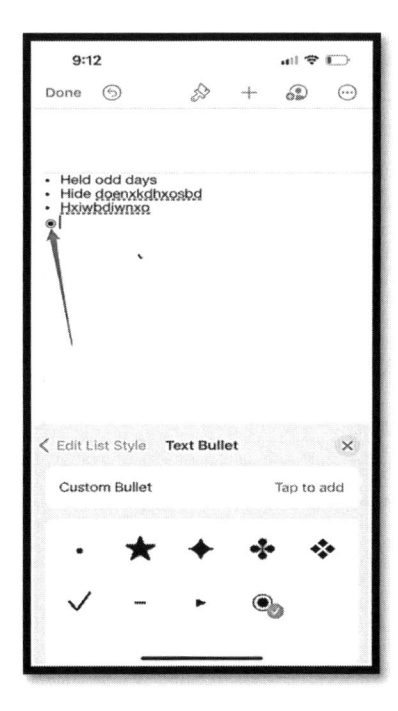

- By choosing **List Type**, you can also change the list's category.

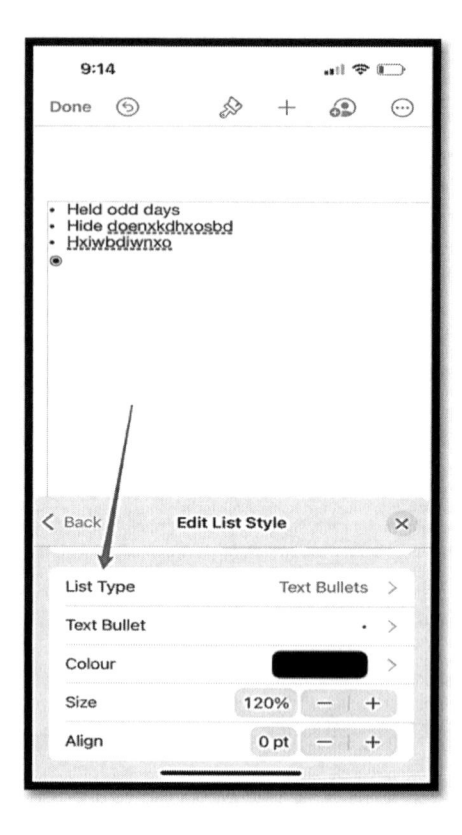

Remember that you can move the cursor next to a previous bullet point, hit the brush icon, and then repeat the process to change the list style.

Insert Lists in Pages App on Mac

You can make changes to your documents while on the road using the Pages app on your iPhone and iPad. You might, for instance, have forgotten to bring your MacBook with you or have been using a Mac at work or school. Then you can easily edit your documents and create a list on your iPhone or iPad.

However, if working on a larger screen is always more convenient for you, here's how Mac users can make lists. Just ensure you're running the most recent version of the application. Take all the necessary steps.

- To open **Spotlight Search**, tap **Command + Spacebar**, then type **Pages** and hit **Return**.

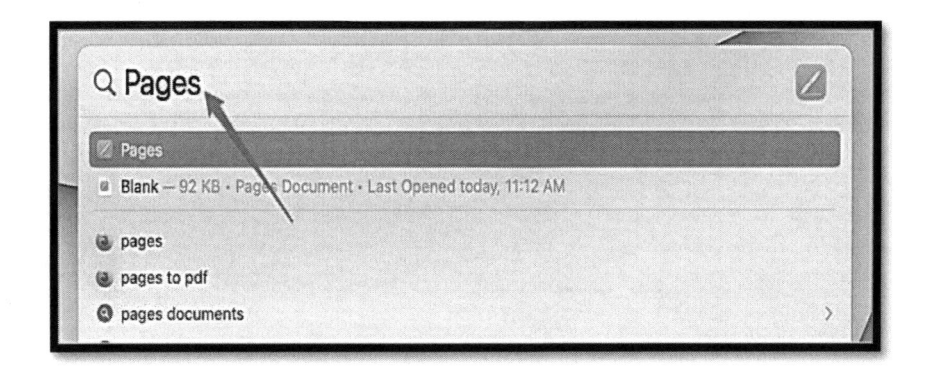

- Open an existing file or start a new blank one.
- Set the cursor where you want the list to go.
- In the top-right corner, select **Format**.

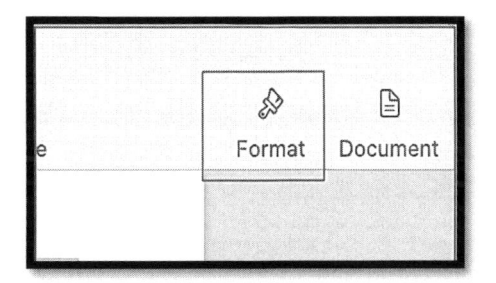

- At the bottom right, select **Bullets & Lists** from the dropdown menu.

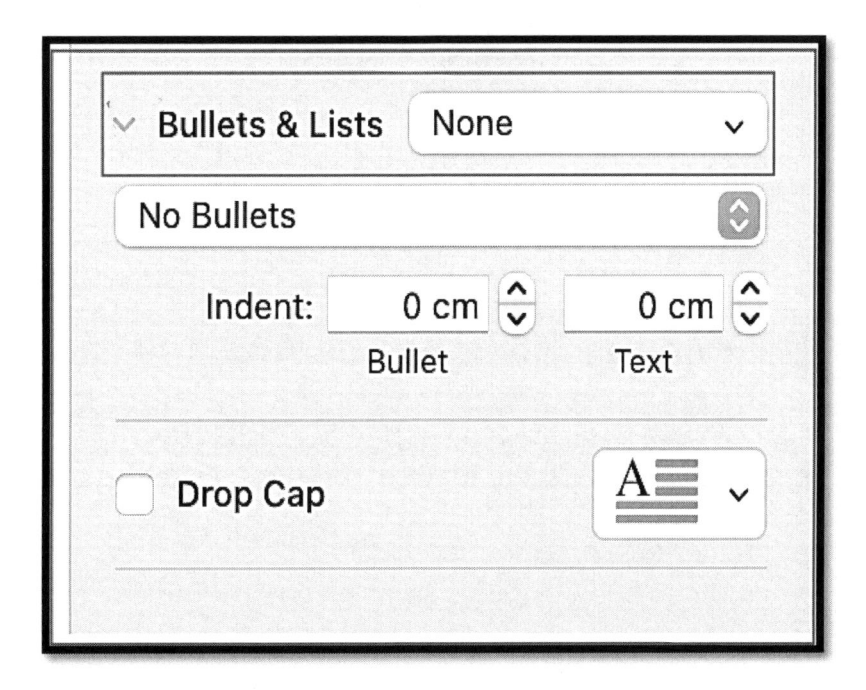

- Choose the list style you like from the available options.

- Type your text and hit **Return** to create a list once your chosen **List Style** has appeared on your document.

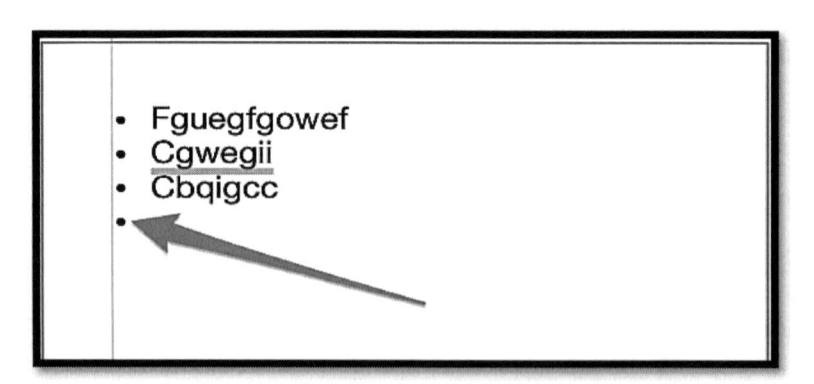

Customize Lists in Pages App on Mac

You can use your Mac to change the look of your lists in the Pages app, just like you do on the iPhone and iPad. Take the following steps.

- Place your cursor beside the list's bullet point.
- In the lower right corner, next to the bullet option, select the dropdown menu.

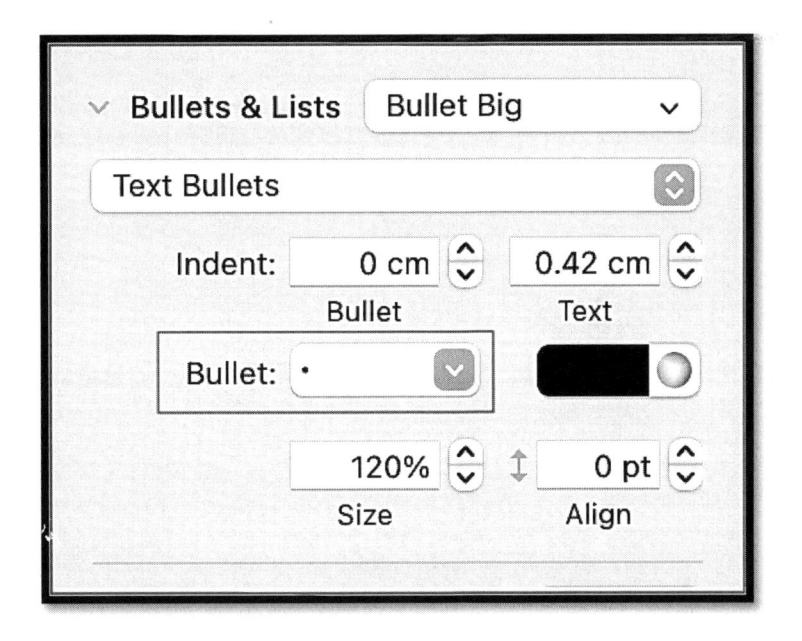

- Choose your preferred bullet style from the available options.

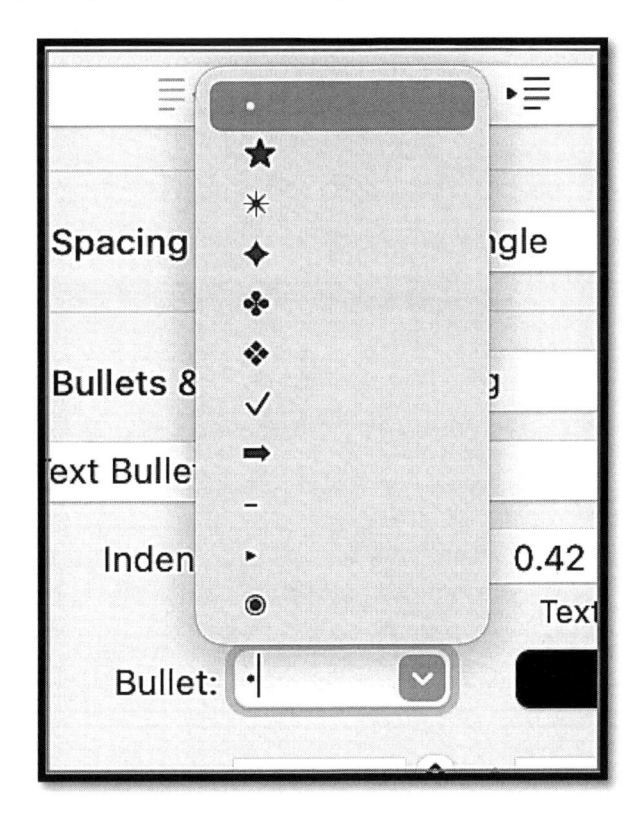

The list's new bullet style will now show on your page.

115

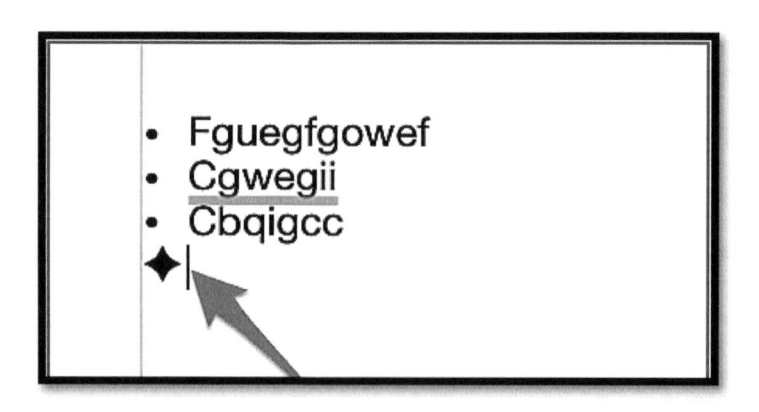

By selecting **List Type** from the drop-down menu next to **Bullets and Lists**, you can also change the list category.

Remember that you can move the cursor beside a previous bullet point, hit the brush icon, and then repeat the process to change the list style.

Conclusion

Making a list of your relevant details can help you grab readers' attention. Based on your document's needs, you can create and customize lists in Apple Pages. Just be sure to consistently update the app across all platforms.

Working With Unique Characters

Apple released the iWork suite of applications, which includes Pages, Keynote, and Numbers, back in 2006. The firm added new features and made other improvements to it over time. These days, Google Docs and Microsoft Office apps can be effectively replaced by applications like Apple Pages and Keynote.

The Apple Pages excels at providing simple editing and word processing features. Even the ability to add charts, special characters, arithmetic equations, and much more is included in the software.

Emojis and other special characters, including Latin words, math symbols, copyright symbols, currency symbols, and more, are now possible to add, thanks to Apple.

We will discuss how to add them to Apple Pages in this section. We'll also cover a few software customizations tips, voice typing features, auto-correcting words to symbols, and more. Let's begin.

1. Add Emojis and Special Characters

The need to insert a copyright symbol, a Celsius character, a new currency, or a basic math symbol can arise while you are editing a document.

Simply navigate to **Edit > Emojis & Symbols** and select the appropriate symbol or emoji from the extensive list. A streamlined menu is also accessible by clicking the **Character Viewer**. Arrows, Latin words, pictographs, punctuation, and other categories are used to categorize it. Finding a symbol from this menu is simpler.

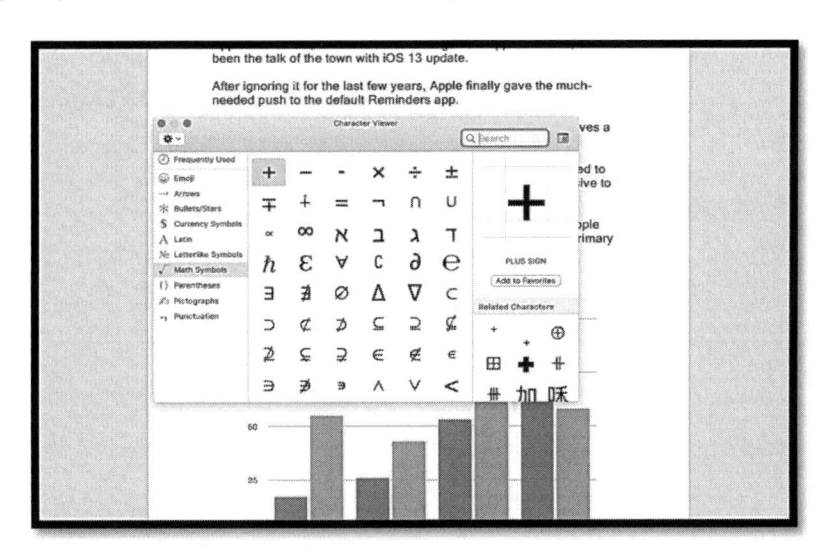

The macOS already has this feature. Therefore, it functions properly in all apps, including Apple Pages, Microsoft Word, Apple Notes, and others. To rapidly access the menu, use the keyboard shortcut **Control + Command + Space**.

2. **Long-Press on Single Words for Suggestions**

This is also included in the default macOS package. You can long-press on keyboard words to bring up appropriate symbol options when you want to add a special character while writing.

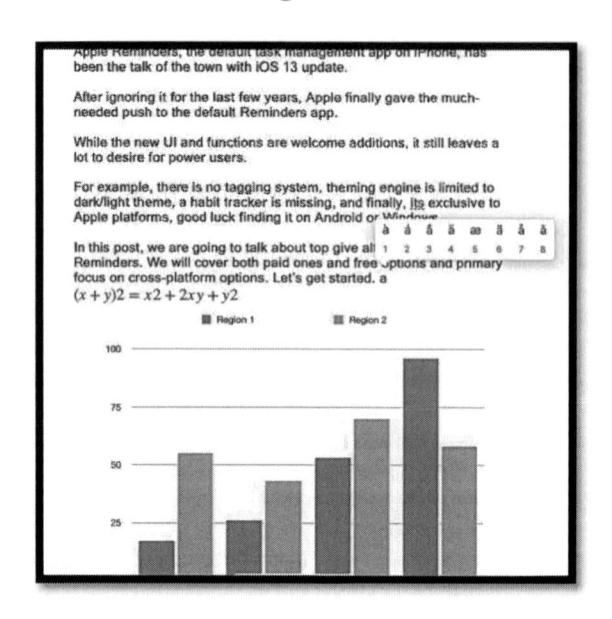

For instance, you can long-press the letter "**C**" to show the available symbols. Similar to this, pressing the letter "**A**" repeatedly will display a long list of options. Use the number shortcuts underneath the character to add them to the document.

3. **Set Auto-Replacement**

You should take into account setting up an auto-replacement for any symbols or special characters that you commonly use. Let's demonstrate how to configure them in Apple Pages.

Click **Pages > Preferences (Command +,)** and then select **Auto-Correction**. A replacement section with two menus can be found here.

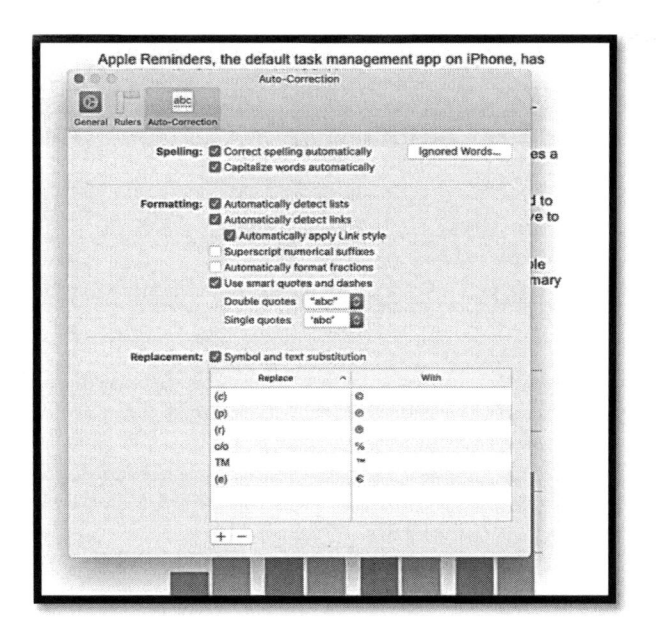

For instance, typing **(C)** will substitute it with a copyright symbol if you typically need one. We have it set to the **(e)** shortcut since we often need to use the Euro currency symbol. Amazingly, Word and OneNote were compatible with the newly introduced shortcuts.

4. Add Math Equation

As previously stated, people who reside in the Apple environment will find Apple Pages to be the ideal word processing application. It's also well-liked in the field of education.

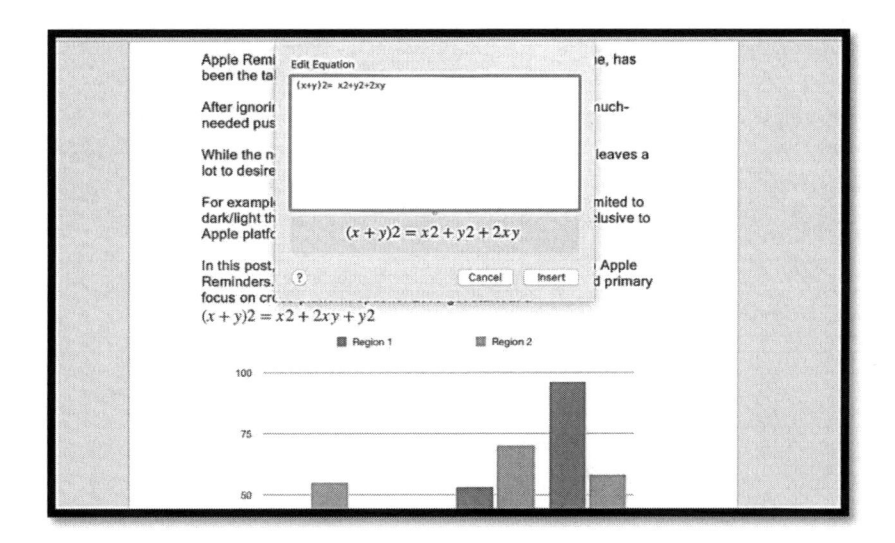

Math equations can now be added to the Pages app by Apple. To add formulas, open the dialog box by selecting **Insert > Equation** (keyboard shortcut: **Option + Command + E**). The formula will now be transformed into a math-friendly version as you type. When you choose Insert, the equation will be added to the document.

5. Insert Charts

When it comes to using graphs to present statistics and numerical data, Apple Pages is just as capable as Microsoft Word.

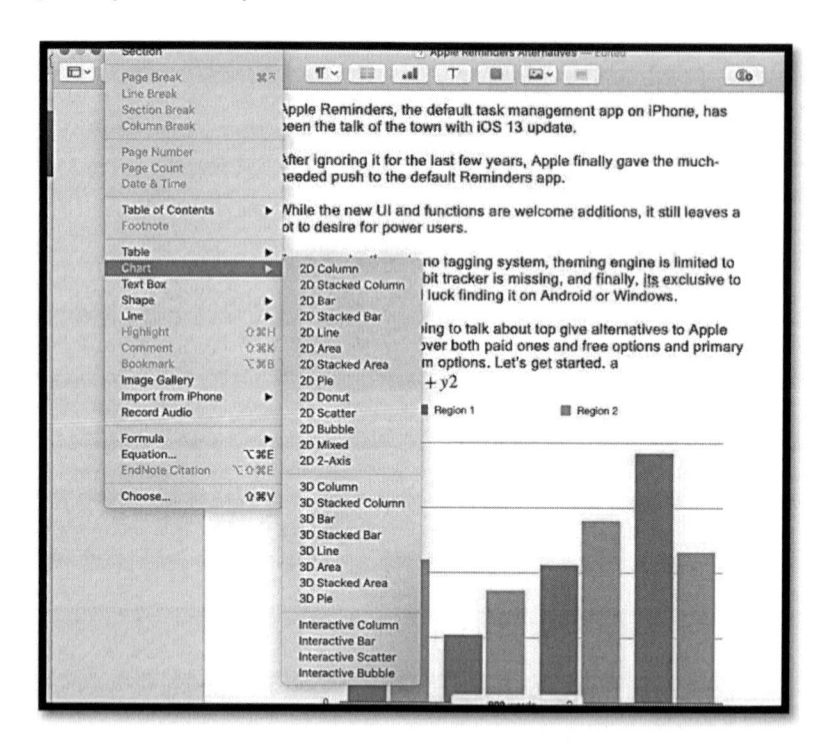

Select a chart from the extensive list of 2D, 3D, and interactive charts by selecting **Insert > Chart**. The only issue we have is that a chart cannot be previewed before being inserted into the document.

6. Customize Toolbar

A standard toolbar for editing and customizing documents is included with Apple Pages. You can, nevertheless, change them to suit your tastes.

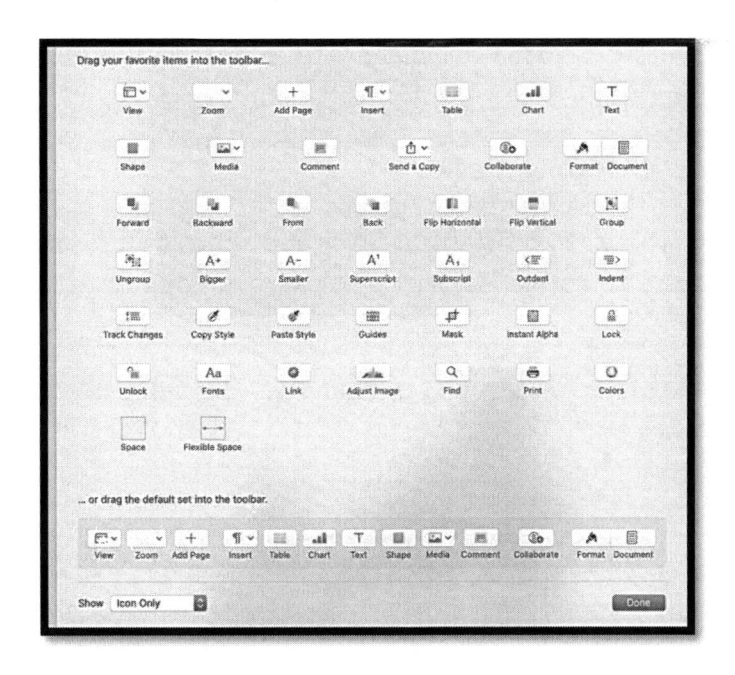

Go to **View > Customize Toolbar** in Apple Pages and adjust the drag & drop functionality as desired. The software can also be configured to display text and icons.

7. Add A Signature From iPhone

Apple has introduced software improvements into its hardware products. The same is true for an iPhone and a MacBook. Users of iPhones can directly add a signature or any sketch made on the device to Apple Pages. They use it to sign documents. This is the procedure.

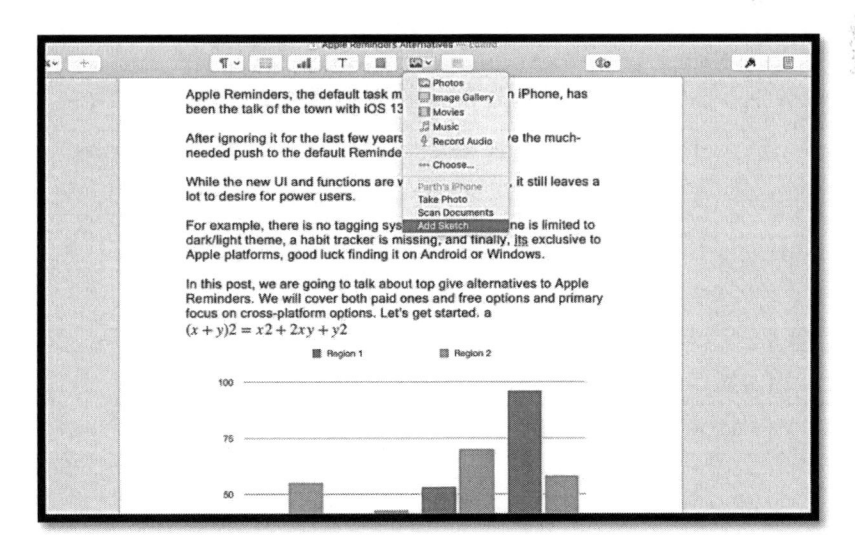

121

Additionally, you may use the phone camera in Apple Pages to scan a document and insert a photo from your iPhone.

8. **Enable Voice to Text**

Do you know that the built-in voice detection feature in Apple Pages allows one to compose complete sentences?

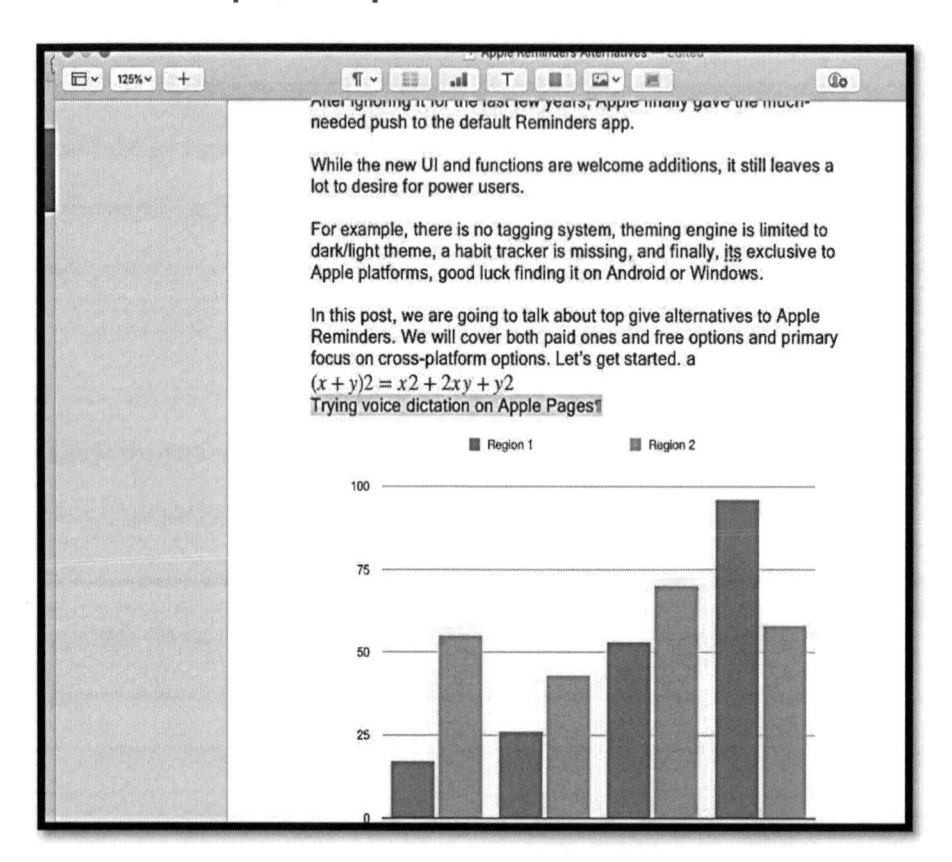

Open a document in Apple Pages, simply select **Edit > Start Dictation**. The software will request authorization before beginning voice typing, and it will receive it. With the English language, it functioned fairly well.

9. **Save A Document Style as A Template**

Professionals will benefit from this one. You might wish to create a letter pad in Apple Pages with your company's logo, address, email, website, and more. This default page can now be saved in Apple Pages as a template. Consequently, you don't need to start from the beginning each time.

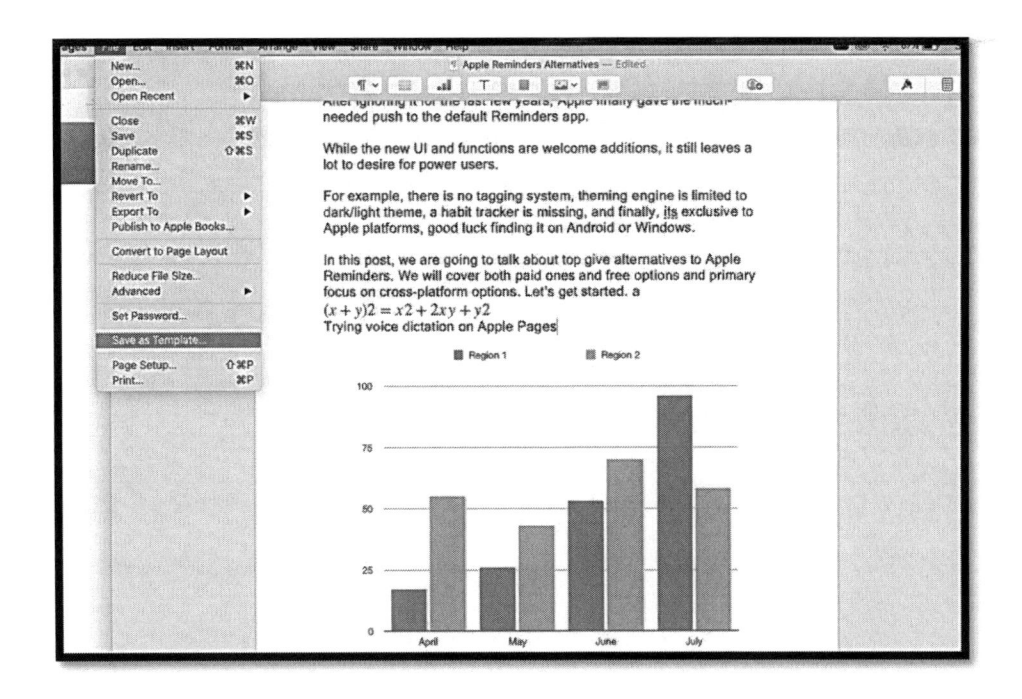

After making the required changes, select **File > Save a Template** and give it a meaningful name.

TEXT FLOW MODIFICATION

On the list of useful Pages features, text boxes come in at number one. They can be used to slap some text anywhere you want in a document. Text boxes are perfect for sidebars, captions, callouts, authorial asides, and any other type of text you need to include on a page that is not part of your document's normal text flow.

By selecting **Insert > Text Box** or the **Text** icon on the toolbar, you may simply create them.

In Pages, you could join text boxes up to 2013. If you link one text box to another, the extra text from the first box will flow into the second one if you enter more text in the first box than the first can show.

A link from that second text box may lead to a third, and so forth. This strategy worked effectively for publications like newsletters where each story could be organized into a separate group of linked boxes.

Text box linking, along with many other features Pages users had become accustomed to and loved, disappeared with the release of Apple's completely rebuilt Pages 5 in 2013. In revisions to Pages, Apple gradually added most of those features back, with a few here and there.

It wasn't until the middle of 2017 that pages once more offered a means to link text boxes, and even then, the feature had changed in both appearance and functionality. And that's helpful.

Linked Text Boxes of The Past

You can skip this section unless you're wondering if, before Pages 5, you never used linked text boxes.

Every new text box you added to a page had two tiny widgets, one on the upper-left edge and the other on the lower-right edge. This was how text box linking functioned. You clicked the upper-left widget (also known as the "**input widget**") of the second box after clicking the lower-right widget (also known as the "**output widget**") of the first box to make text flow from one box to the next.

To make it clear where text was flowing, pages illustrated the links between text boxes by drawing lines connecting the input and output widgets of the boxes.

Up to the point where you had boxes covering numerous pages like you might in a newsletter where an article starting in a box on page 1 might continue in a box on page 6, that's when it didn't work as well. It was tedious to follow that long blue linking line over numerous pages.

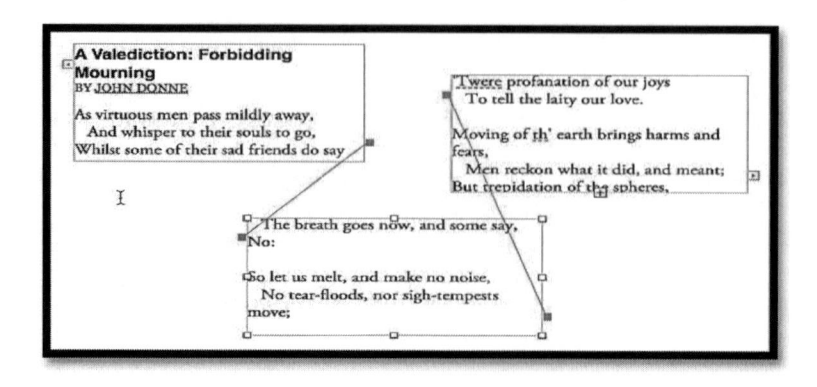

However, the linking feature was sufficient, so when it was removed in Pages 5, the Pages user community was very upset.

Modern Linked Text Boxes

Today's Pages allow you to link numerous text boxes together in a single thread and create multiple threads of linked text boxes within a single document. For example, you might begin several articles on page 1 of a newsletter and then continue each one on a different interior page because each thread would connect with a different article.

These threads aren't displayed as blue lines spanning between boxes like they were in Pages before version 5. Instead, the top of each text box contains a thread control widget that you can use to change how the box links with other boxes.

All three versions of Pages—Pages for Mac, Pages for iOS, and Pages for iCloud—support linked text boxes; in this section, we focus on Pages for Mac, while the feature is the same in the other two.

When the text box is selected, the thread control for an unlinked box is simply an empty circle; for a linked box, however, the thread control is colored and contains a number that shows where the box fits in the thread of linked boxes.

It's easy to add a text box to a thread: just add another text box to the page and click the **Thread Control**. Pages allocate the new box to the most recently modified thread and add additional text if necessary.

When you choose some text or position the insertion point inside a text box, **edit > Select All** will select all of the threaded text, so think of it as a document that is embedded within your Pages project.

Shift-clicking is also functional; for example, you can select text in one box of a thread, then Shift-click text in another box of the same thread to select the text between the first and second clicks.

Rearranging Links

The position of a text box within the page determines where it appears in a thread. In general, Pages places the new box at the end of the thread when you link a newly added box to a thread and that box is on the same page as (or on any page succeeding) the former last box in the thread.

What happens, though, if you add a new box to a page that loads before the beginning of a thread and link that box to that thread? The new box cleverly serves as the thread's starting box, and Pages renumbers the boxes in the thread so that the text flows between them seamlessly.

In other words, by default, there are no hard-coded links in the boxes; rather, the order in which you create them dictates where they appear in the thread.

Using The Thread Control

You don't have to fiddle with box positioning to get the desired threading order. By selecting the box's **Thread Control**, a pop-up menu of options appears, allowing you to change the location of the box inside a thread, remove it from a thread, or use it to create a new thread.

This one work great for those who don't appreciate how Apple frequently designs user interfaces with controls that only show when you're in the proper position.

The thread control widget emerges as soon as you select a text box; it also shows a pop-up **menu > indicator** when you hover over it; and when you click it, it gives you access to both control over the box's links to other boxes and information about those links.

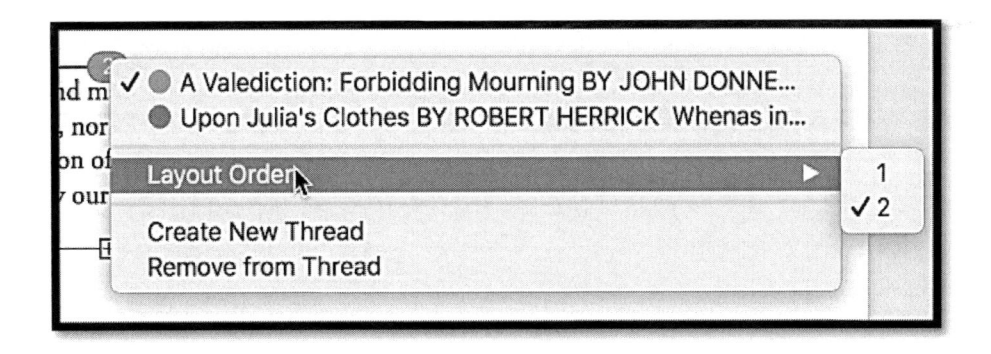

This menu allows you to:

- **Assign any thread to the box**: Each text box thread's opening text and distinguishing color are listed at the top of the menu. Decide the thread you wish to assign the box to.
- **Position the box differently in the thread**: To determine the location of the box in a thread, use the options on the **Layout Order** submenu. Using this option, you may quickly determine how long the thread is.
- **Start a new thread with the box**: Select **Create New Thread**. Starting a new thread and giving the box's thread control a number and a color kicks the box out of its current thread. Nothing is lost because the text from the original thread remains in any additional boxes in the thread even though the original text is no longer displayed in the box.
- **Remove the box from the thread**: Select **Remove from Thread**. As a result, the box is removed from the thread, and the thread control is left blank. No text is lost once more.

Making Threads Look Good

New text boxes in Pages are by default unadorned; they lack color, smell, and borders, and the filler text they hold uses the document's Body text style. **All of that is changeable:**

- **Single text box**: Use the controls on the **Style** tab of the **Format inspector** to change the look of a single-threaded text box by selecting only the box itself and excluding any of its contents. A new fill color or gradient can be applied, the border can be changed to a

range of various line styles or frames, and a shadow and reflection can be added.
- **All linked text boxes in a thread**: Control-click a threaded text box first, and then tap **Select All Text Boxes in Thread** from the menu that displays, to change the look of all linked text boxes in a thread at once. Click the boxes in the thread and change the settings on the Style tab of the Format inspector.
- **Text in threaded text boxes**: Select some or all of the threaded text in the threaded text box before using the options in the **Text Format inspector** to change the style. You can change the text in any Pages document, including setting styles, changing sizes, and more.

As a bonus, you may select **Format > Advanced > Set as Default Text Box Appearance** when you change a text box's appearance, such as its border and fill color. Existing text boxes in your document won't be affected by this command, but any new text boxes you add will have the updated look.

Conclusion

Between the departure of linked text boxes and their reemergence as threaded text boxes, a considerable amount of time had passed. Text box threading is a sleek, user-friendly, and potent replacement for the old linked text box feature, even though it may have appeared like Apple took its time bringing it back.

Users who believed that the release of Pages 5 in 2013 irreparably "dumbed down" the app might want to see how intelligent the most recent version of Pages is in 2022.

MAKING USE OF BIDIRECTIONAL TEXT

You can enter and edit text written from both the left to right (as in English or Chinese) or the right to left (as in Arabic or Hebrew) directions in the same document since Pages supports bidirectional text. Bidirectional text is available in tables, shapes, and paragraphs.

You must create an input source in **Keyboard Preferences** (in **System Preferences** on your Mac) to use another language in your document. In the **Finder**, select **Help > Help Center** and then enter "**input sources**" to learn more.

Any Pages **template** can be used to create a bidirectional document, but to use templates created expressly for a different language, you must first change your computer's primary language in **System Preferences** to that language.

Note: Restart Pages after adding a new input source to your computer so that it can identify it.

Use Another Language in Pages

- On the right side of the menu bar on your computer, select an input source from the Input menu.

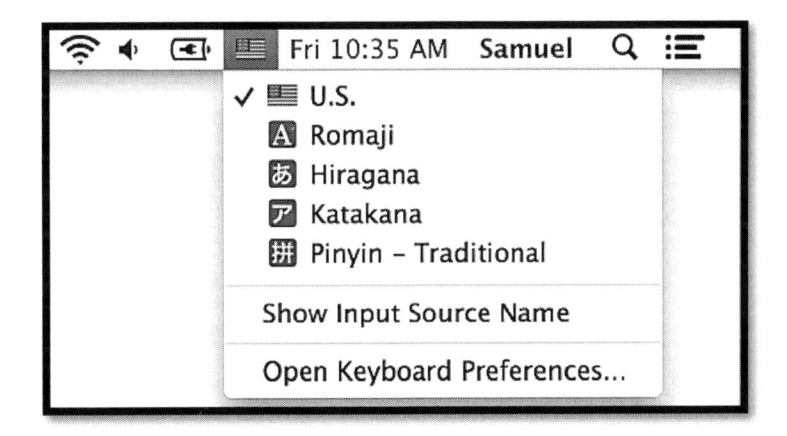

The language you choose causes the insertion point to move to that side of the document. The insertion point goes to the right side of the document and any existing text in the paragraph does the same if, for instance, you change the input source from English to Hebrew.

Change Paragraph Text Direction

When you change the text direction for selected text, the ruler also changes because it always follows the direction of a paragraph.

- A paragraph or list can be selected by clicking on it, or by clicking on the text inside it.

- Use the **Input** menu to switch the language, or use the **Paragraph direction** icon ⇆ in the **Format inspector's Text** pane to enter text in the current language. The paragraph direction changes as the insertion point shifts to the opposite side.

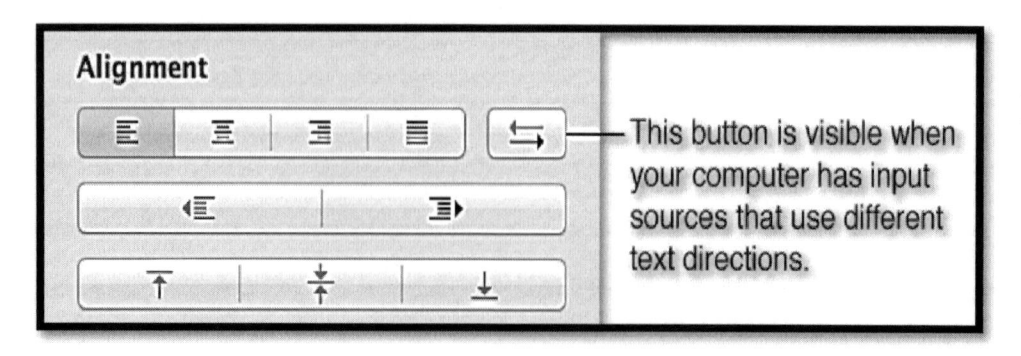

Alignment — This button is visible when your computer has input sources that use different text directions.

- At the end of the paragraph, type text and then click **Return**. The same direction is taken in the following paragraph. The language can be selected from the Input menu or by clicking the **Paragraph direction** icon ⇆.

When you click the **Paragraph direction** icon ⇆ after selecting several paragraphs with different text directions, the paragraphs in your selection are formatted to resemble the first paragraph in your selection. The text in the selected shapes is formatted to match the first shape you choose if you choose multiple shapes that have text inside them with various text directions.

In the **Finder**, select **Help > Help Center**, then type "**bidirectional text**" to discover how to type, edit, and use bidirectional text as well as some of the OS X supporting features.

EXAMINING FORMATTING SYMBOLS

Each time you hit the **Spacebar**, **Tab**, or **Return** key, as well as any time you add a column break, page break, or section break, **formatting symbols** (also known as **Invisibles**) similar to the ones below, are added.

When you select the text that contains Invisibles on your iPhone or iPad, you can usually see them. Click on an open area of the page, then click **Select All**, to quickly display every symbol in your document.

Invisible Character Represents

•	Space
⋮	Nonbreaking space (Option-Space bar)
→	Tab
↵	Line break (Shift-Return)
¶	Paragraph break (Return)
🗋	Page break
⑊	Column break
⊓	Layout break
▤	Section break

↑	Anchor point for objects set to Move with Text and any text wrap option except Inline with Text
Blue box around text	The text is bookmarked

If text goes below the borders of a text box, a **clipping indicator** ⊞ is displayed at the bottom. Up until the text box is resized to display the entire text, this symbol is still visible.

CHAPTER FIVE
ENHANCING YOUR DOCUMENTS WITH PAGES

There is a lot of stuff you can do with documents in Pages and this chapter will treat them.

ADDING IMAGES TO DOCUMENTS

You can find instructions on how to include images and other visuals into your Pages documents in this section.

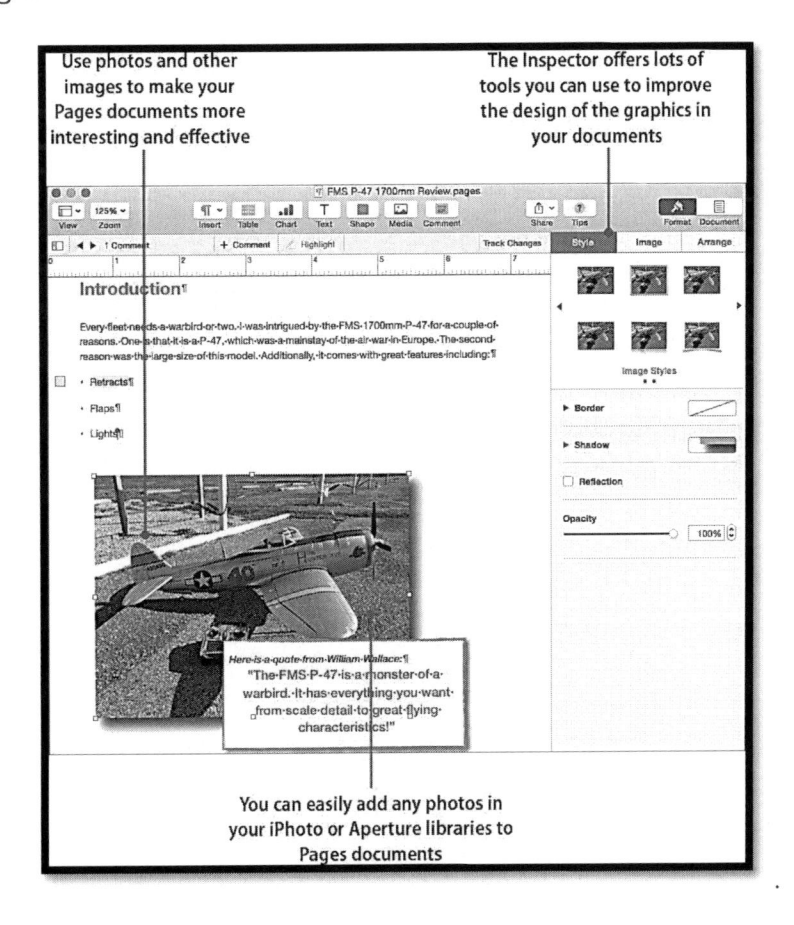

The cliche "A picture is worth a thousand words" is both outdated and overused. The principle that this cliche expresses is that images successfully communicate happens to be accurate, which explains why it is used so frequently. The cliche fails to mention that most often, a story cannot be told entirely through images.

The best communication often combines both written and visual elements. Pages also give you a lot of options for working with text and tables. So, you'll learn how to use visual components, such as images, in your Pages documents to increase their efficacy and aesthetic appeal.

Insert Photos and Other Graphics into Pages Documents

Your iPhoto or Aperture library, other locations on your Mac, pictures you've made and saved on your computer, and images you've downloaded are just a few of the various sorts of graphics you can include in your documents. (If you intend to use a downloaded image in a document, ensure you don't breach any copyright or other use restrictions.)

You can include pictures and other images in your Pages documents in a variety of ways, including the following:

- Replace an image placeholder with a photo from iPhoto.
- Add an image from the Media Browser.
- Drag an image from your desktop into a document.

The following activities provide explanations for each of these options.

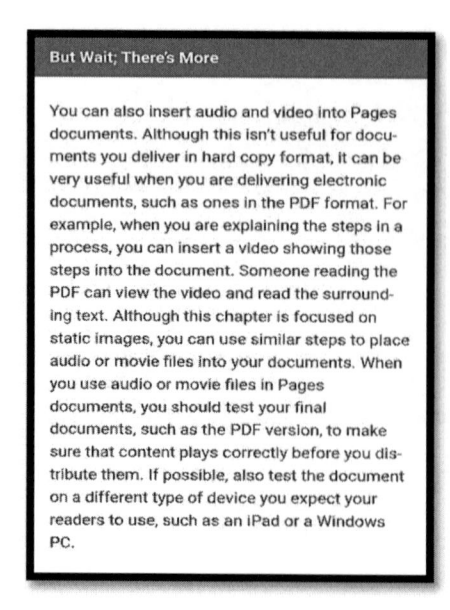

> **But Wait; There's More**
>
> You can also insert audio and video into Pages documents. Although this isn't useful for documents you deliver in hard copy format, it can be very useful when you are delivering electronic documents, such as ones in the PDF format. For example, when you are explaining the steps in a process, you can insert a video showing those steps into the document. Someone reading the PDF can view the video and read the surrounding text. Although this chapter is focused on static images, you can use similar steps to place audio or movie files into your documents. When you use audio or movie files in Pages documents, you should test your final documents, such as the PDF version, to make sure that content plays correctly before you distribute them. If possible, also test the document on a different type of device you expect your readers to use, such as an iPad or a Windows PC.

1. Replace an Image Placeholder with a Photo from iPhoto

You can upload your photographs to many of the image placeholders in Pages document templates.

- For the **image placeholder**, click the symbol in the bottom-right corner. The **Media Browser** is displayed.

- Navigate to the **Photos** tab. The images in your iPhoto **Photo Library** are displayed. The photo sources are displayed on the left side of the browser and are identical to those in iPhoto.

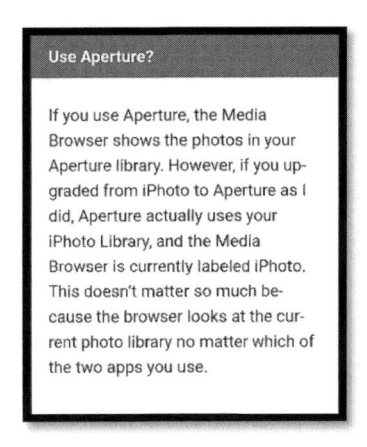

> **Use Aperture?**
>
> If you use Aperture, the Media Browser shows the photos in your Aperture library. However, if you upgraded from iPhoto to Aperture as I did, Aperture actually uses your iPhoto Library, and the Media Browser is currently labeled iPhoto. This doesn't matter so much because the browser looks at the current photo library no matter which of the two apps you use.

- Choose the photo source from which you want to browse. The images from that source are visible.
- View the images in the source you selected.
- To replace the placeholder image, click the image you wish to use. The image stands in for the placeholder. (Note that the placeholder icon for the image vanishes.)

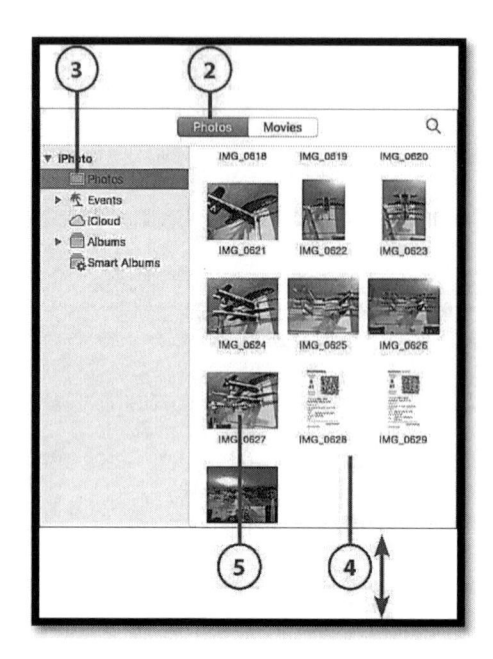

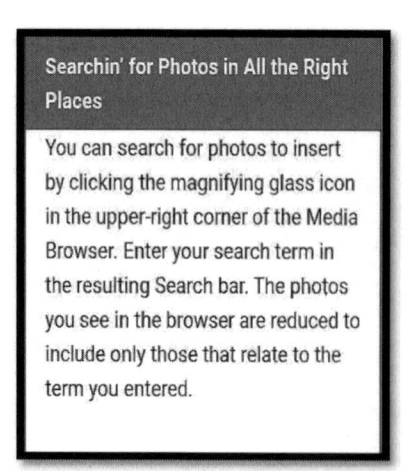

> **Searchin' for Photos in All the Right Places**
>
> You can search for photos to insert by clicking the magnifying glass icon in the upper-right corner of the Media Browser. Enter your search term in the resulting Search bar. The photos you see in the browser are reduced to include only those that relate to the term you entered.

- To design the image, use the **Pages** tools (described in "**Design Photos and Other Images in Pages Documents**" later in this section).

2. Use the Media Browser to Insert Photos into Pages Documents

To insert a picture anywhere in a document, use the Media Browser.

- Put the cursor approximately where you want the picture to be. (You can quickly move it later.)
- From the toolbar, select the **Media** button. The **Media Browser** is displayed.

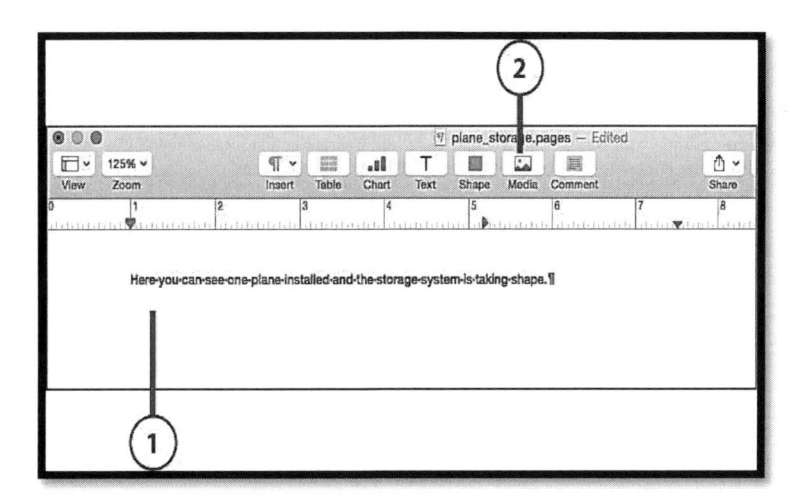

- To choose the photo you wish to insert into the document, follow steps 2 through 5 from the prior task.

137

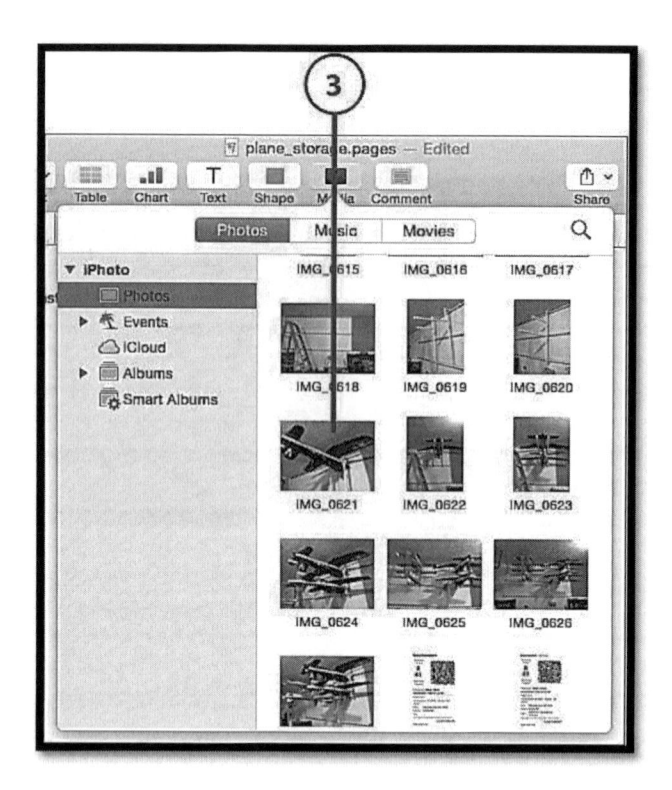

- Use the tools in Pages to design the image (further instructions are provided in the section below under "**Design Photos and Other Images in Pages Documents**").

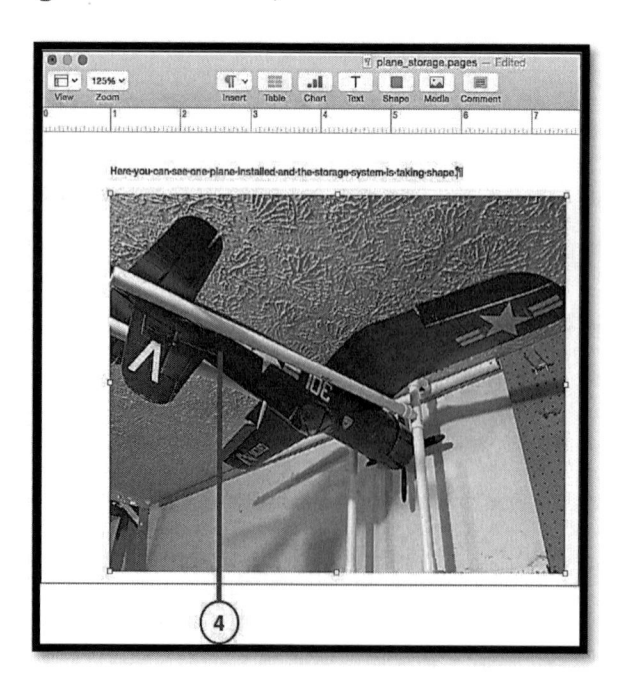

> **>>> Go Further: Add Shapes to Pages Documents**
>
> You can add various kinds of shapes to your Pages documents, such as lines, curves, circles, squares, and stars. You can add shapes from the templates available in Pages and then customize them for your specific use. For example, you can change the fill color, resize them, and so on. Working with shapes is quite similar to other objects you've learned about. Click the Shape button on the Pages toolbar. Then browse the available shapes to find the one closest to the shape you want to add to your document. Click that shape, and it is added at the current location of the cursor. You can then resize the shape, position it on the page, and use the shape tools in the Inspector to format it.

3. Drag Photos and Other Graphics from the Mac Desktop into Pages Documents

Only images and graphics saved in iPhoto or Aperture are accessible through the Media Browser.

Any image that is saved on your Mac can be added to a Pages document by dragging it there from the desktop.

- Put the cursor approximately where you want the picture to be. (You can quickly move it later.)

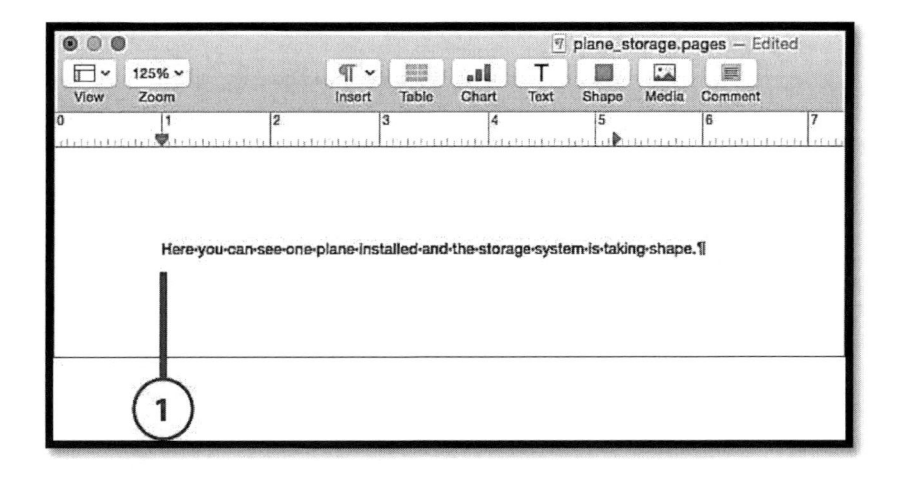

139

- Navigate to the location of the photo you wish to include in the document by opening a **Finder** window.
- Drag the file onto the Pages document from the **Finder** window. A copy of the image is added to the document.

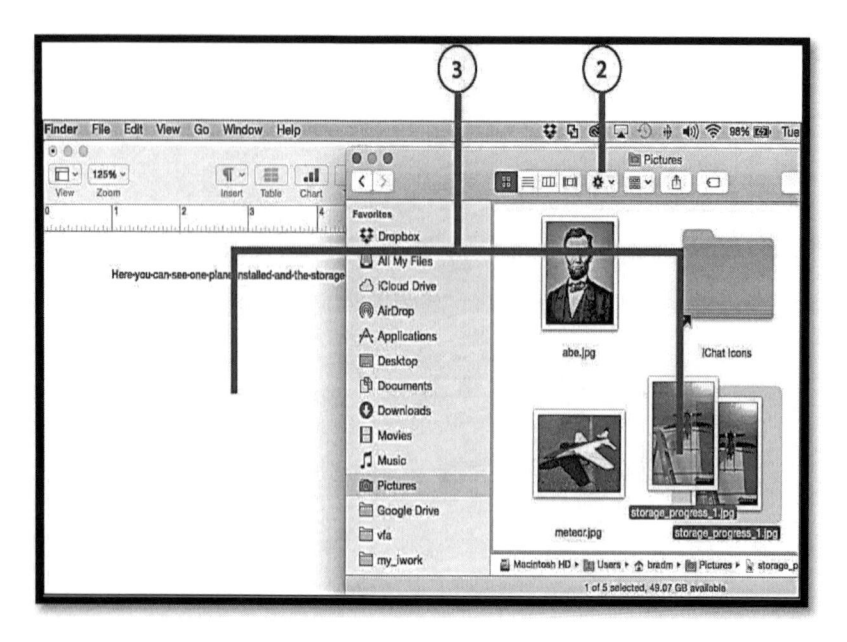

- Use the tools in Pages to design the image (further instructions are provided in the section below under "**Design Photos and Other Images in Pages Documents**").

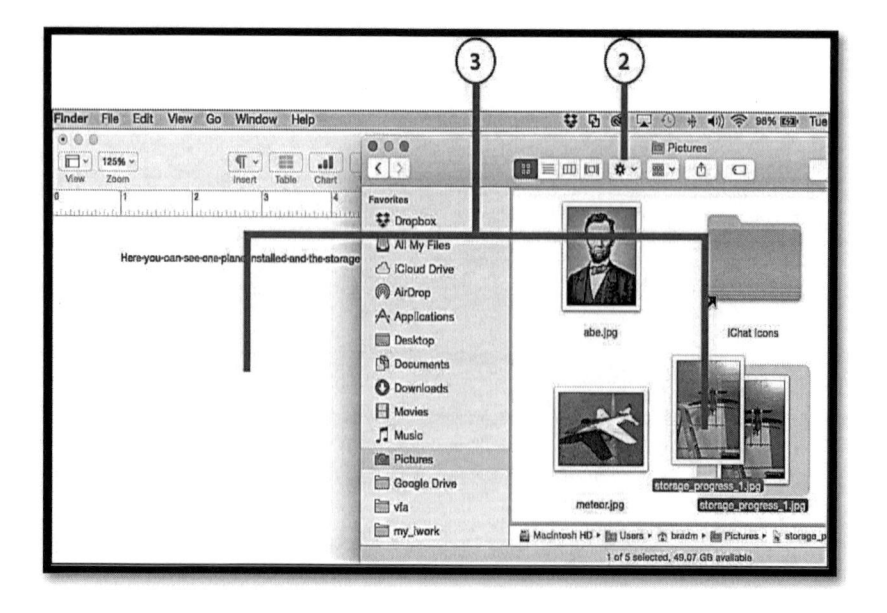

Is Dragging a Drag?

You can also add a photo by selecting **Insert > Other** as an alternative option. Move to and select the photo file you wish to enter using the ensuing dialog, select it, and click **Open**. The image you chose is positioned where the cursor is right now.

The Finder window doesn't need to be placed in a way that it can be seen alongside your Pages document, making this option easier than dragging.

Don't Have the Image Yet?

You might be aware that you want to use a particular image in a document, but you don't yet have the final result available. In this situation, you can make an image placeholder to provide a blank space for a picture and then, when the finished image is ready, replace the placeholder with it.

Add a picture to the document and scale it to the size you want the final image to be to create a placeholder. Select the image, then click **Format > Advanced > Define as Media Placeholder**.

The final image can then be replaced for it as instructed in the assignment "Replace an Image Placeholder with a Photo from iPhoto" previously in this section.

Design Photos and Other Images in Pages Documents

You have a variety of design options for the photos and other images in your Pages documents, including the ones listed below:

- **Resize images or photos**: Images can be resized to fit the page or to reflect their importance or level of detail with the content. The proportion of the images can also be changed, however doing so may have unforeseen effects.
  Therefore, take care when resizing images outside of their proportions to avoid getting squashed or stretched versions.
- **Rotate images or photos**: You can rotate or flip photos in either a horizontal or vertical direction.

- **Style images or photos**: The Inspector lets you add borders, drop shadows, and reflections, then adjust the opacity of photos and images to change how they seem. You can express your creativity while using these tools to create images more impactful and aesthetically pleasing.
  You can use the built-in styles in Pages to style elements like text and tables, or you can build and save your styles.
- **Mask any images or photos**: When creating a document, masking can be used to remove parts of images. In contrast to cropping, masking allows you to select the portion of an image that should be visible while hiding the rest so that it cannot be seen. Masking is similar to cropping, with the exception that it does not change the image.
  Masking is advantageous because it is simple to adjust the mask or to take it off entirely to reveal the entire image once more. (This contrasts with cropping, which removes and makes unavailable a portion of the image.)
- **Remove background from photos or images**: Sometimes the background of an image contains distracting features. To make the main subject of an image stand out more, you can utilize the tools in Pages to remove the background from the image.
- **Adjust photos or images**: Pages have some basic features you can use to enhance the quality of the photographs in your documents, even though it is not a photo-editing app. These involve changing the photos' exposure, contrast, saturation, and other settings.
  Additionally, you may instruct Pages to make manual edits to a photo by using the app's Enhance feature. Starting with the **Enhance tool** is frequently an excellent idea because you can quickly reverse its effects and make manual adjustments to the photo if you don't like them.
- **Manually reposition images or photos**: Generally speaking, images and photos should be placed in the text section to which they pertain. Photos in Pages can be manually positioned on a page much like other objects.
- **For placement of images or photos, use the Arrange tab**: You can utilize the tools on the **Inspector's Arrange** tab to see how images and photos relate to the surrounding text. Photos and images can be

set up to float with the surrounding text or stay on the page. Images can be rotated, layered, and more.

For information on how to complete each of these design activities, see the tasks that follow.

1. Resize images or photos

The following are simple methods for resizing images in documents:

- Choose the image that needs to be resized.
- To resize or enlarge a picture, drag a **selection** handle that can be found on its corners. As you drag, a line crosses the image's diagonal, and the selection handle's current dimensions are displayed beside it.

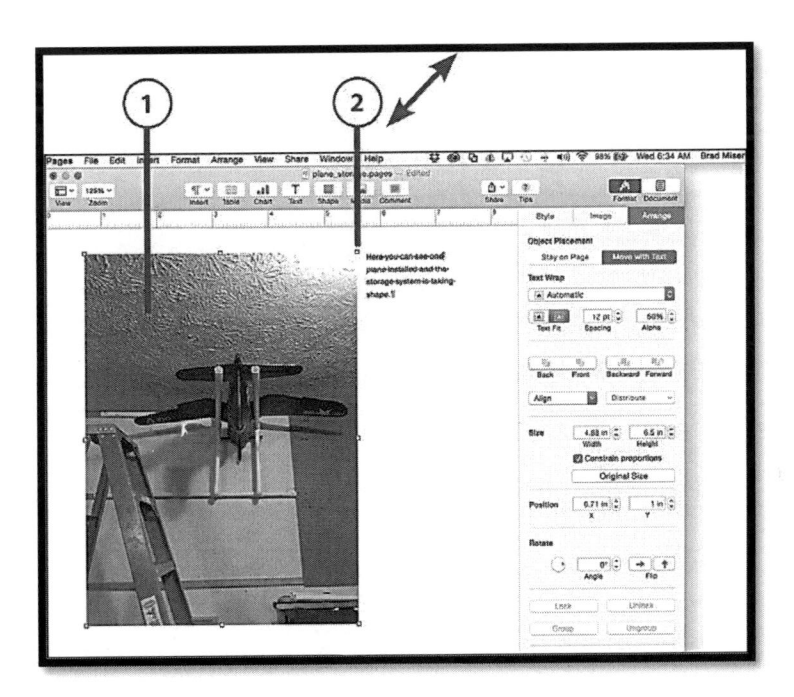

Resizing Other Kinds of Graphics

Pages presume that you wish to keep the number of photos you add to documents the same. Other types of graphics you might utilize do not follow this rule. Hold down the **Shift** key while dragging a corner of the graphic to ensure the proportions are maintained.

As you resize it, its proportions are preserved. Based on the type of graphic you are working with; the proportions could not be preserved if you don't hold down the **Shift** key.

- Release the selection handle once the image is at the desired size.

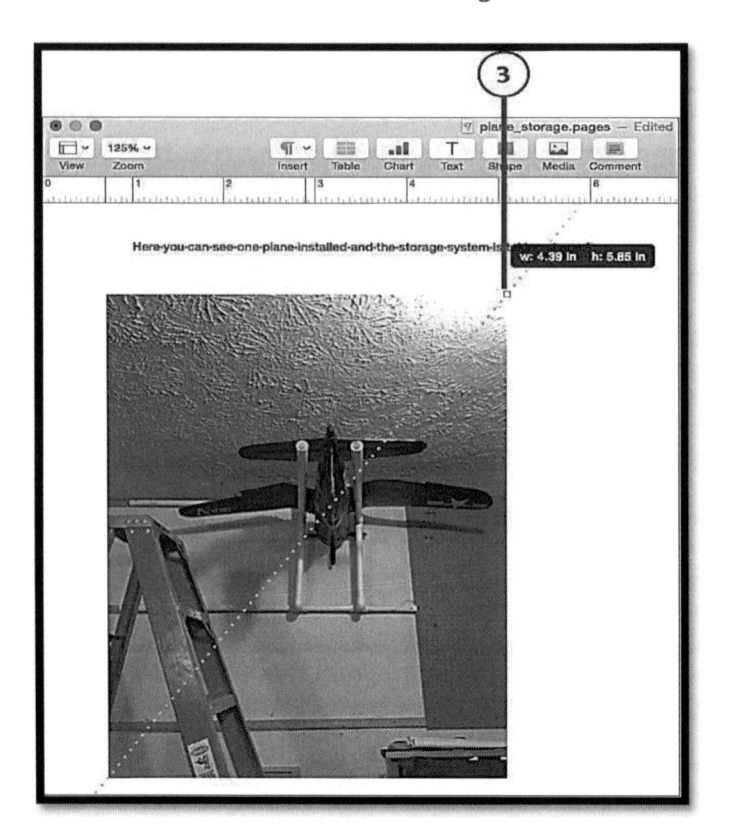

Be Precise

Select the image you wish to resize and select the **Arrange** tab in the **Inspector** to resize it with more precision. To resize the image, use the **Size** tools. The dimensions for Width and Height can be entered or selected.

To maintain the image's proportion when changing dimensions, use the **Constrain proportions** check box. To restore the image to its original size from when you first added it to the document, select **Original Size**.

2. Rotate images or photos

The steps listed below can be used to adjust the orientation of images or photos in your documents:

- Choose the photo that you want to rotate.
- Select the **Inspector's Arrange** tab.
- Type the angle you want to rotate the image by; for instance, to rotate it 90 degrees clockwise, type **-90** in the **Angle** box.

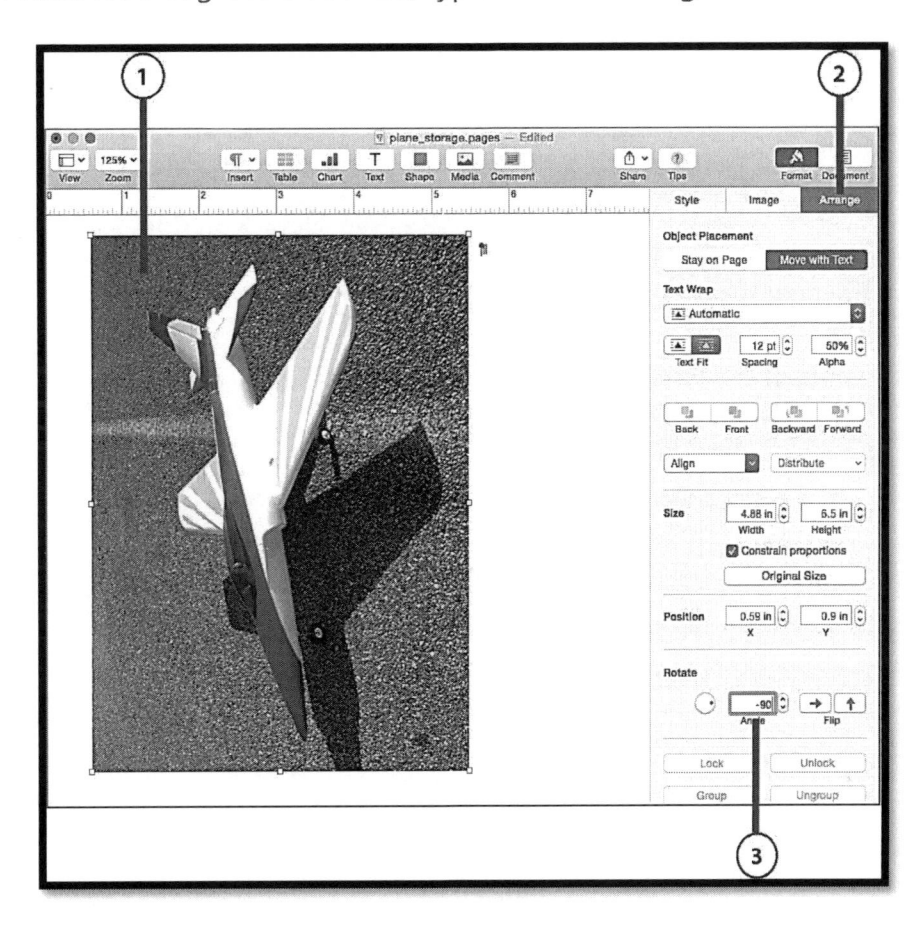

- Hit the **Enter** key. The amount you enter rotates the image.
- Drag the **Rotate wheel** either clockwise or counterclockwise to rotate a picture. The image rotates as you drag, and the **Angle** box updates to show the current angle.
- Press the **horizontal arrow** to turn an image horizontally.
- Press the **vertical arrow** to turn an image vertically.

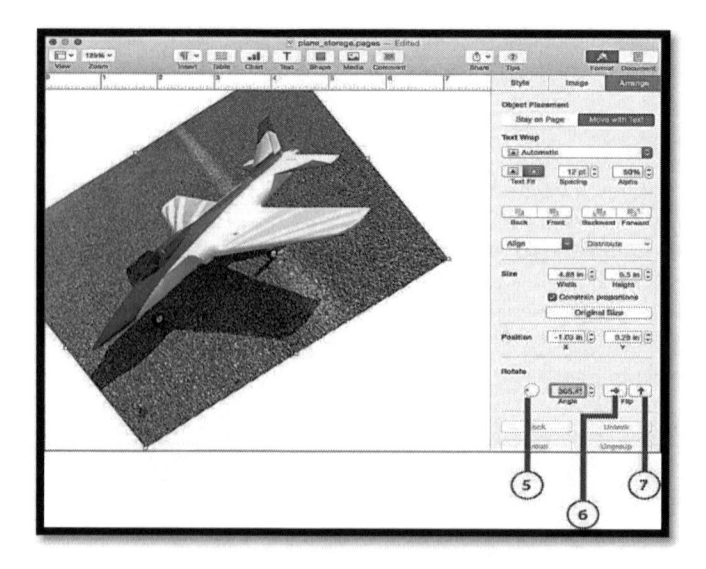

3. Style images or photos

To give pictures and other images in Pages documents more visual interest, use the style tools.

- Choose the image you wish to style.
- In the **Inspector**, select the **Style** tab.
- To view the available styles, use the arrows on the left or right of the screen.
- Choose a style to add to the image by clicking it. The image is styled appropriately. You can skip the remaining steps if you are satisfied with the photo.
- Press the **disclosure triangle** beside **Border** to manually add a border.

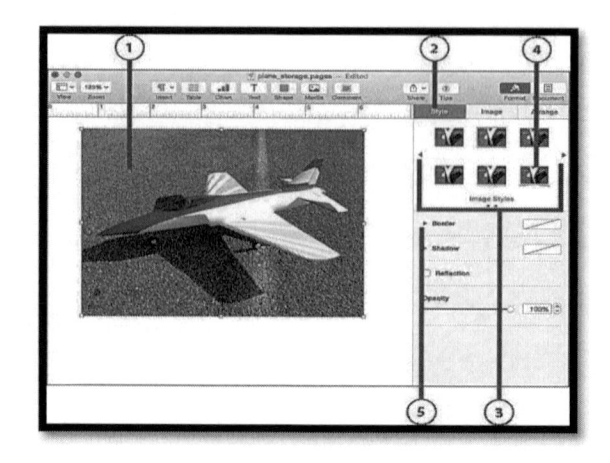

146

- Select the border style you want to use. **Line, Picture Frame,** and **No Border** are the available options.
- Press the **Frame** menu when you click **Picture Frame** to configure the options for that type.

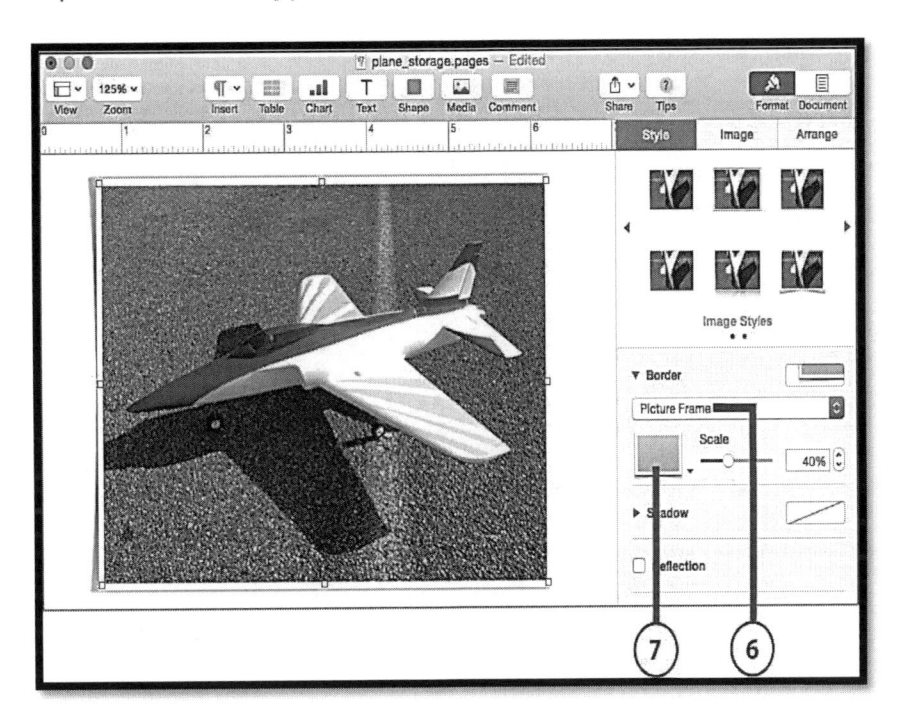

- Select the style of frame you want to apply.

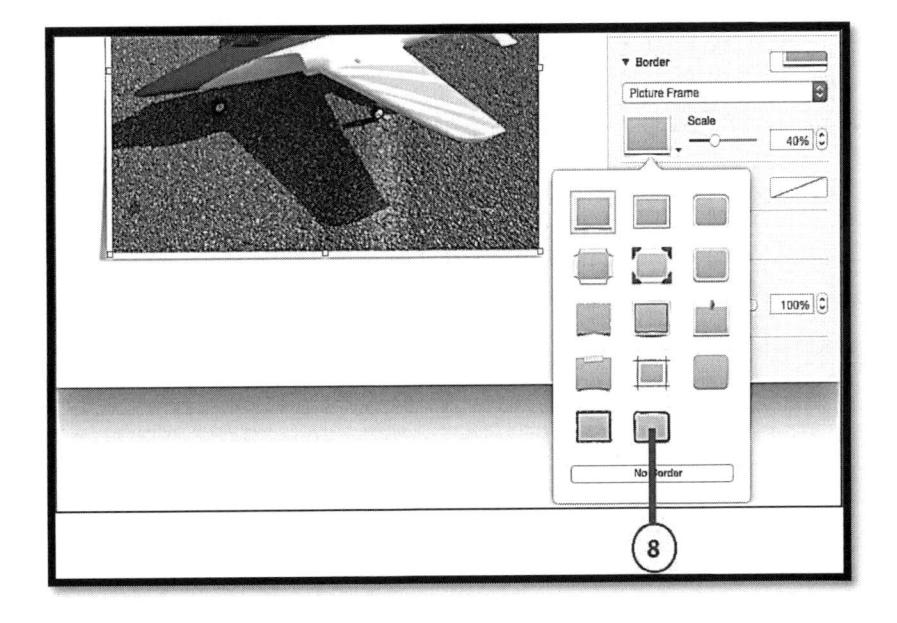

147

- To change the border's thickness, move the **Scale** slider to the left to make it thinner or to the right to make it thicker. You can also enter or select a scale by using the scale box.
- Simply click the **disclosure triangle** beside **Shadow** to add a shadow to the image.

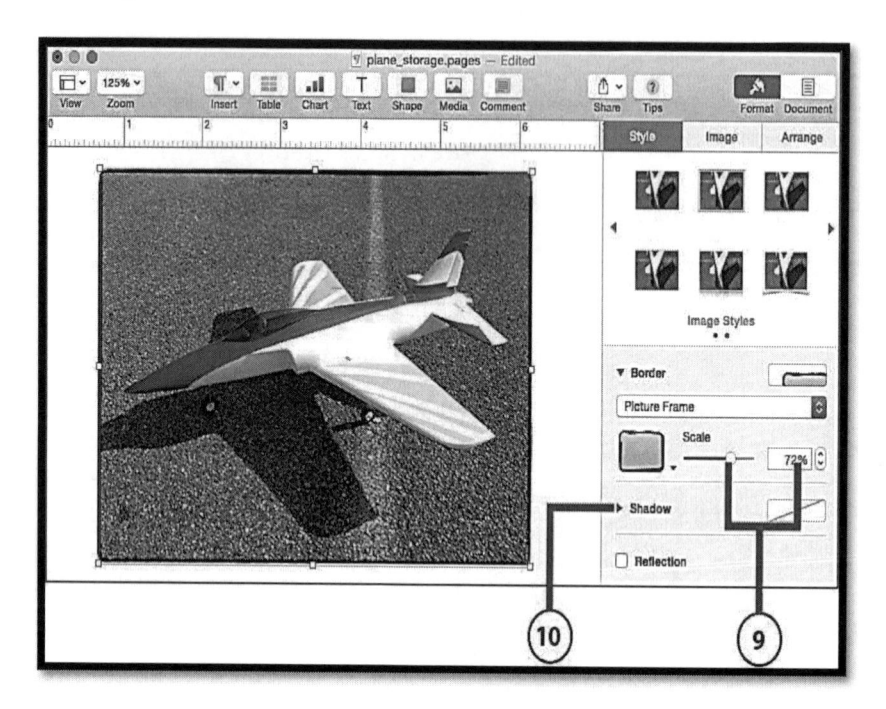

- Select the kind of shadow you want to use from the **Shadow** menu. **None, Drop Shadow, Contact Shadow,** and **Curved Shadow** are the available options. These methods demonstrate the **Curved Shadow** option, although similar procedures apply to the others.
- To choose whether the shadow should curve toward the image or away from it, as well as how much curvature there should be, move the Inward slider to the left or right.
- To adjust the size of the shadow with the bottom (by choosing a **positive offset**) or the top of the image, use the **Offset** slider or box (using a **negative offset**).
- To change how opaque or transparent the shadow is, use the **Opacity** slider or box.
- To change the shadow's angle, use the **Angle** box or **wheel**.
- To change the shadow's color, use the **Color tool**.

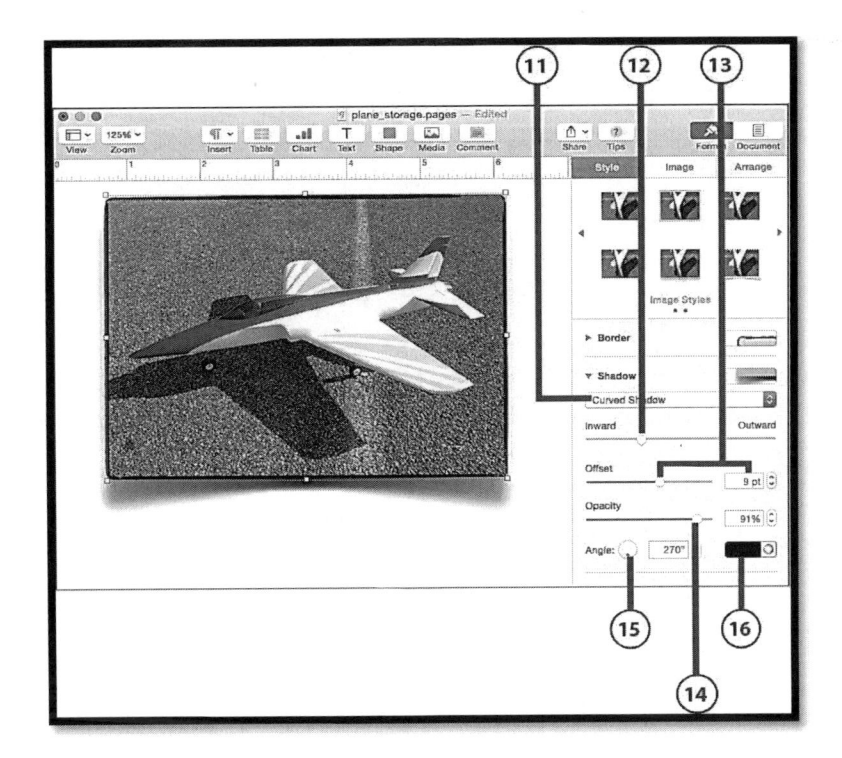

- Check the **Reflection** check box to add a reflection to the image.
- To adjust the amount of reflection, use the **Reflection** slider or box.
- To make the image more opaque or transparent, move the slider or box next to **Opacity**.
- When you see an empty style with the add **(+)** icon, press the right-facing arrow at the top of the **Style** tab to make it possible to reuse the styles you've already applied.

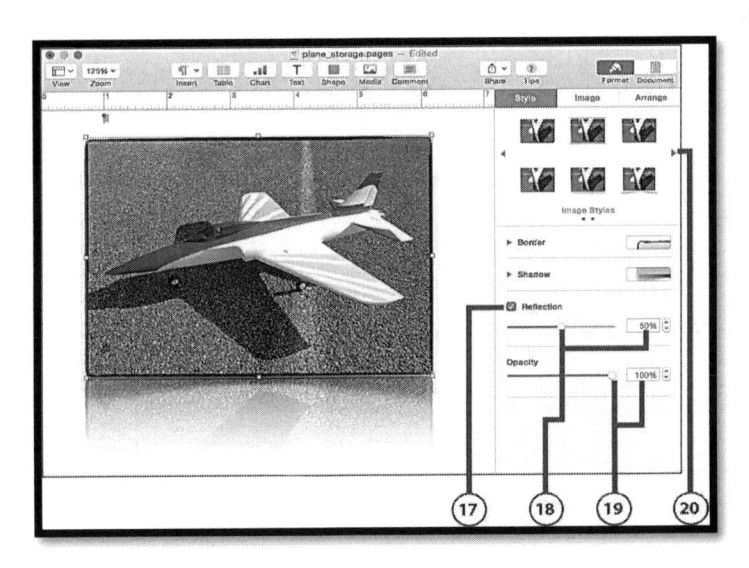

- To save your current style settings, select the **empty style** box.

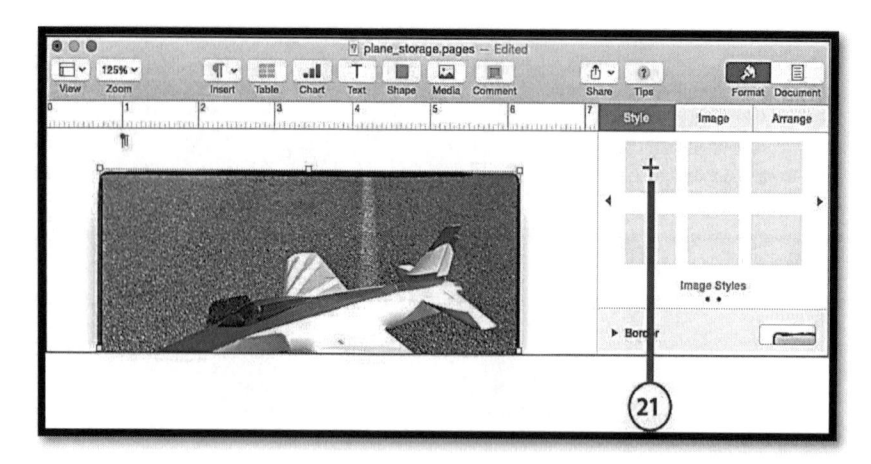

㉑

- Select the image to which you want to apply your style, then click the style you saved.

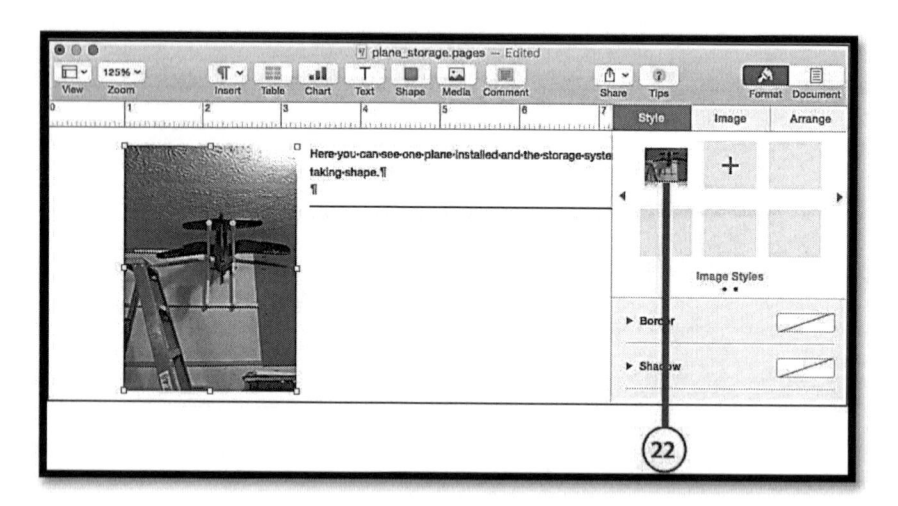

㉒

Delete Custom Styles

You can remove saved styles by performing a secondary click and selecting **Delete Style**. The style that was saved is gone.

4. Mask any images or photos

You can hide any photo parts you don't want to show in a document.

- The image you wish to mask should be selected.
- Select the **Inspector's Image** tab.

- Press **Edit Mask**. The mask tool shows up.

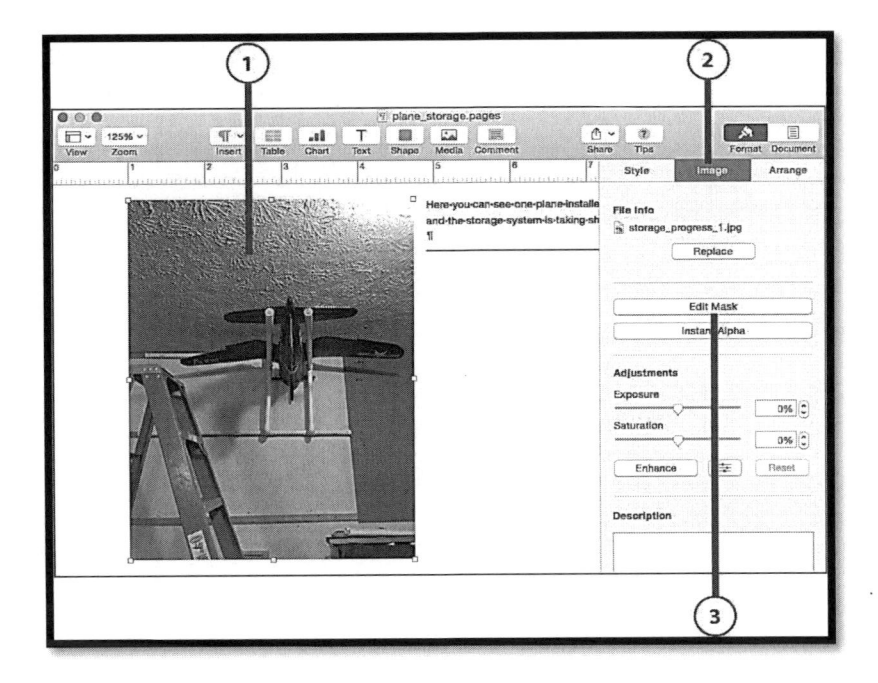

- The size of the image within the frame can be changed by dragging the slider to the left or right. The image's non-displayable portions are highlighted in gray.

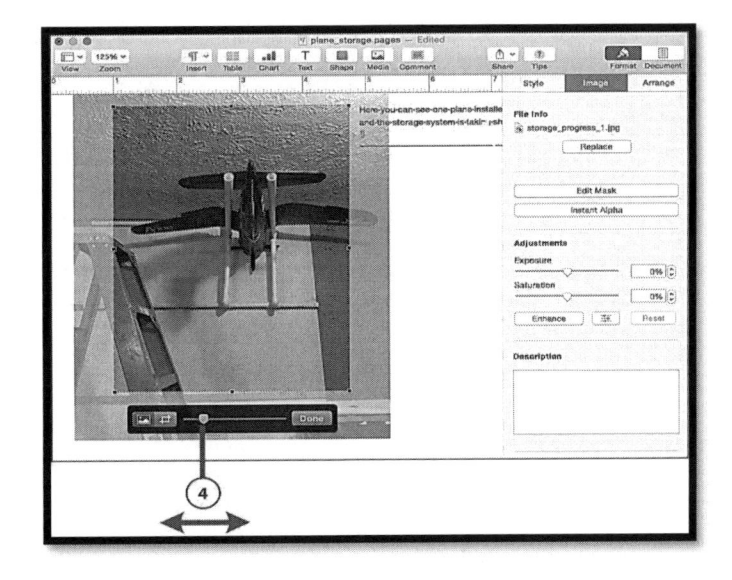

- To change the mask box's proportions, move the selection handles on the box.

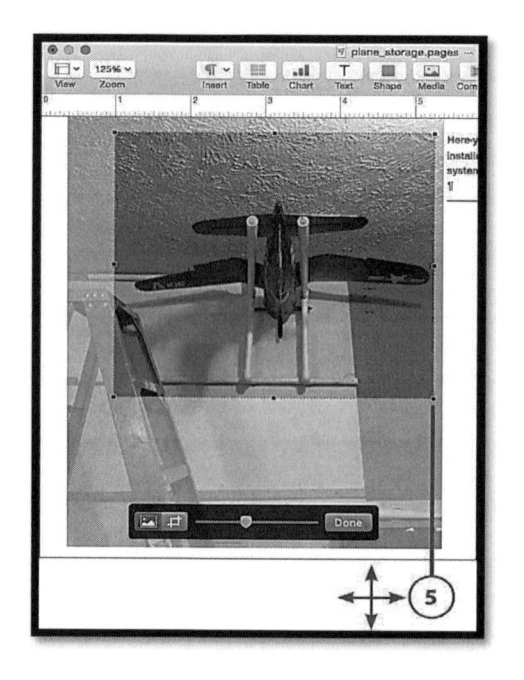

- To change the area of the image that is visible, move the image inside the box.
- Click **Done** once you've finished making changes. The image is masked.

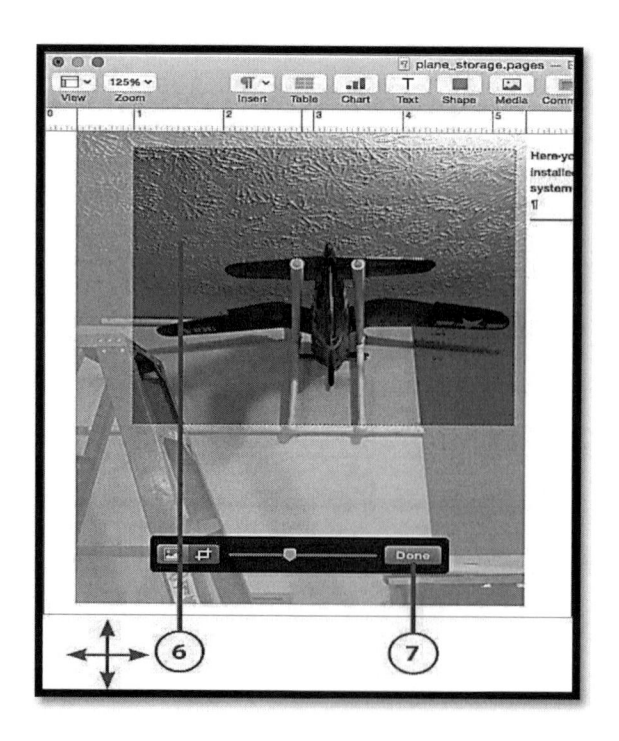

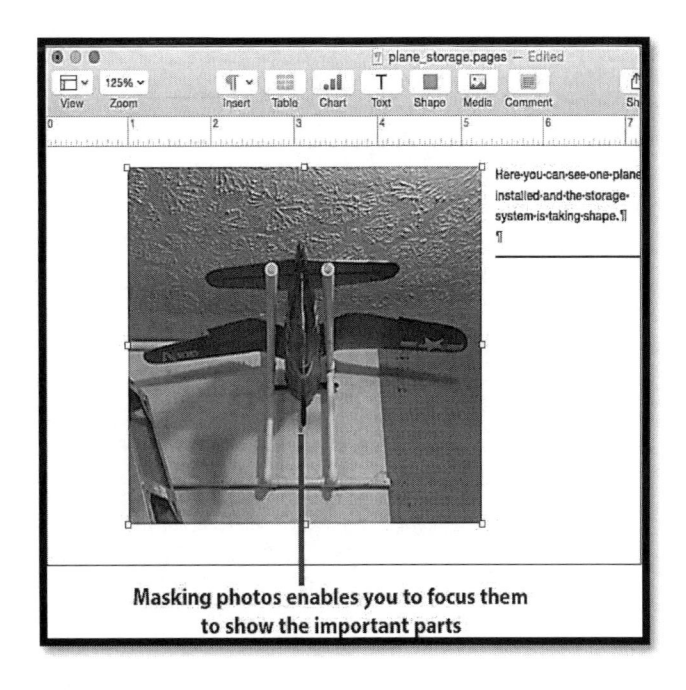

Masking photos enables you to focus them to show the important parts

5. Remove background from photos or images

Use the Instant Alpha tool to erase background components or any color from photographs.

- Select the image you wish to change.
- Go to the **Image** tab.
- Then select **Instant** Alpha.

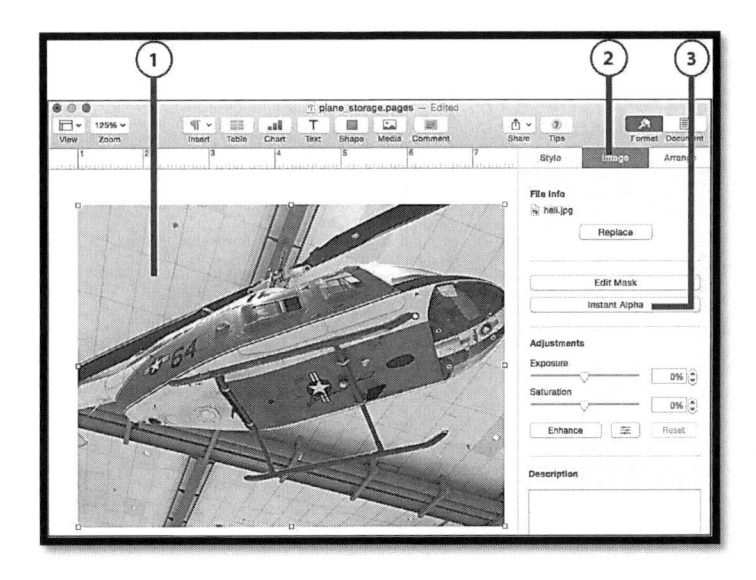

153

- You can remove the color from the image by dragging it over the desired locations. The matching areas of the image that will be hidden are highlighted in blue as colors are selected. (Instead of dragging, simply click on a color to delete it.)

- Select more colors to remove.

- Hit **Done** once the image is displayed in the document as you desire.

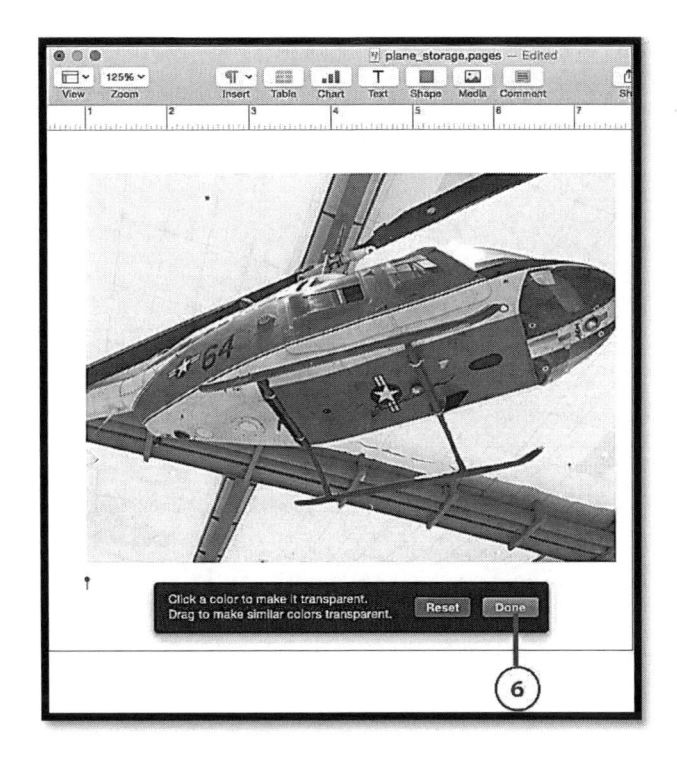

6. Adjust photos or images

Pages isn't an image editing app, but it does allow you to make some simple edits:

- Choose the image you wish to change.
- Toggle to the **Image** tab.
- To have Pages adjust the image for you, select **Enhance**. You're done if you like the results. If not, keep making manual adjustments.

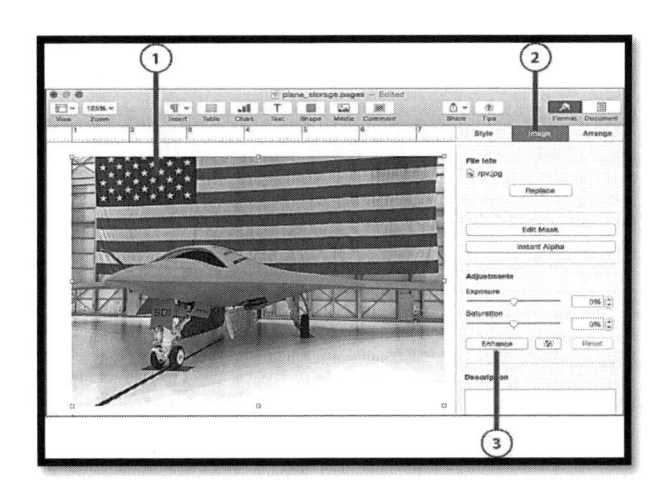

- To change the exposure of the picture, use the **Exposure** slider and box.
- To change the color saturation of the image, use the **Saturation** slider and box.
- Hit the **Adjust Image** icon to access even more options. A palette called **Adjust Image** emerges.

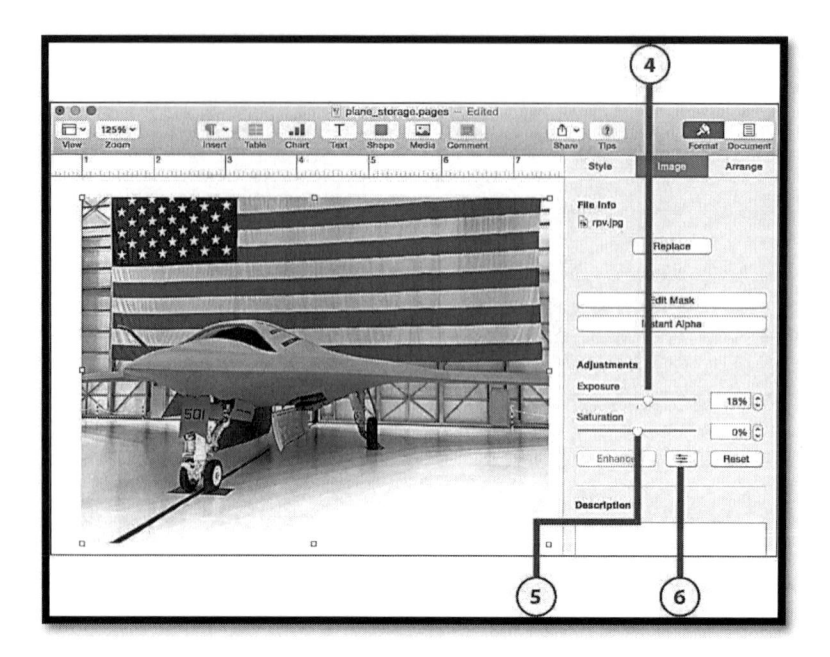

- To add extra adjustments to the image, use the tools on the **Adjust Image** palette.
- When you've finished adjusting the image, close the palette.

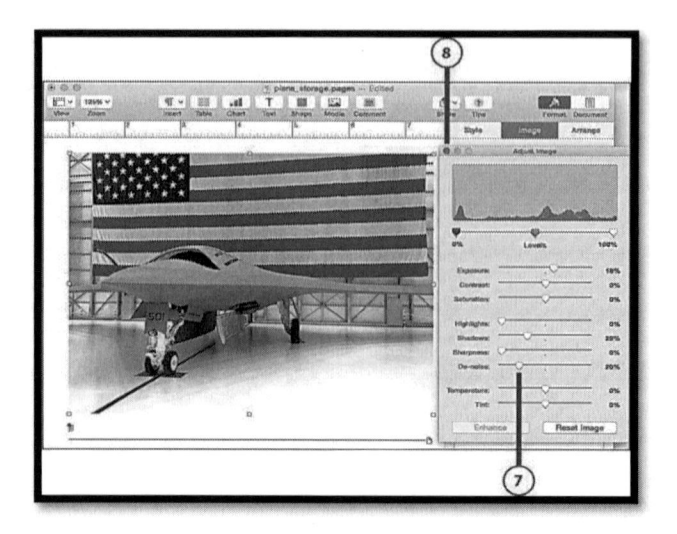

Note: The majority of Pages' photo editing tools provide a reset option that you can utilize to reverse any changes you've made. For instance, click Reset if after making adjustments, you decide that the photo is not better.

7. Manually reposition images or photos

Photos and other images can be moved about in your Pages documents by simply dragging them.

- Select the image that you want to move.
- The image can be moved around the document. Its present location may be seen in the black pop-up box as you move it. When the photo is positioned to something, yellow alignment lines become visible. For instance, if a yellow line runs down the middle of the image, it indicates that the image's centerline and the document's centerline are in line. Alignment lines can also be seen at the top, bottom, or on either side. Based on the photo's **Arrange** settings (covered in the next task), the text flows around it.

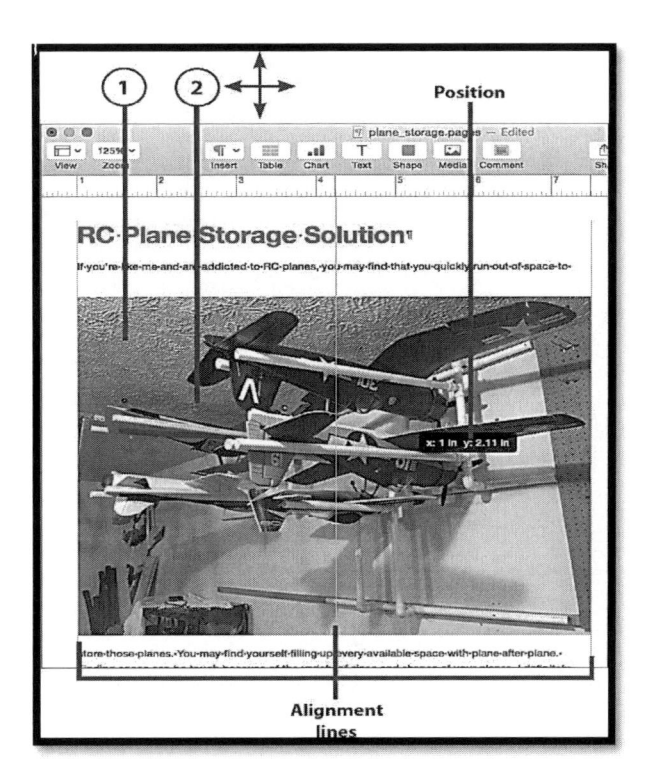

- Release the photo after it is in the desired location.

Distribute Graphics

If you have several graphics, you can arrange them on the page in an even distribution. Simply select the graphics you want to distribute. Click the **Distribute** menu on the **Inspector's Arrange** tab and select how you want the images to be distributed. For instance, select **Horizontally** if you want the graphics to fill the entire width of the page.

8. For placement of images or photos, use the Arrange tab

Decide how a photo relates with the text and other objects on the page where it displays by configuring the **Arrange** settings.

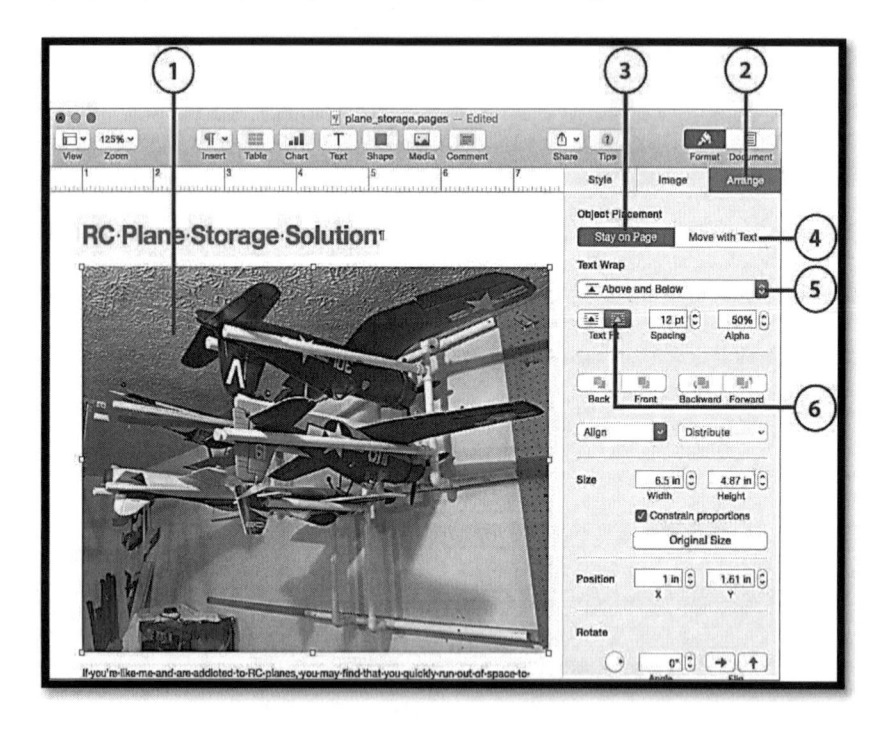

- Select the image that you wish to configure.
- Go to the **Arrange** tab.
- Select **Stay on Page** if you want the image to stay on the current page while the text is placed above it.
- Select **Move with Text** if you want the image to float so that it keeps the context of the text around it when you add text or other content before it.
- Decide how you want the photo to interact with the text surrounding it from the Text Wrap option. To have Pages automatically flow the

text, select **Automatic**. To have the text flow around the top, bottom, and sides of the image, select **Around**.

Alternatively, select **Above and Below** to have text flow along the image's top and bottom but not its sides.

- To control how closely text matches the borders of a picture, use the **Text Fit** button. To make the text match the image's rectangle border, press the button on the left. The text will flow to the shape of the image if you press the button on the right. For shapes and other non-rectangular graphics, this option is most helpful.

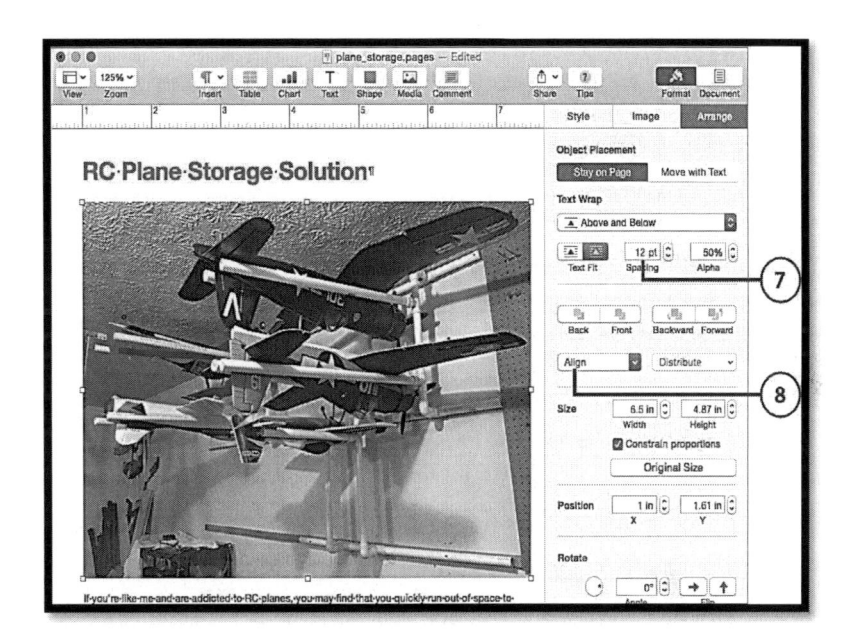

- Set the distance between the photo and the surrounding text using the **Spacing** box.
- To align the image from top to bottom or from left to right, use the **Align** menu.

Lock it

You can lock a photo to keep it from shifting positions. Select the image, then select the **Arrange** tab and **Lock** button.

Go Further: Layer Graphics

Photos and other graphics can be layered on top of each other. For instance, you could want to layer a smaller photo over a larger one so that the smaller one highlights a crucial close-up detail. Place the first graphic in your document to begin the layering process. Place the second one after that.

Drag the subsequent one over the preceding one. You are free to repeat this as often as you wish. Use the **Back, Front, Backward,** and **Forward** icons on the Inspector to change the stack's order.

CHANGING THE COLOR LEVELS IN AN IMAGE

Add a border, a color, a shadow, and other features to an object to make it more unique.

Change The Transparency of An Object

- Select the object.
- Drag the **Opacity** slider in the **Format inspector's Style** window.

Add And Change an Object's Border

- Select an object.
- Select the disclosure triangle beside **Border** in the **Style** pane of the **Format inspector**, then select a border type from the pop-up menu.
- To change the look of the border, use the controls (options differ based on the kind of border you select).

Fill An Object with Color or A Gradient

Shapes, text boxes, and other items can all be filled with either a solid color or a gradient (two or more colors that blend into one another). You have the option of selecting colors and gradients created to match the template or selecting from the entire palette.

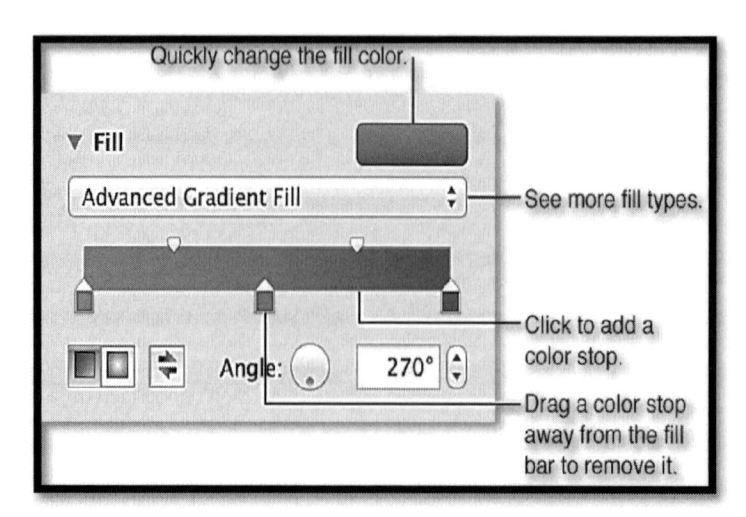

- Select an object.
- **Perform any of the following actions in the Format inspector's Style pane:**
    - **Use a color or gradient that compliments the template**: To select a color or gradient, select the **color well** beside **Fill**.
    - **Use a fill with a two-color gradient**: Select **Gradient Fill** from the pop-up menu by clicking the **Fill disclosure triangle**, then select **colors**. The left color wheel displays the **Colors** window, where you can select any color, and the left color well displays colors that go with the template.
    - **Use a custom gradient**: To select colors, press the **square color wells** underneath the slider after clicking the **Fill disclosure triangle** and selecting **Advanced Gradient Fill** from the pop-up menu. The gradient's blend, angle, and direction can all be adjusted using the color well sliders and other controls.

Add An Image Fill

Shapes, text boxes, and other objects can all be filled with images.

- Choose an object.
- Select the **disclosure triangle** beside **Fill** in the **Format inspector's Style** window.
- From the **Fill** pop-up box, select **Image Fill** or **Advanced Image Fill** if you want to tint the image.
- Select an image by clicking **Choose**, go to your photos, and then double-click it.
- Select a tint color by clicking the color wheel (to the right of the **Choose** button) if you selected **Advanced Image Fill**.
- To change how transparent the tint is, move the **Opacity** slider in the **Colors** box.
- Select **Option** from the pop-up menu above the **Choose** icon to change how the image fills the object:
    - **Original Size**: Inserts the image into the object without changing its original size.
    - **Stretch**: Resizes the image to match the dimensions of the object.

- **Tile**: Repetition of the image inside the object.
- **Scale to Fill**: Enlarges or reduces the image so that there is no space around it.
- **Scale to Fit**: Resizes the image to best match the dimensions of the object.

Save A Custom Fill

A custom fill can be saved so you can use it again.

- Choose the object that has the fill that you want to save.
- Tap the **color well** next to **Fill** in the **Format inspector's Style** window. There is a pop-up menu with additional fill options.
- Replace it by dragging the fill from the **Current Fill well** over a different fill from the pop-up menu. Some fills are irreplaceable.

Add A Shadow

Images, text boxes, and forms can all have shadows added to them.

- Choose an image, text box, or shape.
- Select the **disclosure triangle** beside **Shadow** in the **Style** pane of the **Format inspector**, then select a type of shadow from the pop-up menu.
  - **Drop Shadow**: Gives the impression that the object is soaring above the page.
  - **Contact Shadow**: Gives the impression that the object is standing on the page.
  - **Curved Shadow**: This creates the impression that an object's edges are curved.
- **To change the appearance of the shadow, adjust any of the following:**
  - **Blur**: A shadow's edge's softness.
  - **Offset**: The distance between the shadow and the text or object.
  - **Angle**: The shadow's angle.
  - **Perspective**: The angle at which a contact shadow is cast by a light source.

Add A Reflection

Shapes, text fields, and images can all have reflections added to them.

- Choose an image, text box, or shape.
- Click the **Reflection** checkbox in the **Format inspector's Style** pane.
- To increase or decrease the visibility of the reflection, move the slider.

You can make your object style and reuse it if you wish to apply the same formatting to other objects.

ADDING TABLES TO YOUR DOCUMENTS

Apple's word processing application Pages has more complex capability than just serving as a possible Microsoft Word substitute. Here's how you use the Pages program from Apple to make eye-catching tables and infographics.

The free iWork word processor from Apple, Pages, has remarkably basic tools for including eye-catching tables and charts in documents. By effectively communicating informational aspects and the links between various data sets, tables, and charts, when structured and positioned correctly, offer appealing white space to documents and often eliminate the need for superfluous text.

The Pages application offers beautiful formatting options for tables with vivid, graphical highlights. Additionally, Pages permits the creation of a variety of straightforward or complex 2D, 3D, and interactive bar, pie, bubble, scatter, doughnut, and similar charts. The best part is that tables and charts are simple to add to and edit within a Pages document.

Tables

To add the appropriate element when **Pages** is open, select the **Table or Chart** icon from the menu bar (Figure A).

Figure A

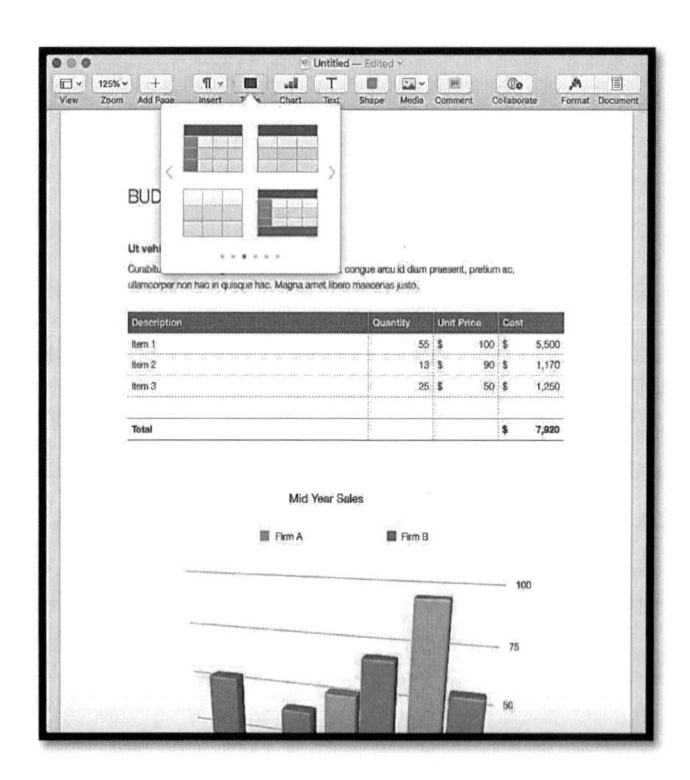

A selection of preformatted charts with a wide range of preformatted colors and layout styles are offered by the **Tables** option.

Place the cursor in a column near the area where you want to add a new column, then click the table within the page to cause Pages to show the table's formatting elements. From the ensuing pop-up menu, click **Add Column Before** or **Add Column After**.

You can also choose **Delete Column** if you want to take away the highlighted column. You can insert column headers or change a column into a header using the same contextual pop-up menu. Simply click inside the appropriate cell to enter the data.

The same procedures can be used to add or remove table rows, add row headers, and turn a row inside a table into a header.

Select the table, then hit the **Format** icon from the **Pages Toolbar** to change the formatting and color of the table. Within the **Inspector**, pages will display multiple relevant table styles. Choose the **New Style** option you want to use, and Pages will make the necessary adjustments without changing the text or data in the table.

ADDING A CHART

Although there are a few minor issues, it's fairly simple to get your data into a stunning and professional-looking chart when using iWork. While some users enjoy Excel for more advanced tasks, others prefer Numbers and Pages for plotting charts and the like. Let's investigate how.

There are several other chart types available in the Chart option (Figure B), such as bar graphs, pie charts, and column graphs. Six various color schemes are offered for each of the more than a dozen preformatted 2D charts, eight preconfigured 3D charts, and four interactive chart templates.

Figure B

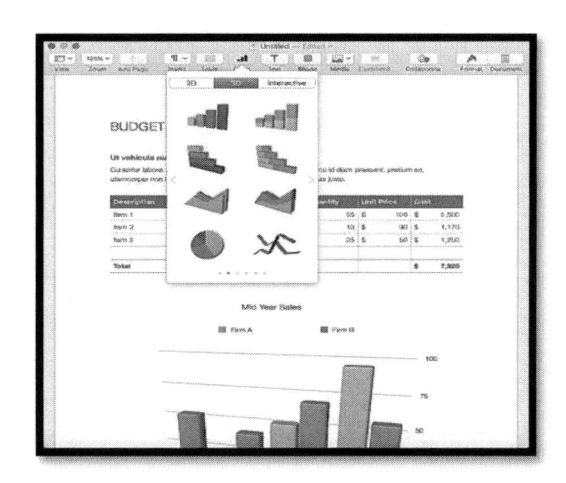

Charts are simple to edit once they have been placed. Charts can be changed, edited, and refined using the **Format** option (Figure C). Select the chart inside the Pages document, then select the **Format** icon from the toolbar to make changes. The **Inspector** will show options for changing the chart's color, style, and particular components that are relevant to the context.

For instance, if you make a pie chart and wish to change it further, you can select the **Wedges** tab and change the name and value labels for the data points, the format of the value data, the locations of the label options, and even the wedge position.

Figure C

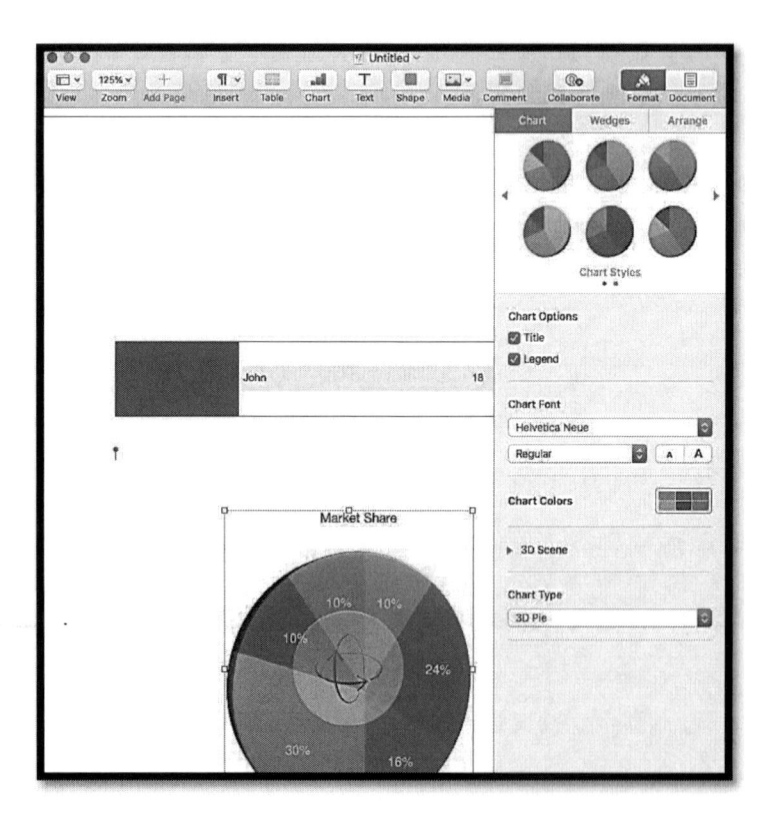

By selecting the relevant chart and then selecting the **Edit Chart Data** icon, you may change various chart settings, such as labels and values. Many charts also let you change the angle and perspective from which they display on the page; to do this, simply click one of these charts and move the cursor to adjust the spin that corresponds to it.

Getting Started

Load **Pages** and then select **New Document** from the bottom left-hand corner. We'll demonstrate how to create a chart on a straightforward, blank page, but keep in mind that you may add charts to any type of Pages documents, such as newsletters, reports, and posters (if you so want!).

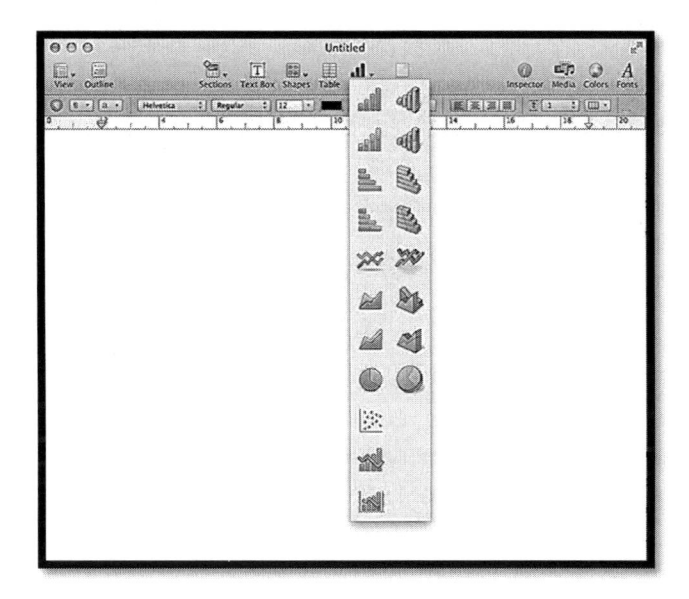

A drop-down box containing a variety of charts is displayed when you select the **Charts** button in the toolbar. You can create scatter graphs, bar, line, and pie charts (as well as combinations of the two, like a bar and line chart) from inside Pages, which should be sufficient for the majority of people's needs.

Placing Your Chart

We're going to start by creating a bar chart with some sample sales information for two different goods over several years. For the sake of clarity, we'll select the first icon in the box, a basic bar chart. The chart is then added to the document by Pages. Even while you always have the option to move your chart after you've finished editing it, it's always best to decide where it should go before you begin. Simply move the cursor (by clicking with the mouse) to the location where you want your chart to appear to accomplish this.

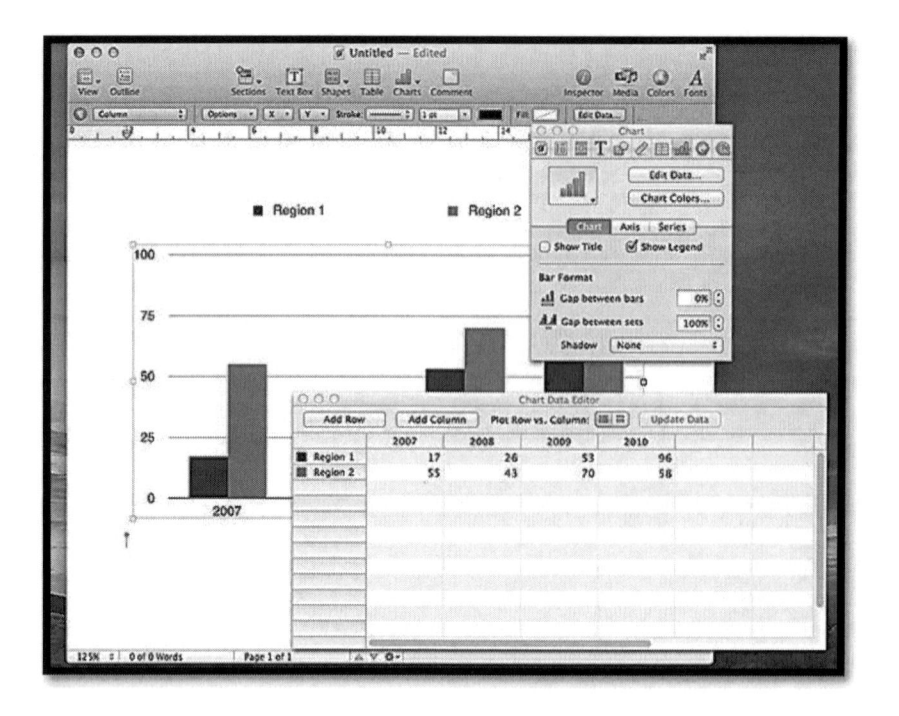

The **Inspector** appears on the **Chart** view (which we'll look at in a moment), as seen in the image above, and you also get the **Data Editor** page, where you may enter your data. Let's do that right away.

Working With Data

There are two methods for working with data while creating charts. The first, and by far the simplest, is to just edit your data in Numbers before pasting it. The advantage of this method is that your chart will update automatically with the new data, allowing you to see exactly how it will appear. Alternatively, you can enter your data directly into the **Editor**.

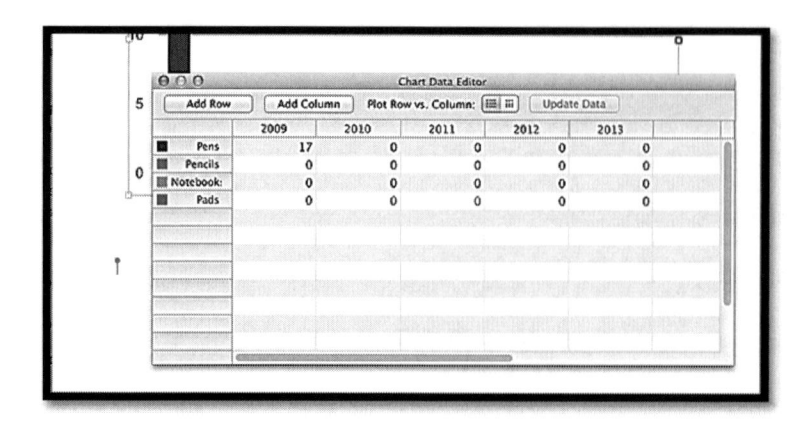

The various years are listed across the top, one year per column, and each sales item is listed down the side, one item per row, for our sample sales data. Take note of how Pages has automatically given each row a different color so you can readily tell them apart. Of course, we can adjust these afterward.

By using the **Add Row** or **Add Column** buttons in the data editor, you may always add more rows or columns as needed. Simply click the right mouse button and choose either **Delete Row** or **Delete Column** after selecting the row or column (Pages will highlight it in blue).

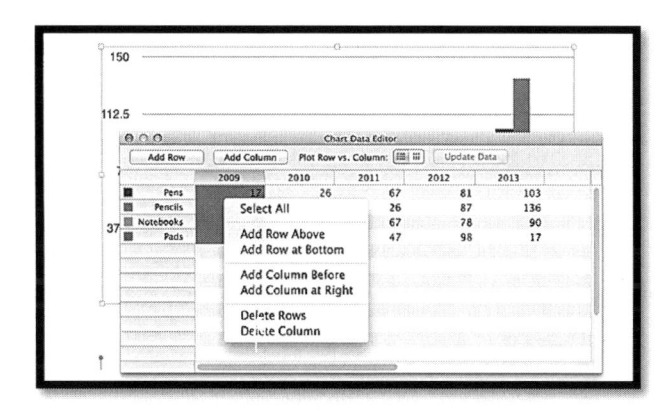

After you've supplied all the essential data, Pages will display your finished chart to you. By selecting the **Edit Data** button in the toolbar above, you can always make changes to the data afterward. This will open the **Data Editor** as we previously saw.

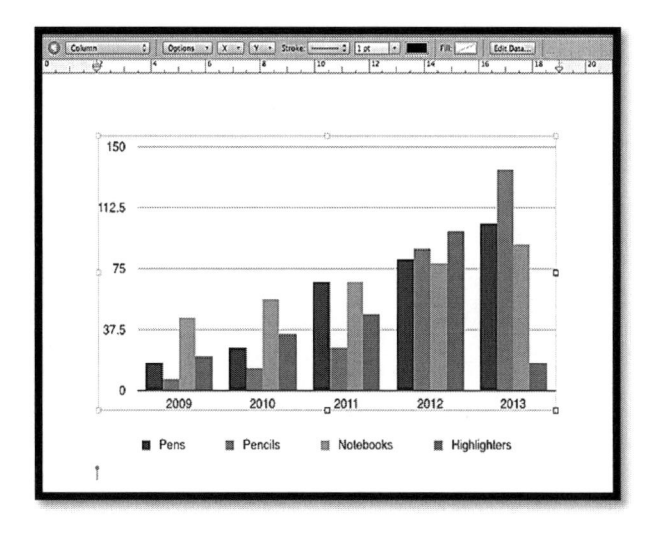

It's time to experiment with our chart now that we have our data in it!

Customizing Your Chart

The Inspector view is your friend when it comes to customizing anything in the iWork suite. Click on the chart you want to use straight away (it's in the upper right corner of the screen). There should be an automatic showing of the **Chart** view.

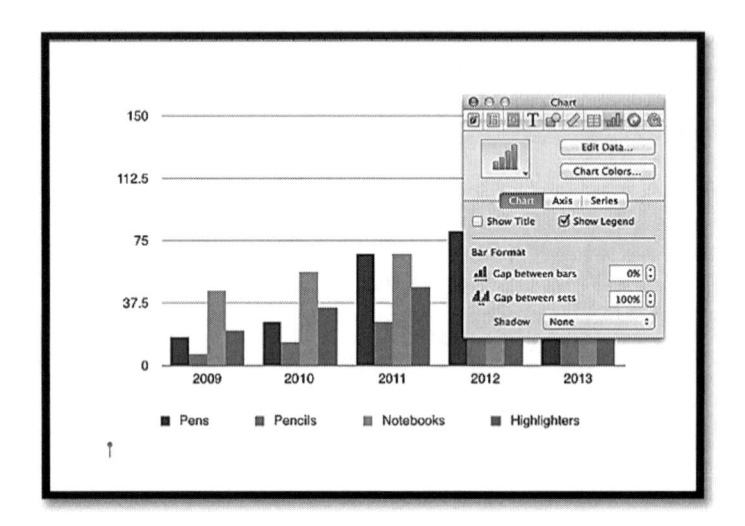

You can choose your chart type and alter the appearance of your chart from the first tab, "**Chart**." Pages will immediately match the data to the new chart type if you change it. When you select the **Show Title** checkbox, a new text box that you may change will display above your chart, allowing you to enter a title.

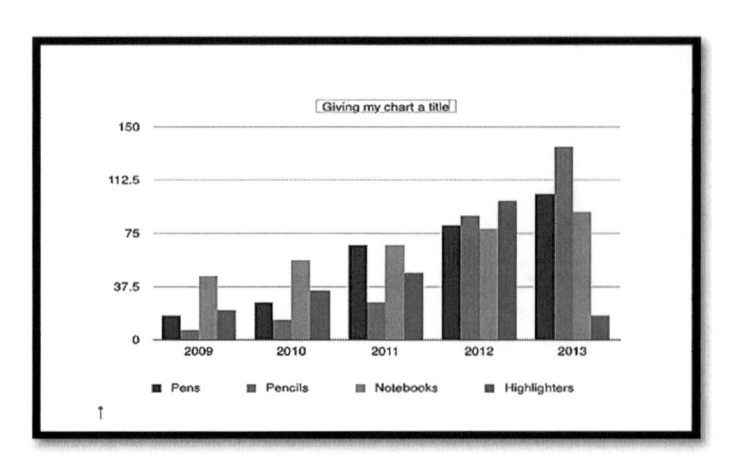

By using the **Show Legend** checkbox, you can also decide whether your chart has a legend or not. By default, it sits beneath your chart, but if you click the legend, you can drag it wherever you want. If you wish to give your graph a caption, you will need to do it manually by adding some text beneath it and formatting it as needed because, unlike Word, Pages does not permit captions on graphs.

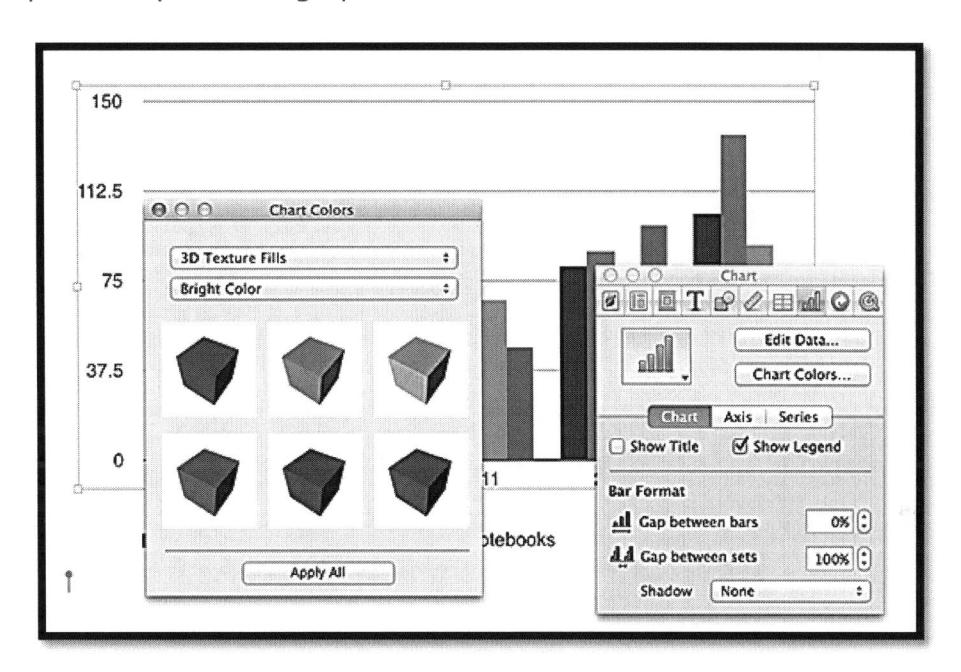

Simply tap the **Chart Colors** icon to open a new dialogue box and change the colors in your chart. Now, you can choose from a variety of color schemes that Pages have pre-built. Tap the **Apply All** icon after selecting the one that appeals to you the best. The new color scheme will automatically be reflected on your chart.

Playing With the Axes

Axes that best fit your data are automatically chosen by Pages, although based on your data, you can get some strange results. The steps in the samples above, as you can see, are 0, 37.5, 75, 112.5, and 150, which seems a little disorganized. Fortunately, there is a simple method for customizing your axes, so go ahead and click on the **Axis** tab in the **Inspector's Chart** view.

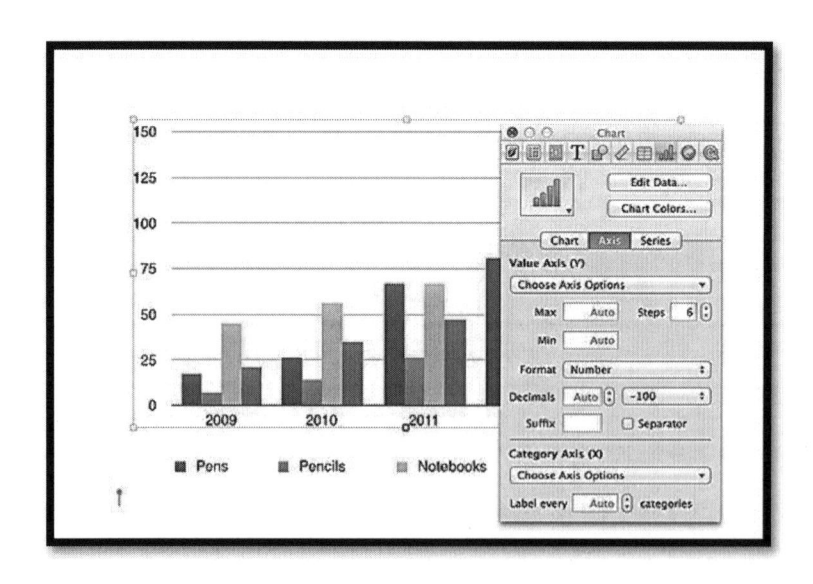

As you can see, the **Value Axis (Y)** section allows you to customize the **Y-axis**, or the one that runs vertically, by choosing the maximum or minimum data value (helpful if, for instance, you don't want your axis to start at 0) and the number of steps. We choose 6 steps for this data since they provide a nice progression (0, 25, 50, 75, and so on).

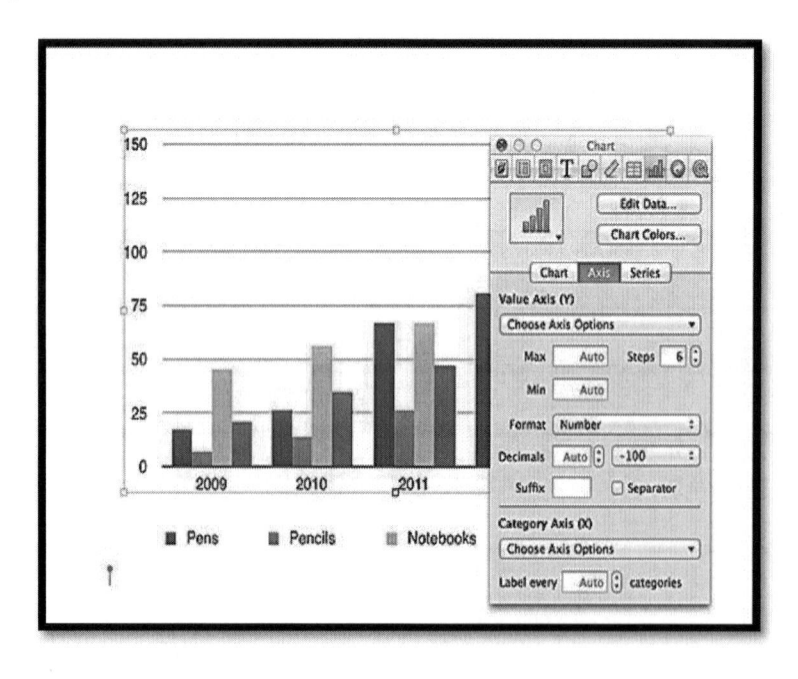

Pages give you some more advanced axis customization options if you select the Choose **Axis Options** drop-down box.

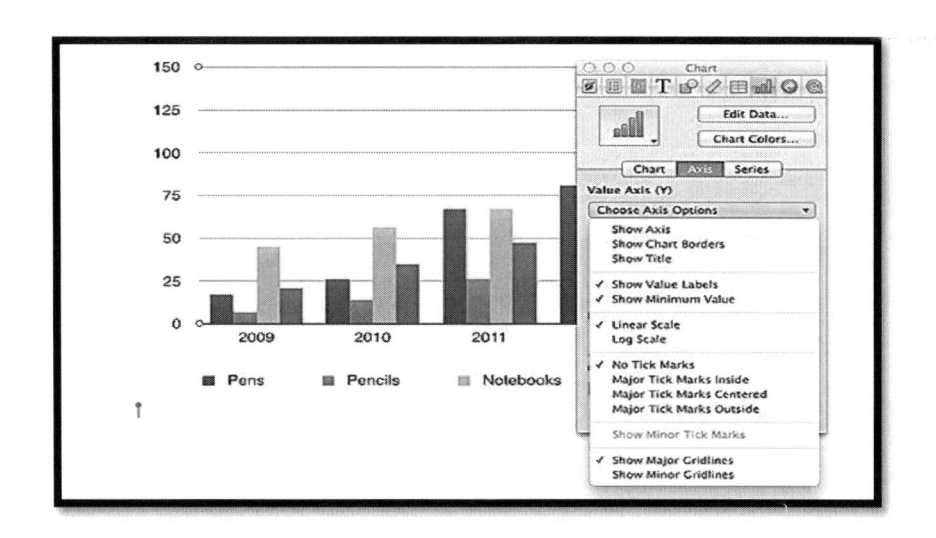

For math nerds, you can select between a linear and log scale here. You can also further customize the look of your graph by adding gridlines and tick marks. You may format the numbers in your graph (much like in Numbers) using the **Inspector**. If you're using a special number format, like a currency or percentage, this feature can be helpful.

Other Stuff

You can further customize your graph by selecting a few more options by clicking the Series tab. To make it simpler for readers to see certain sets of data, you can, for instance, add value labels to each data collection. This functions better in charts with fewer data points. It can start to appear a little disorganized when using scatter graphs, for instance, where there may be 50 pieces of data.

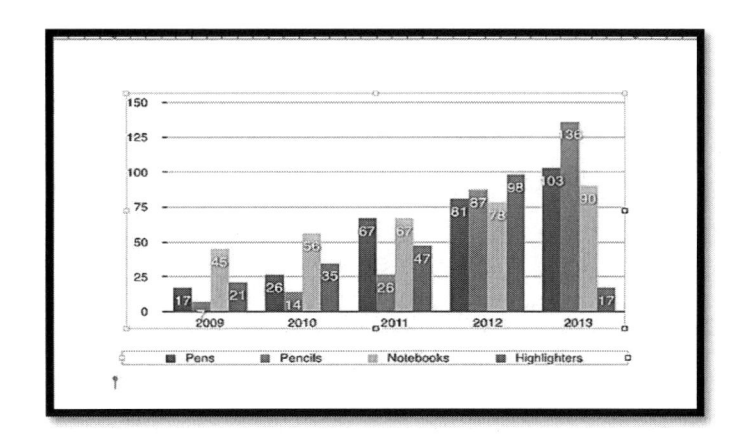

If your chart calls for it, you may also add a variety of trendlines (linear, logarithmic, polynomial, and so forth) and error bars from the **Series** tab.

Exporting Your Charts

You can easily choose your chart by clicking with the mouse, copying it, and then pasting it anywhere you want to apply it in another iWork application, such as Numbers or Keynote.

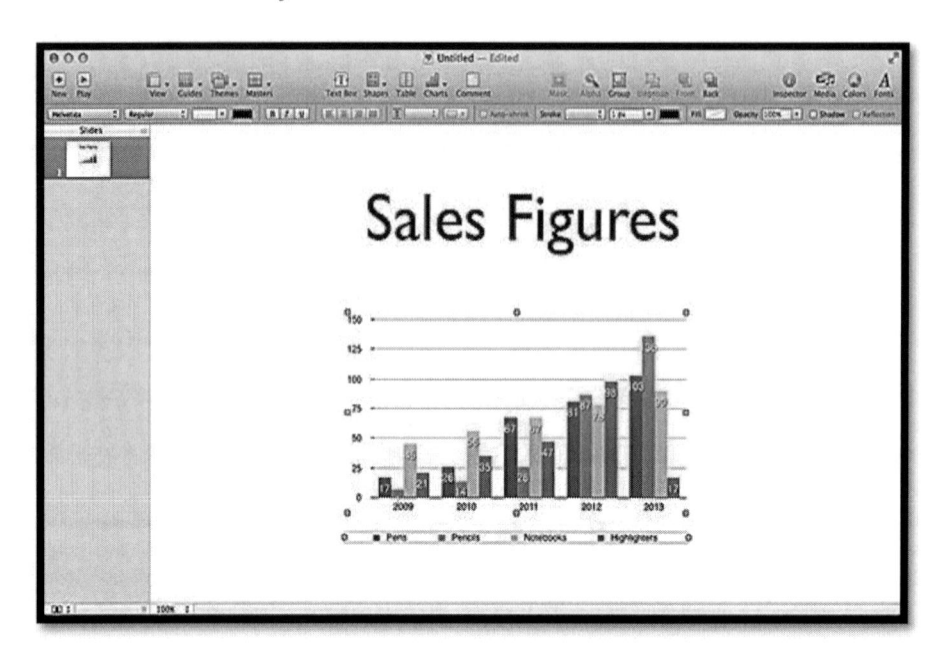

Pages do not permit you to export your chart as an image, contrary to Excel. Therefore, the best approach to achieve this is to take a screenshot of your graph and enter it as a PNG file in another piece of software (like Word, for instance).

Conclusion

Hopefully, this section gave you a thorough overview of how to make some awesome-looking charts in Pages and that it will inspire you to use all of your imagination. Charts are an excellent way to convey data and keep in mind that this lesson is just the beginning. Besides making basic bar graphs like the ones we've seen above; you can do a lot more!

BOOK 2
APPLE NUMBERS

CHAPTER ONE
INTRODUCTION TO NUMBERS

Numbers has recently gotten a complete makeover, along with the rest of iWork, and now features a brand-new design, iCloud synchronization, and much more. Along with a free update for all current users, Apple is now including its office suite for free with every qualified Mac, making iWork available to everyone.

The spreadsheet application Numbers was created by Apple and is included with iWork. Using several templates, Numbers allows you to build robust spreadsheets that can be shared with your coworkers or wirelessly transferred across iDevices via iCloud.

A USER-FRIENDLY INTERFACE

Get started with a template

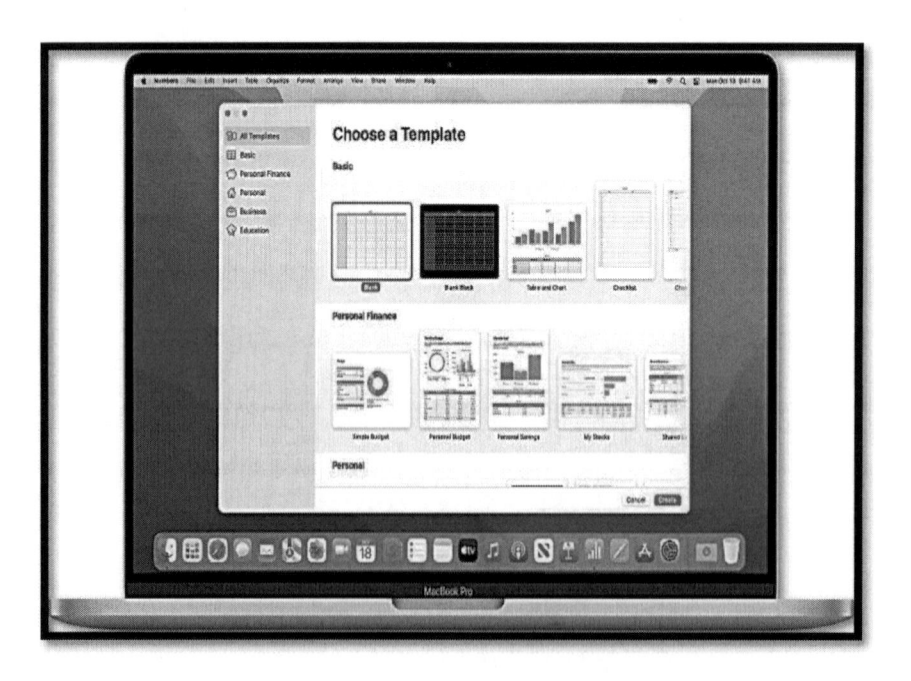

Every spreadsheet starts with a template, which is a sample you can use as a guide. Replace the charts and data in the template with your own, and add additional tables, formulas, and more.

Add data to a table

You can either enter your data or import it from another file. A broad variety of formulas, including sum and average, can be added to any cell. You may apply filters, categorize your data, make pivot tables, and more to organize your data and spot trends.

Create a chart

Utilize a 2D, 3D, or interactive chart to illustrate your data. The chart dynamically updates as you make changes to the data in the table.

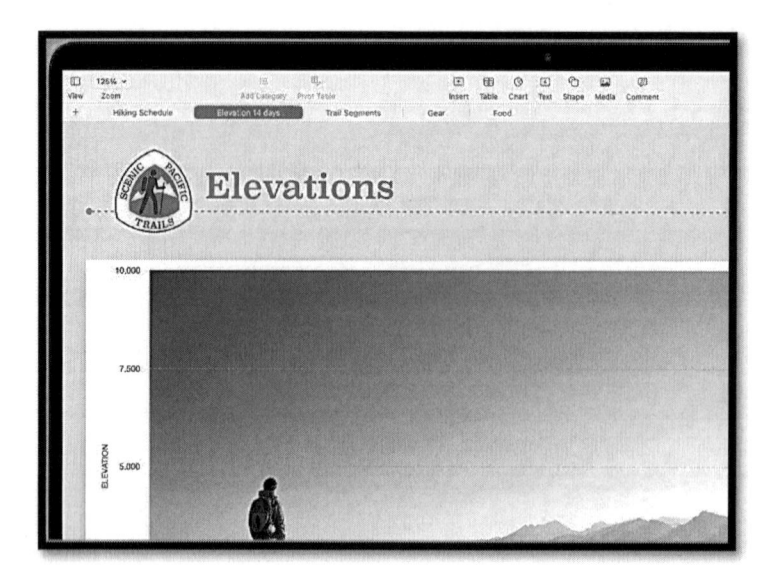

Get organized with sheets

Create separate sheets in your spreadsheet for each kind of data you wish to track, such as income, expenses, and so forth. To switch to the sheet you wish to see, just click a tab at the top of the spreadsheet.

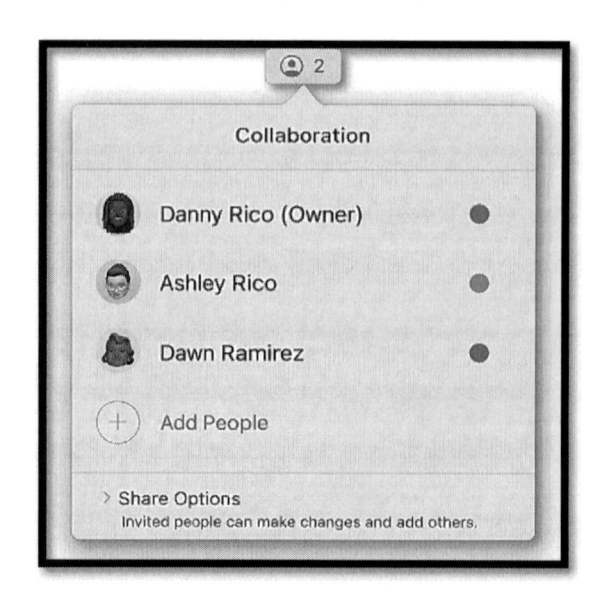

Collaborate in real-time

To collaborate on your spreadsheet with others, invite them. Everyone you invite will be able to see changes as they are made, but you can decide who can edit the spreadsheet or merely view it.

A WIDE RANGE OF TEMPLATES

Templates for Apple products like Pages and Numbers are difficult to locate. Your search might be shortened by using these template websites.

You can get a head start by using a template when creating a document. To make creating your document easier, templates can include sections, formatting, graphics, and built-in calculations.

There simply aren't as many templates available for Apple programs like Pages and Numbers as there are for Microsoft tools like Word and Excel. Finding templates that are either free or moderately priced is also difficult.

Here are five excellent websites that provide Pages and Numbers templates, both for free and for a fee, to aid you in your quest.

1. **Template.net**

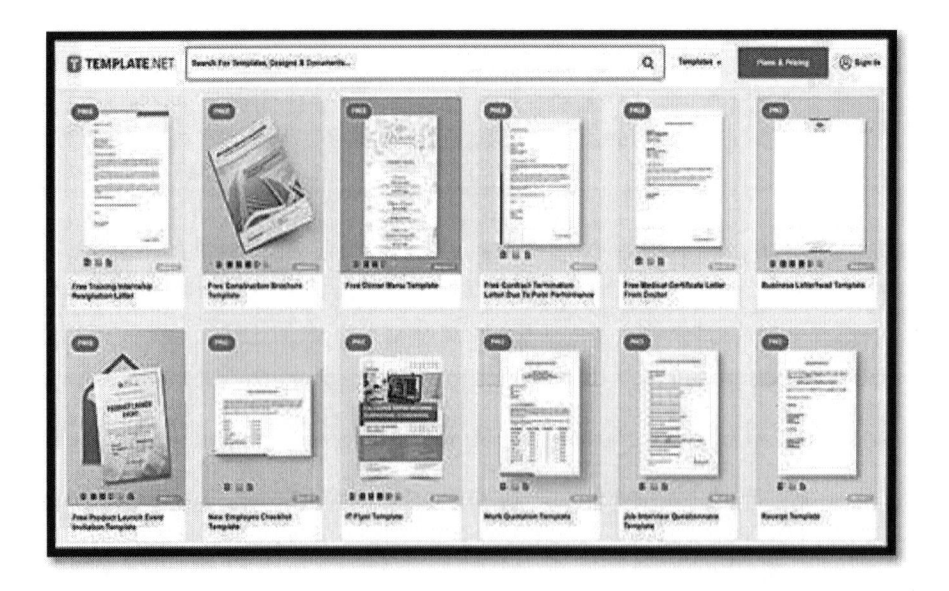

Template.net is an excellent source for templates for numerous programs, such as Pages and Numbers. You can browse or search thousands of free templates, including cards, contracts, budgets, inventory sheets, and certificates.

A scrolling list of applications like Photoshop, Google Docs, Google Sheets, InDesign, and others may be seen at the top of the main screen. Finding templates made specifically for your application is made considerably simpler as a result.

Browse the screens of template options after choosing **Pages** or **Numbers**. You'll observe that the free templates are prominently labeled and that the applications for which they are appropriate are also shown.

You'll get useful information about what it contains, such as the size, file format, and orientation, when you choose a template that piques your interest. You'll also find comparable templates at the bottom, which are great for when you need to create multiple documents for your project.

Check out the Template.net pricing plans for a Pro Membership for unlimited use if you discover that you'll be visiting the site frequently for templates.

You should bookmark Template.net as a reliable resource for Pages and Numbers templates.

2. iWorkCommunity.com

Check out iWorkCommunity.com for some very interesting templates. The templates on this website were made by people using Apple software just like you, which is fantastic. You can even upload your templates to assist others.

Select **Pages, Numbers, Keynote**, or **Script** in the upper-right corner of the home page to browse by application. The options can then be reduced using the tags on the left or the search box at the bottom. Templates are available for a range of document types, including schedules, resumes, and agendas.

You will acquire all the information about a template by selecting it, including a brief description, the file size, and the total number of downloads. You can start downloading the file by clicking its name next to **Download**.

The fact that iWorkCommunity.com now offers all of its templates for free justifies visiting it. And don't forget to use the **Submit New Template** button at the top to assist your fellow document creators if you create a template for Pages or Numbers that you'd like to share.

3. **Stock Layouts**

Stock Layouts is the website for you if you're looking for a template that is based on graphics. Along with Microsoft products, InDesign, Illustrator, Pages, Numbers, and Keynote templates, it also provides free templates.

On the home page, there is a section with free graphic design templates; if you're also interested in paid templates, there are more below. Choose a template to view information such as page size, fold type, and compatibility. Click the **Download Now** button after selecting your preferred file format in the dropdown box.

You can find both paid and free templates for the same kind of document below the template's details.

If you are interested in purchasing templates, Stock Layouts also has a variety of pricing plans. A single template can be purchased for a modest fee, or you can subscribe and receive ten to fifty templates each month.

There is a good selection of graphic design templates on Stock Layouts for flyers, brochures, newsletters, menus, datasheets, and other documents.

4. **Klariti**

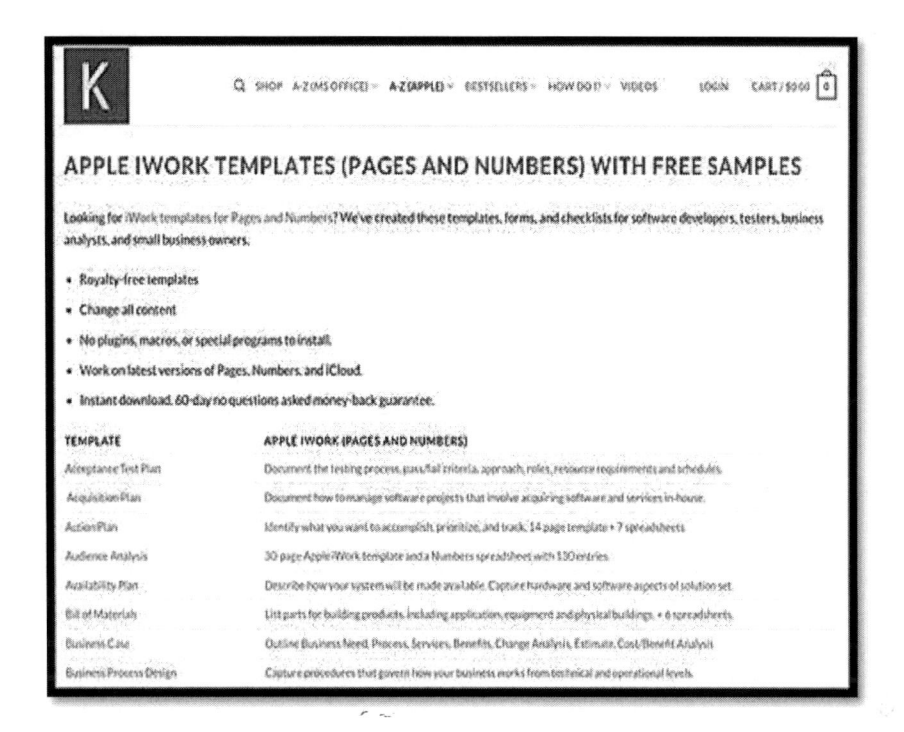

Another website that offers templates for both Microsoft and Apple products is Klariti. There are more than 250 options for Pages and Numbers on Klariti, and if you're not happy, you can get a refund. However, the templates on Klariti are not offered for free.

Simply click the **Apple** icon on the top navigation, choose **Pages** or **Numbers**, and then look through the extensive list of templates. The list is orderly laid out so you can easily notice the template name and a short description.

When you select a template, the full document—all pages, important sections, and useful FAQs—is displayed. When you're prepared to buy, press the **Buy Now** button and adhere to the instructions. The website takes PayPal and all popular credit cards.

Templates for Pages, such as proposals and plans, and those for Numbers, such as requirements and guides, are also available. If you're having trouble finding the ideal template for you and don't mind spending a little money, check out Klariti.

5. **Vertex42**

Vertex42, a website well-known for its fantastic Excel templates, also provides Numbers templates. There are still many excellent options even though Numbers doesn't have a ton of templates.

Go to the Browse Template Categories section on the right side of the home page to access the templates. Click **Numbers Templates** at the very bottom. You can find templates on that page under headings like "**home and family**," "**personal finance**," "**business finance**," and "**office**."

Simply click the **Download** button to download a template. Every file has a Numbers format. However, if you want more information about the template or if you want it for Excel as well, click the "[**Template name] for Excel**" link located above the **Download** button. The filename, which must be in Numbers format, will be displayed on the download page for the template. To get the template, select the **Download** button on that page.

On Vertex42, the templates for Numbers are now free. Also, don't forget to visit the website for Word or Excel templates!

Conclusion

Templates can assist you in focusing on the content of your documents rather than their creation if you own a Mac and use Pages and Numbers as your go-to document-making applications.

CUSTOMIZABLE CELLS

To display numbers, text, and date and time values, you can design your cell formats. You can use your customized formats again because they are available in the Data **Format** pop-up menu.

Create A Custom Number Format

- Click **Create Custom Format** from the **Data Format** pop-up option in the **Cell** pane of the **Format inspector** after selecting the cell or range of cells to which the format should be applied.
- Then, select **Number** from the **Type** pop-up option after entering a name for your format.
- **To specify the format, choose one of the following:**
    - **Enter text into the field**: The cell displays the text you type.
    - **Drag tokens into the field for the custom format**: The type of data you will enter into a cell is represented by a token. For instance, you can use an integer token with five digits when inserting US zip numbers into a custom format. Tokens can be moved around the field by dragging them.
    - **Customize a token element**: To access formatting options, like the type of currency symbol or the number of digits to display, select the arrow on a token.

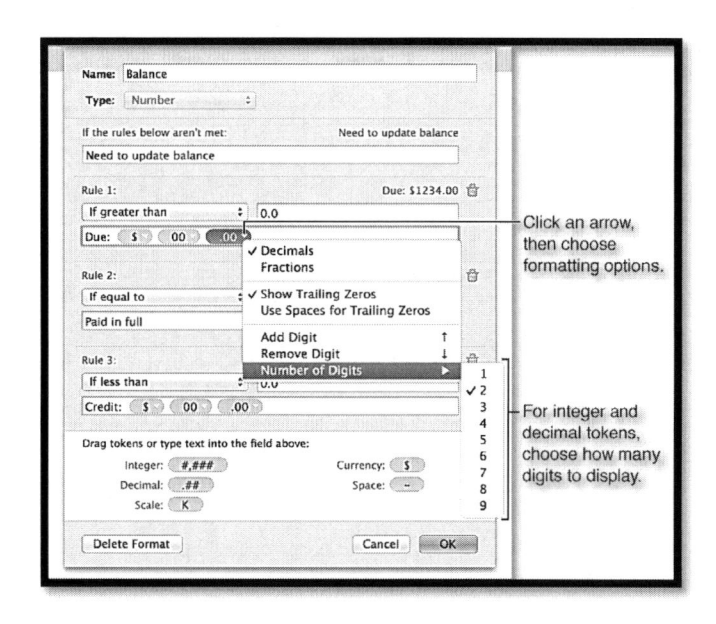

- To format a cell separately based on predefined conditions, add up to three rules.

All positive numbers you enter in this instance are shown as phone numbers with the area code **(952)**. The text "**(952) 555-5103**" appears in a cell when you type "**5555103**." A cell that you enter "**0**" into displays "**No number on file**."

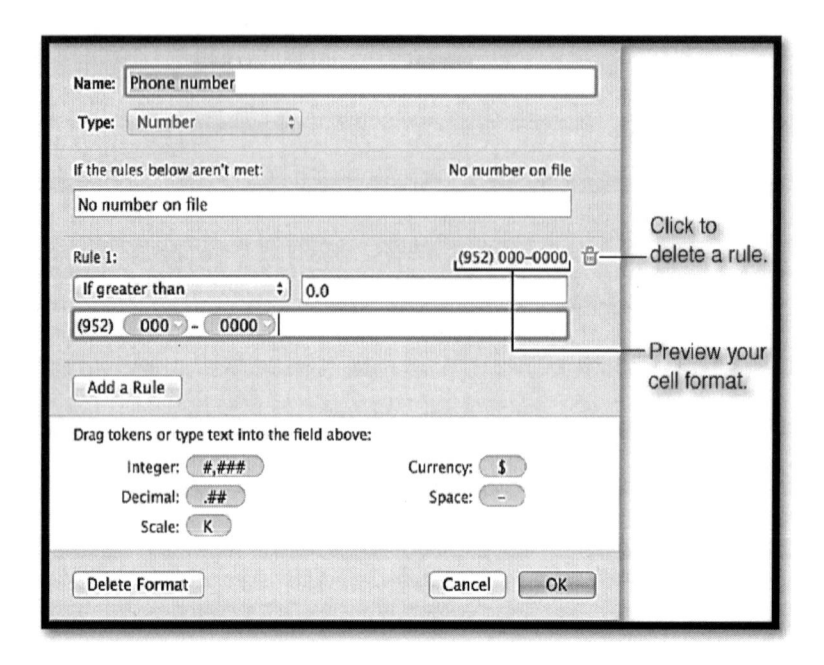

Create A Date and Time Format

- Click **Create Custom Format** from the **Data Format** pop-up menu after selecting a cell or a range of cells in the Cell pane of the Format inspector.
- Select **Date & Time** from the **Type** pop-up menu after entering a name for your format.
- Choose one of the following to define your format:
  - **Enter text into the field**: The cell displays the text you type.
  - **Drag tokens into the field for the custom format**: The type of data you will enter into a cell is represented by a token. Tokens can be moved around the field by dragging them.
  - **Customize a token element**: The formatting options for the data are displayed when you select the arrow on a token.

In this example, the day of the year token **("5")** and custom text are used to make a cell display "**56 days into the year**" when you type "**2/25/2014**" into it.

If you enter a value that involves a hyphen **(-)** or a slash **(/)**, such as "**1/4/2014**," date and time formats are applied to the cell.

Create A Text Format

- Select **Create Custom Format** from the **Data Format** pop-up menu after selecting a cell or a range of cells in the **Cell** pane of the **Format inspector**.
- Then, select **Text** from the **Type** pop-up menu after entering a name for your format.
- Enter the text you wish to automatically display in each cell that follows this format in the text field. The text you enter in the table cell is represented by the blue "**text**" token.

In this example, the text "**Notify customer:**" is displayed before any content you enter in a cell. The table cell says "**Notify customer: Need to update address**" when you enter "**Need to update address**" in it.

187

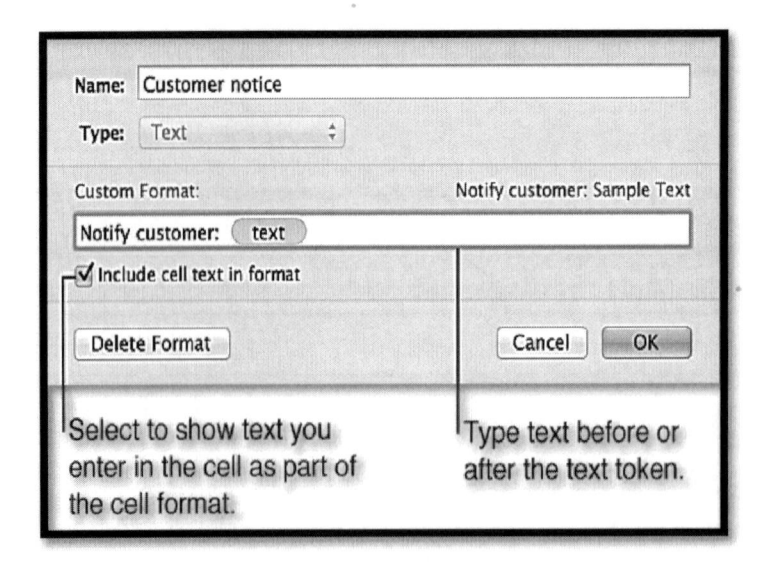

ADVANCE FORMULAS AND FUNCTIONS

A formula executes calculations using specific values you supply and presents the outcome in the cell where the formula is placed.

You can use functions in formulas to carry out calculations, retrieve data, or change it in some other way. For instance, the PRODUCT function multiplies values.

The built-in functions and formulas of spreadsheet programs like Numbers are among their best features. These useful small tools make it much easier to work with numbers. Without performing the math, yourself, you may sum a column, retrieve the maximum number in a row, average a group of cells, and more.

Although there are many built-in formulas, only a few of them are frequently utilized. Apple, therefore, makes these available in the Numbers app. Sum, average, minimum, maximum, count, and product are some of them. This section demonstrates how to use these typical formulas and functions in Numbers on both Mac and iOS.

Using The Formula Editor

It's necessary to get to know the Formula Editor before you start adding formulas and functions to Numbers.

Simply click the **Equal Sign** in the cell where you want to add formula or function to make the process simple. The editor can be accessed in just this manner. You can also enter the **Functions Browser** (which we'll talk about later) by selecting **Insert > New Formula** from the toolbar.

The left side of the **Formula Editor** can be moved, and one of its edges can be moved to change the size by using the double-sided arrow.

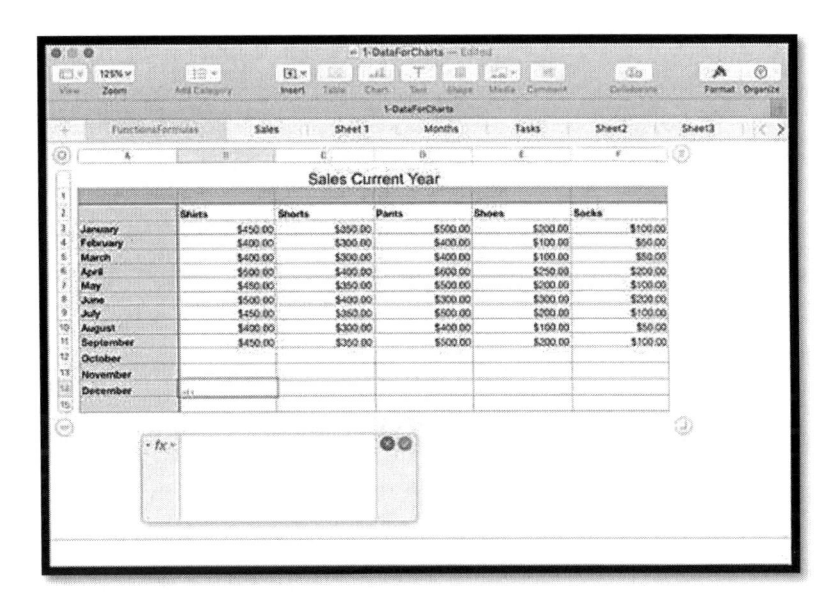

To add a cell range or a single cell to your formula, simply click on it or drag it across the editor. Arithmetic operators can also be used to multiply, divide, add, and subtract. You can enter numbers with or without decimals, of course.

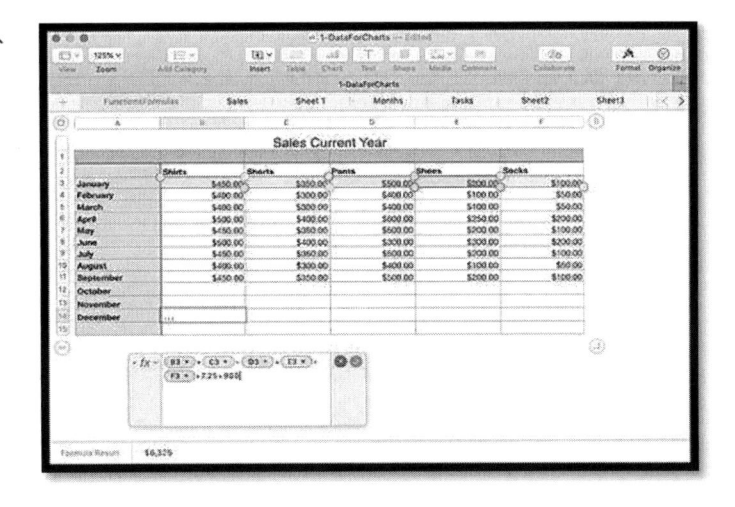

189

When you're done with the editor and wish to apply your formula, click the green checkmark. Additionally, you can close it without saving any changes by clicking the red **X** if you change your mind.

Inserting Formulas in Numbers on Mac

Even though the spreadsheet we're utilizing for our example isn't very large, picture it if it had hundreds of columns or rows. When making calculations, using those formulas is most helpful. No matter if the values are in columns, rows, or a collection of cells, inserting the desired formula is the same process.

Choose the cell that will house the formula and its output in the beginning. Then, choose the formula by selecting **Insert > Formula** from the menu bar or the **Insert** icon from the toolbar. Press **Enter** when it appears in your spreadsheet.

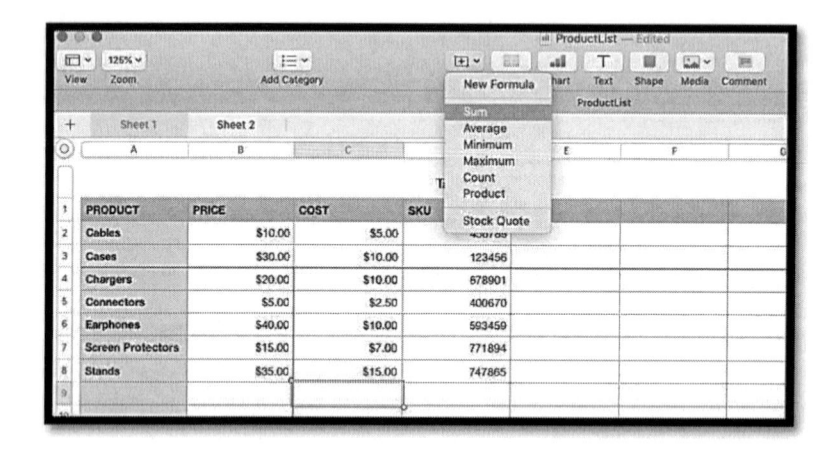

The group of cells to which you want to apply the formula will be assumed by Numbers, but you can readily adjust this.

Editing the formulas

Double-click the cell that the formula is now in. You'll see a little pop-up with the formula and the cells it applies to. Either tap inside the pop-up and adjust the cells by entering the labels or drag the corners of the range of cells to the desired positions. Select the **green checkmark** to confirm when you're done.

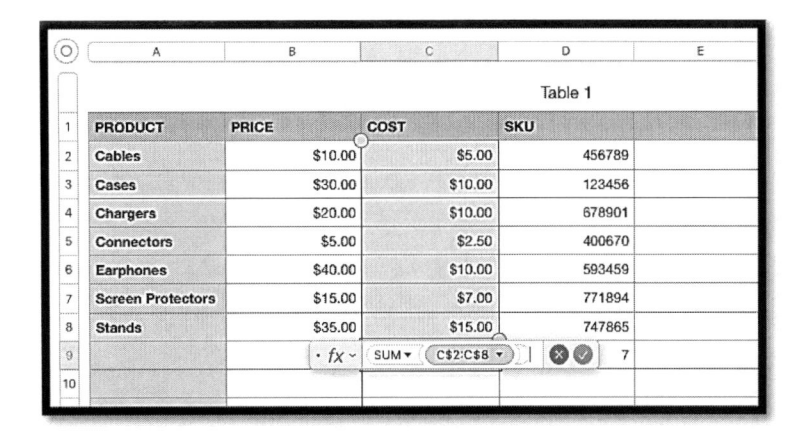

Getting a quick view of formulas

Without actually inserting it as a cell in the spreadsheet, you might just want to view one of the formulas. For example, you might wish to view the average of a column or the highest number inside a collection of cells.

When you select the cells, each of those common formulas will automatically appear at the bottom of the **Numbers** window. Also, you can add a function to the view by clicking the **gear** icon to the right and selecting it.

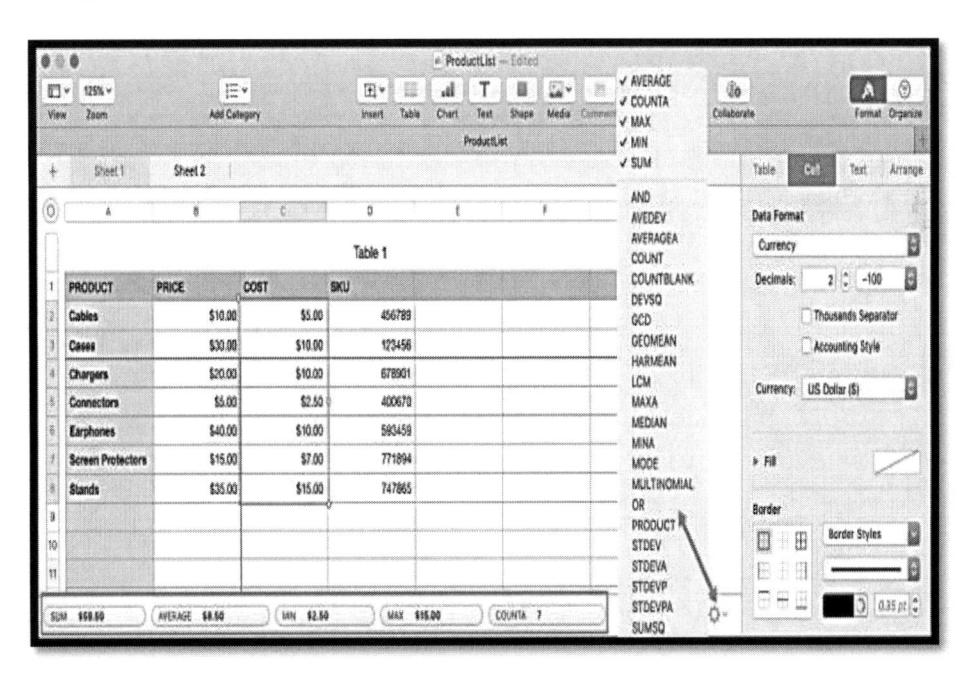

Inserting And Editing Formulas In Numbers On iPhone And iPad

You can add formulas on your iPhone and iPad if you're using your spreadsheet while on the go. Choose the cell where you wish the formula and ensuing result to appear. Select **New Formula** from the pop-up menu by tapping the **Cell** button at the bottom of the screen.

The formula can then be entered manually or, for best results, by tapping the **Function (fx)** button on the left. Then you'll see the same formulas once more. When you tap the one you desire, it will appear in the bottom text box. Drag your finger through the cells you want to include in the formula or type the values into the "**value**" text section. When you're done, click the **green** "**checkmark**" icon.

Numbers make using common functions and formulas much simpler than you may expect. Additionally, using these built-in tools can help you save time and minimize data-related problems. Are you ready to try it?

Review Formula Errors and Learn How to Avoid Them

An icon is shown in the cell when a formula in a table cell is inaccurate, incomplete, has invalid cell references, or generates another error condition in the cell due to an import operation. One or more cautions are shown by a **blue triangle** in the upper left corner of a cell. When a **red triangle** with the **Syntax Error** icon ⚠ appears in the center of a cell, a formula error has taken place.

Review errors and warnings in formulas

- Tap or click the icon to view the issue or warning.
- The cell's error and warning conditions are displayed in a message window.

How to avoid formula errors

- Your cell references and values should be checked for mistakes.
- If the cell is a part of a range, for instance, check that the formula doesn't contain a reference to itself.
- Put the text you want to include in your formula between double quotation marks.

- Ensure the inspector is set to a numeric cell format for any number values you typed or pasted into cells.
- Update your formula to remove the referenced cell if you delete it.
- After adding rows or columns, double-check your formula to make sure your references still relate to the cells you intended to include.

Copy Or Move Formulas and Their Computed Values

Formula-containing cells and cells that are used as references by formulas can be copied or moved between different locations.

- The cell reference in the formula is immediately changed when you copy, paste, or drag a cell to a new position. For instance, if a formula contains a reference to cell A1 and you shift A1 to cell D5, the formula's reference to cell A1 now refers to cell D5.
- The absolute and relative cell references may need to be changed when you copy or move a cell that contains a formula.
- **Choose one of the following actions, then select one or more adjacent cells:**
    - **Move cells to a different location (such as a different table or page)**: You can move the selection by dragging it.
      Values are replaced and those in the original position are removed when you drag them to a different table. A new table is made on the sheet, page, or slide if the selection is moved there.
    - **Copy cells to a different location (such as a different table or page)**: While dragging the selected cells, keep holding down the **Option** key.
      Additionally, you can click or **Control-click** the selection, select **Copy**, and then click or **Control-click** the location where you wish to paste the cells, and select **Paste**.
      Values in the original location are saved while values in the destination cells are replaced. A new table is formed if the selection is copied to a blank space on the sheet, page, or slide.

Refer To Cells in Formulas

All tables contain reference tabs that list the names of each table cell. The reference tabs are located to the left of each row and at the top of each column. They contain a row number and a column letter, respectively (for example, "3"). The values in the reference tabs can be used to reference a cell, row, or column.

Cell references can be used to locate the cells whose values you want to use in calculations. If you're using Numbers, you can refer to cells in the same table as the formula cell as well as cells in separate tables on the same or different sheets.

How to refer to cells in other sheets

You can use a cell in one of the sheets in a Numbers document to calculate values on the other sheets, which are identified by the tabs next to the toolbar.

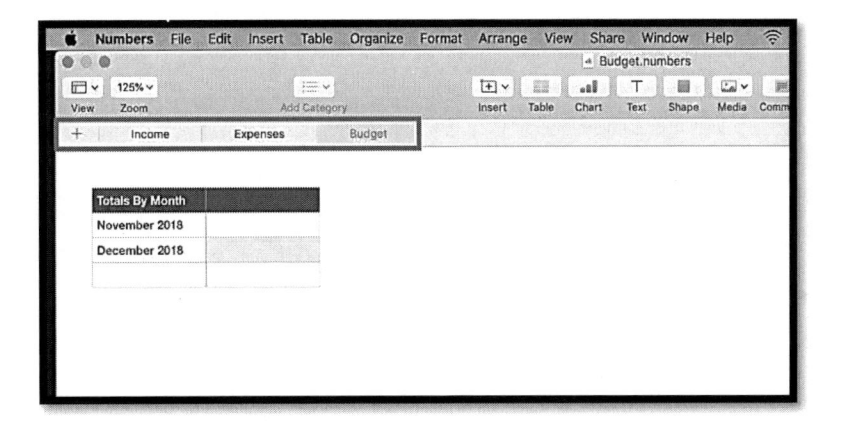

For instance, in the spreadsheet shown above, you might use a figure from the "**Expenses**" tab and another from the "Income" tab to fill in a summary cell beneath the "Budget" cell. That's awesome, and here is how you'll go about it!

The first step is to begin creating the formula that will add up (or average, or do whatever else is necessary) the concerned cells. To achieve this, click on the cell you want your formula to appear in, and then click the "**Insert**" button, a **+** button with a box around it in the toolbar.

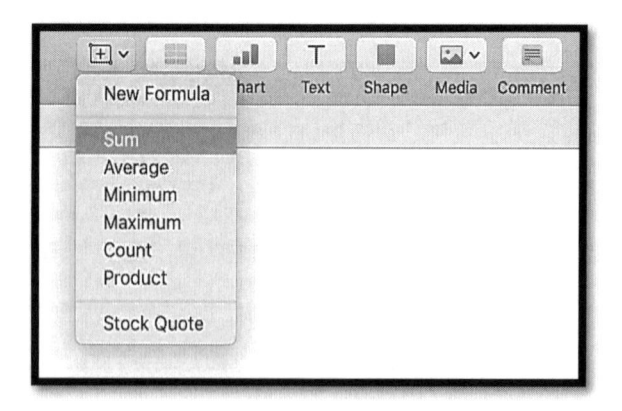

The formula you desire can then be selected, as seen above; we are choosing "**Sum**," which will immediately enter that equation into the selected cell.

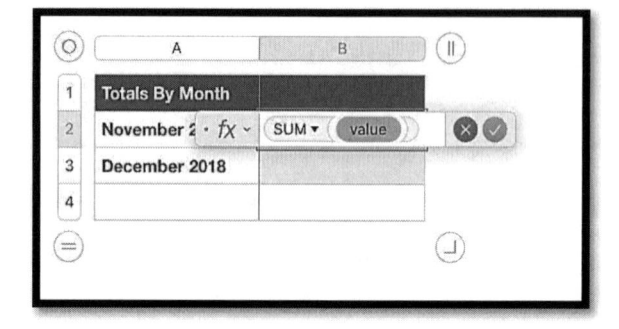

Although the Mac in this instance didn't try to auto-sum anything, if yours does, Numbers might fill that cell with the references nearby:

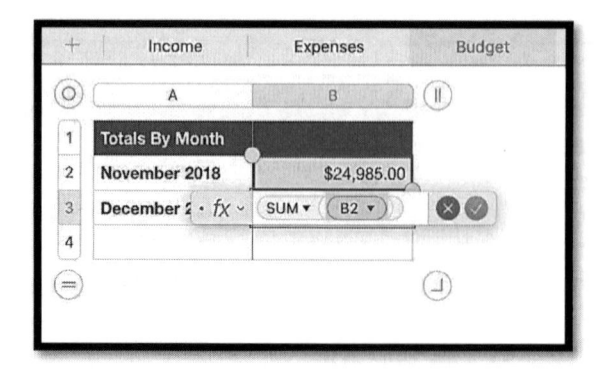

If that applies to you, simply click the cell once more to remove the problematic data, then place your cursor in the center of the empty formula as follows:

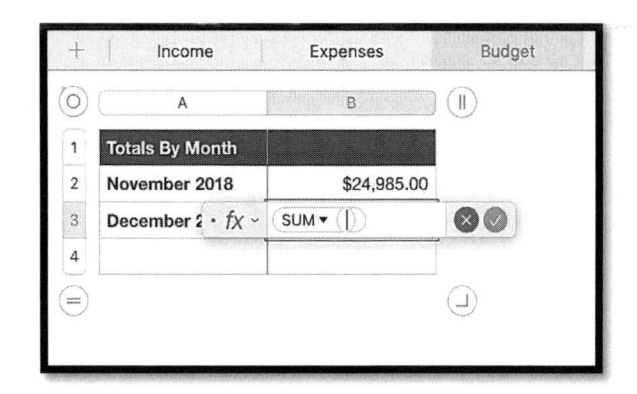

When you're ready to enter the correct data, check to see that the formula is open and ready, possibly with your cursor inside it. Then, select each of the other sheets one at a time, clicking on the cells you want to use from each sheet as you go.

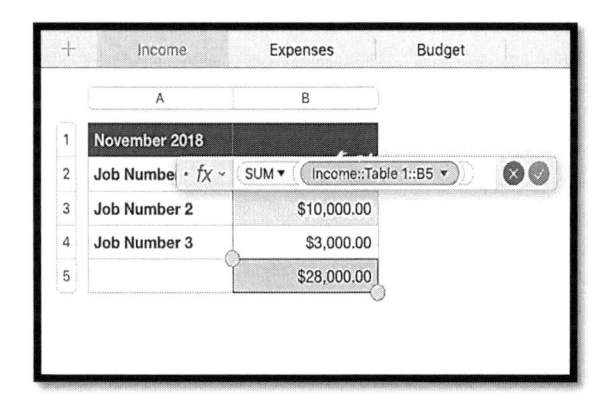

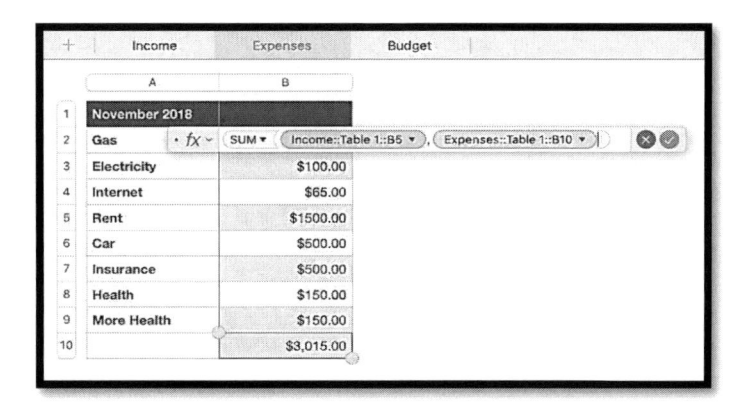

If you've done it right, the formula should remain active while you click around, and the cells you're adding should show up in the box as they do for us above. The result of your calculation will be displayed when you return to the original sheet by pressing **Return** or clicking the **green checkmark** beside the formula box.

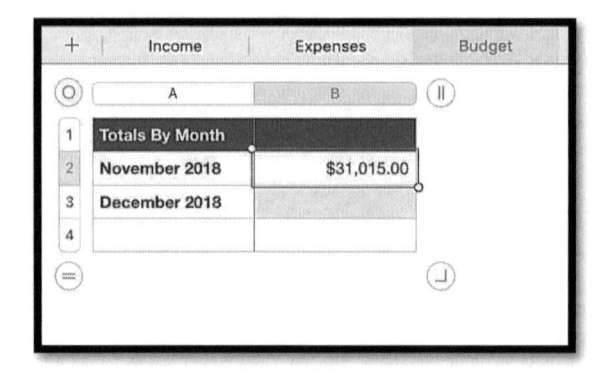

The structure here is **=SUM**, so keep that in mind if you wish to manually enter it in (**Sheet 1 Name: Table Name:Cell Name, Sheet 2 Name::Table Name::Cell Name**). In other words, if you prefer to do things that way, go for it! It will just take you longer than clicking around will.

Now that we're dealing with income and expenses, we should go in and change that formula so that it subtracts expenses from income rather than adding the two values together. Our budget would not be well-understood if we just added our expenses to our income. Let's just double-click the formula cell and enter the minus sign in its place to accomplish this.

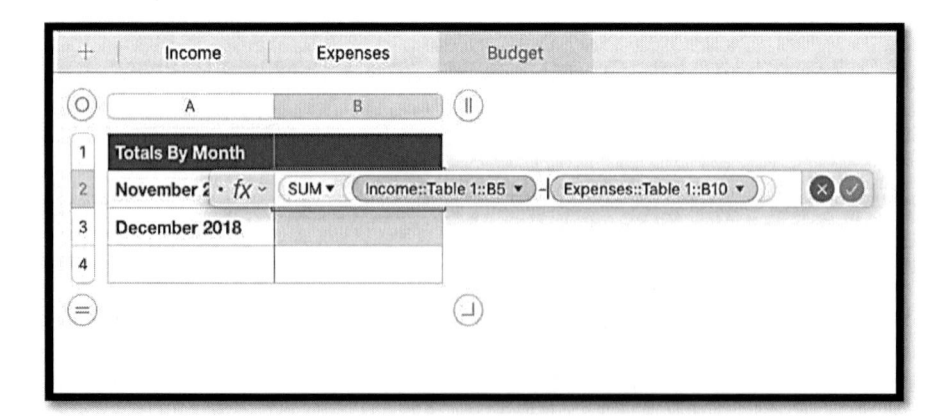

Use String Operators and Wildcards

The concatenation or joining of two or more strings, as well as the contents of referenced cells, is possible with the string operator (&) in formulas.

Wildcards **(*,?,~)** can be used in situations to represent one or more characters.

Concatenate strings or the contents of cells

The concatenation or joining of two or more strings or the contents of referenced cells is done with the **&** character.

The following are some instances of the concatenation operator in use:

- "Abc"&"Def" returns "AbcDef".
- "Abc"&A1 return "Abc2" if cell A1 contains 2.
- A1&A2 returns "12" if cell A1 contains 1 and cell A2 contains 2.
- B2&", "&E2 return "Last, first" if B2 contains "Last" and E2 contains "First".

Use a wildcard to match any single character

In an expression with conditions, the ? character is used to match a single character.

What are some instances of the wildcard character being used? Matching patterns include:

- "Ea?" will match any string that starts with "Ea" and has precisely one extra character, like "Ea2" or "Eac."

- Any string starting with "Th" and including exactly two more characters, such as "Then" and "That," is matched by "Th??"

- A count of the number of cells in the range B2:E7 that have a value that begins with a character followed by "ip," such as "rip" and "tip," is returned by the function COUNTIF(B2:E7,"?ip"). Neither "drip" nor "trip" matches it.

Use a wildcard to match any number of characters

In an expression with conditions, the * character is used to match any set of characters, even none.

The following are some instances when the wildcard character * is used in pattern matching:

- "*ed" will match any string that ends in "ed," including "Ted" and "Treed."
- A count of the number of cells in the range B2:E7 that include a value that ends with "it," such as "bit" and "mit," is returned by the function COUNTIF(B2:E7,"*it"). It doesn't match with "mitt."

Match a wildcard character

In an expression with conditions, the character is used to indicate that the next character ~ should be matched rather than utilized as a wildcard.

Following are some instances of the character being used in matching patterns:

- Instead of using the question mark to match any single character, "~?" matches the question mark.

- The number of cells in column E that have the asterisk character is returned by COUNTIF(E,"~*").

- SEARCH("~?",B2) returns 19 if cell B2 includes "That is a question? Yes, it is!" since the question mark is the string's 19th character.

Use multiple wildcard characters in a condition

Combinations of the wildcard characters (? * ~) are allowed in expressions with conditions. Examples include:

- "*a?" matches any expression that begins with the letter "a" and ends with a single other letter, including the words "That," "Cap," and "Irregular."
- A count of the number of cells in the range B2:E7 that have a value that starts with any number of characters (even none), followed by "on," and then a single character is returned by the function COUNTIF(B2:E7,"*on?"). It matches words like "alone," "bone," "one," and "none." Only (which has two characters after the "on") and eon are not compatible with this (which has no characters after the "on").

How To Use Double Quotations in Formulas

Double quotation marks can be used to denote a string in a formula. The double quotations can also be escaped, which instructs Numbers, Pages, and Keynote to return the quotation marks as a text string rather than treating them as the beginning or end of a string.

The quotation marks in the example below denote the beginning and end of the string; the final result does not contain any quotation marks.

Formula	Result
="My favorite drink is Grape Soda"	My favorite drink is Grape Soda

Additional double quotation marks can be added as escape characters if you want the outcome to contain quotation marks.

The first and last quotations in the sample below denote the beginning and end of the string, respectively. The two sets of double quotation marks denote that the word "Grape Soda" should have a double quotation mark on each side.

Formula	Result
="My favorite drink is ""Grape Soda"""	My favorite drink is "Grape Soda"

In the same formula as cell references, double quotations can also be used to denote a string. Let A1 in the example below say, "My favorite drink is."

Formula	Result
=A1 & "Lemonade"	My favorite drink is Lemonade

The reference to cell A1 (which contains the word "Green Tea") is surrounded by extra double quotation marks that are used as escape characters in the sample below.

Formula	Result
="My favorite drink is """&A1&"""	My favorite drink is "Green Tea"

To specify where to return a double quotation, use the CHAR command and code 34.

List Of Functions by Category

Below is a list of every function covered in Formulas and Functions Help, organized by category.

1. **Date And Time Functions**

How often do you enter the time or date as they are right now on a Numbers sheet? When you open a spreadsheet to track your activities, weight, or work schedule, you may need to enter the current date. Alternatively, you might urge team members or employees to use Numbers and keep track of the time they enter their data.

Numbers' ability to enter the current date and/or time without requiring you to type it in or use a calculation is a useful feature. With the aid of the date and time functions, you may use dates and times to find answers to issues like calculating the number of working days between two dates or determining what day of the week a date will fall on.

Here's how to format both if you want to.

Adding Date or Time in Numbers on Mac

- Select the cell in your spreadsheet where you want the current date or time by opening it in Numbers on a Mac.

- Within the menu bar, select **Table**. Select **Insert Current Date** or **Insert Current Time** from the options at the bottom.

- You can also use **Control + Command + Shift + D** for the current date and **Control + Command + Shift + T** for the current time if you like keyboard shortcuts.

Format The Date and Time on Mac

You might not like the format when the time or date appears on your mobile. For instance, you might choose 24-hour time over 12-hour time or merely want numbers for the date rather than the month written out.

How to modify both to your taste is as follows:

- Select the **Format** button in the upper right corner after selecting the cell that contains the date or time.
- At the top of the sidebar, select the **Cell** tab.
- Use the drop-down boxes in the **Data Format** section to change the **Date or Time** format.

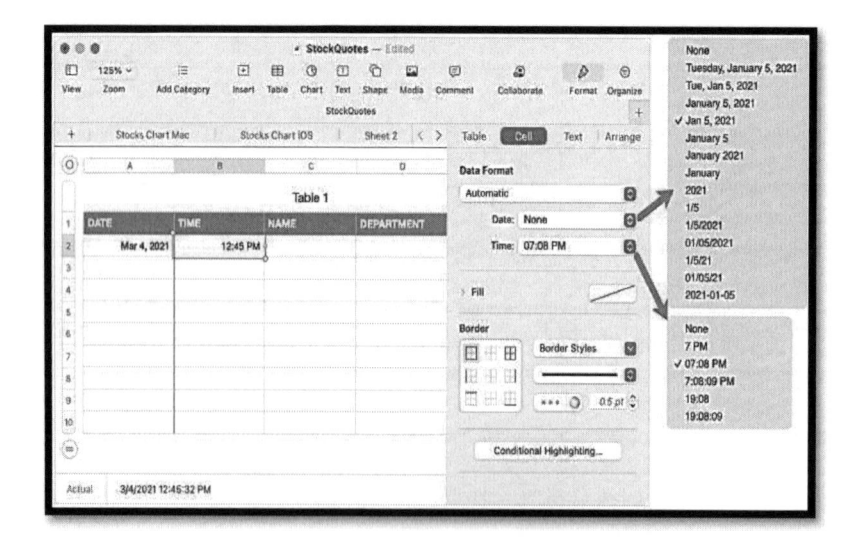

Adding Date or Time in Numbers On iPhone and iPad

The current date or time can be added to a cell on the iPhone and iPad with fewer taps than typing it in.

- Open **Numbers** and choose the cell you want to display the date or time in.
- Click the **Cell** icon when it displays on the bottom right. Go to **Insert** in the pop-up and choose either **Current Date** or **Current Time**.

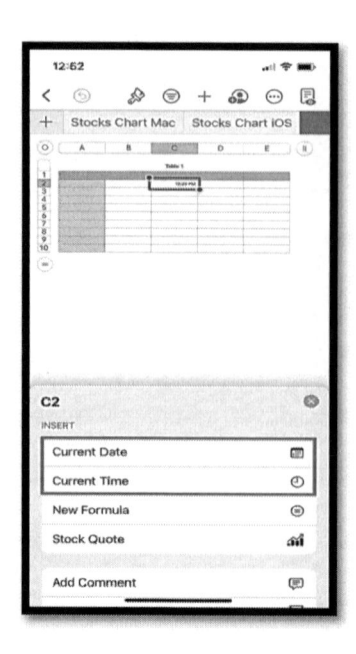

Format The Date and Time On iPhone and iPad

On your iPhone and iPad, Numbers offers a simple method for changing the format of the date and/or time. This is how:

- Select the **Format** icon (paintbrush) at the top after selecting the cell that contains the date or time.
- Select the **Format** tab.
- The **Info** icon (**i**) is located next to **Date & Time**. Tap it.
- Select the **Time format** below and the **Date format** above.

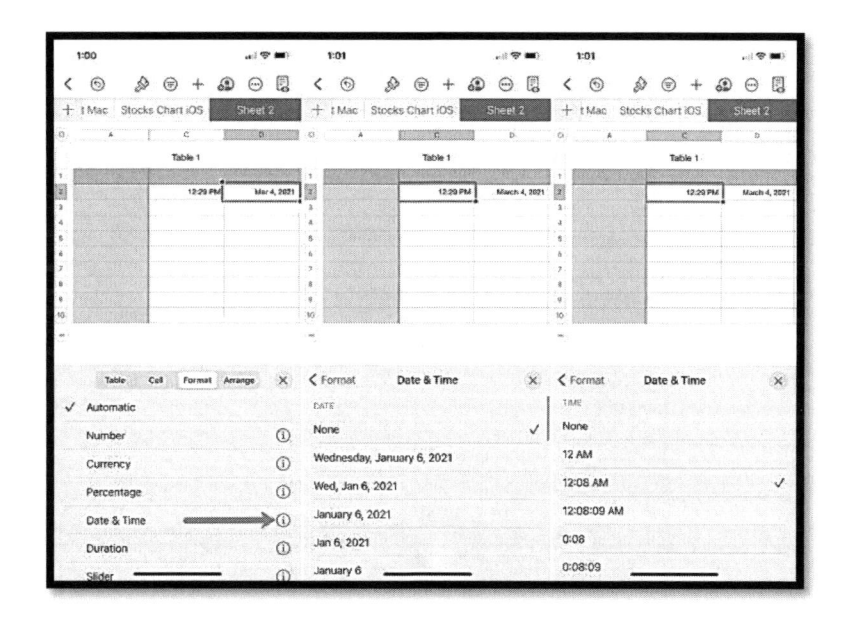

Conclusion

You can make data entering less tedious by using quick features like Numbers' ability to quickly insert the current date or time.

2. Duration functions

The duration functions enable you to work with time intervals (durations) by converting between different time units, including hours, days, and weeks. Here, you'll use it to calculate the duration of financial schedules or projects. It's a great little function to have in your toolbox.

So, as you can see, we have numbers that represent weeks, days, hours, minutes, seconds, and milliseconds. All we did for the formula in the **Duration** section is to type in **= duration** and plugged in these numbers.

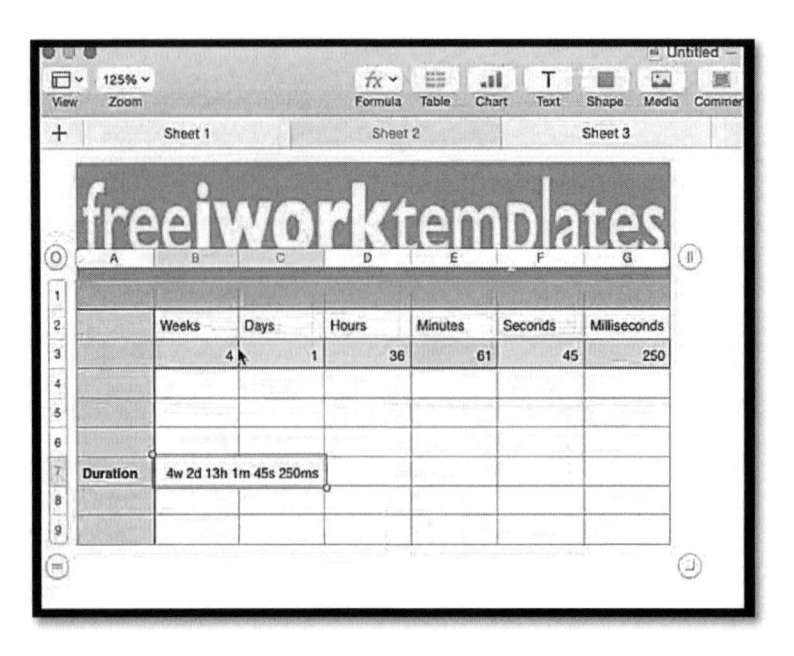

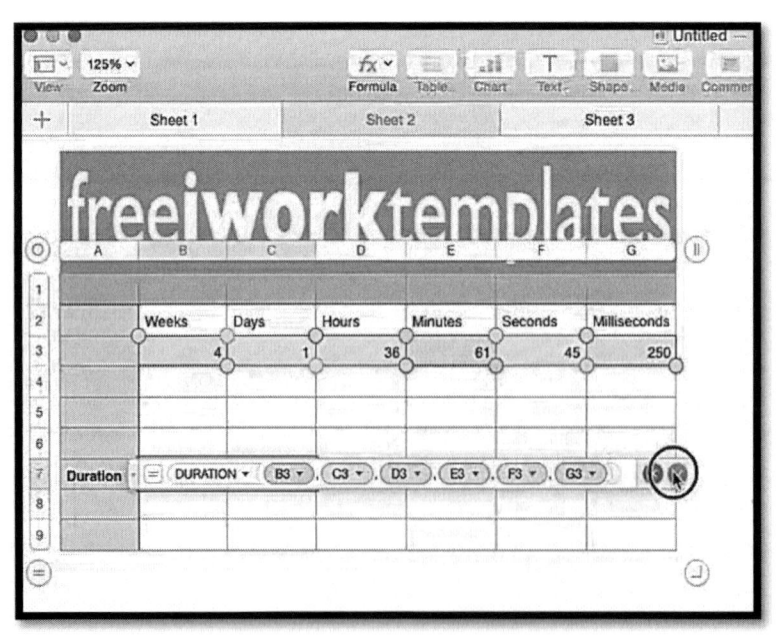

We get this wonderful formatted sequence here that shows exactly how long whatever these are. "Numbers" is great because it does the math for you.

So, let's say this isn't **45** seconds but **15000** seconds and you'll notice that our hours and minutes and seconds jumped dramatically in the **Duration** section because Numbers is doing the calculating for us.

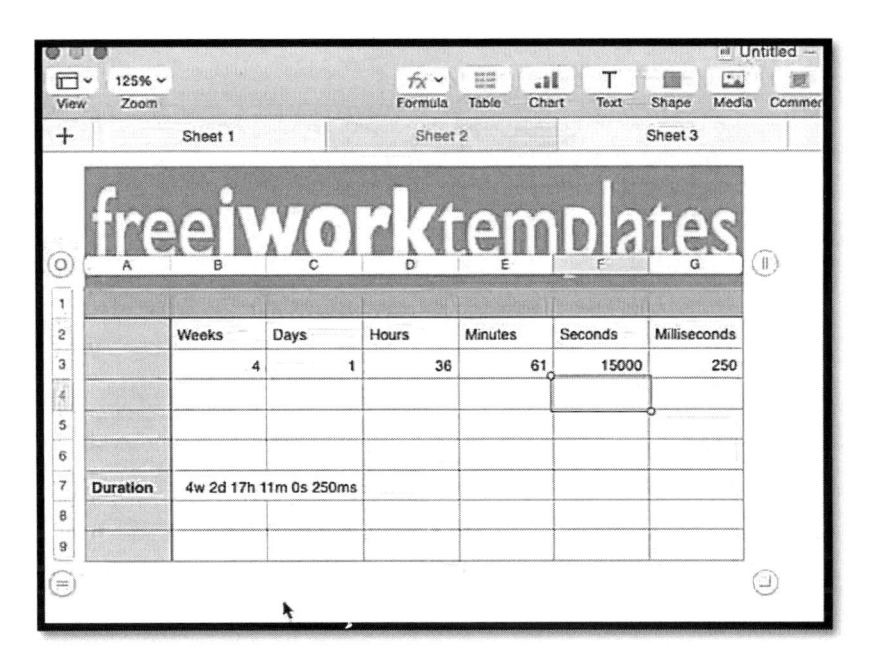

Well, that's the duration function. Use it well it'll treat your right.

3. Engineering functions

The engineering functions assist you in calculating some typical engineering values and performing a base conversion.

4. Financial functions

By figuring out issues like the amount of annual depreciation of an item, the interest generated on investment, and the current market price of a bond, the financial functions assist you in working with cash flows, depreciable assets, annuities, and investments.

Note: Your Language & Region settings (found in System Preferences on macOS, Settings on iOS and iPadOS, and Time Zone/Region in iCloud Settings) determine the currency displayed in the majority of function results.

5. **Logical and information functions**

The logical and information functions enable you to assess the contents of cells and decide how to deal with them or the results of formulas.

6. **Numeric functions**

You can calculate frequently used mathematical numbers using numeric functions.

7. **Reference functions**

You can extract data from cells and find data within tables with the use of reference functions.

8. **Statistical functions**

You can use a range of measures and statistical approaches to manipulate and analyze data sets with the assistance of statistical functions.

9. **Text functions**

You can handle character strings with the aid of the text functions.

10. **Trigonometric functions**

You can work with angles and their components with the aid of trigonometric functions.

More Useful Formulas and Functions

We have some more helpful methods for working with your data if the basic formulas or functions we've covered so far aren't sufficient for what you want to achieve.

Compare Values

To check whether cell values are equal, greater than, less than, or not equal, you can use comparison operators. The formula's output will be shown as True or False. If you want to compare sales, income, or expenses over months or years, this is useful.

For our example, we're looking to determine if our January sales were higher than or equal to those from the year before.

- Open the **Formula Editor** and choose the cell where you want the formula to appear.
- For the formula, select the first cell.
- Type the comparison operator here. Enter <= when the value is greater than or equal to.
- To view the formula, select the second cell.
- Hit the **Return** key or click the checkbox.

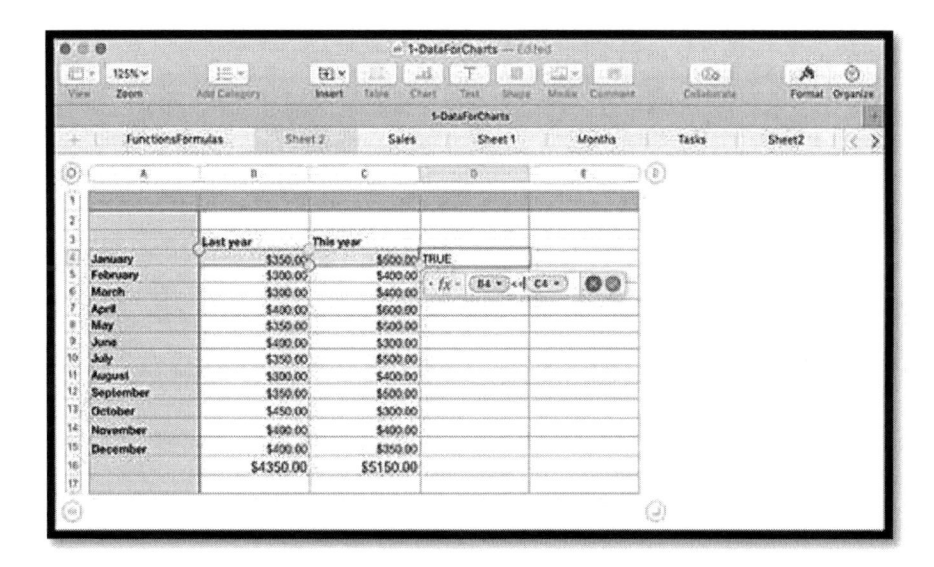

You can see from our example that the result "**True**" in the formula's cell indicates that our sales for this January were higher than or equal to those from last year.

Split Text

If you have more information than you need or wish to extract only certain pieces of information, you can use the Right and Left functions to break up text strings. Area codes from phone numbers, states from cities, or zip codes from address strings can all be extracted using this method.

For this illustration, we have a spreadsheet with data that includes a customer's two-letter state abbreviation and city, such as Chicago, IL.

Each person's state should be extracted and placed in a separate field.

- Open the **Formula Editor** and choose the cell where you want the formula to appear.
- By pressing the **Format** button in the top right corner, you can access the **Functions Browser**.
- Search for "**Right**," click it from the list, and then hit **Insert Function**.
- Click "**source-string**" in the **Formula Editor**, then click the data-containing cell.
- Click "**string-length**" to the right in the editor and enter **2**.
- To use the formula, click the checkmark.

This formula extracts two characters (step 5) from the string's right side (step 3). By using this formula on our column, we are now able to view each customer's individual state's abbreviation.

Remove Extra Spaces

It's possible that the data in your spreadsheet isn't always formatted the way you need it to be if it came from a database. You can have too many spaces between the first and last name of a customer if you use the customer spreadsheet example from above. This can be problematic for mail merging or automated emails that use those names.

We may quickly and easily get rid of those superfluous spaces using the Trim function in numbers.

- Open the **Formula Editor** and **Functions Browser** after selecting the cell where the formula should be entered.
- In the list, look for "**Trim**," tap it, then press **Insert Function**.
- Select "**source-string**" in the Formula Editor, then click the data-containing cell.
- To use the formula, click the checkmark.

Now that there are no excess spaces to mess with our other software, we have a neat, tidy list of the names of our customers.

Concatenate Data

The above situation might not apply to you. It's possible that you want to combine data from two separate cells into one. The **Concatenate function** can be used to accomplish this with both text and numbers.

Let's imagine that the first and last names of a customer are divided across two different cells in the data we got.

Those names must be together for our email program to function.

- Open the **Formula Editor** and **Functions Browser** after selecting the cell where the formula should be entered.
- Select **Insert Function** after doing a search for "**Concatenate**" and selecting it from the list.
- Select "**string**," then select the first name's cell and add the comma.
- Add opening and closing quotation marks, place a space in the middle **("")**, and then a comma.
- The last name's cell should be clicked.
- To use the formula, click the checkmark.

Let's go! Our customers' first and last names are all in one column rather than being dispersed throughout other cells.

Convert To Plain Text

The Plaintext function in Numbers is an additional feature that can be extremely helpful, especially when gathering data from diverse sources. Your spreadsheet might contain rich text-formatted text and numbers. Examples include names that are bold, italicized, or underlined, as well as links that can be clicked.

Your data can be reduced to plain, straightforward text by using the Plaintext function.

- Open the **Formula Editor** and **Functions Browser** after selecting the cell where the formula should be entered.
- Select **Insert Function** after doing a search for "**Plaintext**" and selecting it from the list.
- Click the cell containing the data, then click "source-string."
- To use the formula, click the checkmark.

After that, your data should seem plain, devoid of HTML, rich text, or other formatting.

Types Of Arguments and Values

Many of the terms employed to describe the functions in the Functions Browser are defined in this section.

Any value types

Any argument can be a Boolean value, date/time value, duration value, integer value, or string value if it is stated as such.

Arrays and array functions

An array is a list of values that a function can use or that a function can return. Instead of returning only one value, an array function delivers an array of values. It's usual practice to supply values to another function using array functions.

Boolean expression and value type

An expression that responds to the Boolean values TRUE or FALSE is referred to as a Boolean expression. A reference to a cell that contains or generates a logical TRUE or FALSE value or a logical TRUE or FALSE value is known as a Boolean value.

It is often what happens after a Boolean statement has been evaluated, although a Boolean value can also be given as a function's first argument or as the content of a cell. A Boolean value is frequently used to specify which expression the IF function should return.

Collection value type

A reference to a single table cell range or an array returned by an array function are both acceptable examples of an argument that is provided as a collection. An extra attribute that specifies the kinds of values that can be contained in an argument that is declared as a collection.

Condition expression

A condition is an expression that may contain references, constants, the string ampersand operator, and comparison operators. The condition's contents must produce the Boolean value TRUE or FALSE when the condition is compared to another value.

Constant expression

An expression that is directly referenced in the formula is known as a constant. Neither cell references nor function calls are present. For instance, the string expressions "cat" and "s" are constants in the formula given:

CONCATENATE("cat","s")

Date/time value type

Any of the formats that Numbers supports can be used to represent a date/time value or as a reference to a cell that has that value. All date/time values contain both a date and a time, but you can opt to display only one of the two in a cell.

Duration value type

A duration value is a time value or a reference to a cell that contains a time value. Weeks (W or weeks), days (D or days), hours (H or hours), minutes (M or minutes), seconds (S or seconds), and milliseconds (m or milliseconds) are all types of duration values.

List value type

A list is a series of additional values separated by commas. For instance:

CHOOSE(3,"1st","second",7,"last")

In some instances, a second set of parentheses surrounds the list. For instance:

AREAS ((B1:B5,C10:C12))

Modal argument or value type

There are various stated values that can apply to a modal argument. Modal arguments typically contain information on the kind of calculation or data type the function should do. It is stated in the argument description if a modal argument has a default value.

Number value type

A reference to a cell that contains a numeric expression, a number, or both might be considered a number value. The limit is stated in the argument description if the range of possible values for a number is restricted (for instance, the number must be greater than 0).

Range value type

A reference value refers to a specific cell or a group of cells.

A single colon separates the starting and finishing cells if the range spans more than one cell. For instance:

COUNT (A3:D7).

The reference must include the name of the table if it refers to a cell in another table. For instance:

Table 2: B2.

Keep in mind that a double colon (::) separates the table title from the cell reference. When you choose a cell in a different table while creating a formula, the name of the table is automatically added.

The name of the cell must be given if the reference is to a cell in a table on a different slide, sheet, or page. For instance:

SUM (Slide 2::Table 1::C2:G2).

Double colons are used to demarcate the names and cell references. When you select a cell in another location while creating a formula, the names of the slide (or sheet) and the table are automatically added.

String value type

A string value is defined as a value with zero or more characters or as a reference to a cell with zero or more characters. Any printable character, such as numbers, may be used to create the characters.

Functions That Accept Conditions and Wildcards as Arguments

SUM is one of many functions that work with complete collections. Other functions, like SUMIF, only affect the cells in the collection that comply with a condition.

For instance, the following formula may be used to add all the values in column B that are less than five:

=SUMIF(B,"<5")

Due to the fact that it instructs the function to disregard cells that do not satisfy the criteria, the second argument of SUMIF is known as a condition.

Functions that take conditions go into one of two categories:

- Functions whose names have the IF or IFS suffix (except for the function IF, which does not take a condition; Instead, an expression that should return either TRUE or FALSE is required. Utilizing the comparison operators found in their conditions, such as ">5," "=7," or ">2," these functions can compare numbers.
  Wildcards are also accepted by these functions for defining conditions. For instance, you could use the following formula to determine how many cells in column B start with the letter "a":
  =COUNTIF(B,"a*")
- Functions that accept conditions but cannot do numerical comparisons, such as HLOOKUP. Wildcards are sometimes allowed when using these functions.

All the functions that can receive conditions—whether they be regular expressions, wildcards, numeric comparisons, or a combination of the three—are listed in the image below.

CHARTS AND GRAPHS

Numerous charts are available in Apple's Numbers spreadsheet application to assist in understanding the data in its tables (as does its Pages word processor). However, in order to convey information when converting numbers into images, you must choose the appropriate type of image.

Standard Charts

Everyone is familiar with the usual line, bar, and pie charts, but being familiar with them does not always mean that you will know which one is the most appropriate in a certain circumstance. What about area charts, stacked bars, and donuts, their offspring? If you choose the incorrect one, your viewers might be unable to make any conclusions or, worse still, they might reach the incorrect conclusion.

1. Line Charts

You are aware of what a line chart is and perhaps even that it is mostly used to show the rate of change over time for a single item or when comparing several items.

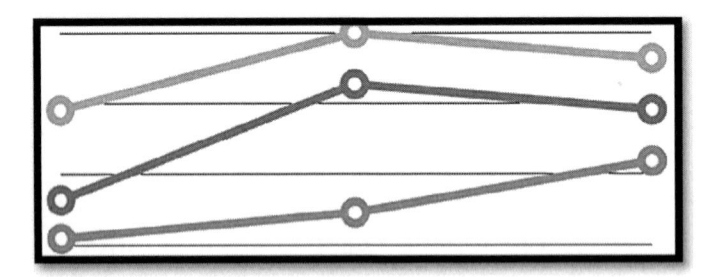

A basic line chart

2. Column And Bar Charts

Compare data by group or category using a column (vertical) or bar (horizontal) chart, such as the output of Widget Factories A, B, and C, the starting salaries of well-known post-graduate degree holders, or the average monthly rainfall in your city for each month last year.

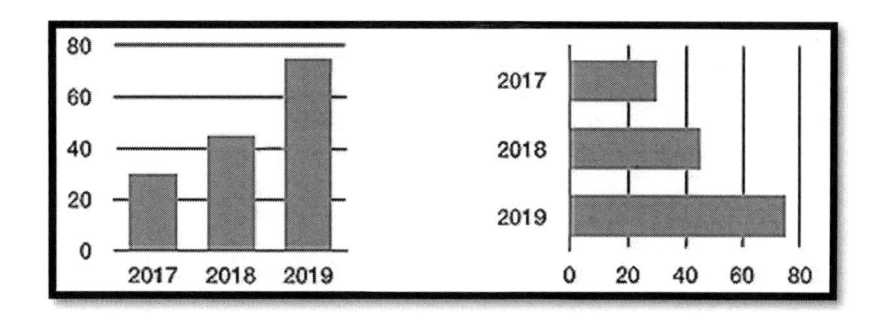

The same data in a column chart and a bar chart

Generally, practical considerations determine which of these fits better on a printed page, a web page, or whether you need to handle a long label.

3. Pie Charts

Pie charts are simple yet beautiful, however they can be used incorrectly. Because the data provided by the slices creates a whole, we refer to them as pie charts rather than "circular graphs." So, instead of examining how a value varies over time, use a pie chart to iilustrate how a whole something is divided up. A pie chart that appears to have been "exploded" simply has one or more of its slices removed for emphasis or for aesthetic purposes.

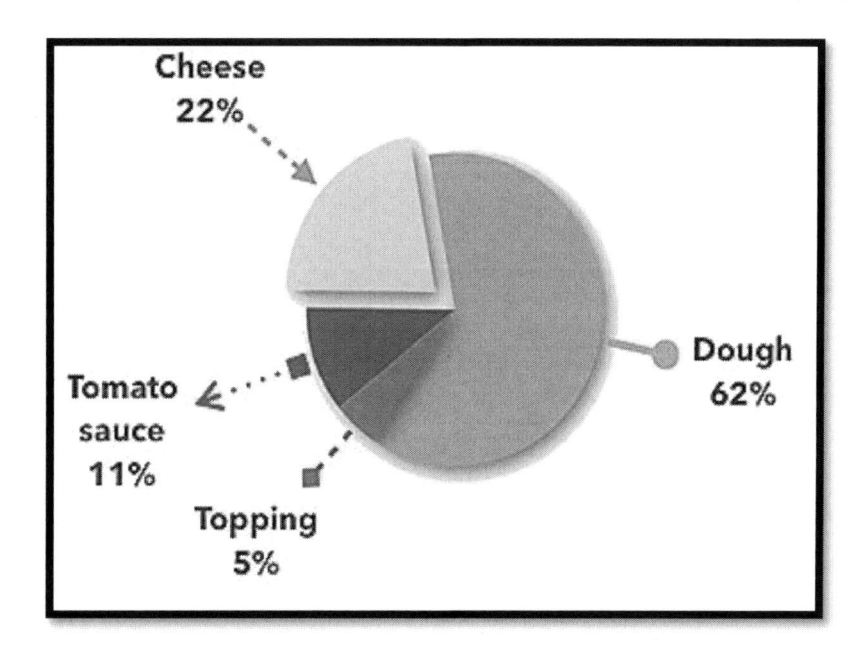

Some have more cheese than others

4. Donut Charts

Donut charts, like pie charts, make it easier for readers to understand how a total item is divided. Whether the arcs of a donut chart's ring are easier or more difficult to comprehend than the pie chart's wedges is up for debate. However, some experts also despise the typical pie chart based on broad interpretational guidelines.

Pie is simpler to comprehend and that you should only use donut charts when the variances between the arcs are significant enough to continue to be visible. For example, it is simpler to see the size difference between the orange and dark blue pie wedges in this figure than it is to see the same colors in the donut ring.

The ability of a chart to visually convey information is what distinguishes a good one from a bad one. Of course, you would label each wedge or arc with the number it represents.

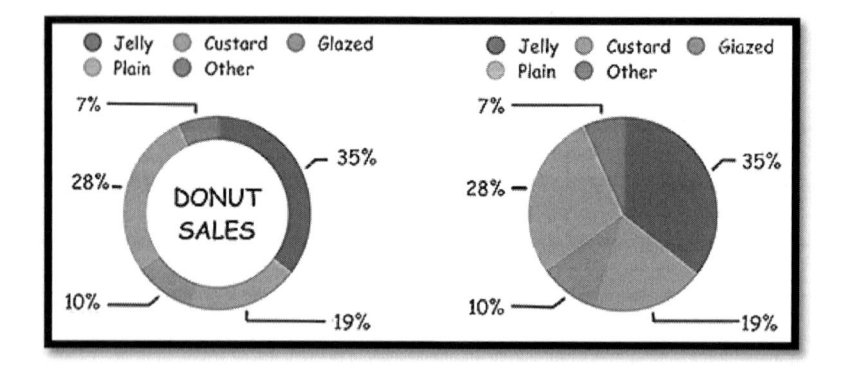

Donut and pie charts illustrating the same data

5. Stacked Column and Bar Charts

Similar to a (misshaped) pie chart, a single stacked column or bar shows how much of a whole something is divided up. You can include data on the overall totals as well as the size of each column's or bar's component by using numerous stacked columns or bars in a chart.

This figure has three charts that provide data for each of three years, a breakdown of the data for those years, and a combination of the data from the first two charts.

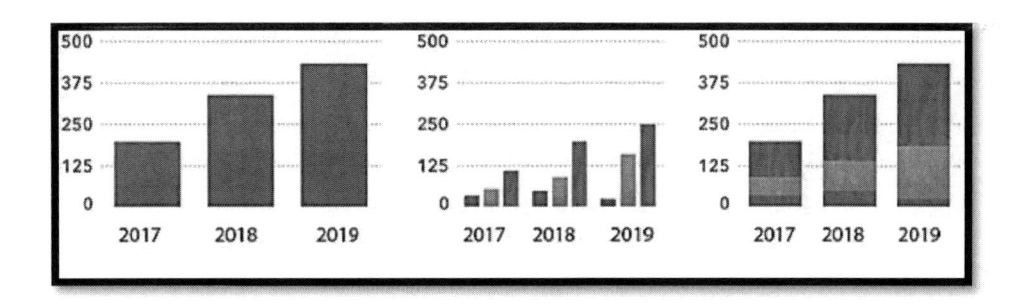

Left to right: Single-year data, a breakdown of that data into its constituents, and a stacked column chart combining the information from the other two charts

You can be unsure of whether to exhibit data in a column/bar chart or a line chart. Use a line chart when you want to highlight changes over time; a column or bar chart when you want to focus on totals at certain periods in time.

6. Area Charts

A line chart with color filling might appear to be an area chart, and in reality, that is what it is. However, unless one piece of data is smaller than the other at every point, avoid using it to represent more than one data set. Think about the situation where there are only two data sets, like in the figure below. Only the first and last years of the background data set are visible. The background data may be substantially different at some or all of its points, or it may be virtually the same but somewhat lower at all of its locations. The slope we can see indicates that there was a progressive increase from the penultimate to the last number, which is the sole clue provided.

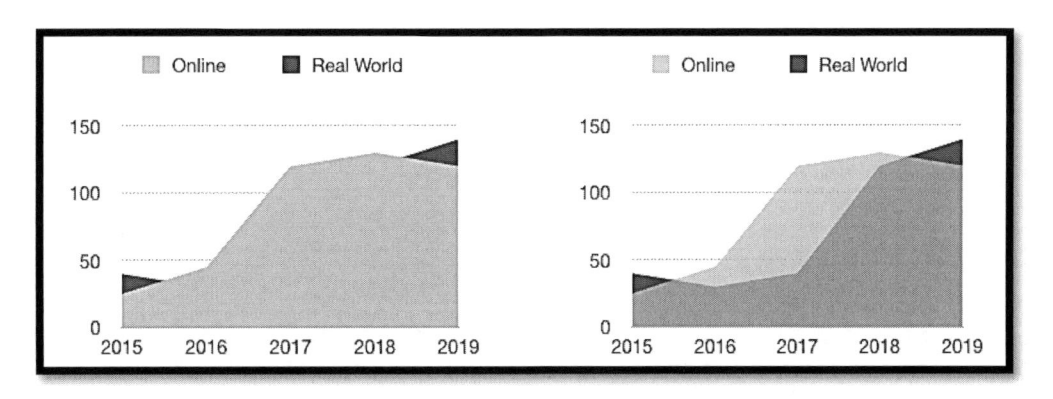

Left: an area chart with most of its second data set hidden. Right, one of many possibilities for the background data set.

Furthermore, area charts using different data sets frequently convey the wrong message. Even if the frontmost set is smaller than the background set overall, since you see much more of it, you can quickly conclude that it has a larger data set than the background set.

Advanced Charts

These less popular chart kinds may not be as well known to you because they are utilized much less often. That might be as a result of the fact that some creators and viewers might misinterpret them more frequently.

1. **Stacked Area and Stacked Bar Charts**

A stacked area chart displays the proportion of the total that each x-axis data value represents, much like a stacked column/bar chart does (although having a different shape). However, this kind of chart has both its own flaws and all the interpretation problems that come with a standard area chart.

Unless you are an expert, avoid using stacked area charts. If you are an expert, stay away from it if your audience is not. Instead, think about a stacked column/bar chart. One issue with this type of chart's interpretation is seen in the figure below. The red band, which you can see, sank in February. Nevertheless, because your eye follows the top of the band normally, you might not realize that it is also compressed from the bottom, which has an impact on how sharp the drop is perceived. Yet, the version with the stacked columns makes it obvious how little of a difference February's red band is in comparison to the months before and after.

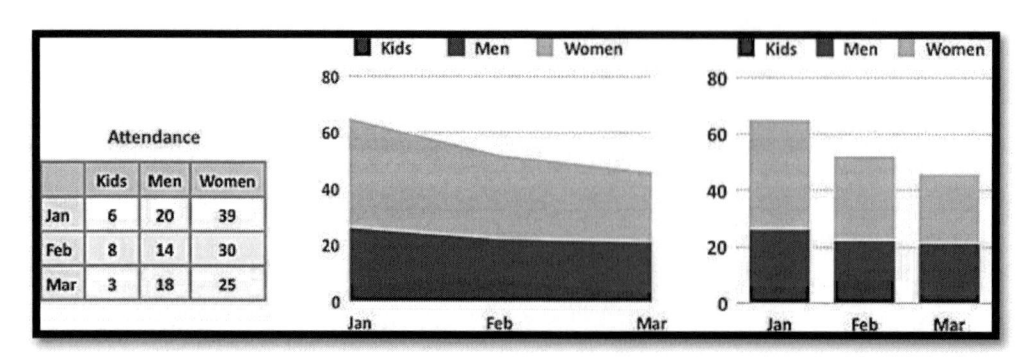

Attendance	Kids	Men	Women
Jan	6	20	39
Feb	8	14	30
Mar	3	18	25

The same data in a stacked area chart and a stacked column chart

2. Dual-Axis Charts

Two y-axes, one on each side of the chart, are used in a dual, or 2-axis, chart. It is intended to compare two items that have completely distinct scales on their y-axes, either because they have different units of measurement (like the weather and popsicle sales displayed above) or because they have vastly different ranges on the same numeric scale.

The main criticism is that because most people don't know how to read these charts or find it difficult to compare the two axes, they commonly misread these charts. Knowing your audience is the key to using a dual-axis chart effectively.

At least, that is the official recommendation. The dual-axis chart, however, was easily understood by everyone who saw it, even non-math friends who aren't geeks (a graphic designer, a professor of German, and sisters who are 16 and 11 years old).

This suggests that you shouldn't instantly be scared away from this chart option, even though it may be due to the small number of data points, the fact that we displayed the original single-axis chart version for comparison, or even their innate knowledge of what would occur to popsicle sales as the temperature increases.

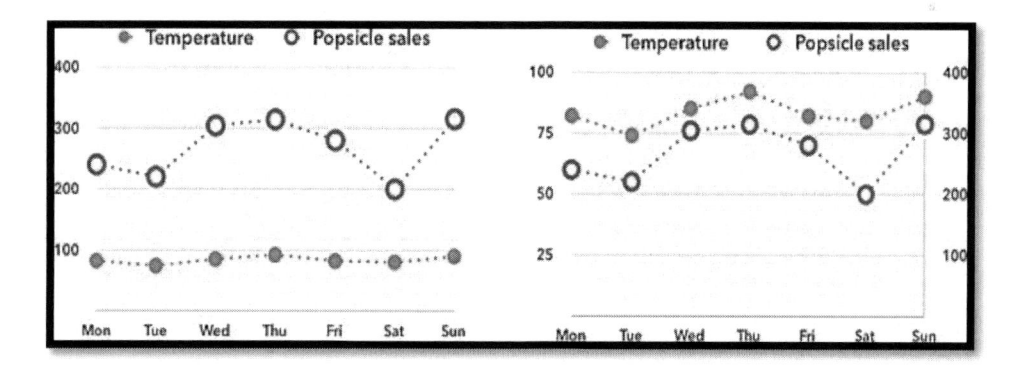

Left: A standard line chart with widely varying data series can't show the variation in the lower-values series (here, the temperature). Right: The same data as a dual-axis chart.

3. Scatter Charts

A scatter chart, often called an x-y plot, plots pairs of coordinates to indicate correlations between variables, such as the association between rain and fungus growth rate or the relationship between average speed and fuel usage.

A scatter chart shows clusters and outliers by plotting the first number from each series together, followed by the second-number pair, and so on, as opposed to two series of data displayed along a line. A best-fit line, or trend line, is frequently drawn between the points on a scatter chart to highlight a trend.

However, stay away from trend lines until you are familiar with all of their implications: For instance, Numbers provides six different types of trend lines, including polynomial, logarithmic, and linear.

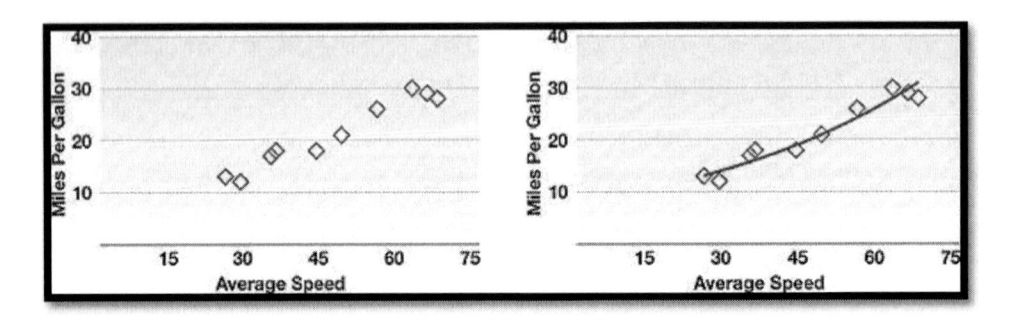

A basic scatter chart; on the right, an added trend line

4. Bubble Charts

A bubble chart is essentially a scatter chart with a third data set contained in the data. The x, y coordinates for a bubble's center point are plotted using the data from the first two data sets, and the bubble's size is represented by the third value (the z value).

Interpreting bubble charts can be challenging. Is the circle's area more important than its diameter? You can't tell how much of a difference in bubble size represents how much of a difference in the data, even when they are mathematically interwoven, if you don't know which one was used for the chart.

Even if we are aware that it is the diameter that matters, a quick study into the topic suggests that humans are unable to resist responding to the area.

These two charts, which make use of the same data, show the significant distinction between the approaches. The number of salesmen and the variety of things offered are indicated by the x and y coordinates. Nevertheless, because the things range in price, the size of a bubble represents the amount of money made. It's the only way to include that information in the chart because the pricing of the various "units" being sold vary. The bubble area on the left corresponds to the same number as the bubble diameter on the right. The bubble on the left serves as an example of a different issue with this type of chart: when two bubbles are touching, it can be difficult to determine how large of a number either one represents. However, this issue pales in comparison to the interpretation issue that arises when bubbles actually overlap.

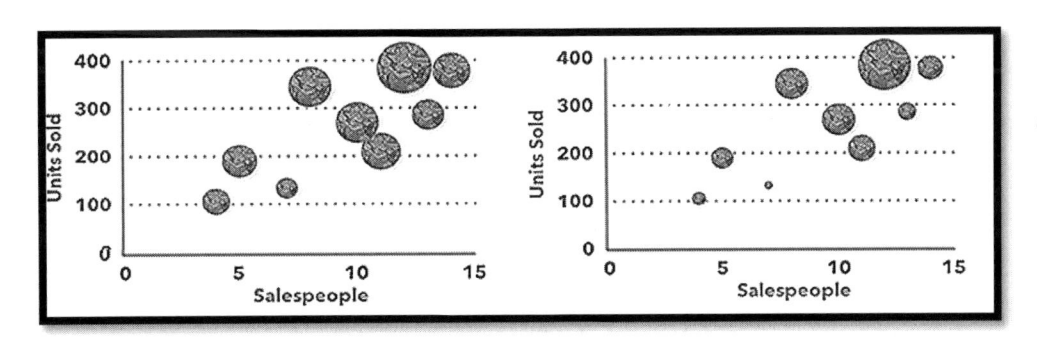

The same data represented by a bubble's area (left) and its diameter (right)

How To Insert, Format, And Edit Charts & Graphs in The Numbers App on Mac, iPad, And iPhone

You have fantastic options for displaying data with graphs and charts. Visuals allow you to examine data quickly, compare it, and even put it into perspective rather than having to read rows and rows of data. The good thing about spreadsheet applications like Numbers is that you only need to choose your data and a chart; the application will do the rest.

Once your chart is created, you can edit it to customize how it looks and include things like a title, labels, and a legend. This offers you the freedom to show your data in whatever way you choose in a graph or chart. To create your Numbers chart, format it how you like, and make any necessary changes, follow these instructions.

Insert A Chart in Numbers on Mac

While inserting a graph or chart before selecting your data is an option, selecting the data first is recommended.

You can then make adjustments after getting a quick glimpse of how your data will appear in the type of chart you select.

- Drag the cursor through the cells, columns, or rows to choose the data for your chart.

- Select the kind of graph or chart to display by clicking the **Chart** button in the toolbar or by selecting **Insert > Chart** from the menu bar. The styles of charts available to you are 2D, 3D, and interactive. We'll use a basic 2D chart in this case. Select from a variety of charts that will effectively display your data, including pie, bar, column, line, and area charts. You can choose a color scheme right away if you click the **Chart** button in the toolbar by using the arrows.

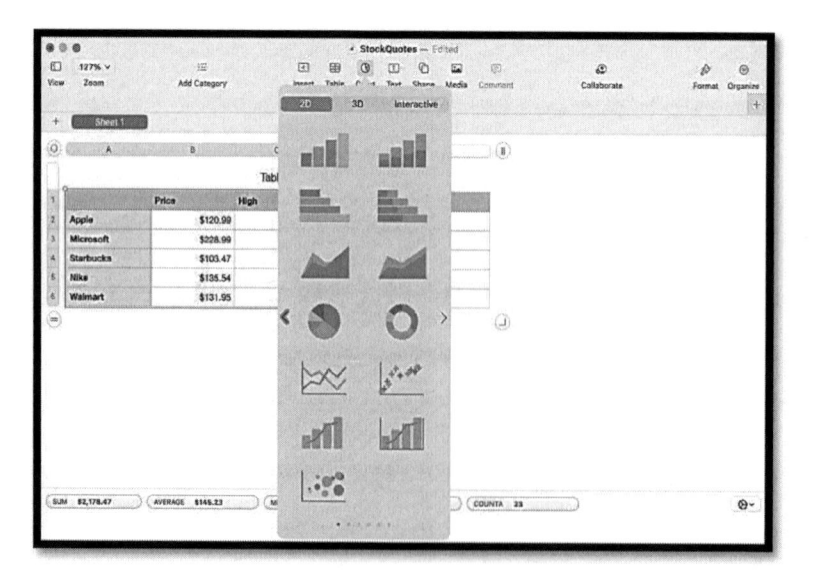

- The chart will automatically appear in your sheet once you've chosen a style. Drag a corner to resize the chart or click and drag it to a new location. You're good to go if you're satisfied with the chart as-is.

However, continue reading if you want to make some changes to the formatting or data references.

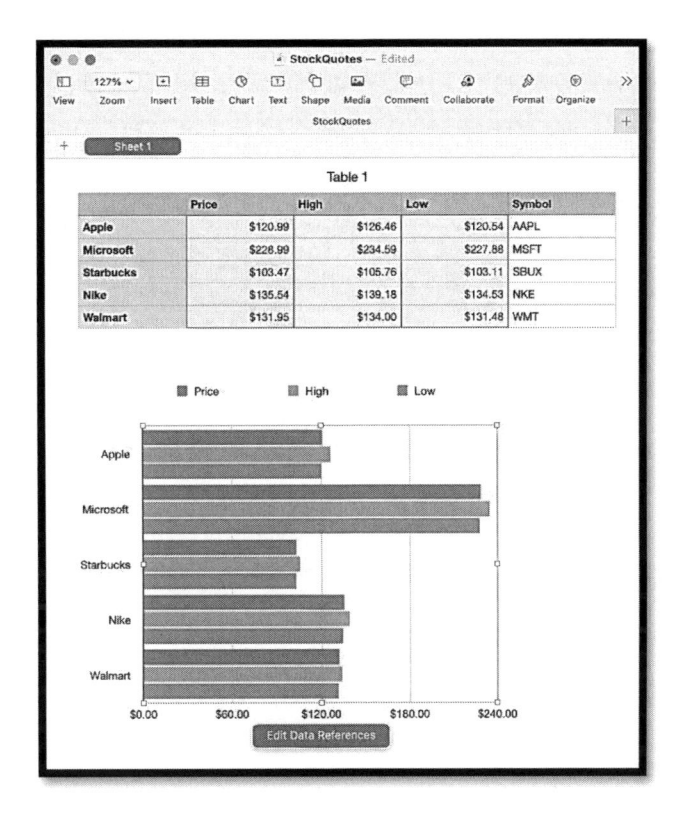

Format A Chart on Mac

You can format your chart in Numbers in a variety of ways. You have a lot of flexibility, from including a title and rounding the corners to changing the axis scale and showing tick marks.

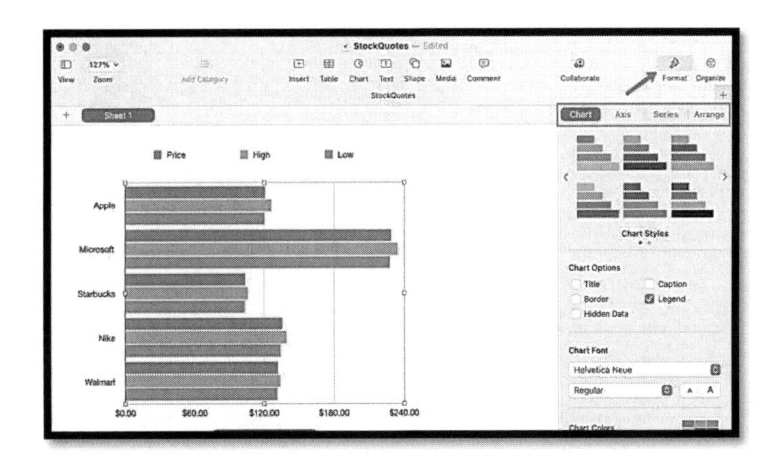

Press the **Format** button in the top right corner after selecting the chart.

By pressing this, the sidebar with tabs for the formatting categories of Chart, Axis, Series, and Arrange is displayed.

- **Chart**: Change the color scheme, add a title or legend, change the font style, size, and color, add a background or border, apply a shadow, round the edges, and change the gap size for the chart.
- **Axis**: Include reference lines and tick marks, change the axis scale, format the gridlines, show the axis name and line, and show the labels.
- **Series**: Include and select the error bars, trendlines, and value labels.
- **Arrange**: Move the chart left or right, change its alignment, size, and position, and lock it.

Edit A Chart on Mac

It's easy to make these adjustments if you want to change the data that's being used in the chart or plot the rows against the columns as the series, or vice versa.

Tap the **Edit Data References** button that appears alongside the chart after selecting the chart. This will make the chart data on your sheet stand out.

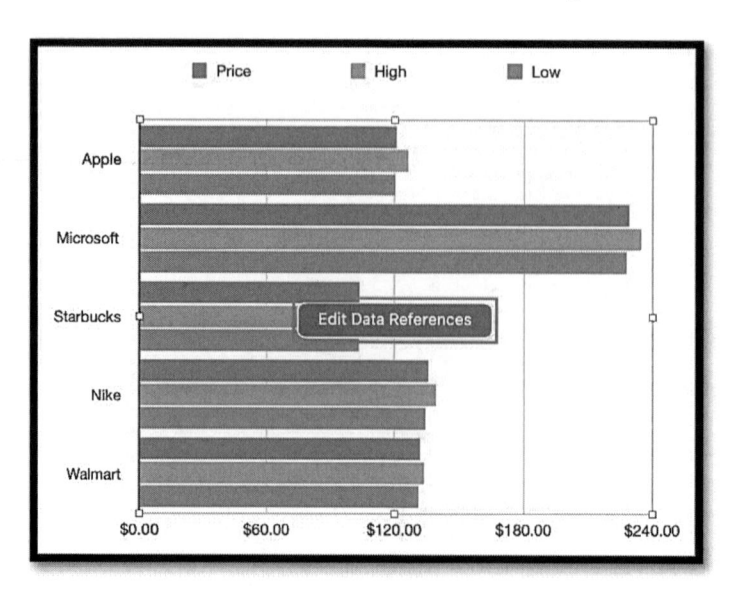

- To change the plot series or remove a series from the chart, click the arrow next to a column or row header.
- To add more data to your chart, select more cells.
- To switch between columns and rows for the plot series, use the drop-down on the bottom left.

Click **Done** at the bottom of the window once you have finished making changes to the chart data.

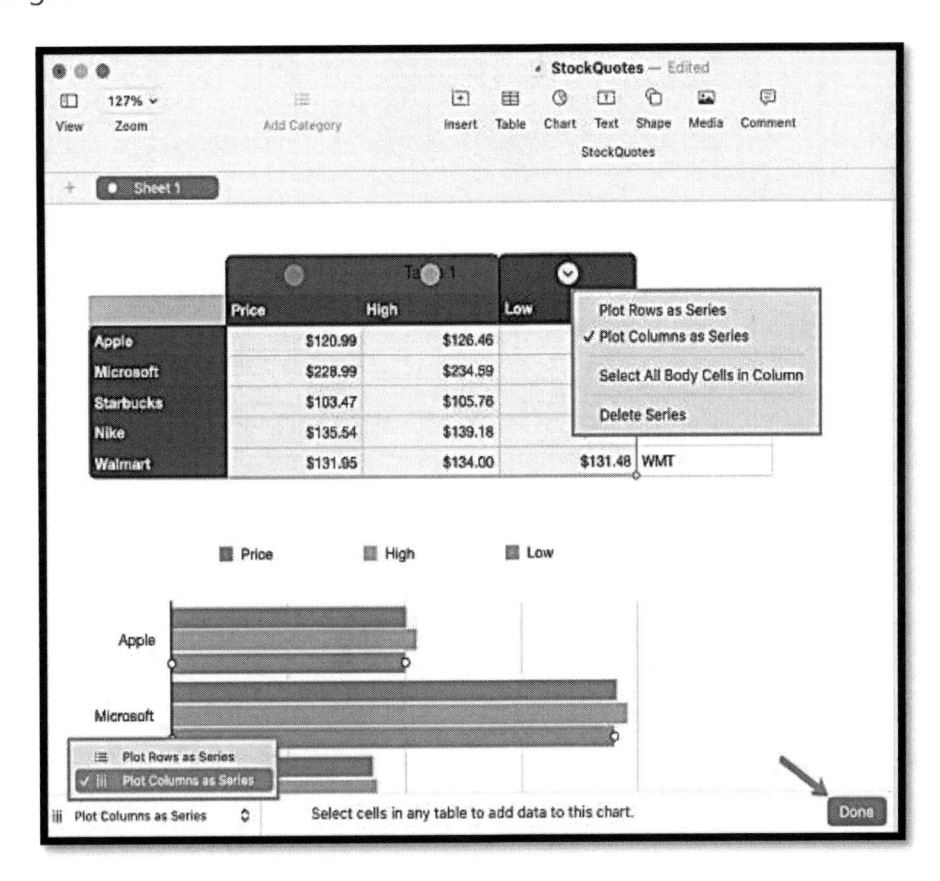

Additionally, you can change the kind of chart you're using. For instance, you might believe that your data would appear better as a column than a bar chart.

- Tap the **Format** button after selecting the chart.
- Select the **Chart** tab from the sidebar's top.
- Use the **Chart Type** drop-down menu at the bottom of the sidebar to select a different chart style.

229

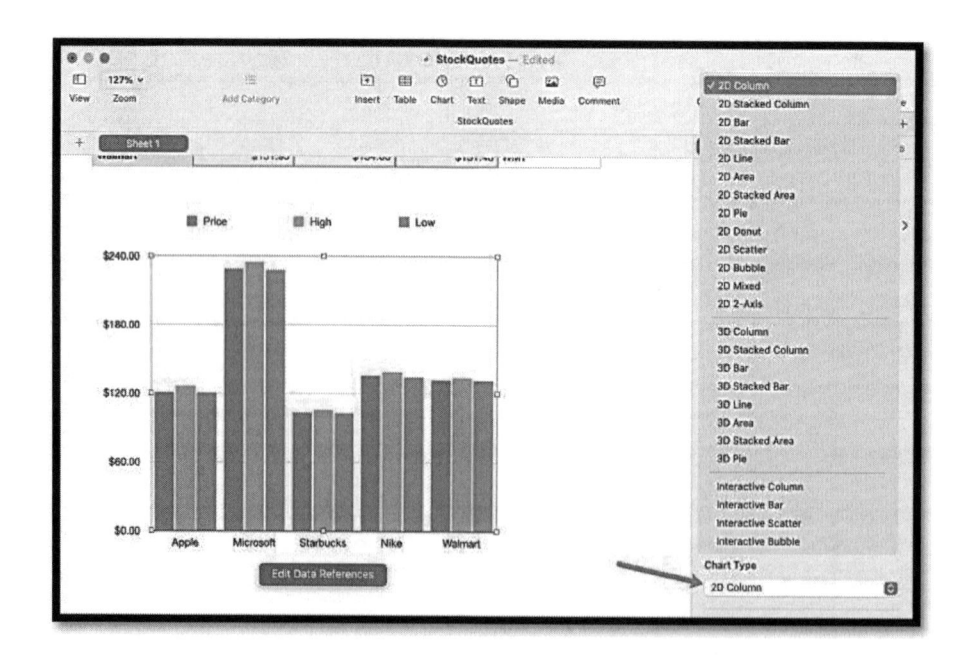

Insert A Chart in Numbers On iPhone and iPad

You can still insert, format, and modify charts in Numbers on iPhone and iPad even though it's a little bit simpler to deal with charts on a Mac. Similar to Mac, iOS makes it simpler to select your data before adding a chart.

- Drag through the cells, columns, or rows to select the data in your chart.
- Select the Chart icon by clicking the + sign at the top. Choose from Interactive, 3D, or 2D. To select a color scheme, swipe left or right.
- Select the chart you want to use, and it will automatically appear in your sheet beneath your data.

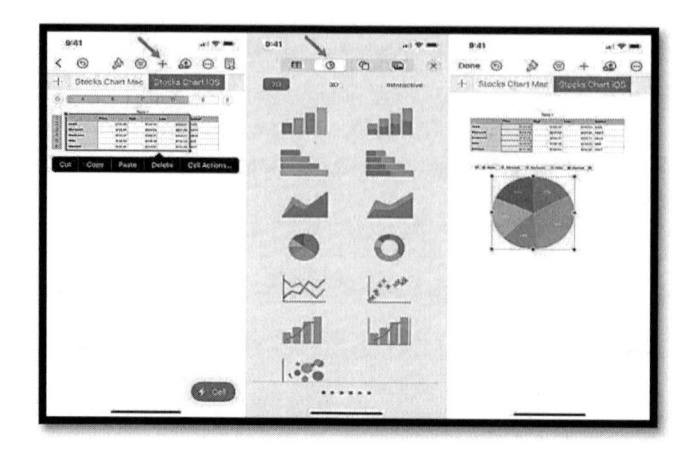

Format A Chart On iPhone and iPad

The majority of the formatting options for a Numbers chart is the same on an iPhone or iPad as they are on a Mac.

Click the **Format** icon (paintbrush) at the top after selecting the chart. Use the Chart, Style, Data, and Arrange tabs to format the chart in the pop-up.

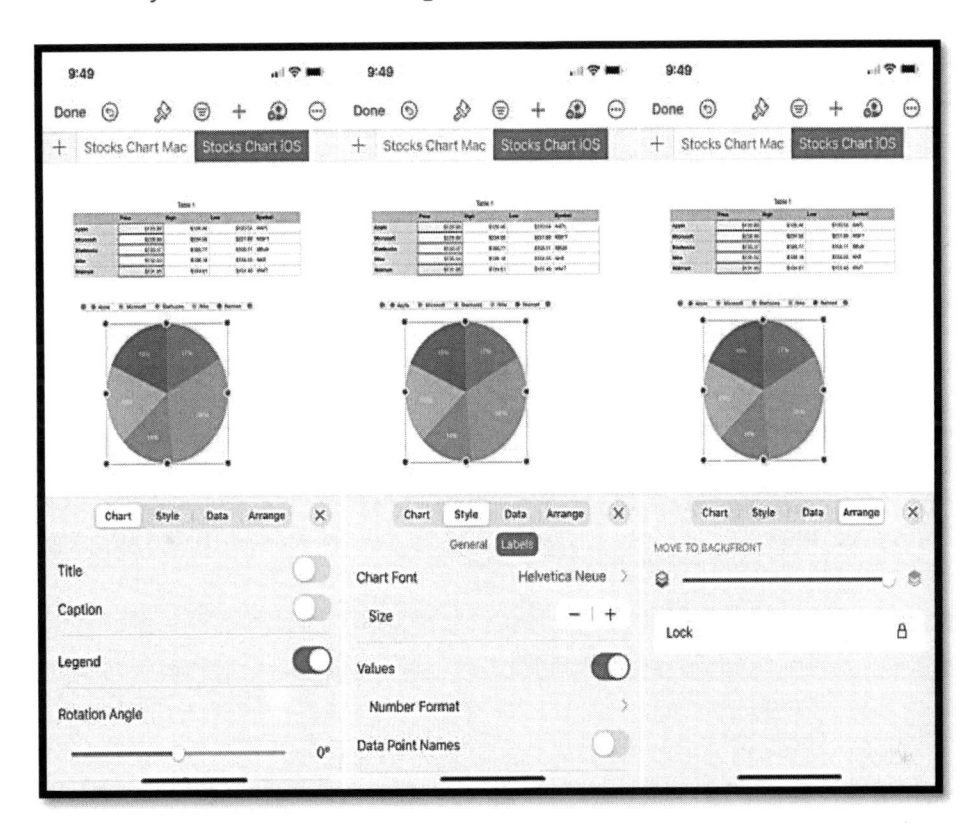

Edit A Chart On iPhone and iPad

Select the chart and press the Format icon (paintbrush icon) at the top to alter the data you're using in your Numbers chart.

- To edit each data series separately, select **Edit Series**.
- To edit or add references to the chart, click **Edit References**.

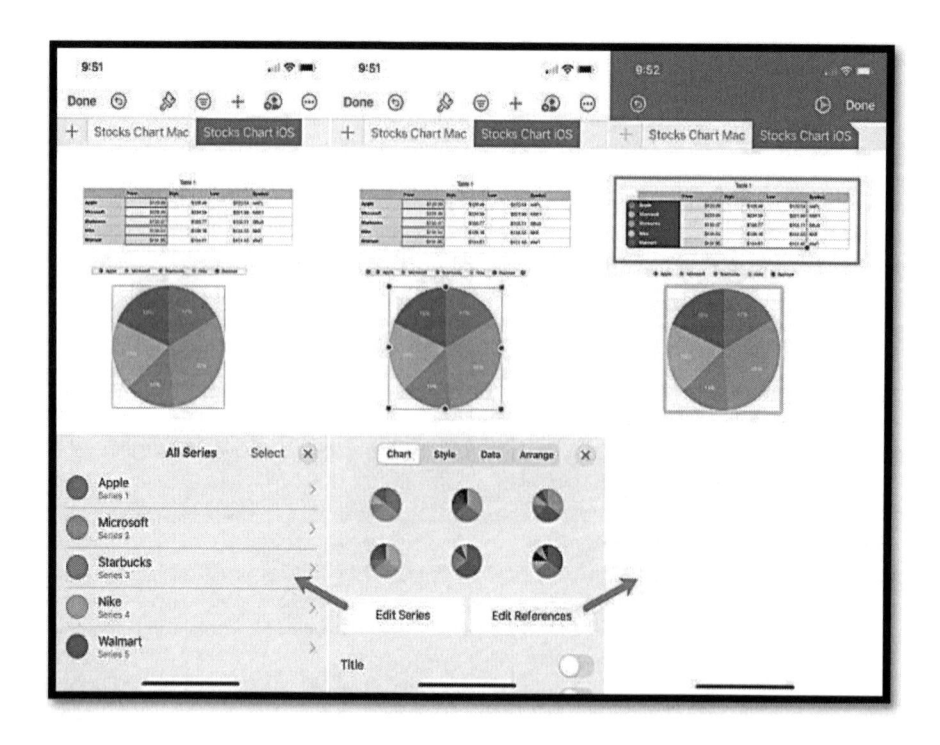

Try it if you think a graph or chart in Numbers would be useful for your sheet. You can pick a straightforward chart or one that has been designed with trendy colors and elegant types. All depends on you!

CHAPTER TWO
FINDING TREND WITH PIVOT TABLE IN NUMBERS

You have likely heard of pivot tables if you want to work as a data analyst. Even if you weren't aware of it, you may have already used a pivot table. In any type of analysis, pivot tables are a must, and if you're pursuing a career in data, you'll use them frequently in your day-to-day job.

New simple "pivot tables" have been added to the Numbers app, an iWork suite productivity tool, making it simpler and faster to summarize, reorganize, and combine data for analysis. Additionally, the brand-new, robust data analytics tool may be shared with others, imported into, or exported from Microsoft Excel, and represented with insightful charts.

WHAT IS A PIVOT TABLE?

A pivot table is a tool for summarizing data that is derived from larger tables. A database, a Numbers spreadsheet, or any other data that is or could be turned into a table-like structure might be these larger tables. A pivot table's data summary may include sums, averages, or other statistics that the pivot table meaningfully groups together.

Given that a pivot is defined in the dictionary as "a central point, pin, or shaft on which a mechanism turns or oscillates," the term "pivot table" actually provides a good indication of the significance of pivot tables and the function they play in analysis. When it comes to conducting data analysis, this concept is crucial.

The information you have been given about a particular subject is often contained in a database or dataset. To derive knowledge from this raw data is the entire purpose of any analysis. A table containing thousands of rows, however, cannot be fully understood by simply looking at it and scrolling up and down.

Drawing insight frequently requires you to exclude certain data points and manipulate how they show their data, for instance through summary statistics. Data analysts use summary statistics to condense a set of observations in order to convey a lot of information as clearly as possible.

What Are Pivot Tables Used For?

Let's examine their potential applications in more detail now that we understand what pivot tables are. As was already established, pivot tables give data analysts the ability to summarize enormous datasets into an easily digestible table.

Let's look at a real-world illustration. The brief table that follows provides details on the different factors that were taken into account while ranking the states in America in terms of quality of life. The raw data shown here refers to the major Florida cities' results in several categories.

	Income	Commute	Job Growth	Physicians	Murder Rate	Rape Rate	Golf	Restaurants	Housing	Median Age	Literacy	Household Income	Recreation
A	26,000	49.2	10.8	1987	5.3	51.3	925	5582	109,400	35.3	5.15	68,000	2620
B	29,300	45.3	9.5	517	6.6	50.8	364	9988	97,000	43.2	5.97	70,400	3066
C	24,800	39.8	8.2	592	8.2	77.7	1627	20511	114,700	29.5	9.41	60,500	1297
D	27,900	46.8	7.6	3310	6.7	51.2	956	8946	99,100	40.5	4.61	65,900	2902
E	37,500	39.9	12.2	975	5.1	40.1	426	4000	122,200	47.1	5.64	84,700	2214
F	31,900	49.5	7.7	2238	6.9	38.0	1459	8970	145,300	39.3	4.80	75,800	1402
G	25,300	44.4	5.4	611	4.5	38.8	1063	9570	99,500	38.6	6.84	62,600	2900
H	22,000	44.8	6.2	272	7.5	65.7	951	19101	76,400	41.6	2.79	54,800	2448
I	29,400	44.9	7.8	381	8.4	48.7	349	12099	112,500	41.8	4.48	72,900	2756
J	42,400	44.7	8.0	1812	8.1	45.4	397	10953	143,500	41.2	5.16	100,000	2508
K	40,500	40.0	10.9	294	8.0	69.6	191	2655	173,800	41.7	6.41	102,000	3000
L	24,700	38.7	9.0	196	2.8	19.0	449	15796	129,200	33.4	1.66	65,300	1570
M	24,400	41.1	8.7	404	7.3	77.2	1590	16001	126,500	30.6	5.60	62,200	1713
N	22,400	42.8	8.3	534	5.7	57.9	1160	16712	102,700	34.5	2.16	59,200	2190
O	22,200	37.8	8.4	166	5.6	50.9	815	11856	110,300	35.4	2.72	57,100	2142
P	27,500	48.4	8.1	1553	14.0	83.6	1195	12348	107,400	34.3	4.03	72,000	2657
Q	23,100	44.5	4.7	502	7.9	42.7	556	65804	116,000	38.5	2.07	59,400	2066
R	25,000	41.4	13.9	172	4.0	17.8	459	36151	120,000	52.7	3.61	57,300	1467
S	25,800	53.5	5.3	4143	16.8	57.4	3054	14310	132,800	36.2	5.03	71,900	3520
T	22,600	45.0	6.5	526	5.5	52.2	861	8878	86,500	41.5	5.29	54,000	2977

The names have been changed to remain anonymous and replaced with letters of the alphabet, but you can still discern that each row represents a distinct city. There is a measure for each row that provides details for a certain criterion (listed in the columns). Now, what would be the simplest method for you to do if you were given this dataset and asked to summarize these qualities for the full state of Florida?

Of course, using a pivot table. You can create a simple summary like the one in the small table below, which displays an average for all the cities dispersed by the metrics in the table, with just a few clicks.

Data	Total
Average of Income	27735
Average of Median Age	38.845
Average of Literacy	4.6715
Average of Commute	44.125
Average of Job Growth	8.36
Average of Physicians	1059.25
Average of Murder Rate	7.245
Average of Rape Rate	51.8
Average of Golf	942.35
Average of Restaurants	15511.55
Average of Housing	116230
Average of Household Income	68800
Average of Recreation	2370.75

This and other shortcuts come in quite handy, especially when comparing multiple things. It would take a lot more time, effort, and concentration if you weren't aware of pivot tables to manually type the **Average ()** formula for each column in the input dataset and then format the final table to look like the one above.

In the aforementioned example, we've simply included data for Florida; however, you might also be given access to a large database containing information on important US states and given the duty of comparing statistical summaries for each state to determine a ranking. Once more, employing a pivot table can help you finish this task quickly.

So, to sum up, the most significant applications of pivot tables include:

- Creating a summary of a sizable database or dataset.
- Completing it quickly and conveniently.

Pivot Table Functionalities

There are four key parts used when users develop pivot tables:

- **Columns**: Only the field's unique values are presented across the top when a field is selected for the column area.

- **Rows**: The first column is filled with data when a field is selected for the row area. All row labels are the unique values, and duplicates are removed, much like the columns.
- **Values**: Each value is retained in a pivot table cell and used to show the information that has been simplified. The sum, average, minimum, and maximum values are the most typical values.
- **Filters**: Filters use the entire table to perform a calculation or restriction.

One of the numerous functions for pivot tables that we explored in the last section was the example we provided. We had to figure averages in the previous example. What other features do pivot tables have, though? To begin with, you can also calculate other descriptive statistics. Measures that demonstrate quantitative aspects of the data, such as count, sum, min, max, product, variance, and standard deviation, are known as descriptive statistics. You may also decide how this summary table will appear; in the Florida example, the summary categories are distributed across the table's rows, but you can also arrange them in the table's columns. Additionally, you can filter the data in the pivot table to provide results that only meet specific requirements.

For instance, we could limit our search to cities with an average personal income of more than $31,900.

By using just one filter, the above table would be transformed into the one below:

Data	Total
Average of Income	38075
Average of Median Age	42.325
Average of Literacy	5.5025
Average of Commute	43.525
Average of Job Growth	9.7
Average of Physicians	1329.75
Average of Murder Rate	7.025
Average of Rape Rate	48.275
Average of Golf	618.25
Average of Restaurants	6644.5
Average of Housing	146150
Average of Household Income	90625
Average of Recreation	2281

You can see that we were able to change the analyses' perspective with minimum effort. Another issue is brought up by this: pivot tables are a great tool for exploratory analysis. Exploring some of the data's baseline statistics and characteristics can help you understand the nature of its contents. This process is known as exploratory analysis. This may include incomplete observations and extreme values in the dataset in addition to descriptive statistics. You may conduct a few brief explorations using a pivot table and some grouping strategies and summary measurements.

Yet another useful tool for exploratory analysis is supported by pivot tables. Once your data has been condensed, you can plot your results using tools like bar charts and scatter plots. Consider the scenario where you obtained similar data for California and wanted to compare the means of a few selected columns for the two states. This is how it would appear:

Data	California	Florida
Average of Household Income	77800	68800
Average of Housing	121909	116230
Average of Income	28520	27735
Average of Restaurants	16856.55	15511.55

Instead of looking at the data in the table, you can quickly make a bar chart like the one below, which makes the contrasts between the two situations much more obvious.

Here are the pivot tables' primary functions once again:

- Calculate different descriptive statistics of the underlying data.
- Filter data based on a specific criterion/criterion.
- Create visualizations of the conducted analysis.

Conclusion

We looked at the use of pivot tables in fundamental analysis in this section. We examined a few instances to show the value of this kind of data pivoting and how it could expedite your work.

Here is a summary of the main ideas so far:

- When using pivot tables to create summary statistics, you can use whatever metrics you choose and apply filters to only display the data you are interested in seeing.
- These summarized metrics from the tables' output could be used in exploratory analysis.
- Through the creation of user-friendly visuals in pivot tables, data analysis is made simple to continue.

The fact that pivot tables behave like dynamic reports is their strongest feature, especially in Numbers. The tables you create include statistics and findings you could share with a stakeholder, but they're also dynamic, so you can make changes whenever you choose without having to start over.

HOW TO CREATE A PIVOT TABLE IN NUMBERS

A pivot table is a useful statistical tool and one of the most important features in Apple Numbers and other spreadsheet apps. If you have a lot of data to evaluate or research, the pivot table is extremely helpful.

Create A Pivot Table

Learning how to create a pivot table is a crucial skill, particularly if you use Apple Numbers frequently.

Making a simple pivot table is explained in the steps that follow.

1. Select the Data

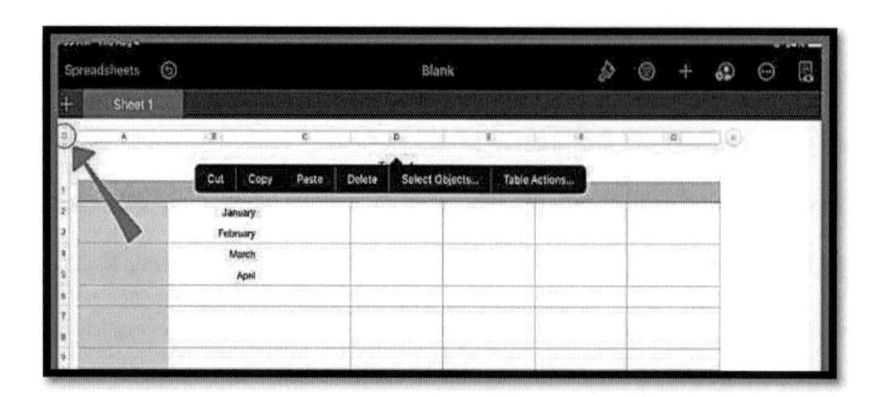

The first step is to select the cells or tables that you wish to use to create a pivot table, supposing that your spreadsheet is already loaded with data. For instance, to select a whole table, just click on the circle next to the first column in your spreadsheet (or above the first row) and choose **Table Actions**.

2. **Click Create Pivot Table**

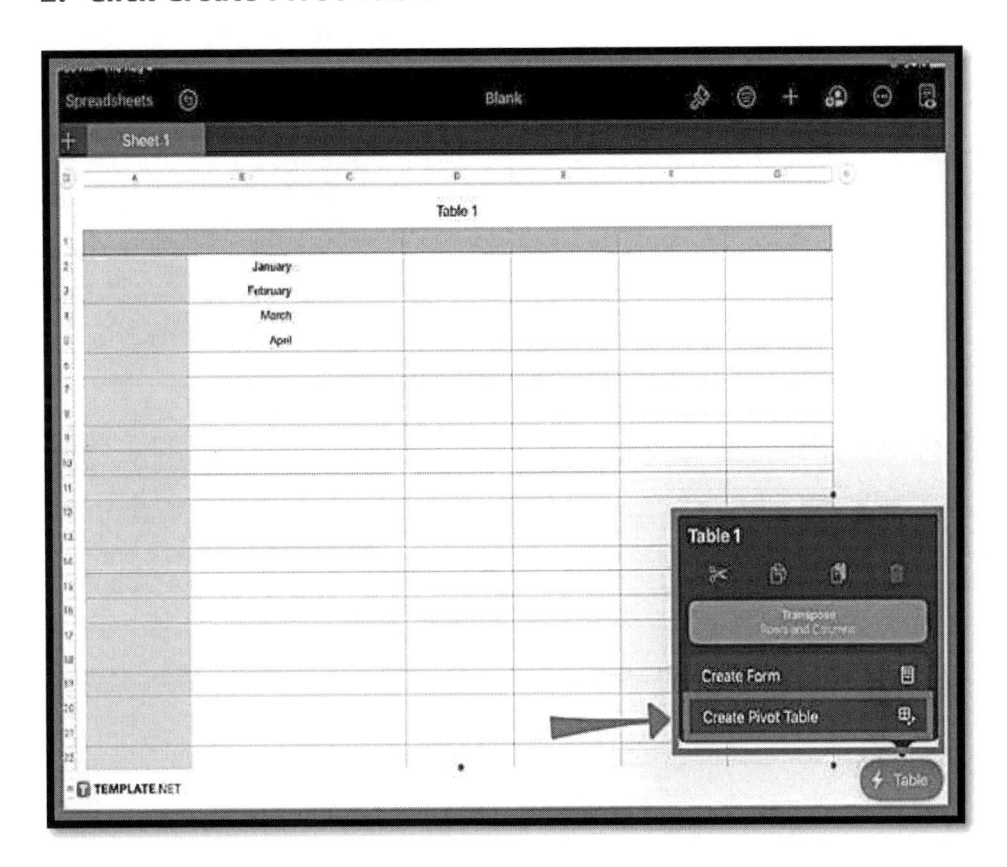

Click **Create Pivot Table** from the pop-up menu after tapping **Table Actions** or the **green Table** icon. In order to create the appropriate report, a pivot table effectively summarizes or arranges particular columns or rows in a spreadsheet. Because they make it possible to spot trends and patterns in your data, pivot tables are great for organizing enormous databases or doing in-depth analyses of large volumes of data.

3. **Customize the Pivot Table**

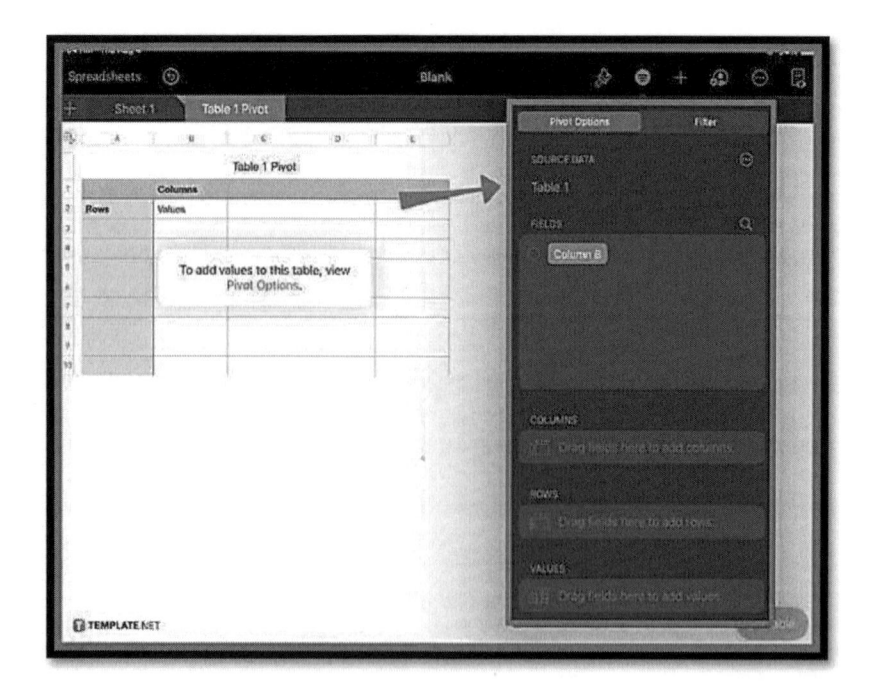

For the purpose of adding or changing values to the selected table, tap **Pivot Options** on the spreadsheet. Additionally, you can arrange the data in your pivot table. You can add fields and values in three distinct sections below **Pivot Options**.

These are the values, columns, and rows. Based on the contents of your table or spreadsheet, you will see a list of all these sections under the heading "**Fields**." The date, revenue, units, etc. are a few common instances of fields.

4. **Apply a Filter**

The Filter option is located beside the Pivot Options. By adding a restriction or calculation to your table, you can utilize this method to further customize your data.

HOW TO TROUBLESHOOT PIVOT TABLE PROBLEMS

In this section, you'll learn how to troubleshoot pivot table problems in Numbers.

Organize Your Data

You might need to organize your data at some point if you use Apple Numbers as your spreadsheet program. To get the information you need fast, you might wish to arrange by cash amount, date, or alphabetically.

You have a few options in the Numbers app for quickly sorting the information in your sheets. The column shortcut menu has quick options as well as rules you can configure for more precise sorting. You'll see both of them right here.

1. **Quick sorting in ascending or descending order**

Sorting can be done in two very basic ways: ascending or descending. Additionally, these can be used with text, numbers, dates, or empty cells. These two sorting options are therefore conveniently located in the shortcut menus for your columns.

The first step is to decide the column you wish to sort by, bearing in mind that this will affect all of the data in your table. By setting up a rule, which we'll cover later in this how-to, you can restrict the effect of the sort order you select to only certain rows.

- Click the arrow by the header after selecting your column.
- Select from the **Sort Ascending** or **Sort Descending** options.

The data in your table will automatically change to reflect the sort order for that column.

If the sort is not what you wanted, keep in mind that you can undo it using the **Edit > Undo** option in the menu bar.

2. **Setting up a sort rule**

You can put up a sort rule to just sort specific rows of your table or to sort it by more than one column.

You can open it in one of the following ways in Numbers' right-hand sidebar.

- From the menu bar, select **Organize > Show Sort Options**.
- From the shortcut menu, select **Show Sort Options** by clicking the arrow beside any column header.
- In Numbers, select the **Sort** tab from the sidebar by clicking the **Organize** button in the top right corner.

It's time to get to work now that you know how to access the location where you can create a sort rule.

Sort An Entire Table

You might want to sort your entire table using different columns.

For instance, you might wish to sort by date, then by name, then by price, then by product, or something along those lines.

- Verify that the **Sort Entire Table** is selected in the top drop-down box.
- In the drop-down box, select the first column you want to sort by.
- For that column, choose **Ascending** or **Descending** order.
- In the following drop-down box, select the second column you wish to sort by before selecting the order as well.
- You should be able to sort the table automatically, but you can check by clicking **Sort Now** at the top of the sidebar.

- Select the **Trash Can** beside a column to remove it from the sort rule.
- Press the **three lines** to the left and drag the column to the new position in the sort order rule to change the order of the columns you're sorting by.

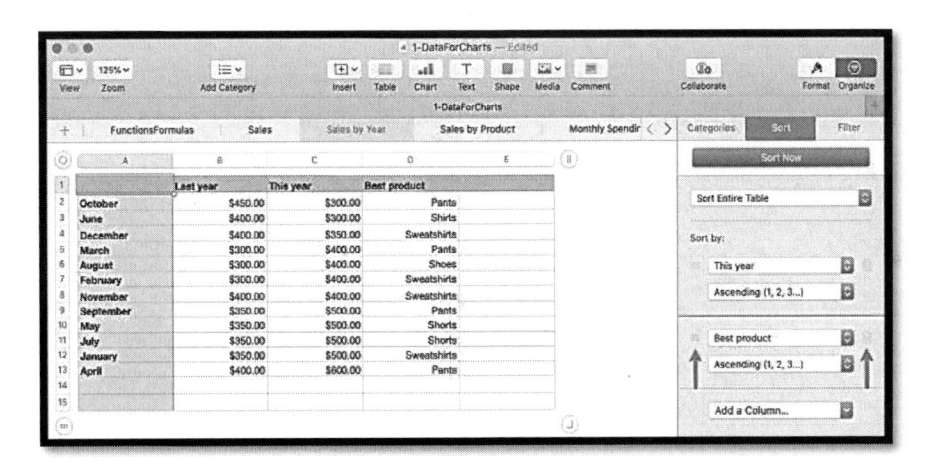

Sort Selected Rows

Just like sorting a table, you can easily create a sort rule to just sort certain rows in your table.

- Select the rows that you want to sort. Drag through neighboring rows or first press, hold down **Shift**, and then tap the final row in the range

to navigate between them. Click the first row while holding down **Command**, then click each of the remaining non-adjacent rows.
- Click **Sort Selected Rows** from the drop-down box in the sidebar.
- Use the same Steps 2 through 5 above to add the columns and order as you did when setting up your rule.

Note: When sorting your table by a few selected rows only, exercise extreme caution because the remainder of your table's data will not be changed. Additionally, be mindful that you may undo the sort by selecting **Edit > Undo** from the menu bar.

It's simple to sort data in Numbers, and you can choose the columns and the order you want to sort by.

Check For Blank Cells

Every user has access to the search feature, right? We need to know what "is empty" means to you in order to determine if a cell "is empty."

Let's assume it means:

=ISBLANK(the cell) returns TRUE if the cell is actually empty.

or

The string in the cell has a length of 0.

The widely used solution is this:

=LEN(the cell)=0

Thus, you could say:

=IF(AND(D2="P1/Us",LEN(P2)>0),P2,"")

A cell is considered empty by Numbers' designers when it is completely empty. A cell that has a string in it with a length of zero is not truly empty.

The key problem is that there is no method to specify a cell's value as (really empty) through a formula.

We must therefore define "empty cell" differently.

CHAPTER THREE

HIGHLIGHTING COMPARISONS WITH RADAR CHARTS IN NUMBERS

In this chapter, you'll learn everything about radar charts and its relationship with the Numbers app.

WHAT IS A RADAR CHART?

A radar chart displays multivariate data that is mapped onto an axis and includes three or more quantitative variables. It has a core axis that contains at least three radiating spokes that give it the appearance of a spider's web.

The values for the data are mapped on these spokes. It is intended to quickly highlight similarities, contrasts, and outliers for that good, service, or other thing of interest.

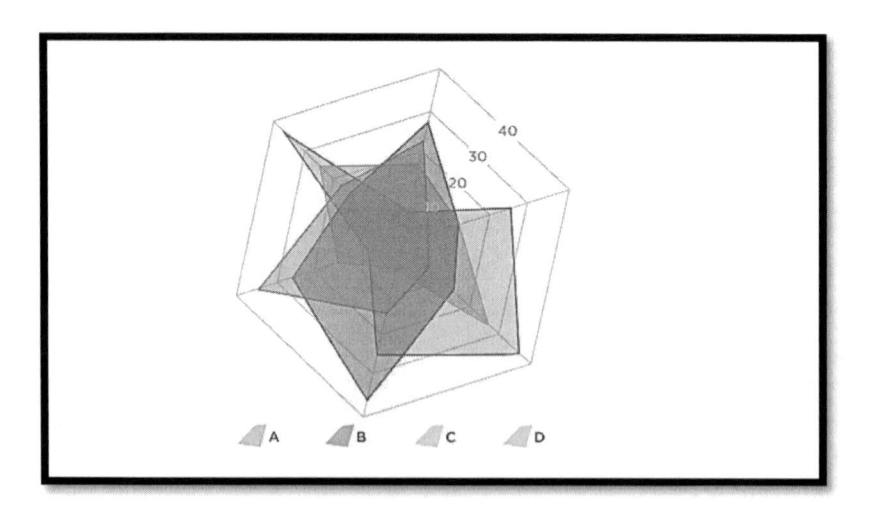

It is also referred to as an irregular polygon, polar chart, spider chart, web chart, star chart, cobweb chart, and Kiviat diagram. Georg von Mayr, a German, is credited with creating this family of charts. He released the first radar chart in 1877.

Consider your favorite brownie for a simple illustration of an application for radar charts. A brownie can have several different features, or variations, including chewiness, chocolatiness, the presence of nuts and other ingredients like cranberries, as well as the crust, moisture, and density.

Each element would have its own "spoke" on a radar chart for brownies, and the measurement for that variable would be marked on the spoke's length. Your mother's brownies, for instance, could be very chewy, but she doesn't add nuts or any unnecessary ingredients.

With walnuts and a cakier texture, your favorite bakery may rank differently. Then, a spider web-like pattern is created by drawing a line from each rating for each variable.

When Should Radar Charts Be Used?

When there are a few things to compare, radar charts are most useful. This can be accomplished by overlaying several product details on a single chart or by using many charts that present the same radii but analyze various products. By placing charts next to one another or by mapping the measures onto one chart, you could, for instance, compare your mom's brownies, those from the bakery, and those from your neighbor.

There are numerous potential possibilities in terms of business use. Consider conducting a staff member skill analysis. They might have their communication, problem-solving, teamwork, deadline management, timeliness, and technical knowledge evaluated. A radar chart rapidly displays how employees are rated in relation to their peers.

Since a radar chart may be used to present performance metrics, managing quality improvement is another application for radar charts in enterprises.

When to use a radar chart:

- Multivariate observations exist.
- Any number of variables may exist.
- Outliers must be identified.
- You must evaluate several goods or services against one another.
- The size of the data sets is small or average.

There are a few excellent practices to follow while creating a radar chart:

- The order of the variables should be meaningful.
- There should be more than three series presented on separate radar charts.
- Avoid using too many variables to avoid making the chart unclear.
- There should be transparency in the filled-in color if there are numerous data series.

Types Of Radar Charts

There are three different types of radar charts: the simple radar chart, the filled radar chart, and the radar chart with markers. We can better grasp all three of them because they are extensions of one another.

Simple Radar Chart

The other two types of radar charts are created by modifying this basic type. By connecting the graph's points, it expresses all data with regard to their origin and shows the value of each entity in a dataset.

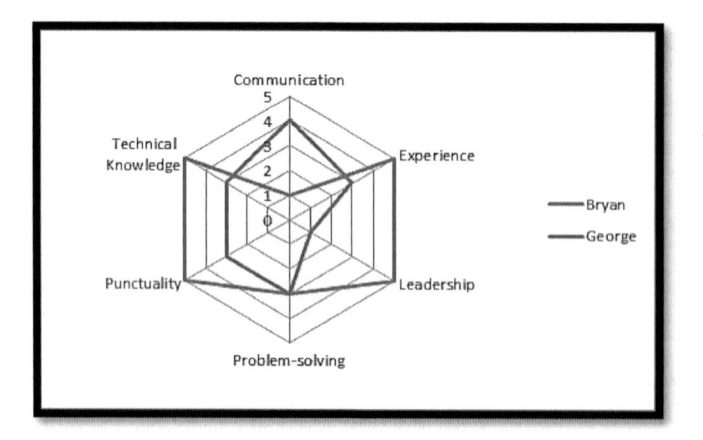

Filled Radar Chart

The term "filled radar charts" refers to an expansion of the simple radar chart that is "filled" with color. Colors are used to fill in the voids between the lines and the web's center in this kind of chart. These are the most attractive charts because they create a visual hierarchy.

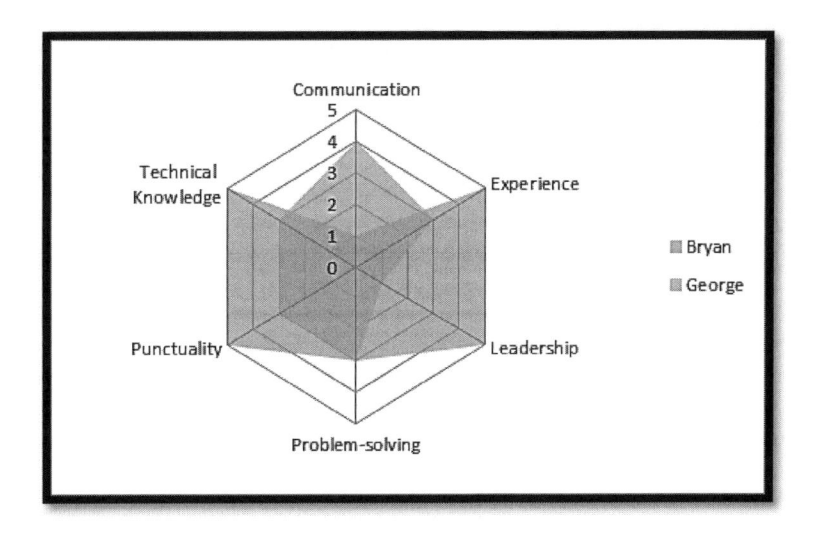

Radar Charts with Markers

The straightforward radar chart and this style of chart are fairly similar. The fact that this radar chart has markers on the data points is the only distinction between the two. Markers are initially used to plot the values, and then lines are used to connect them.

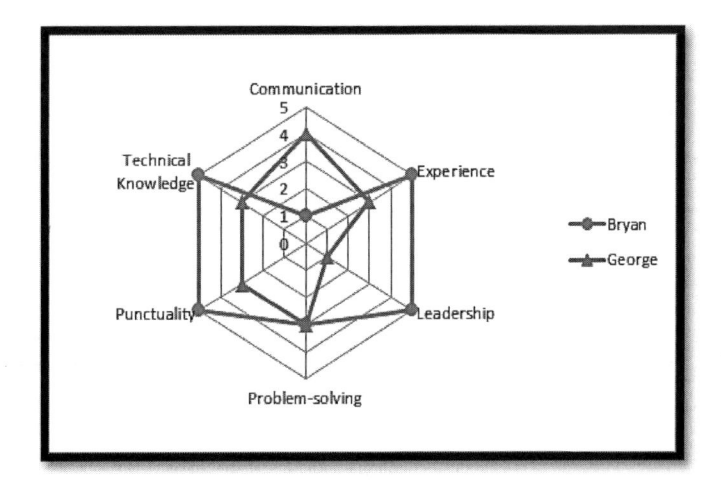

Elements That Make Up a Radar Chart

These star plots, in contrast to many other graphs, simply have a few simple elements that are simple to comprehend and remember.

- **Center point**: The primary point of origin from which the axis starts.

- **Axes**: A radar chart must include at least two axes in order to depict the data in two dimensions. The axes will be circular on one and radial on the other.
- **Grids**: By dividing the whole graph into smaller portions, the data may be plotted and comprehended more quickly.
- **Data**: The data points are displayed to create an array of equiangular spokes after the graph has been drawn. The data is two-dimensional, even though the chart is circular, and each entry is displayed with a unique color.

NUMBERS APP AND RADAR CHART

You can add a chart to a sheet and then choose the table columns containing the desired data to create any type of chart. Alternatively, you can select the data first and then make a chart that shows it. Anytime you change the data in the table, the chart immediately updates.

You can import an Excel spreadsheet with charts into Numbers. The data that the imported charts show is the same, despite the fact that they may not look exactly like the original charts.

Note: The Charting Basics template contains information on many chart types. Double-click the Charting Basics template after selecting **File > New, Basic**, in the left sidebar. Select the tabs at the top of the template to examine the many sheets in Charting Basics; each sheet describes a different kind of chart.

Create A Radar Chart, Pie, Donut, Pie Chart, Bar Chart, Line Chart, Or Column Chart

- Select **2D, 3D**, or **Interactive** after clicking the **Chart** button in the toolbar. For a wider selection of styles, use the left and right arrows.

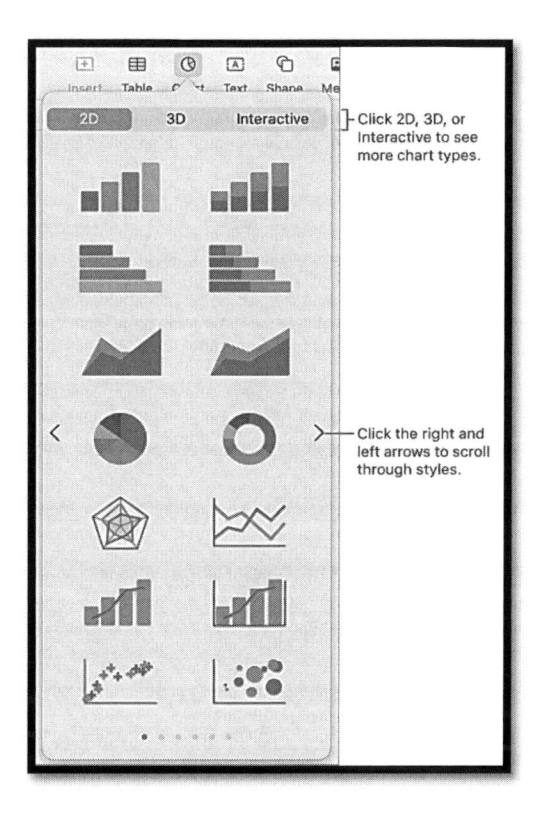

Note: Two or more data series are stacked together in the bar, column, and area charts.

- Drag a chart onto the sheet by clicking on it. The **Rotation control** is located in the middle of a 3D chart if one (3D chart) is added. To change the direction of the chart, drag this control.
- If the **Add Chart Data** icon isn't visible, ensure the chart is selected and then click the icon next to it.
- Select the table cells containing the desired data. Cells from one or more tables, including tables on different sheets, can be selected. A dot displays on the tab for each sheet that has data utilized in the chart when you are editing the chart's data references.
- Decide from the pop-up menu in the bar at the bottom of the window whether rows or columns are plotted as a data series.

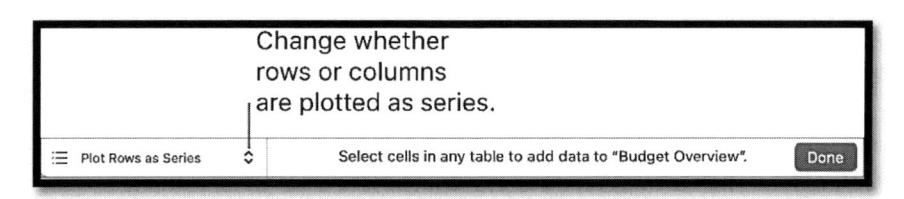

251

- In the bar at the bottom of the window, select **Done**.

HOW TO INTERPRET A RADAR CHART

To interpret a radar chart, take the following steps:

1. Define the category that each axis represents.

Identify which type of data each axis on the radar chart represents by looking at the chart. For instance, lead response time, customer acquisition cost, customer lifetime value, monthly new leads, and time spent selling can be the categories on a radar chart that shows an employee's sales KPIs.

2. Establish the connections between the various categories.

You can identify how each category in the radar chart connects to the others in terms of scales of measurement after you know which category each axis of the chart represents. These scales might apply to all of the categories equally. The radar chart, meanwhile, may also display data quantified in several ways.

The relationship between the categories as a whole depends on knowing if each category uses the same scales of measurement. The scales of calculation, for instance, are different when utilizing the same radar chart from the first step's illustration because some metrics are determined by time while others are calculated by cost or value.

3. Pay attention to the created shape.

Now is the time to examine the general radar chart shape that was created by joining each data point. You can tell if any particular data points are very high or very low in comparison to the other data points by looking at the general shape.

4. Take a look at the wheel.

You can evaluate specific data after reviewing the entire shape by locating the point at the end of each shape's line. The "zero" position is often in the middle of each wheel, and the higher the quantity for a certain data group, the nearer a point is to the chart's edge.

5. Compare data.

You can compare data on a radar chart using one of two main ways. The first step is to arrange several different radar charts next to one another and compare their shapes to search for outliers. The alternative method is to compare shapes by placing them side-by-side and adjusting the opacity so that you can see each one.

The first method might be preferable if you need to compare multiple shapes. It could be simpler to utilize the layover method if you only need to compare two or three shapes.

ADVANTAGES OF USING RADAR CHART

When charting and comparing data, radar charts have a number of advantages, including:

1. A lot of different variables can be compared.

Radar charts' main benefit is its capacity to plot a large number of variables on a chart and then connect each one to form a polygonal shape that symbolizes the group. In contrast to other graphs and charts, this enables you to compare multiple variables in a way that looks less cluttered and is simpler to understand.

2. You are quick to compare things.

Radar charts show data as shapes that may be laid over one another to compare groups' differences rapidly. You can save time by quickly visually comparing each polygon's dimensions.

3. It's easy to spot outliers.

Radar charts make outliers easy to spot because their points won't line up with other chart variables. By examining how each point relates to the others, you can easily determine whether an individual salesperson has metrics that vastly outperform the rest of the team, for instance, if you wish to compare their numbers to your team's overall metrics.

4. You can apply various measurement scales.

The capacity to graph variables using various techniques of evaluation is another significant benefit of radar charts. You could use one variable to assess sales per hour and another variable to monitor customer conversion rate, for instance, if you wanted to compare metrics for your sales staff.

DISADVANTAGES OF USING RADAR CHART

- Even a radar chart might become crowded if there are too many variables to compare.
- Users occasionally struggle to create the right data set to represent a variety of variables collectively.
- They are not the best for weighing trade-offs or comparing variables with a wide range of differences.
- The radial distance can occasionally be challenging to estimate and deliver accurate information.

CHAPTER FOUR

TURN HANDWRITING INTO TEXT IN NUMBERS

In Numbers on the iPad, you can use your Apple Pencil to create drawings, convert handwriting to text, select items, and scroll just like you would with a finger. When using the Apple Pencil in Numbers, you automatically switch to the writing and drawing view. You can override the default behavior if you prefer to scroll and select things using the Apple Pencil.

Note: You need an iPad that is compatible and has iPadOS 14 installed in order to use Scribble to transform your handwriting to text. Not every language is supported by Scribble.

CHANGE THE DEFAULT APPLE PENCIL BEHAVIOR FOR NUMBERS

Change the Apple Pencil's default settings if you want to use it for scrolling and object selection instead of writing or drawing. The Numbers setting for the Apple Pencil is exclusive to Numbers.

While all Numbers spreadsheets are affected by a change you make to one of them, other apps like Pages and Keynote are unaffected.

- Open a spreadsheet in Numbers, then click the **More** button.
- Scroll down to see **Apple Pencil**, then click it to enable **Select and Scroll**. If your Apple Pencil supports it, you can enable Double-Tap to Switch and then double-tap the Apple Pencil's lower portion to enable or disable **Select and Scroll**.

The Apple Pencil can still be used to draw in Numbers if the default setting is changed to **Select and Scroll**. After selecting **Drawing** from the **Media** menu, press the **Insert** button.

TURN HANDWRITING INTO TEXT

The iPad's Scribble feature converts your handwriting to text. Scribble is turned on by default when an Apple Pencil is connected to an iPad that is compatible and has iPadOS 14 installed. Go to **Settings > Apple Pencil** to check the **Scribble** setting or turn it off.

- To write in a text box, shape, table cell, or form field in Numbers, tap there with the Apple Pencil.

  Note: To replace all of the data in a cell in a table, tap the cell. Tap the cell once more to set the insertion point where you wish to start writing in order to edit it.

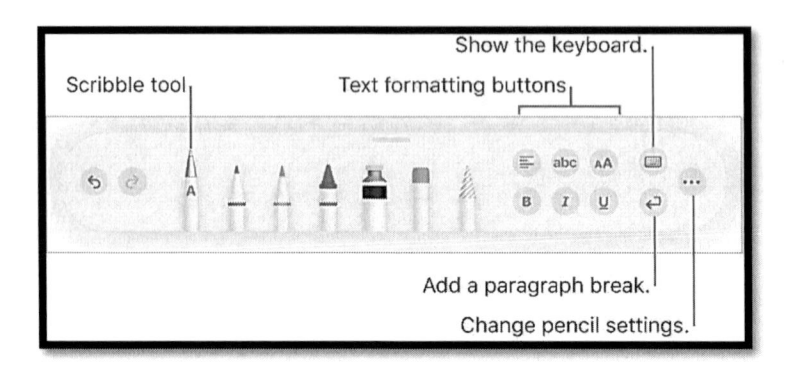

- Then begin writing by tapping the **Scribble tool**. Even if your handwriting stretches outside the text area's borders, Scribble still works.
  Note: The Scribble tool does not show up in the toolbar if Scribble is turned off in Settings or if a language that supports Scribble is not listed in your language list.
- With the Apple Pencil, you can do any of the following as you type text:
    - **Delete a word**: Scratch it out.
    - **Insert text**: When a space appears, tap and hold in a text area and then begin writing.
    - **Add or remove characters**: Draw a vertical line between them.

- **Select text**: Draw a circle around text or a line through it. To change the selection, simply drag the selection handles with your finger.
- **Start a new paragraph**: In the toolbar at the bottom of the screen, tap the **Next Line** button.
- **Show a keyboard**: To edit text, delete characters, add spaces, and more, click the **Keyboard** button in the toolbar and then press the appropriate keyboard keys.
- **Switch to another language that is supported**: You must have previously added the keyboard in **Settings > General > Keyboard > Keyboards**. Tap and hold the **Keyboard** button in the toolbar, then click the language you wish to use. The button momentarily displays the chosen language's initials (for example, EN for English).
- **Undo the previous action**: In the toolbar, click the **Undo** button. Click more than once to reverse all of your previous actions.
- **Create a new text field**: Apart from other text spaces, begin writing (such as another text box or a selected table or table cell). Your text is placed in a brand-new text box.

The toolbar's buttons for text alignment, font and font size changes, bolding, italicizing, underlining, and adding paragraph breaks are also available when the Scribble tool is selected. The buttons for the number keyboard, date keyboard, formula editor, and action menu are substituted for the text icons in table cells.

Drag the toolbar handle down to minimize it for additional writing space. Click the minimized toolbar to bring it back to its full size. Click the **More** icon, then enable Auto-minimize to have the toolbar minimize itself as you start writing.

HOW TO USE SHAPES LIBRARY IN NUMBERS ON AN iPHONE AND iPAD

A closed-path shape can be saved to the shapes library if it was made or edited. The path, flip, and rotation properties of a custom shape are retained when it is saved, but the size, color, opacity, and other properties are not.

Your custom shapes are accessible in any Numbers spreadsheet on all of your devices if you have iCloud Drive enabled and are signed in with the same Apple ID across all of them (but not in Numbers for iCloud).

- To add a custom shape to the sheet, click it and then press **Add to Shapes**. The shape is preserved in the **My Shapes** section of the library of shapes, which only shows up if you have custom shapes. You cannot change the order in which shapes appear in the library once you have created them.
- Tap and hold the newly formed shape in the shapes library, then select **Rename**.
- Put your name in the shape field.

Tap and hold a custom shape in the shapes library, then hit Delete to remove it.

Note: The deletion of a custom shape from an iCloud Drive account affects all of your iCloud Drive-using devices that are logged in with the same Apple ID.

CHAPTER FIVE
CREATING AND CUSTOMIZING A FORM IN NUMBERS

In Numbers for iPad, a form is a convenient way for users to enter data into a single row of a spreadsheet. If you're merely entering data, using a spreadsheet isn't very challenging. However, you can utilize a form if you're gathering data from other individuals or simply want a more straightforward approach to enter data. You'll enjoy the lovely form feature in Numbers 12.1 for the iPhone and iPad.

Basically, you create a form, connect it to a table, and then enter data using the form. Additionally, you can benefit from handwritten data in the form if you use Numbers on an iPad with an Apple Pencil. So, here's how to develop and use forms in Numbers if you're prepared to simplify data entering on your device.

HOW TO CREATE A FORM IN NUMBERS

We'll use Numbers on the iPad to bring you through this course so you can see everything clearly. But if you utilize the app on your iPhone, the procedures remain the same.

To set up the form, launch Numbers and then create a new workbook or access an existing one.

Start with a sheet you've already generated so you can simply connect to the table inside of it.

- Tap the **plus** sign and choose **New Form** from the tab row at the top left of the sheet.
- Select **Blank Form** if you want to create a new table. In a new tab called **Form Data,** this will generate a linked table that is empty. You can select from the sheets and tables you already own if you wish to use an existing table.

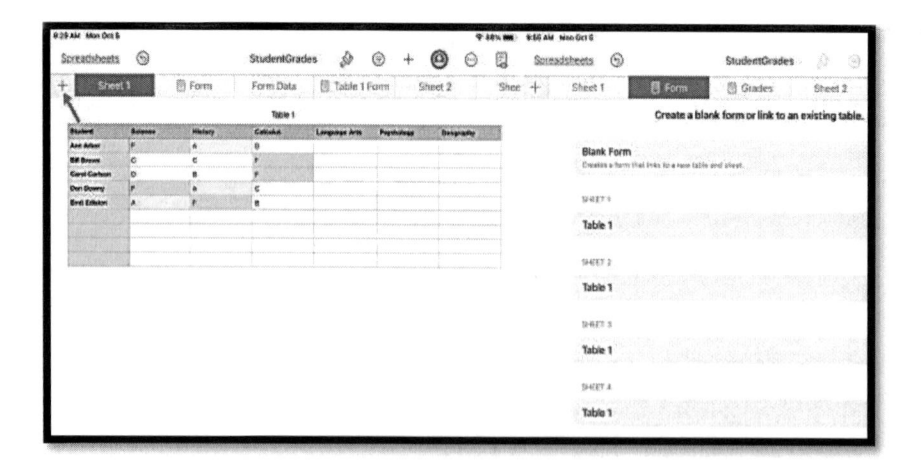

- A new tab containing your form will appear for you to update and personalize with fields and labels. To access the **Form Setup** screen, tap the gear icon.

- **The headers for the rows and columns will be visible. Thereafter, you can:**

    - Drag to change the order.
    - To remove one, click the **minus** sign.
    - To change the format, click the **Info** icon.
    - To change a label, tap it.
    - Add one more field. Your linked table will also gain a new column as a result of this.

- Tap Done once you've finished setting your form.

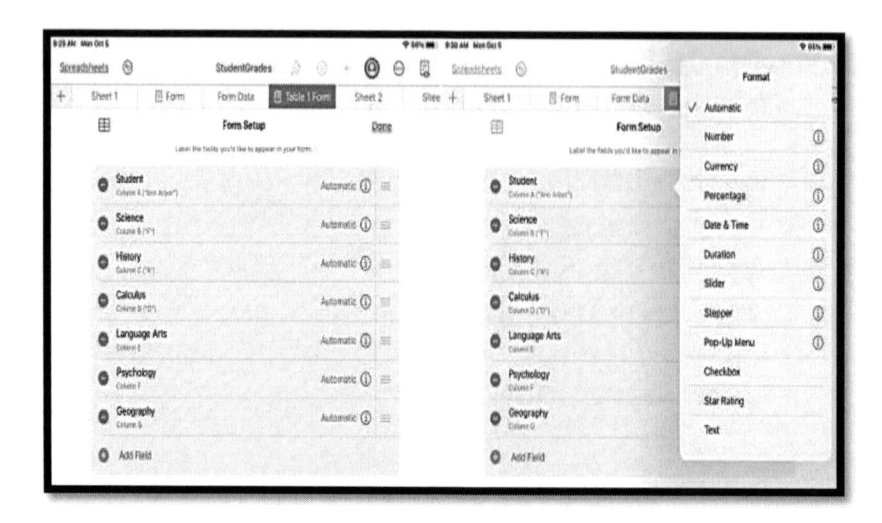

Double-press your form's name in the tab, give it a new name, and then click **Done** on the keyboard to finish.

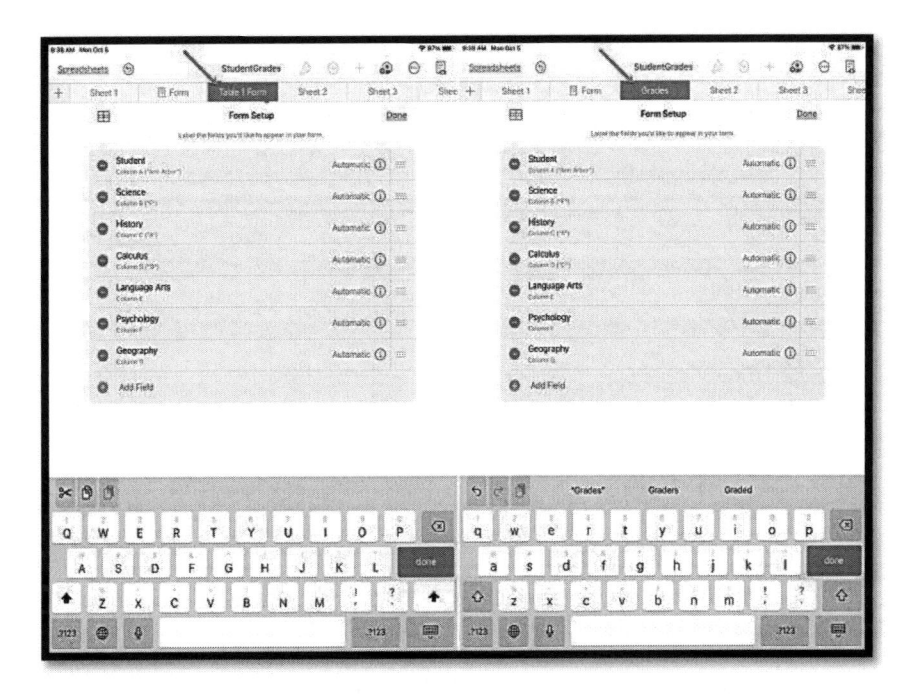

USE YOUR FORM IN NUMBERS

Simply press the form name in the tab row to start entering data into your form. The linked table's first record will be shown to you.

- To navigate between each record, use the arrows at the top or the dots along the right side.
- To add a record, click the **plus** symbol. This will immediately add a record (and table row) after the current one. Use the arrows or dots to navigate to the last record, then press the + sign, if you want the record that is at the end of the form and the table.
- To erase a record, click the **Trash can** icon.

Each record's number in your form matches the record's number in the linked table. Note that your first row is a header row, therefore this is not the row number.

Click the **Table** icon on the upper left of the form, beside the gear icon, to see the data in the linked table.

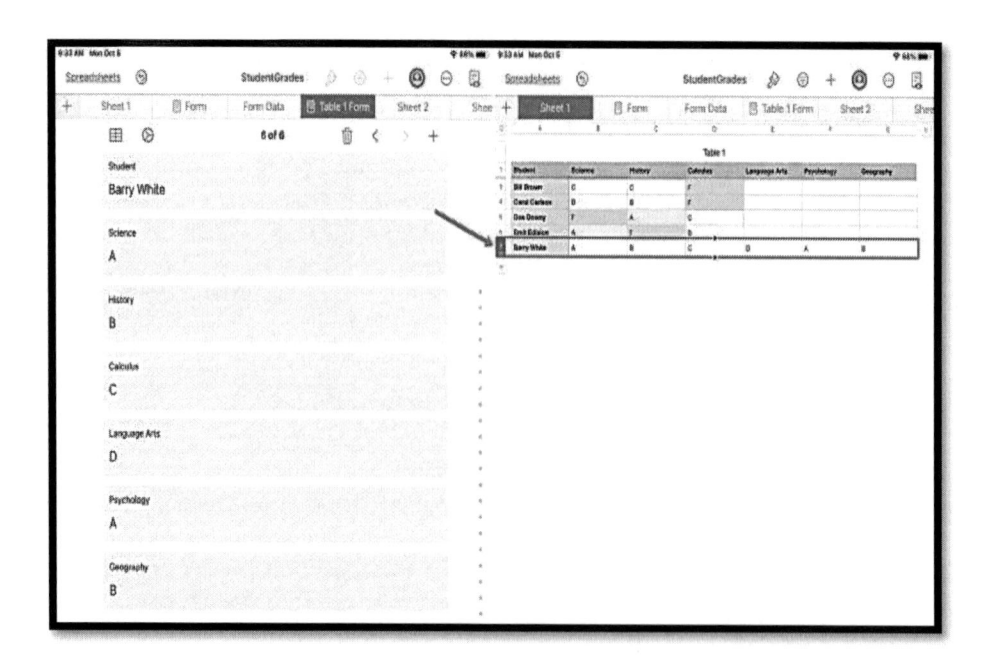

Notes On Forms in Numbers

Here are a few more tips for working with forms in Numbers.

- By clicking the **gear** icon, you can change the settings of any form at any moment.
- Data will also be added to or modified in the form if changes are made directly in the linked table. Therefore, if you'd like, you can still interact with the data in the sheet's table.
- Using an iPad and an Apple Pencil? It will automatically convert handwritten data into typed language and fill up your form and table as though you had entered it using a keyboard if you enter data into the form fields by hand.

Conclusion

Numbers allows you to create forms that may be used for many types of data entering. A form makes it simple and quick to add your data for contact information, money, weight tracking, client information, and in the examples above, grade tracking.

CHAPTER SIX
COLOR, GRADIENTS, AND IMAGES IN NUMBERS

This chapter will explain everything you need to know about color, gradients, and images in Numbers.

ADDING COLOR, GRADIENTS, AND IMAGES TO CELL IN NUMBERS

When your spreadsheet includes subtotals or logical divisions, shading the contents of a cell, row, or column can be useful.

To color cells, rows, or columns, follow the steps given:

- You can format cells, rows, or columns by clicking in or dragging them.

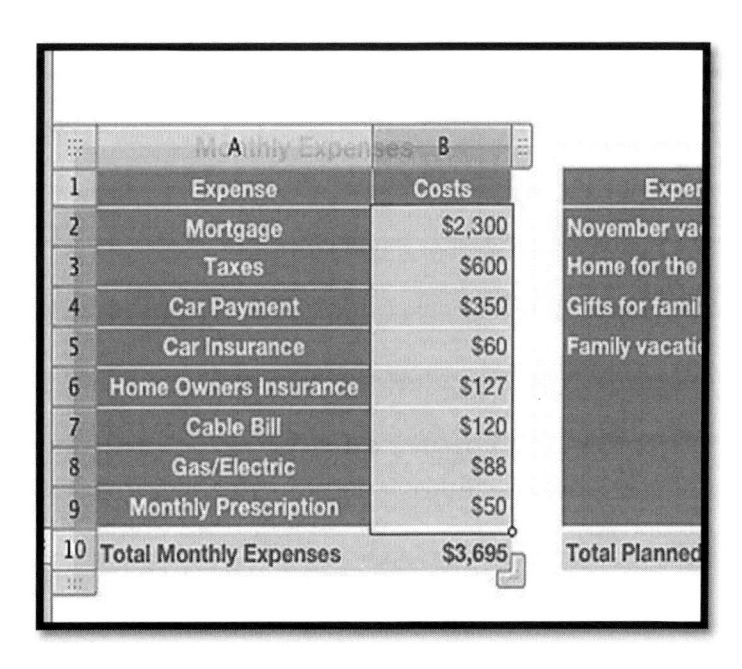

- The cells appear to be highlighted. To move about the spreadsheet, use the scroll bars. Select the **Inspector toolbar** icon.

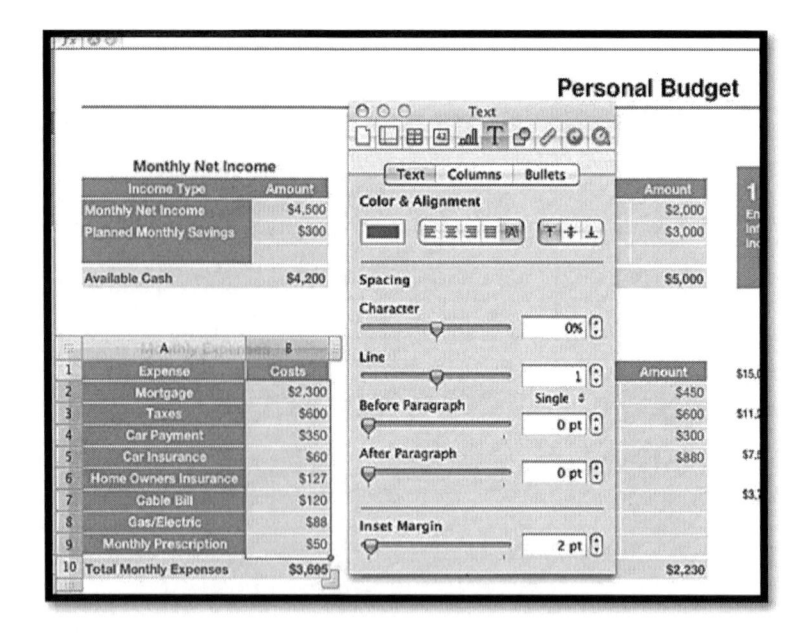

- Inspector starts up. In the **Inspector toolbar**, select the **Graphic Inspector** icon.

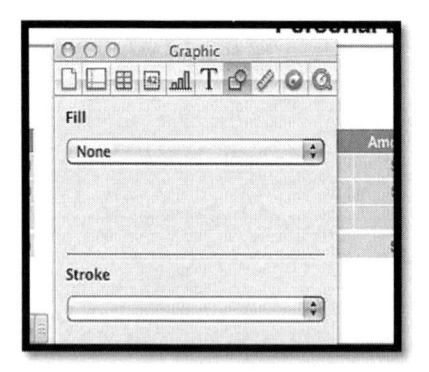

- Numbers show the settings. Select **Fill** from the pop-up menu.

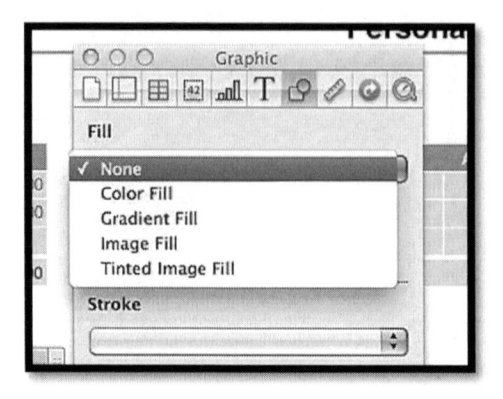

264

- Choose a shading option. To choose a color for your shading, tap the color box.

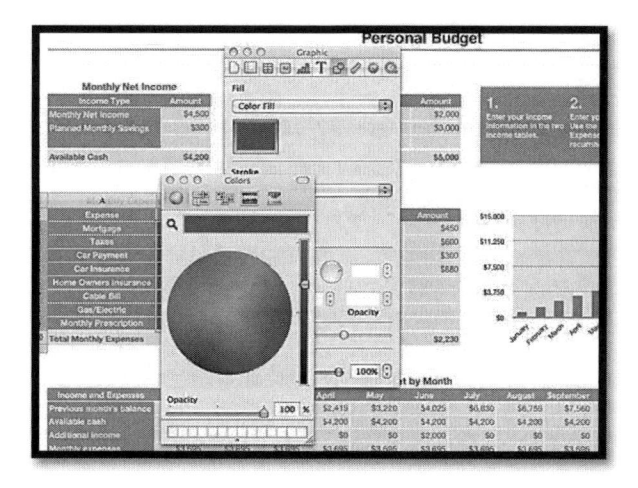

- Numbers show the color picker. To choose a color, click. In the color picker, click the **Close** icon. Select "**Close**" on the Inspector's toolbar.

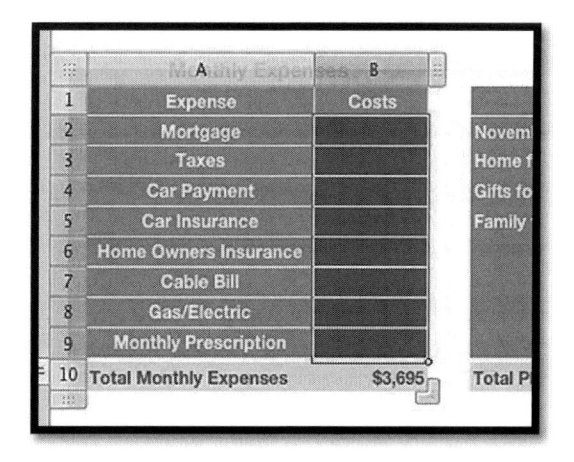

The shading and colors you selected are now applied when you return to the spreadsheet.

APPLYING COLOR AND GRADIENT FILLS TO SHAPES IN NUMBERS

Shapes and text boxes can be filled with images, plain colors, or gradients (two or more colors that blend into one another).

Fill with a color or gradient

- To select one or more shapes or text boxes, click them.
- Select the **Style** tab in the **Format** sidebar.
- **Select from the following:**
    - **A color or gradient designed to go with the template**: To select a color or gradient, click the color well beside Fill.
    - **Any color**: Select Color Fill from the Fill pop-up menu by clicking the disclosure arrow beside Fill. Select a color from one of the color palettes after clicking the color wheel.
    - **A two-color gradient fill**: Select Gradient Fill from the Fill pop-up menu by clicking the disclosure arrow beside Fill, then select colors. The color wheel opens the Colors window, where you can select any color, and the color well displays colors that go with the template. The gradient's angle and direction can be adjusted using the controls.
    - **A custom gradient**: To select colors, click the color stops below the slider after selecting Advanced Gradient Fill from the Fill pop-up menu by clicking the disclosure arrow next to Fill. To add an additional color stop, slide the slider. To alter the gradient's blend, angle, and direction, move the color stops and make use of the other options.

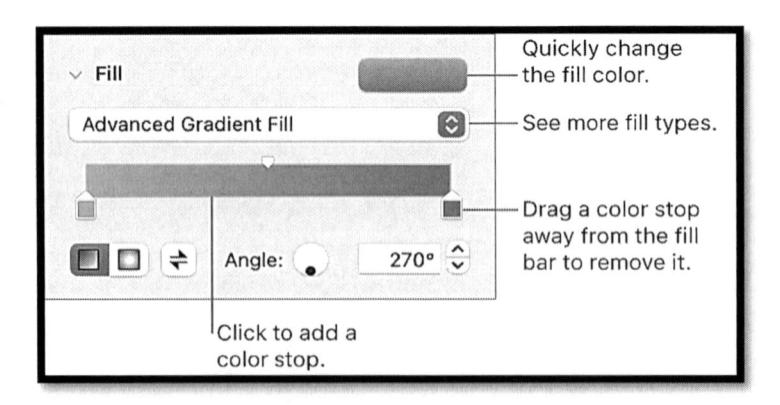

Fill with an image

- To select one or more shapes or text boxes, click them.
- Select the **Style** tab in the **Format** sidebar.
- To add a tint to the image, select **Advanced Image Fill** from the **Fill** pop-up menu by clicking the **disclosure** arrow beside **Image Fill**.

- Double-click a photo with the **.jpg, .png,** or **.gif** filename extension after clicking **Choose** and selecting a photo from your photos.
- If you choose **Advanced Image Fill**, select a tint color by clicking the **color well** (located to the right of the **Choose** button). You may adjust the transparency of the tint by using the **Opacity** slider in the **Colors** box.
- **Select the pop-up menu above the Choose button and select an option if the image isn't what you expected or if you want to change how the image fills the object:**
    - **Original Size**: Adds the image without changing the object's original proportions. Drag the **Scale** slider to change the image's size.
    - **Stretch**: Reshapes the image to the object's dimensions, potentially changing its proportions.
    - **Tile**: Repetition of the inside image. Drag the **Scale** slider to change the image's size.
    - **Scale to Fill**: Enlarges or reduces the image to fill the entire surface of the object.
    - **Scale to Fit**: Resizes the image while keeping its proportions to fit the dimensions of the object.

Save a custom fill

A custom fill can be saved so you can use it again.

- Tap the **Style** tab in the Format sidebar after selecting the shape or text box with the fill you want to save.
- Drag the fill from the **Current Fill** well over another well to replace it by clicking the **color well** beside **Fill**. Only a well of the same type is accessible by drag. Drag the fill from the **Current Fill** well over a well in the **Gradient** section, for instance, if the custom fill is a gradient.

Select a different option from the **Fill Type** pop-up menu to change the fill types that you can replace. For instance, to save a gradient fill, click **Gradient Fill** from the pop-up menu, drag the fill from the **Current Fill** well to a well in the **Gradient Fills** section, and then release the mouse button.

Remove A Fill

- To select one or more shapes or text boxes, click them.
- Select the **Style** tab in the **Format** sidebar.
- Select **No Fill** by clicking the color well beside **Fill**.

ADD AND EDIT IMAGES

Any sheet can have images and graphics added, and you can then change how they look in various ways.

Numerous prebuilt image styles that are created to coordinate with a spreadsheet's template are available in Numbers. These styles include coordinating borders, reflections, and shadows. Applying one of these styles will allow you to quickly edit an image. Alternatively, you can give it a unique look by adding your own border, shadow, and other elements. Additionally, you can crop an image by masking out unwanted portions and adjust its background and exposure.

Add a picture

Follow any of the following steps to add an image:

- Select an image from your Aperture or iPhoto library by clicking the **Media** button in the toolbar. Drag the picture onto the sheet.
- Drag a picture to the sheet from the **Finder** or a website.
- Select an image to add by selecting **Insert > Choose** from the **Insert** menu at the top of your computer screen.
- Select the image you wish to add by clicking the **Placeholder** icon in the bottom-right corner of an image placeholder. Templates make use of image placeholders to show you how to space and arrange objects.

Crop or mask a picture

Without actually cropping the image, you can conceal undesirable areas. **Just the portions of the image that you want to be visible can be framed using the mask controls.**

- Click the image twice. The mask controls are displayed. The size of the default mask matches that of your image.
- Change the areas of the image that are visible by using the controls.

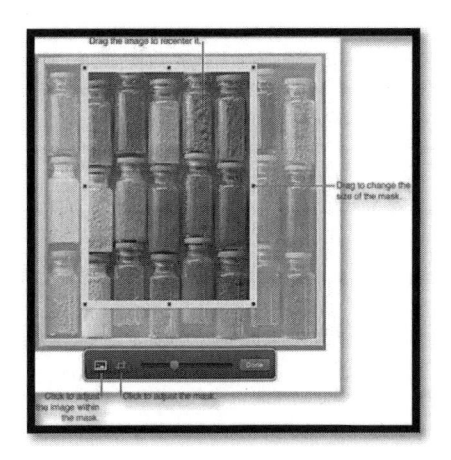

- Select "**Done**."

By double-clicking the image to bring up the options, you can adjust the mask whenever you like. Alternatively, you can select the picture and click **Edit Mask** in the **Format inspector's Image** pane.

Take a picture and crop out the background and extras

To make certain areas of an image transparent, use the Instant Alpha tool. Using this tool, you can get rid of an image's undesired background or color.

- Select the image.
- Select **Instant Alpha** in the **Format inspector's Image** pane.
- Drag gently over the color you wish to remove after clicking it. As you drag, more similar-colored areas are added to the selection. To remove several colors, click and drag numerous times.
    - Remove all instances of the color, even in neighboring areas of the image: While dragging, keep holding down the Option key.
    - **Add colors back to the image**: Restore the image's colors by dragging while holding down the Shift key.

- Select "**Done**."

Change the image's saturation, exposure, and other settings

- Select the picture.
- **Use the controls to make changes in the Format inspector's Image pane:**
    - **Exposure**: Changes how light or dark the entire image is altogether.
    - **Saturation**: Changes the image's color richness. To make the colors richer or more brilliant, drag to the right.
    - **Enhance**: The image is automatically adjusted by distributing the histogram's red, green, and blue tones equally.
- Select the **Advanced image** option to access the image histogram and other sophisticated features like levels, gamma, temperature, and tint.

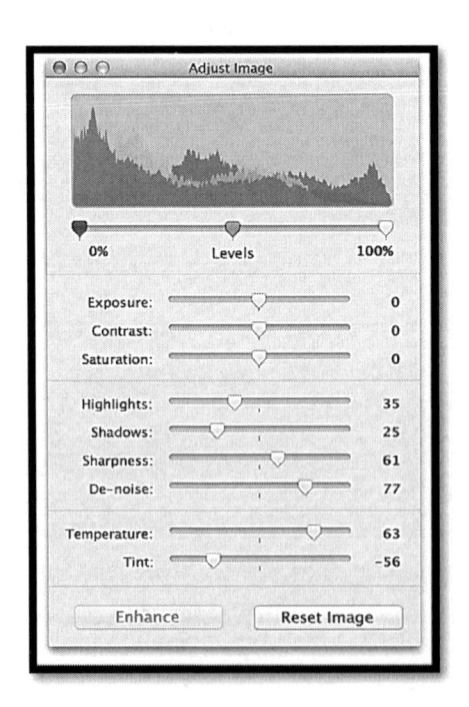

Select **Reset Image** to return to the default settings.

RESIZING AND MOVING CELLS IN NUMBERS

Controls that allow you to select, move, resize, and lock tables are displayed when you click one.

Select a table

- In the top-left corner of the table, select **Table handle** ⊙ after clicking anywhere else in the table. When the table is selected, three selection handles (the white squares) emerge on the edge of the table.

Resize a table

A table's size can be changed by resizing it, but its row and column numbers are unaffected.

- To enlarge or reduce the size of the table, select it and then drag any of the selection handles (the white squares) on its edge. Drag the dot in the corner to resize the rows and columns simultaneously. Shift-drag the white square in the corner of the table to resize it accordingly.

Move a table

- Click anywhere on the table. To move the table to the desired location on the sheet, drag the **Table handle** ⊙ in the top-left corner.

Lock or unlock a table

A table can be locked such that no changes, moves, or deletions can be made to it.

- Select **Lock** in the **Format inspector's Arrange** pane after selecting the table.
- Click the table, then select **Unlock** to make it accessible.

CHAPTER SEVEN
CAPTIONS AND TITLES IN NUMBERS

In this chapter, you'll learn how to add and edit captions and titles in Numbers.

ADDING CAPTIONS AND TITLES IN NUMBERS

The majority of objects, such as diagrams, equations, pictures, image galleries, movies, forms (aside from lines), tables, eight-handled text boxes, and graphs, can have titles or informative captions added. If you have organized your spreadsheet's objects into groups, you may additionally give each group a caption and title.

Add A Caption

- Choose the object to which a caption should be added.
- Choose one of the following options in the **Format** sidebar:
    - **For equations, text boxes, pictures, and shapes**: Tap the **Style** tab, then check the box beside **Caption**.
    - **For drawings**: Select the **Caption** checkbox by clicking the **Drawing** tab.

- o **For tables**: Select the **Caption** checkbox by clicking the **Table** tab.
- o **For graphs**: Select the checkbox next to **Caption** by clicking the **Graph** tab.
- o **For image galleries**: Select the **Caption** checkbox under the **Gallery** tab, then decide whether to use a unique caption for each image or the same caption for all of the pictures.
- o **For grouped objects**: Select the checkbox beside **Caption** in the **Arrange** tab.
- Enter your caption by clicking the blank caption placeholder underneath the object (a blue outline around the caption field indicates it is selected).

To edit the caption, click it (a blue outline appears), then type.

- Click the caption (or select the object, then select the caption), then make your selections on the Caption tab of the Format sidebar to change the font, size, style, or other formatting.
- Uncheck the box beside Caption to make the caption invisible. The previous caption is displayed again if you select the checkbox once more.

Add A Title

- Choose the object to which a title should be added.
- Choose one of the following options in the **Format** sidebar:
  - o **For equations, text boxes, pictures, and shapes**: Tap the **Style** tab, then check the box next to **Title**.
  - o **For drawings**: Select the Title checkbox by clicking the Drawing tab.

- **For tables**: Select the Title checkbox by clicking the Table tab.
- **For graphs**: Select the checkbox beside Title by clicking the Graph tab.
- **For image galleries**: Select the check box next to Title by clicking the Gallery tab.
- **For grouped objects**: Select the checkbox beside Title in the Arrange tab.

- Select the dropdown beside **Title** and select "**Top**" or "Bottom" to change the title's position. If "**Bottom**" is selected and a caption is added, the caption will always be displayed below the title.
  For doughnut charts, select "**Top**" or "**Center**" from the dropdown menu beside **Title**. A title can only display on top of some objects, including tables and the majority of graphs.
- Type your title after selecting the placeholder title (which is indicated by a blue outline around the title field).

- Click the title (or select the object, then select the title), then make your selections in the **Title** tab of the **Format** sidebar to change the font, size, style, or other formatting.
- Uncheck the box beside **Title** to make the title invisible. The previous title is displayed once more when you select the checkbox.

EDITING CAPTIONS AND TITLES IN NUMBERS

When you add a table, its title (for instance, Table 1) is automatically shown. The title can be edited or hidden. In a spreadsheet, no two tables can share the same name.

Show or hide a table title

- After selecting the table, select the **Format** icon.
- Turn **Title** on or off by tapping **Table** first.

Edit a table title

- Tap the table's title twice to make a selection. The name contains the insertion point.
- Make your changes after dragging the insertion point to the area you want to edit.

Note: A border can be used to enclose the table title. To make a box surround the table, first tap the table, then tap the table title. Turn on **Border** after tapping the **Format** icon.

CHAPTER EIGHT
ADDING AUDIOS TO NUMBERS

On the Apple iPhone, iPad, and Mac, the Numbers app is pre-installed. It is a fantastic solution for displaying data like spreadsheets. However, there are situations when using numbers alone will not adequately convey your true intentions. If you wish to convey more information about your spreadsheets, you can add audio files using the Numbers app.

Numbers alone can get boring after a while, so adding explanation to the data can spice things up. We'll demonstrate how to add an audio file in the Apple Numbers app in this chapter. Users of the iPhone, iPad, and Mac can use these steps.

ADD AUDIO FILE IN NUMBERS APP ON IPHONE AND IPAD

Consider going to a meeting where you are expected to present a spreadsheet. An audio clip had to be downloaded and added to that file. However, that clip is on your iPad or iPhone. That audio clip can be added right from your iPad or iPhone.

Take these actions. Although we are using an iPhone, iPad owners can also follow these instructions.

- Open the **Numbers** app.

- Launch your spreadsheet.
- At the top of the menu bar, click the **Plus** icon.

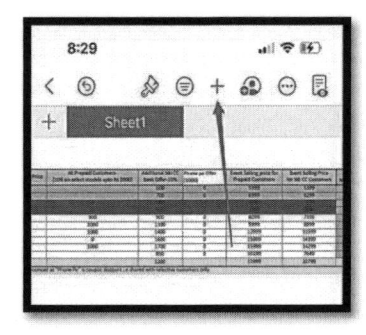

- In the top right corner, click the **Media** icon.

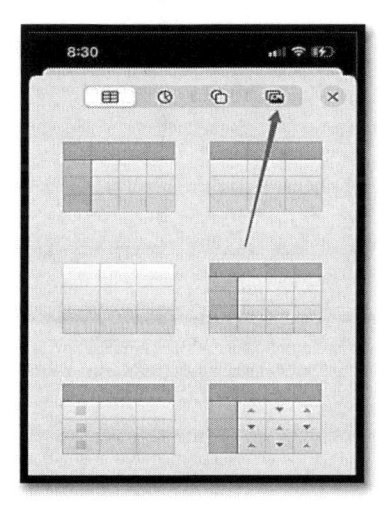

- To choose the file, click on **Insert from**.

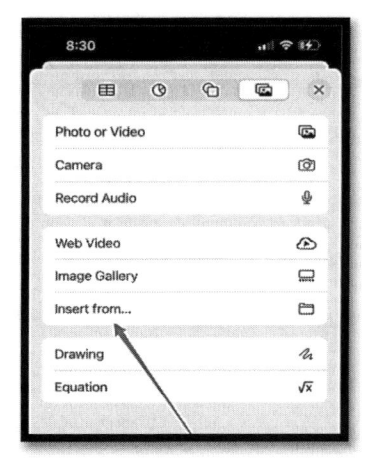

- Your screen will automatically open to the **Recents** tab.
- To access the iCloud drive, click **Browse**.

- The spreadsheet will be updated after you have selected the audio file.

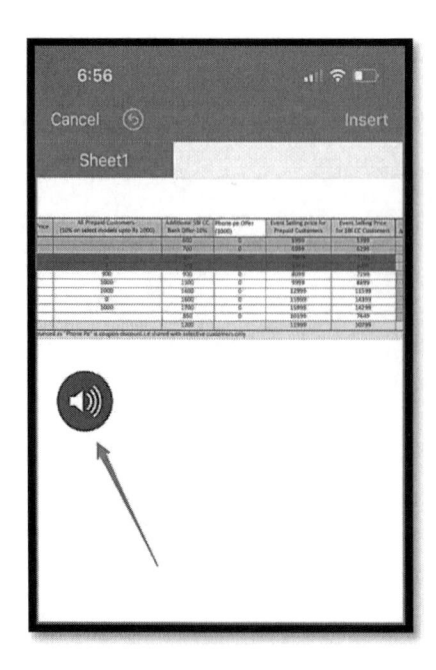

You can add an audio file using this method. To play your audio clip both before and during your presentation, click the **Audio** icon.

Follow these instructions if your file is not on the iCloud drive.

- In the top left corner, select **Browse**.

- From the list, choose the location of your folder.

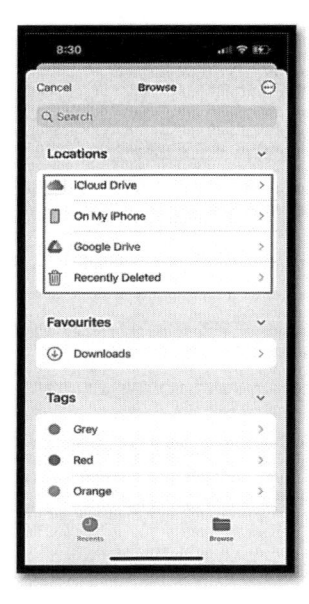

To add a file to your spreadsheet, select it.

RECORD AND ADD AN AUDIO FILE

On your iPhone and iPad, you may even record audio and add it immediately to your spreadsheet. If you want to add another audio clip to the file, this will also be helpful. **Here's how.**

- In the **Numbers** app, open your spreadsheet file.

- Select the **Media** tab by tapping the **Plus** sign.

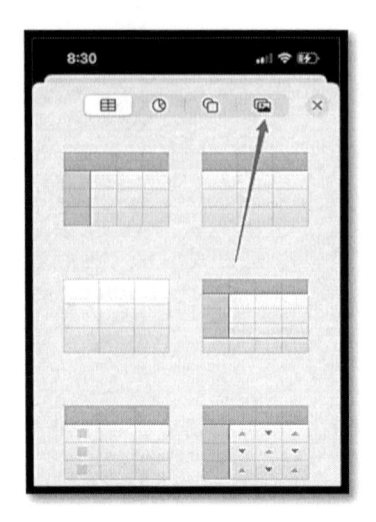

- Click on **Record Audio**.

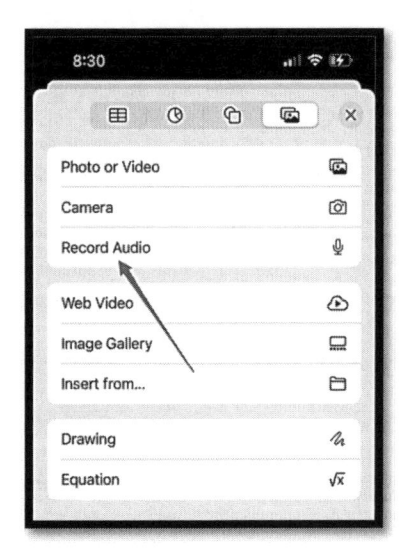

- To begin recording, click the **Record** icon.

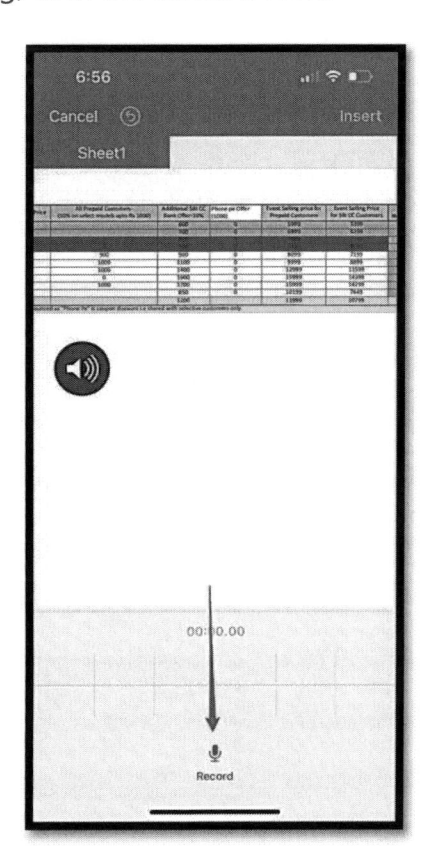

- Give Numbers permission to use the microphone.

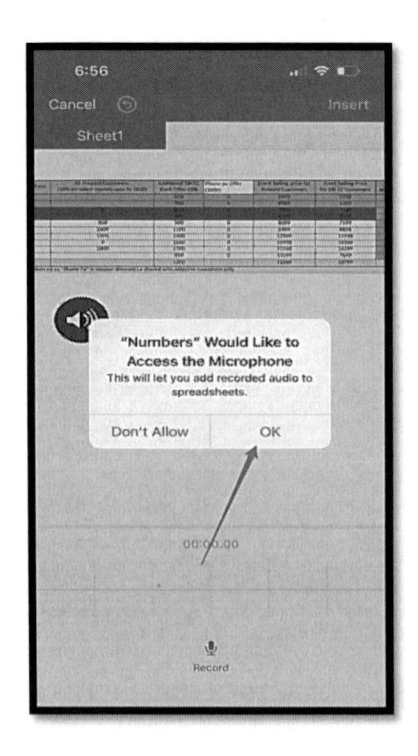

- To end the recording, click the **Stop** icon.

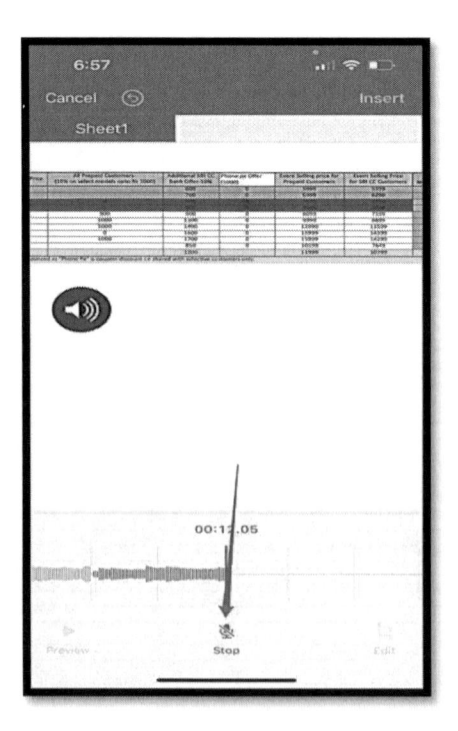

- Before adding the sheet, you can either **Preview** or **Edit** your recording.

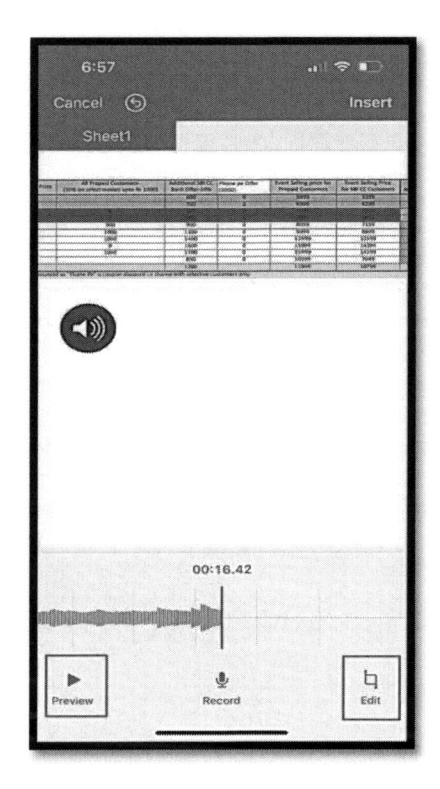

- To add the clip, select **Insert** in the top right corner.

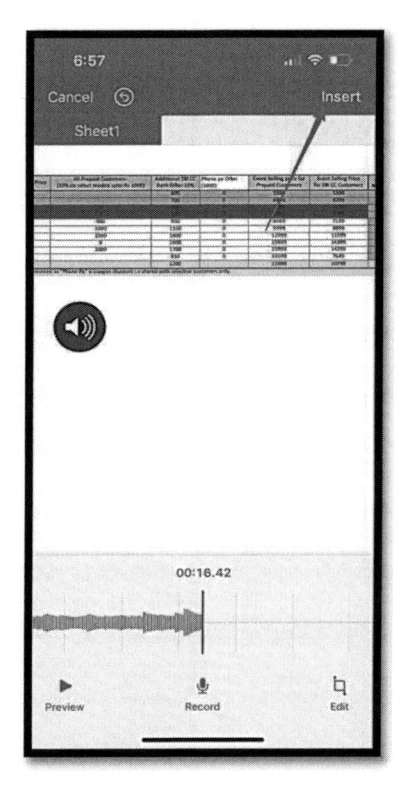

ADD AUDIO FILE IN NUMBERS APP ON MAC

If your audio files are solely on your Mac, adding them to Numbers on your Mac is simple. This feature can assist you in clarifying a certain metric if you teach a subject like financial planning. Take these steps.

- On your Mac, open the **Numbers** app.

- Open a new document or your spreadsheet.
- On the top menu bar, select the **Media** icon.

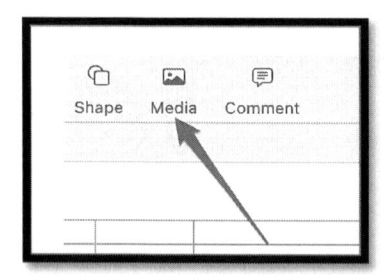

- Select **Choose** from the drop-down menu.

- Hit **Insert** after selecting your audio file.

The audio clip has been successfully added to your spreadsheet. By choosing the Edit Audio option from the right menu, you can edit that clip.

You can record a new audio clip on your Mac and add it, just like you can on an iPhone or an iPad. You can capture high-quality audio for your presentation using your Mac and studio-quality microphones. How? Read on.

- Tap on the **Media** icon once more after opening the document or starting a new one.

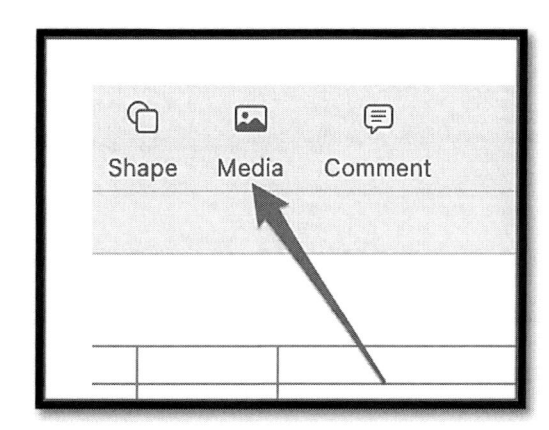

- Then select **Record** Audio.

- To begin recording audio, select the **Record** button.

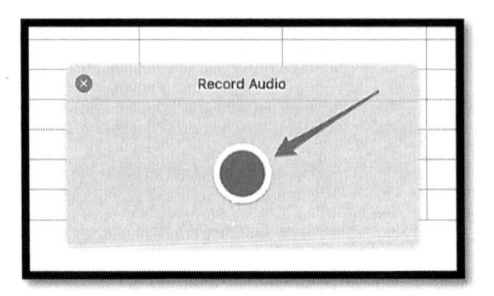

- To pause your recording, click once more.

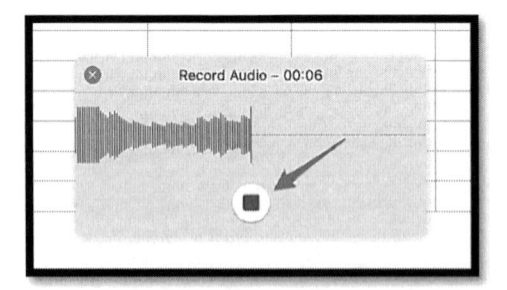

- Additionally, you have the option to **Preview** and **Edit** your clip here.

- After doing so, select **Insert** to add your recorded clip.

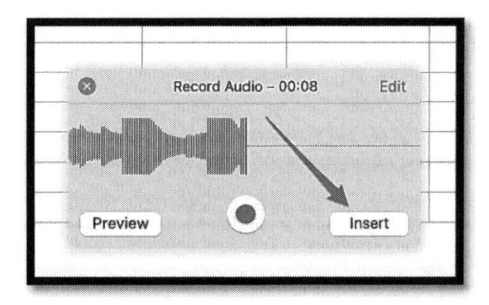

Conclusion

The Apple Numbers app's feature can improve the impact of your presentations. To make your point clearer, you can include a lot more details and stats. To use this feature, you don't need to use any additional spreadsheet applications. Apple undoubtedly has given its users' needs a lot of attention. All users have free access to this facility for adding audio clips.

CHAPTER NINE
CUSTOM TEMPLATES IN NUMBERS

In this chapter, you'll learn how to use custom templates in Numbers.

CREATING A CUSTOM TEMPLATE

You can save a spreadsheet as a template if you make one that you want to use repeatedly as a model for other spreadsheets. You can create your own template by simply adding your business logo on an already existing one, or you can create a brand-new template from scratch.

Your custom template can be added to the template chooser, or you can save it as a file to install and use on your iOS device or share with others. Save your template to iCloud, iTunes, a WebDAV server, or send it as an email attachment before installing it on your iOS device.

SAVE A SPREADSHEET AS A TEMPLATE

- Select **"File" > "Save as Template"** (from the **File** menu at the top of your computer screen).
- **Select an option:**
    - **Add to template chooser**: After entering a name for the template, hit Return. Your template can be found in the template chooser's My Templates section.
    - **Save**: Give the template a name, then decide where to save it. If you save it to iCloud, the template will be available for download in the spreadsheet manager the next time Numbers is launched on your iOS device.

You must compress the file before uploading it to webmail or saving it to a web server. It must have the ".nmbtemplate.zip" file extension in order to be installed and used in Numbers on your iOS device.

Install A Template on Your Mac

If you selected **Add to Template Chooser** when you saved your template, you may skip this step. The installed template is already available in **My Templates**.

By adding it in the template chooser, you can install a unique template that you have saved on your computer or that someone else supplied you.

- Select **Add to Template Chooser** after double-clicking the "**.nmbtemplate**" file extension-containing template.

Instead of opening a new spreadsheet via the template chooser, Numbers can be configured to do it automatically. Select **Preferences > Numbers** (from the Numbers menu at the top of your computer screen). Tap "**Use template**" in the General pane, then press **Change Template** to choose a template.

Install A Template on Your Device

You must compress the template file in order to install a template from a WebDAV server or email attachment (so it has the filename extension.nmbtemplate.zip). The template is automatically compressed for you if you send it via Mail. In the Finder, Control-click the file and select Compress if you use another email service or WebDAV server.

Install a template on your iOS device by performing the following steps:

- **From iCloud**: Your template will automatically show up in the spreadsheet manager and be identifiable by a template badge if iCloud is enabled. Click Install, then tap the file.
- **From a WebDAV server**: Click **Share** (you might need to press the screen to see the Share icon), then click Open in Numbers after downloading the template from the server. Hit **Add**.
- **From email**: To open an attachment in Numbers, click the attachment in Mail, then tap Share (you might need to tap the screen to reveal the **Share** symbol). Hit **Add.**

The template can be found in the **Template Chooser's My Templates** section.

RENAME OR DELETE A CUSTOM TEMPLATE

A template that has been installed can be found in the My Templates section of the template chooser.

- Control-click the template name in the template chooser, then select **Rename** or **Delete**.
- When renaming, enter the new name, then hit **Return**.

Templates can never be rearranged; they always appear in the order they were inserted.

EDIT A TEMPLATE

After you save a template, you cannot alter it. On the other hand, you can build a new template based on the previous one.

To make the custom template visible in the template chooser, you must first install it (see instructions above).

- Double-click the template you want to edit after selecting **File > New**. The **My Templates** section of the template chooser contain customized templates.
- After making your changes, save the spreadsheet as a new template.

After creating the new template, you can remove the old one.

CHAPTER TEN
FUNCTIONS IN NUMBERS

Do you track, log, manipulate, and analyze data using Numbers on your Mac? Whether you are aware of it or not, the application comes with several features that can help you manage your data more effectively.

You can stop wasting hours performing tasks manually and put the calculator aside. We're here to show you how to use the functions and formulae in Numbers to make working with your data simpler.

MAKING USE OF THE FORMULA EDITOR

It's necessary to get to know the Formula Editor before you start adding formulas and functions to Numbers.

Simply click the Equal Sign in the cell where you want to add a formula or function to make the process simple. The editor can be accessed in just this manner. You can also enter the Functions Browser (which we'll talk about later) by selecting **Insert > New Formula** from the toolbar.

The left side of the **Formula Editor** can be moved, and one of its edges can be moved to change the size by using the double-sided arrow.

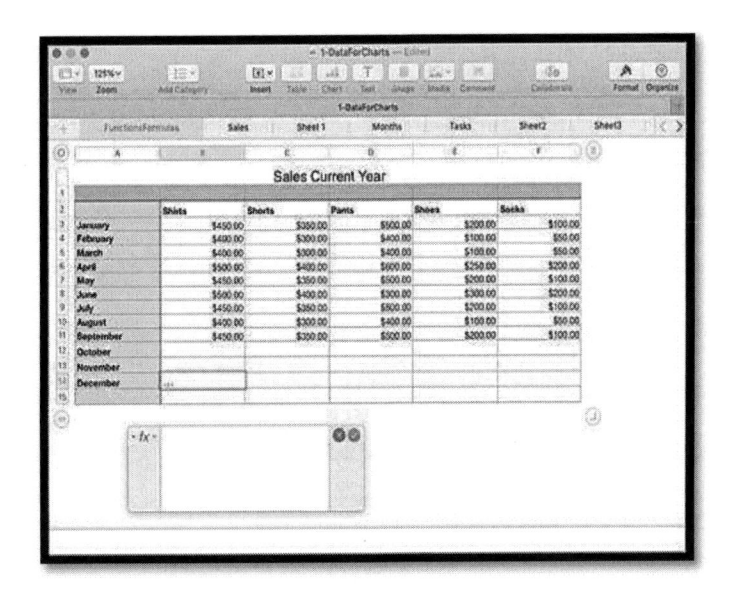

To add a cell range or a single cell to your formula, simply click on it or drag it across the editor. Arithmetic operators can also be used to multiply, divide, add, and subtract. You can enter numbers with or without decimals, of course.

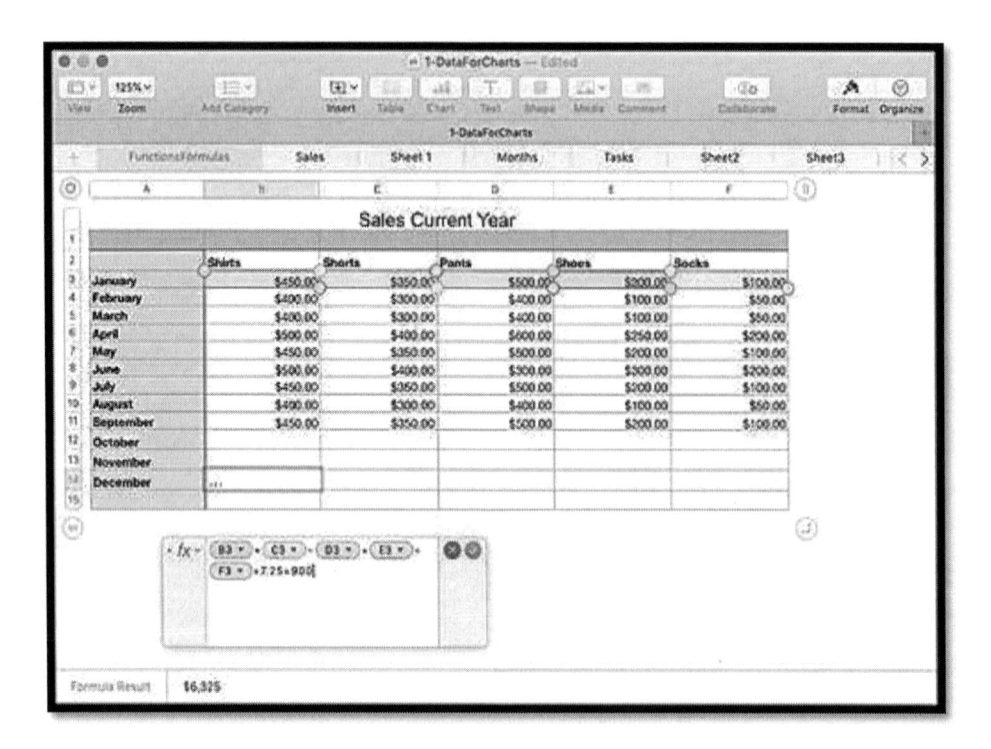

When you're done with the editor and wish to apply your formula, click the green checkmark. Additionally, you can close it without saving any changes by clicking the **red X** if you change your mind.

To ensure your data is accurate before moving forward, you should be aware of how to erase duplicates in Numbers.

SIMPLE AND QUICK FORMULAS

Numbers include certain simple formulas that you can apply without manually entering them, which is convenient.

Choose the cell where you want to enter a formula. Select sum, average, minimum, maximum, count, or product by clicking the **Insert** button on the toolbar.

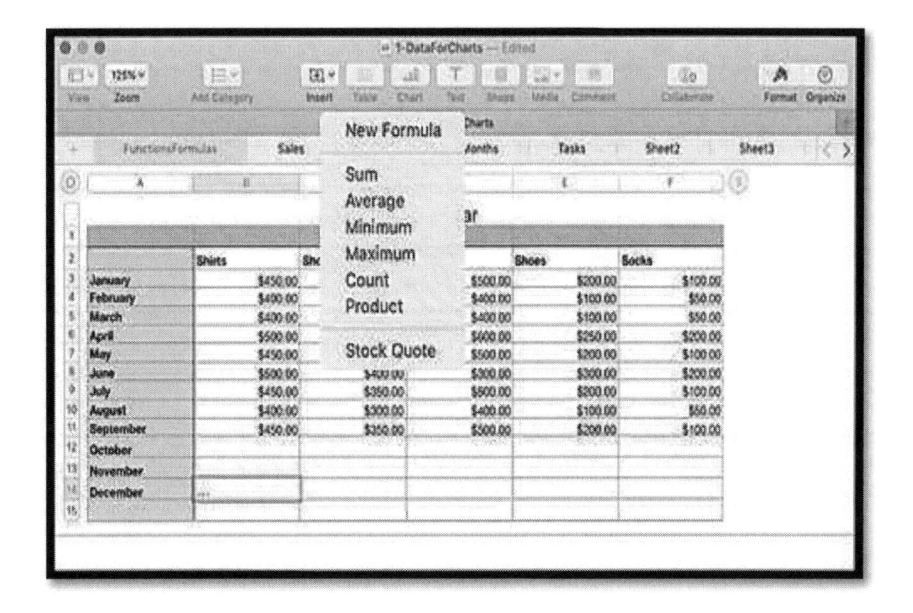

Based on the information in your spreadsheet, Numbers will make a decent guess about which cells to utilize and highlight them for you. And while the Numbers app is frequently accurate, it is not always. Hit the **Return** key to apply the formula if the cells that are highlighted are the right ones.

Click the cell holding the formula to bring up the **Formula Editor** if the highlighted cells are not the ones you want to use. Then, choose the appropriate cells so that they appear in the editor. Clicking the checkbox will apply the formula in its entirety.

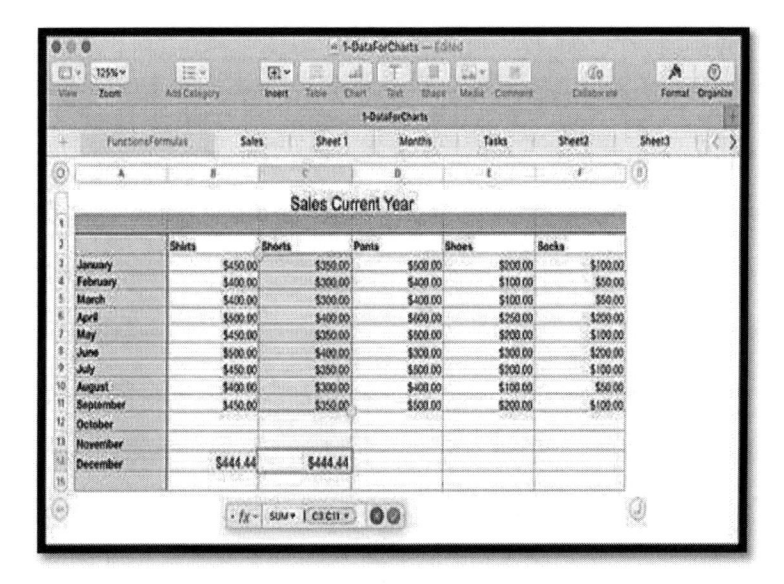

ADDITIONAL FORMULAS AND FUNCTIONS

We have some more helpful methods for working with your data if the fundamental equations or functions we've covered so far aren't sufficient for what you want to achieve.

Compare Values

To check whether cell values are equal, greater than, less than, or not equal, you can use comparison operators. The formula's output will be shown as True or False. If you want to compare sales, income, or expenses over months or years, this is useful.

For our example, we're looking to determine if our January sales were higher than or on par with those from the year before.

- Open the **Formula Editor** and choose the cell where you want the formula to appear.
- For the formula, select the first cell.
- The comparison operator in text form, enter <= to indicate greater than or equal to.
- For the formula, select the second cell.
- Hit the **Return** key or click the checkbox.

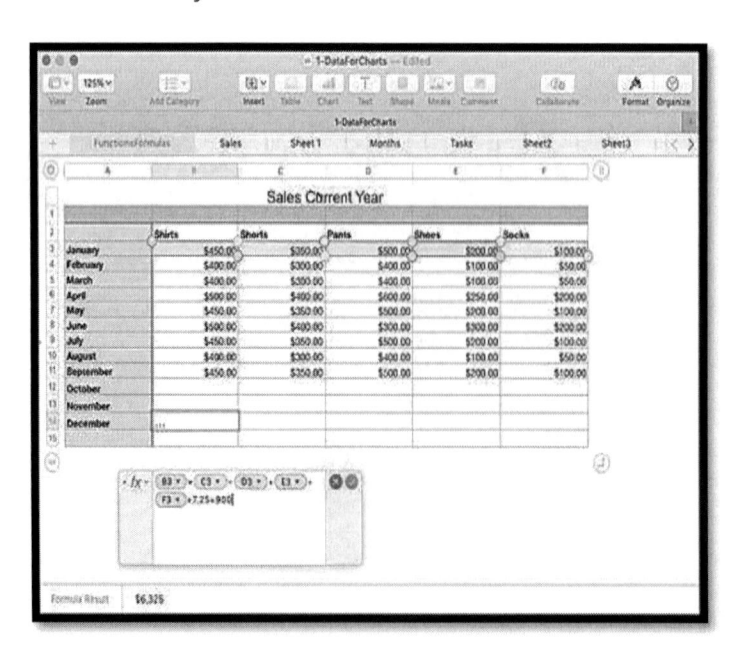

You can see from our example that the result "True" in the formula's cell indicates that our sales for this January were greater than or equal to those from last year.

Split Text

If you have more information than you need or wish to extract only certain pieces of information, you can use the Right and Left functions to break up text strings. Area codes from phone numbers, states from cities, or zip codes from address strings can all be extracted using this method.

For this illustration, we have a spreadsheet with customer information that includes both a city name and a two-letter state abbreviation, such as Chicago, IL.

Each person's state should be extracted and placed in a separate field.

- Open the **Formula Editor** and choose the cell where you want the formula to appear.
- By pressing the **Format** button in the top right corner, you may access the **Functions Browser**.
- Select "**Right**" from the list by searching for it, then click **Insert Function**.
- Select "**source-string**" in the **Formula Editor**, then select the data-containing cell.
- Click "**string-length**" to the right in the editor and enter **2**.
- To use the formula, click the checkmark.

This formula extracts two characters (step 5) from the string's right side (step 3). By using this formula on our column, we are now able to view each customer's individual state's abbreviation.

Remove Extra Spaces

It's possible that the data in your spreadsheet isn't always formatted the way you need it to be if it came from a database. You can have too many spaces between the first and last name of a client if you use the customer spreadsheet example from above. This can be problematic for mail merging or automated emails that use those names.

We may quickly and easily get rid of those superfluous spaces using the Trim function in numbers.

- Open the **Formula Editor** and **Functions Browser** after selecting the cell where the formula should be entered.
- In the list, look for "**Trim**," click it, then click **Insert Function**.
- Click "**source-string**" in the **Formula Editor**, then click the data-containing cell.
- To use the formula, click the checkmark.

Now that there are no unnecessary spaces to mess with our other software, we have a neat, tidy list of the names of our customers.

Concatenate Data

The above situation might not apply to you. It's possible that you want to integrate data from two separate cells into one. Concatenate is a function that can be used to combine text and numbers.

Let's imagine that the first and last names of a customer are divided across two different fields in the data we got.

Those names must be together for our email program to function.

- Open the **Formula Editor** and **Functions Browser** after selecting the cell where the formula should be entered.
- Click **Insert Function** after conducting a search for "**Concatenate**" and selecting it from the list.
- Click "**string**," then click the first name's cell and press the comma.
- Add opening and closing quotation marks, place a space in the middle (""), and then a comma.
- Select the last name's cell by clicking it.
- To use the formula, click the checkmark.

Let's go! Our customers' first and last names are all in one column rather than being dispersed throughout other cells.

Convert To Plain Text

The Plaintext function in Numbers is an additional feature that can be extremely helpful, especially when gathering data from diverse sources. Your spreadsheet might contain rich text-formatted text and numbers. Examples include names that are bold, italicized, or underlined, as well as links that can be clicked.

Your data can be reduced to plain, straightforward text by using the **Plaintext function**.

- Open the **Formula Editor** and **Functions Browser** after selecting the cell where the formula should be entered.
- Click **Insert Function** after conducting a search for "**Plaintext**" and selecting it from the list.
- Click the cell containing the data, then click "**source-string**."
- To use the formula, click the checkmark.

After that, your data should seem plain, devoid of HTML, rich text, or other formatting.

COPY YOUR FUNCTIONS AND FORMULAS

You'll probably want to apply the formula or function to more than one cell with the examples we've provided here. Consequently, depending on how your data is organized, you can simply drag to replicate your formula to adjacent cells in rows or columns.

Choose a cell that contains the formula you wish to duplicate. Click the **yellow dot** on the cell's edge, move it to the cells you want to duplicate it to, then let go.

That formula or function ought to immediately apply to the related data in addition to copying to those cells.

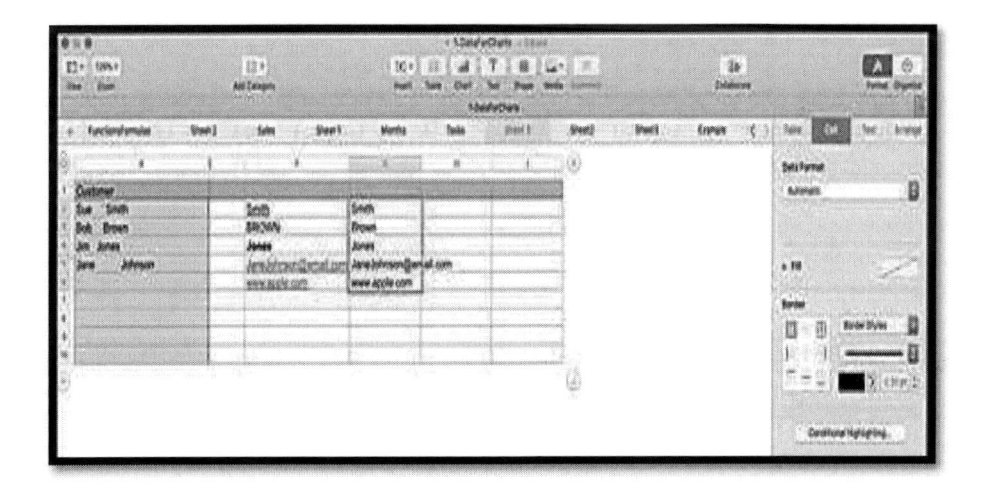

SIMPLER METHODS FOR DATA ANALYSIS IN NUMBERS

Formulas and functions make it considerably simpler to manipulate and analyze the data in your Numbers spreadsheets. Try out these formulas and some of the additional built-in functions Numbers has to offer for managing both numbers and text. You simply can't know which one would be of great assistance until you give it a try.

ADDING FORMULAS IN MAC NUMBERS

Even though the spreadsheet we're utilizing for our example isn't very large, picture it if it had hundreds of columns or rows. When making computations, using those formulae is most helpful. No matter if the values are in columns, rows, or a collection of cells, inserting the desired formula is the same process.

First, select the cell that will display the formula's result. Then, choose the formula by selecting **Insert > Formula** from the menu bar or the Insert button from the toolbar. Press **Enter** when it appears in your spreadsheet.

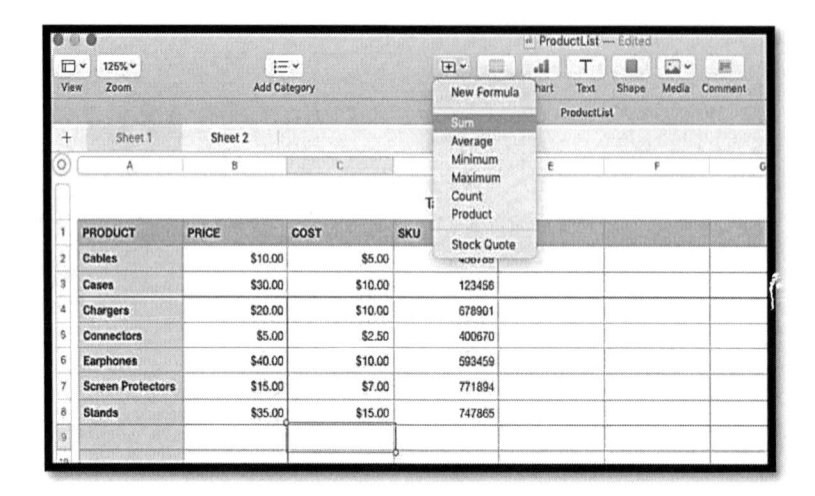

The group of cells to which you want to apply the formula will be assumed by Numbers, but you can readily adjust this.

EDITING THE FORMULAS

Double-click the cell that the formula is now in. You'll see a little pop-up with the formula and the cells it applies to. Either click inside the pop-up and adjust the cells by entering in the labels, or drag the corners of the range of cells to the desired positions. Click the green checkmark to confirm when you're done.

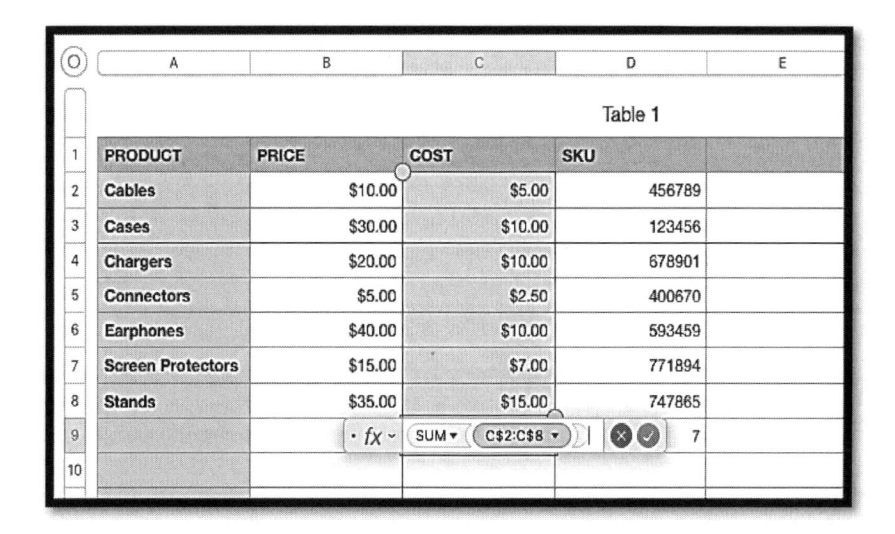

GETTING A QUICK VIEW OF FORMULAS

Perhaps you want to view a formula without actually entering it as a cell in the spreadsheet. For instance, you might want to view the largest number in a set of cells or the average of a column.

When you choose the cells, each of those typical formulas will automatically display at the bottom of the Numbers window. Click the **gear** icon to the right and pick the function if there is one you want to add to the view.

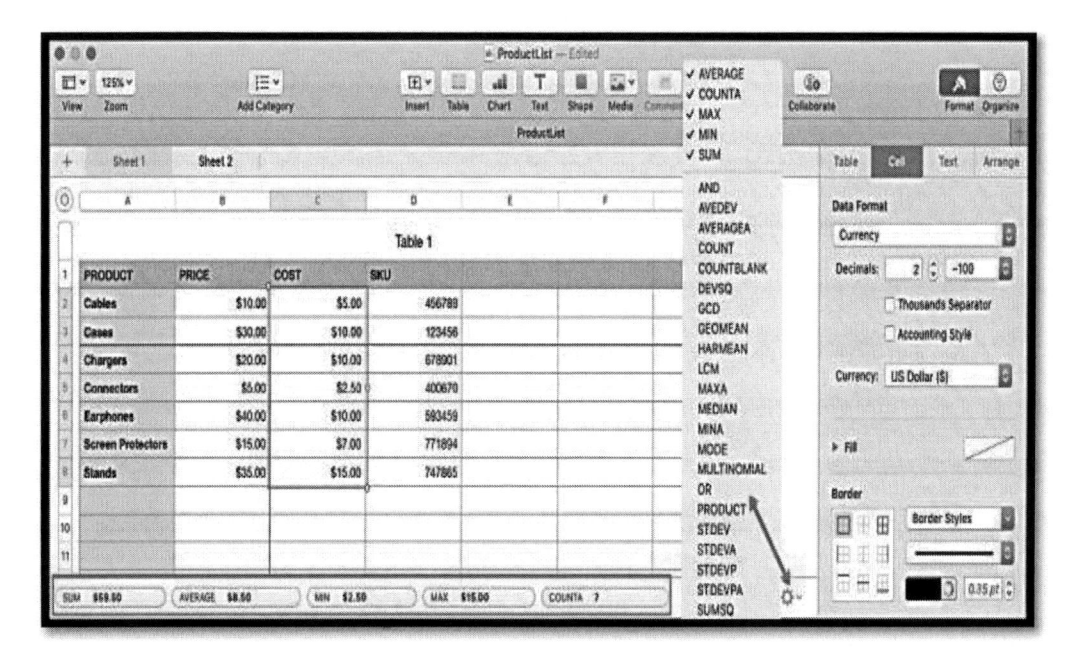

ADDING AND EDITING FORMULAS IN NUMBERS ON THE IPAD AND IPHONE

You can insert formulas on your iPhone and iPad if you're using your spreadsheet while on the go. Select the cell where you wish the formula and ensuing output to appear. Select **New Formula** from the pop-up menu by tapping the **Cell** button at the bottom of the screen.

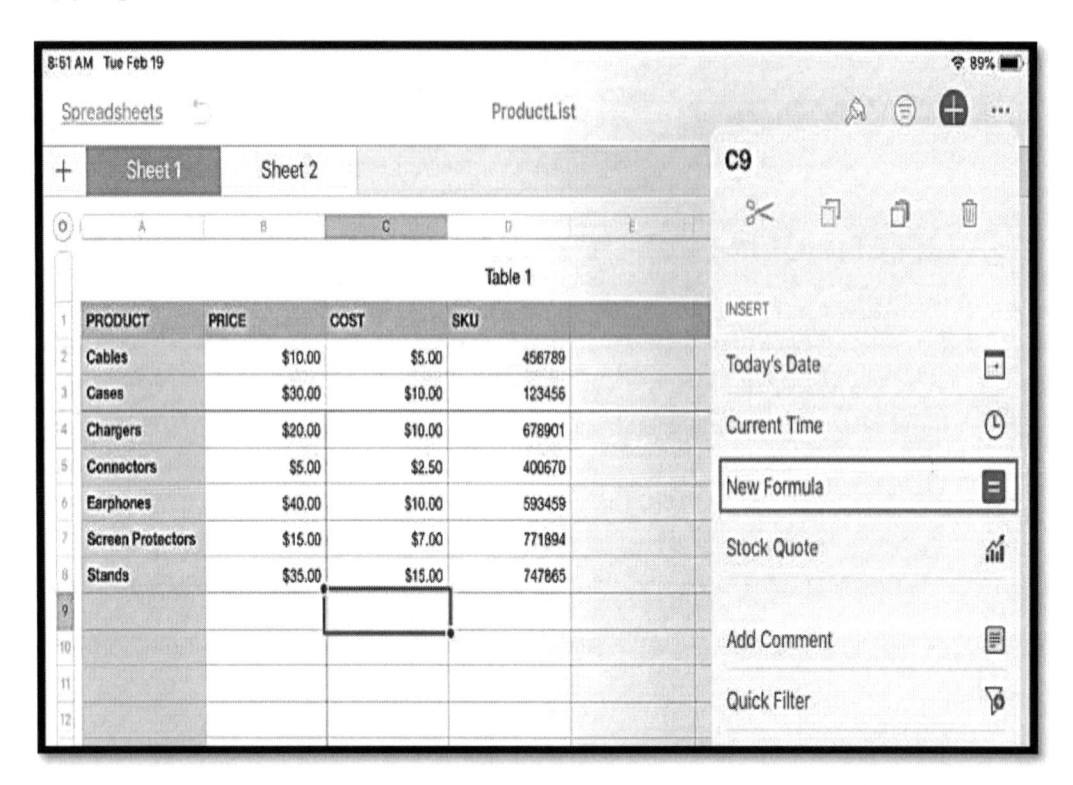

The formula can then be entered manually or, for best results, by tapping the **Function (fx)** button on the left. Then you'll see the same formulas once more. When you tap the one you desire, it will appear in the bottom text box. Drag your finger through the cells you want to include in the formula or write the values into the "**value**" text section. When you're done, click the green "**checkmark**" icon.

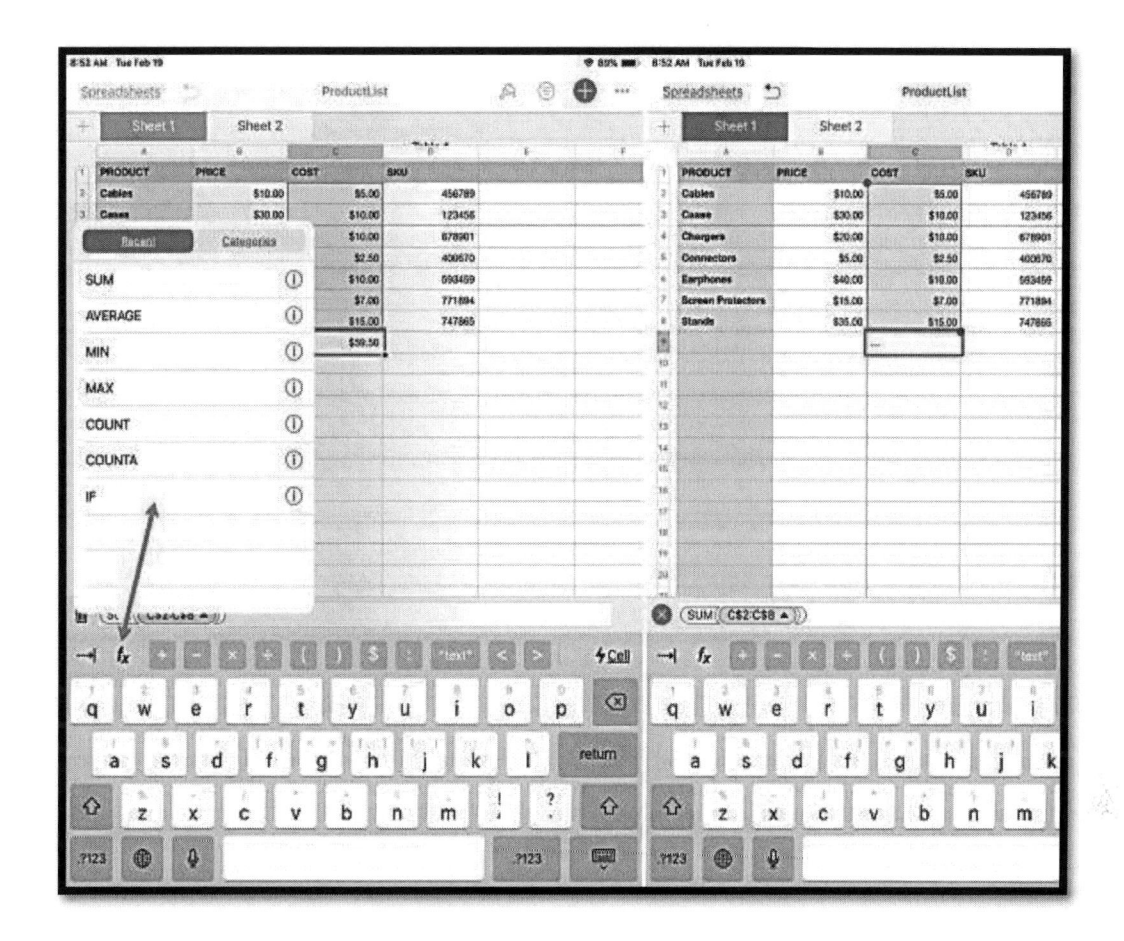

Numbers make using common functions and formulas much simpler than you may expect. Additionally, using these built-in tools can help you save time and minimize data-related problems. Are you prepared to try it?

CONCLUSION

We have come to the end of the road with iWork 2023 and it was an interesting experience. With all the information passed across in this manual, you're sure to be a pro in using Pages, Numbers, and Keynote for any purpose. If there's any aspect you don't quite understand, you can go back to it and your imaginary teacher will guide you.

BOOK 3
APPLE KEYNOTE

CHAPTER ONE
INTRODUCTION

An outstanding presentation is easy to achieve with **Keynote**. With this tool, you can easily and quickly add charts, edit photos, and incorporate cinematic effects, colored backgrounds, good theme designs, videos, audio, etc. to your slides for an excellent and impressive presentation. It is mostly pre-installed on most Apple products and can also be used on Macs, iPad, iPhone, or PCs.

In this chapter, we will cover an introductory session of the Keynote. It will cover what the keynote is about, its basic features, the current version, what's new in the latest version, how to start a presentation, and many more interesting sub-topics.

Let's Begin...

What is Keynote?

Keynote is a **presentation program from Apple** similar to PowerPoint for Microsoft that allows users to make, edit, and manage presentations that include multiple types of media. It has a lot of graphics and editing tools that allow its users to add charts, change pictures, and add cinematic effects to slides. Users can also make their slides using photos as backgrounds and themes that can be changed. You can go as far as adding animated objects and live video feeds to slides with Keynote. It gives you options like textures, color gradients, and photos to use as transitions.

Another interesting thing about this is that teams can work on projects together in real-time and share ideas and comments on a single platform thanks to the built-in collaboration feature. There are also custom captions and titles, math equations, a reading mode, an image gallery, the ability to export a presentation, and more. One big difference between **Keynote** and **PowerPoint** is that Keynote makes presentation files that can be opened, edited, and played on your Mac, iOS device (iPhone, iPad, or iPod Touch), and even on a web browser through icloud.com. Therefore, If you just bought a new Mac or iOS device, Keynote is already on it (if not, you can get it from the App Store or the Mac App Store). Keynotes also use **iCloud** to make sure that all of your devices have the latest versions of your presentations. You have everything you need to make a great presentation quickly and easily with Keynote.

Basic Features of Keynotes

1. **Amazing Creative Tools**

With **Keynote** you can picture an **excellent presentation**. This is because of its nice creative tools. You can add pictures or videos, add frames, reflections, and shadows, use interactive charts to make your data more interesting, use smooth transitions like in a movie to join everything together, etc. This software has an amazing tool to give you an excellent presentation.

2. Developed with Simplicity

The keynote sets up an interesting presentation right from the start. All the tools you need are right in front of you on a clean, easy-to-use interface. And it's made to work well on different devices no matter how large or graphically rich it is.

3. Impressive Charts

Another feature of the keynote is the **Chart**. A chart is worth a thousand words when it comes to explaining data. You can pick from columns, bars, pies, scatter, bubbles, and other types of charts. Use animation to make something stand out. Make your charts interactive to draw people's attention to key parts of the story. This is an intriguing feature of the keynote.

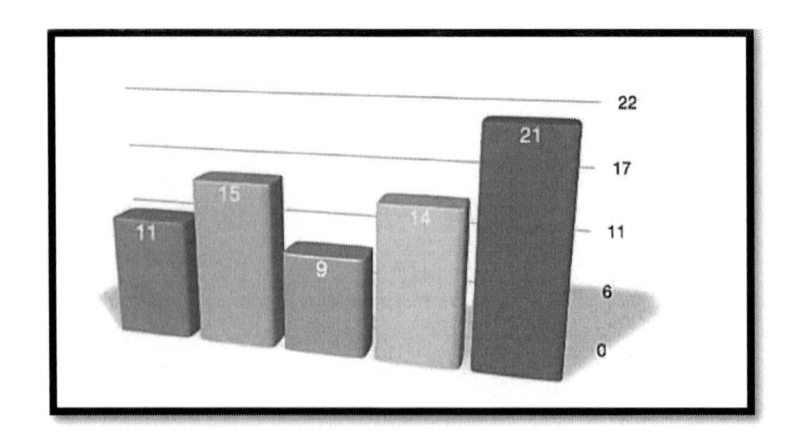

4. Keynote Everywhere

Another feature of the keynote is the fact that you can save or carry your work anywhere at any time. When you make a presentation on your Mac, it looks the same on your iPhone or iPad. And moving your work from one device to another is easy. You can even access your presentations from the web, share them, and work with others in real-time.

5. Simple to Share

With the app, it's easy to share your presentation with lots of people through various means which will be discussed later in this book. You can send a copy of your file right from the toolbar, you can give anyone you want a link to your presentation, you can give them access to edit and make comments, and you can send presentations using services like Gmail or Dropbox. It makes it easier to connect with your team and, in the end, with your audience.

6. Friendly with Microsoft PowerPoint

One amazing feature of the keynote is that it works well with Microsoft PowerPoint. The files can be saved as PowerPoint files, or you can import PowerPoint files and edit them right in the app. Most of the most popular features of PowerPoint are also supported making everyone work on the same project without any trouble even if you use different apps.

Other Features include:

- Keynotes have amazing **backgrounds with gorgeous color** and visual intrigue to your slides.
- **Keynotes add live video streams** to any slide and can also make a presentation using a video chat. When used in conjunction with video conferencing, Keynote for Mac provides a smooth experience. Run a presentation slide show in its window so you may multitask. You can view your presenter notes, current and upcoming slides, and slide navigation in a different window as well.
- **Keynotes outline your presentation easier**: iPhone and iPad users now have a new method to see their presentations with the introduction of an outline view.
- **Keynote can turn handwriting into text magically:** iPadOS and Apple Pencil make it easy to convert your handwriting to text so you can get back to work without stopping to retype.
- **Audio** can be recorded, edited, and played back straight from a slide.
- It's simple to **apply text overlays to any graphic,** video, or form. When you reposition an object, the associated text will follow suit.
- With **keynote, you can apply color, gradient**, or image to the background of any presentation, to your text, or any object.
- **Enable Black Mode** to give Keynote a dramatic dark effect and emphasis your material.
- **iCloud Drive folder sharing:** Add a Keynote presentation to a shared iCloud Drive folder, and automatically start collaborating.
- With Keynote, you can use **offline collaboration t**hat is, you can make changes to shared presentations even when you don't have internet access, and they'll be uploaded.
- **Streaming videos on the web:** Embedding a video from a site like YouTube or Vimeo allows you to play it directly within your presentations, negating the need to download and open the video in a separate media player.
- **Modified Toolbar:** Keynote for the iPad allows you to quickly insert objects, find settings, and use your preferred tools via a configurable toolbar.

What's New in Keynote?

For iPhone, iPad, and Mac

View the most recent activity in a shared presentation in iPad Keynote.

In a presentation that has been shared, it is simple to obtain updates.

The activity list records when anyone invited to your presentation performs any of the following actions:

- Performs alterations, such as adding, editing, resizing, relocating, and pasting (but not style changes).
- Adds new comments and responds to existing ones.
- The first participant to join a shared presentation.

Collaborate in Messages

Easily share your presentation and view updates in Messages. Send a message or initiate a face time call directly from a group presentation.

Eliminate Backgrounds

For a dramatic effect, choose your live video background, or rapidly isolate an image's topic.

Restructured Toolbar

With the iPad's Keynote's customized toolbar, you can quickly insert objects, find settings, and use your favorite tools.

For iCloud

Keynote for **iCloud** is a web application for creating and editing presentations on a Windows or Mac computer (using a supported browser). Keynote for iCloud presentations are automatically accessible in the Keynote app on any Mac, iPhone, or iPad signed in with the same Apple ID. You can create or modify a Keynote presentation on a computer, iPhone, iPad, or the web, and the changes will appear everywhere. You can also share a link to a presentation with others and then edit it in real-time.

Beginning with a Theme

Every presentation begins with a theme, which is a collection of pre-design slide layouts that serve as a starting point. Replace the graphics and text of the theme with your own, and then add additional slides as necessary.

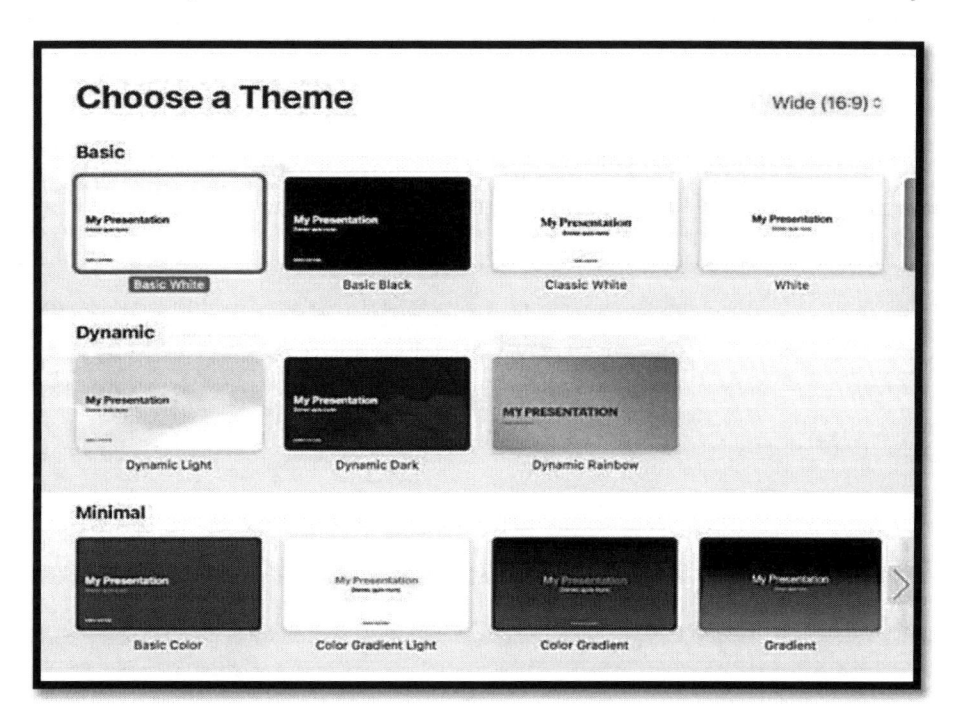

Create a Presentation

In the toolbar are the Tables, Charts, Text, Shapes, and Image object buttons. At the top of the Charts pop-up menu is the 2D and Interactive buttons. When the 2D button is clicked, a choice of 2D chart thumbnails is displayed for selection.

Add Photos, Shapes, Charts, and more

Images, videos, audio, charts, shapes, and tables can be added to any slide. In your presentation, you can layer objects, resize them, and link them to websites or other slides.

Intro to Text Boxes, Images, and Other Objects

The selected image on the slide has a picture frame border, and Picture Frame is selected from the border menu on the Style tab of the Format sidebar.

Personalize Every Detail

Customize the look of any object added to a slide. Choose a new hue, add a drop shadow, modify the opacity, and more.

Alter the Appearance of Objects

A text box is selected on a slide, and the Build In tab is selected at the top of the animate sidebar on the right. The Drift motion is selected from a pop-up menu and choices for tweaking the animation are shown below it in the sidebar.

Animation

Add visual effects or animations to engage your viewers. Add a transition so that one slide dissolves into the next, or float each letter of a word onto the slide.

Play your Presentation Anywhere and Anytime

Your presentation can be seen on your computer, on a separate screen, or over the internet. You can open the presenter display in a separate window while the presentation is playing to examine and amend your presenter notes; time your presentation, and more.

Work together in Real Time

Invite others to assist you in creating your presentation. Everyone you invite can observe updates as they are made, but you choose who can modify the presentation and who can only view it.

Keynote 12.2.1 for MAC

The most recent version of Keynote on mac Informer is 12.2.1. It is an ideal presentation option for both the Design and Photo categories.

Keynote, which comes pre-installed on most Apple devices, makes it simple to create stunning and memorable presentations with its robust tools and dazzling effects. Utilize Apple Pencil on your iPad to bring your slides to life with diagrams and illustrations.

And with real-time collaboration, your team can collaborate regardless of whether they are using a Mac, iPad, iPhone, or PC. Delivers sophisticated presentations with the ability to customize the output and even connect additional devices, such as the iPad and Apple Pencil, to draw directly on the slides. Incredible ease in creating presentations.

Keynote's potent yet user-friendly tools and mesmerizing effects put the show in a slide show.

Conclusion

With Keynote, you have access to all the tools you need to make creating an impressive presentation incredibly straightforward. Stunning presentations in minutes, Apple-designed themes, Advanced Theme Chooser, Slide Navigators, Tables, 2D and 3D charts and chart animations, Typography options such as smart quotes, ligatures, and automatic scaling Reviewer comments, Alignment guides, and rulers, Cinema-quality animations, Magic Move for creating sophisticated animations with simple transitions, Text transitions, Object-driven transitions, etc. However, note that certain features may require Internet connectivity; additional fees and conditions may apply.

CHAPTER TWO
CREATE A PRESENTATION

As already established in Chapter one of this book **Keynote** is a **presentation program** that allows users to make, edit, and manage presentations that include multiple types of media. It is all about making a presentation on your slides. This chapter is going to therefore include how to create a presentation, group and ungroup slides, reorder the slides, and skip and unskip the slides. Then we will go over to the redo and undo buttons and finally the hyperlinks.

You can also re-use a text, copy or cut it and move it to another location, etc., therefore, how to cut copy, and paste text on the keynote will be discussed in this chapter also.

How to Create a Presentation in Keynote

For Mac

- To create a Keynote presentation, you must first select a **theme**, which consists of a collection of predesigned slide layouts.

Note: Each slide layout features a unique arrangement of text and images that corresponds to the theme, while **a theme** is a collection of elements used to create a presentation, such as a placeholder text and images, coordinated color schemes, etc.

Note: After creating a new presentation, you can modify themes however you like, and you can change the presentation's theme at any time.

- First, Click the **Keynote icon** in the Dock, Launchpad, or Applications folder to launch **Keynote**.
- Open **Keynote** by clicking the **Keynote icon** in the Dock, Launchpad, or Applications folder.
- After the opening keynote, the **theme chooser** appears. The **theme chooser** displays thumbnails of the available presentation templates.

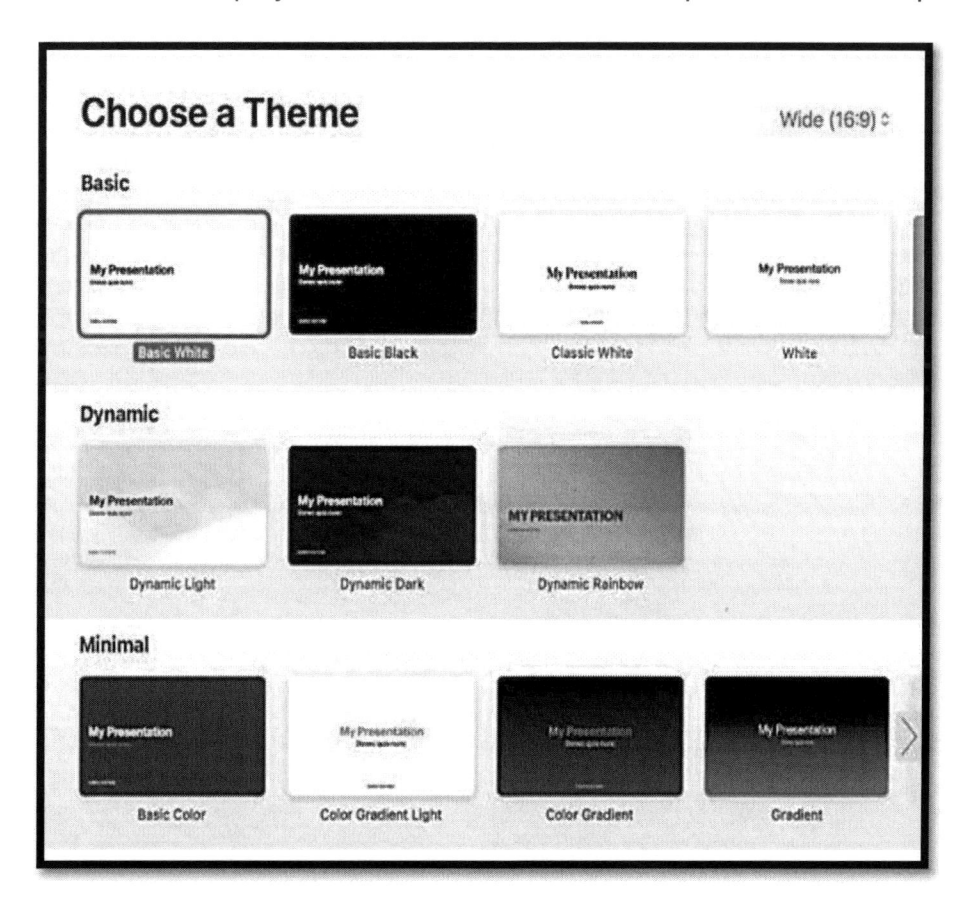

Note: If the theme chooser does not appear, proceed as follows:

You can also select **File** and then **New** to view additional **themes**.

315

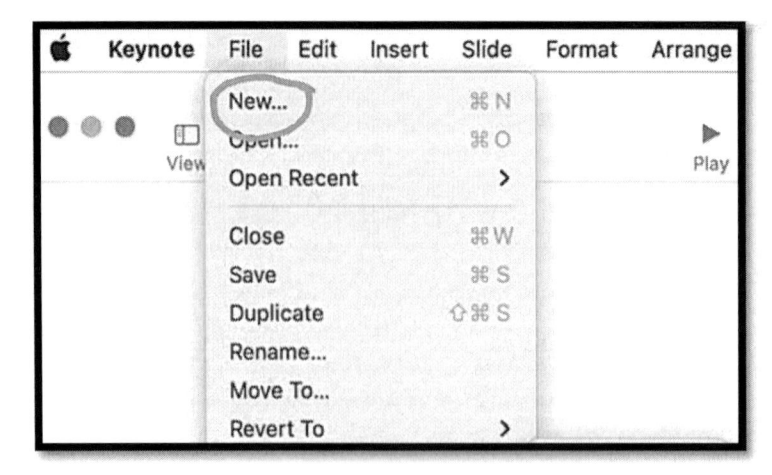

- Move the cursor over a row and then click the **left or right arrow button**.
- **Double-clicking** a theme will launch it.

Note: To change the slide layout for the first slide, click the **Slide Layout button** in the **Format sidebar** on the right, then chooses a **different layout.** Each slide layout features a unique arrangement of text and images that serves as a starting point for your presentation's content.

- To add content to the presentation, you can either:

Add a slide: Select a layout by selecting the (+) Add Slide button in the toolbar.

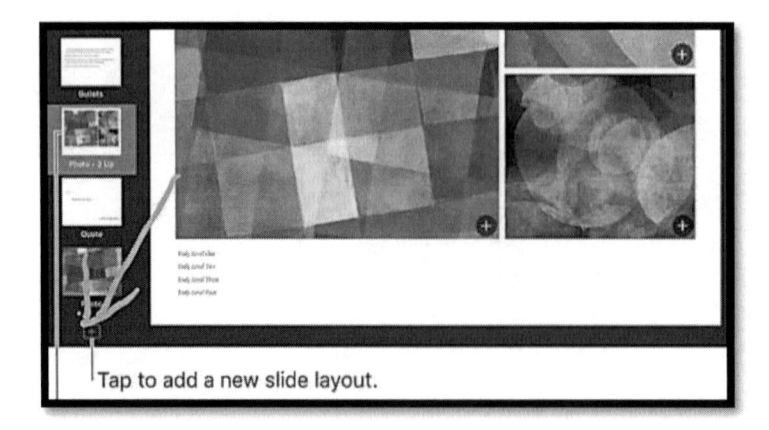

Add text: Double-click placeholder text and add your text.

316

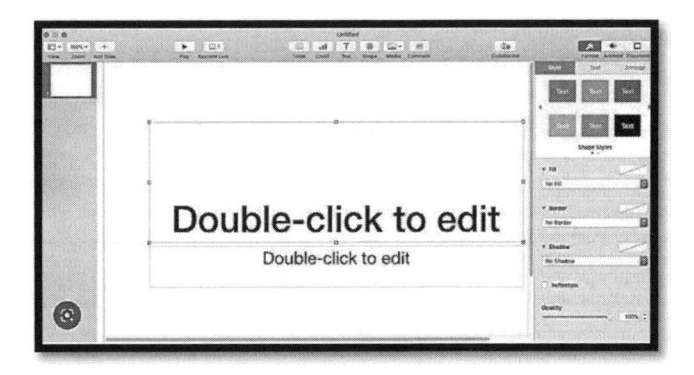

Add an image: **Drag** an image from your Mac or a website onto a placeholder image, or click the **Replace** Image button in the lower-right corner of a placeholder image, to replace it.

- Click **Save** after selecting **File > Save**, entering a name, and selecting a location.

Note: If **iCloud Drive** is configured on your Mac, Keynote will automatically save the presentation to iCloud Drive. However, you can modify the presentation's name and storage location at any time.

iCloud Drive stores your presentations, spreadsheets, PDFs, images, and other document types so that you can collaborate in real time on the same file across multiple apps. iCloud Drive is compatible with Apple's Pages, Keynote, Numbers, and GarageBand, as well as some third-party applications.

You can access iCloud Drive through the Files app on iOS and iPadOS, the Finder on macOS, File Explorer on Windows, or iCloud.com.
- To play the presentation, press the **arrow keys** to advance through the slides after clicking the **Play button >** in the toolbar.
- To conclude the presentation, press Esc (Escape).
- When you are finished working on the presentation, click the **red close button** in the upper-left corner of the window.
- Keynote automatically saves your changes, ensuring that none of your work is lost.

Choose a Default Theme for your Presentation

You can configure Keynote to always open a new presentation with a specific theme rather than the theme chooser.
- Choose **Keynote** > **Settings** from the Keynote menu at the top of your screen.
- Select "**Use theme**" from the "**For New**" Presentations controls by clicking **General** at the top of the window.
- The name that shows after "**Use theme**" is the name of the currently selected theme.
- Select a theme by clicking the **Change** Theme button and then click **Choose**.
- Click the **red close button** in the upper-left corner to close the window.

Save and name a Keynote presentation on Mac

When saving a presentation for the first time, you type in the name and choose a location to save it, such as on your desktop or in a folder.

Keynote saves your presentation automatically as you continue to work. You can rename a presentation or create a copy with a different name at any time.

Save and Name your Presentation

- Click anywhere in the presentation window to make it active.
- Select **File** and click **Save**

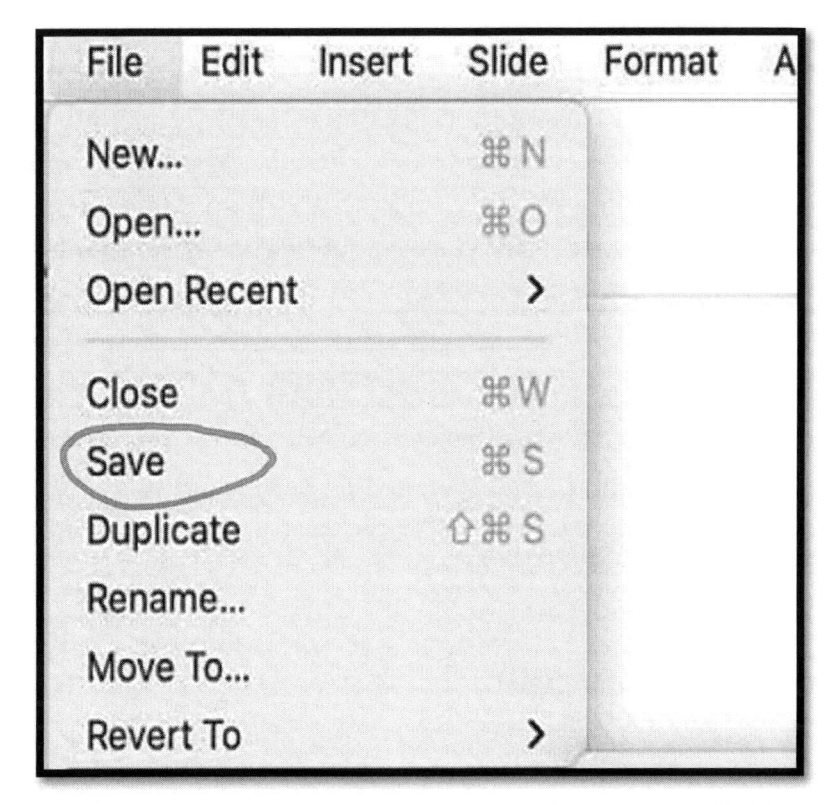

- Enter a **name** and one or more tags in the **Save As** field (optional).
- Click the **Where** menu and select a **location**.

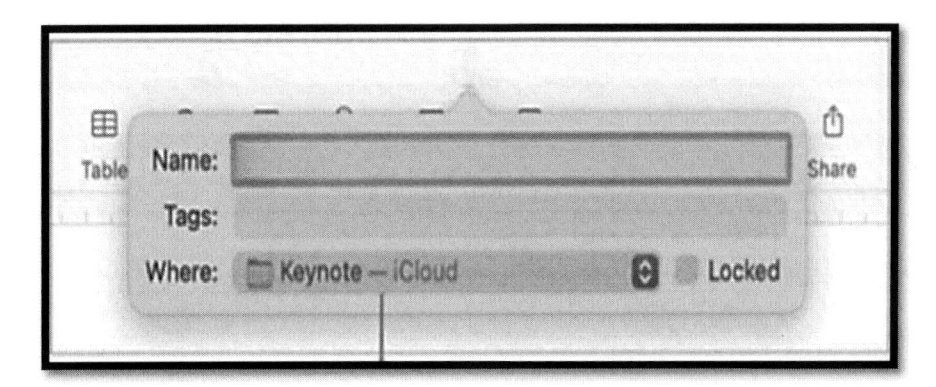

- The Save dialog for a Keynote presentation with iCloud in the Where drop-down menu.
- Select **Save**.

To Rename your Presentation

- Click the name of the presentation at the top of the Keynote window, then type a new name.
- Click outside the dialogue box to dismiss it.

Save a Copy of your Presentation

- While the presentation is open, select **File** > **Save As** while holding the Option key (from the File menu at the top of your screen).
- Enter a name for the duplicate and then press **Return**.
- The duplicate is saved in an identical location as the original. You can change the location where the copy is saved or send it to someone else.

Change where a Presentation Copy is saved

To change where a presentation copy is saved, you can choose to move it to another folder or a different location.

To do this:
- Click on the Presentation and select **File** and next press "**MoveTo**" from the menu bar.
- Select a new location by clicking the "**Where**" pop-up menu.
- Choose **other** at the bottom of the menu for additional locations, and then select a location.
- Select **Move**.

Note: To create a new folder for the presentation, click **New Folder** in the window's lower-left corner, enter a **name for the folde**r, and then click **Create**.

For iPad/iPhone

Creating a Keynote presentation is similar to that of a Mac with a very slight difference in the interface. First, you choose a **theme** or enter content using the default theme into an outline.

To create a Presentation from a Theme

- To access the theme selector, launch Keynote, tap the **Add +** button in the presentation manager, and then select Choose a **Theme**

- Tap the **category names** at the top of the screen to view different themes in the theme selector, and then tap a theme to open it.

Note: To change the slide layout for the first slide, tap the **slide** in the slide navigator on the left, tap **Format**, tap **Layout**, and then **tap a layout**.

- Utilize any of the following to create your presentation:

Add a slide: Tap the slide you want the new slide to follow in the slide navigator, then tap the **Add** Slide button and a **layout**. If the slide navigator is not visible, pinch the screen to zoom out.

Add text: Double-tap the placeholder text to replace it.

Add an image: To replace placeholder images with your own, click the **Replace** Image button.

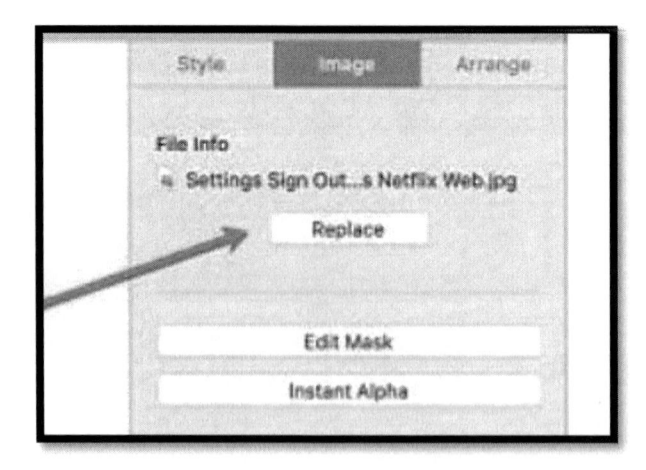

- To begin the presentation, tap the **Play** button, then tap a slide to move to the next, and so on.
- To conclude the presentation, pinch anywhere on the screen to close it.

Play a Keynote presentation on iPhone

- Tap to select the desired slide in the slide navigator, and then tap the **Play** button.
- To proceed with the presentation, perform one of the following:
- **Go to the following slide: Click the slide.**
- **Return one slide or reset the slide's builds: Select right.**
- **To advance to a different slide: Tap the screen's left edge** to display the slide navigator, and then tap the desired slide.
- To view all slides, you may need to swipe **up or down.**
- To hide the slide navigator, tap **anywhere** on the slide.
- Touch and hold anywhere on the screen to **reveal the toolbar,** then tap a button to display the slide navigator, live video sources, more multipresent slideshow, or drawing and laser pointer controls.
- To dismiss the toolbar, tap away from it.
- To stop a presentation from playing, pinch anywhere on the screen.

Add and Delete a Slide

While creating your Presentation, there may be a need to add more slides or maybe delete and remove some slides. Let's dive into how to add and remove a slide. A presentation slide can be added in several different ways.

You have the option to create a new slide, duplicate an existing one, or import slides from another presentation.

For iPhone/iPad

To Add a Slide

You can create a new slide in both the slide and light table views:
- Select a slide format by tapping it and then tapping the **Add** Slide button.
- When you get to the bottom of a slide and want to add another one, just hit Return twice.

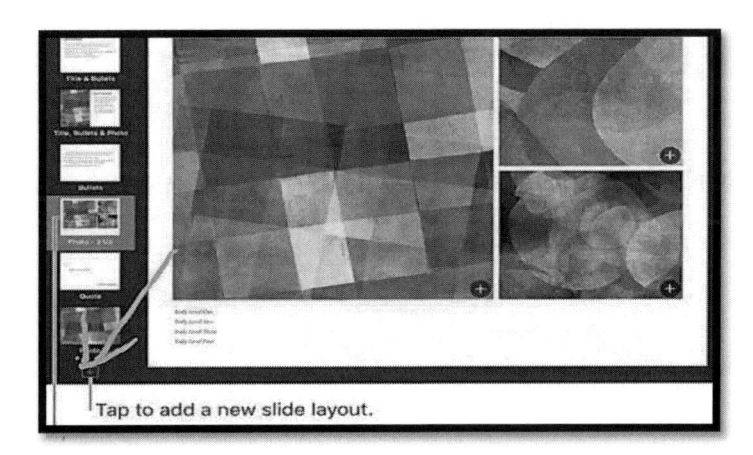

To Duplicate a Slide

When in **slide** view, tap the slide navigator to select it, tap it again to select it, and then tap **Duplicate**.

To duplicate multiple slides at once while in slide view, tap and hold one slide in the slide navigator, tap and hold any additional slides you'd like to duplicate, and then release all slides except the first.

To make a copy of a slide while in light table mode, tap the slide you want to copy, and then tap the Duplicate button.

Light table duplication of multiple slides: You can duplicate slides by tapping Select at the bottom of the screen, selecting them, then tap Duplicate.

Insert a Slide from another Slide

- To view the desired slide, launch the presentation.
- Once you're in slide view, you can tap the slide navigator to choose a specific slide to view.
- To zoom out of a slide and reveal the navigation controls, pinch the screen.
- Repeatedly tapping the slide and then selecting "Copy" will copy the slide.
- Select "Back" from the menu bar.
- Select the presentation into which you wish to insert the slide by tapping on it in the presentation manager.
- With slideshow mode active, tapping anywhere on the slide navigator is followed by a second tap.
- Select the **Paste** option.

Delete a Slide

To delete a slide while in slide view, tap the slide in the slide navigator, tap it again, and then tap the **Delete** button.

To cancel multiple slides at once while viewing them: Tap one slide, touch and hold it while tapping others with a different finger, then release all

324

fingers. Light table view slide deletion: Select the slide you want to delete by tapping it, and then tap the **Delete** button.

Multiple slides can be removed at once in the outline view: The slides you want to remove can be marked by tapping the checkboxes on them, then the Delete button, and finally the done button at the bottom of the screen.

Slide deletion while viewing an outline: To delete a slide, select it by tapping the top row, dragging its handle, and then selecting Delete. Removing multiple slides at once while in outline mode: To remove a slide from the text outline, tap the row at the top of the slide's thumbnail image and then tap the **drag handle**. Select the slides you want to remove by dragging their white resizing handles, and then hit the **Delete button.**

Drag Handle:

Delete Button:

For Mac

To Add a Slide

Select an action from the list below:

To add a new slide, open the **toolbar** and click the **Add Slide button**. When you create a new slide, it will be added beneath the currently active slide in the slide navigator.

To use the desired layout, select it in the slide navigator and hit Return. The new slide will show up under the selected one.

The slide can be rearranged in the sidebar by dragging it there.

Note: Slides can be customized with text, shapes, tables, charts, photos, and videos after they've been added.

Duplicate a Slide

Once you've made edits to the layout and content of a slide, you can make a copy of it again by selecting it and clicking the "**Duplicate**" button.

To duplicate a slide, select it (or select multiple slides at once) in the slide navigator and press **Command-D.**

The duplicate slides follow the selected slides in the presentation.

Note: Slides that you've copied can be moved to a different presentation by dragging them.

Insert a Slide into another Slide

A slide or multiple slides can be selected in one presentation's slide navigator and dragged to the other presentation's slide navigator.

Delete a Slide

Select the slides you want to delete by clicking on them in the slide navigator, and then hitting the **Delete** key on your keyboard.

Reorder Slides

You can reposition the slide in the presentation outline, light table view, or the slide navigator.

Click the first slide you want to move, then hold down the **Command** key and click the additional slides you want to move.

Drag the slide to a new location in the slide navigator, presentation outline, or in a light table view.

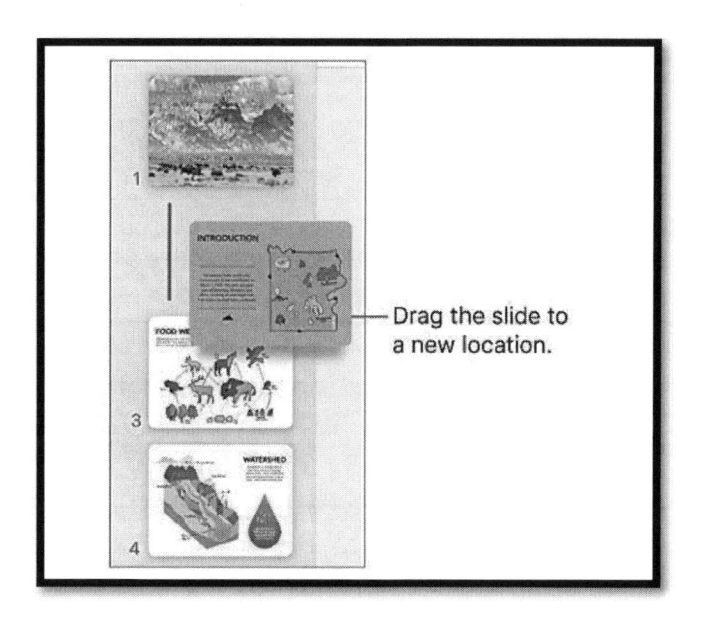

Skip a Slide

You can easily skip a slide in your presentation if you don't want it to appear. If you have two versions of a slide but only want to present one of them, skipping is a useful tool. Slides you have already skipped can be selected and edited in the same way as any other slide. Slides that have been skipped can be seen as grayed-out thumbnails in light table view or as horizontal bars in the slide navigator.

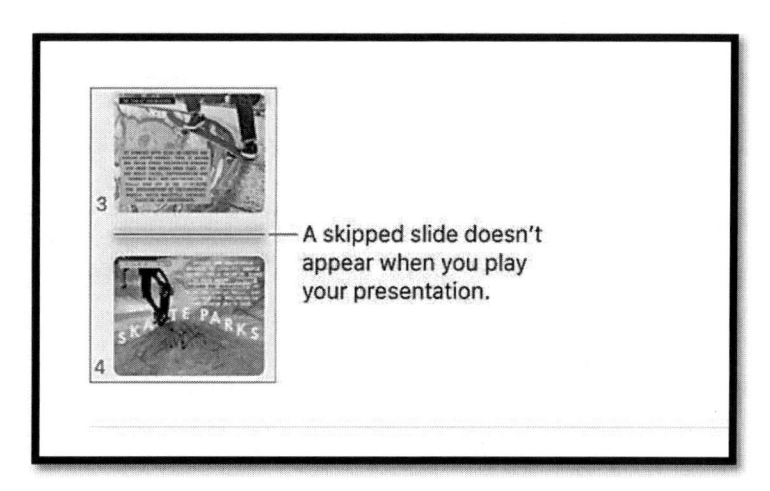

Note:

Keep in mind that the presentation will skip the entire collapsed group if the first slide in the group is skipped.

A previously skipped slide can be "unskipped" if the presenter decides they want to show it.

Slides that have been skipped are represented by a horizontal line in the slide navigator.

Select one or more slides in the slide navigator and go to **Slide > Skip Slide** to quickly advance through your presentation from the Slide menu at the top of your screen. In addition, you can use Control-clicking a slide in the slide navigator and selecting Skip Slide to skip a slide.

To return to a previously skipped slide, select it (or them) in the slide navigator and then go to **Slide > Unskip Slide** from the Slide menu at the top of your screen. In addition, you can use the Control key to right-click a slide in the slide navigator and select Unskip Slide.

Group and Ungroup Slides

For iPhone/iPad

Slides can be more efficiently organized and presented if they are grouped. Slides can be moved collectively in presentations, and you can expand or collapse groups to see the structure of your slides more clearly. To create a group slide, select the slides and indent them below another slide in the slide navigator. If you choose to skip a collapsed group's first slide, the presentation will skip over the entire group.

Group Slides

To do this, first, open your presentation

Select **Slide** View from the menu that appears after you tap the **three** dots.

Select **Slide View > Done**.

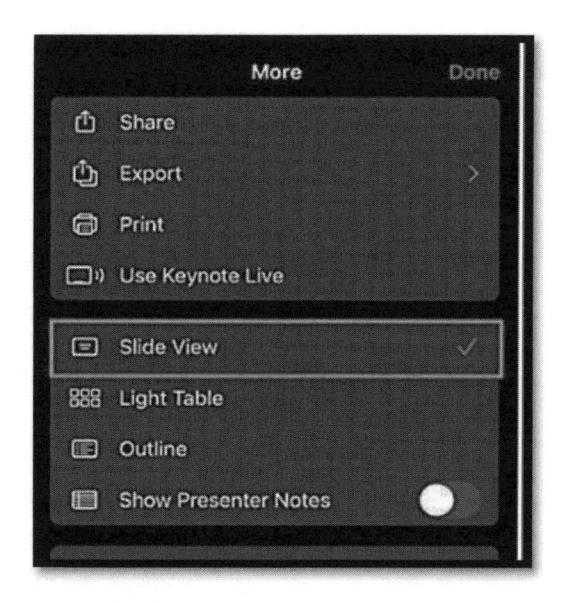

Select and hold on a slide you want to group below the slide above.

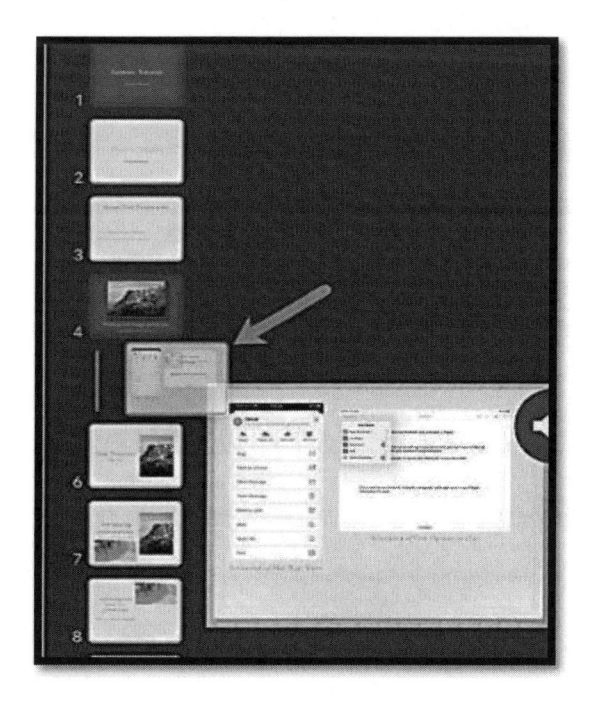

Slowly move the slide to the right until the line appears on the left, and then let go.

You can continue to group slides in this fashion, and the arrow on the parent slide will let you collapse or expand the group as needed.

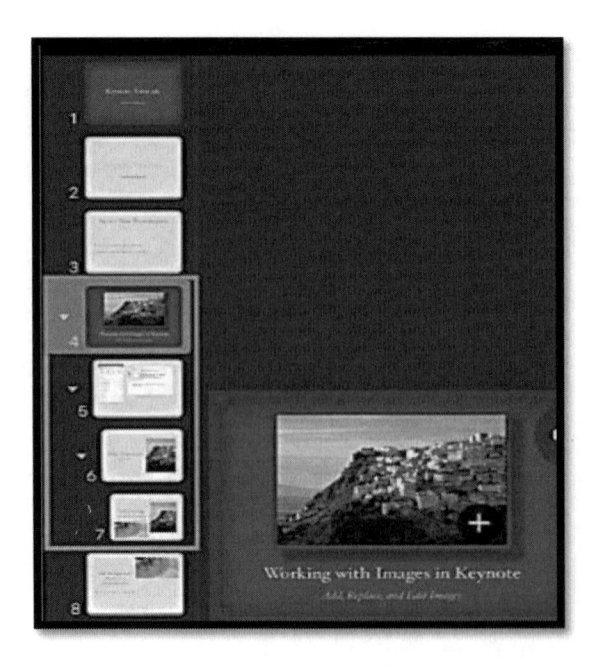

Ungroup Slides

To undo the indentation, tap a slide or multiple slides in the slide navigator and drag them to the left.

Reorder Slides

To reorder slides while in slide view, touch and hold a slide in the slide navigator until it appears to lift, and then drag it to the desired location.

Touch and hold a slide in the slide navigator, then tap additional slides to select them all.

Drag a slide to a new position by touching and holding it in light table view until it appears to lift.

To reposition a slide in outline view, touch and hold the drag handle until the slide appears to lift, and then drag it to a new location.

When the slides appear to rise when you touch and hold the drag handle, you can move them to a new location by dragging them.

Skip or Un-skip a Slide in Keynote

- You can easily skip a slide in your presentation if you don't want it to appear.
- To skip or un-skip a slide in the slide navigator, tap the slide you want to skip or un-skip and tap it again.
- To zoom out of a slide and reveal the navigation controls, pinch the screen.
- To see Skip Slide or Un-skip Slide, you might have to rotate your iPhone or tap the Show More Items button.
- To illustrate, on a light table: To skip or un skip a slide, tap the corresponding button at the bottom of the screen after tapping on a slide or slides to select them.
- To skip or un-skip a slide while in outline view, tap the row at the top of the text outline, tap the drag handle, and then tap Skip Slide or Un-skip Slide.
- Keep in mind that the presentation will skip the entire collapsed group if the first slide in the group is skipped.
- Once a slide has been skipped, a horizontal line appears in the slide navigator.

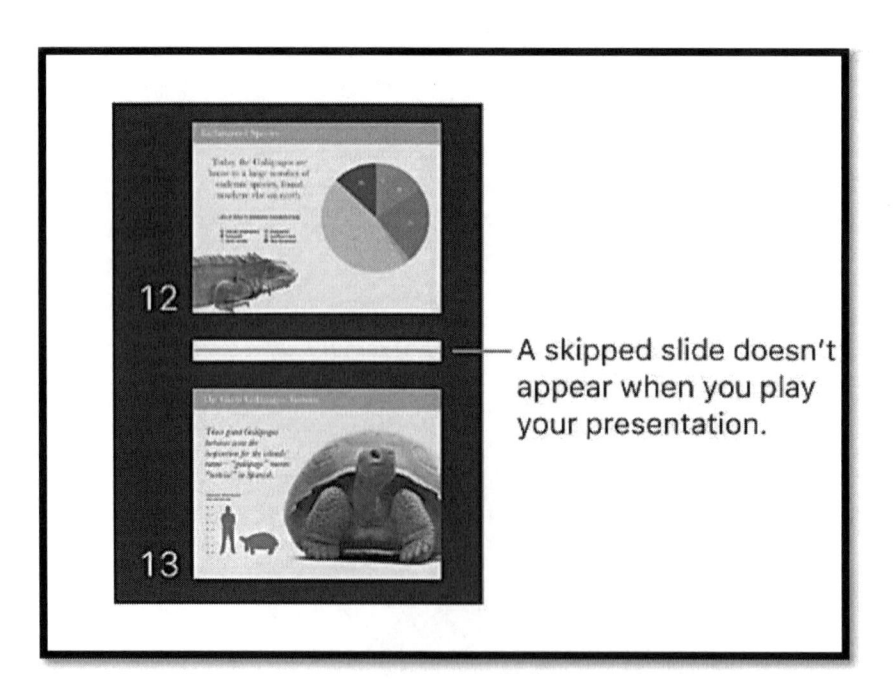

A skipped slide doesn't appear when you play your presentation.

For Mac

The Keynote window's left side, in navigator view, displays thumbnails of the slides that make up your presentation; you can organize these slides into groups using the slide navigator. Clicking the slide navigator button in the presenter display will open or close the slide navigator when playing your slideshow in a window. You can navigate between slides by clicking their thumbnails, rearranging them with the drag-and-drop feature, or using the Down Arrow and Up Arrow keys on your keyboard, respectively.

The slide navigator will show the first five slides in a vertical sequence, with the option to scroll down to see the rest of the slideshow. Slides can be navigated by indenting them one level below the current slide and clicking the View menu button on the toolbar, then selecting Navigator. Slides can be more efficiently organized and presented if they are grouped. Slides can be moved collectively in presentations, and you can expand or collapse groups to see the structure of your slides more clearly. If you choose to skip a collapsed group's first slide, the presentation will skip over the entire group.

Group Slides

- Select one or more slides in the slide navigator and click the button to move them to the bottom of the presentation.
- Keep swiping the slides to the right until you see a line appear on the left.
- Up to six levels of indentation are allowed within individual slides, but only one level of indentation is allowed between slides.

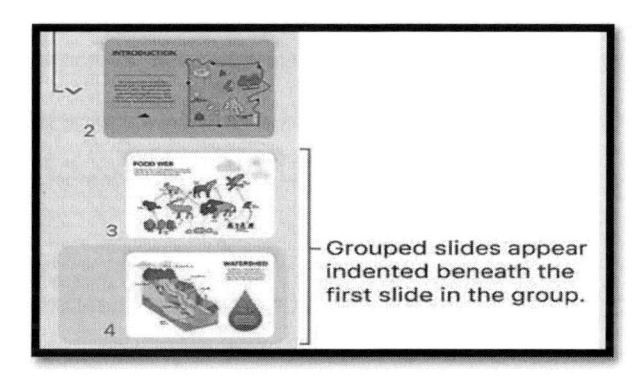

Grouped slides appear indented beneath the first slide in the group.

Ungrouped Slides

To remove the indentation, click and drag a slide or multiple slides in the slide navigator to the left.

Undo/Redo

To undo is to cancel or reverse the effects or results of something and the Redo is to do it over again.

To Undo or Redo changes in Keynote on iPad/iPhone

To Undo an Action: Simply click the **undo** button. Repeated tapping will undo the last set of changes. Swiping three fingers to the left will also undo the current operation.

Redo the previous step: If you accidentally tapped Redo instead of Undo, just press and hold the Undo button. Repeat these procedures numerous times to undo everything you've done recently. Alternatively, you can undo a move by swiping three fingers to the right.

Note: The Undo button

Undo or Redo Changes in Keynote on Mac

Undo the last action:

- Click on **Edit** >and select **Undo** (from the Edit menu at the top of your screen), or click **Command-Z** on your keyboard.

Redo the Previous or Last action:

- Select **Edit** > **Redo** from the menu bar, or use the keyboard shortcut of **Shift-Command.**

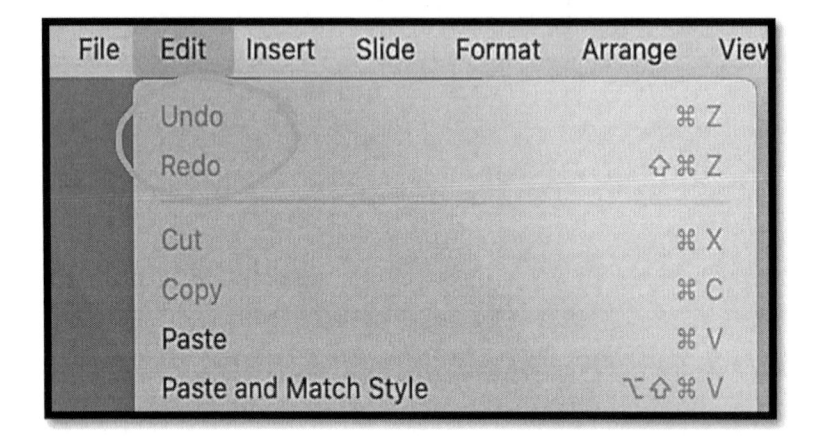

Hyperlinks

For Mac

Shapes, lines, images, image galleries, movies, drawings, text boxes, equations, groups of objects, and animated drawings are all examples of the types of things that can be turned into links. Quickly advances to the next slide Displays a webpage or email when clicked. Makes a telephone call you can make changes to the link text or destination, or remove the links entirely, to make the text act like regular text again.

334

Inserting a Link

- Control-click whatever you want to a link (text, object, etc) Click on **Add Link** and select the location you want the link to go to (Slide, Webpage, Email, or Phone Number).

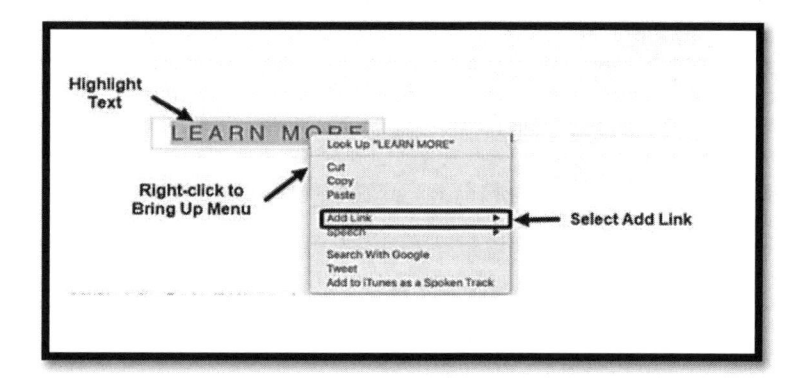

- Location information is required.

Website: Launches a specified website in a user's default web browser. Copy and paste the web address (URL) into the Link field. When creating a text link, use the Display field to type the exact words you want visitors to see. When displaying a website, you may only want to display the domain name.

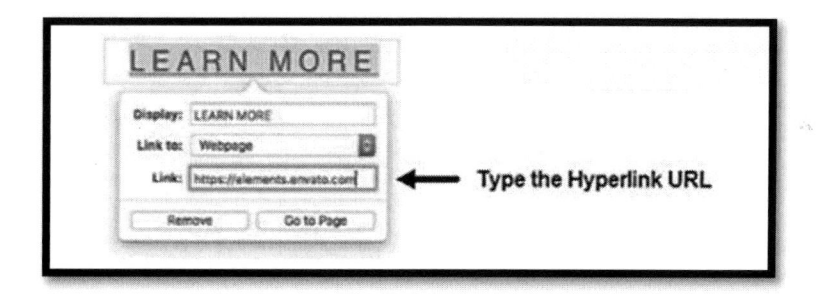

Email: To send an email, simply enter the recipient's address in the "**To field**" and hit the Enter key. To customize the text that viewers see when clicking on a text link, edit the Display field. As an illustration, you could just display the recipient's name instead of their full email address. Fill out the Subject field with relevant information or leave it blank.

Phone Number: Put your phone number in the "Number" box. Type your desired visible text into the Display field. You may, for instance, wish to identify the owner of a given phone number.

- **Stop the presentation:** Completes the slideshow.
- Click the **Go to Slide,** Open Link, Compose Email, or Call buttons to preview the link's target; once you're satisfied, click the slide to dismiss the link editor.
- A link button on a shape.

A link button indicates the object has a link.

To access the linked content, either clicks the linked text, the link button on the linked object, or the linked cell in the table.

Edit or Remove a Link

- Click the linked text or the link button on the linked object, or double-click a link in a table cell.
- You can edit the link or delete it in the link editor.
- The text of the removed link remains intact, but the link's formatting disappears and the link itself becomes inactive.
- When you're done, the link editor can be closed by clicking the slide.

On iPhone/iPad

To add a Link

- You can create a link by tapping an object, text box, or the selected text and then tapping the **Link button.**
- Select a link by tapping the **Link To button** (Slide, Webpage, Email, or Phone Number).

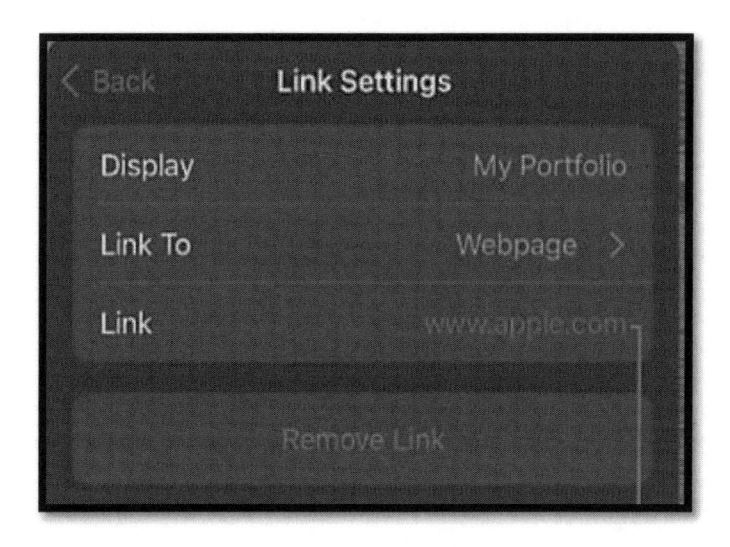

Display, Link To (when a webpage is selected), an**d Link** make up the Link **Settings tab**. There's a Delete Link option near the foot of the page.

- Location information is required.

This slideshow transitions to the next available slide. Select a slide from the drop-down menu, or use the **Link to** Slide button to select a specific slide. **The different locations are:**

Website: Launches a specified website in a user's default web browser. Copy and paste the web address (URL) into the Link field. To customize the text that viewers see when clicking on a text link, edit the Display field. When displaying a website, you may only want to display the domain name.

Email: To send an email, simply enter the recipient's address in the "**To field"** and hit the Enter key. To customize the text that viewers see when clicking on a text link, edit the Display field. As an illustration, you could just display the recipient's name instead of their full email address. Fill out the Subject field with relevant information or leave it blank.

Phone Number: Put your phone number in the "Number" box. Type your desired visible text into the Display field, for example, the name of the owner of the phone number.
- Stop the presentation when you're done.

- You can double-check where you're going by tapping Back and then the appropriate button for Going to Presentation, Opening Link, Creating Email, or Making a Phone Call.

Note: The shape's button functions as a link.

Edit or Remove Link

- Select the link by touching it or the text that contains the link.
- When a link is located in a table cell, tapping the cell itself is required before tapping the link button.
- Choose Link Settings from the editor's menu.
- Modify the text or select the **Remove Link** option.
- The text of the removed link remains intact, but the link's formatting disappears and the link itself becomes inactive.
- The slide can be closed by tapping it when you're done with Link Settings.

Copy and Paste Text into Keynote

On Mac

Start by selecting the text you want to copy

Note: If the text you want to select is in a table cell, you'll need to click the cell first, and then select the text. If it's a word, double-click on it, and if it's a paragraph, triple-click on the paragraph.

After selecting, click **Edit>Copy** or press the **Command + C** keyboard shortcut.

File	Edit	Insert	Slide	Format	Arrange	View
	Undo				⌘ Z	
	Redo				⇧⌘ Z	
	Cut				⌘ X	
	Copy				⌘ C	
	Paste				⌘ V	
	Paste and Match Style				⌥⇧⌘ V	

To Cut: To cut a text, you remove the test from its original location and put it in another location. To do this:

Select the text

Select **Edit** > **Cut** to remove the text from its original location.

To Paste: **This is to insert the copied text at the location where you want it to be. To do this:**

Select the location where you want to insert the text and go to **Edit** > **Paste** or use **Command-V**.

Note: You can click **Paste and Match style** which helps to preserve the formatting of the original text. You can also copy and paste objects, shapes, boxes, etc.,

Copy and Paste a Text Style

It is possible to just copy the style of the selected text and apply that style to other text. Rather than copying the actual words, you can just copy the formatting and paste it wherever you like.

To do this:

Select the text with the style or formatting you want to copy.

Place the Insertion point (a blinking vertical line or I-beam in the text that denotes the location of the next character you type) in the text whose format you wish to copy.

Next, select **Format** > **Copy Style** from the Format menu at the top of your screen).

Choose **Format** > **Paste Style** after selecting or inserting the text to which you want to apply the style.

The current paragraph or character style is overwritten if the insertion point is placed inside a paragraph or if you select an entire paragraph, text box, or shape.

Note: If you place the insertion point in a paragraph or you select full paragraphs, text boxes, or shapes, existing paragraph or character styles are replaced with what you paste.

Copy, Cut, and Paste Text in Keynote for iCloud

Copying and pasting text is a quick way to reuse previously typed material. To copy or cut text on iCloud:

Click on the text you want to copy.

To copy press Command-C, and to **cut it, press Command-X** on a Mac

To **copy pres**s **Control-C** and or cut **press Control-X** on a Windows computer

To Paste:

Insert the insertion point (or select some text) at the location where you want the pasted text to appear, and then do one of the following:

Click **Command-V** on a Mac and **Control -V** key on a window computer.

Find and Replace Text

You can replace search results automatically with new content that you specify, and it works for words, phrases, numbers, and characters. Presentation notes and content on slides that were previously viewed are also indexed in a search.

On Mac

Search for Specific Text

Select **Find & Replace** by clicking the **View menu** button in the toolbar

In the **Search Field,** enter the word or phrase you want to find.

Select Whole Words or Match Case from the Find and Replace Options drop-down menu to search for only exact matches of the case you specify or to limit the search to the exact phrases you typed.

Matches will appear as you enter text.

To find words that match the capitalization you specify, or to restrict search results to the whole words you entered, click the Find and Replace Options menu button, then choose Whole Words or Match Case.

Click the arrow buttons to find the next or previous match.

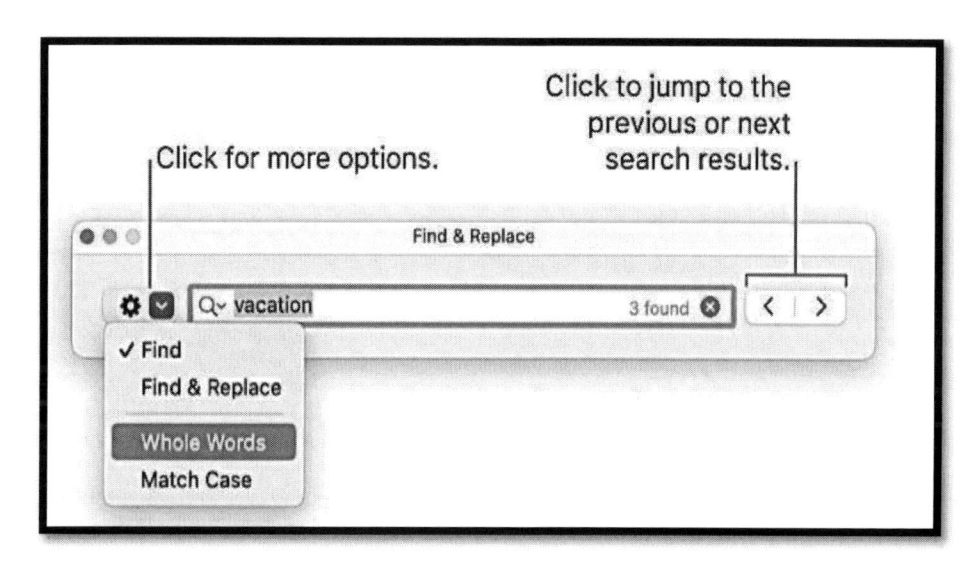

Replace Found Text

Click the **View menu button** in the toolbar, and then choose **Show Find & Replace**.

Click the **Find and Replace Options** menu button in the Find & Replace window

Choose **Find & Replace.**

Note: You can also select other options, such as Whole Words and Match Case, to refine your search.

Enter a word or phrase in the first field.

As you type the entered text, matches words appear.

Type in the replacement word in the second field.

341

If you leave the Replace field blank, all instances of the found text are deleted when you replace the found text.

The Find and Replace dialog box highlights the Expand all button.

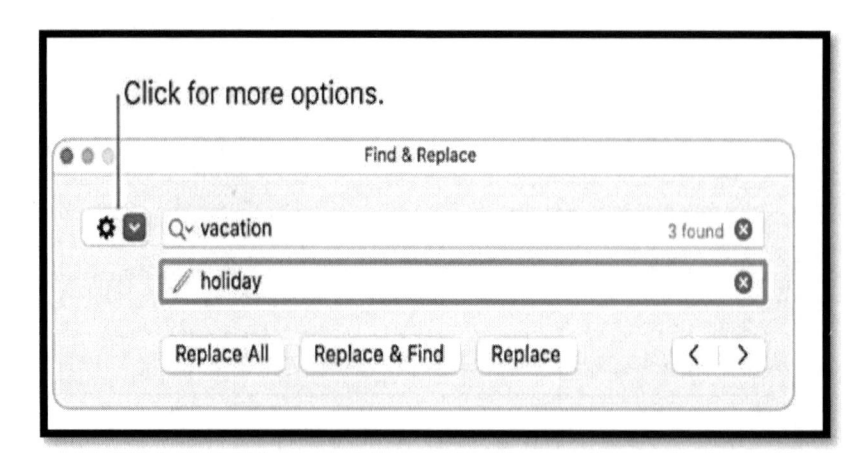

You can go over the text matches and make adjustments using the buttons at the bottom of the Find & Replace window.

With Replace All, the matched text is completely swapped out for the replacement text.

Selecting Replace & Find instead of just Find will replace the current match and continue searching for the next one.

Replace: Substitutes the specified text for the selected match without proceeding to the next possible match.

Use the back or forward arrow to go back one match or forward one match, respectively, without altering the results.

Find and Replace Text in Keynote for iCloud

You can search for your presentation for a specific phrase or word, and then choose whether or not to replace it with new text. To reveal the Find and Replace field, select **View** and click **Find & Replace** from the menu bar.

Note: Be aware that you can use the Find button in the toolbar even if the presentation you're viewing is set to View Only. It's possible to look for specific words or phrases, but you can't change them.

To search for something specific, type it into the **Find** field.

Simply select a setting from the drop-down menu next to the search bar to narrow your results:

Use "**Match Case**" to locate phrases that use the same case as the text you've entered.

This option "**Whole**" limits search results to only those that contain whole words.

When you use **Find and Replace,** any occurrences of a search term are replaced with whatever you type into the Replace field.

Use the navigational arrows to move to the next or previous matching text.

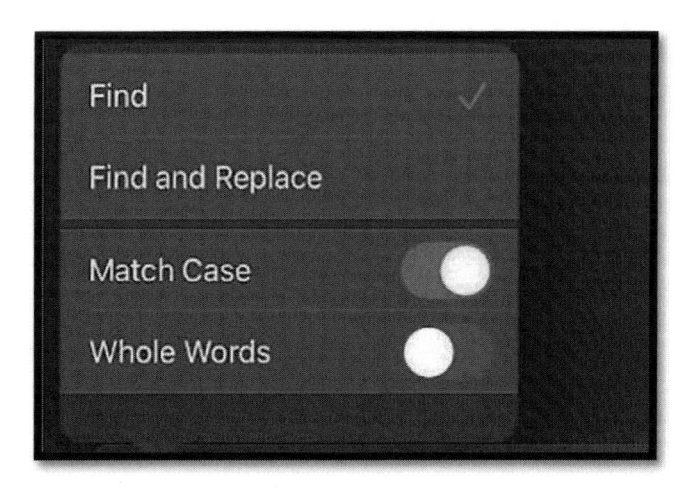

Note: Use one of the following methods, depending on what you want to alter when you come across the text:

Replace: To replace the selected text

Leave the Replace field empty to have the selected text **deleted**.

Replace the highlighted words with new ones: Simply replace the existing text with the new one and click **Replace**.

After you're done, you can either click the done button or hit the Esc (Escape) key on your keyboard.

For iPhone and iPad

Finding and Replacing Text

Go to the toolbar's Tools menu, and then tap **Find**

The Find window will open as a popover at the screen's bottom.

Simply enter the text you're looking for and hit the **Return** key to locate it.

 Keynote immediately locates the first occurrence of the text.

To **replace** the found text, open the Find popover's Settings

Select **Find & Replace**, and then enter the new text in the Replace field

To edit the text, press the **Replace** button.

Type your search terms into the left field and your replacement into the right.

Note: Holding down the Replace button gives you a Replace All popover, which makes it easy to change text throughout your presentation.

To Replace Text From the Dictionary:

- Pick a slide with a word on it.
- The option to **edit** appears in a pop-up.
- To see further, click More.
- More popover appears.
- Select the Replace option.
- Keynote's built-in dictionary provides suggestions that pop up in a floating window.
- If you select some text and then tap on a suggestion, the text will be replaced with that suggestion.

LockUp a Text

On Mac

A presentation can be locked to prevent unauthorized changes, such as those made when copying, deleting, or renaming the file. When you lock something, no one else can alter it in any way, either physically or digitally. When you lock a text box, for instance, you won't be able to modify its dimensions or the text it contains.

To Lock or Unlock a Presentation

To lock or unlock a presentation, click the name of the presentation in the presentation window and then click the **Locked** checkbox.

Alert that can be used to either secure or unlock a presentation.

Click outside the window to close it.

Lock up for iCloud

Pick some stuff to lock or unlock.

Click Arrange at the top of the **Format** sidebar on the right, then click **Lock or Unlock.**

Conclusion

If you have had a presentation slide before, you can now get started. Any number of hyperlinks can be included in a Keynote presentation. Before sending out your slideshow, make sure every link works by testing them.

CHAPTER THREE
MANAGING DOCUMENT WITH KEYNOTE

Managing your documents on keynote is key in every of your presentation. You must learn how to save your work, sync your presentation across various devices, share or export your document, edit your presentation while offline, collaborate, how invite people to edit your document, how to print, among others, all these will be discussed in this chapter,

Saving a Document

On Mac

After creating your presentation, click on the **save** button on the file menu.

As you work continuously on that presentation on Keynote, your presentation will be saved automatically and given a name by default.

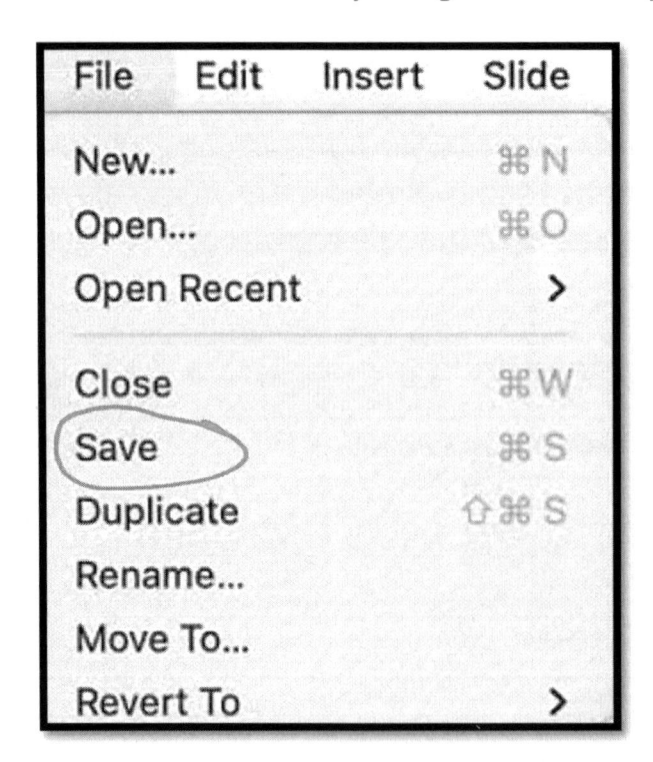

Note: You can give the presentation a new name at any time, or make a copy of it.

Rename a Document or Presentation

A presentation can be renamed. To do this:

- First, **open** the document
- Select "**Rename**" from the toolbar's Actions Menu.

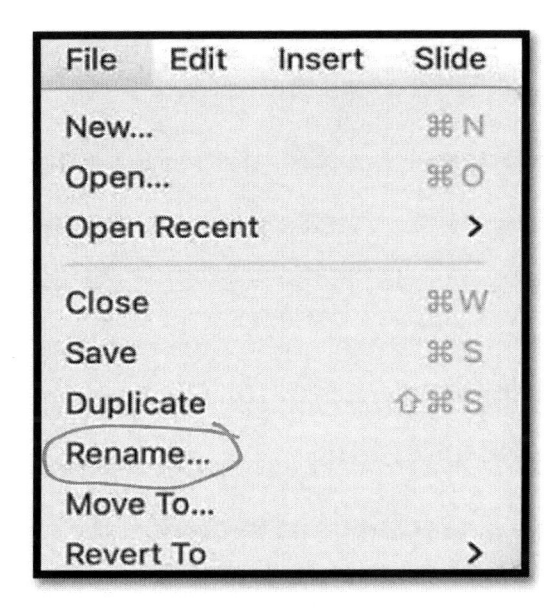

Then type your preferred name to save the document

Click **Done**

There is an **x** button next to the name box that can be used to swiftly remove the current name if you wish to delete it,

For iPad/iPhone

Save a presentation

When you create a new presentation on your iPad/iPhone, it is given a generic name like "**Untitled 1,**" and it is saved in the default folder.

To rename it;

Select "**File**" > "**Save As**" while holding down the Option key (from the File menu at the top of your screen).

The Save As field requires a file name, type in your preferred title for that presentation

Input a tag or multiple tags (optional).

To specify a location to store the presentation, click the **Where** drop-down menu.

And choose a location to save it

Lastly, click **Save**

Alternatively, click the presentation name at the top of the Keynote window, then type a new name.

You can also open the presentation, choose **File** > **Rename** (from the File menu at the top of your screen), then enter the new name and click **save**

Duplicate a Presentation

Select **Duplicate** under the **File** menu.

When you click on the tab labeled "**New Presentation**," a blank presentation with the selected title will open.

Input a **new** name

To Revert a Previous Presentation

Bringing a presentation back to a previous version.

Select **File** > **Revert to** (found under the File menu) and then make a selection: **Last Viewed** or **All Versions Browsed.**

Last Opened: If you close a presentation after making edits, those edits will be lost until you reopen it.

Browse All Versions: Once you've selected Browse All Versions, you can navigate between different iterations by clicking the corresponding checkboxes along the timeline.

When you locate the desired version, you can:

Click **Restore,** to bring back your presentation to this version.

Press the Option key, and then select "**Restore a Copy**" to use this version as a template for a new presentation.

Simply clicking the "**Done**" button will save your current presentation without allowing you to make any changes.

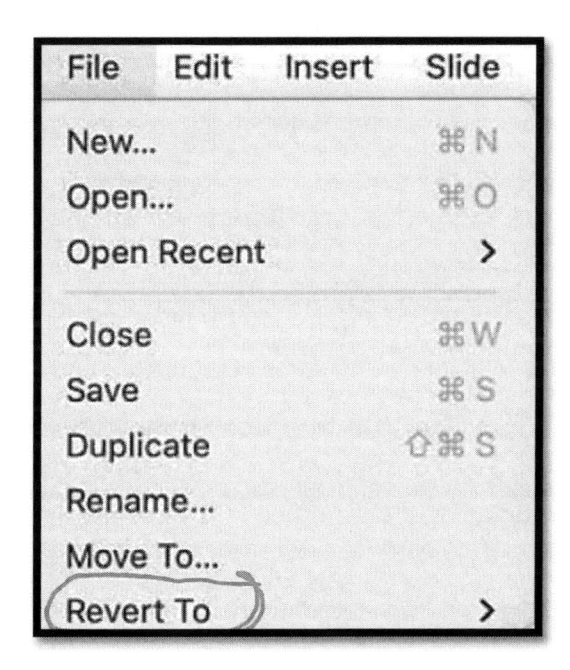

Locate a Presentation

A presentation can be difficult to find if you can't remember where you saved it.

To find your Presentation on Mac or iCloud:

- If you have recently opened the file: The presentation can be accessed by opening Keynote and selecting **File** > **Open Recent** from the File menu at the top of the screen. Your ten most recently viewed presentations are listed in Keynote.

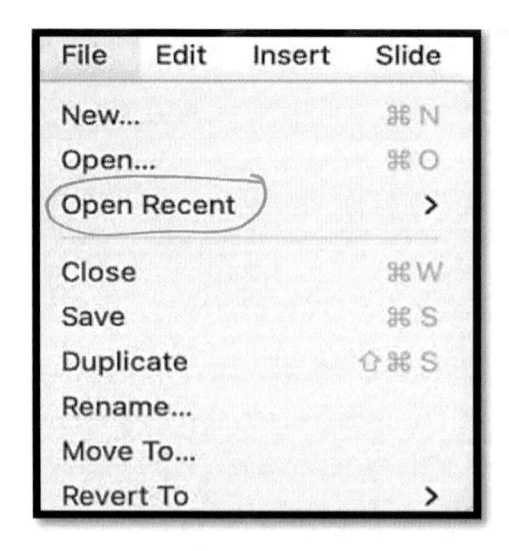

If you can remember the title of your presentation, then click **File > Open** and then type in the title or any part you can remember. All presentation that matches it will pop up. As soon as you find the presentation, double-click it to open it.

If you can't remember the title but know you want to look through email attachments or a presentation: To search for a specific word or phrase within a presentation's title or body, use the "**Spotlight**" icon (a magnifying glass) in the menu bar at the top right of your screen. When you find any presentation that matches it in the search results, click on it to see a preview and double-click on the presentation file to view it.

Save a Presentation in another Format

A presentation can be saved in a different file format. With Keynote, your presentations can be exported to PDF, Microsoft PowerPoint, QuickTime, HTML, and Images, among other formats.

Note: The exported version is completely independent of the original.

To export your presentation:

Select **File** > **Export To** > from the main menu.

Note that the export options vary by file format, so you'll need to specify which one you're using (PDF, PowerPoint, QuickTime, HTML, Image, Keynote 09

Click **next** and type in a name for your presentation

Whenever you save a presentation, the. pptx extension (file extension) will be added to the end of the name.

Select a destination folder from the **Where** drop-down, then click **Export** to save the presentation.

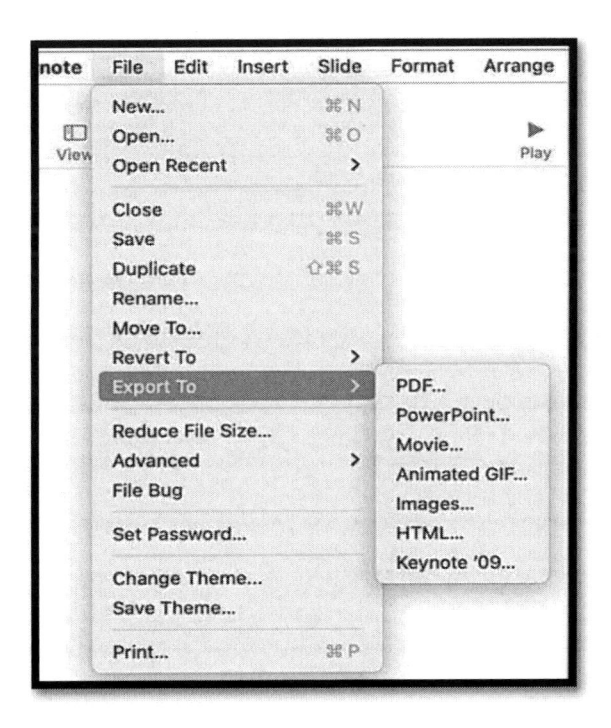

Save a Presentation in Package or Single-File Format

Your presentation will be saved as a single file in Keynote. However, consider using a package file to store your presentation if it is large or contains many media files. A package files in Keynote can be converted also into a single file, because it's difficult to send or attach a package file to some websites or email accounts.

To change your file type:

Select **File** > **Advanced** > **Change file type**

Then select Package from the File menu (or Single File).

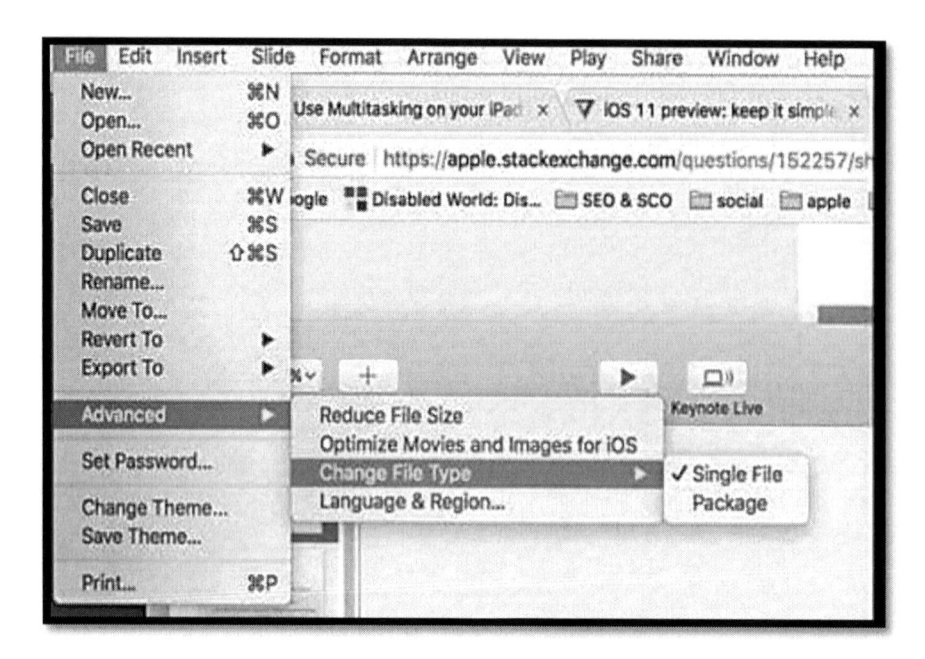

Using iCloud to Sync Documents

Your presentations are synced and kept up-to-date on **iCloud**, accessible from any iOS device, the web, or your computer. Whatever device you're currently using to make changes is irrelevant; you'll always have access to the most recent versions. If you want to easily collaborate on and update your presentations, you need to use iCloud Drive.

Keynote presentations made on your Mac, iPhone, and iPad will be synchronized with Keynote for iCloud if you have iCloud set up on those devices. So, whether you're using Keynote on a Mac, iPhone, iPad, or the web to create or edit a presentation, you'll always be working with the most up-to-date version.

To Use iCloud with Keynote

Select **iCloud** from the System Preferences menu.

Create a new Apple ID and sign in with it, or sign in with your existing Apple ID. A new menu will appear; from there, select **iCloud Drive** and click **Options**. Choose Keynote and then click the button labeled "**Done**."

Set up iCloud on your iPhone, iPad, or iPod touch

Download and install iCloud on your iPhone, iPad, or iPod touch.

In the **Setting** on your iPhone, iPad, or iPod touch, tap your **name**.

Note: If [your name] isn't there, select "Sign in to your [device], then enter your Apple ID (Apple ID) and password.

Select iCloud, and then activate the desired app or function you want to use.

To view additional options, select **Show All.**

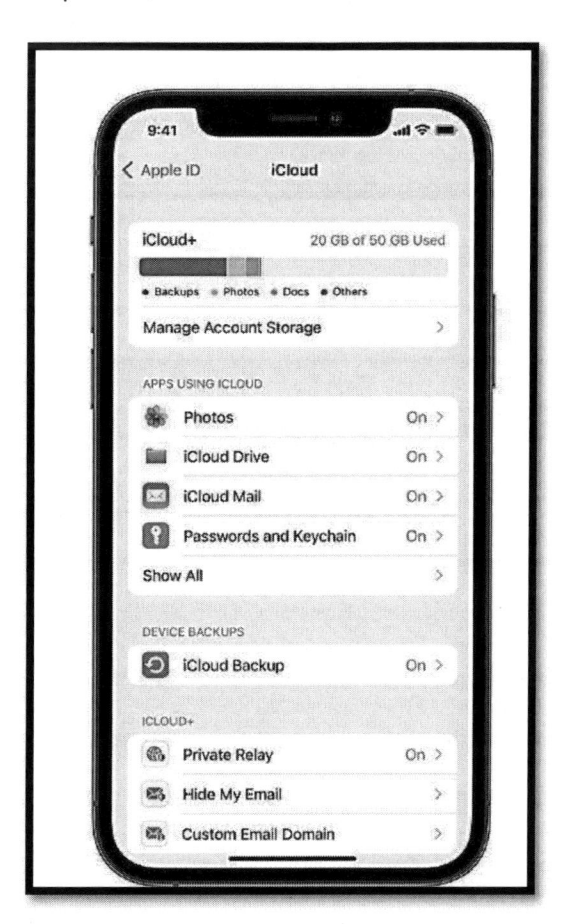

Set up iCloud on Mac

You can access iCloud by selecting **Apple** > **System Settings**, then clicking [**your nam**e] at the top of the sidebar, and finally clicking **iCloud** on the right.

Note: If you don't see your name, select iCloud and then click Sign in with your Apple ID.

Activate and pick each option or program.

Sync a Presentation from a Mac

For iCloud to work properly on your Mac, you'll need to have installed macOS 11 or later and have iCloud set up.

Open the iCloud presentation you'd like to share on your Mac.

To access a previously downloaded presentation: Select File > **Move To,** then click the **Where** pop-up menu and select **iCloud**.

If your presentation is not saved, Select **File** > **Save**, then click the **Where** pop-up menu and select iCloud.

Note: Any edits you make in Keynote for iCloud will be reflected in the Mac version, and vice versa.

Note: If you want to use iCloud, you should have a device that can at least run the software, updating to the most recent version of macOS is a must also.

Start using **iCloud** with account login.

Sync a Presentation from an iPhone/iPad

iCloud requires that your iPhone or iPad be set up with iCloud and running iOS 14 or iPadOS 14. Use the Keynote app on your iPhone or iPad to put together a presentation. Keynote for iCloud will immediately update you with your presentation. Any edits you make in Keynote for iCloud will be reflected in the presentation on your device, and vice versa.

Understanding Syncing Symbols in Keynote for iCloud

The presentation manager's thumbnail sometimes displays syncing icons. Keynote for iCloud takes you straight to the presentation manager, where you can make and access presentations saved to your iCloud Drive.

The most recently modified presentations are displayed by default in the presentation manager.

- To see all of your presentations, select **Browse** from the menu.
- To see only the presentations you have shared with others, select **Shared**.
- The presentation's **More** button **(three dots)** can be found in the presentation's bottom right corner.

When you see this symbol, upload to iCloud is in progress and data is being uploaded to iCloud when you see this, the upload failed.

If you can't open a presentation in the presentation manager, and either symbol appears in the presentation's thumbnail, make sure the device used to create the presentation is connected to the internet and set up with iCloud.

Setting up iCloud Drive on your Mac

With **iCloud Drive,** you and your team can simultaneously edit the same presentation, spreadsheet, PDF, image, or other file type using any of your devices' supported apps.

When enabled, **iCloud Drive** syncs your presentations across all of your computers, iOS devices, and iPadOS devices that are signed into iCloud with the same Apple ID. No matter where you are, you will always be viewing the most up-to-date versions of your presentations.

To Set Up iCloud Drive

Select **Apple menu** > **System Setting**s (or System Preferences). Then click Apple ID if you're already logged into your Mac with an Apple ID

Select **iCloud** from the menu. Sign in with your Apple ID and password by clicking Sign In and then proceeding with the on-screen prompts. Make sure the box next to **iCloud Drive** is checked. Select the **Keynote** option by clicking the **Options** button next to iCloud Drive.

Note: Keynote presentations created or edited on a Mac without iCloud Drive enabled will not be uploaded to the cloud. Keynote on your Mac won't reflect any presentations you've made or changes you've made on other platforms.

Emailing a Keynote Document

One can share a Keynote presentation via various means such as **AirDrop, Mail, Messages,** or any other method. You can email the file in a variety of formats, including a Keynote presentation, a Portable Document Format (PDF) file, a Microsoft PowerPoint presentation, a movie, and more.

To Send a Copy of your Presentation in another format

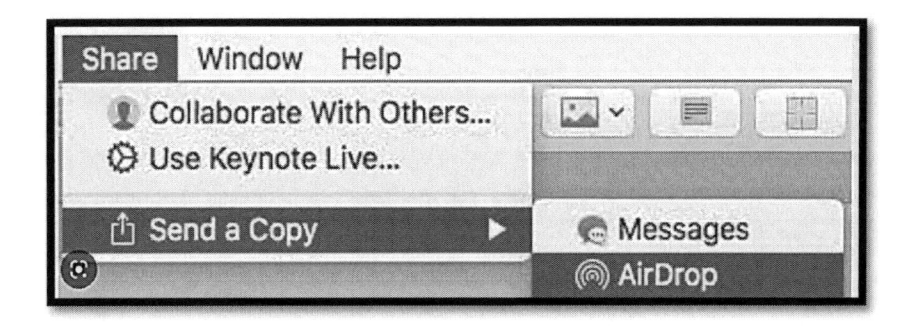

If you're using version 13 or later of macOS Ventura: Select **Share** > **Send Copy** from the menu that appears after you click the Share button in the toolbar. Macs running a version of OS X before version 12 You can send a duplicate by selecting **File** > **Copy** (from the File menu at the top of your screen).

Select a sending option.

Airdrop: This is sharing presentations with anyone close by and on the same Wi-Fi network. AirDrop can be used immediately without entering any password or configuring any additional settings. You can see who is online and ready to receive your files via their profile pictures and computer names in AirDrop. The file can only be sent if the recipient is willing to open it.

Mail and Messages: The recipient will receive a direct copy of the file. To control who can view your presentation, you can lock it down by selecting the "Require password to open" box if it appears.

If you have password protected the presentation, the password will be applied to the copy you send.

To continue, click the **Next** button and then enter your information (an email address if you're writing an email).

To proceed, please log in to your account with the selected sending method and send.

Note: You can also export your presentation in another format for safekeeping before sending. You can export to PowerPoint, movies, images, etc. This is helpful if you plan on sharing the presentation with recipients who are using different programs. The original presentation is unaffected by any edits made to the one being exported

To save the presentation in another format:

Open the presentation and click on **File** > **Export To** > [format] (from the File menu at the top of your screen). Selecting Export To from the File menu brings up a submenu with several different export formats, including PDF, PowerPoint, Movie, HTML, Images,

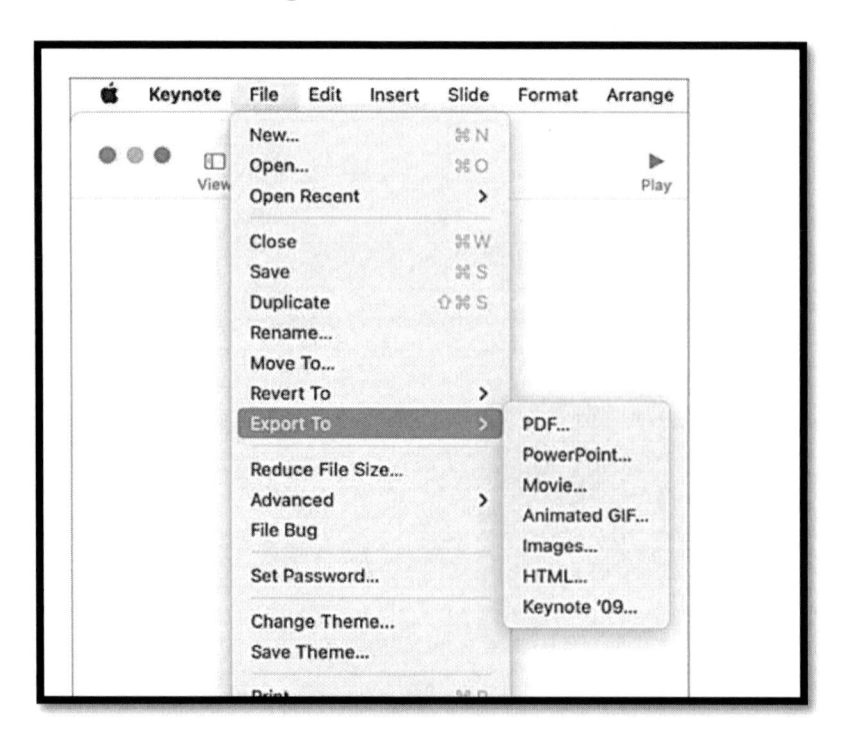

PDF: The PDF contains one page for each slide. Adobe Acrobat can read and edit PDF documents.

PowerPoint: To save a PowerPoint presentation in a format that can be opened by versions of PowerPoint, select **Advanced** Options and then .ppt from the resulting menu.

Movies: Select **From**, and then enter the slide numbers for which you want to export the movie: To listen to your recorded narrated slideshow, click the Playback drop-down menu and select Slideshow Recording. A self-playing presentation, on the other hand, advances automatically to the next slide or builds at the intervals you specify. Time intervals do not affect animations that are programmed to play automatically after a certain build or transition has finished.

Animated GIF: Exported as an animated GIF, your chosen slideshow is ready for sharing online. Using the presentation slides as a starting point, you can make an animated GIF and send it via text, email, or upload it to a website

To Create GIF:

- Open your presentation and go to **File** > **Export To** (from the File menu at the top of your screen).
- Enter the slide numbers of the first and last slides you wish to include.

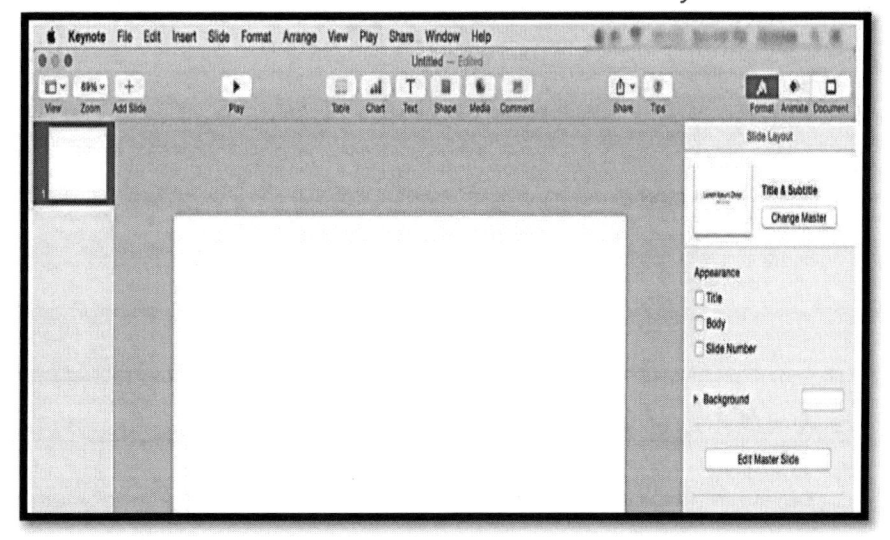

- Select a desired **resolution** and **frame rate** using the respective drop-down menus.
- To adjust the rate at which the animation proceeds after a click, move the Auto-advance slider.
- To give the GIF a name, click "**Next**" and start typing it.
- Simply select a destination on the **Where** pop-up menu, and then click **Save**.
- Select **Export**.

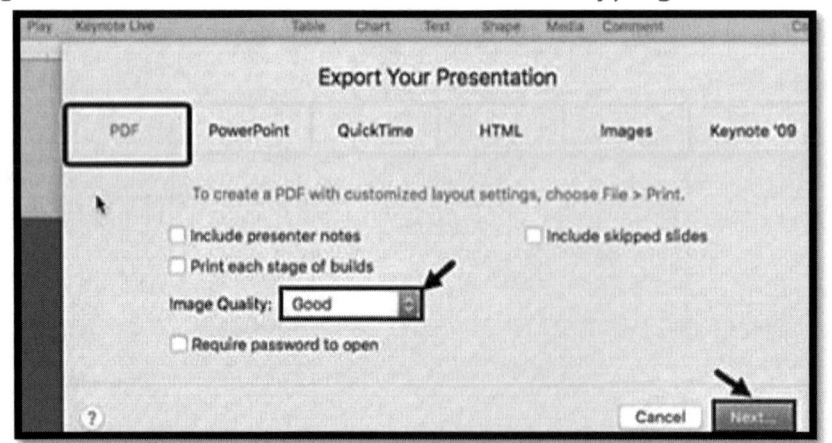

Note: Use transparent backgrounds for your animated GIF if the slide backgrounds employ **No Fill** or have transparency.

Images: Select the slides you want to save as images, and then choose the appropriate image format. The larger the file size, the higher the image quality.

HTML: To view your presentation online, simply open the index.html file in any web browser. Your entire presentation, including any animations or builds, can be exported.

Note: To make your presentation easier to send, post, or share, you can reduce its file size.

Reduce a Presentation's File Size in Keynote

You can reduce the size of your presentation's file if it contains media like an audio file, video, or image slideshow.

To do this:

Select **File** > **Reduce File Size** (from the File menu at the top of the screen).

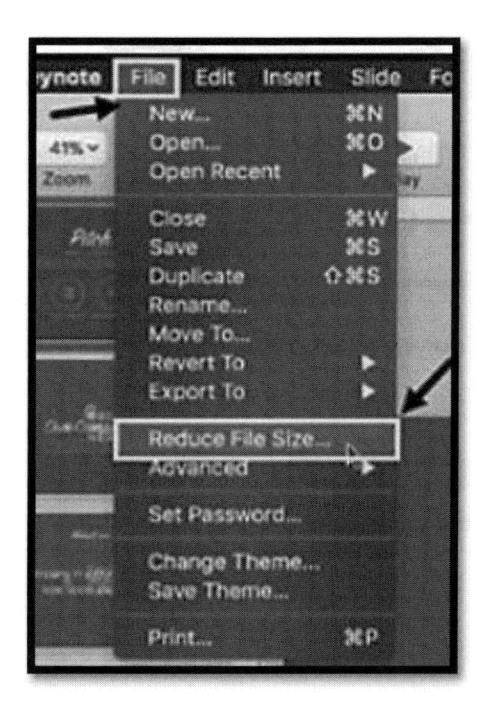

You can select the changes/adjustments from the list that pops up:

- Scale down large images
- Remove trimmed parts of movies and audio
- Most compatible (H.264)
- High efficiency (HEVC)
- Preserve original format

- Reduce the size of high-resolution images without compromising quality.
- To implement the modifications, select anyone to apply the adjustment

How to Quickly Email and Share Keynote Presentations

- Reduce the size of the file: You should compress your Keynote presentation before sending it to others.
- Create a Copy to Email: Create a copy of your Keynote presentation to email or share
- Share the Keynote presentation in PDF format.

It's best to simply attach the file to your preferred email program from here.

Collaborating

With keynote, you can collaborate with your team to work on a presentation together and at the same time. Since iCloud stores all versions of a presentation, anyone working on a shared presentation will be able to see any updates that have been made in real-time.

Access: Also, you can decide who can view it and what they can do after viewing it.

Permission: They can edit the work

Invitation: You can also invite selected users who will need to access the presentation using their Apple ID.

You can stop sharing a presentation with others or modify its sharing settings at any time.

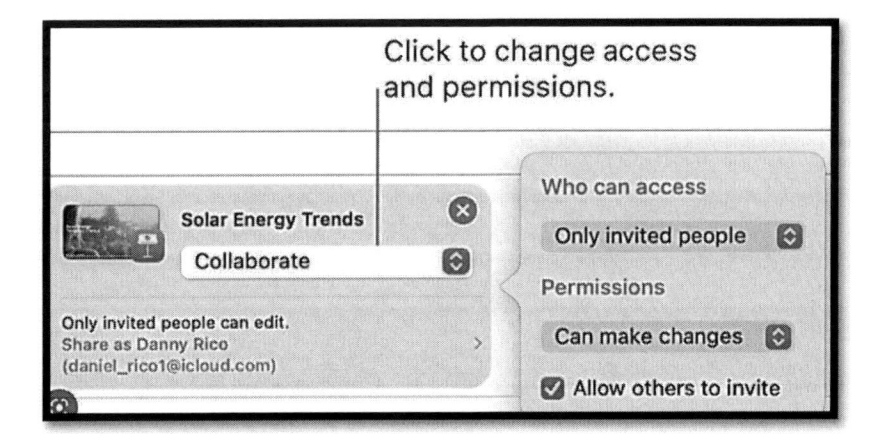

iCloud Requirement

Using your Apple ID and with iCloud Drive enabled, you can invite others to work with you on a presentation.

Your invitee won't be able to accept your invitation until they add your invited email or phone number to their Apple ID, so be sure to use an address or number that is already associated with their Apple ID. Instructions will be displayed after they tap or click the link in the invitation.

Minimum System Requirements

You and the people you share with will need any of the following to view or make changes to a shared presentation and to invite others to participate in the presentation:

An Apple Mac running Keynote 12.2 or later on an OS X version of OS X (higher than 12)

An iOS 15-capable iPhone, as well as a Keynote 12.1-capable Mac

To use Keynote 12.2, you'll need an iPad running iOS 15 or later.

Anyone you share a presentation with must use a Mac or Windows computer running a browser that is compatible with the presentation format.

Note: A presentation can be viewed, but not edited, on any device running Android or an iOS version that falls short of the requirements.

Work offline

You can keep working on a collaborative presentation even if you are not online. Any alterations you've made will be synced with iCloud the next time you go online. Refer to Offline-Only Editing for more information.

Edit While Offline

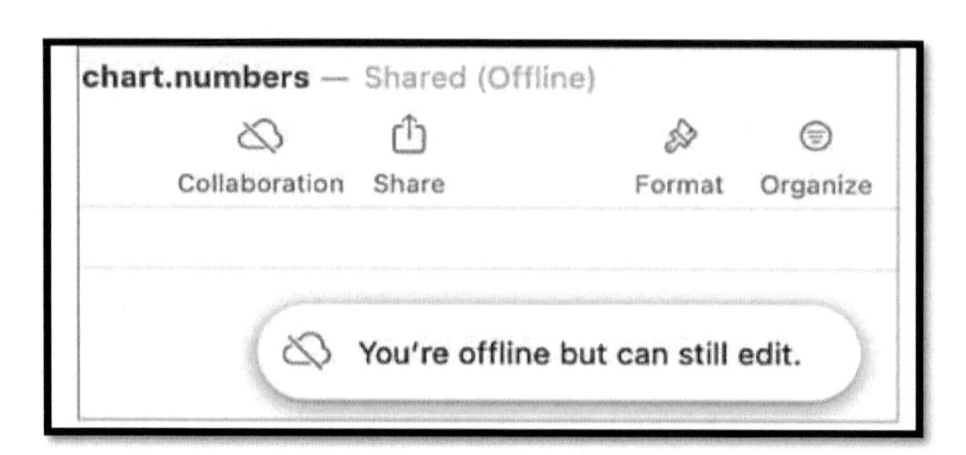

When you're not connected to the internet, the Collaborate button will change to a cloud with a diagonal line through it. When you next connect to the internet, your presentation will be updated with your most recent work. Once you're back online, you can check out the most recent updates to the group's presentation. You are currently offline but can make changes, according to a pop-up message.

Take Note of the following when making edits while offline

Before uploading your edited document, you can send a copy to another user by clicking Share in the toolbar or going to File > Share (in the main menu). You can verify the progress of your updates by looking at the sync status. To see the synchronization status, go to View > Show Sync Status (from the View menu at the top of your screen).

Slides or objects you are editing offline will not be updated when you reconnect to the online session if other participants have deleted them. Having just one person working on a project that needs information from various areas of expertise may not be enough. So, it's crucial to have software that allows multiple people to work on the same project at once, while also keeping track of changes and facilitating version control and comments.

Invite People from Your Mac

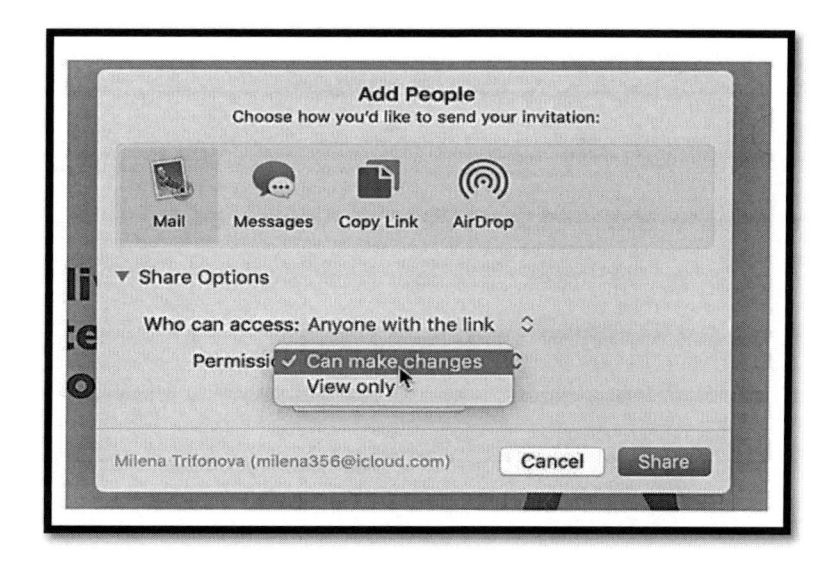

Open the file you intend to share.

To begin working together, select the plus sign from the toolbar and then click the Collaborate icon. To control who can see and make changes to your document, go to **File** > **Share** > Options. If you choose to share your document with others, they will automatically be granted editing permission. Select a sharing method to let others contribute to your document. Share the event details via email, text, AirDrop, or a link.

To forward or publish the message, select the **Share** button. As soon as you enable collaboration, a checkmark will appear on the Collaboration icon at the top of your document, turning it green. This symbol also indicates how many users, excluding you, currently have the document open.

You can set restrictions on your document like:

Select "**Anyone with the link**" if you want the document to be accessible by anyone who has the link to it. You have the option of allowing them editing privileges, or restricting their access to reading only. The Collaboration menu is where you'll go to modify your Share Settings at any time. In addition, by selecting the ellipsis (...) next to a user's name, you can **grant or remove access** privileges for that person individually.

The color next to their name corresponds with the color of the edit tracker at the time of the edit.

Note: To hide or reveal the real-time monitoring of collaboration actions, select **View** > **Hide Collaboration Activity/Show Collaboration Activity** from the menu bar.

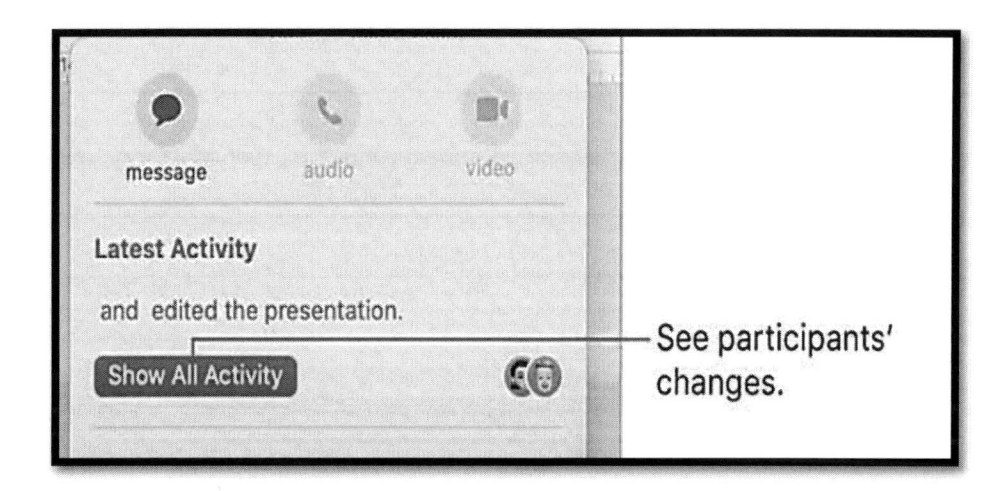

Note: To make changes to a coworker's document on a Mac or iOS device, you'll need to be online. If the device loses network connectivity or you go offline during a collaborative session, the app will prompt you to choose whether or not you would like to work on an offline copy of the document. If you're working on a project with others in iCloud.com and you lose Internet connection, your changes won't be visible to them until you reconnect to the Internet.

Stop Sharing a Document

To stop sharing a document, open it, tap or click the Collaborate icon with a checkmark, then select **Stop Sharing**. Finally, tap or click OK.

Note: When you stop sharing a document, it disappears from everyone's iCloud Drive.

Invite People to collaborate on iPhone/iPad

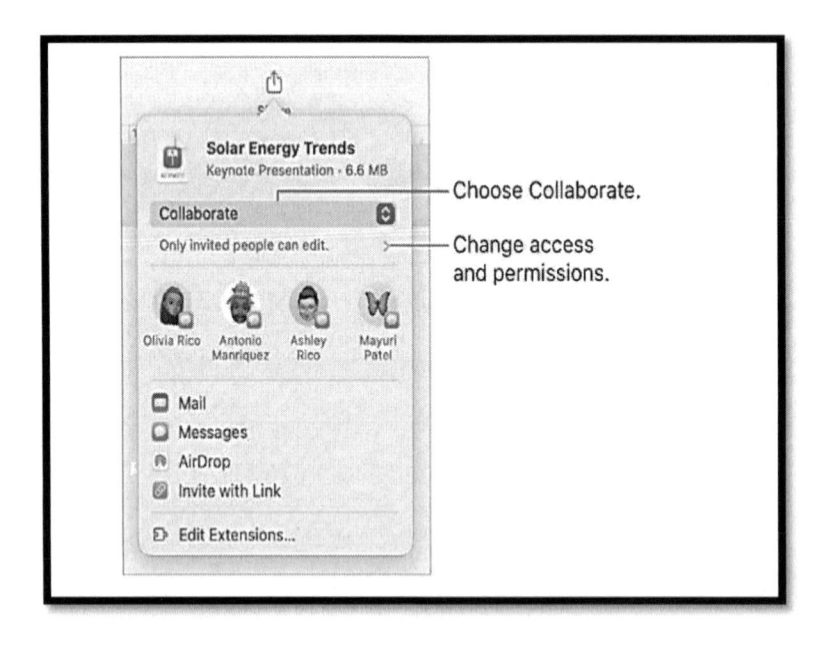

Putting a presentation in iCloud is the first step in asking others to collaborate with you. You'll need to be logged in with your Apple ID and have iCloud Drive enabled for Keynote for this to work

You can then **share** your work by selecting the Share button from the menu bar.

Note: A message appears to suggest you upload the presentation to iCloud Drive if it isn't already there.

Select a user group from the **"Who can access?"** drop-down menu.

People you invite: Only those you've invited who also have an Apple ID will be able to view the presentation. To view your shared presentation, recipients must first obtain an Apple ID.

Your invitee won't be able to accept your invitation until they add your invited email or phone number to their Apple ID, so be sure to use an address or number that is already associated with their Apple ID. Instructions will be displayed after they tap or click the link in the invitation.

Anyone with the Link: presentation can be viewed by anyone who has the link to it, which can be done either by tapping the link or by clicking it.

Select a means of invitation delivery:

Use **AirDrop** to send a presentation to someone who is also on the same network and can view it.

Both **Mail and Messages** allow you to include a personalized note and send a copy directly to one or more email addresses or phone numbers.

Select Share when you're ready to send the invite.

Note: The Collaborate button gets checked once you've invited others to view the presentation. When invited people accept, a counter showing how many people have accepted your invitation will appear to the right of the button.

Invite More People

Depending on the presentation's settings, you can add more people to work on it by adding them or sending them a link. To do this; pick one of the options below:

Navigate to **File > Manage Shared Presentation** (from the File menu at the top of your screen).

Click the **Collaborate button** in the toolbar, and then choose **Manage Shared Presentation.**

Simply right-click the file in iCloud Drive and select **Manage Shared Presentation** from the menu.

Alternatively, if you are the owner of a shared presentation with access set to "**People you invite**," or if the owner of the presentation has permitted you to add more people, you can use this method to invite them to collaborate. To invite someone to participate, go to **Add more People > Select Invite Method** and click **Share**

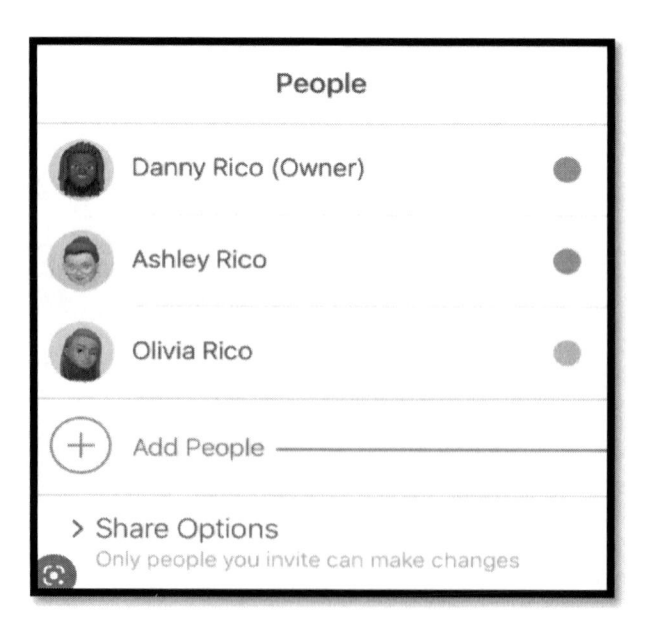

Also, If your presentation's settings allow access to "**Anyone with the link**," you can use this method to distribute the link to a wider audience. **Select the link, right-click** and select "**Copy Link**," and then paste it where desired. Select **Paste** from the **Edit** menu (located in the top-right corner of the screen) or use the keyboard shortcut **Ctrl+V.**

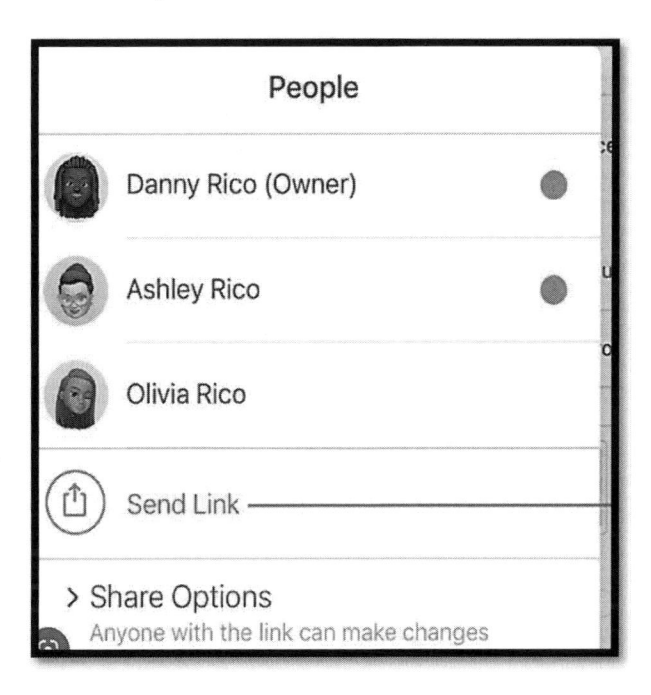

Note: Keep in mind that the presentation title and a stylized graphic containing the link may appear in the message body; you should not alter or remove either of these elements.

Change Access or Permission for Everyone

Access can be changed for all participants if you are the owner of a shared presentation with "**People you invit**e" access, or if the owner has permitted you to invite others. To do this:

Select the **Collaborate** button in the toolbar, and then click **Manage Shared Presentation.**

Change Access: Select a user group from the "**Who can access**?" drop-down menu.

The original invitees will still be able to access the presentation along with anyone else who has the link if you change the setting from "People you invite" to "Anyone with the link." They don't need to log in with the email or phone number you used to send the link.

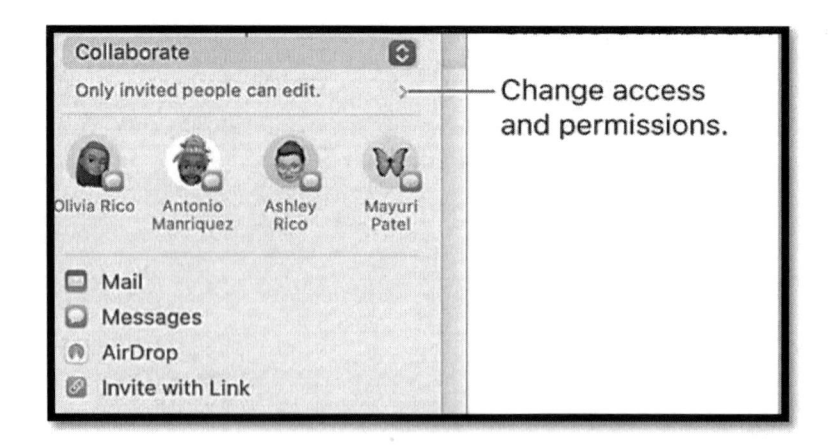

```
Collaborate
Only invited people can edit.          ──── Change access
                                            and permissions.
Olivia Rico  Antonio  Ashley  Mayuri
             Manriquez  Rico   Patel
☐ Mail
☐ Messages
☐ AirDrop
☐ Invite with Link
```

Those you choose to invite as opposed to "**Anyone with the lin**k" Unfortunately, the old link is now useless. Access to the presentation is restricted to those who have been sent an invitation from you and have signed in with their Apple ID.

Change Permission: There will be a drop-down menu titled "Permission." Select one of the following.

Can make Changes: People with access to the shared presentation can make edits and even print their copies.

View Only: The shared presentation can only be viewed and printed, but no changes can be made by any of the participants. No notifications appear when they join a presentation, and they can't respond to or delete comments from the activity list.

Allow other users to invite People: Leave it up to other people to send out invitations: To allow all attendees to invite new people to the presentation or modify the access and permission settings, select the "**Anyone can add more people**" checkbox.

Change Access or Permission for Individual Participants

If you limit viewing of a presentation to "**People you invite**," you can customize access to each individual.

To manage a group's shared presentation, select the **collaboration** button and select **manage shared presentation.**

Hover over their name and select more and select any of the following:

Allow to add other People: When enabled, this option gives the user the power to modify the presentation's access and permission and add new people.

Can make changes: Allows the user to make changes to and print the shared presentation.

View Only: When this setting is activated, viewers can still open and read the presentation, but they will be unable to make any changes or add any comments.

Remove Access: The presentation is deleted from the user's iCloud Drive and the link is disabled. The presentation is unaltered by their changes.

Click **Done**

Accept an Invitation to Collaborate

What happens when you click a link to a shared presentation depends on the access and permissions set by the owner, the version of Keynote and macOS installed on your computer, and whether or not you're using iCloud Drive. Before you begin, make sure you meet the minimum system requirements for collaborating. Click (or tap, if you're viewing the invitation on iPhone or iPad) the link in the email, message, or post you received.

If the email address or phone number used to invite you is not associated with your Apple ID, follow the instructions that appear to add that email or phone number to your Apple ID.

Note: If you don't want to associate another email address with your Apple ID, you could instead ask the owner of the shared presentation to invite you again using an email address or phone number that's already associated with your Apple ID.

If prompted, enter your Apple ID password or continue with the on-screen instructions.

Based on the following, the presentation will begin:

If you're using a Mac and have macOS 12 and Keynote 12.2 or later, the presentation will open in Keynote for iCloud if you're signed into iCloud Drive on your Mac. If you're not signed into iCloud Drive, the presentation will open in Keynote for Mac if you click the link in Mail on your Mac or a website. If you have an iPad running iPadOS 15.0 or later and Keynote 12.2 or later, the presentation will open in Keynote and be saved in your presentation manager. If you're using an older version of iOS, iPad, or Keynote on an Android device: Your presentation will load in a new tab in your browser, where you can view it but not make any changes.

Collaborate on Shared Documents

Open the shared presentation. For help viewing the presentation, click **Accept an invitation to collaborate** Edit the Presentation.

Any changes you and your collaborators make to the presentation will be instantly reflected for all to see. When multiple users are editing the same document, their cursors and selected text or objects will appear in a different color. Click or tap a cursor to see the editor's name appear in the edit summary.

Any of the following will do:

See who is currently working on the Presentation: To see who has joined the presentation and is either editing it or viewing it at the moment, click the **Collaborate** button in the toolbar.

When viewing a presentation as its owner, if the access setting is "**Only people you invite,**" you will only see the email address or phone number of anyone who has been invited but has not yet accessed the file.

Follow's Someone Edit: To view who is working, simply click the dot next to their name. If you don't see a dot, the person doesn't have the presentation open.

Hide or Show Activity: Click the View button in the toolbar, and then choose Hide Collaboration Activity or Show Collaboration Activity.

Invite others: Select how you'd like to send the invitation, and then click Share if you're using a Mac running macOS 12.0 or later and have permission to invite others to collaborate on the shared presentation.

Opt out of shared Documents

It is possible to opt out of a presentation by deleting your name from the list of people who have access to it.

To do this:

When the presentation is active, select the **Collaborate** menu item from the toolbar. Select the presentation by clicking **Shared** (located on the left). Select Collaboration Details after clicking the More button.

To delete your account, just hover over your name, click the ellipses (...), and select **Remove Me**.

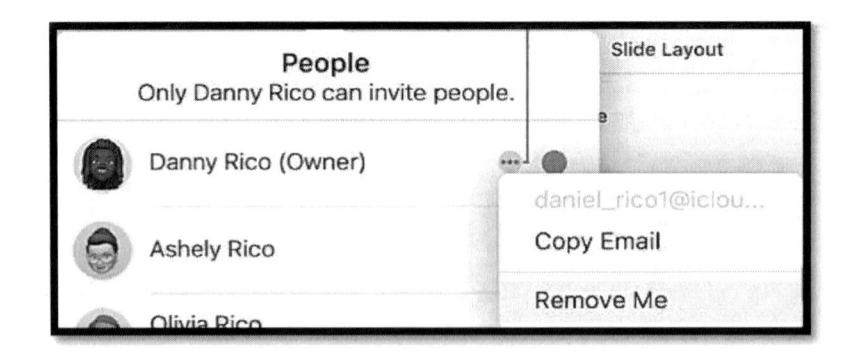

Locate the Presentation others have shared with you

Locate the link to the shared presentation

Click **share** on the left side of the presentation manager to find the presentation if you have previously viewed it.

If there are more slideshows than can be displayed in the current view, select See All from the menu on the top right.

If you delete a presentation from the presentation manager and then wish to view it again, you can do so by visiting the original link you were sent. The presentation will reappear in the presentation manager as long as its owner is still sharing it.

Exporting a Keynote Presentation

Export to MP4 File: Converting a Keynote Presentation into a QuickTime Video

Open up your Keynote presentation and choose "**File**" from the menu that appears.

Select Export **To** and click on **QuickTime**.

Adjust the settings to your desired outcome and select **Next**

Click **Save** to save your File

Converting a Keynote Presentation into a Voiceover QuickTime Video

To export your slides as a video with voiceover for the QuickTime video version of your presentation, please follow the steps below.

- **Open** your Keynote presentation.
- Choose **Play** from the menu that appears.
- Select Record Slideshow.
- To begin recording, tap the **red** button at the bottom of your screen.
- Use the up and down arrow keys on your keyboard to move through the slideshow.
- When you are finished, press the **red** button once more to stop recording.
- Go to the menu bar, then click **File and s**elect **Export To,** and then select **QuickTime**.
- Then **Save** your file.

Exporting

Export as a Movie

Choose **File** > **Export To** > **Movie**.

Choose a **Playback** option

If your recording is a slideshow in which you click through slides while narrating, select the **Slideshow Recording** option.

Choose Self-Playing to export the presentation with set timings.

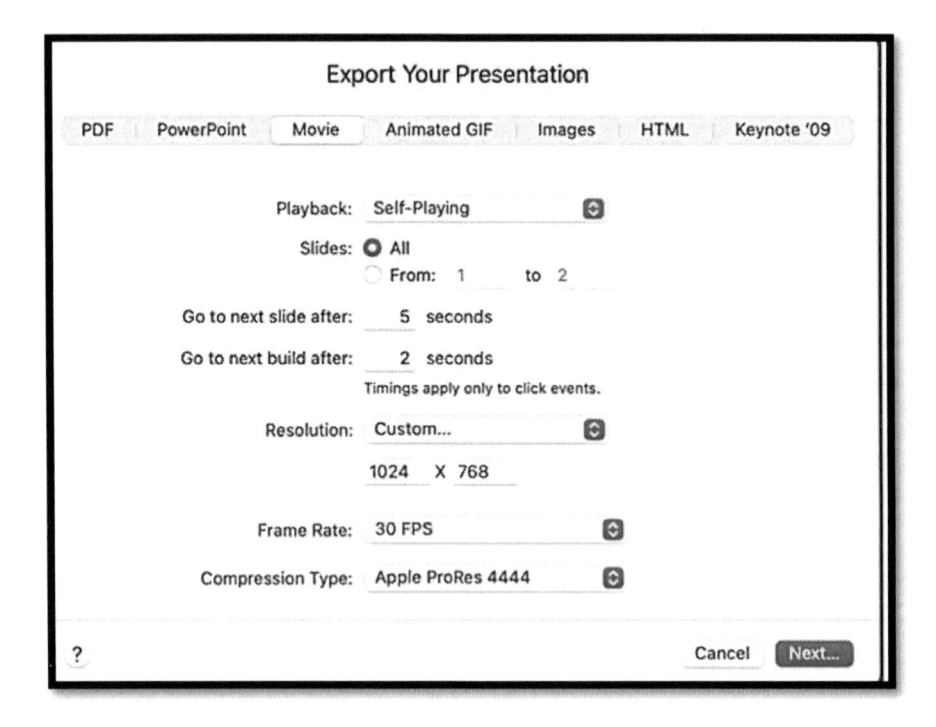

Select the slides that you want to export

Set Resolution: Select either **720p or 1080p** as the default **resolution**, or go to **Custom** and enter your values. You can select a compression method (only available when choosing Custom).

Finish the Exporting

Select **next**, give the file a name and save it somewhere, then select **Export**.

Note: You will receive either an m4v or a movie file, depending on the settings you've selected. Your presentation is now in a form that can be viewed and shared with ease, regardless of the method you used to create it. It's

Printing

A Keynote presentation can be printed in multiple formats, with or without any notes or comments. To access Printers & Scanners, select **System Preferences** from the Apple menu (found in the upper-left corner of your screen) and then click **Printers & Scanners.**

To Print:

Select "**File**" > "**Print**" from the menu bar (from the File menu at the top of your screen).

If you want just one page printed or a whole document, please specify.

Select Keynote from the drop-down menu that appears when you click the arrows on the bottom of the page selector.

To reveal the menu, select **Show Details** from the print dialogue's button bar.

Select the checkboxes next to the options you want to print, and then click one of the print formats (Slide, Grid, Handout, or Outline).

Depending on the format you select, the available options will change.

Click the **Print** button.

Conclusion

As a way of concluding this chapter, here are some tips for Managing Presentations across Devices

While offline, the Open dialog on a Mac will show "Syncing" below the presentation thumbnail. You can save your edited presentation to iCloud the next time you connect to the web.

Conflicts will appear if you try to make changes to a presentation on more than one computer or device before saving. Be sure to let the app sync with iCloud before attempting to make changes to the presentation on a different device.

In the event of a conflict, you may choose to keep only some of the presentations you have modified or keep them all.

A presentation must be saved or transferred to iCloud before it can be shared there.

If you remove a presentation from Keynote, it will also be removed from iCloud and from any other devices on which you have installed Keynote.

The folder structure you use on one device will apply to all of your devices if you choose to use folders to organize your presentations.

A presentation password set on one device will be needed to access it on any other device.

CHAPTER FOUR
LOCKING PRESENTATIONS

While you can edit, share or even create Keynote presentations, you can also lock your presentations on the keynote, so that others cannot make changes to it.

Therefore, the presentation can be password-protected so that only those who know the password can view it or make changes to it. 8n this chapter, we are going to look at how to use passwords to lock your Presentations, remove or change passwords, and how to transfer presentations using finder and AirPods.

Using Password to Lock Presentation

Password can be any word that can be used to access anything known to the owner, therefore restricting access to other persons, almost any combination of numbers, upper- and lowercase letters, and special keyboard characters can be used as a password. There can be only one password for a given presentation.

Password-protected presentations can be unlocked with just a fingerprint if your computer has the fingerprint detection feature known as Touch ID.

Require a Password to Open a Presentation
For iPhone/ iPad

- Tap the **More** buttons
- Click on **Presentation** Options

- Click on **Set Password**.
- Type in your Password
- And Click **Done**

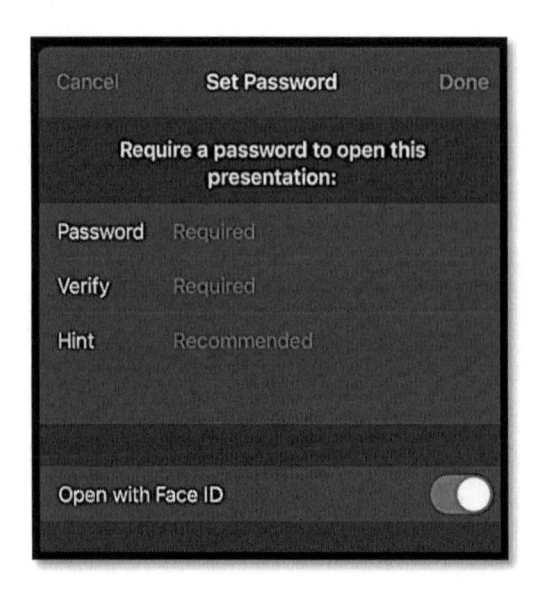

For Mac:

Select **File** > **Set Password** from the main menu

- Type in your password
- Click **Set** Password

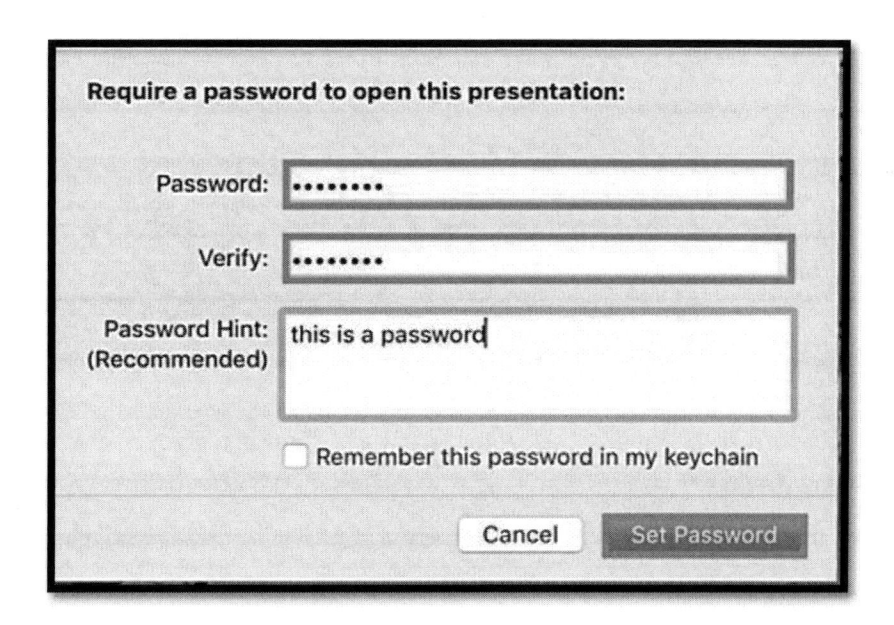

Note: If your computer is set up for Touch ID, "Open with Touch ID" appears. You can select the checkbox to turn on Touch ID for the presentation.

Change or Remove a Password

For iPhone/iPad

Open the presentation and then do one of the following:

To **Change** a password, you can: Select **More > Presentation Options > Change Password**.

After filling in the blanks, tap the button labeled "**Done**."

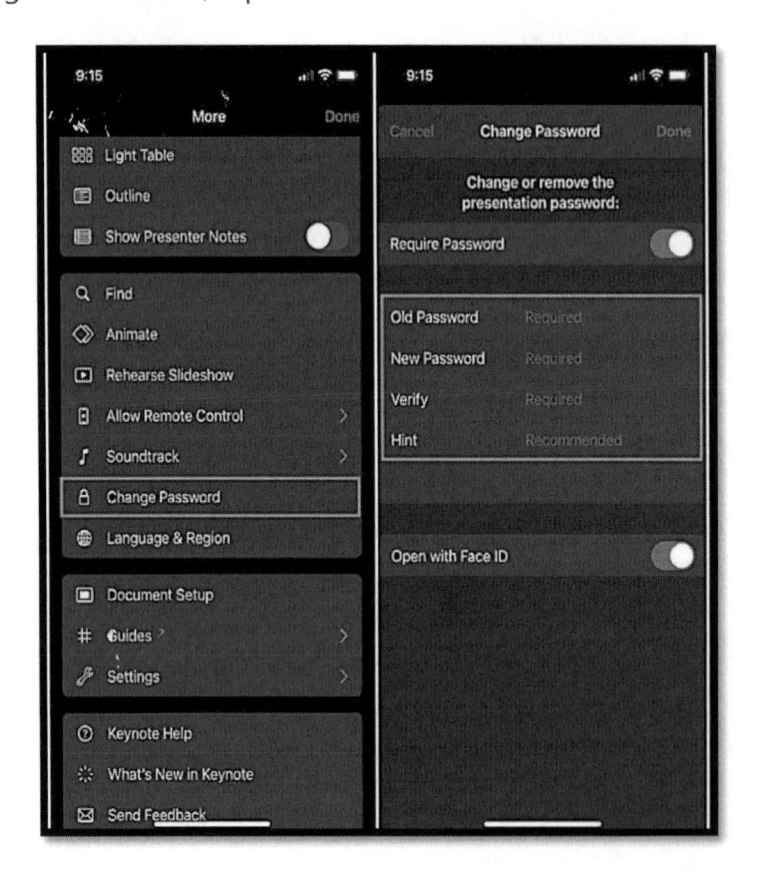

To **Remove** a password: Select **More > Presentations Option**s **> Change Password.** To remove the password, turn off Require Password and enter the previous one, and tap **done**.

For Mac

Open the presentation and then do one of the following:

To Change a password, you can: Go to **File** > **Password Change** (from the File menu at the top of your screen). Enter the requested information, then click **Change Password.**

To Remove a password: Select **File** > **Change Password** to modify your current password. Enter the previous password and select **Remove password.**

> Please enter the password to disable protection for this document.
>
> Password: [ ]
>
> Cancel   Remove Password

Note: When a password is added to a presentation, or an existing password is changed, it is only valid for that version of the presentation and any subsequent versions.

Set up Touch ID to Open Password Protected Presentation

To use Touch ID to Open Password protected presentations, you must first enable Touch ID on your computer before you can use it to access password-protected presentations.

On Mac:

To activate the Touch ID:

As of version 13 of macOS Ventura: Choose **Apple menu** > **System Settings**, click **Touch ID & Password**, click **Add Fingerprint**, then follow the onscreen instructions.

macOS 12 or earlier: Choose **Apple menu** > **System Preference**s, click **Touch ID**, click **Add Fingerprin**t, then follow the onscreen instructions.

Note: It's important to know that if you don't see Touch ID, your Mac doesn't support it.

Set up Touch ID for Pages: To enable Touch ID in Pages,

Go to the **Pages** > **Settings menu** (via the main Pages menu) and tick the appropriate box.

On iPhone:

You can either use Face ID or Touch ID on iPhone

Open with Face ID: Click on **Presentation,** If prompted to allow Keynote to utilize Face ID, press **OK**

Note: Facial ID can be disabled or enabled in Keynote at your discretion. The Keynote toggle may be found in the Settings menu under **Face ID** & **Passcode** > **Other Apps, then enable or disable keynote**

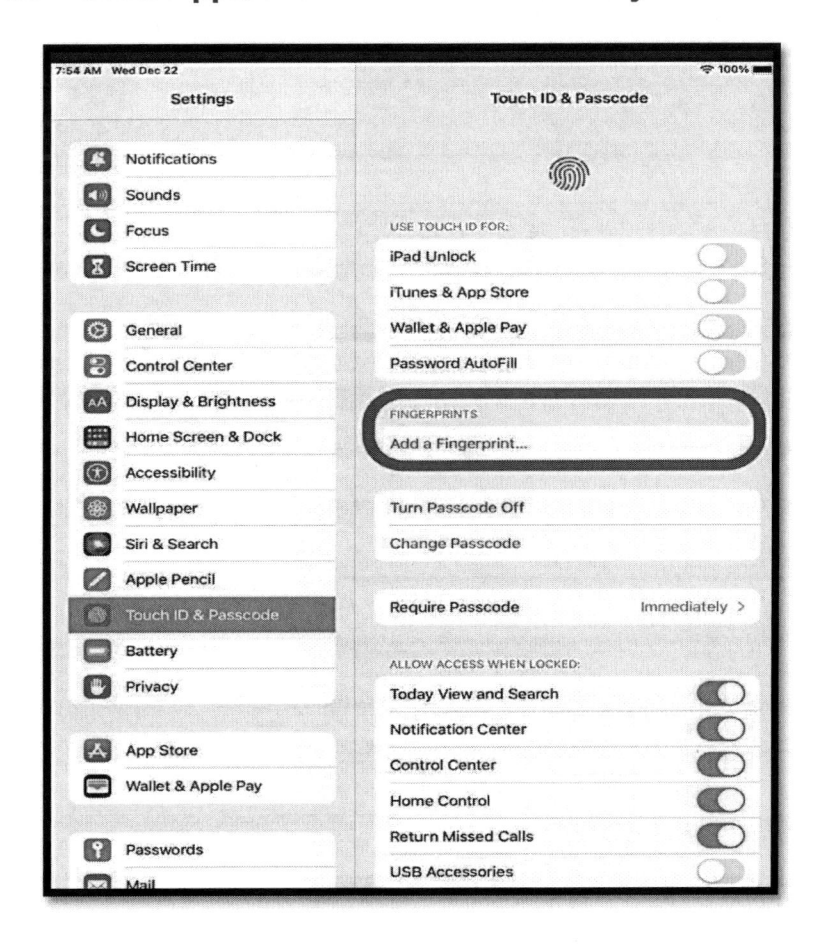

Use Touch ID to unlock: Start by touching the presentation, then place your finger on Touch ID.

Lock or Unlock a Presentation

Presentation locking is not the same as password protection; anyone can regain access to a locked presentation.

To lock or unlock a presentation, click its name at the top of the window and then the **Locked** checkbox.

Close this window by clicking anywhere outside of it.

Transferring Presentation using Finder and Airpod

Keynote presentations can be transferred via the Finder. The Finder can be used to move presentations between gadgets. When iCloud isn't an option, this method comes in handy. Presentations also created in Microsoft PowerPoint can also be transferred in this way and viewed in Keynote.

Transfer the presentation from your computer with the finder

Simply Open the **Finder** on a computer and plug in your iOS device.

The device shows up in the sidebar of the Finder window shortly.

Click the device's name in the sidebar, and then click **Files** in the main window's drop-down menu.

Simply drag the desired presentation file into the Keynote folder.

Once the presentation is finished, you can find it in the Finder, just below Keynote.

Initiate sync by clicking **Sync** and then waiting for it to finish.

Open the Files **app** from the Home screen, then select Browse at the bottom of the screen, and finally On My iPhone or my iPad.

You can access the presentation by selecting the **Keynote folder**, and then tap the presentation's thumbnail.

Note: Keynote allows you to open and make changes to PowerPoint presentations. If you are unable to open an encrypted PowerPoint presentation in Keynote, you can try modifying the encryption method and saving the presentation again.

Transfer the presentation to your computer with the finder

Move the presentation to your device if it's not saved on your device.

Simply **Open** the Finder on the computer and plug in your iOS device

The device shows up in the sidebar of the Finder window shortly.

Click the device's name in the sidebar, and then click Files in the main window's drop-down menu.

Note: To move a Keynote presentation to a new location, open the Keynote folder, find the presentation you want to move and then click and drag it.

Using Airpod to Transfer Keynote Presentation

Using AirDrop, presentations can be wirelessly sent to an iOS device or Mac on the same Wi-Fi network. To do this:

- **Open AirDrop:**

To use AirDrop on a **Mac: G**o to the **Finder** by clicking on the desktop and selecting **Go** > **AirDrop** (from the Go menu at the top of the screen).

A new AirDrop screen loads. Bluetooth and Wi-Fi connectivity can be toggled on and off as needed.

On iPhone/iPad: Open the iOS **Control Cente**r, select AirDrop, and then decide whether you want to accept items from anyone or just those in your Contacts list.

- **Choose the presentation you wish to send:**

To send a copy of an open presentation via AirDrop on a Mac: Select **Share** > **Send a copy** from the Share menu at the top of the screen. Or, right-click a presentation file and select **Share** > **AirDrop** from the menu that appears.

For iOS devices: Launch the presentation and click **Share** and then **AirDrop** from the list of sharing options.

- Pick a recipient to send it to.

Use Handoff to transfer Keynote presentations

Handoff can be used to send Keynote presentations from one device to another if your Mac, iPhone, iPad, and Apple Watch are all to one another, you can use Handoff to transfer your current presentation from one device to the next.

Enable Handoff

You must enable Handoff on all of your devices before you can use it. To do this:

Using a Mac: Go to **Apple menu** > **System Settings** > **General** > **AirDrop** & **Handoff on the right,** then enable "**Allow Handoff between this Mac and your iCloud devices**".

Note: If you're using an older version of macOS (previous than 12.1): The option to "Allow Handoff between this Mac and your iCloud devices" can be found in the General section of System Preferences (accessible via the Apple menu).

For iOS devices: Turn on Handoff by selecting **Settings** > **General** > **Handoff**.

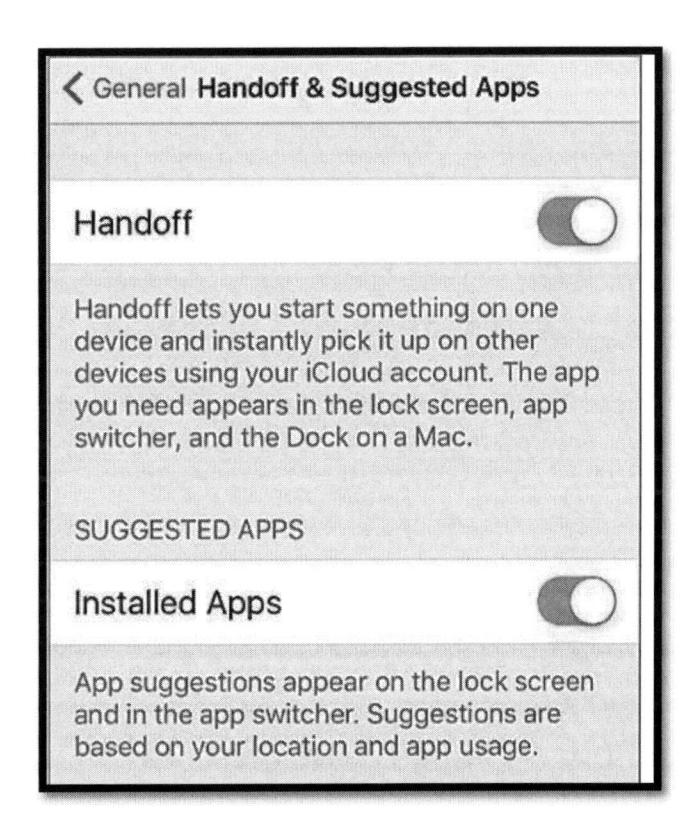

Hand off a Presentation to iPhone or Ipad

Open your Presentation

When your Mac is close to a device, a Keynote Handoff icon appears in the lower-left corner of the device's Lock screen.

When you double-click the Home button or swipe up from the bottom of the screen, the multitasking screen will appear, and the Handoff icon will be one of the visible options.

Select Keynote from the screen's bottom to resume your presentation from where you left off.

Handoff a Presentation to Mac

Open up a presentation on your Apple device of choice (iPhone, iPad, or another Mac).

The Handoff icon will appear on the left side of the Dock when the device or other Mac is close to the Mac you want to hand off to.

The presentation can be accessed by selecting the Handoff icon.

Note: If you're giving a presentation on a Mac, you can use Handoff to control it from your iOS device.

Use a Remote to Control a Presentation in Keynote on Mac

To use this, both the mobile device and the Mac must have Keynote installed and be connected to the internet via Wi-Fi. The remote device must have Keynote running to be used as a remote.

To use the remote control, open the presentation manager and then select Continue. Keynote needs permission to connect to other local networks and devices. To do this: Click Settings > **Privacy** > **Local Network** and then enable Keynote

Set Up iPhone/iPad as a remote control

Both the device and the Mac must have Keynote installed and Wi-Fi enabled.

Launch Keynote on the device you wish to use as a remote control.

Click on the **Remote** button in the **presentation manager, and then** click **Continue**.

The **Setup Remote screen** is displayed.

Note: Click **OK** if prompted to allow Keynote to discover and connect to local network devices.

Launch Keynote on a Mac then navigates to **Keynote** > **Settings** (from the Keynote menu at the top of your screen).

Select **Enable** after clicking **Remotes** at the top of the settings box.

Click the **Link** beside the device you wish to use as a remote control.

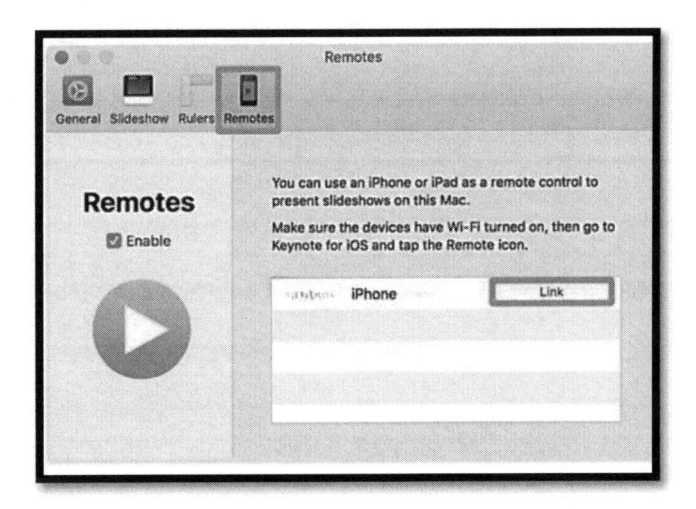

A four-digit code is displayed on the Mac and smartphone.

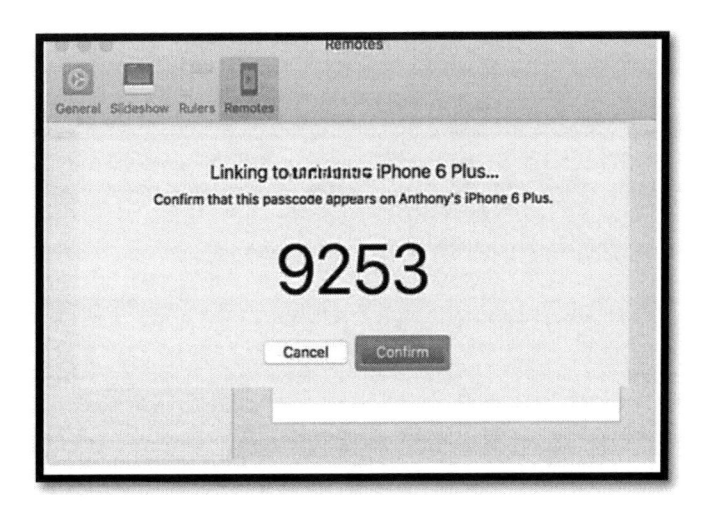

Confirm that the four-digit codes match, click the **Confirm** button, and then close the Keynote settings.

After linking the devices, the remote can be used to control the presentation.

Use iPhone or iPad as a remote control

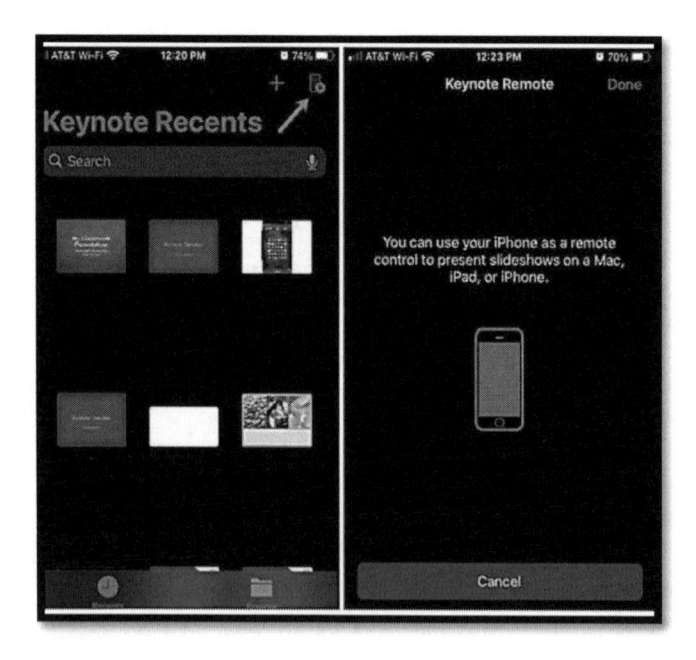

The iPhone or iPad must first be configured as a remote control, as stated above.

To use Handoff to transform your device into a remote, Handoff must be enabled on both the Mac and the device, and the presentation you wish to control must be stored in iCloud Drive.

The presentation can be seen on a Mac.

Transform the device into a remote: Launch **Keynote** on the remote device, hit the **Remote** button in the presentation manager, and then click **Play**.

Using Handoff, you can transform an iPad into a Mac remote: Swipe up on the Keynote button on the Lock screen's lower-left corner. Additionally, you can double-click the Home button or swipe up from the bottom of the screen (for devices without a Home button) to access the multitasking screen, and then tap Keynote at the bottom of the screen.

- To control the presentation, you can:

- Proceed to the next slide or structure: Tap the slide or swipe to the left across it.
- Go back to the prior slide: Swipe over the slide to the right.
- Skip to a particular slide: Tap the slide number located in the upper-left corner, then tap the desired slide.
- Immediately stop the presentation: Tap the icon labeled Close.

Change the presentation device linked to a remote control device

- Open Keynote on the iOS device you're using as a control center.
- To use the remote, click the **remote** button in the Presentation Manager Menu item.
- **To use, click devices and then one of the following:**
- **To Add Another to Device:** Click the "**Add a Device**" button and then follow the on-screen prompts.
- **Change to another presentation device:** Select another device name and then confirm by selecting done.

Remove a Device: You can delete a device by swiping left on its name and then tapping the **Delete** button.

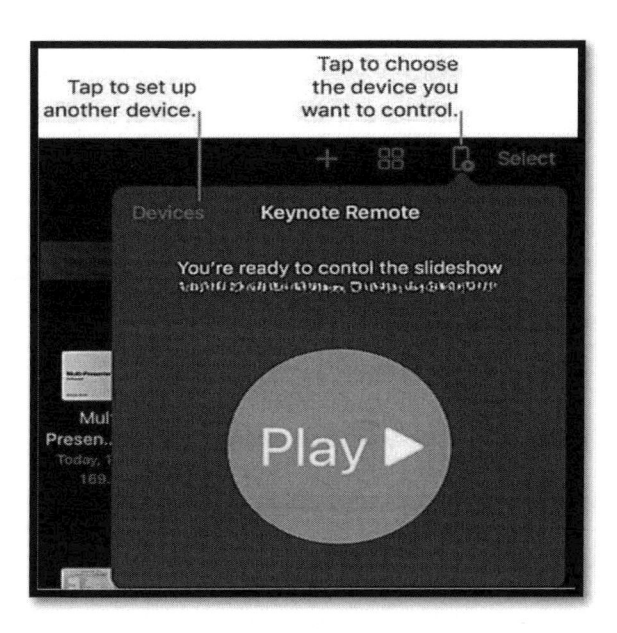

395

Conclusion

To conclude this chapter, know that you can also unlink the remote control. Open Keynote, go to Settings and select Remote, and click **Unlink**.

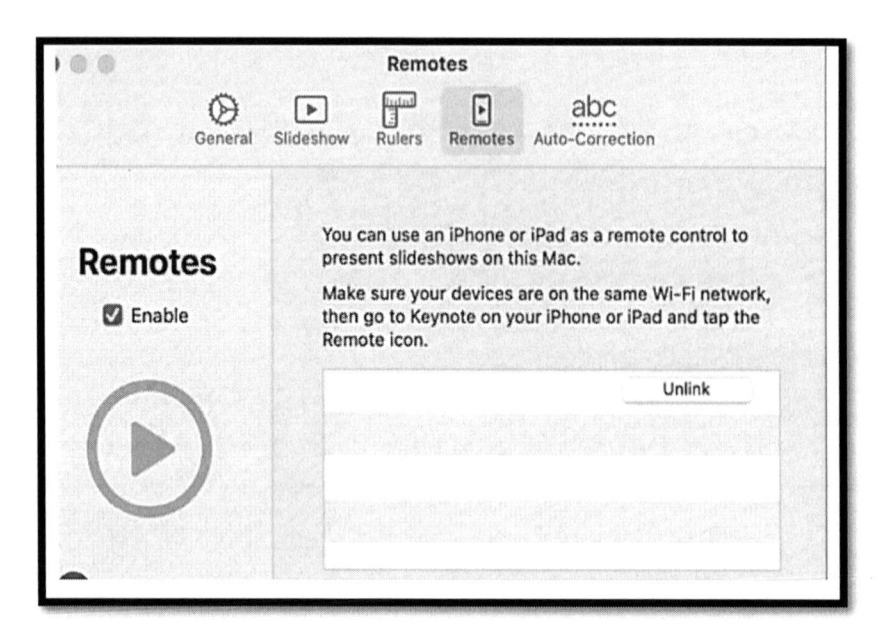

CHAPTER FIVE
WORKING WITH PHOTOS ON THE KEYNOTE

No doubt, we can say the Keynote program is both user-friendly and powerful. It has become increasingly fashionable as a means of creating effective visual aids to back up your presentation.

Your presentations can include pictures to catch the audience's interest or to back up your claim and enhance your presentation. In this chapter, we are going to discuss how you can use images in your presentation, covering how to add images, edit, rotate, resize, and enhancement to these images among others.

How to add an image to your Keynote Presentation

Open Keynote on your Mac and navigate to the slide you'd like to modify.

Then, upload it using one of the following methods:

Drag the image from your Mac's file browser to the desired location on the slide. Alternatively, select the desired option from the drop-down menu after clicking the Media button in the toolbar: **Photos**, **Image Gallery**, Choose (to find the image), or **Take** Photo.

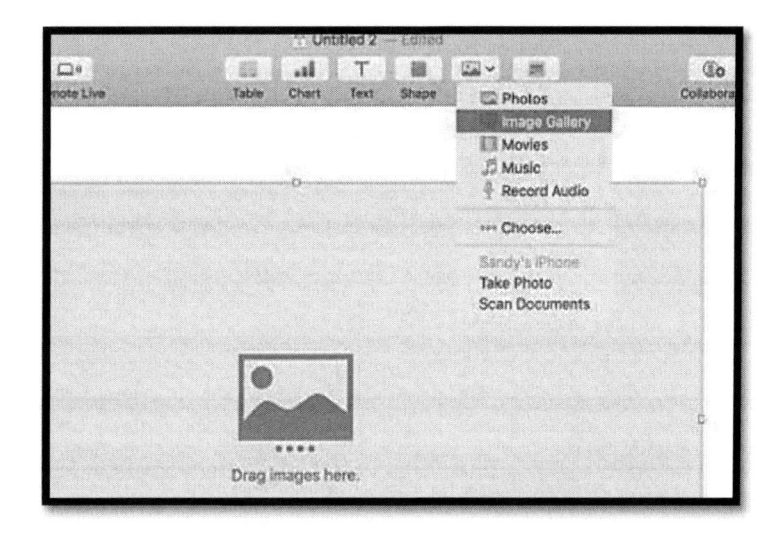

If the slide has a media placeholder: To insert an image into a media placeholder, click the Media button in the slide's lower right corner and select one of the following:

Images can be dragged into media placeholders on slides from your computer or the web.

Select an image from your gallery by clicking the **Replace** Image button that appears at the media placeholder's lower-right corner.

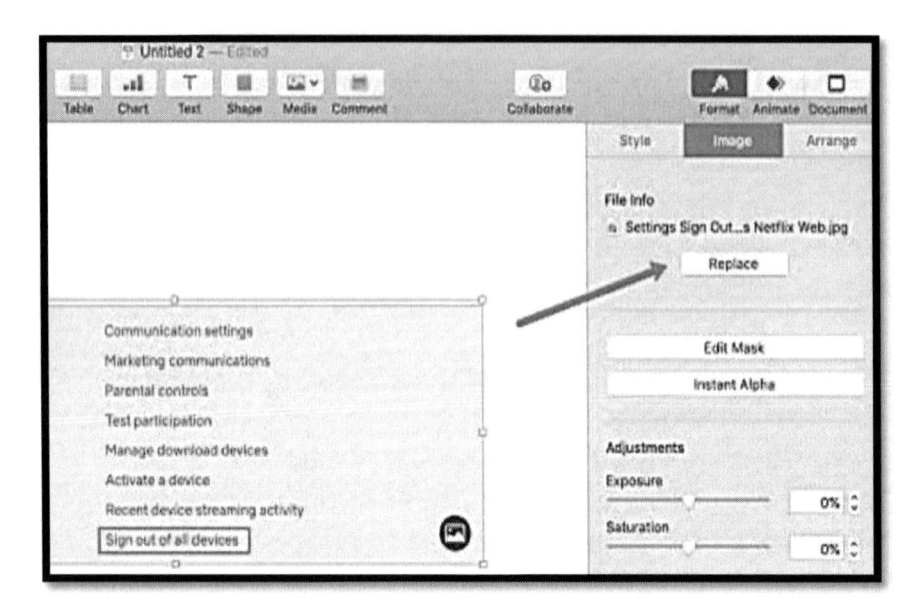

You can add a picture to the slide or a media placeholder by clicking the **Media** button in the toolbar, selecting Photos, and dragging the picture from your photo library. Select the image you wish to replace by clicking on it, and then on the Image tab in the Format sidebar. Select a new image by clicking the **Replace** button. The original dimension of the image has been retained in the new one.

Add an Image on iPhone

- To insert an image into a presentation slide, select **Add**, then the **Media button.**
- Select **Photo or Video** and Select "**Insert from**" to upload an image or video from iCloud or another service.
- Select the image by navigating to it.
- To resize the image, drag and drop any blue dot, then select **done**.

Use an Image Gallery Placeholder in your Presentations

An image, video, or audio file can be inserted into a presentation using a media placeholder. If you use a media placeholder, you can swap out the media without having to reposition anything else on the slide.

Insert an image onto your slide and format it to match the style of the rest of the visuals in your presentation. The image can be cropped, resized, rotated, and masked, among other manipulations.

To use the image as a placeholder, select it by clicking on it, then going to **Format** > **Advanced** > **Define as Media Placehold**er (from the Format menu at the top of your screen).

Note; In case you have an image in mind for your presentation but aren't quite ready to include it just yet, you can use the Image Gallery feature as a stand-in until you're ready to use it. When you're ready, you can use the final method above to insert your image with ease. The advantage of this is that you can keep working on your presentation and add images at a later date without having to redo any of the slides or other elements.

Here's how to insert an Image Gallery as a Placeholder:

On Mac:

Find the slide and position on the slide where you'd like the placeholder to appear.

Select Image Gallery from the Media menu in the top navigation.

At any time, you can add images to that placeholder by dragging them there or by clicking the Media icon in the lower right corner and selecting them from your computer's storage.

On iPhone

To do this: Insert an image onto your slide and format it to match the style of the rest of the visuals in your presentation.

The image can be cropped, resized, rotated, and masked, among other manipulations.

To use an image as a placeholder, tap the image once to select it, then click on the **Format** button, **Image**, and finally **set as Placeholder.**

Replace an image in your Keynote presentation

Inserting an image into a Keynote presentation and then deciding you'd rather use a different one is easy.

On Mac:

Decide on the picture that will be changed.

Open the sidebar by clicking the **Format** button in the top right.

Select "**Image**" at the top of the available options.

Go to **Edit** > **Replace**, and then find your picture to replace, and click Open.

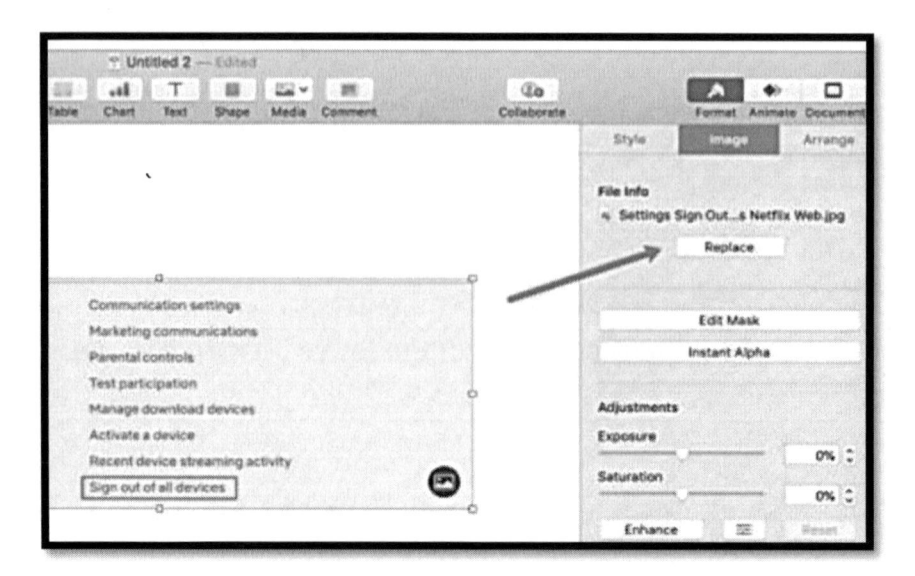

On iPhone

Select a media placeholder, and then in its lower-right corner click the **Replace** Image button.

Get to the image and select "**Insert from**" below the album selection to use a photo from iCloud or another service.

Pick the picture you'd like to upload by tapping it.

To insert a picture saved to iCloud or another service, select the desired photo from the folder list.

To resize the image, drag and drop any blue dot, then select **Done**.

Edit images in your Keynote presentation

One good feature of the keynote is the ability to edit your images to your desired taste while on the app. Let's check out the following Keynote image editing features.

- **Make parts of an image stand out**

Using an image mask, you can hide parts of your image to highlight others. If you want to draw attention to a specific area of an image, this is a useful tool.

Double-click your image or navigate to **Image** > **Edit Mas**k in the Format menu bar.

Use the size slider to modify the mask when the mask controls appear.

Next, adjust the size with the slider when the mask control shows and then adjust the image with the Image button and the mask with the Crop-like button. You can grab the mask and the image separately and reposition them however you like.

To conclude, select the **done** option.

- **Remove background color**

Sometimes the background color in an image isn't necessary. The Instant Alpha function can eliminate this:

Select an image

In the Format menu, select **Image** > **Instant Alpha.**

Select the color you wish to remove by clicking on the image and dragging slowly over it. Shades of similar colors will be incorporated.

When you're done, hit the "**Done**" button.

- **Additional image editing options**

The images you use in Keynote can be edited in a variety of ways. You can find the most used **ones** in the Format menu, which are:

Select Style in the Format menu to change the image's style, add a border, shadow, or reflection, and play with the opacity.

To edit the image's exposure, saturation, contrast, temperature, and alt text, select **Image** from the sidebar.

If you click the **Arrange** button, you'll be able to reposition the image in a variety of ways, including rotating it 90 degrees or flipping it horizontally or vertically. There is also the option to group and ungroup selected images.

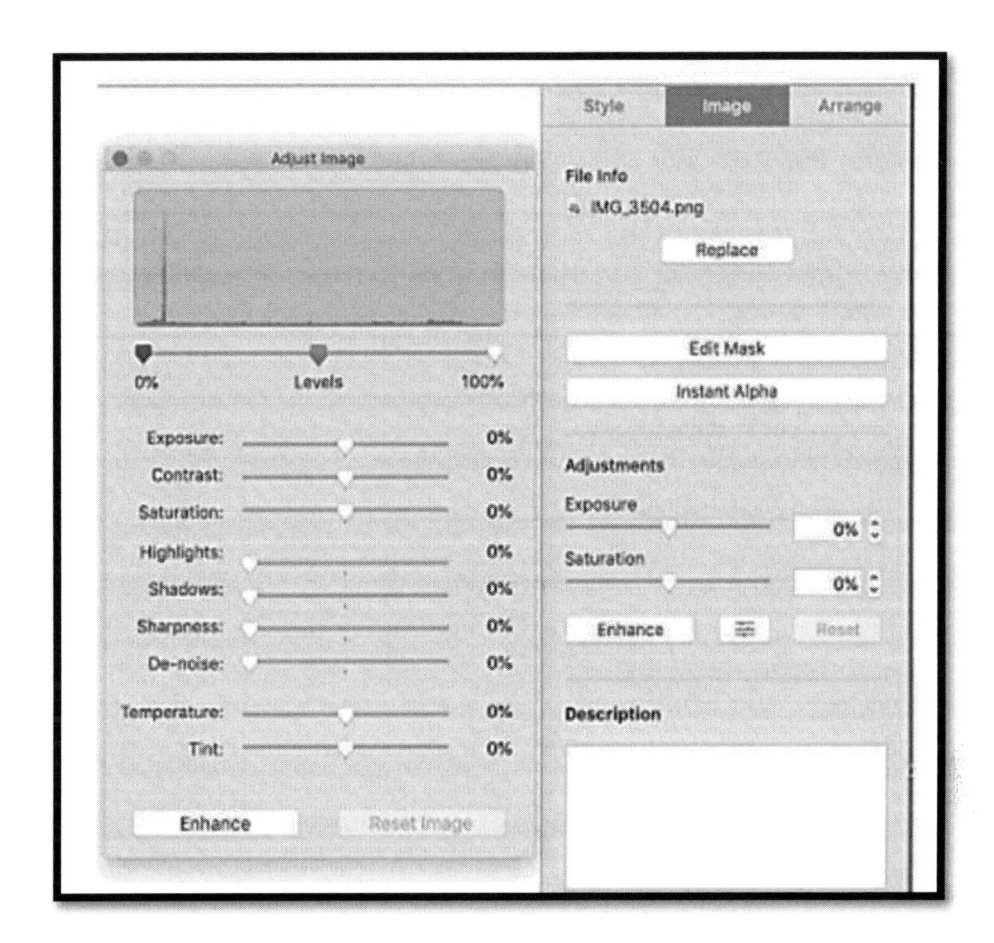

3. **Take a Photo or Scan with an iPhone or iPad and add it to your presentation**

If you have an iOS device on hand, such as an iPhone or iPad, you can use it to snap a picture or scan an item and then import it into your Mac presentation.

Note: Make sure your Mac, iPhone, or iPad meets the system requirements

To add a photograph or scanned document to a presentation slide, select the **Media** menu button in the toolbar and then either **Take Photo** or **Scan Document**s under your device's name.

You can do one of the following on your iOS device:

Take a Photo: To take a picture, first press the Camera button, then select **Use Photo** (tap **Retake** to retake the photo).

Auto-scan a document: Keep the document facing the camera and it will take a picture of the page, crop it, and fix the perspective for you. After saving the scan, you can use it in your presentation.

Scan a Page Manually: Select the desired scanning area by dragging the frame after tapping the Take Picture button. Select **Keep Scanning,** and then **Save**.

You can **reposition** the image on your slide simply by dragging it, and you can resize it by dragging any of the selection handles.

- **Add an image Description**

Every picture in your presentation can have its caption. When someone uses a screen reader to access your presentation, the image descriptions are read aloud. To do this:

Select the image with a click, and then go to the **Image tab** in the **Format** panel.

Simply enter your text into the **Description text box** and **save**

- **Add an image gallery in Keynote on Mac**

An image gallery allows multiple photographs to be displayed sequentially on a single slide. Playing the presentation allows you to cycle through the images before moving on to the next slide. As we move from one image to the next, we see a visual effect.

To open an image gallery, select **Media** from the toolbar's menu.

You can **resize** and **reposition** the image gallery by dragging its selection handles.

Simply drop your image files into the gallery from your computer.

The image gallery must be selected for any of the following to take effect:

Adjust the position or zoom level of an image: To reposition an image on a slide, double-click it to select it and drag it to a new location. To zoom in or out, simply drag the slider.

Reorder images: Drag the thumbnail images to rearrange them after selecting the **Gallery** tab in the **Format** sidebar.

Change the transition between images: In the Animate sidebar, select the **Action tab**, and then select **Change** to modify the transition that plays between slides.

To navigate through the image gallery, click the Previous Item button or the Next Item button.

To remove an image from the gallery, in the Format sidebar, click the Gallery tab, click the image thumbnail, then press Delete.

- **Add a caption or title to objects in Keynote on Mac**

You can also add a title to an image gallery, as well as add captions to individual images or all images.

Adding a Caption

- To add a caption to your image, select the image
- Choose an option from the list below to change the format in the sidebar:
- To add a **caption** to a **shape, image, movie, text box, or equation,** go to the **Style tab** and check the box labeled Caption.

For Drawing: Choose the Caption checkbox by going to the Drawing menu item.

For Tables: Tables can have captions added by clicking the **Table tab** and marking the box that says Caption.

For Charts: Select the Caption checkbox by going to the Chart menu item.

For Image Gallery: To add a caption to a gallery of images, select the option to do so from the Gallery tab by checking the box to the right of Caption.

For Grouped Object: Select the Caption checkbox in the Arrange menu for grouped objects.

- **Add a Title**

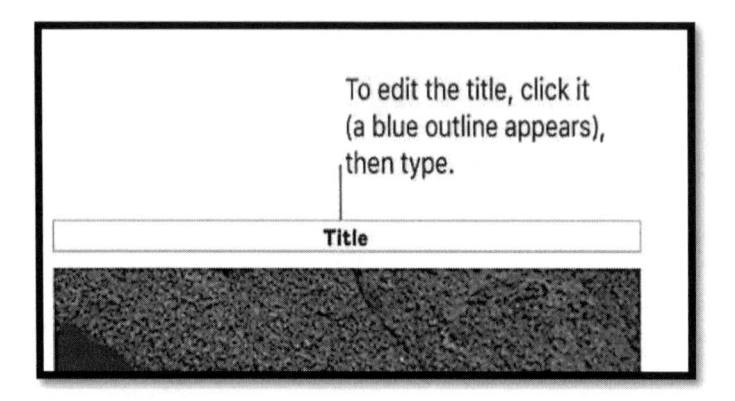

Choose the object with which you want to enter a title.

Choose an option in the Format menu:

Shape, image, movie, text box, or equation can have its title by clicking the Style tab and checking the box labeled Title.

For Drawing Select the Title checkbox by clicking the Drawing tab.

For Tables: Select the checkbox beside Title on the Table tab to add a title to your tables.

For Chart: To change the chart's title, go to the **Chart** tab and click the Title checkbox.

For Image Gallery: When creating an image gallery, choose the **Gallery** menu item, and then select the Title checkbox.

For Grouped Object: To assign a title to a group of objects, select the checkbox labeled Title on the **Arrange** tab.

Note: The title can be moved to the top or bottom by using the corresponding drop-down menu next to the Title.

If you add a caption and then select "**Bottom**," it will always appear under the subtitle.

Select "**Top**" or "**Center**" from the drop-down menu next to the **Title** to generate a donut chart.

Select the title (or the object, then the title), and then use the options on the Title tab of the Format sidebar to alter the font, size, style, and other formatting features.

Mask (Crop a Photo)

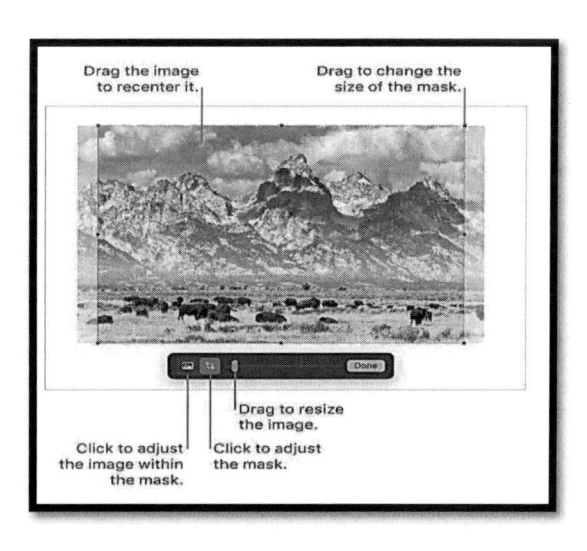

A mask, also called photo cropping, allows you to hide unwanted details in an image without permanently altering the original.

Simply double-click the image to view it at its full resolution.

The mask's setting screen loads. Initially, your mask will have the same proportions as your image.

If your Mac is equipped with a Force Touch track pad, you can activate the mask settings by pressing down hard on the image (press firmly on the track pad until you feel a deeper click).

The controls allow you to hide or reveal specific regions of the image.

The next photo you take will be entirely up to this mask's artistic direction.

When you're done, click the Finish button.

To Alter the shape: Using the shape you want to use as a mask, select the image you want to mask by right-clicking it and going to **Format** > **Image** > **Mask with Shape.** Simply by pulling the shape's handles, you can make it smaller or larger.

For iPhone

To crop a photo on your iPhone, just tap and hold the picture for a moment.

The mask's settings menu opens. The default size of the mask is the same as your image. To see only the parts of the picture you want to see, adjust the frame size and position. The mask adjustment bar is located at the image's footer. When you are finished, tap the done button.

Adjust Saturation, Exposure, and Other Settings

Select the image with a click, and then go to the **Image ta**b in the **Format panel.** Make alterations to the control

Exposure: Changing the exposure of a photo means adjusting the level of brightness or darkness throughout the image.

Saturation: Image saturation can be adjusted to modify the intensity of colors. As you drag to the right, the colors will become deeper and more vibrant.

Enhance: Using the histogram, the image is enhanced automatically by balancing the red, green, and blue tones.

Just click **Reset** or the **Reset Imag**e button in the Adjust Image window to undo your changes.

Resize, Rotate, and Flip Objects in Keynote

Resizing an object allows you to change the size of the object however you like, while proportional resizing maintains the object's original shape. The dimensions can be customized to your needs. Except for tables, charts, and image galleries, you can flip or rotate any item.

Object Resizing

Select an object by clicking on it.

The object is locked if there are no white squares around it; to resize it, you must first unlock it.

By clicking **Arrange** in the Format sidebar, you can decide whether the object should be resized freely or proportionally:

Freely Resize: Select the "Constrain proportions" box and deselect it (below Size).

Resize Proportionally: Make sure the box labeled "Constrain proportions" is checked.

Note: Please take note that only proportional resizing is allowed for groups containing specific objects. Images and videos that have been rotated and shapes that turn green when selected fall into this category.

Rotate an Object

- Select the image you want to rotate by clicking on it.
- Select the **Arrange** button in the **Format** toolbar.
- To set the desired rotation angle, either drag the rotate wheel or enter a number in the degree field.
- You can also rotate an object by dragging it while holding down the Command key and pointing to a white square on it.

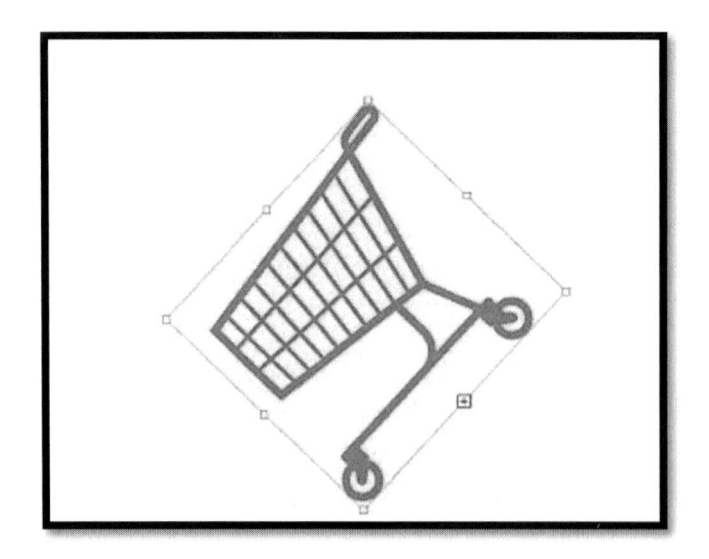

For iPhone:

Select the object, then hold it with two fingers and rotate it by turning your hand.

Once you've started the rotation, you can keep going by dragging with one finger. To indicate the degree of rotation, a compass appears.

With just two fingers, you can spin this thing around.

Alternatively, Select an image, go to the **Format** menu, select **Arrange**, and finally select **Rotate**. To change the object's rotation angle, either clicks and drag the wheel next to Rotate or type in the desired number of degrees.

Flip an Object

- Select the image
- Select the **Arrange** button in the **Format** toolbar.
- To perform a vertical or horizontal flip, use the Flip button (located close to the rotate wheel).

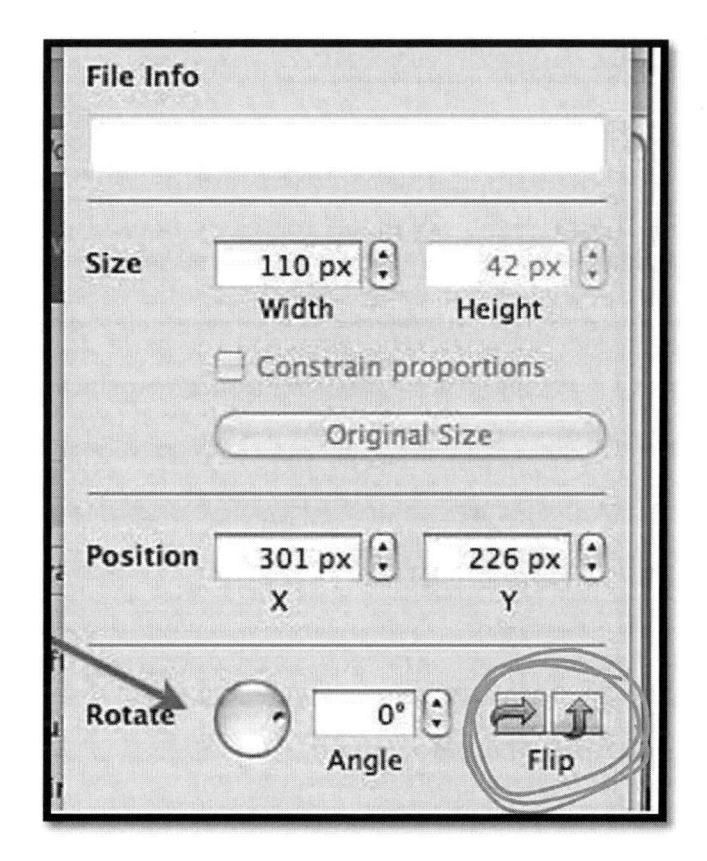

Position and Align objects well

Multiple objects can be aligned with one another, or the location of a single object can be specified by entering its x and y coordinates.

Align an object using x and y coordinates

To do this:

- Select an object
- Select the Arrange button in the Format toolbar.
- Fill in the X and Y coordinates in the appropriate fields.
- For X, we use the distance from the left side of the slide to the object's top left corner.
- The Y coordinate is the distance from the top of the slide to the object's top left corner.
- The x and y coordinates of the object are shown when you drag it.

Align objects vertically and horizontally

- Select an image
- Select the Arrange button in the Format toolbar.
- The Align menu will appear; select a setting from the drop-down menu.

The selected object will be centered on the slide. If more than one item is selected, they will all move to be in the same position relative to the object with the greatest alignment in the direction you chose. If you try to align three things to the left, for instance, the object on the far left stays put and the other two adjust themselves to fit.

Equally space objects

Both horizontal and vertical, or, object spacing, can be adjusted independently.

- Select an object, three or more
- Select the Arrange button in the Format toolbar.
- Select an option from the Distribute drop-down menu and select any of the following.

Evenly: Objects are evenly spaced in all three dimensions (horizontal, vertical, and diagonal).
Horizontally: Along the horizontal axis, objects are evenly separated.
Vertically: Along the vertical axis, things are evenly spaced.

Image Enhancement

If you're making a presentation in Keynote, you can choose from a wide range of image formats.

You can make changes or edits to your images after you've added them to your slides. The "**Adjust Image**" window, which contains a wide variety of controls, is where you need to go to accomplish this.

To do this:

Open the presentation and navigate to the slide containing the image. Select "**View**" via the drop-down menu. To access the "**Adjust Image**" panel, select "**Show Adjust Image.**" Changes can be made more or less drastic by dragging the slider to the right or left, respectively. Move the "**Brightness**" or "**Contrast**" slider to modify the image's luminance and darkness, respectively. The "**Saturation**" slider allows you to alter the color's intensity. Adjust the "**Temperature**" slider to make the image cooler or warmer. Set the image's overall **hue** by dragging the "**Tint**" slider. The image can be made more or less sharp using the "**Sharpness**" slider. Adjust the image's brightness by dragging the "Exposure" slider up or down. The "**Levels**" slider lets you modify the contrast between the scenes' darkest and brightest areas. To instantly make the colors sharper, just hit the "**Enhance**" button. To undo any changes you've made to the image, select "Reset Image."

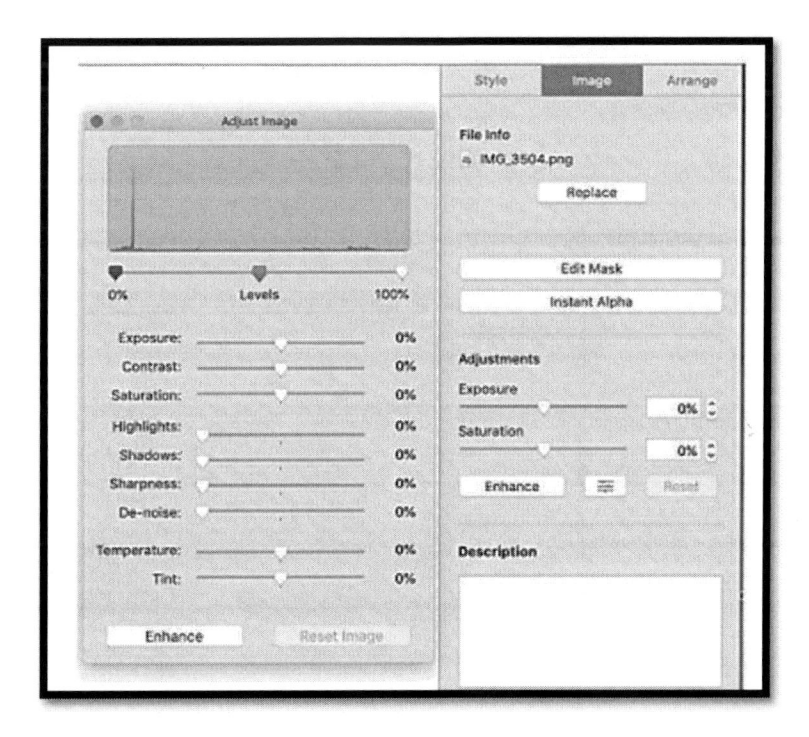

Add a Reflection:

- Select an image or object
- Select the Style tab in the Format toolbar.
- Activate the **Reflection** toggle and adjust the visibility of the reflection using the slider.

Add a Shadow

- Select an object or image
- Select the **Style tab** in the Format toolbar.
- Choose a shadow by clicking the revealing arrow next to it and then selecting it from the resulting menu.

Drop Shadow: The effect of a drop shadow is to give the impression that the object in question is floating above the slide.
Contact Shadow: The effect of a contact shadow is to give the impression that the object is resting on the slide.
Curve Shadow: Curved shadow gives the impression that the edges of the object are rounded off.

You can alter the appearance of the shadow by modifying any of the following:
Blur: The blurring of the edges of a shadow.
Offset: The offset is the distance between the object or text and the shadow.
Angle: Shadow cast at an angle, or an angle.
Perspective: A contact shadow's angle of illumination is a key factor in determining its perspective.

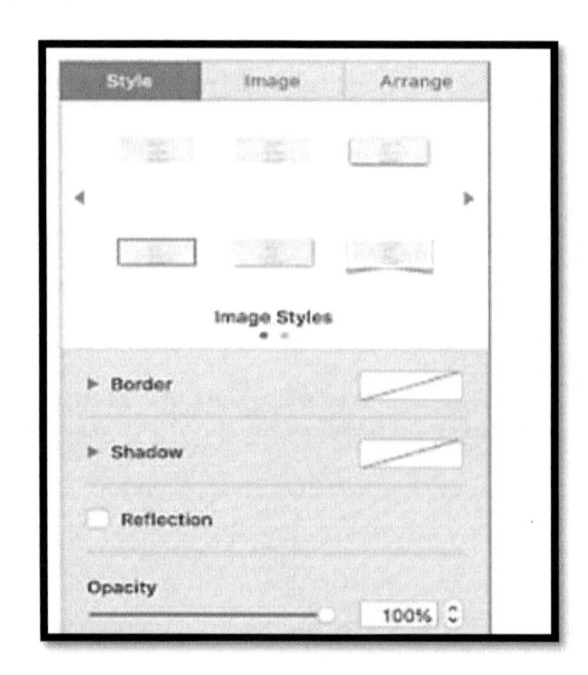

Change Object Transparency in Keynote

Making things more or less transparent can lead to some fascinating results. A low-opacity object, for instance, allows the underlying object to be seen when placed on top of it.

To do this **on Mac**:

Select the image or object

Selecting a text box will alter the entire contents of the text box, including the text and any background color.

To adjust the transparency of a drawing, use the Opacity slider in the Format sidebar; to adjust the transparency of other items, use the Style tab.

In conclusion, you can create interesting effects by making objects more or less opaque. When you put a low-opacity object on top of another object, for example, the bottom object shows through. Editing can change the overall look of your image or object.

CHAPTER SIX
WORKING WITH TABLES IN KEYNOTE

Tables can be useful not only for including data in your presentation but also for neatly arranging items such as text in groups, images, or objects. When creating a Presentation on Keynote, you should consider using a table to format your data especially when you have lots of data to deal with. In this chapter we are going to discuss working with tables, which include how to insert tables, format tables, merge and unmerge tables, columns, rows, etc.

Add a Table

You have two options for inserting your table into Keynote on Mac. 4

Option 1: Open your presentation and navigate to the slide where you want the table to appear. Click the Table button in the toolbar, and a neat little drop-down box appears, allowing you to choose the style and color scheme.

Note: The color schemes available for the table are determined by the theme.

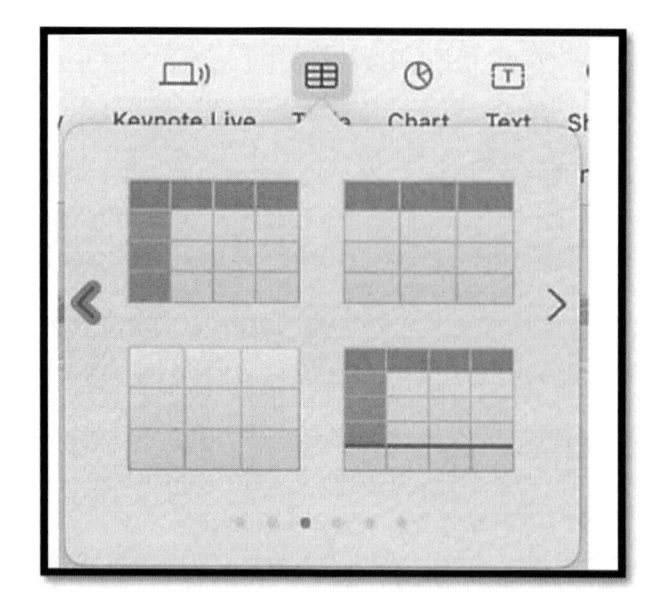

Option 2: You can also insert a table from the menu bar by selecting **Insert** > **Table**. You have the same options for the style of table you want in the pop-out menu, except they're listed as text rather than visually. So, choose between Headers, Basic, Plain, and Sums.

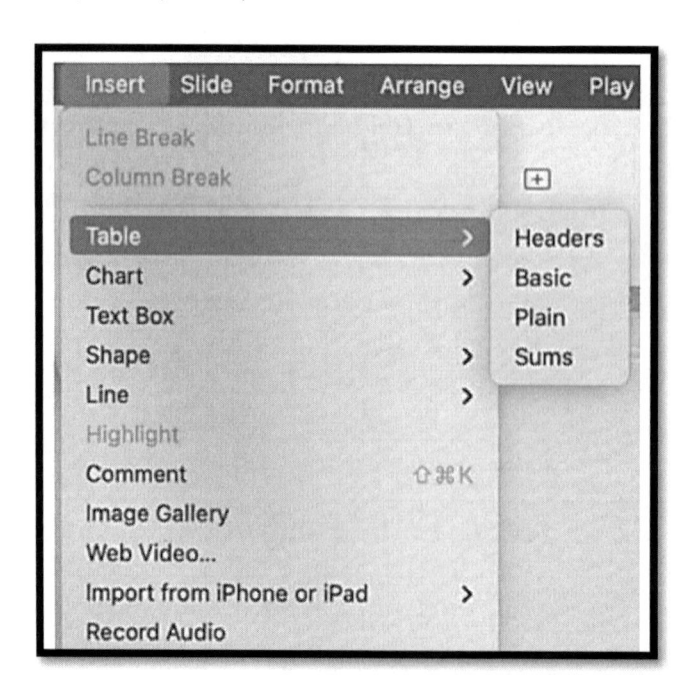

416

Delete a Table

Click the table, then click the Table handle in the top-left corner, and finally press the Delete key on your keyboard.

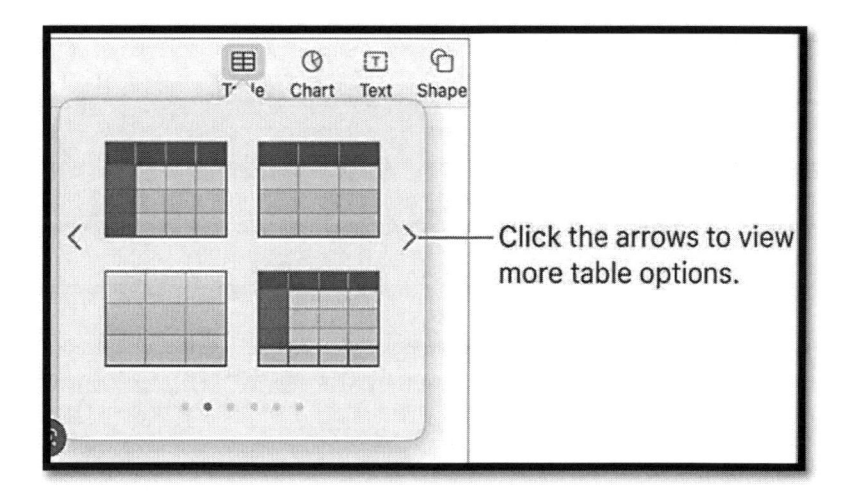

Edit a Table

You can edit a table in various forms. Let's discuss some ways to edit a table on the keynote

- **Change table gridlines and colors in Keynote on Mac**

A table's appearance can be altered by changing its outline, showing or hiding gridlines, adding borders and color to cells, and alternating row colors.

To do this:

Click the table, and then select the **Table tab** from the **Format sidebar.**

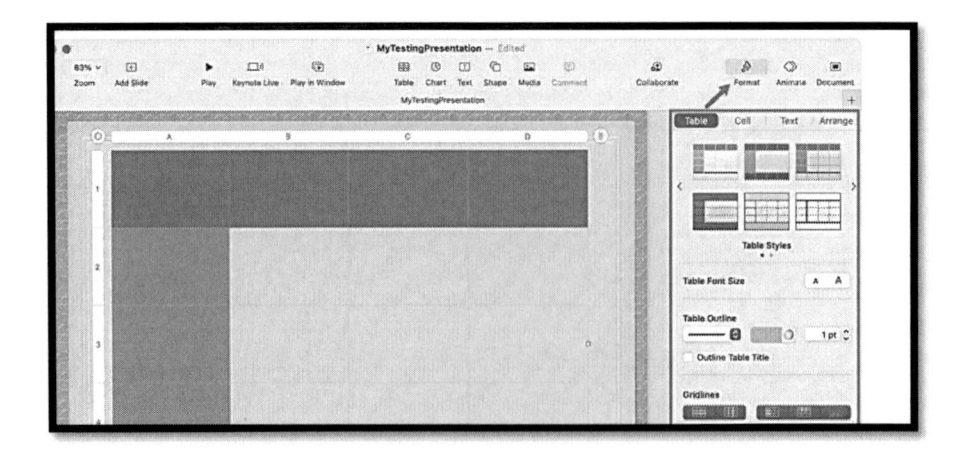

Perform any of the following:

Change the outline: Use the controls in the Table Outline section of the sidebar to change the line type, thickness, and color.

Change the gridlines: Click the buttons in the Gridlines section of the sidebar to show or hide gridlines from the table body, header rows and columns, and footer rows.

- **Change the Borders and Background of the Table Cells**
- You can change the border and background of any table cell selection.
- Choose the cells you want to modify.
- Click the Cell tab in the Format sidebar.

Perform any of the following:

Change cell borders: In the Border section, click a border layout button below the border to select which borders you want to format, then select a border style for the selected borders from the Border Styles pop-up menu. After you select a border style, additional controls appear to allow you to select a line color and thickness, as well as a dotted or solid border.

Click a border layout button, then Command-click additional borders to select multiple borders.

The Sidebar contains controls for changing the appearance of cell borders.

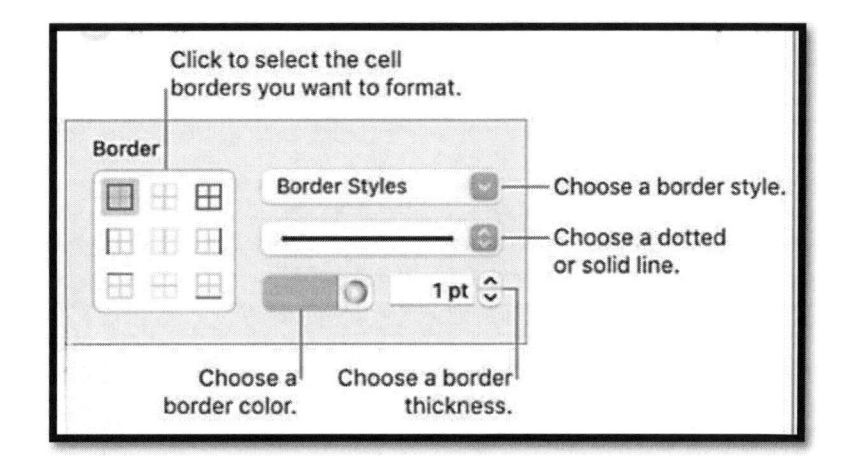

[Diagram: Border formatting options with labels: "Click to select the cell borders you want to format.", "Choose a border style.", "Choose a dotted or solid line.", "Choose a border color.", "Choose a border thickness."]

Change the background by clicking the **color well** in the Fill section, then selects a color option.

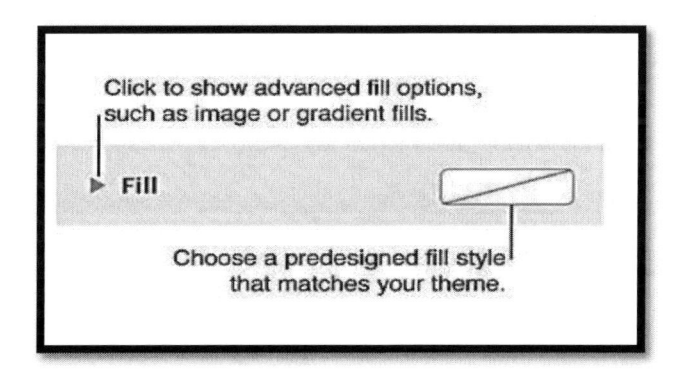

[Diagram: Fill options with labels: "Click to show advanced fill options, such as image or gradient fills.", "Choose a predesigned fill style that matches your theme."]

Alternate the row colors

Click the table, and then select the Table tab from the Format sidebar.

Select the Alternating Row Color checkbox in the sidebar and then click the **color well** to choose a color.

Use Table Styles in Keynote

The simplest way to change the appearance of a table is to apply a different table style to it at any time. You can create a new table style if you customize the look of a table and want to apply the same formatting to other tables. The new style is saved alongside the theme's other styles.

Apply a Different Style to a Table

Click the table, and then select the Table tab from the Format sidebar.

Choose a different style from the drop-down menu at the top of the sidebar.

Note: If you made changes to the appearance of your table before applying a different table style, the new table style keeps those changes. Control-click the new table style, then select Clear Overrides and Apply Style to override those changes when you apply a new style.

Revert Changes to a Table Style

If you changed the look of a table, for example, by changing the border of table cells, you can undo your changes by reapplying the original table style.

Click the table, and then select the Table tab from the Format sidebar.

Control-click the table style to be reapplied, and then select **Clear Overrides and Apply Style.**

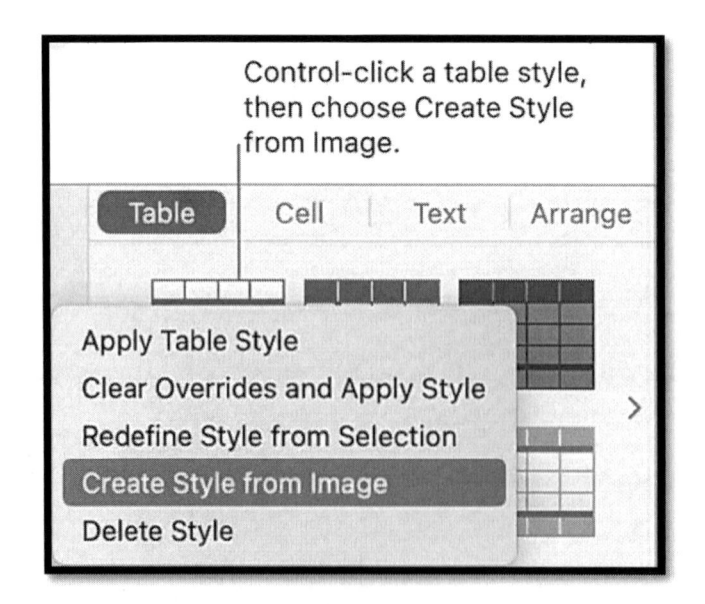

Save a Table as a New Style

- If you make changes to the appearance of a table and want to save them, you can create a new table style that you can use again later.

- Click the table that contains the formatting that you want to save as a new style.
- Click the Table tab in the Format sidebar.
- To add your style, navigate to the last group of styles by clicking the arrow to the right of the table styles, then click the Add button.
- The new table style is now available in the table styles section at the top of the sidebar.
- You can arrange styles however you want by dragging them.

Table Style that uses the Color in an Image

You can make a table style that matches the colors in an image. When you want to make a visual connection between the data in the table and the subject of the image, this can be useful. The new style includes a table title, a header row and column, and a footer row, all of which match the image's colors. When you apply the new style to a specific table, it adds colors to the table's features.

- Click any table in your presentation, or add a table by clicking the Table button in the toolbar.
- Click the **Table tab** in the Format sidebar.
- Navigate to any image on your computer.
- Click the Media menu button in the toolbar to browse your photos.
- Drag the image to the sidebar's table styles.
- To make a new style, drag an image into the table styles.
- Control-click a table style in the sidebar.
- Select Create Style from Image from the shortcut menu, and then browse for an image.
- The shortcut menu is in the table style.
- A new table style with the image's colors is added to the table styles at the top of the sidebar; it does not replace the style you Control-clicked to open the pop-up menu with.
- Click the style in the sidebar to apply it to the selected table—it isn't applied automatically when you create it.

Redefine a Table

- You can redefine the style to quickly change the appearance of all tables that use the same style.
- Choose a table that uses the style you want to change, and then change its appearance to look the way you want.
- If the table you just modified is no longer selected, click it.
- Click the Table tab in the Format sidebar.
- Control-click the style you want to redefine at the top of the sidebar, and then select Redefine Style from Selection.
- Select one of the following:
- All objects that use the current style should be updated: This alters the appearance of all tables that currently use this style.
- Don't update objects or remove them from the style: This only affects the table you've chosen. Because the style was replaced, the style for the tables that aren't updated is removed from the Style tab.
- Select OK.
- The style in the sidebar is updated, as are all tables that use it.

Organize a Table

You can rearrange the table styles in the sidebar to make it easier to find the ones you use the most.

- Select a table from your presentation.
- Click the **Table tab** in the **Format sidebar**.
- Click and hold the style to be moved, and then drag it to a new location.
- If you have multiple style panes and want to move a style between them, drag it over the left or right arrow to open the other pane.

Add or Remove Rows and Columns in Keynote

A table's rows and columns can be added, deleted, and rearranged. Rows and columns are classified into three types:

The table data is contained in the body rows and columns.

The table's header rows and columns (if any) appear at the top and left side. They typically have a different background color than the body rows and are used to indicate what the row or column contains.

Footer rows (if present) are located at the bottom of a table and can have a different background color than the body rows.

A table with header, body, and footer rows and columns, as well as handles for adding and removing rows and columns.

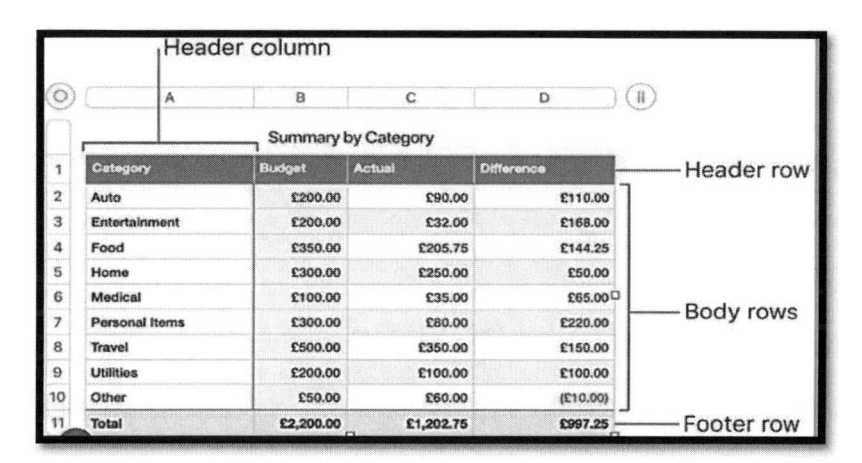

Add or Remove row and column

Select the table.

Perform any of the following:

Columns on the right side of the table can be added or removed: In the top-right corner of the table, click the Add Column button, then an arrow to increase or decrease the number of columns.

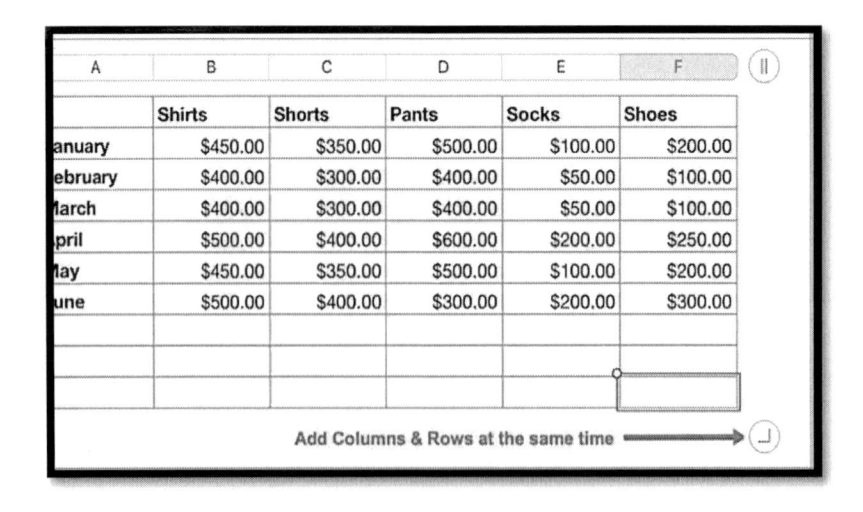

	A	B	C	D	E	F
		Shirts	Shorts	Pants	Socks	Shoes
anuary		$450.00	$350.00	$500.00	$100.00	$200.00
ebruary		$400.00	$300.00	$400.00	$50.00	$100.00
arch		$400.00	$300.00	$400.00	$50.00	$100.00
pril		$500.00	$400.00	$600.00	$200.00	$250.00
ay		$450.00	$350.00	$500.00	$100.00	$200.00
une		$500.00	$400.00	$300.00	$200.00	$300.00

Add Columns & Rows at the same time

Add or remove rows from the table's bottom: In the bottom-left corner of the table, click the Add Row button, then an arrow to increase or decrease the number of rows.

Insert a row or column wherever you want in the table: Control-click a cell, then select where you want the row or column to be added (above, below, before, or after the selected cell). You can also move the pointer over the row or column number or letter next to where you want to add the row or column, click the down arrow, and then select where to add the row or column.

Delete any row or column in the table: Control-click a cell in the row or column to be deleted, and then select Delete Row or Delete Column. You can also move the pointer over the row or column number or letter you want to delete, click the down arrow, and then select Delete Row or Delete Column.

Insert multiple rows or columns at the same time: Select several rows or columns equal to the number of rows or columns you want to insert anywhere in the table. Select Add Rows Above or Add Rows Below by clicking the arrow next to one of the selected row numbers or column letters (or Add Columns Before or Add Columns After).

Delete multiple rows or columns at the same time: Click the arrow, then choose Delete Selected Rows or Delete Selected Columns after the command-clicking the rows or columns.

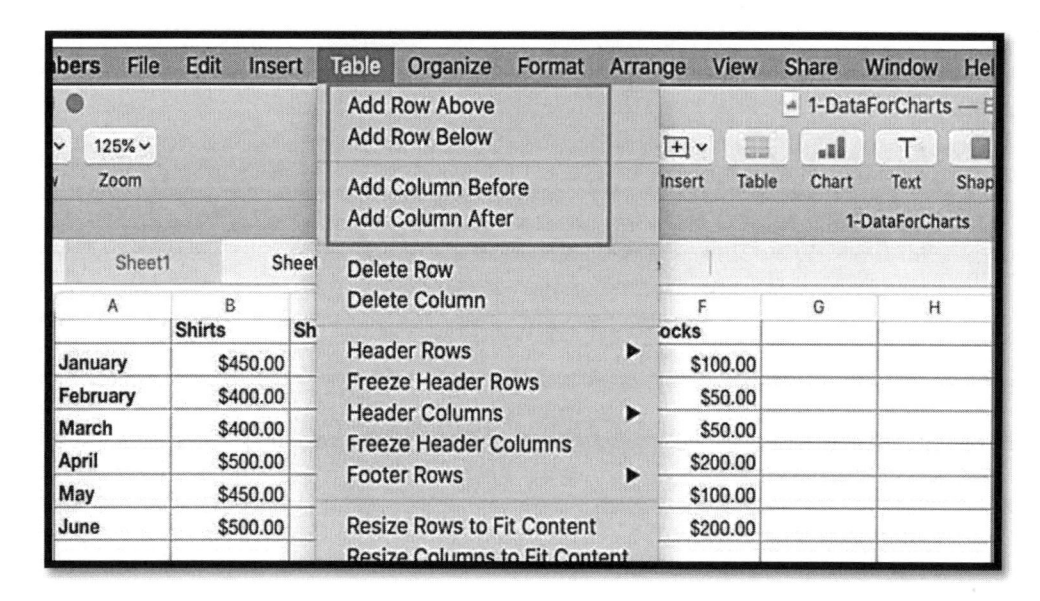

Add or Remove Header Rows and Column

By adding header rows, header columns, and footer rows, existing rows or columns are converted to headers or footers. If you have data in the first row of a table and add a header row, the first row is converted to a header with the same data.

The information in header cells is not used in calculations.

- Click the table, and then select the Table tab from the Format sidebar.
- Select the number of header rows, header columns, or footer rows you want from the pop-up menus below Headers & Footers.

Merge and Unmerge Cells

Merging adjacent table cells creates a single cell. Unmerging previously merged cells keeps all of the data in the new top-left cell.

Note:

Nonadjacent cells or cells from different areas of the table, such as cells from the body and the header, cannot be merged.

Columns and rows cannot be merged.

A cell cannot be split. A cell cannot be unmerged if it has never been merged with another cell.

Merge Cells

- Choose two or more cells that are adjacent.
- Control-click the cells and select **Merge** Cells.
- If the Merge Cells command is grayed out, you may have selected entire columns or rows, or a header cell and a body cell that cannot be merged, even if they are adjacent.

Note:

If only one of the cells had content before merging, the merged cell retains that cell's content and formatting.

If multiple cells contain content before merging, all of the content is preserved; however, cells with a specific data format, such as numbers, currency, or dates, are converted to text.

If you apply a fill color to the top-left cell, the merged cell will inherit that color

Unmerge cells

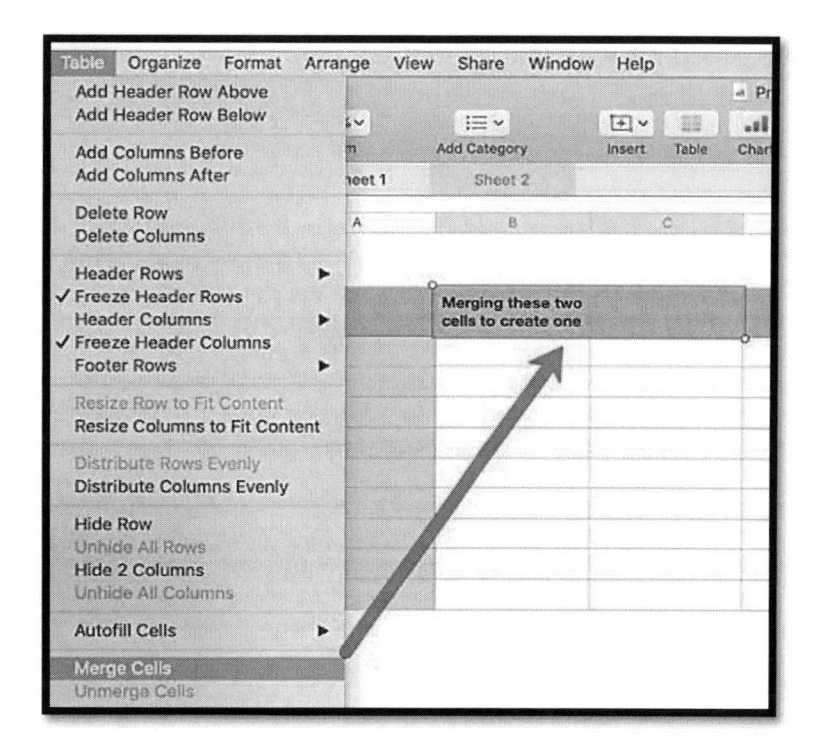

- Unmerge cells by right-clicking the cells and selecting Merge Cells.
- The first unmerged cell receives all of the content from the previously merged cell.
- Merged cells are treated differently in formulas:
- In a formula, use the address of the merged cell's top-left corner to refer to the cell directly.
- A cell range used in a formula cannot contain only a portion of a merged cell.
- If you refer to a cell in a formula and then merge that cell with cells outside the formula's intended range, the formula may fail.

Add and edit cell content in Keynote on Mac

There are several ways to add content to a table. You can enter new content directly into cells or copy and paste content from elsewhere. After you've added content to a cell, you can always edit or clear it.

Make sure a table is unlocked if you can't add content to it. Select Arrange > Unlock after clicking the table (from the Arrange menu at the top of your screen).

Add content to cells

- Fill in the blanks with content.
- **Fill in the blanks with the following text:** Start typing after clicking the cell.
- Copy the paragraphs you want to paste into a cell, then double-click the cell and select **Edit > Paste** (from the Edit menu at the top of the screen).
- **Content should be edited:** Double-click the cell to bring up the insertion point, then type. Click where you want the insertion point to be, then type.
- **Replace the following content**: Start typing after clicking the cell. The previous content is overwritten.
- **Delete everything**: Click inside the cell, then press the Delete key on your keyboard.

Wrap text to fit in a cell

If a cell is too narrow to display all of the text in the cell, you can wrap the text so that it appears on multiple lines in the cell.

Text in a single cell can be wrapped or unwrapped: Control-click the cell, then select Wrap Text from the shortcut menu. When wrapping is enabled, a checkmark appears. Deselect Wrap Text to unwrap text.

Wrap text for a row, column, or entire table as follows: Choose the row or column, or table. Click the Text tab in the Format sidebar, then the Style button near the top of the sidebar. Check or uncheck the "Wrap text in cell" box.

Clear Content from a range of cells

- Choose the cells to be deleted.
- **Perform one of the following:**
- Remove the content while keeping the data format, text style, and cell style of the cells: Press the Delete key.

- All data, formatting, and styling should be removed: Select Edit > Clear All (from the Edit menu at the top of your screen).

Autofill Cells

Fill cells, rows, or columns quickly with the same formula, data, or logical sequence of data—for example, a series of numbers, letters, or dates.

Perform any of the following:

- **Fill one or more cells with content from neighboring cells:** Select the cells that contain the content you want to copy, and then move the pointer over the selection's border until a yellow autofill handle (a dot) appears. Drag the handle over the cells where you want the content to be added.
- A cell with a yellow handle that you can drag to autofill cells.
- Comments are not added, but any data, cell format, formula, or fill associated with the selected cells is. Autofill replaces existing data with the content you're entering.
- **Fill in cells with sequential content or patterns from neighboring cells:** Fill in the first two body cells (not header or footer cells) of the row or column you want to fill with the first two items in the series; for example, type A and B. Move the pointer over a selection border until a yellow autofill handle (a dot) appears, then drag the handle over the cells you want to fill.
- You can also use a value pattern to autofill cells. For example, if two selected cells have the values 1 and 4, dragging over the adjacent two cells adds the values 7 and 10. (Values are incremented by 3).
- Auto-filling does not establish an ongoing relationship between cells in a group. After auto filling, the cells can be changed independently of one another.
- When you autofill cells, any formulas that use those cells are automatically updated to use the new value.

Drag the yellow handle to autofill cells.

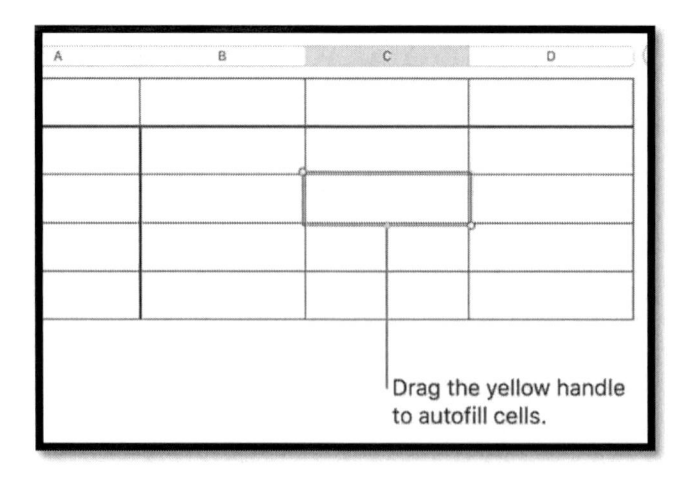

Add an object to a cell

- Images, shapes, lines, charts, and equations can be pasted into table cells. When you paste an object into a cell, it is added to the cell as an image fills (background). You can change the way the object fills the cell or add text in front of the object.
- When you paste a shape with text, only the text is pasted into the cell.
- Choose **Edit > Cut or Edit > Copy** after selecting an object in your presentation (or another document) (cut removes it from its original location).
- Select the cell to which you want to add the object by clicking it (it can be a cell that already has text).
- Select **Edit > Paste.**
- The keynote scales the object to fit in the cell by default. To change the size of the object, in the Format sidebar, click the Cell tab, then click the disclosure arrow next to Fill, and then selects another option from the "Scale to Fit" pop-up menu.

Delete an object from a cell

You can delete an object without deleting the text if a cell contains both text and an object.

Click the cell, and then select the Cell tab from the Format sidebar.

- Click the reveal arrow next to Fill.

430

- Select No Fill from the Image Fill pop-up menu.
- The object removal control for the selected cell.

Show a Cell Row and Column

When you move the pointer over a table, you can temporarily highlight the row and column of a cell in blue. This can help you identify column and row references for specific cells in a large table.

While moving the pointer over a cell, hold down the Option key.

Copy or Move Cells

Cells can be copied or moved.

When you copy or move a cell's data to a new location in the table, all of the cell's properties, including its data format, fill, border, and comments, are copied.

Choose which cells to copy or move.

Perform one of the following:

Move the data: After selecting the cells, click and hold the selection until the cells rise off the table, then drag them to a different location in the table. The new data replaces the old data.

Copy and replace existing content: Select Edit > Copy (from the Edit menu at the top of your screen). Choose Edit > Paste, then select the top-left cell where you want to paste the data (or an area with the same dimensions as the cells you're pasting).

Choose Paste Formula Results if your data range contains formulas but you only want the results.

To paste a cell style, select the cells where you want to paste the style, then choose **Format > Paste Style** (from the Format menu at the top of your screen).

Copy and paste the cell contents without the style: Select the cells where you want to paste, then select **Edit > Paste and Match Style**. The formatting of the new location is applied to the pasted cells.

To make a new table, copy and paste the following code outside of an existing table: Select the cells, and then drag them to the desired location. The pasted cells are pasted into a new table.

When you copy a range of cells that contain hidden data (either hidden or filtered), the hidden data is copied as well. When you paste to a range of cells that contains a matching arrangement of hidden cells, the hidden data is also pasted. The hidden content is not pasted otherwise.

Resize rows and columns in Keynote on Mac

In a table, you can change the width of selected columns and the height of selected rows, or you can resize all rows or columns at once.

Individual cells cannot be changed in width or height.

Resize rows and columns manually

Select the table.

Perform one of the following:

To resize a column or row, move the pointer to the right of the column letter or below the row number until you see the Resize pointer, then drag to resize.

Multiple rows or columns can be resized: Select the rows or columns, and then move the pointer to the right of the rightmost column letter or below the bottommost row number until you see the Resize pointer, then drag to resize. They've been proportionally resized.

Resize all of the rows and columns in a table: Drag the white square at the bottom edge of the table to resize rows; drag the square on the right edge of the table to resize columns; or drag the square in the bottom-right corner to resize both rows and columns.

When the rows or columns of one table align with the rows or columns of another table on the canvas, yellow alignment guides may appear as you drag.

Note: If the content of cells does not fit after resizing, you can adjust the rows or columns. See the task below to find out how.

Resize rows and columns precisely

- To resize a cell in a row or column, click it.
- Click the Table tab in the Format sidebar.
- Click the Height and Width arrows in Row & Column Size to set the desired size.
- The controls for determining the exact row or column size.
- The row or column as a whole is resized. When you select cells from more than one row or column, all of the rows or columns in the selection are resized.

Size a row or column to fit its content

- Select the table.
- Click the arrow to the right of the row number or column letter, then choose Fit Height to Content or Fit Width to Content from the menu that appears.

Make Rows and columns the same size

Select the rows or columns to make them the same size; to make all the rows or columns the same size, click the table, then click the Table handles in the top-left corner.

Select **Format > Table > Evenly Distribute Rows or Evenly Distribute Columns** (from the Format menu at the top of your screen).

Resize a table

Resizing a table makes it larger or smaller, but it does not affect the number of rows and columns it contains.

Then, in the top-left corner of the table, click the **Table handle.**

To make the table larger or smaller, drag any of the white squares on the table's edge:

Resize the rows and columns at the same time: Drag the white square in the corner to the right.

Resize the table in proportion: Shift-drag the white square in the corner to the right.

A chosen table with resizable white squares.

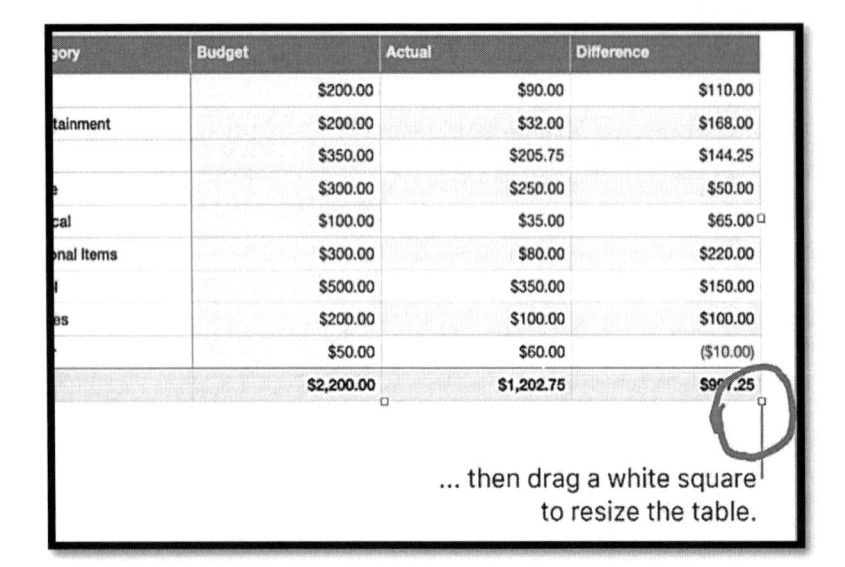

ory	Budget	Actual	Difference
	$200.00	$90.00	$110.00
tainment	$200.00	$32.00	$168.00
	$350.00	$205.75	$144.25
	$300.00	$250.00	$50.00
cal	$100.00	$35.00	$65.00
nal Items	$300.00	$80.00	$220.00
	$500.00	$350.00	$150.00
es	$200.00	$100.00	$100.00
	$50.00	$60.00	($10.00)
	$2,200.00	$1,202.75	$997.25

... then drag a white square to resize the table.

Move a table

Drag the Table handle in the top-left corner of the table after clicking it.

Lock or unlock a table

- A table can be locked so that it cannot be edited, moved, or deleted.
- **Tables should be locked:** Select Arrange > Lock after clicking the table (from the Arrange menu at the top of your screen).
- **To unlock a table, do the following:** Select Arrange > Unlock after clicking the table.
- In Keynote for Mac, select tables, cells, rows, and columns.
- You must first select tables, cells, rows, and columns before you can edit or rearrange them.

Select tables, cells, rows, and columns in Keynote on Mac

To complete a task, you may need to select rather than simply click a table. Selecting ensures that the table is in the proper state for the next steps.

Select a table

To select the table, first, click outside of it to ensure it is not selected, then click inside it.

Select a cell

- Click the table once, then the cell once.
- To edit the contents of a cell, select it: Click the cell twice.
- Click the table, then click the cell once, then drag a white dot in any direction across the range of adjacent cells.
- When you drag the yellow dot, the cell contents are copied to the rows you are dragging over. If you inadvertently do this, drag the yellow dot back to its original position or press Command-Z on the keyboard to undo the action.
- Select nonadjacent cells by clicking the table once, then Command-clicking any other cells.

Select rows and columns

- Select the table.
- Above the columns, letters appear, and numbers appear to the left of the rows.

Perform one of the following:

- Choose just one row or column: Click the row or column number or letter.
- Choose several adjacent rows or columns: Drag a white dot across the adjacent rows or columns after clicking the number or letter for a row or column.
- Choose rows or columns that are not adjacent: Command-click any row or column number or letter.

Change the look of table text in Keynote on Mac

Both the entire table and individual cells inside the table can have their text formatted differently.

Change the font, size, and color of the table text

Pick the table to edit all of the table's text at once, or select individual cells to edit just those cells' text.

The Text tab can be found on the Format toolbar.

To modify the font, size, color, and character style select the Style menu item and then utilize the text controls in the font area (such as bold or italic).

The formatting options for text in tables.

Please take note that you must choose the specific text you wish to alter before applying a character style from the Character Style pop-up menu. Selecting a cell, row, column, or full table prevents you from making a style selection from this menu.

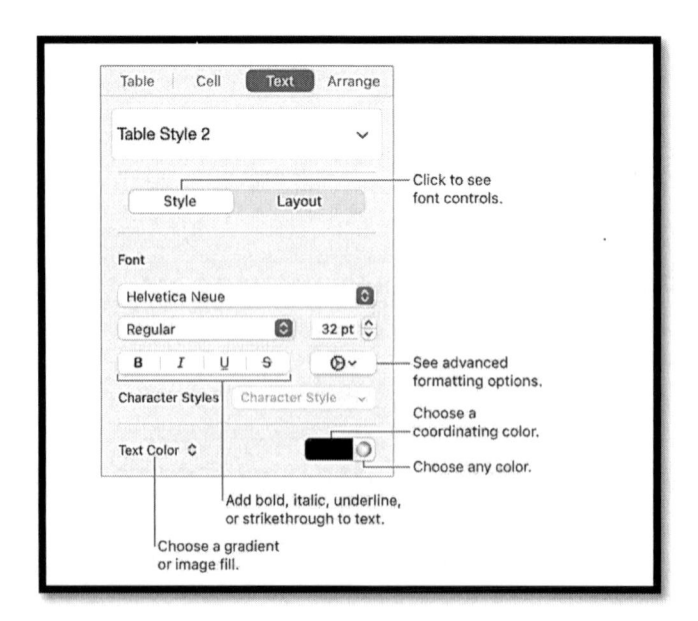

Change the font size of all table text

- You can change the font size proportionally for all text in the table.

436

- Select the table.
- Click the Table tab in the Format sidebar, then the Table Font Size buttons.
- The sidebar contains controls for changing the font size of the table.

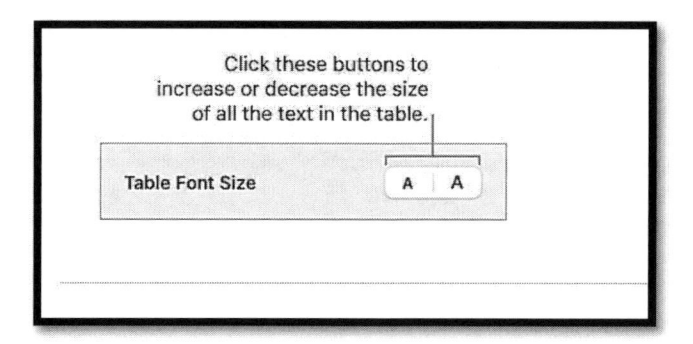

Conclusion

Tables can be useful not only for including data in your slideshow but also for neatly arranging items such as images or objects. Will you use tables in your next Keynote presentation?

CHAPTER SEVEN

WORKING WITH CHARTS AND SHAPES ON KEYNOTE

In making your presentation look unique and well-presentable, you can add charts to your presentation especially when you have lots of scattered data, using charts will help your data be more presentable. In this chapter, we will look at how to add chart to your presentation, how to edit charts, and also how to add shapes to your presentation.

Note: Keynote's Chart Data editor is where your data will go when you're making a chart (not in the chart itself). Making modifications in the Chart Data editor results in an immediate refresh of the chart.

Types of Charts on Keynote

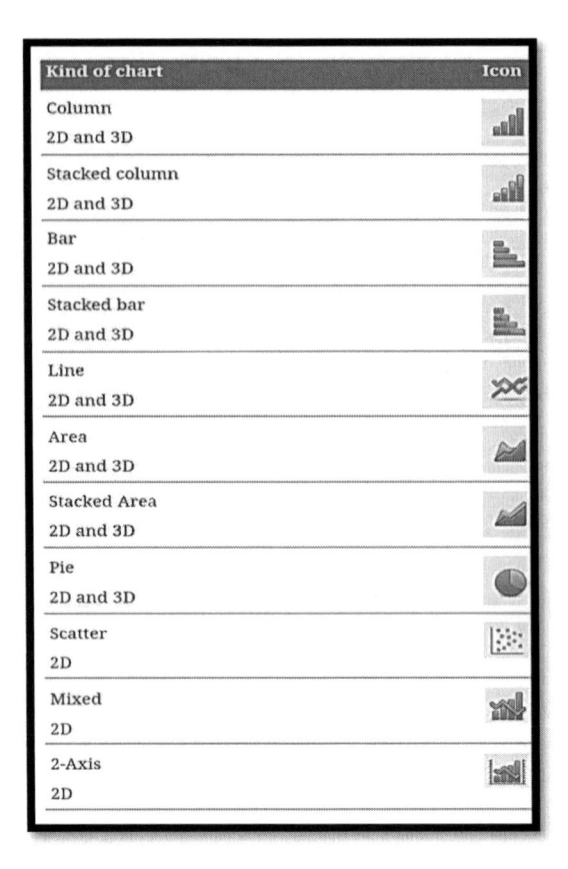

Kind of chart	Icon
Column 2D and 3D	
Stacked column 2D and 3D	
Bar 2D and 3D	
Stacked bar 2D and 3D	
Line 2D and 3D	
Area 2D and 3D	
Stacked Area 2D and 3D	
Pie 2D and 3D	
Scatter 2D	
Mixed 2D	
2-Axis 2D	

Add Chart on Keynote

There are different types of charts on Keynote. The bar chart, line chart, pie chart, area chart, or radar chart.

To switch between different kinds of charts, just hit the Chart button on the toolbar and then select 2D, 3D, or Interactive. To view additional options, use the left and right arrow keys.

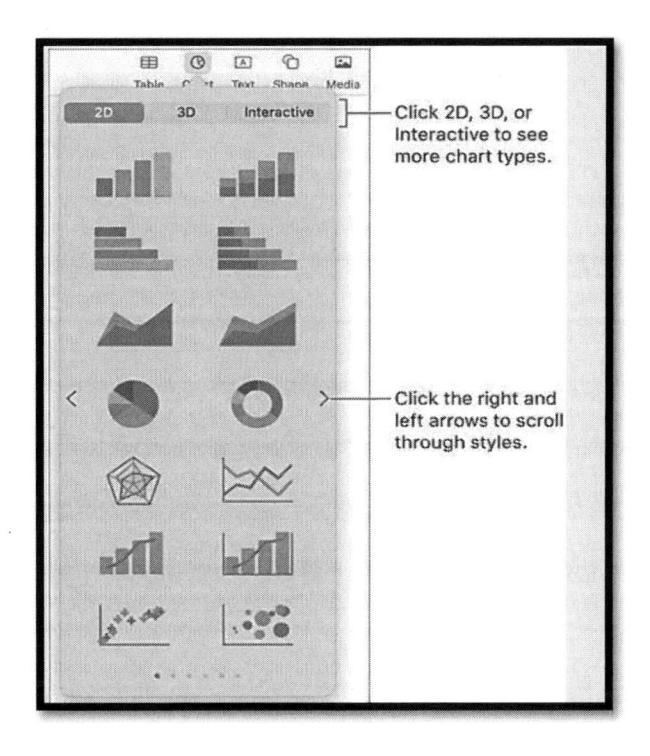

To Add a Chart:

- Select a chart and add it to the slide.
- You can input data in the chart by clicking the chart, then clicking the **Edit Chart Data** button next to the chart.
- The Chart Data editor shows column headers and buttons to select rows and columns for the data
- Use the buttons in the top right corner of the table to switch between plotting rows and columns as data series.
- To return to the chart, close the Chart Data editor.

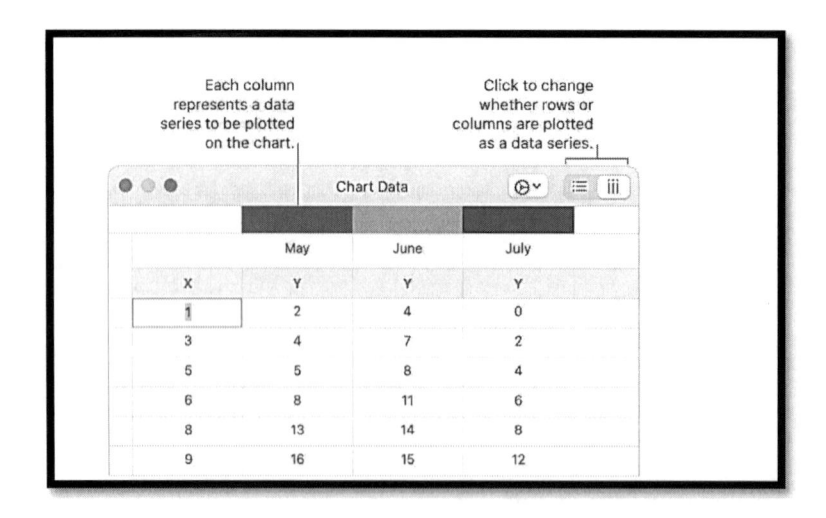

To insert data into the Chart Data Editor, choose one of the following options:

- To edit row and column labels, **double-click a label** and then start typing.
- To add or modify a number in a cell, **double-click the cell** and then start typing.
- Drag a row or column label to a new position to reorder rows or columns.
- Click **Add Row or Add Column** to add a row above the selected row or a column to the left of the selected column, respectively.
- Click the "**Row vs. Column**" option in the Chart Data Editor to pick whether the chart's data series are represented by rows or columns.

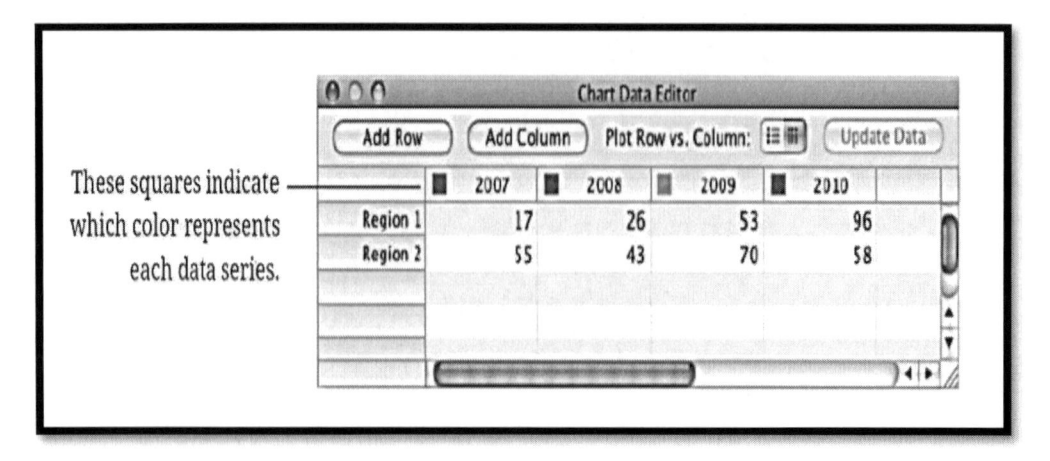

Delete a Chart

Select the Chart by clicking on it, and then hit the **delete** key on your keyboard.

Modify a Chart

Changes can be made at any time to the chart data references (numbers, dates, and times). All or part of a data series can be added or removed, and a series can be modified by the addition or removal of data.

After selecting the chart and clicking the Edit Chart Data button, you can:

- **Add new data set:** You can enter data into the Chart Data editor by clicking a cell in a new column or row, typing, and pressing Return or Tab.
- **Delete a data set**: To delete a row or column, select it by clicking its bar, then clicking the arrow that appears, and finally clicking **Delete Row or Delete Column**.
- **Reorder Data Series:** You can rearrange the order of the data series by dragging the bars in the appropriate places.
- **Currency symbols and other formatting options:** This can be accessed by selecting the Series tab at the top of the right-hand sidebar and then adjusting the corresponding controls.

The chart can be viewed again by closing the Chart Data window.

Switch rows and columns as data series

When you add a chart, Keynote sets its default data series. If a table is square or wider than it is tall, the table rows are usually the default series

You can choose whether the data series is rows or columns.

After selecting the chart, click the **Edit Chart Data** button.

In the Chart Data editor's top-right corner, click a row or column button.

Plot rows and Plot columns buttons are available in the Chart Data editor.

When you're finished, close the Chart Data editor.

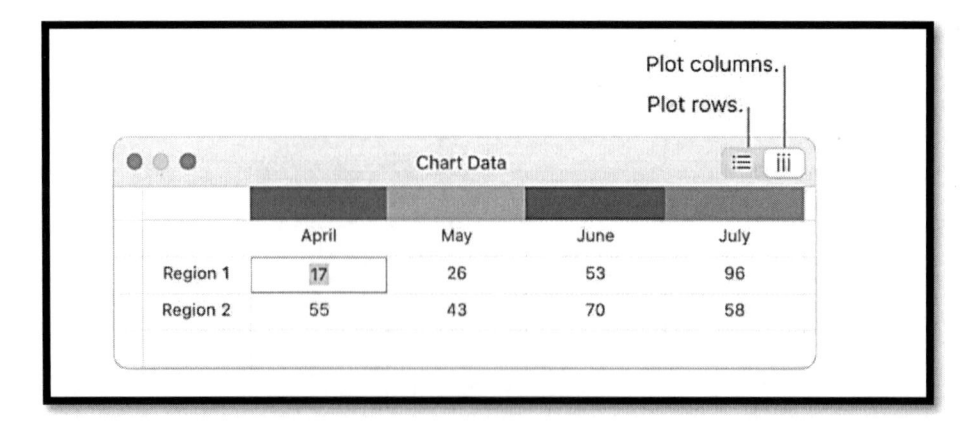

About Chart down Sampling

When a column, bar, line, or area chart refers to a table with a large number of data points, the chart displays a representative sample of each series to improve Keynote performance, this is known as down sampling. Down sampling does not affect the data in your table and only affects the visible data points in the chart.

When you click Large Data Set in the Chart tab of the Format sidebar, a message appears if your chart data is being down sampled.

If you want to see specific data points in your chart, you must build it from a smaller table or a smaller subset of data from a larger table.

Change the look of chart text and labels in Keynote on Mac

You can change the appearance of chart text by applying a different style, changing the font, adding a border, and other options.

Change the font, style, and size of a chart text

Click the chart, and then select the **Chart tab** from the **Format sidebar**.

To do any of the following, use the controls in the Chart Font section of the sidebar:

- **Modify the font**: Select a font from the Chart Font pop-up menu.

- **Modify the character's style:** Select an option from the pop-up menu located beneath the font name (Regular, Bold, and so on).
- **Reduce or increase the font size**: Select the small or large A.
- All of the text in the chart increases or decreases in proportion (by the same percentage).

Edit the Chart Title

- Charts have a default placeholder title (Title) that is hidden. The chart title can be displayed and renamed.
- Click the chart, and then select the Chart tab from the Format sidebar.
- Choose the Title checkbox.
- Double-click the chart's placeholder title, and then type your own.
- To change the font, size, and color of the title, double-click it again, and then use the controls in the Chart Title section of the sidebar to make changes.
- To move the title to the center of a donut chart, select Center from the Title Position pop-up menu.

Designing your Bar Chart

You can design your bar chart to any look of your choice. There are various ways to design your bar chart.

- **Change Color and Shadows in Chart Element**

Adding colors, textures, shadows, and other things can change how a chart looks. You can change the way a chart looks as a whole, or you can change individual data series to make them stand out...

To do this:

- Click on the chart.
- **Click the Chart tab in the Format column, then do one of the following:**
- **Apply a coordinated color palette to all the data series in the chart**: Click one of the small pictures at the top of the Chart tab. Every color on the chart changes at the same time.
- **Apply colors, images, or textures to all the data series in the chart**: Click the Chart Colors button, click Colors, Images, or Textures,

and then click a set of colors to use them. Hold the pointer over a color combination to see what the colors will look like in your chart.
- To change how one data series looks, click on a part of it (like a bar, column, pie wedge, or scatter point) and then click **the Style tab** in the Format sidebar. To make changes, use the controls in the sidebar. The changes only affect the element or data series that was chosen. To change a different series, click on one of its parts, then make the changes you want.

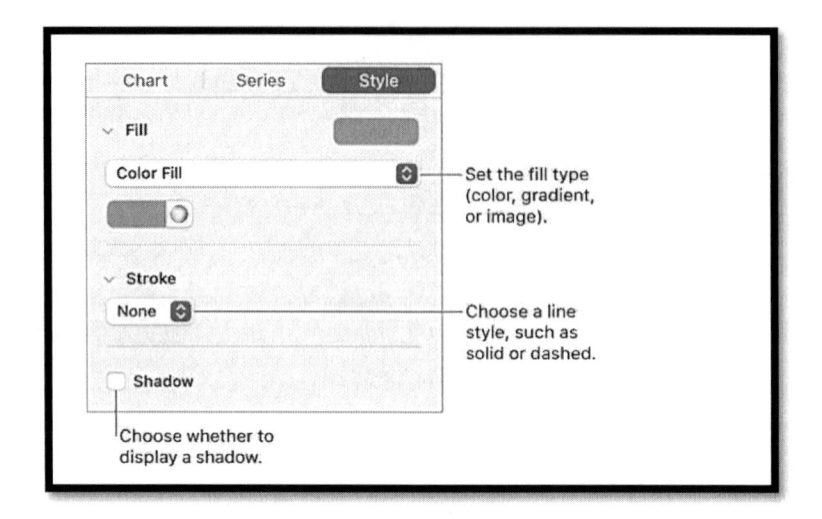

Change the spacing in the bar or column chart

- Click the chart, and then click the **Chart tab** in the Format sidebar.
- Click the arrow next to Gaps that says "Show more," then set the amount of space.
- A column chart that shows how far apart the columns are compared to how far apart the sets are.

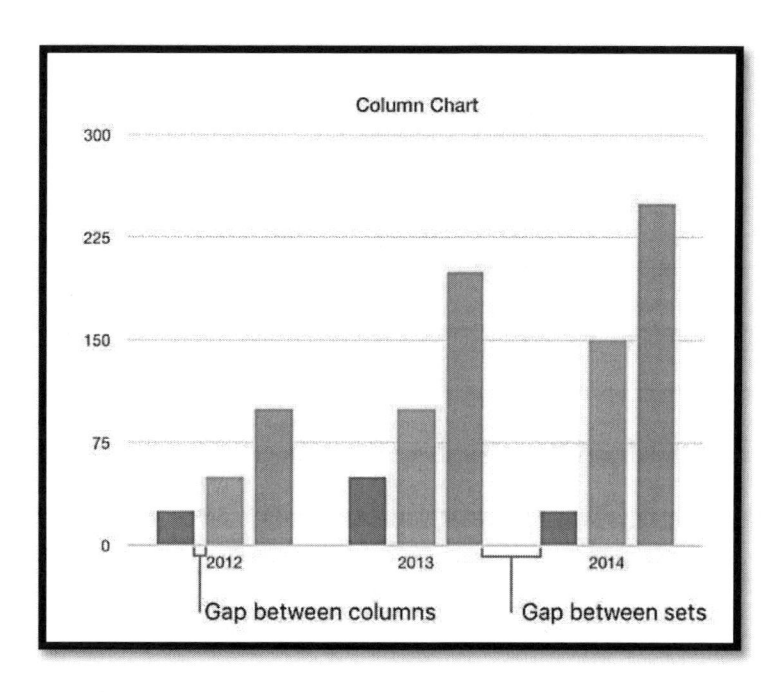

Add Rounded corners to the bar, column, mixed, and 2 axes

- To choose the chart, click on it.
- Click Chart in the Format column.
- Click the arrow next to Rounded Corners that says "Show more," then move the slider or type in a value.
- Click **Done**

Use chart styles in Keynote on Mac

You can change how a chart looks and then use that changed chart to make a new style. You can also make a new chart style that uses the same colors as a picture you like. You can use the new styles on other charts, and they are saved along with the styles that come with the theme.

The small images at the top of the Chart tab show chart styles that have already been made and are made to look good with the theme you're using. At any time, you can change the style of a chart.

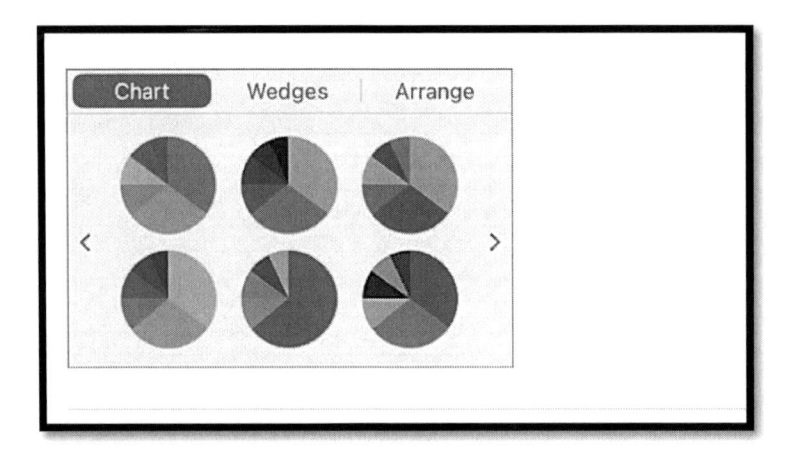

Apply a different style to a chart

- Click the chart, and then in the Format sidebar, click the Chart tab.
- Click one of the chart styles at the top of the sidebar to apply it

Save a chart as a new style

If you changed how a chart looks and want to keep those changes, you can make a new chart style that you can use again later. To do this

- Click the chart whose style you want to save as a new one.
- Click the Chart tab in the Format box on the right.
- Click the arrow to the right of the chart styles to move to the last group of styles.
- To add your style, click the "**Add**" button.
- Choose an option from the menu that pops up:
- **All series styles:** Keep all of the styles of series that can be used with the chart.
- **Only visible series styles**: Only keep the styles of the series that can be seen on the chart.
- Select **OK**.
- The new chart style is added to the list of chart styles at the top of the sidebar. You can drag styles around to put them in any order you want, or you can change them.

Create chart styles that uses the color in an image

You can make a new chart style whose colors match those of an image. This can help you see a connection between the data in the chart and the picture.
To do this:

- To add a chart, click a chart or the Chart button in the toolbar.
- Click the Chart tab in the Format box on the right.
- Pick a picture whose colors you like. Any picture on your computer will work.
- Click the Media menu button on the toolbar to look through your photos.
- Move the picture to the styles of charts in the sidebar.
- To make a new style, you drag an image to the chart styles.
- You can also Control-click a chart style, choose to Create Style from Image from the shortcut menu, and then browse for an image.
- The new chart style is added to the list of chart styles at the top of the sidebar. The new style doesn't replace the style you clicked Control-click on.
- Click the style in the sidebar to use the new style on the chart you chose.
- The new chart style is added to the list of chart styles at the top of the sidebar.

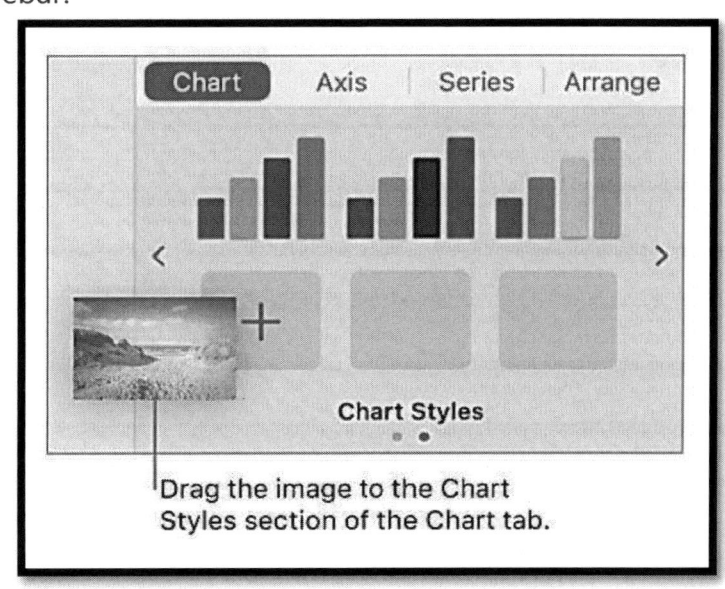

Drag the image to the Chart Styles section of the Chart tab.

Redefine a chart style

You can modify the look of a chart—by changing its fonts, colors, and so on—then update that chart's style to incorporate the changes.

Any other charts using that style are also updated.

- Click a chart that uses the style you want to update, and then modify its appearance so it looks the way you want.
- Click the chart you just modified (if you deselected it).
- In the Format sidebar, click the Chart tab.
- At the top of the sidebar, Control-click the style you want to redefine, then choose **Redefine Style** from Selection.
- If your chart has fewer than six data series, a dialog appears. Choose an option:
- **All series styles:** Keep all available series styles associated with the chart.
- **Only visible series styles:** Keep only the series styles currently visible in the chart.
- Click OK.
- To update charts of the same type that use that style to the latest version, click the chart you want to update, and then select the chart style in the sidebar.

Delete a chart style

Control-click the style, and then choose Delete Style.

Working with Shapes in Keynote

The shapes library has a lot of shapes from many different categories. When you add a shape to a slide, you can change it in several ways.

Add a Shape

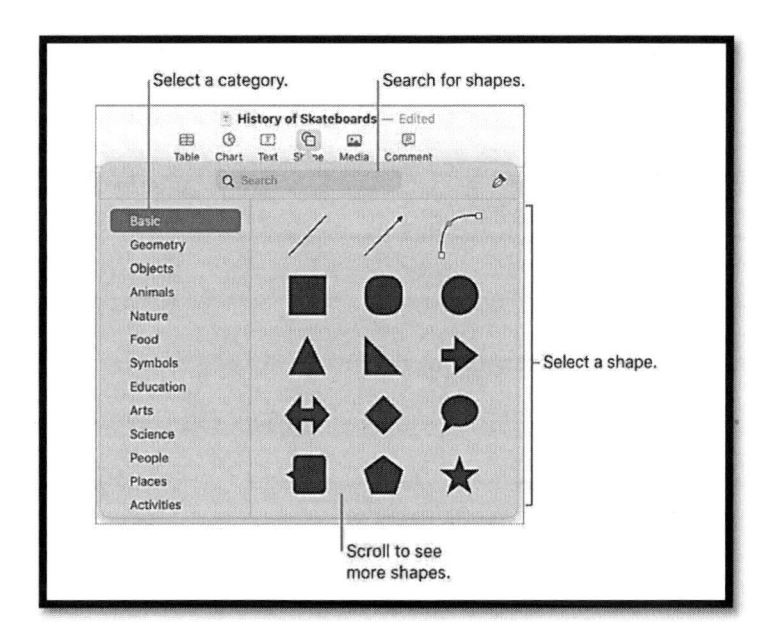

You can put a shape anywhere on a slide or in the workspace around it, and then change it however you want.

- In the toolbar, click the **Shape** button.
- The library of shapes, with the categories on the left and the shapes on the right. You can search for shapes in the box at the top, and you can scroll to see more.
- Choose a category from the list on the left, then click or drag a shape onto the slide (or the area around it) to add it.
- Move the pointer over the shapes pane and scroll down to see all the shapes.
- Type a shape's name into the search box at the top of the shapes library to find it. Move the pointer over a shape to find out what it's called.
- Move the shape around on the slide by dragging it.

Adjust the curve along the edge of a shape

- Select a shape by clicking on it.
- Choose **Format > Shapes and Lines > Make Editable** (from the Format menu at the top of your screen).

- Navigate to **Shapes and Lines** under **Format.**, then click **Make Editable**
- Lines can be made straight or curved by double-clicking their white handles.
- Line types are represented by their respective handles:
- **A square with red lines denotes a very sharp line**. All lines radiating from here are straight.
- **A circle with red-outline**d represents a curved line. Curved lines lead to this location.
- The point-based shape can be edited.
- When you're finished making changes to the shape, press the escape key.

Select Keynote > Settings (found in the top-right corner of the program window) and then click the General tab. From there, select "Curves default to Bezier." Using the point's handles, you can modify the Bezier curve as you edit the shape.

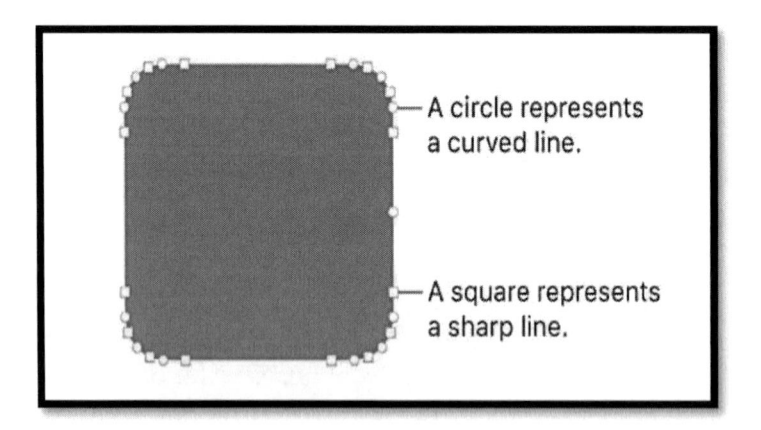

Adjust the features of a shape

The green dot indicates that the selected shape can have its properties modified, so you can edit any basic shape from the Basic category in the shapes library. A five-pointed star, for instance, can have its arms extended to form even more complex shapes.

Select a shape by clicking on it.

To take any action:

Reshape the corners of a rounded rectangle: By dragging the green dot closer to a corner to sharpen it and farther away from a corner to make it rounder, you can change the shape of the corners of a rounded rectangle.

Change the number of points on a star: To adjust the number of stars' facets, click and drag the outer green dot in either direction (clockwise to add, or counterclockwise to remove). The number of points on a star can range from three to twenty.

Change the shape of the points on a star: If you want the star's points to be longer and narrower, drag the inner green dot toward the star's center; if you want the points to be shorter and wider, drag the dot away from the center.

Change the shape of a callout or speech bubble: Simply by dragging the green dot around the bubble's main body, you can alter its form. To modify the length and orientation of the point, drag the green dot at its tip. To modify the width of the point, move the green dot at its base.

Change the number of sides in a polygon: Modifying a polygon's symmetry by adding or removing sides: Simply by dragging the green dot in either direction (clockwise or counterclockwise), you can change the number of sides.

Adjust the proportions of arrows: Drag the green dot closer to the arrow's tip to make the arrowhead shallower, or drag it closer to the arrow's side point to make the trunk thicker.

See more editing handles to make a shape abstract: Check out these additional and abstract shape editing tools: Format > Shapes and Lines > Make Editable (from the Format menu at the top of your screen). To create a drag handle, hover the mouse cursor in the space between any two already established points. After resizing the shape to your liking, release all mouse buttons.

Draw a Shape in Keynote

You can draw a shape by using your pen tool. To access the Pen Tool, first, select Shape from the toolbar's drop-down menu.

Select a starting point for your custom shape by clicking anywhere on the slide (or the blank space around it). Click and drag the pointer to make a new dot; you can add as many as you like.

To make a curved line, click and drag, and then release the mouse button to complete the line. To remove a newly created segment, select it by clicking on a point and then pressing the Delete key.

Make one of the following selections to finish the picture:

Close the shape: Join the ends of the shape with a straight line.

Open the shape: You should not close off the shape by connecting the last and first points with a line. You can use the Return or Esc key.

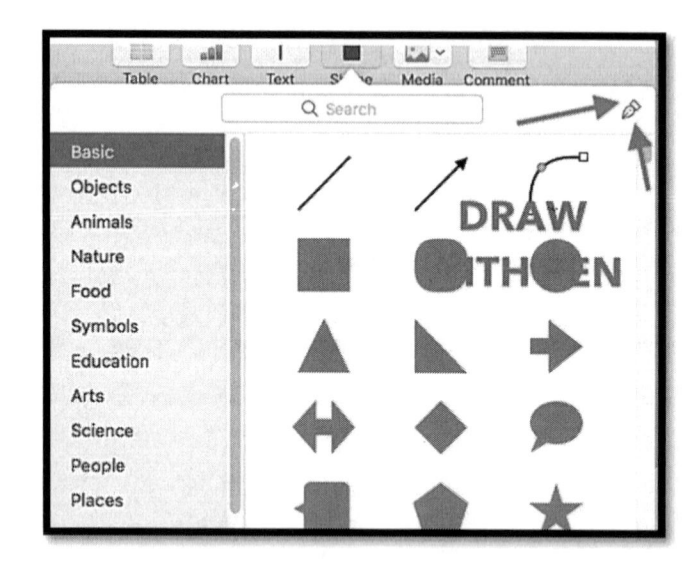

Save a shape to the shapes library in Keynote: You can add a closed-path shape to the library if you create or modify one. The only properties of a custom shape that are preserved during saving are the shape's path, flip, and rotation.

Select a unique shape with a click, then go to **Format > Shapes and Lines > Save to My Shapes to** store it (from the Format menu at the top of your screen).

My Shapes is a subcategory of the Shapes Library that appears only when custom shapes are present, and this is where the shape will be saved. You cannot alter the order in which shapes are added to the library after they have been created.

Name the shape in the field that appears below it, or edit the name by clicking on it.

Simply Control-click on the shape you want to remove from the shapes library, and then select Delete Shape from the context menu.

When you delete a custom shape in iCloud Drive, it will be removed from all of your devices that are signed into iCloud Drive with the same Apple ID.

Fill shapes and text boxes with color or an image in Keynote

Select one or more shapes, text boxes, or other objects by clicking on them.

Select the Style tab in the Format panel's sidebar.

Pick one of the following explanations:

A color or gradient designed to go with the theme: To change the Fill's color or gradient, simply click the well to the right of the word.

Any Color: Highlight Fill by clicking its disclosure arrow, then select Color Fill from the Fill pop-up menu. Choose a hue from the color wheel, and then use it to select a palette.

A two-color gradient fill: To pick a gradient fill color scheme, open the Fill pop-up menu, click the disclosure arrow next to Fill, and then select Gradient Fill. The color will display complementary hues while clicking the color wheel brings up the Colors window from which you can select any color. Adjust the knobs to modify the gradient's inclination and direction.

A Custom Gradient: To pick your colors, open the Fill pop-up menu, select Advanced Gradient Fill, and then use the arrow down next to the slider to reveal the color stops. To introduce a new color step, just click the slider. By dragging the color stops and adjusting the other sliders and dials, you can modify the gradient's intensity, angle, and even direction.

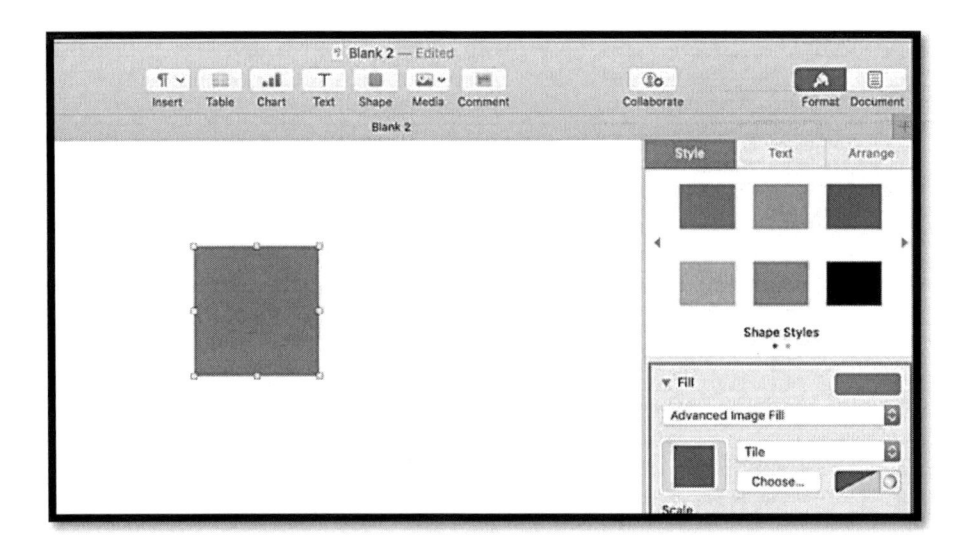

Fill with an image

- Select one or more shapes, text boxes, or other objects by clicking on them.
- Select the Style tab in the Format panel's sidebar.
- To add a tint to an image, select **Advanced Image Fill** from the Fill pop-up menu by clicking the disclosure arrow next to Fill.
- Double-click an image with a .jpg, .png, or .gif filename extension from your photo library after clicking Choose.
- When using Advanced Image Fill, pick a tint color by clicking the well to the right of the Choose button.
- You can adjust the level of transparency of the tint by clicking the color wheel and dragging the Opacity slider.
- If the image doesn't appear as expected, or if you want to adjust how the image fills the object, select an alternative from the menu that appears when you click the Choose button.

Original Size: Places the image inside the object at its actual size. Adjust the image's size by dragging the Scale slider.

Stretch: Image proportions may be altered as the image is stretched to fit the object's dimensions.

This object uses a tiling effect, which means that the image is repeated multiple times inside it. Just by dragging the Scale slider, you can make the image any size you want.

Scale to Fill: Enlarges or reduces the image so that it fills the frame.

Scale to Fit: If you select Scale to Fit, the image will be resized to fit the dimensions of the object without distorting its proportions.

Save a custom

It's possible to save a customized fill and use it later.

To save a fill, select the desired shape or text box by clicking on it, and then from the Format menu, choose the Style tab.

To alter the fill of a well, simply click the color well next to Fill, then drag the fill from the Current Fill well to the well you'd like to alter.

When dragging, only wells of the same type will work. If the custom fill is a gradient, for instance, you'll want to move the fill from the Current Fill well to a well in the Gradient Fills section.

Simply by clicking the Fill Type drop-down menu and choosing a new option, you can modify the replaceable fill types. Select Gradient Fill from the drop-down menu, and then move the fill from the Current Fill well to a well in the Gradient Fills section to save it.

Remove a fill

- Select one or more shapes, text boxes, or other objects by clicking on them.
- Select the Style tab in the Format panel's sidebar.
- Select "No Fill" from the color picker that appears next to "Fill."
- Type in some text in Apple's Keynote presentation software.

Add text inside a shape

To add text to a shape, double-click the shape and when the insertion point appears, you can start typing in your text.

Note: If the text doesn't contain the shape then resize the shape by dragging the selection handle till all the text fit in the shape

Conclusion

Keynote provides a great deal more than simple shapes for use in presentations. You can choose from a variety of shapes in various categories, as well as create and save your own.

CHAPTER EIGHT
ENHANCING A PRESENTATION WITH KEYNOTE

When you play your presentation, a Magic Move transition creates the illusion of objects moving from their positions on one slide to new positions on the next slide. Transitions are visual effects that play as you navigate between slides. In this chapter, we will discuss how to enhance your presentation using transitions and animations.

Add a Transition

When you add a slide transition in Keynote, you get a nice preview of each effect.

To add a transition to your slide:

- Select the first slide to which you want to apply the transition. This must be done for each slide where you want to use a transition.
- On the top right, click the **animate** button.
- Click the **Add an Effect** button to bring up a drop-down menu of options.
- Hover your mouse over an effect and click **Preview** when it appears to see how it will appear. Choose it if you like it.

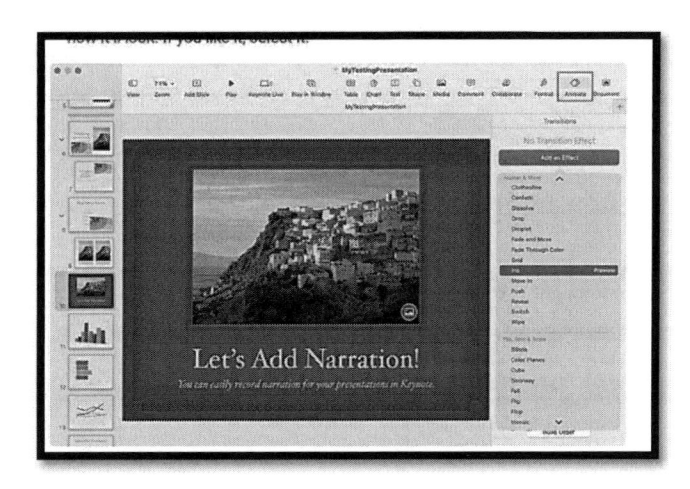

After selecting a transition, you can modify it depending on which one you use. You can alter the direction, duration, and timing. Change and Preview buttons are located at the top of the sidebar.

- Use the **Change** button to select a different effect or to remove the current one.
- Use the **Preview** button to see a preview of your changes as you make them.
- In the sidebar, select the Start Transition option from On Click or automatically, as desired.

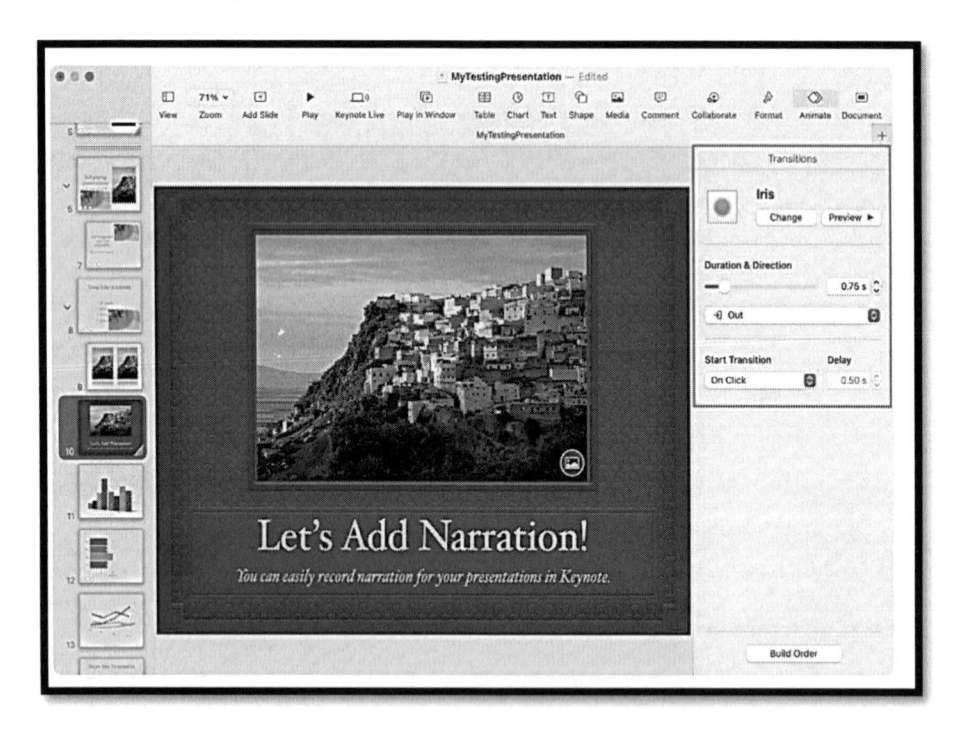

- After you've added a transition, go to the next slide in your presentation and repeat the process. This allows you to use different transitions for your slides if you want to spice up the show.

Add a Magic Move Transition

The easiest way to create a Magic Move transition is to create a slide with objects, duplicate the slide, and then rearrange, resize, or reorient the objects on the duplicated slide.

To add a magic move transition:

- Tap the slide you wish to add a Magic Move transition to in the slide navigator, click the slide again, and then tap **Transition.**
- Tap **Add Transition**, and then click **Magic Move**, before clicking **done.**
- Select **Duplicate** to duplicate the slide, or **Cancel** if it has already been duplicated.
- Change the position or appearance of objects on one or both slides by dragging them to new locations, rotating or resizing them, adding or deleting them, and more.
- To preview the transition, tap the first slide in the slide navigator, followed by the **Play** button.

To modify how objects move between slides:

- **Select Delivery and Acceleration and then choose one of the following options:**

Magic Place acceleration and delivery options in the Acceleration pane.

459

Transfer text fluidly between slides: Select a Text Match option:

By Object: Reposition one or more text boxes from the first slide to the second slide.

By Word: Transfer one or more words from the first slide to the second slide. This animation can be used to simulate how words rearrange themselves to form a new sentence.

By Character: Transfer one or more of the characters from the first slide to the second slide. This animation can be used to create the illusion of letters rearranging themselves to form a new word.

Change a Slide Transition

- Select the slide in the navigation pane.
- Select the transition at the bottom of the display, and then click **Change.**
- Select a new transition.

Remove Transition

- Click on the **More** button, and select **Animate.**
- Click the slide again and select **Delete Animation**.

Animate objects onto and off a slide in Keynote

To add dynamism to your presentation, you can animate the text and objects on a slide so that they appear, disappear, or both.

Note: The term for object animations is **built effects**. Depending on whether the object is a text box, chart, table, shape, or media, unique build effects can be applied to it.

Animate an object onto and off a slide

Click the object or text box you wish to animate on the slide, and then click **Animate.**

Do any of the following:

Animate the object onto the slide: At the bottom of the display, select **Add Build In**.

Animate the object off the slide: At the bottom of the display, select **Add Build Out**.

- Select an animation (swipe left to see them all).
- A preview of the animation is played.
- Tap the Left Back button to dismiss the options.
- Tap the animation's name at the bottom of the screen to configure options such as duration and direction
- Select **Done** in the upper-right corner of the display.

Create a motion path

A motion path can be created for an object so that it moves around the slide. To do this:

- On the slide, click the object you wish to animate to select it.
- In the Animate sidebar, click the tab labeled **Action**.
- Select **Move** from the **Add Effect** menu, and then click **Add Effect.**
- Drag the opaque object to where you want the movement to begin, and then drag the transparent ghost object to where you want it to end.
- If you don't see the transparent object, click the object, then click the red diamond below it.
- Dragging the white dots along the line will add curves to the path.
- An opaque object indicates the beginning position, while a translucent object indicates the end position.
- Utilize the controls on the **Action tab** of the animate sidebar to modify the duration and acceleration of the animation.
- To make the object pivot to match the curve of the movement path as it moves, select **Align to the path.**
- To view an animation preview, click **Preview**.

Conclusion

As a way of concluding this chapter, here are some basic tips to create a unique presentation on keynote:

- Get creative with photos
- Simplify charts and graphs
- Use tables for large data
- One theme should be used per slide
- Create a visual experience with data
- Practice always
- Use a good color combination.
- Keep your presentation short and simple.

Thank you so much for your order and for taking your time to read this book. We are constantly striving to improve our customer satisfaction, hence, we are curious to find out how helpful this book is to you, if you can spare us a minute to leave us a review, we'd be super grateful.

INDEX

1

1. Resize images or photos, 142

2

2D, 119, 163, 164, 177, 225, 229, 249
2D and 3D charts, 312
2D and Interactive, 310
2D and Interactive buttons, 310
2D chart thumbnails, 310

3

3D, 119, 163, 164, 177, 225, 229, 249, 250
3G contract limit, 48

9

90 Apple-designed templates, 4

A

A basic line charts, 217
A circle with red-outlined, 449
A column chart, 443
A Custom Gradient, 452
A table with header, 422
A table's appearance, 416
A table's rows and columns, 421
A two-color gradient fill, 452
A USER-FRIENDLY INTERFACE, 175
A WIDE RANGE OF TEMPLATES, 178
Abc, 198
AbcDef, 198
ability to export a presentation, 305
About Chart down Sampling, 441
Access, 362, 370, 371, 372
access iWork documents, 1
access **System Preferences**, 15
account ID, 14
Action tab, 404, 460
Actions Menu., 346
actual size, 453
add a caption, 404, 405, 406
Add a caption, 404
ADD A COMMENT, 43
add a Link, 335
Add a Magic, 457
Add A Reflection, 162
Add a Shadow, 413
Add A Shadow, 161
Add a Shape, 448
Add a slide, 315, 320
Add a Slide, 322, 324
Add a Table, 414
Add a Title, 405
Add a Transition, 456
Add an image, 316, 320, 403
Add An Image Fill, 160
Add an object to a cell, 429
Add and Delete a Slide, 321
Add and edit cell, 426
Add and edit cell content, 426
Add Build In, 460
Add button, 20
Add Chart, 437
add charts, 304, 436
Add Column button, 422
Add content to cells, 427
add curves, 460
Add data to a table, 176
Add Emojis and Special Characters, 116
Add Fingerprint, 385
Add images, 4
Add Math Equation, 118
Add more People, 369
Add new data set, 440
Add or Remove Header Rows and Column, 424
Add or Remove row and column, 422

Add or Remove Rows, 421
Add or Remove Rows and Columns, 421
Add Photos, 310
Add Rounded corners, 444
Add Rounded corners to the bar, 444
Add Slide button, 315, 320, 322, 324
Add Text in A Text Box, 99
Add text inside a shape, 454
Add Text Inside a Shape, 100
Add to Template Chooser, 94, 288
Add Transition, 458
Add visual effects, 311
Add visual effects or animations, 311
added to a slide, 311
adding, 304, 309, 369, 416, 422, 424, 441, 450, 458
Adding a Caption, 404
ADDING A CHART, 164
adding animated objects, 304
ADDING IMAGES TO DOCUMENTS, 132
ADDING TABLES TO YOUR DOCUMENTS, 162
adding the number, 30
additional 50GB, 53
additional devices, 312
ADDITIONAL FORMULAS, 293
Additional image, 401
additional options, 352, 437
additional settings, 356
additional slides, 310, 322, 325, 329
additional **themes**, 314
Additional visual elements, 16
address (URL), 334, 336
Adds new comments, 309
Adjust Image, 155, 407, 411, 412
Adjust Image window, 407
Adjust Saturation, 407
Adjust the curve, 448
Adjust the features of a shape, 449
Adjust the image's size, 453
Adjust the position, 403
Adobe Acrobat, 358
Adobe Reader, 56
ADVANCE FORMULAS, 187
Advanced, 312, 351, 358, 398, 452, 453
Advanced Theme, 312

Advanced Theme Chooser, 312
Airdrop, 356
AirDrop, 88, 355, 356, 365, 368, 388, 389
AirPods, 380
Align an object using x and y coordinates, 410
Align menu, 411
Align objects, 411
Align objects vertically, 411
Align objects vertically and horizontally, 411
Align to the path, 460
Alignment guides, 312
All series styles, 445, 447
Allow other users, 371
Allow to add other People, 372
Alter the Appearance, 311
Alternate the row, 418
alternating row, 416
Alternating Row, 418
Alternating Row Color, 418
Alternating Row Color checkbox, 418
Amazing Creative Tools, 305
amazing tool, 305
An Apple Mac running, 363
An iOS 15-capable, 363
Angle, 413
Animate an object onto and off a slide, 459
Animate objects, 459
Animate objects onto, 459
Animate objects onto and off, 459
animate sidebar, 311, 460
Animate the object, 460
animated GIF, 358, 360
Animated GIF, 358
animation, 306, 311, 359, 459, 460
Animation, 311
Another feature, 306, 307
another format, 356, 357
Any Color, 452
Any value types, 213
Anyone with the link, 365, 369, 370, 371
Anyone with the Link, 368
App Store, 2, 58
appearance of a table, 419
appearance of cell borders, 417

Apple, 1, 2, 3, 4, 7, 9, 10, 15, 24, 25, 40, 43, 46, 48, 49, 51, 52, 53, 54, 56, 57, 58, 61, 64, 65, 67, 69, 70, 76, 77, 81, 84, 85, 90, 93, 97, 104, 115, 116, 117, 118, 119, 120, 121, 123, 125, 127, 162, 175, 178, 180, 182, 187, 217, 237, 240, 254, 255, 257, 258, 261, 275, 286

Apple Books, 2, 4, 40

Apple Books publishing., 4

Apple devices, 3, 85

Apple ID, 309, 352, 353, 355, 362, 367, 368, 371, 373, 452

Apple ID. Instructions, 362, 368

Apple Inc, 1, 2

Apple products, 304

Apple-designed themes, 312

Apple's Pages, 316

Apple's Services business, 40

AppleScript automation framework, 1

application **Keynote**, 1

Applications folder., 314

Apply a Different Style to a Table, 419

apply a new style., 419

Apply A Paragraph Style, 101

Apply colors, 442

apply text overlays to any graphic, 308

appropriate box., 386

appropriate symbol, 116, 117

area chart, 437, 441

Arrange button, 401, 408, 409, 410, 411

Arrange menu, 405, 427, 433

arrange styles, 420

Arrange tab., 144, 157, 272, 273

arrangement of text and images, 313, 315

Arrays and array functions, 213

arrow buttons, 340

Assign A Shortcut Key to A Style, 101

asterisk, 101, 102, 103, 199

attractive documents, 1, 3

audio, 304, 310, 360, 361, 398

Audio, 308

Auto-advance slider, 359

Auto-Correction, 15, 24, 117

autofill cells, 428

Autofill Cells, 428

autofill cells., 428

Autofill replaces, 428

Autofill replaces existing data, 428

automatic scaling, 312

automatic scaling Reviewer, 312

automatic spelling check, 15

Auto-scan a document, 403

Axis Options drop-down box., 171

B

background, 308, 309, 400, 401, 414, 417, 418, 422, 429

backgrounds, 304, 308, 360

backgrounds and themes, 304

bars, 306, 326, 440

Basic, 305, 415, 449

Basic category, 17, 18

basic features, 304

Basic Features of Keynotes, 305

Basic section, 99

basic tips, 461

Beginning with a Theme, 310

BIDIRECTIONAL TEXT, 127

blank page, 8, 99, 166

blank template, 18, 98

blanks with content, 427

Blur, 161, 413

blurring of the edges, 413

blurring of the edges of a shadow, 413

body rows and columns, 421

book-creation program, 4

Bookmark, 35

BOOKMARKS, 35

Books, 17, 40

Boolean expression and value type, 213

border layout, 417

border layout button, 417

border menu, 311

borders, 16, 126, 131, 141, 158, 255, 267

borders and color, 416

borders and color to cells, 416

bottom of the page., 32

bottom-left corner of the table, 423

Browse All Versions, 74, 347
browse folders, 11
browser, 9, 10, 50, 51, 52, 63, 77, 84, 90, 134
brush icon, 30, 105, 108, 111, 115
bubbles, 306
build effects, 459
built effects, 459
built-in collaboration feature, 305
built-in functions, 187, 298
business adds a feature, 76
business finance, 183
button on the file menu, 345
By Character, 459
By Object, 459
By Word, 459

C

Can make changes, 372
Capacity, 53
Caption checkbox, 404, 405
Card under Contacts., 17
Cell Name, 197
cell values, 207, 293
cells, 417, 419, 424, 425, 426, 427, 428, 429, 430, 431, 432, 433, 434, 435
cell's content and formatting, 425
Change a Slide, 459
Change a Slide Transition, 459
Change all notes, 42
Change automatic hyphenation, 23
Change button, 457
Change cell borders, 417
Change Color and Shadows, 442
Change document types, 17, 18
Change file type, 351
Change Numbering for Notes, 43
Change Object, 414
Change Object Transparency, 414
Change one note, 42
Change or Remove a Password, 383
Change Password, 383, 384, 385
change pictures, 304
Change Share Options, 63, 64
Change table gridlines, 416

change the appearance, 418, 421, 441
change the border, 417
Change the Borders, 417
Change the Borders and Background, 417
Change the font, 435, 441
Change the gridlines, 417
Change The Look of Note Text, 42
Change the look of table text, 435
Change the outline, 417
Change the spacing, 443
Change the spacing in the bar, 443
Change the spacing in the bar or column, 443
Change the spacing in the bar or column chart, 443
Change The Symbol for Notes, 43
character spacing, 22
character style, 102, 338, 435
Character Viewer, 116
chart animations, 312
Chart Data, 436, 438, 439, 440, 441
Chart Data editor, 436, 438, 440, 441
Chart Data Editor, 439
Chart Data editor results, 436
Chart Element, 442
Charts, 165, 166, 173, 217, 218, 219, 220, 221, 222, 223, 224, 246, 247, 248, 310, 405, 437, 442
CHARTS AND GRAPHS, 217
charts interactive, 306
checkboxes, 324, 347, 379
Choose A Document Type, 16, 18
Choose a new hue, 311
choose Delete Style, 447
Cinema-quality, 312
Cinema-quality animations, 312
Clear Content from a range of cells, 427
Clear Overrides, 419
Clear Overrides and Apply Style, 419
Click on **Set Password.**, 381
click **Reset**, 407
Clicking **Start Writing**, 18
clipping indicator, 99, 100, 131
Close the shape, 451
CloudConvert, 89

466

Collaborate, 309, 364, 365, 366, 368, 369, 370, 372, 373, 374
Collaborate button, 46, 60
Collaborate icon, 58, 60, 61, 63, 64, 65, 66, 68, 69
Collaborate in Messages, 309
Collaborate on A File, 58
Collaborate" icon, 66
Collaborating, 362
COLLABORATING, 57
Collaboration menu, 365
Collaboration screen, 65, 66
collaborative approval, 52
collapse groups, 327, 331
collapsed group, 326, 327, 330, 331
Collection value type, 213
color, 4, 16, 39, 68, 99, 100, 103, 126, 127, 147, 152, 153, 155, 159, 160, 161, 164, 165, 168, 170, 220, 225, 227, 229, 247, 249, 256, 262, 264, 265, 266, 267, 268, 269
color gradients, 4
Color in an Image, 420
COLOR LEVELS IN AN IMAGE, 159
Color tool, 147
color well, 418, 454
colored backgrounds, 304
Command key, 325, 408
Command-click, 417, 434
Command-click additional, 417
Command-click additional borders, 417
Command-Z, 17
Command-Z on the keyboard, 434
company logo, 94
Compare Values, 207, 293
Computed Values, 193
computer, 309, 311, 339, 351, 356, 363, 372, 379, 380, 382, 385, 387, 388, 397, 398, 403, 420, 446
Concatenate strings, 198
Conclusion, 12, 35, 46, 57, 97, 115, 127, 173, 183, 204, 236, 261, 286, 312, 344, 379, 395, 436, 455, 461
CONCLUSION, 302
Condition expression, 214
CONFIGURING PAGES PREFERENCES, 14
Constant expression, 214

Constrain proportions, 408
Contact Shadow, 147, 161, 413
contact shadow's angle, 413
Content should be edited, 427
contents of cells, 198, 207
contrast, 401, 412
Control-click a table style, 420
Control-clicking, 327
controls, 317, 321, 323, 330, 400, 407, 411, 417, 432, 435, 436, 440, 441, 442, 443, 460
Convert Notes from One Kind to Another, 42
convert Pages files, 89
Convert to Page Layout, 17
Convert To Plain Text, 212, 297
Copy and Paste a Text Style, 338
Copy and Paste Text, 337
Copy and replace existing content, 430
Copy Link,", 369
Copy or Move Cells, 430
Copying A File, 14
COUNTIF, 198, 199, 216
covering note, 52
Create a basic document, 16, 18
Create a chart, 177
Create A Date and Time Format, 185
Create a motion path, 460
Create a Presentation, 310, 313
CREATE A PRESENTATION, 313
Create A Text Format, 186
Create chart styles, 446
Create Custom Format, 184, 185, 186
Create GIF, 358
Create Internal Links, 35
Create Style from Image, 420, 446
creating presentations, 312
currency, 425
Currency symbols, 440
Curve Shadow, 413
Curved Shadow, 147, 161
Custom Number Format, 184
Custom Paper Size, 20
CUSTOM TEMPLATE, 95, 287, 289
CUSTOMIZABLE CELLS, 184
customization, 171
Customize a token element, 184, 185
customize the output, 312

Customize Toolbar, 119, 120
Customizing Your Chart, 169
Cut or Edit, 429

D

Dashlane, 77
data series, 438, 439, 440, 442, 443, 447
Date And Time Functions, 201
Date/time value type, 214
dazzling effects, 312
decimal places, 1
Default, 22, 127
Default Theme, 317
Delete a Chart, 440
Delete a chart style, 447
Delete A Custom Template, 96
Delete a data set, 440
Delete a Slide, 323, 325
Delete A Style, 103
Delete a Table, 416
Delete an object from a cell, 429
Delete Animation, 459
Delete any row or column, 423
Delete Button, 324
Delete Custom Styles, 149
Delete everything, 427
Delete multiple rows or columns, 423
Delete Row or Delete Column, 423, 440
Delivery and Acceleration, 458
Designing your Bar Chart, 442
desired file, 14
desktop publishing, 1
Developed with Simplicity, 306
device shows up, 387, 388
device's name, 387, 388, 402
different layout, 315
different style, 419, 441, 445
different style from the drop-down, 419
different table style, 418, 419
dimensions, 344, 408, 411, 430, 453, 454
Display field, 334, 336
Display, Link, 336
Distribute Graphics, 157
Dock, 314, 391

document, 2, 3, 7, 8, 9, 14, 15, 16, 17, 18, 19, 20, 21, 22, 23, 24, 25, 26, 31, 32, 34, 36, 37, 38, 39, 41, 42, 43, 44, 45, 46, 47, 48, 49, 50, 52, 53, 54, 55, 56, 58, 60, 61, 64, 65, 68, 69, 70, 71, 72, 73, 74, 75, 76, 77, 78, 79, 80, 81, 83, 84, 85, 86, 89, 93, 94, 95, 96, 97, 98, 99, 100, 103, 104, 105, 107, 110, 113, 115, 116, 117, 119, 121, 122, 124, 125, 126, 127, 128, 129, 133, 134, 136, 138, 139, 140, 141, 143, 149, 153, 156, 158, 163, 165, 166, 178, 180, 181, 182, 183, 194, 283, 284
Document, 16, 18, 19, 20, 21, 23, 26, 27, 34, 38, 47, 71, 73, 75, 76, 77, 84, 85, 93, 98, 100, 121, 166
DOCUMENT, 16, 19, 54, 70, 72, 76
document based, 16
Document Body, 18, 19
DOCUMENT CONFIGURATION, 16
Document Manager, 47
Document Manager screen, 47
Document radio button, 23
Document Setup, 18, 21, 26, 27
DOCUMENT SETUP USING PAGES, 16
Document tab, 18, 19, 34
Document's Text, 38
documents, 1, 2, 3, 4, 6, 9, 12, 13, 14, 15, 16, 19, 24, 32, 35, 36, 40, 43, 46, 48, 50, 53, 54, 69, 70, 71, 72, 76, 82, 83, 85, 89, 90, 93, 97, 104, 111, 119, 120, 132, 133, 140, 141, 142, 144, 145, 156, 162, 166, 179, 181, 183
Documents box, 48
DOCX, 4
Double hyphens, 23
double-click a label, 439
Double-click placeholder text, 315
double-click the Home button, 390, 393
Double-clicking, 315
Down Arrow, 331
Down Arrow and Up Arrow, 331
Down Arrow and Up Arrow keys, 331
download, 9, 12, 51, 83, 85, 90, 183, 287
Download button, 83, 183
Download Files, 83
drag and drop, 397, 400
Drag files, 83
Drag Handle, 324

Drag the image to the sidebar's table styles, 420
dragging, 324, 325, 329, 397, 398, 401, 403, 408, 409, 412, 420, 428, 434, 440, 448, 450, 452, 453, 454, 455, 458
Dragging, 460
Dragging the white dots, 460
dramatic effect, 309
Draw a Shape, 450
draw people's attention, 306
Drive On iCloud.com, 83
drop shadow, 311, 413
Drop Shadow, 147, 161, 413
drop-down menu, 318, 336, 339, 342, 347, 358, 368, 370, 371, 378, 387, 388, 396, 406, 411, 412, 419, 450, 454, 456
Duplicate, 322, 325, 347, 458
Duplicate a Slide, 322, 325
Duplicate button, 322
Duration value type, 214
dynamism, 459

E

easily skip a slide, 326, 330
Easily write reports., 8
eBook with Pages, 40
eBooks, 4, 40
edge of a shape, 448
EDIT, 61, 95, 267, 289
Edit a Table, 416
edit appears, 343
Edit Chart, 438, 440
Edit Chart Data, 438, 440
Edit Chart Data button, 438, 440
Edit icon, 80
Edit images, 400
Edit menu, 333, 370, 427, 428, 430
Edit or Remove a Link, 335
Edit or Remove Link, 337
edit PDF documents, 358
Edit While Offline, 363
editing, 304, 309, 364, 365, 373, 374, 400, 401, 450
Editing for more information, 363

Editing the formulas, 189
effects to slides, 304
Eliminate Backgrounds, 309
Email, 334, 335, 336, 337, 361
email address, 334, 336, 357, 373, 374
email address or phone number, 373
email addresses or phone, 368
email addresses or phone numbers, 368
email or phone number, 370, 373
EMAILING, 54
Emojis & Symbols, 116
Enable Black Mode, 308
Enable Handoff, 389
Enable Voice to Text, 121
endnote sign, 41
Endnotes, 41, 42
engage your viewers, 311
Engineering functions, 206
Enhance, 407, 412
ENHANCING A PRESENTATION, 456
ENHANCING A PRESENTATION WITH KEYNOTE, 456
ENHANCING YOUR DOCUMENTS WITH PAGES, 132
Enter key, 144
EPUB, 4
Equal Sign, 188, 290
Equally space objects, 411
EXAMINING FORMATTING SYMBOLS, 129
Excel, 1, 47, 164, 173, 178, 183, 232, 249
excellent presentation, 305
excellent presentation., 305
Existing iWork Files, 81
explaining data, 306
Export, 47, 70, 73, 85, 87
EXPORT, 70
Export as a Movie, 376
Export Document, 47
Export Presentation, 47
Export Spreadsheet, 47
Export to MP4 File, 375
Exporting, 375, 376, 377
EXPORTING DOCUMENTS, 46
Exposure, 407, 412

F

Face ID, 76, 77, 78, 79, 386
FaceID, 68
Facial ID, 386
facing the camera, 403
FAQs, 69, 182
favorite tools, 309
feature of the keynote, 306, 307, 400
Figure A, 163
Figure B, 164
Figure C, 165
File menu, 17, 40, 73, 287, 319, 346, 347, 348, 351, 356, 357, 358, 360, 369, 378, 384
File option, 17
File Sharing, 46, 47, 48, 90
File Sharing feature, 46
File Sharing feature in iTunes, 46
File Sharing folder, 47
File Sharing option, 47
File Sharing section, 48
files and folders, 13
files via their profile pictures, 356
Fill An Object with Color or A Gradient, 159
Fill section, 418
Fill with an image, 453
filling in the blanks, 383
Financial functions, 206
Find & Replace, 339, 340, 341, 343
Find and Replace, 339, 340, 341, 342
Find and Replace dialog, 341
Find and Replace dialog box, 341
Find and Replace Options, 339, 340
Find and Replace Options menu button, 340
Find and Replace Text, 339, 341
find settings, 308, 309
Find window, 343
Finder and Airpod, 387
Finding and Replacing Text, 343
Fit Height to Content, 432
Flip an Object, 409
Flip button, 409
flipping, 401

Follow's Someone Edit, 374
FONT SELECTION AND FORMATTING, 100
footer boxes, 28
footer row, 420
Footer rows, 422
Footers options, 27
footnote, 41, 42
footnotes, 41, 42, 43
FOOTNOTES AND ENDNOTES, 41
For a paragraph style, 101
For Mac, 313, 324, 331, 333, 381, 384
Format, 311, 315, 320, 338, 344, 349, 350, 355, 397, 398, 399, 400, 401, 403, 404, 405, 406, 407, 408, 409, 410, 411, 412, 413, 414, 416, 417, 418, 419, 420, 421, 424, 427, 429, 430, 432, 435, 436, 441, 442, 443, 444, 445, 446, 447, 448, 449, 450, 451, 452, 453,454
Format button, 22, 202, 209, 227, 228, 294
Format icon, 164, 165, 204, 230, 274
Format inspector, 39, 100, 101, 102, 103, 126, 127, 129, 159, 160, 161, 162, 184, 185, 186, 268, 269, 270
Format sidebar, 311, 315, 344, 397, 404, 406, 408, 414, 416, 417, 418, 419, 420, 421, 424, 427, 429, 432, 436, 441, 442, 443, 445, 447
formatting, 335, 337, 338, 406, 418, 420, 428, 431, 435, 440
formatting features, 406
formatting options, 435, 440
formatting symbols, 129
Formula Editor, 187, 188, 208, 209, 210, 211, 212, 290, 292, 293, 294, 295, 296, 297
Formula-containing cells, 193
forward or publish, 365
frame border, 311
free iWork word processor, 162
Friendly with Microsoft, 307
full table prevents, 435
FUNCTIONS, 187, 290, 293, 298
fundamental equations, 293

G

gallery, 305, 397, 403, 404, 405
gear icon, 190, 259, 260, 261, 300

General, 15, 256, 288
general idea, 16
Get creative with photos, 461
Get started with a template, 175
Getting a quick view of formulas, 190
Getting Started, 166
GIF a name, 359
Gmail, 307
Gmail or Dropbox, 307
good color, 461
good color combination, 461
good theme designs, 304
gorgeous color, 308
gradient fill color scheme, 452
gradients, 305
grant or remove access, 365
graphically rich, 306
graphics, 1, 3, 4, 133, 138, 142, 157, 158, 178, 181, 267
graphics and editing tools, 304
graphics and text, 310
graphics APIs, 1
Group and Ungroup Slides, 327
Group Slides, 327, 332
Grouped Object, 405, 406
grouped objects, 405
group's first slide, 327, 331
Guidelines, 32

H

Handoff, 389, 390, 391, 393
handwriting. Magically, 7
hardcopies, 4
header, 28, 32, 34, 164, 228, 240, 241, 260
Headers, 27, 415, 424
Heading, 37, 100
Heading 3, 37
Hide Collaboration Activity, 366, 374
Hide or Show Activity, 374
High efficiency (HEVC), 361
highlighted words, 342
hit **Cancel**, 17
home page, 10, 180, 181, 183

Home screen, 2
horizontal and vertical, 411
horizontal axis, 411
How to avoid formula errors, 192
How to refer to cells in other sheets, 194
HTML, 349, 350, 357, 360
hyperlink, 35
hyperlinks, 313, 344
Hyperlinks, 333
Hyphenation checkbox, 23
Hyphenations, 22
hyphens, 23, 24

I

iBooks Author, 4
iCloud, 1, 9, 10, 11, 12, 36, 38, 44, 46, 48, 49, 50, 53, 58, 61, 63, 69, 73, 77, 81, 82, 83, 84, 85, 89, 90, 104, 124, 175, 206, 257, 277, 278, 287, 288, 305, 308, 309, 316, 317, 318, 339, 341, 344, 348, 351, 352, 353, 354, 355, 362, 363, 366, 367, 369, 372, 373, 379, 387, 389, 393, 397, 400, 452
iCloud account, 10, 50, 53, 58, 73, 84
iCloud Drive, 308, 316, 351, 354, 367, 373, 452
iCloud presentations, 309
iCloud website, 1
ideal environment, 3
Ideal for businesses, 7
iDevice, 91
iDevices, 175
iDisk, 13, 14, 49
If You See a Warnings Window, 74
illumination, 413
Image Enhancement, 411
Image from the sidebar, 401
image galleries, 4, 271, 272, 273, 333, 408
Image Gallery, 396, 398, 405
image of the inspector, 35
Images, 310, 311, 349, 357, 360, 397, 408, 429, 442
image's exposure, 401
image's topic., 309
implement the modifications, 361
Impressive, 306

Impressive Charts, 306
impressive presentation., 304
incorporate cinematic, 304
incorporate cinematic effects, 304
indentation, 329, 332
individual images, 404
individual images or all images, 404
Individual Participants, 371
Input a tag, 347
Input a tag or multiple tags, 347
Input menu, 128, 129
Insert a row or column, 423
Insert Charts, 119
Insert Function, 209, 210, 211, 212, 294, 295, 296, 297
Insert multiple rows, 423
insert objects, 308, 309
Insert Page Number, 33
Inserting a Link, 334
Inserting A Note, 41
Inserting an image, 399
Inserting Formulas, 189
Inspector window, 35
Inspector's Chart view, 170
installed macOS 11 or later, 353
Instant Alpha., 152
interactive charts, 305
interesting, 304, 305, 306, 414
interesting sub-topics, 304
Intro to Text Boxes, 311
INTRODUCTION, 304
INTRODUCTION TO NUMBERS, 175
introductory session, 304
Invisible Character Represents, 130
Invitation, 362, 372
Invite More People, 369
Invite others, 311, 374
Invite People from Your Mac, 364
invited email or phone number, 362, 368
iOS, 1, 2, 4, 13, 36, 38, 39, 40, 46, 48, 49, 50, 52, 53, 58, 76, 78, 79, 85, 88, 90, 124, 187, 206, 229, 287, 288
iOS device, 305, 351, 366, 387, 388, 391, 394, 402
iOS devices, 355, 389, 390

iOS iWork apps, 40
iPad, 3, 9, 13, 14, 18, 19, 21, 25, 40, 46, 47, 50, 58, 61, 63, 64, 65, 66, 67, 68, 69, 70, 73, 79, 81, 83, 85, 90, 91, 104, 111, 129, 191, 224, 230, 254, 255, 258, 261, 275, 284, 304, 305, 307, 308, 309, 312, 319, 322, 327, 332, 335, 343, 346, 351, 352, 354, 363, 367, 373, 380, 383, 388, 389, 391, 393, 402
iPad and Apple Pencil, 312
iPadOS, 7, 85, 206, 254, 255
iPadOS and Apple Pencil, 308
iPhone, 2, 3, 6, 8, 9, 18, 19, 21, 25, 32, 47, 50, 58, 61, 63, 64, 65, 66, 67, 68, 69, 73, 79, 81, 83, 85, 89, 90, 91, 104, 107, 111, 113, 120, 121, 129, 191, 203, 204, 224, 229, 230, 258, 275, 279, 284, 301, 304, 305, 307, 308, 309, 312, 319, 321, 322, 327, 330, 332, 335, 343, 346, 351, 352, 354, 363, 367, 373, 380, 383, 386, 388, 389, 390, 391, 393, 397, 399, 400, 402, 407, 409
iPhone and iPad, 8, 25, 32, 58, 85, 89, 104, 107, 111, 113, 191, 203, 204, 229, 230, 258, 279, 301
iPhoto **Photo Library**, 134
iTunes, 14, 47, 48, 50, 51, 90, 91, 287

"**iWork**", 50

I

iWork 2022, 24, 302
iWork app, 14, 45, 63, 70
iWork applications, 1
iWork Collaboration, 69
iWork office suite, 1, 57, 58
iWork.com, 13, 52
iWorkCommunity.com, 180

J

juggle and polish, 3

472

K

Keep Scanning, 403
Keeper, 77
keeping track, 364
keynote, 304, 306, 307, 308, 313, 314, 345, 362, 380, 386, 416
Keynote, 1, 14, 47, 48, 49, 52, 54, 58, 60, 61, 63, 64, 65, 66, 67, 69, 70, 71, 74, 81, 83, 90, 99, 115, 173, 180, 181, 200, 254, 302, 304, 305, 307, 308, 309, 311, 312, 313, 314, 316, 317, 318, 319, 321, 330, 331, 332, 333, 337, 339, 341, 343, 344, 345, 347, 348, 349, 350, 351, 352, 354, 355, 360, 361, 363, 367, 372, 373, 375, 376, 378, 379, 380, 386, 387, 388, 389, 390, 391, 392, 393, 394, 395, 396, 399, 400, 401, 403, 404, 408, 411, 414, 416, 418, 421, 426, 431, 433, 434, 435, 436, 437, 440, 441, 444, 447, 449, 450, 451, 452, 454, 455, 456
Keynote 12.2 or later, 373
Keynotes, 305, 308
Keynotes add live video streams, 308
Keynotes outline, 308
Klariti, 182

L

Landscape, 17, 21
Last Opened, 347
later of macOS Ventura, 356
later on an OS X version, 363
later on an OS X version of OS X, 363
latest version, 304, 447
Launches a specified website, 334, 336
Launchpad, 314
Layer Graphics, 158
layer objects, 310
Left Back button, 460
legacy Pages '09, 4
Ligatures, 22, 23
LIGATURES AND HYPHENATIONS, 22
Light table, 322, 324
Light table duplication, 322
Light table view, 324
Light table view slide, 324

Light table view slide deletion, 324
line chart, 437
line color and thickness, 417
link button, 335, 337
Link field, 334, 336
Linked Text Boxes of The Past, 123
List Of Functions by Category, 201
list style, 101, 102, 109, 110, 111, 113, 115
List Type, 111, 115
List value type, 214
Location information, 334, 336
Lock or Unlock, 344, 387
Lock or unlock a table, 433
Locked checkbox., 344, 387
LOCKIN, 76
LOCKING PRESENTATIONS, 380
LockUp a Text, 344
Logical and information functions, 207
Long-Press on Single Words for Suggestions, 117

M

Mac, 1, 2, 3, 9, 13, 14, 16, 19, 25, 32, 36, 38, 39, 40, 45, 46, 47, 48, 50, 58, 63, 64, 66, 67, 68, 69, 73, 74, 79, 81, 82, 83, 85, 93, 104, 111, 113, 124, 127, 133, 138, 175, 183, 187, 189, 195, 201, 202, 224, 225, 226, 227, 229, 230, 275, 283, 284, 288, 290
Mac or iOS, 305, 366
Mac or iOS device, 305
Mac users, 1, 111
Mac. 4, 414
macOS, 1, 4, 13, 58, 79, 90, 117, 206
macOS 12, 373, 374, 385
macOS and iOS, 1
macOS Ventura, 385
Macs, 304, 356
Magic Move, 312, 456, 457, 458
Magic Move for creating sophisticated, 312
Magic Move for creating sophisticated animations, 312
Magic Place, 458
Magic Place acceleration, 458
Magic Place acceleration and delivery, 458

Magic Place acceleration and delivery options, 458
Mail and Messages, 356, 368
mail merge, 6
Make alterations, 407
Making Lists, 104
Making Threads Look Good, 126
Making Use of Paragraph Styles, 100
MAKING YOUR TEMPLATES, 94
Manage Custom Sizes, 20
manage presentations, 304, 313
Manage Shared, 369, 370
MANAGING DOCUMENT WITH KEYNOTE, 345
MANAGING DOCUMENTS, 13
managing the files, 53
Managing your documents, 345
margins, 16, 19, 20, 21
MARGINS, 19
Mask, 400, 406, 407
Mask (Crop a Photo), 406
Match Case, 339, 340, 342
match the image's colors, 420
Matches, 340
math equations, 4, 305
Media Browser, 133, 136, 138
Media menu button, 402, 420, 446
media placeholder, 397, 398, 400
menu bar, 26, 80, 94, 128, 163, 189, 202, 225, 241, 243, 276, 283, 299
Menu Bar, 44
menu bar., 319, 323, 341, 366, 367, 400
Merge and Unmerge, 424
Merge and Unmerge Cells, 424
Merge Cells, 425, 426
Merging adjacent, 425
Merging adjacent table, 425
Merging adjacent table cells, 425
Microsoft Office, 1, 13, 54, 55, 57, 85, 116
Microsoft Office applications, 1
Microsoft Office formats, 1
Minimum System Requirements, 363
MobileMe iDisk, 13
Modal argument or value type, 215
Modern Linked Text Boxes, 124
modifications, 436

Modified Toolbar, 308
Modify a Chart, 440
modify the intensity of colors, 407
modify the opacity, 311
modify the transition, 404
MONITOR CHANGES, 45
More button, 18, 21, 23, 254, 354, 374, 459
More buttons, 380
More icon, 18, 256
More Useful Formulas and Functions, 207
Most compatible (H.264), 361
Move a table, 433
Move Files from PC, 91
Move Formulas, 193
Move the data, 430
multipage documents, 35
multiple apps, 316
multiple borders., 417
multiple cells, 425
Multiple objects, 410
Multiple rows or columns, 431
multiple slides, 322, 323, 324, 325, 329, 332
Multiple slides, 324
multiple types, 304, 313
multiple types of media, 304, 313
multipresent slideshow, 321
multitask, 308
multitasking screen, 390, 393
My Card from Contacts, 17
My Documents, 14, 47, 70, 71
My Presentations page, 14
My Spreadsheets, 14, 47, 71

N

Native format, 47
native formats, 1
native Pages application, 9
Navigable Table of Contents, 36
navigation pane, 459
navigational arrows, 342
Navigators, 312
negative offset, 147
new coding certificate, 5

New Features, 5
new location, 319, 325, 329, 388, 403, 421, 430, 431
new sentence, 459
new style, 418, 419, 420, 444, 445, 446
New Style option, 164
new table, 418, 419, 420, 431
new table style, 418, 419, 420
Newsletters, 17
Next Item button, 404
next major event invitations, 5
Nonadjacent cells, 425
Note, 313, 314, 315, 316, 319, 320, 324, 325, 326, 333, 337, 338, 339, 340, 341, 342, 343, 345, 349, 350, 352, 353, 354, 355, 357, 360, 363, 364, 366, 367, 368, 370, 373, 377, 382, 385, 386, 388, 389, 391, 398, 402, 406, 408, 415, 419, 425, 432, 436, 455, 459
notifications appear, 371
number of characters, 198, 199
number of columns, 422
Number value type, 215
Numbers, 1, 6, 14, 25, 28, 32, 44, 47, 48, 49, 52, 54, 58, 60, 61, 63, 64, 65, 66, 67, 69, 70, 71, 74, 76, 81, 83, 90, 99, 115, 164, 167, 172, 173, 175, 178, 179, 180, 181, 182, 183, 187, 189, 190, 191, 194, 195, 200, 201, 203, 204, 205, 206, 212, 214, 217, 223, 224, 225, 226, 229, 230, 231, 232, 237, 239, 240, 241, 243, 244, 245, 249, 254, 255, 257, 258, 261, 262, 263, 264, 267, 271, 275, 279, 280, 283, 286, 287, 288, 290, 291, 292, 297, 298, 299, 300, 302
number's font style, 33
Numeric functions, 207

O

object animations, 459
Object Resizing, 408
Object-driven transitions, 312
Objects, 311, 408, 411
Office format, 47
offline copy, 366
Offset, 147, 161, 413
Older iWork, 75

On Mac, 337, 339, 344, 345, 385, 398, 399
One amazing feature, 307
Only people you invite, 374
on-screen instructions, 373
on-screen prompts, 355, 394
Opacity slider, 414, 453
Opacity slider or box, 147
opaque object, 460
Open Password, 385
open the document, 346
Open the shape, 451
Open with Touch ID, 382
OPENING EXISTING FILES, 74
Opening Locked Documents, 79
OPENING PAGES FROM ICLOUD, 9
operating systems, 1, 70
Opt out of shared Documents, 374
Option key, 319, 346, 348, 430
option or program, 353
Organize a Table, 421
ORGANIZING PAGES AND DOCUMENTS, 80
original document, 17, 75
original invitees, 370
original shape, 408
Original Size, 143, 160, 266, 453
OS X, 13, 129
Other Features, 307
Other Settings, 407
Other Stuff, 172
other types of charts, 306
output widget, 123
outstanding presentation, 304
Overrides, 102

P

page layout document, 16, 17, 18, 19, 21, 98
page number appears, 33
Page Number format, 29
Page Number style, 33
page numbers, 24, 25, 26, 30, 32, 35, 39
Page Setup, 20
Page Thumbnails, 81

Pages, 1, 2, 3, 4, 5, 6, 9, 10, 12, 13, 14, 15, 16, 17, 18, 19, 22, 23, 24, 25, 31, 32, 34, 35, 36, 37, 38, 40, 45, 47, 48, 49, 51, 52, 54, 55, 56, 58, 60, 61, 63, 64, 65, 66, 67, 69, 70, 71, 72, 73, 74, 76, 77, 78, 80, 81, 82, 83, 84, 85, 86, 88, 89, 90, 93, 95, 96, 97, 98, 100, 104, 107, 111, 113, 115, 116, 117, 118, 119, 120, 121, 122, 123, 124, 125, 126, 127, 128, 132, 133, 134, 135, 136, 137, 138, 139, 140, 141, 142, 145, 154, 156, 157, 162, 163, 164, 165, 166, 168, 169, 170, 171, 173, 178, 179, 180, 181, 182, 183, 200, 217, 254, 302

Pages app icon, 2
PAGES EXPORTING FILES, 85
pages file, 11, 77, 85
pages files, 13
Pages files, 9, 12, 85, 89, 90
Pages for iOS, 2
PAGES NUMBERS AND HEADERS, 24
Pages Preferences, 15
paper size, 16, 19, 20, 21
PAPER SIZE, 19
Paragraph, 100, 101, 102, 103, 104, 128, 129
paragraph styles, 36, 37, 39, 100, 102
Paragraph Styles, 101, 102, 103, 104
paragraphs, 20, 23, 36, 37, 39, 101, 127, 129
Passcode, 386
Password, 67, 68, 76, 79
PASSWORD, 76
Password Change, 384
Password to Lock, 380
Password-protected, 380
Paste and Match style, 338
Paste Formula Results, 430
Paste Style, 338, 430
Paste Text, 339
pasting, 309, 339, 430
PC in a compatible format, 12
PCs, 304
PDF, 1, 4, 12, 24, 47, 51, 54, 56, 57, 70, 104, 349, 350, 355, 357, 358, 361
PDF files, 1
PDF icon, 47
penning Aunt Peg, 3
People to collaborate, 367

People you invite, 368, 369, 370, 371
Performs alterations, 309
Permission, 362, 370, 371
PERMISSION, 62, 64
Permissions, 59
Personalize Every Detail, 311
personalized note, 368
perspective, 403, 413
Perspective, 161, 413
Phone Number, 334, 335, 336
photo card templates, 5
photograph, 402
photograph or scanned document, 402
photos, 304, 324, 420, 446
Photos tab, 134
photos to use as transitions, 305
Pick a slide, 343
pick from columns, 306
Picture Frame, 311
pie chart, 437
pies, 306
pivot table, 232, 233, 234, 235, 236, 237, 238, 239
PIVOT TABLE IN NUMBERS, 232, 237
pivot tables, 176, 232, 233, 234, 235, 236, 237, 238
placeholders, 94, 97, 134, 267
Placing Your Chart, 166
Plain, 415
plain text, 4
platforms, 1, 12, 115
Play from the menu, 376
play videos, 9
Play Vimeo and YouTube videos, 9
Play your Presentation, 311
Play your Presentation Anywhere and Anytime, 311
Playback drop-down, 358
Playback option, 376
Playing With the Axes, 170
Plot columns, 440
Plot rows, 440
Plot rows and Plot columns buttons, 440
pop-out menu, 415

476

popular features, 307

pop-up menu, 19, 42, 43, 45, 94, 101, 102, 103, 104, 125, 159, 160, 161, 163, 164, 184, 185, 186, 191, 238, 250, 263, 265, 266, 301, 310, 311, 319, 353, 359, 417, 420, 429, 430, 435, 441, 442, 452, 453

Portable Document, 355

Position and Align objects, 410

Position and Align objects well, 410

positive offset, 147

potential readers, 36

PowerPoint, 1, 47, 304, 305, 307, 349, 350, 355, 357, 358, 387, 388

PowerPoint files, 307

PowerPoint for Microsoft, 304

Practice always, 461

preferences, 15, 20, 24, 33, 60

Preferences, 15, 17, 23, 58, 117, 127, 128, 206, 288

preferences section, 15

Prerequisites, 58

Pre-selected table-of-contents styles, 37

presentation, 304, 305, 306, 307, 308, 309, 310, 311, 312, 313, 314, 315, 316, 317, 318, 319, 320, 321, 323, 325, 326, 327, 330, 331, 332, 335, 336, 341, 343, 344, 345, 346, 347, 348, 349, 350, 351, 353, 354, 355, 356, 357, 358, 360, 361, 362, 363, 364, 367, 368, 369,370, 371, 372, 373, 374, 375, 376, 377, 378, 379, 380, 382, 383, 384, 385, 386, 387, 388, 389, 390, 391, 392, 393, 394, 396, 397, 398, 399, 400, 402, 403, 411, 412, 414, 420, 421, 429, 436, 454, 456, 457, 459, 461

Presentation, 317, 318, 319, 321, 337, 339, 344, 346, 347, 348, 349, 350, 353, 354, 356, 360, 369, 370, 373, 374, 375, 376, 380, 383, 385, 386, 387, 388, 390, 391, 394, 396, 414

presentation manager, 323, 354, 373, 375

presentation program, 304, 313

presentation program from Apple, 304

presentation short and simple., 481

presentations, 305, 307, 308, 309, 312, 316, 327, 331, 348, 349, 351, 354, 355, 356, 379, 380, 385, 387, 388, 389, 396, 455

presenter display, 311, 331

Preserve original format, 361

press **Documents**, 18

press the Delete key, 416, 427

Preview button, 457

previous matching text., 342

Printers & Scanners, 378

Printing, 378

Proportionally, 408

Q

Quickly translate text., 7

QuickTime Video, 375, 376

QuickTime., 375, 376

R

radar chart., 437

Range value type, 215

Rearrange Page Layout pages, 81

Rearranging Links, 125

rearranging themselves, 459

red close button, 317

Redefine a chart style, 447

Redefine a Table, 421

Redefine Style, 421, 447

Redo the previous step, 332

Reduce File Size, 360

Refer To Cells in Formulas, 194

Reference functions, 207

Reflection check box, 148

relocating, 309

remote control, 391, 392, 393, 394, 395

Remove a Collaborate, 64, 65

Remove A Collaborator from The File, 64

Remove a Device, 394

Remove a fill, 454

Remove A Note, 43

Remove Access, 64, 65

Remove Extra Spaces, 209, 295

Remove Header Rows, 424

Remove Me., 374

Remove password., 385

remove rows, 423

Remove Transition, 459

Remove trimmed parts, 361

removing rows and columns., 422
Rename, 318, 346, 347
Rename A Custom Template, 95
Rename a Document, 346
Rename A Style, 103
Rename Style, 103
Reorder Data, 440
Reorder Data Series, 440
Reorder images, 404
Reorder Slides, 325, 329
Repeated tapping, 332
Replace an image, 399
Replace button., 343, 397
Replace field empty, 342
Replace Found Text, 340
Replace Image button, 316, 320, 397, 400
Replace option, 343
Replace placeholder text, 98
replace search results, 339
Replace Text, 343
Replace Text From the Dictionary, 343
Replace the following content, 427
replacement, 340, 341, 343
replacement word, 340
Require a Password, 380
Requirement, 362
Reset Image, 407, 412
Reset Image button, 407
Resize, 408, 431, 432, 433
resize and **reposition**, 403
resize them, 310
resizing, 309, 324, 408, 432, 450, 458
Resizing Other Kinds of Graphics, 142
resolution and **frame rate**, 359
Return key, 129, 208, 292, 293, 343
Revert a Previous, 347
Revert Changes to a Table Style, 419
Review Formula Errors, 192
rich font library, 1
rich text, 4, 212, 297, 298
Rotate, 408, 409
Rotate wheel, 144
row colors, 416, 418
Row vs. Column, 439

rows and columns, 417, 422, 431, 432, 433, 434, 438, 440
Rows and columns, 421, 432
rows or columns, 423, 424, 431, 432, 434, 439, 440
RTF, 4
Rulers, 15

S

saturation, 401, 407
Saturation, 407, 412
Save a chart, 445
Save A Custom Fill, 161
Save a Table, 419
Save a Table as a New Style, 419
Save to Files, 89
Saving a Document, 345
SAVING AND RENAMING, 72
Scale down large images, 361
Scale to Fill, 454
Scale to Fit, 429, 454
Scan a Page Manually, 403
Scan Documents, 402
scatter, 306, 443
Screen View, 6, 18
Scribble, 7, 254, 255, 256
Search Field, 339
second slide, 459
second text box, 122
Security Options, 70
select a border style, 417
Select a cell, 434
Select a layout, 315
Select a new transition., 459
Select a sending option., 356
select a setting, 342, 411
Select a table, 421, 434
Select an image, 397, 401, 409, 411, 412
Select an object, 408, 410, 411, 413
Select Folder icon, 48
Select Image, 398
select Package, 351
Select Record Slideshow., 376
Select rows, 434

478

Select tables, 434
selected borders, 417
selection border, 428
selects a color option, 418
Send a Copy, 356
Send via Mail, 54, 57
sequential content or patterns, 428
Set Auto-Replacement, 117
Set Password, 381, 382
Set Password from the main menu, 382
Setting up, 355
Settings menu, 386
Settings tab, 336
Setup Remote screen, 391
Shadow cast, 413
Shadow cast at an angle, 413
Shapes, 99, 159, 160, 162, 257, 264, 310, 333, 447, 448, 449, 450, 451
shape's button functions, 337
Share button, 356, 365, 367
Share File dialog box, 59
Share Options, 61, 63, 64, 66
Shared Documents, 373
SHARING, 46
sharing method, 365
sharing settings, 362
Sharpness, 412
Shift-Command, 333
shortcut menu, 420, 427, 446
Shortcuts app, 1
Show a Cell Row, 430
Show a Cell Row and Column, 430
Show Adjust Image, 412
Show Collaboration Activity, 366, 374
Show Comments, 45
Show Comments & Changes pane, 45
Show Details, 378
Show Find & Replace, 340
showing or hiding gridlines, 416
sidebar, 19, 23, 36, 41, 42, 43, 45, 81, 99, 202, 227, 228, 241, 243, 249, 265, 266, 267, 271, 272, 273
Sidebar, 417
Simple batch mailing., 6
simple transitions, 312

Simplify charts and graphs, 461
simulate how words, 459
single platform, 305
Size a row or column, 432
Size a row or column to fit its content, 432
Skim through in style., 8
Skip a Slide, 326
Skip or Un-skip a Slide, 330
Skip Slide or Un-skip Slide, 330
Slide from another Slide, 323
slide in Keynote, 459
slide layout features, 313, 315
slide navigator, 320, 321, 322, 323, 324, 325, 326, 327, 329, 330, 331, 332, 458
slide numbers, 358
Slide View, 327
slides for an excellent, 304
slideshow, 323, 331, 335, 336, 344, 358, 360, 376, 377, 436
Smart Dashes checkbox, 24
smart quotes, 312
smooth experience, 308
smooth transitions, 305
sophisticated presentations, 312
Spacebar, 32, 111, 129
specific paragraphs, 23
specific section, 44
spell checker, 1
Split Text, 208, 294
Spotlight Search, 32, 111
spreadsheet, 1, 6, 49, 57, 58, 69, 175, 177, 178, 187, 189, 190, 191, 194, 201, 208, 209, 212, 217, 224, 232, 237, 238, 239, 240, 249, 254, 257, 258, 262, 264, 267, 271, 274, 275, 276, 277, 279, 283, 284, 286, 287, 288, 289, 292, 294, 295, 297, 299, 300, 301
spreadsheet application **Numbers**, 1, 175
spreadsheets, 1, 46, 175, 254, 275, 287, 298
standard format, 4
start a presentation, 304
Statistical functions, 207
Stay on Page, 157
Steve Jobs, 1
Stock Layouts, 181
stop sharing a document, 366

479

Stop Sharing a Document, 366
Stop Sharing button, 66
storage and backup, 53
straightforward, 312
Stretch, 453
String value type, 216
Stunning presentations, 312
style in the sidebar, 420, 421, 446, 447
Style menu, 30, 31
style selection, 435
Style tab, 126, 127, 145, 148, 265, 266, 267, 271, 272, 311, 404, 405, 412, 413, 414, 421, 443, 452, 453, 454
Style-based tables, 36
Style-based tables of contents, 36
stylized graphic, 370
stylized graphic containing, 370
Submit New Template button, 180
Substitutions, 24
Sums, 415
swift in-document translation, 7
Switch rows, 440
symbol appears, 354
Sync Documents, 48, 351
synchronization status, 364
System Preferences, 15, 127, 351, 355, 378, 385, 390

T

Tab, 129
Table Cells, 417
table data, 421
Table handle, 416, 432, 433
table in proportion, 433
table of contents, 36, 38, 39
Table of Contents, 36, 37, 38, 39, 40
TABLE OF CONTENTS, 36
Table of Contents view, 36, 37, 38, 39, 40
Table of Contents view., 37, 38, 39, 40
Table or Chart icon, 163
Table Outline, 417
Table Outline section, 417
Table Style, 420

table style that matches, 420
table styles, 420, 421
Table tab, 405, 416, 418, 419, 420, 421, 424, 432, 436
table text, 435
Tables, 163, 233, 310, 312, 405, 414, 433, 436
table's bottom, 423
table's features, 420
tables for large, 461
tables for large data, 461
table's header rows and columns, 422
Take Photo, 396, 402
tap Keynote, 393
tap the button, 383
temperature, 401
Template Chooser, 94, 95, 96, 289
Template Chooser., 94, 95, 96
Templates, 16, 93, 178, 180, 182, 183, 267, 287, 288, 289
term for object, 459
text box, 21, 22, 23, 41, 99, 122, 123, 124, 125, 126, 127, 131, 161, 162, 169, 191, 255, 256, 266, 301, 311, 335, 338, 344, 403, 404, 405, 414, 454, 459
Text Box, 122, 127
Text box linking, 123
text boxes, 16, 98, 122, 123, 124, 126, 127, 159, 160, 161, 264, 265, 267, 271, 272
Text Bullet., 109
Text Direction, 128
text fields, 162
TEXT FLOW MODIFICATION, 122
text flows, 16, 125, 156
Text functions, 207
Text in a single cell, 427
TEXT INSERTION, 98
text layout, 16
Text Match option, 459
Text pane, 101, 102, 103, 129
Text panel, 100
Text transitions, 312
text with color gradients, 4
textures, 305, 442
the App Store, 305
the App Store or the Mac App, 305

the App Store or the Mac App Store, 305
the Chart tab, 405, 441, 442, 443, 444, 445, 446, 447
The color schemes, 415
The Drift motion, 311
The editor displays, 37
The File to Prevent Unauthorized Access, 67
The folder structure, 379
The green dot, 449
the **image placeholder**, 134
the **Image** tab, 152, 154
The keynote, 306, 429
The keynote sets, 306
The keynote sets up, 306
The **Media Browser**, 134, 136
The offset, 413
The PDF, 358
The selected image, 311
The shapes library, 447
The small images, 444
the style and color scheme, 414
The Text tab, 435
The x and y coordinates, 410
The Y coordinate, 410
theme chooser, 314, 317
thousand words, 306
thread of linked boxes, 124
thumbnail, 51, 77, 81
Time intervals, 358
toolbar, 19, 23, 35, 42, 45, 46, 58, 63, 64, 66, 83, 84, 119, 122, 136, 165, 166, 168, 188, 189, 194, 225, 249, 255, 256, 262, 263, 264, 267, 290, 291, 299, 307, 308, 309, 310, 315, 317, 321, 324, 331, 339, 340, 341, 343, 346, 356, 364, 365, 369, 370, 374, 396, 397, 402, 403, 408, 409, 410, 411, 412, 413, 414, 420, 435, 437, 446, 448, 450
top of the page, 10
top of the screen, 320, 348, 360, 388, 389, 427
top right corner, 34, 85, 209, 227, 241, 276, 282, 294
top-left corner, 15, 18, 62, 71, 270, 416, 426, 432, 433
top-right corner of the table, 422

Touch ID, 76, 77, 78, 79, 380, 382, 385, 386
TouchID, 68
Transfer, 387, 388, 459
Transfer Files, 90
Transfer text, 459
TRANSFERRING DOCUMENTS, 81
Transform the device, 393
transition, 311, 358, 404, 456, 457, 458, 459
transition at the bottom, 459
translucent object, 460
transparency of a drawing, 414
transparent, 360, 414, 460
Trigonometric functions, 207
triple-dot icon, 86
Turn ligatures, 22
Turn off **Document Body**, 18, 19
Turn smart dashes on or off, 23
TXT, 4
Type in your password, 382
Type in your Password, 381
Types Of Arguments and Values, 213
Typography, 312
Typography options, 312

U

UNDERSTANDING PAGES, 3
Understanding Syncing Symbols, 354
Undo an Action, 332
Undo or Redo Changes, 333
Undo/Redo, 332
ungroup selected images, 401
ungroup slides, 313
Ungroup Slides, 329
Ungrouped Slides, 332
unique presentation, 461
unique presentation on keynote, 461
unlock a table, 433
Unmerge cells, 426
unskip the slides, 313
unskipped, 327
Update Style, 103
Upgrade, 75
Upload Files, 83
uploaded file, 11

upper-right corner, 460
Use chart styles, 444
use interface, 306
Use String Operators and Wildcards, 197
Use Table Styles, 418
user group, 368, 370
Using Airpod, 388
Using iTunes, 90
Using The Formula Editor, 187
Using The Thread Control, 125
UTILIZING PRE-EXISTING TEMPLATES, 93

V

Value Axis (Y) section, 171
version 13, 356, 385
version of iOS, 373
Vertex42, 183
vertical axis, 411
vertical or horizontal flip, 409
vertical sequence, 331
video feeds to slides, 305
video feeds to slides with Keynote, 305
videos, 304, 305, 308, 310, 324, 408
View menu, 331, 339, 340, 364
View menu button, 331, 339, 340
View Only, 341, 371, 372
visible series, 445, 447
visual experience, 461
visual intrigue, 308
VoiceOver, 1, 2
Voiceover QuickTime, 376

W

web browser., 9, 63
Web-based Distributed Authoring and Versioning, 13
WebDAV, 13, 14, 287, 288

Website, 334, 336
WHAT DO PAGES DO, 3
WHAT IS A PIVOT TABLE?, 232
Wi-Fi network, 356, 388
wildcard, 198, 199
window, 11, 15, 20, 24, 28, 35, 44, 50, 74, 83, 84, 93, 103, 139, 140, 159, 160, 161, 190, 192, 228, 250, 251, 265, 300
Windows, 9, 12, 13, 48, 58, 63, 85, 89, 90
Word, 1, 4, 12, 13, 17, 47, 51, 54, 55, 73, 76, 80, 85, 88, 89, 90, 98, 117, 118, 119, 162, 170, 173, 178, 183
word processing, 1, 4, 12, 13, 16, 17, 18, 19, 20, 21, 41, 57, 70, 80, 98, 99, 116, 118, 162
Work offline, 363
Work together in Real Time, 311
WORKING WITH CHARTS, 436
WORKING WITH CHARTS AND SHAPES, 436
WORKING WITH CHARTS AND SHAPES ON KEYNOTE, 436
Working With Data, 167
WORKING WITH PHOTOS ON THE KEYNOTE, 396
WORKING WITH TABLES, 414
WORKING WITH TABLES IN KEYNOTE, 414
WORKING WITH TEMPLATES ON PAGES, 93
WORKING WITH TEXT ON PAGES, 98
Working With Unique Characters, 115
Wrap text for a row, 427
Wrap text to fit in a cell, 427

Y

yellow alignment guides, 432
yellow autofill handle, 428
YouTube links, 4
YouTube or Vimeo, 308

Z

zoom level of an image, 403

INDEX

1

1. Resize images or photos, 143

2

2D, 120, 164, 165, 178, 226, 230, 250
2D and 3D charts, 313
2D and Interactive, 311
2D and Interactive buttons, 311
2D chart thumbnails, 311

3

3D, 120, 164, 165, 178, 226, 230, 250, 251
3G contract limit, 49

9

90 Apple-designed templates, 5

A

A basic line charts, 218
A circle with red-outlined, 450
A column chart, 444
A Custom Gradient, 453
A table with header, 423
A table's appearance, 417
A table's rows and columns, 422
A two-color gradient fill, 453
A USER-FRIENDLY INTERFACE, 176
A WIDE RANGE OF TEMPLATES, 179
Abc, 199
AbcDef, 199
ability to export a presentation, 306
About Chart down Sampling, 442
Access, 363, 371, 372, 373

access iWork documents, 1
access **System Preferences**, 16
account ID, 15
Action tab, 405, 461
Actions Menu., 347
actual size, 454
add a caption, 405, 406, 407
Add a caption, 405
ADD A COMMENT, 44
add a Link, 336
Add a Magic, 458
Add A Reflection, 163
Add a Shadow, 414
Add A Shadow, 162
Add a Shape, 449
Add a slide, 316, 321
Add a Slide, 323, 325
Add a Table, 415
Add a Title, 406
Add a Transition, 457
Add an image, 317, 321, 404
Add An Image Fill, 161
Add an object to a cell, 430
Add and Delete a Slide, 322
Add and edit cell, 427
Add and edit cell content, 427
Add Build In, 461
Add button, 21
Add Chart, 438
add charts, 305, 437
Add Column button, 423
Add content to cells, 428
add curves, 461
Add data to a table, 177
Add Emojis and Special Characters, 117
Add Fingerprint, 386
Add images, 5
Add Math Equation, 119
Add more People, 370
Add new data set, 441
Add or Remove Header Rows and Column, 425

Add or Remove row and column, 423
Add or Remove Rows, 422
Add or Remove Rows and Columns, 422
Add Photos, 311
Add Rounded corners, 445
Add Rounded corners to the bar, 445
Add Slide button, 316, 321, 323, 325
Add Text in A Text Box, 100
Add text inside a shape, 455
Add Text Inside a Shape, 101
Add to Template Chooser, 95, 289
Add Transition, 459
Add visual effects, 312
Add visual effects or animations, 312
added to a slide, 312
adding, 305, 310, 370, 417, 423, 425, 442, 451, 459
Adding a Caption, 405
ADDING A CHART, 165
adding animated objects, 305
ADDING IMAGES TO DOCUMENTS, 133
ADDING TABLES TO YOUR DOCUMENTS, 163
adding the number, 31
additional 50GB, 54
additional devices, 313
ADDITIONAL FORMULAS, 294
Additional image, 402
additional options, 353, 438
additional settings, 357
additional slides, 311, 323, 326, 330
additional **themes**, 315
Additional visual elements, 17
address (URL), 335, 337
Adds new comments, 310
Adjust Image, 156, 408, 412, 413
Adjust Image window, 408
Adjust Saturation, 408
Adjust the curve, 449
Adjust the features of a shape, 450
Adjust the image's size, 454
Adjust the position, 404
Adobe Acrobat, 359
Adobe Reader, 57
ADVANCE FORMULAS, 188
Advanced, 313, 352, 359, 399, 453, 454

Advanced Theme, 313
Advanced Theme Chooser, 313
Airdrop, 357
AirDrop, 89, 356, 357, 366, 369, 389, 390
AirPods, 381
Align an object using x and y coordinates, 411
Align menu, 412
Align objects, 412
Align objects vertically, 412
Align objects vertically and horizontally, 412
Align to the path, 461
Alignment guides, 313
All series styles, 446, 448
Allow other users, 372
Allow to add other People, 373
Alter the Appearance, 312
Alternate the row, 419
alternating row, 417
Alternating Row, 419
Alternating Row Color, 419
Alternating Row Color checkbox, 419
Amazing Creative Tools, 306
amazing tool, 306
An Apple Mac running, 364
An iOS 15-capable, 364
Angle, 414
Animate an object onto and off a slide, 460
Animate objects, 460
Animate objects onto, 460
Animate objects onto and off, 460
animate sidebar, 312, 461
Animate the object, 461
animated GIF, 359, 361
Animated GIF, 359
animation, 307, 312, 360, 460, 461
Animation, 312
Another feature, 307, 308
another format, 357, 358
Any Color, 453
Any value types, 214
Anyone with the link, 366, 370, 371, 372
Anyone with the Link, 369
App Store, 2, 59
appearance of a table, 420
appearance of cell borders, 418

Apple, 1, 2, 4, 5, 8, 10, 11, 16, 25, 26, 41, 44, 47, 49, 50, 52, 53, 54, 55, 57, 58, 59, 62, 65, 66, 68, 70, 71, 77, 78, 82, 85, 86, 91, 94, 98, 105, 116, 117, 118, 119, 120, 121, 122, 124, 126, 128, 163, 176, 179, 181, 183, 188, 218, 238, 241, 255, 256, 258, 259, 262, 276, 287

Apple Books, 2, 5, 41

Apple Books publishing., 5

Apple devices, 4, 86

Apple ID, 310, 353, 354, 356, 363, 368, 369, 372, 374, 453

Apple ID. Instructions, 363, 369

Apple Inc, 1, 2

Apple products, 305

Apple-designed themes, 313

Apple's Pages, 317

Apple's Services business, 41

AppleScript automation framework, 1

application **Keynote**, 1

Applications folder., 315

Apply a Different Style to a Table, 420

apply a new style., 420

Apply A Paragraph Style, 102

Apply colors, 443

apply text overlays to any graphic, 309

appropriate box., 387

appropriate symbol, 117, 118

area chart, 438, 442

Arrange button, 402, 409, 410, 411, 412

Arrange menu, 406, 428, 434

arrange styles, 421

Arrange tab., 145, 158, 273, 274

arrangement of text and images, 314, 316

Arrays and array functions, 214

arrow buttons, 341

Assign A Shortcut Key to A Style, 102

asterisk, 102, 103, 104, 200

attractive documents, 1, 4

audio, 305, 311, 361, 362, 399

Audio, 309

Auto-advance slider, 360

Auto-Correction, 16, 25, 118

autofill cells, 429

Autofill Cells, 429

autofill cells., 429

Autofill replaces, 429

Autofill replaces existing data, 429

automatic scaling, 313

automatic scaling Reviewer, 313

automatic spelling check, 16

Auto-scan a document, 404

Axis Options drop-down box., 172

B

background, 309, 310, 401, 402, 415, 418, 419, 423, 430

backgrounds, 305, 309, 361

backgrounds and themes, 305

bars, 307, 327, 441

Basic, 306, 416, 450

Basic category, 18, 19

basic features, 305

Basic Features of Keynotes, 306

Basic section, 100

basic tips, 462

Beginning with a Theme, 311

BIDIRECTIONAL TEXT, 128

blank page, 9, 100, 167

blank template, 19, 99

blanks with content, 428

Blur, 162, 414

blurring of the edges, 414

blurring of the edges of a shadow, 414

body rows and columns, 422

book-creation program, 5

Bookmark, 36

BOOKMARKS, 36

Books, 18, 41

Boolean expression and value type, 214

border layout, 418

border layout button, 418

border menu, 312

borders, 17, 127, 132, 142, 159, 256, 268

borders and color, 417

borders and color to cells, 417

bottom of the page., 33

bottom-left corner of the table, 424

Browse All Versions, 75, 348
browse folders, 12
browser, 10, 11, 51, 52, 53, 64, 78, 85, 91, 135
brush icon, 31, 106, 109, 112, 116
bubbles, 307
build effects, 460
built effects, 460
built-in collaboration feature, 306
built-in functions, 188, 299
business adds a feature, 77
business finance, 184
button on the file menu, 346
By Character, 460
By Object, 460
By Word, 460

C

Can make changes, 373
Capacity, 54
Caption checkbox, 405, 406
Card under Contacts., 18
Cell Name, 198
cell values, 208, 294
cells, 418, 420, 425, 426, 427, 428, 429, 430, 431, 432, 433, 434, 435, 436
cell's content and formatting, 426
Change a Slide, 460
Change a Slide Transition, 460
Change all notes, 43
Change automatic hyphenation, 24
Change button, 458
Change cell borders, 418
Change Color and Shadows, 443
Change document types, 18, 19
Change file type, 352
Change Numbering for Notes, 44
Change Object, 415
Change Object Transparency, 415
Change one note, 43
Change or Remove a Password, 384
Change Password, 384, 385, 386
change pictures, 305
Change Share Options, 64, 65
Change table gridlines, 417

change the appearance, 419, 422, 442
change the border, 418
Change the Borders, 418
Change the Borders and Background, 418
Change the font, 436, 442
Change the gridlines, 418
Change The Look of Note Text, 43
Change the look of table text, 436
Change the outline, 418
Change the spacing, 444
Change the spacing in the bar, 444
Change the spacing in the bar or column, 444
Change the spacing in the bar or column chart, 444
Change The Symbol for Notes, 44
character spacing, 23
character style, 103, 339, 436
Character Viewer, 117
chart animations, 313
Chart Data, 437, 439, 440, 441, 442
Chart Data editor, 437, 439, 441, 442
Chart Data Editor, 440
Chart Data editor results, 437
Chart Element, 443
Charts, 166, 167, 174, 218, 219, 220, 221, 222, 223, 224, 225, 247, 248, 249, 311, 406, 438, 443
CHARTS AND GRAPHS, 218
charts interactive, 307
checkboxes, 325, 348, 380
Choose A Document Type, 17, 19
Choose a new hue, 312
choose Delete Style, 448
Cinema-quality, 313
Cinema-quality animations, 313
Clear Content from a range of cells, 428
Clear Overrides, 420
Clear Overrides and Apply Style, 420
Click on **Set Password.**, 382
click **Reset**, 408
Clicking **Start Writing**, 19
clipping indicator, 100, 101, 132
Close the shape, 452
CloudConvert, 90

Collaborate, 310, 365, 366, 367, 369, 370, 371, 373, 374, 375
Collaborate button, 47, 61
Collaborate icon, 59, 61, 62, 64, 65, 66, 67, 69, 70
Collaborate in Messages, 310
Collaborate on A File, 59
Collaborate" icon, 67
Collaborating, 363
COLLABORATING, 58
Collaboration menu, 366
Collaboration screen, 66, 67
collaborative approval, 53
collapse groups, 328, 332
collapsed group, 327, 328, 331, 332
Collection value type, 214
color, 5, 17, 40, 69, 100, 101, 104, 127, 128, 148, 153, 154, 156, 160, 161, 162, 165, 166, 169, 171, 221, 226, 228, 230, 248, 250, 257, 263, 265, 266, 267, 268, 269, 270
color gradients, 5
Color in an Image, 421
COLOR LEVELS IN AN IMAGE, 160
Color tool, 148
color well, 419, 455
colored backgrounds, 305
Command key, 326, 409
Command-click, 418, 435
Command-click additional, 418
Command-click additional borders, 418
Command-Z, 18
Command-Z on the keyboard, 435
company logo, 95
Compare Values, 208, 294
Computed Values, 194
computer, 310, 312, 340, 352, 357, 364, 373, 380, 381, 383, 386, 388, 389, 398, 399, 404, 421, 447
Concatenate strings, 199
Conclusion, 13, 36, 47, 58, 98, 116, 128, 174, 184, 205, 237, 262, 287, 313, 345, 380, 396, 437, 456, 462
CONCLUSION, 303
Condition expression, 215
CONFIGURING PAGES PREFERENCES, 15
Constant expression, 215

Constrain proportions, 409
Contact Shadow, 148, 162, 414
contact shadow's angle, 414
Content should be edited, 428
contents of cells, 199, 208
contrast, 402, 413
Control-click a table style, 421
Control-clicking, 328
controls, 318, 322, 324, 331, 401, 408, 412, 418, 433, 436, 437, 441, 442, 443, 444, 461
Convert Notes from One Kind to Another, 43
convert Pages files, 90
Convert to Page Layout, 18
Convert To Plain Text, 213, 298
Copy and Paste a Text Style, 339
Copy and Paste Text, 338
Copy and replace existing content, 431
Copy Link,", 370
Copy or Move Cells, 431
Copying A File, 15
COUNTIF, 199, 200, 217
covering note, 53
Create a basic document, 17, 19
Create a chart, 178
Create A Date and Time Format, 186
Create a motion path, 461
Create a Presentation, 311, 314
CREATE A PRESENTATION, 314
Create A Text Format, 187
Create chart styles, 447
Create Custom Format, 185, 186, 187
Create GIF, 359
Create Internal Links, 36
Create Style from Image, 421, 447
creating presentations, 313
currency, 426
Currency symbols, 441
Curve Shadow, 414
Curved Shadow, 148, 162
Custom Number Format, 185
Custom Paper Size, 21
CUSTOM TEMPLATE, 96, 288, 290
CUSTOMIZABLE CELLS, 185
customization, 172
Customize a token element, 185, 186
customize the output, 313

Customize Toolbar, 120, 121
Customizing Your Chart, 170
Cut or Edit, 430

D

Dashlane, 78
data series, 439, 440, 441, 443, 444, 448
Date And Time Functions, 202
Date/time value type, 215
dazzling effects, 313
decimal places, 1
Default, 23, 128
Default Theme, 318
Delete a Chart, 441
Delete a chart style, 448
Delete A Custom Template, 97
Delete a data set, 441
Delete a Slide, 324, 326
Delete A Style, 104
Delete a Table, 417
Delete an object from a cell, 430
Delete Animation, 460
Delete any row or column, 424
Delete Button, 325
Delete Custom Styles, 150
Delete everything, 428
Delete multiple rows or columns, 424
Delete Row or Delete Column, 424, 441
Delivery and Acceleration, 459
Designing your Bar Chart, 443
desired file, 15
desktop publishing, 1
Developed with Simplicity, 307
device shows up, 388, 389
device's name, 388, 389, 403
different layout, 316
different style, 420, 442, 446
different style from the drop-down, 420
different table style, 419, 420
dimensions, 345, 409, 412, 431, 454, 455
Display field, 335, 337
Display, Link, 337
Distribute Graphics, 158
Dock, 315, 392

document, 2, 4, 8, 9, 10, 15, 16, 17, 18, 19, 20, 21, 22, 23, 24, 25, 26, 27, 32, 33, 35, 37, 38, 39, 40, 42, 43, 44, 45, 46, 47, 48, 49, 50, 51, 53, 54, 55, 56, 57, 59, 61, 62, 65, 66, 69, 70, 71, 72, 73, 74, 75, 76, 77, 78, 79, 80, 81, 82, 84, 85, 86, 87, 90, 94, 95, 96, 97, 98, 99, 100, 101, 104, 105, 106, 108, 111, 114, 116, 117, 118, 120, 122, 123, 125, 126, 127, 128, 129, 130, 134, 135, 137, 139, 140, 141, 142, 144, 150, 154, 157, 159, 164, 166, 167, 179, 181, 182, 183, 184, 195, 284, 285
Document, 17, 19, 20, 21, 22, 24, 27, 28, 35, 39, 48, 72, 74, 76, 77, 78, 85, 86, 94, 99, 101, 122, 167
DOCUMENT, 17, 20, 55, 71, 73, 77
document based, 17
Document Body, 19, 20
DOCUMENT CONFIGURATION, 17
Document Manager, 48
Document Manager screen, 48
Document radio button, 24
Document Setup, 19, 22, 27, 28
DOCUMENT SETUP USING PAGES, 17
Document tab, 19, 20, 35
Document's Text, 39
documents, 1, 2, 4, 5, 7, 10, 13, 14, 15, 16, 17, 20, 25, 33, 36, 37, 41, 44, 47, 49, 51, 54, 55, 70, 71, 72, 73, 77, 83, 84, 86, 90, 91, 94, 98, 105, 112, 120, 121, 133, 134, 141, 142, 143, 145, 146, 157, 163, 167, 180, 182, 184
Documents box, 49
DOCX, 5
Double hyphens, 24
double-click a label, 440
Double-click placeholder text, 316
double-click the Home button, 391, 394
Double-clicking, 316
Down Arrow, 332
Down Arrow and Up Arrow, 332
Down Arrow and Up Arrow keys, 332
download, 10, 13, 52, 84, 86, 91, 184, 288
Download button, 84, 184
Download Files, 84
drag and drop, 398, 401
Drag files, 84
Drag Handle, 325

Drag the image to the sidebar's table styles, 421
dragging, 325, 326, 330, 398, 399, 402, 404, 409, 410, 413, 421, 429, 435, 441, 449, 451, 453, 454, 455, 456, 459
Dragging, 461
Dragging the white dots, 461
dramatic effect, 310
Draw a Shape, 451
draw people's attention, 307
Drive On iCloud.com, 84
drop shadow, 312, 414
Drop Shadow, 148, 162, 414
drop-down menu, 319, 337, 340, 343, 348, 359, 369, 371, 372, 379, 388, 389, 397, 407, 412, 413, 420, 451, 455, 457
Duplicate, 323, 326, 348, 459
Duplicate a Slide, 323, 326
Duplicate button, 323
Duration value type, 215
dynamism, 460

E

easily skip a slide, 327, 331
Easily write reports., 9
eBook with Pages, 41
eBooks, 5, 41
edge of a shape, 449
EDIT, 62, 96, 268, 290
Edit a Table, 417
edit appears, 344
Edit Chart, 439, 441
Edit Chart Data, 439, 441
Edit Chart Data button, 439, 441
Edit icon, 81
Edit images, 401
Edit menu, 334, 371, 428, 429, 431
Edit or Remove a Link, 336
Edit or Remove Link, 338
edit PDF documents, 359
Edit While Offline, 364
editing, 305, 310, 365, 366, 374, 375, 401, 402, 451
Editing for more information, 364

Editing the formulas, 190
effects to slides, 305
Eliminate Backgrounds, 310
Email, 335, 336, 337, 338, 362
email address, 335, 337, 358, 374, 375
email address or phone number, 374
email addresses or phone, 369
email addresses or phone numbers, 369
email or phone number, 371, 374
EMAILING, 55
Emojis & Symbols, 117
Enable Black Mode, 309
Enable Handoff, 390
Enable Voice to Text, 122
endnote sign, 42
Endnotes, 42, 43
engage your viewers, 312
Engineering functions, 207
Enhance, 408, 413
ENHANCING A PRESENTATION, 457
ENHANCING A PRESENTATION WITH KEYNOTE, 457
ENHANCING YOUR DOCUMENTS WITH PAGES, 133
Enter key, 145
EPUB, 5
Equal Sign, 189, 291
Equally space objects, 412
EXAMINING FORMATTING SYMBOLS, 130
Excel, 1, 48, 165, 174, 179, 184, 233, 250
excellent presentation, 306
excellent presentation., 306
Existing iWork Files, 82
explaining data, 307
Export, 48, 71, 74, 86, 88
EXPORT, 71
Export as a Movie, 377
Export Document, 48
Export Presentation, 48
Export Spreadsheet, 48
Export to MP4 File, 376
Exporting, 376, 377, 378
EXPORTING DOCUMENTS, 47
Exposure, 408, 413

F

Face ID, 77, 78, 79, 80, 387
FaceID, 69
Facial ID, 387
facing the camera, 404
FAQs, 70, 183
favorite tools, 310
feature of the keynote, 307, 308, 401
Figure A, 164
Figure B, 165
Figure C, 166
File menu, 18, 41, 74, 288, 320, 347, 348, 349, 352, 357, 358, 359, 361, 370, 379, 385
File option, 18
File Sharing, 47, 48, 49, 91
File Sharing feature, 47
File Sharing feature in iTunes, 47
File Sharing folder, 48
File Sharing option, 48
File Sharing section, 49
files and folders, 14
files via their profile pictures, 357
Fill An Object with Color or A Gradient, 160
Fill section, 419
Fill with an image, 454
filling in the blanks, 384
Financial functions, 207
Find & Replace, 340, 341, 342, 344
Find and Replace, 340, 341, 342, 343
Find and Replace dialog, 342
Find and Replace dialog box, 342
Find and Replace Options, 340, 341
Find and Replace Options menu button, 341
Find and Replace Text, 340, 342
find settings, 309, 310
Find window, 344
Finder and Airpod, 388
Finding and Replacing Text, 344
Fit Height to Content, 433
Flip an Object, 410
Flip button, 410
flipping, 402

Follow's Someone Edit, 375
FONT SELECTION AND FORMATTING, 101
footer boxes, 29
footer row, 421
Footer rows, 423
Footers options, 28
footnote, 42, 43
footnotes, 42, 43, 44
FOOTNOTES AND ENDNOTES, 42
For a paragraph style, 102
For Mac, 314, 325, 332, 334, 382, 385
Format, 312, 316, 321, 339, 345, 350, 351, 356, 398, 399, 400, 401, 402, 404, 405, 406, 407, 408, 409, 410, 411, 412, 413, 414, 415, 417, 418, 419, 420, 421, 422, 425, 428, 430, 431, 433, 436, 437, 442, 443, 444, 445, 446, 447, 448, 449, 450, 451, 452, 453, 454,455
Format button, 23, 203, 210, 228, 229, 295
Format icon, 165, 166, 205, 231, 275
Format inspector, 40, 101, 102, 103, 104, 127, 128, 130, 160, 161, 162, 163, 185, 186, 187, 269, 270, 271
Format sidebar, 312, 316, 345, 398, 405, 407, 409, 415, 417, 418, 419, 420, 421, 422, 425, 428, 430, 433, 437, 442, 443, 444, 446, 448
formatting, 336, 338, 339, 407, 419, 421, 429, 432, 436, 441
formatting features, 407
formatting options, 436, 441
formatting symbols, 130
Formula Editor, 188, 189, 209, 210, 211, 212, 213, 291, 293, 294, 295, 296, 297, 298
Formula-containing cells, 194
forward or publish, 366
frame border, 312
free iWork word processor, 163
Friendly with Microsoft, 308
full table prevents, 436
FUNCTIONS, 188, 291, 294, 299
fundamental equations, 294

G

gallery, 306, 398, 404, 405, 406
gear icon, 191, 260, 261, 262, 301

General, 16, 257, 289
general idea, 17
Get creative with photos, 462
Get started with a template, 176
Getting a quick view of formulas, 191
Getting Started, 167
GIF a name, 360
Gmail, 308
Gmail or Dropbox, 308
good color, 462
good color combination, 462
good theme designs, 305
gorgeous color, 309
gradient fill color scheme, 453
gradients, 306
grant or remove access, 366
graphically rich, 307
graphics, 1, 4, 5, 134, 139, 143, 158, 159, 179, 182, 268
graphics and editing tools, 305
graphics and text, 311
graphics APIs, 1
Group and Ungroup Slides, 328
Group Slides, 328, 333
Grouped Object, 406, 407
grouped objects, 406
group's first slide, 328, 332
Guidelines, 33

H

Handoff, 390, 391, 392, 394
handwriting. Magically, 8
hardcopies, 5
header, 29, 33, 35, 165, 229, 241, 242, 261
Headers, 28, 416, 425
Heading, 38, 101
Heading 3, 38
Hide Collaboration Activity, 367, 375
Hide or Show Activity, 375
High efficiency (HEVC), 362
highlighted words, 343
hit **Cancel**, 18
home page, 11, 181, 182, 184

Home screen, 2
horizontal and vertical, 412
horizontal axis, 412
How to avoid formula errors, 193
How to refer to cells in other sheets, 195
HTML, 350, 351, 358, 361
hyperlink, 36
hyperlinks, 314, 345
Hyperlinks, 334
Hyphenation checkbox, 24
Hyphenations, 23
hyphens, 24, 25

I

iBooks Author, 5
iCloud, 1, 10, 11, 12, 13, 37, 39, 45, 47, 49, 50, 51, 54, 59, 62, 64, 70, 74, 78, 82, 83, 84, 85, 86, 90, 91, 105, 125, 176, 207, 258, 278, 279, 288, 289, 306, 309, 310, 317, 318, 319, 340, 342, 345, 349, 352, 353, 354, 355, 356, 363, 364, 367, 368, 370, 373, 374, 380, 388, 390, 394, 398, 401, 453
iCloud account, 11, 51, 54, 59, 74, 85
iCloud Drive, 309, 317, 352, 355, 368, 374, 453
iCloud presentations, 310
iCloud website, 1
ideal environment, 4
Ideal for businesses, 8
iDevice, 92
iDevices, 176
iDisk, 14, 15, 50
If You See a Warnings Window, 75
illumination, 414
Image Enhancement, 412
Image from the sidebar, 402
image galleries, 5, 272, 273, 274, 334, 409
Image Gallery, 397, 399, 406
image of the inspector, 36
Images, 311, 312, 350, 358, 361, 398, 409, 430, 443
image's exposure, 402
image's topic., 310
implement the modifications, 362
Impressive, 307

Impressive Charts, 307
impressive presentation., 305
incorporate cinematic, 305
incorporate cinematic effects, 305
indentation, 330, 333
individual images, 405
individual images or all images, 405
Individual Participants, 372
Input a tag, 348
Input a tag or multiple tags, 348
Input menu, 129, 130
Insert a row or column, 424
Insert Charts, 120
Insert Function, 210, 211, 212, 213, 295, 296, 297, 298
Insert multiple rows, 424
insert objects, 309, 310
Insert Page Number, 34
Inserting a Link, 335
Inserting A Note, 42
Inserting an image, 400
Inserting Formulas, 190
Inspector window, 36
Inspector's Chart view, 171
installed macOS 11 or later, 354
Instant Alpha., 153
interactive charts, 306
interesting, 305, 306, 307, 415
interesting sub-topics, 305
Intro to Text Boxes, 312
INTRODUCTION, 305
INTRODUCTION TO NUMBERS, 176
introductory session, 305
Invisible Character Represents, 131
Invitation, 363, 373
Invite More People, 370
Invite others, 312, 375
Invite People from Your Mac, 365
invited email or phone number, 363, 369
iOS, 1, 2, 5, 14, 37, 39, 40, 41, 47, 49, 50, 51, 53, 54, 59, 77, 79, 80, 86, 89, 91, 125, 188, 207, 230, 288, 289
iOS device, 306, 352, 367, 388, 389, 392, 395, 403
iOS devices, 356, 390, 391

iOS iWork apps, 41
iPad, 4, 10, 14, 15, 19, 20, 22, 26, 41, 47, 48, 51, 59, 62, 64, 65, 66, 67, 68, 69, 70, 71, 74, 80, 82, 84, 86, 91, 92, 105, 112, 130, 192, 225, 231, 255, 256, 259, 262, 276, 285, 305, 306, 308, 309, 310, 313, 320, 323, 328, 333, 336, 344, 347, 352, 353, 355,364, 368, 374, 381, 384, 389, 390, 392, 394, 403
iPad and Apple Pencil, 313
iPadOS, 8, 86, 207, 255, 256
iPadOS and Apple Pencil, 309
iPhone, 2, 4, 7, 9, 10, 19, 20, 22, 26, 33, 48, 51, 59, 62, 64, 65, 66, 67, 68, 69, 70, 74, 80, 82, 84, 86, 90, 91, 92, 105, 108, 112, 114, 121, 122, 130, 192, 204, 205, 225, 230, 231, 259, 276, 280, 285, 302, 305, 306, 308, 309, 310, 313, 320, 322, 323, 328, 331, 333, 336, 344, 347, 352, 353, 355, 364, 368, 374, 381, 384, 387, 389, 390, 391, 392, 394, 398, 400, 401, 403, 408, 410
iPhone and iPad, 9, 26, 33, 59, 86, 90, 105, 108, 112, 114, 192, 204, 205, 230, 231, 259, 280, 302
iPhoto **Photo Library**, 135
iTunes, 15, 48, 49, 51, 52, 91, 92, 288

"iWork", 51

---

iWork 2022, 25, 303
iWork app, 15, 46, 64, 71
iWork applications, 1
iWork Collaboration, 70
iWork office suite, 1, 58, 59
iWork.com, 14, 53
iWorkCommunity.com, 181

J

juggle and polish, 4

492

K

Keep Scanning, 404
Keeper, 78
keeping track, 365
keynote, 305, 307, 308, 309, 314, 315, 346, 363, 381, 387, 417
Keynote, 1, 15, 48, 49, 50, 53, 55, 59, 61, 62, 64, 65, 66, 67, 68, 70, 71, 72, 75, 82, 84, 91, 100, 116, 174, 181, 182, 201, 255, 303, 305, 306, 308, 309, 310, 312, 313, 314, 315, 317, 318, 319, 320, 322, 331, 332, 333, 334, 338, 340, 342, 344, 345, 346, 348, 349, 350, 351, 352, 353, 355, 356, 361, 362, 364, 368, 373, 374, 376, 377, 379, 380, 381, 387, 388, 389, 390, 391, 392, 393, 394, 395, 396, 397, 400, 401, 402, 404, 405, 409, 412, 415, 417, 419, 422, 427, 432, 434, 435, 436, 437, 438, 441, 442, 445, 448, 450, 451, 452, 453, 455, 456, 457
Keynote 12.2 or later, 374
Keynotes, 306, 309
Keynotes add live video streams, 309
Keynotes outline, 309
Klariti, 183

L

Landscape, 18, 22
Last Opened, 348
later of macOS Ventura, 357
later on an OS X version, 364
later on an OS X version of OS X, 364
latest version, 305, 448
Launches a specified website, 335, 337
Launchpad, 315
Layer Graphics, 159
layer objects, 311
Left Back button, 461
legacy Pages '09, 5
Ligatures, 23, 24
LIGATURES AND HYPHENATIONS, 23
Light table, 323, 325
Light table duplication, 323
Light table view, 325
Light table view slide, 325
Light table view slide deletion, 325
line chart, 438
line color and thickness, 418
link button, 336, 338
Link field, 335, 337
Linked Text Boxes of The Past, 124
List Of Functions by Category, 202
list style, 102, 103, 110, 111, 112, 114, 116
List Type, 112, 116
List value type, 215
Location information, 335, 337
Lock or Unlock, 345, 388
Lock or unlock a table, 434
Locked checkbox., 345, 388
LOCKIN, 77
LOCKING PRESENTATIONS, 381
LockUp a Text, 345
Logical and information functions, 208
Long-Press on Single Words for Suggestions, 118

M

Mac, 1, 2, 4, 10, 14, 15, 17, 20, 26, 33, 37, 39, 40, 41, 46, 47, 48, 49, 51, 59, 64, 65, 67, 68, 69, 70, 74, 75, 80, 82, 83, 84, 86, 94, 105, 112, 114, 125, 128, 134, 139, 176, 184, 188, 190, 196, 202, 203, 225, 226, 227, 228, 230, 231, 276, 284, 285, 289, 291
Mac or iOS, 306, 367
Mac or iOS device, 306
Mac users, 1, 112
Mac. 4, 415
macOS, 1, 5, 14, 59, 80, 91, 118, 207
macOS 12, 374, 375, 386
macOS and iOS, 1
macOS Ventura, 386
Macs, 305, 357
Magic Move, 313, 457, 458, 459
Magic Move for creating sophisticated, 313
Magic Move for creating sophisticated animations, 313
Magic Place, 459
Magic Place acceleration, 459
Magic Place acceleration and delivery, 459

Magic Place acceleration and delivery options, 459
Mail and Messages, 357, 369
mail merge, 7
Make alterations, 408
Making Lists, 105
Making Threads Look Good, 127
Making Use of Paragraph Styles, 101
MAKING YOUR TEMPLATES, 95
Manage Custom Sizes, 21
manage presentations, 305, 314
Manage Shared, 370, 371
MANAGING DOCUMENT WITH KEYNOTE, 346
MANAGING DOCUMENTS, 14
managing the files, 54
Managing your documents, 346
margins, 17, 20, 21, 22
MARGINS, 20
Mask, 401, 407, 408
Mask (Crop a Photo), 407
Match Case, 340, 341, 343
match the image's colors, 421
Matches, 341
math equations, 5, 306
Media Browser, 134, 137, 139
Media menu button, 403, 421, 447
media placeholder, 398, 399, 401
menu bar, 27, 81, 95, 129, 164, 190, 203, 226, 242, 244, 277, 284, 300
Menu Bar, 45
menu bar., 320, 324, 342, 367, 368, 401
Merge and Unmerge, 425
Merge and Unmerge Cells, 425
Merge Cells, 426, 427
Merging adjacent, 426
Merging adjacent table, 426
Merging adjacent table cells, 426
Microsoft Office, 1, 14, 55, 56, 58, 86, 117
Microsoft Office applications, 1
Microsoft Office formats, 1
Minimum System Requirements, 364
MobileMe iDisk, 14
Modal argument or value type, 216
Modern Linked Text Boxes, 125
modifications, 437

Modified Toolbar, 309
Modify a Chart, 441
modify the intensity of colors, 408
modify the opacity, 312
modify the transition, 405
MONITOR CHANGES, 46
More button, 19, 22, 24, 255, 355, 375, 460
More buttons, 381
More icon, 19, 257
More Useful Formulas and Functions, 208
Most compatible (H.264), 362
Move a table, 434
Move Files from PC, 92
Move Formulas, 194
Move the data, 431
multipage documents, 36
multiple apps, 317
multiple borders., 418
multiple cells, 426
Multiple objects, 411
Multiple rows or columns, 432
multiple slides, 323, 324, 325, 326, 330, 333
Multiple slides, 325
multiple types, 305, 314
multiple types of media, 305, 314
multipresent slideshow, 322
multitask, 309
multitasking screen, 391, 394
My Card from Contacts, 18
My Documents, 15, 48, 71, 72
My Presentations page, 15
My Spreadsheets, 15, 48, 72

N

Native format, 48
native formats, 1
native Pages application, 10
Navigable Table of Contents, 37
navigation pane, 460
navigational arrows, 343
Navigators, 313
negative offset, 148
new coding certificate, 6

New Features, 6
new location, 320, 326, 330, 389, 404, 422, 431, 432
new sentence, 460
new style, 419, 420, 421, 445, 446, 447
New Style option, 165
new table, 419, 420, 421, 432
new table style, 419, 420, 421
Newsletters, 18
Next Item button, 405
next major event invitations, 6
Nonadjacent cells, 426
Note, 314, 315, 316, 317, 320, 321, 325, 326, 327, 334, 338, 339, 340, 341, 342, 343, 344, 346, 350, 351, 353, 354, 355, 356, 358, 361, 364, 365, 367, 368, 369, 371, 374, 378, 383, 386, 387, 389, 390, 392, 399, 403, 407, 409, 416, 420, 426, 433, 437, 456, 460
notifications appear, 372
number of characters, 199, 200
number of columns, 423
Number value type, 216
Numbers, 1, 7, 15, 26, 29, 33, 45, 48, 49, 50, 53, 55, 59, 61, 62, 64, 65, 66, 67, 68, 70, 71, 72, 75, 77, 82, 84, 91, 100, 116, 165, 168, 173, 174, 176, 179, 180, 181, 182, 183, 184, 188, 190, 191, 192, 195, 196, 201, 202, 204, 205, 206, 207, 213, 215, 218, 224, 225, 226, 227, 230, 231, 232, 233, 238, 240, 241, 242, 244, 245, 246, 250, 255, 256, 258, 259, 262, 263, 264, 265, 268, 272, 276, 280, 281, 284, 287, 288, 289, 291, 292, 293, 298, 299, 300, 301, 303
number's font style, 34
Numeric functions, 208

O

object animations, 460
Object Resizing, 409
Object-driven transitions, 313
Objects, 312, 409, 412
Office format, 48
offline copy, 367
Offset, 148, 162, 414

Older iWork, 76
On Mac, 338, 340, 345, 346, 386, 399, 400
One amazing feature, 308
Only people you invite, 375
on-screen instructions, 374
on-screen prompts, 356, 395
Opacity slider, 415, 454
Opacity slider or box, 148
opaque object, 461
Open Password, 386
open the document, 347
Open the shape, 452
Open with Touch ID, 383
OPENING EXISTING FILES, 75
Opening Locked Documents, 80
OPENING PAGES FROM ICLOUD, 10
operating systems, 1, 71
Opt out of shared Documents, 375
Option key, 320, 347, 349, 431
option or program, 354
Organize a Table, 422
ORGANIZING PAGES AND DOCUMENTS, 81
original document, 18, 76
original invitees, 371
original shape, 409
Original Size, 144, 161, 267, 454
OS X, 14, 130
Other Features, 308
Other Settings, 408
Other Stuff, 173
other types of charts, 307
output widget, 124
outstanding presentation, 305
Overrides, 103

P

page layout document, 17, 18, 19, 20, 22, 99
page number appears, 34
Page Number format, 30
Page Number style, 34
page numbers, 25, 26, 27, 31, 33, 36, 40
Page Setup, 21
Page Thumbnails, 82

495

Pages, 1, 2, 4, 5, 6, 7, 10, 11, 13, 14, 15, 16, 17, 18, 19, 20, 23, 24, 25, 26, 32, 33, 35, 36, 37, 38, 39, 41, 46, 48, 49, 50, 52, 53, 55, 56, 57, 59, 61, 62, 64, 65, 66, 67, 68, 70, 71, 72, 73, 74, 75, 77, 78, 79, 81, 82, 83, 84, 85, 86, 87, 89, 90, 91, 94, 96, 97, 98, 99, 101, 105, 108, 112, 114, 116, 117, 118, 119, 120, 121, 122, 123, 124, 125, 126, 127, 128, 129, 133, 134, 135, 136, 137, 138, 139, 140, 141, 142, 143, 146, 155, 157, 158, 163, 164, 165, 166, 167, 169, 170, 171, 172, 174, 179, 180, 181, 182, 183, 184, 201, 218, 255, 303

Pages app icon, 2
PAGES EXPORTING FILES, 86
pages file, 12, 78, 86
pages files, 14
Pages files, 10, 13, 86, 90, 91
Pages for iOS, 2
PAGES NUMBERS AND HEADERS, 25
Pages Preferences, 16
paper size, 17, 20, 21, 22
PAPER SIZE, 20
Paragraph, 101, 102, 103, 104, 105, 129, 130
paragraph styles, 37, 38, 40, 101, 103
Paragraph Styles, 102, 103, 104, 105
paragraphs, 21, 24, 37, 38, 40, 102, 128, 130
Passcode, 387
Password, 68, 69, 77, 80
PASSWORD, 77
Password Change, 385
Password to Lock, 381
Password-protected, 381
Paste and Match style, 339
Paste Formula Results, 431
Paste Style, 339, 431
Paste Text, 340
pasting, 310, 340, 431
PC in a compatible format, 13
PCs, 305
PDF, 1, 5, 13, 25, 48, 52, 55, 57, 58, 71, 105, 350, 351, 356, 358, 359, 362
PDF files, 1
PDF icon, 48
penning Aunt Peg, 4
People to collaborate, 368

People you invite, 369, 370, 371, 372
Performs alterations, 310
Permission, 363, 371, 372
PERMISSION, 63, 65
Permissions, 60
Personalize Every Detail, 312
personalized note, 369
perspective, 404, 414
Perspective, 162, 414
Phone Number, 335, 336, 337
photo card templates, 6
photograph, 403
photograph or scanned document, 403
photos, 305, 325, 421, 447
Photos tab, 135
photos to use as transitions, 306
Pick a slide, 344
pick from columns, 307
Picture Frame, 312
pie chart, 438
pies, 307
pivot table, 233, 234, 235, 236, 237, 238, 239, 240
PIVOT TABLE IN NUMBERS, 233, 238
pivot tables, 177, 233, 234, 235, 236, 237, 238, 239
placeholders, 95, 98, 135, 268
Placing Your Chart, 167
Plain, 416
plain text, 5
platforms, 1, 13, 116
Play from the menu, 377
play videos, 10
Play Vimeo and YouTube videos, 10
Play your Presentation, 312
Play your Presentation Anywhere and Anytime, 312
Playback drop-down, 359
Playback option, 377
Playing With the Axes, 171
Plot columns, 441
Plot rows, 441
Plot rows and Plot columns buttons, 441
pop-out menu, 416

popular features, 308
pop-up menu, 20, 43, 44, 46, 95, 102, 103, 104, 105, 126, 160, 161, 162, 164, 165, 185, 186, 187, 192, 239, 251, 264, 266, 267, 302, 311, 312, 320, 354, 360, 418, 421, 430, 431, 436, 442, 443, 453, 454
Portable Document, 356
Position and Align objects, 411
Position and Align objects well, 411
positive offset, 148
potential readers, 37
PowerPoint, 1, 48, 305, 306, 308, 350, 351, 356, 358, 359, 388, 389
PowerPoint files, 308
PowerPoint for Microsoft, 305
Practice always, 462
preferences, 16, 21, 25, 34, 61
Preferences, 16, 18, 24, 59, 118, 128, 129, 207, 289
preferences section, 16
Prerequisites, 59
Pre-selected table-of-contents styles, 38
presentation, 305, 306, 307, 308, 309, 310, 311, 312, 313, 314, 315, 316, 317, 318, 319, 320, 321, 322, 324, 326, 327, 328, 331, 332, 333, 336, 337, 342, 344, 345, 346, 347, 348, 349, 350, 351, 352, 354, 355, 356, 357, 358, 359, 361, 362, 363, 364, 365, 368, 369, 370, 371, 372, 373, 374, 375, 376, 377, 378, 379, 380, 381, 383, 384, 385, 386, 387, 388, 389, 390, 391, 392, 393, 394, 395, 397, 398, 399, 400, 401, 403, 404, 412, 413, 415, 421, 422, 430, 437, 455, 457, 458, 460, 462
Presentation, 318, 319, 320, 322, 338, 340, 345, 347, 348, 349, 350, 351, 354, 355, 357, 361, 370, 371, 374, 375, 376, 377, 381, 384, 386, 387, 388, 389, 391, 392, 395, 397, 415
presentation manager, 324, 355, 374, 376
presentation program, 305, 314
presentation program from Apple, 305
presentation short and simple., 482
presentations, 306, 308, 309, 310, 313, 317, 328, 332, 349, 350, 352, 355, 356, 357, 380, 381, 386, 388, 389, 390, 397, 456
presenter display, 312, 332
Preserve original format, 362

press **Documents**, 19
press the Delete key, 417, 428
Preview button, 458
previous matching text., 343
Printers & Scanners, 379
Printing, 379
Proportionally, 409

Q

Quickly translate text., 8
QuickTime Video, 376, 377
QuickTime., 376, 377

R

radar chart., 438
Range value type, 216
Rearrange Page Layout pages, 82
Rearranging Links, 126
rearranging themselves, 460
red close button, 318
Redefine a chart style, 448
Redefine a Table, 422
Redefine Style, 422, 448
Redo the previous step, 333
Reduce File Size, 361
Refer To Cells in Formulas, 195
Reference functions, 208
Reflection check box, 149
relocating, 310
remote control, 392, 393, 394, 395, 396
Remove a Collaborate, 65, 66
Remove A Collaborator from The File, 65
Remove a Device, 395
Remove a fill, 455
Remove A Note, 44
Remove Access, 65, 66
Remove Extra Spaces, 210, 296
Remove Header Rows, 425
Remove Me., 375
Remove password., 386
remove rows, 424
Remove Transition, 460
Remove trimmed parts, 362

removing rows and columns., 423
Rename, 319, 347, 348
Rename A Custom Template, 96
Rename a Document, 347
Rename A Style, 104
Rename Style, 104
Reorder Data, 441
Reorder Data Series, 441
Reorder images, 405
Reorder Slides, 326, 330
Repeated tapping, 333
Replace an image, 400
Replace button., 344, 398
Replace field empty, 343
Replace Found Text, 341
Replace Image button, 317, 321, 398, 401
Replace option, 344
Replace placeholder text, 99
replace search results, 340
Replace Text, 344
Replace Text From the Dictionary, 344
Replace the following content, 428
replacement, 341, 342, 344
replacement word, 341
Require a Password, 381
Requirement, 363
Reset Image, 408, 413
Reset Image button, 408
Resize, 409, 432, 433, 434
resize and **reposition**, 404
resize them, 311
resizing, 310, 325, 409, 433, 451, 459
Resizing Other Kinds of Graphics, 143
resolution and **frame rate**, 360
Return key, 130, 209, 293, 294, 344
Revert a Previous, 348
Revert Changes to a Table Style, 420
Review Formula Errors, 193
rich font library, 1
rich text, 5, 213, 298, 299
Rotate, 409, 410
Rotate wheel, 145
row colors, 417, 419
Row vs. Column, 440

rows and columns, 418, 423, 432, 433, 434, 435, 439, 441
Rows and columns, 422, 433
rows or columns, 424, 425, 432, 433, 435, 440, 441
RTF, 5
Rulers, 16

S

saturation, 402, 408
Saturation, 408, 413
Save a chart, 446
Save A Custom Fill, 162
Save a Table, 420
Save a Table as a New Style, 420
Save to Files, 90
Saving a Document, 346
SAVING AND RENAMING, 73
Scale down large images, 362
Scale to Fill, 455
Scale to Fit, 430, 455
Scan a Page Manually, 404
Scan Documents, 403
scatter, 307, 444
Screen View, 7, 19
Scribble, 8, 255, 256, 257
Search Field, 340
second slide, 460
second text box, 123
Security Options, 71
select a border style, 418
Select a cell, 435
Select a layout, 316
Select a new transition., 460
Select a sending option., 357
select a setting, 343, 412
Select a table, 422, 435
Select an image, 398, 402, 410, 412, 413
Select an object, 409, 411, 412, 414
Select Folder icon, 49
Select Image, 399
select Package, 352
Select Record Slideshow., 377
Select rows, 435

Select tables, 435
selected borders, 418
selection border, 429
selects a color option, 419
Send a Copy, 357
Send via Mail, 55, 58
sequential content or patterns, 429
Set Auto-Replacement, 118
Set Password, 382, 383
Set Password from the main menu, 383
Setting up, 356
Settings menu, 387
Settings tab, 337
Setup Remote screen, 392
Shadow cast, 414
Shadow cast at an angle, 414
Shapes, 100, 160, 161, 163, 258, 265, 311, 334, 448, 449, 450, 451, 452
shape's button functions, 338
Share button, 357, 366, 368
Share File dialog box, 60
Share Options, 62, 64, 65, 67
Shared Documents, 374
SHARING, 47
sharing method, 366
sharing settings, 363
Sharpness, 413
Shift-Command, 334
shortcut menu, 421, 428, 447
Shortcuts app, 1
Show a Cell Row, 431
Show a Cell Row and Column, 431
Show Adjust Image, 413
Show Collaboration Activity, 367, 375
Show Comments, 46
Show Comments & Changes pane, 46
Show Details, 379
Show Find & Replace, 341
showing or hiding gridlines, 417
sidebar, 20, 24, 37, 42, 43, 44, 46, 82, 100, 203, 228, 229, 242, 244, 250, 266, 267, 268, 272, 273, 274
Sidebar, 418
Simple batch mailing., 7
simple transitions, 313

Simplify charts and graphs, 462
simulate how words, 460
single platform, 306
Size a row or column, 433
Size a row or column to fit its content, 433
Skim through in style., 9
Skip a Slide, 327
Skip or Un-skip a Slide, 331
Skip Slide or Un-skip Slide, 331
Slide from another Slide, 324
slide in Keynote, 460
slide layout features, 314, 316
slide navigator, 321, 322, 323, 324, 325, 326, 327, 328, 330, 331, 332, 333, 459
slide numbers, 359
Slide View, 328
slides for an excellent, 305
slideshow, 324, 332, 336, 337, 345, 359, 361, 377, 378, 437
Smart Dashes checkbox, 25
smart quotes, 313
smooth experience, 309
smooth transitions, 306
sophisticated presentations, 313
Spacebar, 33, 112, 130
specific paragraphs, 24
specific section, 45
spell checker, 1
Split Text, 209, 295
Spotlight Search, 33, 112
spreadsheet, 1, 7, 50, 58, 59, 70, 176, 178, 179, 188, 190, 191, 192, 195, 202, 209, 210, 213, 218, 225, 233, 238, 239, 240, 241, 250, 255, 258, 259, 263, 265, 268, 272, 275, 276, 277, 278, 280, 284, 285, 287, 288, 289, 290, 293, 295, 296, 298, 300, 301, 302
spreadsheet application **Numbers**, 1, 176
spreadsheets, 1, 47, 176, 255, 276, 288, 299
standard format, 5
start a presentation, 305
Statistical functions, 208
Stay on Page, 158
Steve Jobs, 1
Stock Layouts, 182
stop sharing a document, 367

Stop Sharing a Document, 367
Stop Sharing button, 67
storage and backup, 54
straightforward, 313
Stretch, 454
String value type, 217
Stunning presentations, 313
style in the sidebar, 421, 422, 447, 448
Style menu, 31, 32
style selection, 436
Style tab, 127, 128, 146, 149, 266, 267, 268, 272, 273, 312, 405, 406, 413, 414, 415, 422, 444, 453, 454, 455
Style-based tables, 37
Style-based tables of contents, 37
stylized graphic, 371
stylized graphic containing, 371
Submit New Template button, 181
Substitutions, 25
Sums, 416
swift in-document translation, 8
Switch rows, 441
symbol appears, 355
Sync Documents, 49, 352
synchronization status, 365
System Preferences, 16, 128, 352, 356, 379, 386, 391

T

Tab, 130
Table Cells, 418
table data, 422
Table handle, 417, 433, 434
table in proportion, 434
table of contents, 37, 39, 40
Table of Contents, 37, 38, 39, 40, 41
TABLE OF CONTENTS, 37
Table of Contents view, 37, 38, 39, 40, 41
Table of Contents view., 38, 39, 40, 41
Table or Chart icon, 164
Table Outline, 418
Table Outline section, 418
Table Style, 421

table style that matches, 421
table styles, 421, 422
Table tab, 406, 417, 419, 420, 421, 422, 425, 433, 437
table text, 436
Tables, 164, 234, 311, 313, 406, 415, 434, 437
table's bottom, 424
table's features, 421
tables for large, 462
tables for large data, 462
table's header rows and columns, 423
Take Photo, 397, 403
tap Keynote, 394
tap the button, 384
temperature, 402
Template Chooser, 95, 96, 97, 290
Template Chooser., 95, 96, 97
Templates, 17, 94, 179, 181, 183, 184, 268, 288, 289, 290
term for object, 460
text box, 22, 23, 24, 42, 100, 123, 124, 125, 126, 127, 128, 132, 162, 163, 170, 192, 256, 257, 267, 302, 312, 336, 339, 345, 404, 405, 406, 415, 455, 460
Text Box, 123, 128
Text box linking, 124
text boxes, 17, 99, 123, 124, 125, 127, 128, 160, 161, 162, 265, 266, 268, 272, 273
Text Bullet., 110
Text Direction, 129
text fields, 163
TEXT FLOW MODIFICATION, 123
text flows, 17, 126, 157
Text functions, 208
Text in a single cell, 428
TEXT INSERTION, 99
text layout, 17
Text Match option, 460
Text pane, 102, 103, 104, 130
Text panel, 101
Text transitions, 313
text with color gradients, 5
textures, 306, 443
the App Store, 306
the App Store or the Mac App, 306

the App Store or the Mac App Store, 306
the Chart tab, 406, 442, 443, 444, 445, 446, 447, 448
The color schemes, 416
The Drift motion, 312
The editor displays, 38
The File to Prevent Unauthorized Access, 68
The folder structure, 380
The green dot, 450
the **image placeholder**, 135
the **Image** tab, 153, 155
The keynote, 307, 430
The keynote sets, 307
The keynote sets up, 307
The **Media Browser**, 135, 137
The offset, 414
The PDF, 359
The selected image, 312
The shapes library, 448
The small images, 445
the style and color scheme, 415
The Text tab, 436
The x and y coordinates, 411
The Y coordinate, 411
theme chooser, 315, 318
thousand words, 307
thread of linked boxes, 125
thumbnail, 52, 78, 82
Time intervals, 359
toolbar, 20, 24, 36, 43, 46, 47, 59, 64, 65, 67, 84, 85, 120, 123, 137, 166, 167, 169, 189, 190, 195, 226, 250, 256, 257, 263, 264, 265, 268, 291, 292, 300, 308, 309, 310, 311, 316, 318, 322, 325, 332, 340, 341, 342, 344, 347, 357, 365, 366, 370, 371, 375, 397, 398, 403, 404, 409, 410, 411, 412, 413, 414, 415, 421, 436, 438, 447, 449, 451
top of the page, 11
top of the screen, 321, 349, 361, 389, 390, 428
top right corner, 35, 86, 210, 228, 242, 277, 283, 295
top-left corner, 16, 19, 63, 72, 271, 417, 427, 433, 434
top-right corner of the table, 423

Touch ID, 77, 78, 79, 80, 381, 383, 386, 387
TouchID, 69
Transfer, 388, 389, 460
Transfer Files, 91
Transfer text, 460
TRANSFERRING DOCUMENTS, 82
Transform the device, 394
transition, 312, 359, 405, 457, 458, 459, 460
transition at the bottom, 460
translucent object, 461
transparency of a drawing, 415
transparent, 361, 415, 461
Trigonometric functions, 208
triple-dot icon, 87
Turn ligatures, 23
Turn off **Document Body**, 19, 20
Turn smart dashes on or off, 24
TXT, 5
Type in your password, 383
Type in your Password, 382
Types Of Arguments and Values, 214
Typography, 313
Typography options, 313

U

UNDERSTANDING PAGES, 4
Understanding Syncing Symbols, 355
Undo an Action, 333
Undo or Redo Changes, 334
Undo/Redo, 333
ungroup selected images, 402
ungroup slides, 314
Ungroup Slides, 330
Ungrouped Slides, 333
unique presentation, 462
unique presentation on keynote, 462
unlock a table, 434
Unmerge cells, 427
unskip the slides, 314
unskipped, 328
Update Style, 104
Upgrade, 76
Upload Files, 84
uploaded file, 12

upper-right corner, 461
Use chart styles, 445
use interface, 307
Use String Operators and Wildcards, 198
Use Table Styles, 419
user group, 369, 371
Using Airpod, 389
Using iTunes, 91
Using The Formula Editor, 188
Using The Thread Control, 126
UTILIZING PRE-EXISTING TEMPLATES, 94

V

Value Axis (Y) section, 172
version 13, 357, 386
version of iOS, 374
Vertex42, 184
vertical axis, 412
vertical or horizontal flip, 410
vertical sequence, 332
video feeds to slides, 306
video feeds to slides with Keynote, 306
videos, 305, 306, 309, 311, 325, 409
View menu, 332, 340, 341, 365
View menu button, 332, 340, 341
View Only, 342, 372, 373
visible series, 446, 448
visual experience, 462
visual intrigue, 309
VoiceOver, 1, 2
Voiceover QuickTime, 377

W

web browser., 10, 64
Web-based Distributed Authoring and Versioning, 14
WebDAV, 14, 15, 288, 289

Website, 335, 337
WHAT DO PAGES DO, 4
WHAT IS A PIVOT TABLE?, 233
Wi-Fi network, 357, 389
wildcard, 199, 200
window, 12, 16, 21, 25, 29, 36, 45, 51, 75, 84, 85, 94, 104, 140, 141, 160, 161, 162, 191, 193, 229, 251, 252, 266, 301
Windows, 10, 13, 14, 49, 59, 64, 86, 90, 91
Word, 1, 5, 13, 14, 18, 48, 52, 55, 56, 74, 77, 81, 86, 89, 90, 91, 99, 118, 119, 120, 163, 171, 174, 179, 184
word processing, 1, 5, 13, 14, 17, 18, 19, 20, 21, 22, 42, 58, 71, 81, 99, 100, 117, 119, 163
Work offline, 364
Work together in Real Time, 312
WORKING WITH CHARTS, 437
WORKING WITH CHARTS AND SHAPES, 437
WORKING WITH CHARTS AND SHAPES ON KEYNOTE, 437
Working With Data, 168
WORKING WITH PHOTOS ON THE KEYNOTE, 397
WORKING WITH TABLES, 415
WORKING WITH TABLES IN KEYNOTE, 415
WORKING WITH TEMPLATES ON PAGES, 94
WORKING WITH TEXT ON PAGES, 99
Working With Unique Characters, 116
Wrap text for a row, 428
Wrap text to fit in a cell, 428

Y

yellow alignment guides, 433
yellow autofill handle, 429
YouTube links, 5
YouTube or Vimeo, 309

Z

zoom level of an image, 404

Printed in Great Britain
by Amazon